Traditional Bowyers Encyclopedia

Traditional Bowyers Encyclopedia

The Bowhunting and Bowmaking World of the
Nation's Top Crafters of Longbows and Recurves

Dan Bertalan

Skyhorse Publishing

www.skyhorsepublishing.com

10 9 8 7 6 5 4 3 2 1

Bertalan, Dan.
  The traditional bowyers encyclopedia : the bowhunting and bowmaking world of the nation's top crafters of longbows and recurves / Dan Bertalan.
       p. cm.
  Originally published: East Lansing, Mich. : Envisage Unlimited, c1989.6
  ISBN-13: 978-1-60239-046-1 (alk. paper)
  ISBN-10: 1-60239-046-0 (alk. paper)
  1. Bow and arrow making—United States. 2. Bowhunting—United States. 3. Bowyers—United States. I. Title.

GV1189.5.B47 2007
688.7'920285--dc22
                                              2007015365

Printed in the United States of America

To bowmakers throughout time

Contents

A lot has changed since Dan Bertalan first wrote *Traditional Bowyers of America* in 1989. So when Dan asked me to write the foreword for his updated book I was both honored and humbled. The late Jay Massey, who was a hero of mine both for what he accomplished and what he stood for, had penned the original foreword. Re-reading Jay's thoughts brought back memories of where we were back in 1989—when traditional archery was setting the archery and bowhunting world on fire. Jay noted the interest and surge of traditional archery back then. It was a special time for all of us. Some of us were just learning to leave the modern bow behind, while many others were wondering what took us so long.

Looking back over the past eighteen years is bittersweet. While the number of bowyers peaked in the nineties, there are far more today than there were when *Traditional Bowyers of America* was released. Countless businesses were spawned by the upsurge in traditional archery and every one of them, without exception, was driven by a passion for the traditional bow. Most of the bowyers spotlighted in the 1989 book are still going strong and turning out more bows now than ever before. A few of the bowyers profiled in Dan's original book have retired, passed the torch on to their children and apprentices, or simply closed shop for good. A precious few have gone to be with God. Reading *Traditional Bowyers of America* brought back memories of people I greatly admire and many I sorely miss.

While advances in traditional archery materials, bow-building techniques, and shooting styles have advanced since 1989, nothing has changed the archery and bowhunting world as profoundly as the availability of today's information. In the late eighties there was pretty much one source of information available to the traditional archer—a small number of general bowhunting magazines which produced a handful of articles on traditional archery. That all changed in the nineties when *Traditional Bowhunter Magazine* was unveiled by a handful of passionate traditional bowhunters who knew the growing interest in traditional archery was more than just a fad. On the heels of that information breakthrough came the strangest bedfellow yet for those archers looking to move away from technology. The Internet flattened the world and provided traditional archers with huge, searchable knowledge bases of information just a click away.

Through all of this change there has been one constant, and that is my friend Dan Bertalan, who has never wavered in his love and commitment to traditional archery. This book, updated some eighteen years later, is a reflection of that commitment. A finer ambassador to those who shoot sticks you won't find.

I suppose Dan is young enough to think about edition three some twenty years from now. I'm sure many of us will be interested to see how our world has changed in 2027. But for me, I'm just keeping up with the changes since 1989 and Dan's new edition, the *Traditional Bowyers Encyclopedia*, reflects much of that. The future of traditional archery is bright and this book will undoubtedly be looked back on as a reference for the point in time that is 2007. It's as much a historical treasure for us who love this sport so dearly as it is a source of information. And I can't think of anyone better to bring it to all of us.

Pat Lefemine
Founder, Bowsite.com and Stickbow.com
Union, Connecticut, 2007

Dan Bertalan's book, *Traditional Bowyers Encyclopedia,* couldn't come at a better time, what with the back-to-the-basics archery movement sweeping the country today. All across the U.S. and Canada — and in many other foreign countries, too — archers and bowhunters are rediscovering the archery of old: the time-tested longbow and recurve. Archers everywhere are suddenly wanting more information on traditional archery gear.

It wasn't always that way. For nearly two decades now traditional archery has taken a back seat to the glitz and glitter of high-tech archery gadgetry.

Advertisements and feature stories in archery publications provide a fair index of what sort of archery tackle is being used at a particular time. For example, of the eight bowhunting articles in a 1979 issue of *Bowhunter Magazine,* seven featured compound devices. The magazine contained dozens of pages of four-color advertisements touting the latest in high-tech archery gear. By contrast, only four small black and white ads were run by traditional bowmakers.

It was clear that in 1979, archery trends were being dictated not by traditional bowyers, but by gadget manufacturers — large corporations whose primary objective was not to promote archery, but to strengthen their financial "bottom line."

But now, ten years later, the pendulum is starting to swing in the other direction. In the July, 1989 issue of the same national magazine, nearly half of the bowhunting articles featured traditional bows. This same issue contained advertisements from roughly two dozen traditional bowmakers.

And in a recent survey of the Professional Bowhunters Society — which represents nearly 2,000 of the most experienced bowhunters in the world — nearly 70 percent shoot traditional recurves and longbows. In other words, among the expert bowhunters, archery traditionalism has already arrived.

To whom do we owe thanks for reviving old-time archery? We are indebted to the untold thousands of archers — men and women who cared enough to keep the old traditions alive. We also can thank the hundreds of small, independent American bowyers who swam against the tide and kept on producing quality, handmade traditional bows and arrows.

In this important book, Dan Bertalan — an expert bowhunter and archery traditionalist himself — has presented an in-depth look at some of these bowyers and their work. Not all of America's traditional bowyers are illustrated, of course. To do so would require a book of two thousand pages. But the bowyers written about here do generally represent the best in the field of custom bowmaking today.

The bowyers written about in *Traditional Bowyers Encyclopedia* also represent something else: American independence and originality, and perhaps even more important, early American values.

Dan Bertalan has made an important contribution to traditional archery with this book, one which traditional archers everywhere will be certain to appreciate.

Jay Massey, author, *The Bowyer's Craft*
Girdwood, Alaska, 1989

The author gratefully acknowledges the openness and help of the bowyers profiled in the following pages. The author is also grateful to Linda Peckham, Mary Brown, and Mark Woodbury for their encouragement and editorial assistance.

Introduction

It's been almost two decades since I traversed the nation, literally from the Atlantic to the Pacific, interviewing thirty of America's top traditional bowyers during the summer of 1987 and early into 1988. My goal back then was to capture a thick slice of traditional bowmaking history rich in the heritage and technical aspects that make it so intriguing to true toxophilites.

Despite being in awe while interviewing archery legends such as Fred Bear and Earl Hoyt, Jr. back then, it was still difficult to truly appreciate the magnitude of how quickly chapters in even modern history can change. And although those individual slices of time are fragile things that are here one day and gone the next, like the passing of those true pioneers of the sport, the overall continuum that makes a broader history remains unbroken. Because really, the older chapters merely gather some more of time's dust while a few new ones add to the overall volume. In the end, the greater history of bowmaking and archery in America hasn't changed its foundation other than the addition of a newer chapter here and there.

If you think about it, this particular subject matter alone, "traditional bowmaking" and old-time archery, lends itself to becoming locked in something of a time capsule. Yew wood longbows today are handcrafted much the same way they were five hundred years ago in England. Composite recurves are made essentially the same way Fred Bear and Earl Hoyt made them sixty years ago during the birth of modern bowhunting.

Perhaps the most significant changes aren't in the technical aspects of traditional bowmaking or the overall history. No, the real change lies more within the people who choose to shoot traditional bows.

Twenty years ago saw the first big resurgence in traditional archery. The deviation from popular compound archery to old-time archery seemed a huge leap at the time. But let's put that into today's perspective. Over the past two decades we have seen phenomenal changes in compound bow technology with improvements in let-off, speed, design and overall performance. Arrows have also changed in their construction and impacts on both modern and old-time archery. We have witnessed dramatic changes in everyday life too, like the Internet, cloning, cell phones, plasma screens, iPods, smart-bombs, and technology that seemed like science fiction not so long ago. So the people today who choose to step back in time into the world of traditional archery in fact take a bigger leap than we did decades ago.

However, the main reason why today's traditional archer makes that leap remains essentially the same. If you sample a cross section of people who shoot traditional gear today, you'll still get a core who have loved traditional bows forever and will never stray from that path. Then there's that wider audience of those who have sampled the challenges and rewards of shooting compound bows and eventually have been lured into trying the magic of shooting old-time bows, with its richer, longer history and whole new range of challenges. Whether they choose to shoot those longbows or recurves during a certain hunting trip or archery event, or for that matter, switch back and forth to their compound, doesn't take away from their interest in traditional archery or remove them from the ranks. In fact, it may broaden their scope of archery altogether. Either way, shooting a variety of bows shouldn't "disqualify" someone from being a "traditional archer" in an ever-shrinking realm of interest in today's shooting sports. As Ron Pittsley so aptly points out in a new chapter in his classic philosophical style, "In my experience in promoting archery within large and small archery companies, I never tried to let myself get pigeonholed as an archer. That's one reason I welcome all archers, including compound archers. I think it's important to gain a much broader view of how the shrinking sport of archery is functioning within our world, and the open-mindedness that it takes to promote it."

So young or old, new or experienced, transitional from compound or not, traditional archers are still traditional archers. And this book offers all of them a wholesome chunk of American archery history. Within these pages you'll discover centuries of cumulative bowmaking and bowhunting adventures. In fact, you're holding the single most comprehensive text on the subject. It contains individual chapters on the original thirty bowyers profiled years ago, plus a new chapter on Ron Pittsley, who symbolizes the bridging and unification of the past twenty years within traditional bowmaking. When reading the new chapter on Predator traditional bows, don't be surprised if you sense a different style from the following ones. Two decades can change a great many things, including the pen of the writer. This new chapter also focuses on the essence of traditional archery for many shooters and perhaps even offers the secret to happiness in the sport. To bring you up to date on the past twenty years, we have included an update on the recent status of the original thirty bowyers and their companies. We've even included some changes in the author's professional life.

Because of its depth, this book can be used to fulfill a vast variety of interests in traditional archery. For the historian, it tracks the birth of archery in America and follows its growth into modern bowhunting. It profiles the heydays of traditional archery and the changes over seventy years. For the archer exploring traditional archery for the first time, it holds a treasure chest of information on what to look for in gear and how to use it effectively. For the budding or experienced traditional bowyer, these chapters hold the detailed bowmaking techniques and experience of a nation. Since the first penning of this book, thousands have used it as a detailed guide to building their longbows and recurves. For traditional shooters who want to improve their shooting skills it reveals more sage instinctive shooting advice than any four other books on the subject. And that's vital because a single book or video on instinctive shooting technique can't begin to fulfill the broad instructional arena of instinctive shooting for the masses.

As an added bonus for instinctive shooters, there's a new section in the chapter on Predator traditional bows that reveals detailed information on the latest in conquering target panic and honing instinctive shooting form. For archers shopping for the ultimate traditional bow to help them achieve the most gratification in the sport, these pages hold a wealth of secrets to knowing what properties to look for in a longbow or recurve then how to make that bow perform to your expectations. That alone is a tall order. For the traditional bowhunter, there are enough stories and bowhunting tips to help you hone every aspect of your adventures afield—from what gear to use to outwit those elusive antlered trophies.

Finally, for the entire audience of traditional archery buffs, these pages hold something that's seldom found anywhere else. If you look past the printed words and absorb the true meaning from the pages you read, you'll discover the biggest treasure of all. It's the often ethereal, yet very real secret to finding your personal fulfillment in something that you love—traditional archery.

As you read these pages for the first time or as a repeat, you'll find that the spirit within each chapter remains the same. All of the bowyers reveal their detailed bowmaking techniques that helped spawn the first big revolution in traditional archery that lives on today. They offer their perspectives and philosophy on bowmaking, delving into the tricks of the trade and innovations that make up traditional bowcrafting. In fact, much of the book wades into the technical aspects of almost every part of crafting a traditional bow—from cutting the trees in the forest to the bow's final finish. To help you with all the bowmaking terminology, this book also contains a comprehensive glossary and bow diagram reference. You'll even find an index to aid in locating specific items or points of interest.

Because the information here is so technical relative to bow performance, each bow profiled includes draw/force measurements and qualified hand-shot arrow speeds. A dual-cell chronograph was used to record the hand-shot arrow speeds. Results vary with a shooter's draw and release. To minimize these shooter inconsistencies, only the top three arrow speeds from a sampling of many were used to obtain an average relative chronographed arrow speed. Of course, there are significant variables affecting arrow speed, such as the draw length of the shooter, arrow weight, arrow length, fletching, nock type, bowstring type, bowstring accessories, bow specifics, and shooter characteristics—all of which are noted along with the arrow speeds from the bows measured. So as you browse through the information, try to qualify the results with these human and physical variables.

Besides the wealth of information about selecting a bow and what makes different styles of bows perform, the sage of bowyers in this book offer valuable advice on how to care for your bow. And they all give advice on how to shoot with distinctive and often diverse insights on instinctive form, including both the mental and physical sides of the challenge — from trick shooting to arrowing big game when your nerves are frayed.

As with every meaty archery book, you'll also be served a hearty helping of bowhunting adventure here, blended with solid how-to hunting information. With more than seven hundred years of cumulative bowhunting experience, these bowmakers offer hunting stories aplenty, and few are shy about telling how to bag the big ones or telling about the big ones that almost bagged them. These wry bowmen discuss specific hunting techniques, including what gear they use and why — from boots to broadheads.

Though you might not expect it from the title, this book will also take you on a grand travel adventure of sorts. It starts near the granite shores of the Atlantic along the Hudson River and ends at the misty beaches of the northern Pacific coast. So as you turn the pages, absorb the feel of the passing countryside, linger in the historic towns, stroll through the dusty bow shops, tour the factories and homes as you discover each bowmaker's special world of traditional archery.

Unlike the chapters that follow it, chapter two is historical fiction that recreates a segment in the lives of the Yana Indians who once carved out a niche of existence in northern California. Although fictional in part, the spirit of this chapter, "The Early Ones," represents a magical thread that transcends time and space between today's traditional bowyers and that lost race. For Ishi and his people, bowmaking was a way of life, a way of death, and remained the ultimate craft that reflected the spirit of a person.

Now, a hundred years later, for the men in the following thirty-one chapters, bowmaking remains the ultimate craft.

So sit back long into the nights as you share and savor their tradition within these pages—a tradition that now runs through your veins too.

Dan Bertalan
Madison, Wisconsin, 2007

Chapter One

TRADITIONAL ARCHERY IN THE NEW MILLENNIUM

It's ironic that the new millennium is perhaps the best time in the history of mankind to become a traditional archer.

Primitive hunters roaming the late Paleolithic landscape may have had good hunting opportunities in an unspoiled wilderness with their crude bows and arrows. But they were also on the menu of warm-blooded prey and hunted by a host of predators that had developed a long-standing taste for human flesh. Until stone points came along, nasty carnivores such as saber-toothed lions commonly made short work of us fangless, clawless, shrieking bipeds. However, the development of the bow and atlatl quickly changed all that. In no time, we spear and arrow-flinging humans wiped out most of the large predators, and many of the large herbivores for that matter. For some 10,000 years, the bow and arrow impacted which species lived or perished across the land.

Despite the havoc that predators inflicted on primitive archers, other primitive cultures with their archers posed an even bigger threat. The forgotten history of mankind around the world is littered with the bone dust of societies that were blotted off the face of the earth with bows and arrows. Since the first time that an arrow stopped a beating human heart, more cultures have been wiped out using bows and arrows than perhaps any other single type of weaponry. For thousands upon thousands of years, man killed man using bows and arrows in almost every corner of every continent. The bow was a daily companion in defending life and delivering death.

Thankfully, times have changed for today's archer. Unless they live in the deepest recesses of the Amazon, archers no longer kill each other with their bows and arrows. Oh sure, mankind still openly kills his fellow man because of religious, cultural, or political differences. We simply use more civilized means of destroying mass life nowadays. The bow has been removed from the equation.

So in the end, today's archer no longer faces the lethal threats from wild beasts and fellow archers that they endured for eons. Other than hunting in bear country, or the rare cougar encounter, we no longer have to look over our shoulder in fear of being picked off by some predator. We take our bows afield with little worry of being eaten by lions or bears. And modern fatalities from arrows are as rare as hen's teeth, or about one in three million, annually—and accidentally. Based on those qualifications of safety alone, this is the "best" time of all to be a traditional archer.

Even with the mortal dangers removed from the formula, it's still the best time to be a traditional archer—especially for those interested in bowhunting. We can roam the woods and mountains freely in quest of bowhunting adventure. And oh what adventure awaits us there.

More deer inhabit North America today than at anytime in recorded history. In addition to the estimated thirty million out there now, the number keeps growing by almost one million animals a year. With each yearly jump in populations, more and more bowhunting opportunities spring up across the nation from overpopulated parks and neighborhoods filled with deer to the open prairies where hunters can see a dozen trophy bucks a day. But today's bowhunter's feast afield doesn't end with deer alone. Black bear, elk, pronghorn, and turkey have all surpassed one-hundred year highs in many parts of the country. Combine this wildlife boom with a shrinking number of hunters pursuing them, and you have the best hunting opportunities in species, seasons, bag limits, and distribution seen by modern archers. Fred Bear once commented that he was happy when he saw one buck during a hunt back in the 1940s. In contrast, today's recurve or longbow shooter can see more than fifty deer a day in some areas. The recent boom in bowfishing with traditional gear also reflects changing times. Expanded access to waterways, plus refinements in today's bowfishing gear, have opened up more bowfishing opportunities for archers than ever before.

If Fred Bear were still alive today, he would also have to agree that traditional bows, arrows, and broadheads are better than ever. The shrinking availability of quality cedar and the blossoming growth of the carbon arrow industry have provided traditional archers with the straightest, strongest and most indestructible arrows that have ever been launched from a bow. Admittedly, today's carbon arrows don't hold the same nostalgic value as cedar. But they unquestionably allow a traditional archer to shoot more accurately and deliver more of the bow's stored kinetic energy into speed, arrow flight, and penetration. Top that off with today's broadhead designs and sharpness, and you have the most effective combinations to ever jump from the string of a traditional hunting bow.

Though they haven't changed as much as arrows in the past twenty years, today's traditional bows represent the cumulative evolution of seventy years of modern bowmaking. The design, materials, and craftsmanship of the longbows and recurves being made today have never been better. And the end results are bows that shoot better and are more durable than ever before. The only drawback is perhaps that the selection has never been more daunting. The combination of materials and designs from some bowyers alone is enough to confound any budding archer. Compound that with hundreds of bowyers and you have the widest selection of traditional bows to ever complicate or delight the marketplace. Despite these complications, it's still the best time ever to be shopping for or shooting one of today's traditional bows.

This isn't just opinion either. It's a scientific fact.

Norb Mullaney, a professional engineer from Wisconsin, has tested more recurves and longbows over the past forty-seven years than anyone in the country. His technical knowledge of bow design and performance is unsurpassed, his opinions unbiased. And although he has seen more dramatic changes in compound bow design over the past twenty years, he still marvels at the progression of traditional bow designs.

"The newer generation of hybrid longbows with their deflex-reflex design," says Mullaney, "have made the greatest strides in shooting and performance over the years. They are still classified as a longbow yet they are now as nice to shoot as a recurve. And more bowyers are making these hybrids. They are actually superior in performance to many of the older high performance recurves of thirty years ago."

Norb notes that in his testing of bows, a 540-grain arrow is typically shot from a sixty-pound bow drawn 28.25 inches from low point of the grip to bowstring. He recalls that many of the "classic" recurves from the 1960s and 1970s tested in the 180 to 190 FPS (feet per second) range. Many of today's recurves, and longbows for that matter, shoot arrows in the 200 to 206 FPS range. Some of this can be attributed to improvements in bowstring materials, some to bow design and materials.

Unidirectional fiberglass backing and facing over limb corewoods has been the standard within the traditional bowmaking industry for nearly 60 years. Fiberglass provides the external rigidity and durability of a working bow limb. Nonetheless, as today's bowyers push the technology envelope, some are trying new materials and designs that leave traditional fiberglass and typical limb cross sections in the past.

"Some bowyers, such as O.L. Adcock," says Norb, "have designed some unique varying limb cross sections that result in a lighter limb with increased dynamic limb performance. The limb design of the Adcock bow makes it very shootable by taking out the typical hand-shock of a longbow with lightening the limb. The result is a longbow that shoots an impressive 210 FPS."

Besides new approaches to limb cross section design, some bowyers such as veteran bowyer Arvid Danielson at Black Swan Archery, have broken the tradition of using fiberglass for limb backing and facing. "Most attempts at carbon facing on bow limbs," Norb explains, "had to be covered with a layer of fiberglass to protect the more fragile carbon. That just added more mass weight to the limb. But Arvid's designs have overcome this, which has resulted in less limb weight and superior tension qualities. It improved performance up into the 210 FPS category. The only other traditional bow design with that kind of performance was one of Mike Fedora's recurves that was also in the 210 FPS range. That was an exceptionally fine bow."

Mullaney notes that most of the higher performance recurves today top out around 206 FPS. And even though bowyers still strive for innovations that will set them apart in the race for speed, Norb doubts that many will be able to exceed the 210 FPS speeds that appear to be the upper reaches of materials and design of a "traditional" bow.

Perhaps the final arena where traditional archers enjoy the best times ever is in archery information. The concept of Gutenberg's printing press pretty much dominated archery information and lore for some five hundred years until Howard Hill's archery exploits hit the movie screens in the mid-1900s. Adding to books and movie shorts, Fred Bear later inspired a nation of sportsmen with his movie and television adventures. Years later, bowhunting magazines and videos followed with a flood of archery and bowhunting topics, adding to the growing volume of books. By the late 1980s, there seemed more than enough information to wet the appetites of those interested in old-time archery and traditional bowhunting.

But then two things happened.

Closely following the heels of the renewed interest in traditional archery, a band of traditional archers from Oregon decided to publish the first magazine dedicated exclusively to traditional bowhunting. The first issue of *Traditional Bowhunter Magazine* hit the newsstands in the fall of 1989 with a run of 20,000 magazines. Today, they publish 65,000 and the magazine is recognized as the definitive resource for traditional archery, bowhunting, bowyers, and gear. "Traditional archery has gained a lot of respect within the archery community," says Larry Fischer, one of the founders of the magazine. "In fact, traditional archery has become so popular that even the mainstream archery magazines now have special sections on traditional bowhunting. We can't claim that we grew traditional archery, but we can claim that we are the printed catalyst that brought those interested in traditional archery together."

Larry notes that the spark of interest that ignited the new trend in traditional archery twenty years ago has grown into a full-fledged fire of interest in recent years. "The fifty or so bowyers that we had back in the late 1980's has grown to perhaps five hundred today. Half of those are relatively small workshop businesses. Even the number of overseas and European bowyers has been growing leaps and bounds."

The biggest change Larry has seen is in the participation at the traditional archery gatherings. In the late 1980s, the Great Lakes Longbow Invitational in Michigan, was the biggest gathering in the country, drawing about two old-time archers for the shooting events and festivities. Though that seemed big at the time, today's numbers at traditional archery gatherings such as Denton Hills in Pennsylvania and the Compton in Berrien Springs, Michigan can draw crowds of up to 10,000 participants. "Not only that," adds Larry, "you now have lots of states that have their own traditional archery clubs and host lots of smaller shoots that pull in five hundred to a thousand shooters. And the best part within this growth is seeing all the new young people getting into traditional archery as their first attempt in archery. Anytime you get young people involved it's good for the future of the sport."

Like others with their finger on the traditional archery pulse of America, Larry estimates that about 10 percent of the three million archers in the nation regularly shoot traditional gear, while maybe as many as 30 percent own and occasionally shoot traditional bows.

Although *Traditional Bowhunter Magazine* made a resounding impact on the printed information gap within traditional archery circles, the explosion of the Internet over the past decade has changed the lives of everyone on the planet—including archery information buffs.

Today, Internet browsers have instant access to more information on traditional archery and bowhunting than could have been imagined twenty years ago. A Web search on traditional archery nets 1,250,000 results while a search on traditional bowhunting nets 257,000 results. The range and volume of information on the subject is suddenly overwhelming. Now, instead of waiting for magazines or catalogs to come in the mail then sifting through printed information about shopping for or shooting traditional bows, Internet users can wade through the full spectrum of multimedia where they can read information, view images, listen to audio presentations, and even watch videos—all for free.

One of the most popular traditional bow sites is www.stickbow.com, the traditional counterpart of www.bowsite.com, which were both created by Pat Lefemine. Joining the list of traditional archery and bowhunting information Web sites are www.bowhuntinginfo.com, www.bowhunting.net/traditionalarchery, http://www.huntingnet.com, and a host of others. Searches on related topics such as traditional bows, recurve bows, longbows, and instinctive shooting could fill truckloads if they were printed. And when it's all said and done, today's traditional archer has never had more vivid and comprehensive information at his or her fingertips. Whether shopping for the ultimate bow or looking for accessory gear, the information is simply a click away.

As we look from our electronic Internet world back over the past 10,000 years of man shooting sticks and stings for a variety of reasons, today, right here and now, is by far the very "best" time to be a traditional archer. Primitive hunters may have had grand days to recount around the campfire about the great beasts they felled with their bows. But their days were also tainted with stories of hunters who didn't return because the beasts ultimately proved too great to slay. Native Americans locked in tribal battle with hostile foes for decades had many a bad day with bow in hand, arrow in flesh. Ancient skeletons from primitive cultures with flint, copper, and bronze arrowheads imbedded in bone only hint at the many bad days afield with bows and arrows. For the legions of Roman archers on the battlefields during the Byzantine era, their glory was tainted with blood and pain. For waves of Crusaders who ventured east to reclaim the Holy Land for the pope, the hiss of an arrow was perhaps the final sound to reach their ears. For the longbowmen on the killing grounds at Agincourt, shooting their yew bows was gruesome business that blurred with mud and blood over countless days in the Hundred Year's War that consumed nations. For Ishi and the last of his native tribe, the precious bow proved insufficient to defend their final strongholds in a virgin continent against the land lust of the endless waves of white men. Nonetheless, Ishi passed on his great love for the bow to a white doctor named Pope. And Pope, with his crude homemade gear, ultimately inspired our fathers of modern bowhunting.

So really, when put in the vivid perspectives of time, circumstance, and space, this is unquestionably the best time ever to be a traditional archer. Hopefully, with full appreciation of that fact, you can now sit back and enjoy the following pages to help you savor the history and richness of today's world of bows and arrows.

Venture onward friend, and share the spirit that has brought you this far.

Chapter Two

THE EARLY ONES

A faint rustle from the brush ahead sent the two boys diving among the broken rocks near the creek. It was a poor place to hide, but circumstance gave them little choice. Their naked bodies were covered with red dust that clung in patches to the sweat-lined wrinkles around their necks and frightened eyes. Neither one dared breathe as they heard the padded footfalls approaching.

Straining, in slow snakelike movements, the boys contorted their bronzed bodies to conform with crevices in the broken rocks. Their brown eyes exchanged expressions of fear and excitement. Suddenly, a menacing shadow darkened their faces and paused near their hiding place.

Like their little brother the rock lizard, the boys slowly squinted and stopped all outward expression of life. Tightened stomachs ached as they breathed in harmony with the distant floating clouds. To become one with the lifeless red rocks was their only hope.

Soon, the feared one resumed her steady pace up the narrow trail to the woods. She was carrying her wood gathering harness and water skin. Today, they would be safe. The boys emerged from the rocks, grinning in triumph, and continued down the path to the base of the great cliff.

The feared one was Uni-na, the old crazy hag. Her ancient withered face held deep-set, blackened eyes that could cast a wicked curse on a child. The evil spirits that haunted the distant singing caves sometimes traveled on the north winds and entered the old woman's head, sending her into a rage. When touched by these spirits, she wandered about casting evil curses on children reckless enough to get caught in her path.

The adults in the village paid little attention to her odd behavior. They knew she was the harmless crazy one. The children, however, ran wild-eyed into the hills, hiding until the old woman tired and wandered back to her hut near the overhang of the great cliff.

Uni-na was forced to live there, isolated from the rest of the village, where her crazy antics wouldn't disrupt the harmonious tribe. Even though she was struck by the spirits, the old crazy one could not be completely banished from the tribe. She was the woman of the tribe's creator of man-nee, Chu-no-wa-yahi, the crafter of the bow.

Like two graceful deer, the boys trotted down the trail to the base of the great cliff where the bowmaker lived. There, squatting next to a smoldering morning fire, the old man stirred the embers. The boys saw past the ragged furs, the matted grey hair, and the leathery skin draped over the hunched pile of gnarled bones. In their eyes he would remain the mighty warrior Chu-no-wa-yahi.

From the corner of his eye the old man saw the boys approaching, but ignored them and began a low guttural chant while he continued working on an unborn bow. The boys knew the chant was the old warrior's special way of greeting them. Even though he cherished their bright faces near his fire, the old bowmaker was too proud to openly greet the boys. With eyes full of admiration, the two slowly crept near the fire pit, kneeling in the reddish dust near the old man.

When his audience settled, the bowmaker's chant turned into the broken song of an ancient tribal tale. Chu-no-wa-yahi's story was of the great hunter Yano-ni-yahi, who discovered the hidden valley of the white deer. As his quivering, rhythmic song entranced the boys, Chu-no-wa-yahi continued his meticulous crafting of the bow cradled over his shoulder. Spellbound, the youths wondered if the ancient magic from the story was flowing from the old man's hands into the emerging bow.

Several high pitched fawn bleats passed from Chu-no-wa-yahi's pressed lips, as he recounted how Yano-ni-yahi lured the snow white doe into bow range by imitating a distressed fawn. As the old man fashioned the bow, the growling rasps of sandstone against juniper intensified the description of Yano-ni-yahi's pounding heart and the final gasps of the great white deer. When the old bow crafter finally reached the legend's climax, the boys were amazed to see that he had transformed the rough juniper stave into the fine outline of a young bow.

The old bowmaker saw in their eyes that the boys were anxious to become men and receive their tribal bows, but two acorn harvests would pass before they could enter the men's lodge and become young warriors. Chu-no-wa-yahi tried to quiet their restless spirits by telling them that the staves they had helped gather would be ready to become bows when they became men.

Earlier that spring, the boys had helped the old bowmaker gather straight juniper staves from the shadowed slopes of Waganupa, the great mountain two days north of the village. Chu-no-wa-yahi would slowly wander through the stands of juniper, carefully selecting the straightest and strongest branches. Usually, these were the lower branches which grew slowly from lack of sunlight. After spying a perfect branch, he would have the agile youths carefully whittle off the stave.

Their young arms knotted in pain during the endless job of gently whittling free the tough branch. Although they were tempted to hack at the stubborn wood with the flint hand axe, they knew it was strictly forbidden by the old bow crafter. Hacking at the branch or attempting to break it could cause unseen lengthwise cracks that would make the stave useless for crafting a fine bow. The boys learned that prized staves were to be treated with the same gentleness as a helpless newborn.

Once gathered, the staves were taken back to the village near the base of the great cliff. There they were carefully split in half and bundled together with straight pieces of seasoned wood to keep them straight during aging. With the sapwood facing down, the staves were laid on wooden racks deep in a crevice at the base of the cliff. Protected from rain and sun, the winds of many seasons would slowly age the staves until it was their time to become bows.

The old bowmaker knew when a piece of juniper was ready to be crafted into a bow. He carefully inspected a prospective stave, first with searching eyes, and then with his calloused, tactile hands. He flexed it between his powerfully outstretched arms, and tested the sapwood with his thumbnail. Finally, he smelled the split portion of the juniper, searching for the telltale aroma of a ripely seasoned piece. Chu-no-wa-yahi told the boys how a piece of juniper, ready to be born into a bow, whispers softly to the eyes, nose, and hands: "I am strong. I am worthy. I am ready."

After the staves were cut and seasoned, the boys would not touch them. Soon they would be bows and tribal custom strictly forbade children and women from touching man-nee. If by some careless act the bow was touched by a woman or child, it was taken to the river and washed thoroughly in sand and water. This cleansing from the earth removed any bad luck cast on man-nee by forbidden hands.

Using small flint or obsidian scraping tools and pieces of sandstone, Chu-no-wa-yahi fashioned the rough staves. He never wasted a movement. His withered hands glided gracefully back and forth like winging cliff swallows as he shaped the emerging bow. He preferred crafting during the mornings when the sun reflected off the great cliff and illuminated the wood, revealing the fine grain within, guiding his skilled hands along the emerging lines of power and grace.

Once a flatbow was rough shaped, the old warrior trimmed both ends until the bow spanned from his outstretched hand to his opposite hip. Using a small piece of rounded sandstone, he gently smoothed all surfaces until they flowed together in one harmonious contour. The old crafter taught the boys that the power and smoothness within man-nee depended on the perfect blending of the flat limbs into the rounded, narrower ends, and the thicker handle.

During the final sanding, Chu-no-wa-yahi would string a bow with a long sinew cord and gently draw back the string with his hand while holding the center of the bow with his outstretched foot. By raising his leg, his skilled eye could easily survey the bending arc of man-nee to ensure the balance and symmetry of both limbs. He taught the boys that the limbs must be shaped to bend in a perfect arc and in harmony, like the sweeping wings of the great eagle in flight.

When finished sanding, the bowmaker would lean into the glowing embers of the fire and scrape away smoldering coals from two large rocks near the edge of the pit. Squinting from the hot smoke, his ancient face sometimes looked more frightening than the crazy old hag. After the embers were cleared, the old man would wedge one end of the bow between the closely spaced rocks and gently begin bending the tip until it weakened from the heat. Once the tip was bent into a slight recurve, it was held in place between two cool rocks in the shade of the wood pile. When both ends were bent and set, the tips were slightly trimmed on the edges to accept the deer sinew bowstring.

Once man-nee was shaped into its final form, it was time for both bow and crafter to rest. Chu-no-wa-yahi would gently lay the emerging bow flat on a grass mat near the back of his crowded hut. There, the bow rested, face upward, for a full day before the tedious work of backing the new weapon began. He told the boys that man-nee, like the newborn fawn, must rest after the first day of creation.

The old man often employed the energies of tribal children to chew dried sinew from deer leg tendons into a soft workable form. While the children sat near the fire with puffed mouths full of fibrous sinew, the old bow crafter would prepare a fresh pot of salmon skin glue. The pungent aroma from the bubbling mixture and the constant chewing of dried deer tendons quieted both the appetite and the conversation of the youths squatted around the fire.

Before summoning the children to his fireside, the old man would send Uni-na, the crazy one, down river for the day to collect fresh willow bark for wrapping the bow. Although she had been his woman since their youth, he could not have her near his fire when he needed unworn teeth and tireless jaws to help prepare the sinew.

Once chewed, the sinew was separated into soft fibers, and soaked in a diluted mixture of salmon glue while the old man roughened the bow back with a coarse piece of sandstone. Chu-no-wa-yahi would then apply overlapping layers of the sticky sinew along the back of the bow. His glue-covered hands looked like two squat spiders spinning the sticky strands of sinew up and down the bow. After gluing several layers of sinew, he tightly wrapped the bow in fresh willow bark.

Protected in the back of Chu-no-wa-yahi's hut, the new bow rested for several weeks while the sinew and glue mixture cured. When it was dried, the bowmaker removed the willow bark and sanded the ragged edges of the sinew with a small piece of red sandstone. He would then hand-rub more hot salmon glue over the entire bow until it shined smooth like a wet snake. Finally, he wrapped a buckskin thong around the handle section. Chu-no-wa-yahi fashioned the leather grip with great care to exactly fit the hand of the new owner, allowing the bow and the hunter to function as one.

As a young man, Chu-no-wa-yahi had been praised as one of the most skillful hunters of the village. While hunting, his bow was a part of him; an extension of his spirit. His shots at running deer and flying fowl were already entwined into the village's evening fireside stories. Over the years, his great love and respect for the bow had grown into a fascination for crafting the finest bows in the land. And now, every hunter in the village owned and treasured one of Chu-no-wa-yahi's magical creations. Although other men in the village made adequate bows, none matched the beauty or performance of those that emerged from the fireside of Chu-no-wa-yahi. In the hands of a patient hunter, his bows seldom failed to bring home needed game for the village. They were truly magic.

The old man's skill at crafting bows was also respected by tribes in the far hills to the east and north. Although others from different villages had tried to make bows similar to Chu-no-wa-yahi's, they failed to achieve the mystical performance of the old crafter's bows. They somehow lacked the special combination of knowledge, skill, patience, and the great love for bows that Chu-no-wa-yahi held in his heart. To the old man, creating a bow was not a labor — it was his love, it was his spirit, it was his existence.

The two boys yearned to create bows like Chu-no-wa-yahi and spent hours watching as he passed on more of his sacred craft to them. They, in turn, brightened his heart with their youthful, sparkling faces at his fireside. Surprisingly, the days passed without the disturbing thoughts or fire-side talk of Saltu, the hated white men who were beginning to invade the lowlands to the west. Like a dark cloud within his heart, the old man feared that it was a matter of time before the dreaded white men came into the hills and forced the tribe back into the harsh canyons that only the deer and the eagle called home.

But days with the young boys were peaceful and comforting. They reminded him of his youth, and at night he dreamt of hunting deer when he was young, and in his sleep, his arms drew the imaginary bow intertwined with his spirit.

After leaving Chu-no-wa-yahi each evening, the two boys walked up the trail back to the village, and carried in their hearts a special bond with the old man. At day's end, they renewed their vows to one another: they would continue to learn the sacred crafting of man-nee from Chu-no-wa-yahi, they would also pass the craft on to their sons.

As they said a silent good-night to one another with a meeting of the eyes, they knew in their hearts that someday they too would be the pride of the village like old Chu-no-wa-yahi, the legendary Yana crafter of man-nee, the creator of the bow.

Chapter Three

PREDATOR TRADITIONAL BOWS

TWO SHOTS TO REMEMBER

It happened years ago and the mists of time should have clouded the memory. Yet I can still see it as if it had happened yesterday. I can still hear the whack of the arrow as it hit.

It was at one of the big sportsman shows held at the Novi Expo center near Detroit. A few hundred spectators crowded behind the shooting line where some of the nation's top archers had been gathered for a shooting demonstration. The master of ceremonies stood behind the shooters with his microphone, announcing their credentials and giving a terse description of their archery gear. Four new foam deer targets with three-inch red paper dots in the kill zone stood 25 yards down range.

The first up was some IBO champ or pro staffer who zinged two arrows from his compound into one of the 3-D deer. The arrows pinned the edges of the red dot on the side of the target. The man swaggered away from the line with the confidence that most pros need to take home their prize money. Polite applause filtered through the crowd.

Another pro shooter of some ranking stepped up and repeated the feat with his compound. His long stabilizers hummed with each slap of the bow-string. This time the two arrows huddled in one another's shadow. More applause.

Murmurs rippled through the spectators as a young lady on the U.S. Olympic team stepped to the shooting line. She drew her graceful recurve, poised in perfect form until she drew the tip of the arrow past the clicker on her riser and the arrow leaped from the bow. It sailed into the fresh dot on another target. A hush settled over the crowd as she drew her second arrow. Her next shaft creased the outside edge of the dot. The applause rose into a mix of hoots and cheers. Yeah, a recurve bow with the right person behind it was really something worth watching. She smiled and waved to the onlookers. They smiled and waved back. The gal and her shooting were both things of beauty to behold.

Finally, the announcer introduced the last shooter, a bowhunter shooting a 70-pound recurve of all things. He was some last-minute fill-in to show the crowd that some people still bowhunteddeer with an old-fashioned stick 'n' string. And to top it off, the guy had made his own bow and was displaying them at a booth in the show.

Snickers arose from the throng. I could almost feel the poor guy's guts twisting as he shuffled up to the line. His eyes nervously flicked back and forth from the remaining 3-D target to the floor near his feet as if he were hoping some hole would suddenly open up so he could escape the trap he was in. The only thing visibly remarkable about the guy was the apparent state of shock of being cast into the limelight plus having to perform with homemade traditional gear in front of world-class shooters. No, this wasn't going to be pretty.

I'd shot enough bows in competition to see a man defeated before he even tried. He hardly looked stout enough to handle the heavy draw weight. Shoulders slumped, he nocked an arrow and sighed heavily. He lifted his chin and gazed at the target, almost squinting. Then in a heartbeat he was someplace else, someone else from the shaken man who had stood there only seconds before.

With fluid moment, he drew, held a rock-solid anchor, exhaled and pulled cleanly through the string with back tension until a little string clicker on his limb made a barely audible "tick." The arrow smacked dead center in the small dot. He didn't appear to hear the cursing and gasps of surprise that came from the crowd as he drew his second arrow. He held this one at full draw even longer than the first, until his muscles began to tremble. Ah ha, now the truth would come out. But as he pulled on the bowstring, the quiver in his arm locked for a second, the clicker clicked, and the arrow jumped from the bow.

From a 70-pound recurve at 25 yards it's hard to clearly see the arrow in flight. But it was clear for everyone to see it when it rattled tightly against the first arrow in the dead center of the dot. Everybody in the place that day appeared shocked that some frumpy looking average Joe with a recurve could outshoot two pro compound shooters with release aids and an Olympic shooter, all using sights and stabilizers. The only person who didn't look stunned was the recurve shooter who pulled his arrows quickly and with relief, shrugged almost apologetically to the pros, then vanished off to the side.

Two things struck me that day about Ron Pittsley shooting his "home-made" Predator recurve in front of all those people — the honed shooting skills of the instinctive archer and his classic recurve were perhaps the two most impressive traditional things I had ever seen in public.

"There was so much pressure with all those people watching me," recalled Pittsley, over fifteen years later, "that I felt pretty inferior because I was trying to perform at something where I wasn't even in the same league as those pro target shooters.

"So I pretty much escaped into a tunnel vision and tried to focus on the shot. Somehow I managed to make two good shots into the target. They looked pretty good in comparison to the pros but I think it was because I was so stressed that I became more focused than anyone else shooting.

"But without question, I couldn't have done that in front of all those people without the clicker making me go through all the steps of proper shooting form that required 110 percent of my concentration. Those steps are drawing the bow, reaching full draw, establishing a solid anchor, aiming, holding on the target, and increasing back tension until that clicker went off and told me it was time to shoot the arrow. I think that consistently good shots need to be partially "mindless" and the Crick-It allows that to happen."

THE ESSENCE OF SHOOTING

Ask a dozen traditional shooters what they want to achieve more than anything else in the sport and they will likely say they "want to shoot the perfect arrow." For most archers, that simple, single act is the essence of shooting traditional gear. But of course it's not so simple to achieve. Then if you ask them to define what shooting a perfect arrow means, they will include a few cornerstones such as being in control of the shot, having perfect form, and hitting exactly where they're aiming. That all makes sense. However, if you watch that same dozen shooters on the practice line, few if any can achieve what they want most from shooting their bows—because few are in control of their shot, or demonstrate perfect form, or end up hitting where they're aiming. Sorry, but it's true. That fact alone is the biggest fundamental reason why so many people drop out of traditional archery. That's also why the same number who enthusiastically try traditional archery each year almost equals the same number who drop out from shooting frustration. And that's why the number of traditional archers who actively shoot traditional gear remains relatively constant. Perhaps the saddest part of all is that most of them who eventually drop out could actually learn how to shoot that perfect arrow if they had the right help. Recognizing that, then getting the help they need is the key to someone finding either fulfillment or disappointment in the essence of shooting. *(If you read nothing else in this entire book, and wish to remain a traditional archer, take a moment to re-read this pivotal paragraph then honestly ask yourself where you fit in and what you want from traditional archery.)*

Even legends such as Fred Bear and Ben Pearson both had the malady of *target panic*, which is the psychological inability to reach full draw and aim at a target. In fact, the vast majority of archers shooting longbows and recurves eventually struggle with this affliction that prevents them from becoming fulfilled at something they so desperately want fulfillment in. At one time Ron Pittsley was also overcome with target panic. Yet unlike the thousands who have abandoned the sport because they couldn't conquer it, Pittsley not only beat it to become one of the best instinctive shots in the nation, he perfected ways for everyone to beat it—and achieve the essence of shooting in traditional archery.

"The biggest challenge facing most traditional archers," says Pittsley, "is becoming proficient enough with their choice in bows to remain gratified with the sport over time. In traditional archery it's definitely harder to make the arrow go where you want because of all the things the shooter has to do right every time. There's a whole lot of open space around that target and a lot of places to hit other than the bull's-eye. And it's all just waiting for you to hit anywhere when you to do anything wrong. Those are some of the things that make traditional archery so unforgiving.

"So first, you have to realize that archery, like a lot of shooting disciplines, requires practice and form. Shooting well doesn't come from a mood or a good feeling. It requires proper and very deliberate physical actions to get the desired results. And that's not a very easy concept for the masses to get a hold of. They tend to approach it more from an attitude of, hey, let's just grab this thing to go shoot it and have fun. Sure, it's fun hitting what you're aiming at and that sometimes becomes a real distraction for most shooters.

"The solution is first getting a realistic grasp on what it takes to 'feel good' about a shot. In part, if you want to feel good about picking up that bow and going out the door, you have to embrace practice habits with defined goals and make it a true discipline. Too many people approach their shooting with the attitude of *hoping* to be good at it. But few ever become really good with the *I hope I can* attitude."

During medieval times, it was common for archers in warfare to shoot 90-pound longbows—about the physical limits of a robust man back then. Of course, they were tough dudes who didn't work in an office all day. They lived or died by their ability to shoot heavy bows long distances. But today's archer doesn't need to shoot a heavy bow to survive. In fact, shooting too heavy of a draw weight inhibits the accuracy of most archers. Even though bow weights have come down since we stopped going to war with them, many archers have been over-bowed with too much draw weight since the resurgence of traditional archery. And that contributes greatly to causing target panic and poor shooting. The good news for traditional archery however is that bows weights have been coming down in recent years. Most bowyers, including Pittsley, note that the average bow going out the shop door has dropped 10 to 12 pounds in draw weight. This coming out of the Dark Ages in bow weight is good news for shooters and their form.

"To shoot really well," says Pittsley, "you need to learn to anchor, aim, release with back tension, and follow through. But you can't do all that when you're over-bowed like so many shooters have been over the years. That prevents you from getting to step two, which is perfecting proper shooting form. Because without that, you can't refine your confidence and you can't acquire the skills to become gratified with shooting. That's why so many people get frustrated and quit."

CRICK-IT TO THE RESCUE

Pittsley openly admits that he too was struggling desperately once with becoming the traditional shooter he wanted to be. However, the more he struggled, the worse his shooting got, until he almost threw in the towel. "Like many people in their early years of bowhunting, I wanted to succeed so badly. But there wasn't any chance of that because I was trying to learn to shoot well exclusively while bowhunting. And bowhunting is not a good arena to learn how to shoot a bow because you're under tremendous pressure that causes you to screw up, which manifests itself into more self-doubt. I was so frustrated as a bowhunter I was ready to go out and buy a bowling ball.

"I had heard of a draw check that helped people reach and maintain an anchor and execute back tension. So I made my own draw check using a toggle switch from the dashboard of a junk car that I duct-taped to my bow. The toggle switch clicked when I reached full draw and it instantly took my mind off what I was doing wrong and made me start to focus on what I needed to do right. Suddenly for the first time, I could see and feel what it was like to shoot a bow properly. From that point on, it's just a matter of perfecting form and execution.

"I still shoot with a draw check that I've redesigned and I always will. It's a good device for maintaining shooting form. At this point in my shooting career it's second nature and like an old friend. For most traditional shooters it's an absolute must to help them get on track because so many archers don't even know what it feels like to truly draw a bow all the way to anchor, hold it, and aim it solidly, then release with proper back tension. But a Crick-It can definitely help someone get into that shooting mode almost instantly."

After Pittsley discovered how the draw check clicker changed his shooting, he began selling the ones made at the time. Almost

Perhaps one of the most unknown truly great traditional shots in the country, Pittsley uses a combination of high anchor, a slight bow cant, and full concentration on form—with the psychological help of his Crick-It.

overnight, many of the shooters at his local archery club using clickers and his Predator recurves became some of the top shots in the state. Yet as good as the clicker was, Pittsley saw some ways to make it better. "With the help of a buddy, I refined the design to one that was more aesthetically pleasing and less intrusive on the bow. The new design also worked a little better with less foot-pounds of pull to make it click. After we made the refinements, we began making them as the Crick-It draw check and the product is still going strong."

Always coming from his soft-sell perspective, Pittsley focuses mostly on helping other people to enjoy the sport more and not drop out. "No, the Crick-It isn't for everyone. First, you need to ask yourself honestly if you're fully satisfied or dissatisfied with your shooting. If you're dissatisfied or want to improve, by all means consider everything to help you improve. That can be either good instruction from a qualified shooter or a draw check like a Crick-It. Unfortunately for most people, instruction alone can't conquer the target panic that is causing their poor shooting. It's almost impossible in fact. So the Crick-It offers an opportunity for any archer to instantly see and feel the proper shot. But it isn't a magic bean. It's simply a little tool that will help shooters achieve a path of success in learning how to draw, anchor, aim, and shoot an arrow with back tension. And man, that catapults you way ahead in the archery game.

"The real gratification in making the Crick-It is seeing people who are frustrated with archery getting this simple little device, putting it on their bow, and suddenly seeing how to achieve what they have been trying to accomplish for so long. Then they have the choice of setting a goal of shooting a Crick-It their whole life like me, or just putting it on their bow for three months until they learn how to shoot a bow with proper, consistent form."

The Crick-It draw check has proven a simple and effective cure for thousands of archers conquering target panic.

Despite its redeeming remedies for poor shooting and target panic, the Crick-It still comes under fire from certain traditionalists. How can you put a small piece of metal and string on a traditional bow and still call it "traditional"? For those caught up more in idealistic definitions and less in learning how to shoot a bow with consistent confidence there will always be that debate. However, a growing number of traditional bowhunters who are honest about their shooting skills under pressure and ethics afield believe that it's more important to shoot the best arrow they can from their traditional bow rather than risk a poor shot that could haunt them for years. Nonetheless, the debate continues, and in the end, all individuals must wrestle with their value systems and ethics to ultimately guide themselves to a decision that makes them feel right about their approach to shooting traditional style bows. Heck, some people still debate whether fiberglass on bow limbs or Fastflight bowstrings are really "traditional."

UNCOMMON MARKET VIEW

Unlike most of his bowyer counterparts, Ron Pittsley has worked professionally in both small and large scale within the bowmaking industry. He began making his Predator takedown recurves in the late 1980s after building a few bows with his friend Mike St Johns. After perfecting his limb and riser designs, Pittsley began selling the first prototypes of the Predator in 1988. Making the bows in the back room of a radiator auto shop that he owned at the time, he began selling them locally.

Almost overnight, their classic look combined with the way they shot made them commonplace at his local archery club. Soon word spread nationally and the Predator takedown recurve became firmly established as a top performing bow.

By 1995 the owner of Darton Archery in Michigan, a bow company with a long history in recurves, took a special interest in Pittsley's design. They were so interested in fact, that in 1996 Darton hired Pittsley to head up their reviving recurve manufacturing business, and to make the Predator for their recurve line of bows. By the year 2000, it became clear that trying to introduce custom recurves into a compound-dominated dealer market was fraught with too many challenges. However, Pittsley continued marketing Darton's full line of bows until 2005. Then it was time to return to his roots in archery. He left Darton and resumed his custom bowmaking business in a small shop near his home in East Tawas, located in northeast Michigan. There, under the new name "Hunter's Niche," and with the help of business partner, Mike Hoadley, Pittsley makes Predator bows, Flemish weave bowstrings, and the Crick-It draw check. And through all the changes in the past twenty years, Pittsley has gained an uncommonly broad perspective of the archery industry.

"All shooting sports are declining," notes Pittsley with a genuine tone of concern in his voice, "and blood sports are on the chopping block more than any. However, archery is somewhat insulated from that because it has become more of a family sport and a form of weekend entertainment. As people shoot their bows for fun, it's natural for them to think, hey, I can use this thing for hunting. Then they quickly graduate from carp to elk. So really, archery has perhaps the strongest foundation of any of the shooting sports for the future.

"Within the sport of traditional archery, you have two main groups of people. First there are those who have done it forever and have no interest in doing it any other way. Then there's the transitional archer who has moved to traditional archery from the high-tech side from boredom. There are also a few new to the sport who feel

A younger Ron Pittsley field testing an early Predator design on this dandy Iowa whitetail.

that traditional archery is where they should begin. But no matter how they get into it, the bottom line is that shooting a traditional bow draws people's interest because they are just so much fun to shoot."

FUN TO SHOOT — PRETTY TO LOOK AT

The foundation of a traditional bow that is fun to shoot hinges on a bow design that best converts the archer's energy into launching an arrow accurately at the target. That's sounds simple enough. However, the characteristics that make an ideal design can become pretty complex. The Predator recurve is a takedown bow, so the actual working portion is confined to the limbs. The limb design evolved during the early years of development of the Predator and hasn't changed since Pittsley discovered the ideal balance between speed (AMO speed of 204 feet-per-second, independently tested) and shooting stability. "The limb we build now is essentially the same Predator design that I took into Darton Archery years ago and came back out the door with. It's been proven by others that it's going to store energy well and be efficient in delivering that energy with good arrow speed. So from that point of the view, it's a very good working limb from a pack of

Despite his experience within a large archery company, Pittsley still uses good old elbow grease and a skilled eye to put the custom finishing touches on shaping his risers.

many.

"That's important because what makes any bow perform is 90 percent in the limb design of how those limbs store your physical energy and how it delivers that energy to the arrow in efficiency. Without the mechanical advantages that you get shooting a compound bow, the traditional archer can actually feel and see all of the bow's function when they shoot it. So if you have a design that works well, the remaining quality of a bow is about how pretty you can make it look and your understanding about everything with materials and construction so that it holds up over time."

In making his bow limbs, Pittsley follows a combination of convention and modern manufacturing techniques. The workhorses of his limb manufacturing are his huge limb presses. They appear like Goliath things compared to a few simple metal bands and C-clamps used by some old-time bowyers. His big industrial presses weigh over 1500 pounds each and use a two-stage operation. First, they hydraulically come together to encase the limb laminates, then use air pressure in an air hose to exert the final uniform pressure across the limb composites. "It's important to have limb presses that are large and rigid." Pittsley notes. "After the air hose presses the forms together, a uniform heat-strip heats the laminations evenly to cure the glues."

Though the huge limb presses look like overkill for a small custom bowmaking operation, Ron points out that they are simply part of an overall procedure that requires knowledge and attention to production standards that he honed at Darton. "Making a composite laminated bow these days is

Making limbs and riser in perfect alignment is a critical process. Here Pittsley uses a special machined metal riser and machinist's table with some custom jigs in making perfectly aligned interchangeable limbs.

The massiveness of Predator's industrial-strength limb presses insure the integrity of the valuable limb forms and solid lamination of the composites.

pretty common knowledge and overall it hasn't changed much in the past 20 years. What has changed for me is the technical knowledge I've gained of how to produce a bow more proficiently and understand when those procedures are right or wrong. In short, when you're in more control of all the various techniques and materials of making a bow, you make a better bow. And the biggest challenge there is laminating up layers of wood and fiberglass with the proper glues and techniques that are designed for this industry—because it's pretty tough to hold those pieces together in a working bow over time."

For limb core materials under clear or black fiberglass, Pittsley often uses laminated maple Actionwood or solid maple. Bamboo has also become a popular corewood of choice. They also offer limb cores in some exotics,

Predator risers blend 21st century materials such as black Phenolic and resin-impregnated woods with classic lines from the 1950s.

red elm and black locust. "If you just want stable performance, maple is technically the best corewood. If you want a combination of good looks and stability, red elm and black locust are my two top choices."

Ron builds his riser sections with multiple laminated layers of woods with stripes and strips that offer good looks blended with strength. Unlike many traditional bowmakers, Pittsley also uses various synthetics such as Phenolic and Mycarta, which are paper and cloth resin materials common to other manufacturing industries. "They're really different and fun stuff to work with," says Pittsley. "Most people are looking for things that are different and we blend them with exotic woods such as bubinga, which is African rosewood. It's a good, heavy, strong, durable wood, and it's reasonable to work with. We also use other exotics such as bocote, cocobolo, ebony, and a host of others. One thing I've used that most bowmakers don't is maple impregnated with acrylic resin. It really stabilizes the wood and gives it mass weight, more strength, and neat colors. The nice thing is that with so many good choices in materials, we can match those variations to the beauty in the eye of the beholder."

Despite some of the high-tech production techniques and materials that go into a Predator, its classic appearance harkens back to the heydays of traditional archery. So does Pittsley's recommendation on bow weight. He notes that one of the reasons that archers from the 1950s and 60s shot so well, was that they usually shot recurves in the 45-pound range. During the first big resurgence of traditional archery in the 1980s, archers upped their draw weights to between 60 and 70 pounds. Perhaps it was a macho thing or the image of big men like Howard Hill who could handle heavy bows. Whatever the reason, being so over-bowed resulted in a lot of archers not being able to accurately and comfortably handle their bows. Today, the average Predator going out the door is in the 50-pound range. And ideally, having a second pair of limbs in the 40-pound range is a smart option for archers to use to comfortably hone there shooting form.

HEROES AND DREAMS

Even Pittsley admits that trying to emulate the heroes in traditional archery decades ago caused most shooters to reach beyond their practical physical limits, including himself. But those heroes also offered us the tantalizing allure of shooting recurves and longbows. They also made us reach for our dreams of bowhunting adventure. "There are a lot of people who have made notable contributions to archery since its modern inception in the 40s and 50s. However, the heroes from yesteryear like Fred Bear, Ben Pearson, and Howard Hill actually created our sport. They defined it and made it what it is today. They functioned by vision rather than by ego. And you can't really reproduce that kind of hero in archery today. Those founding fathers of archery and bowhunting only come around once in a lifetime."

Inspired by the movie adventures of his long-time Michigan hero, Fred Bear, Ron Pittsley dreamed of chasing massive antlered creatures across North America with his recurve. And when his Predator started to sell in the early years, he began feeding that thirst for grand adventure by diving headlong into his bowhunting.

One such trip took him to the wilderness of Quebec where he got to prove both his nerve and the ability of his Predator bow. It was late September and moose were full in the rut. Despite a long week in the bush traversing lakes and rivers in canoes and calling in earnest, only one small bull sauntered within bow range. Before Pittsley and his hunting buddies knew it, the week was almost over. They packed up and headed back to the main outpost for a shower and hot meal before heading home.

With only a few hours remaining before he had to leave, Pittsley and his partner headed out into the darkness for one final morning hunt near the lodge. Only days before, an elderly bear hunter had been watching a setup down a logging trail when he was supposedly "chased off" by an angry bull moose. So Pittsley and his partner walked down that trail at first light under the glow of a cloudless sky.

The air hung still in dead silence. His partner bellowed into the dawn with a homemade moose call. Immediately a bull answered. "Wouka!" It was less than 200 yards and coming, so the hunters set up a quick ambush. On the second bellow from the call, a chorus of moose talk echoed through the timber from the valley below. The angry calls of two cows in heat told the unfolding story. They didn't want their boyfriend wandering off from his duties. Despite a heated exchange of cow calls, the soft grunting of the bull confirmed that he was not only staying with his cows, but moving off in the opposite direction.

Pittsley and his buddy quickly changed tactics. If the bull wouldn't come for love, perhaps he'd come for a fight. By the sounds of their calls, the moose had already moved off several hundred yards so the hunters quickly closed the gap to within 100 yards. Using a slab of wood from a lightning-shattered tree, Ron's buddy began raking the brush while letting out some

Point-blank bull — Pittsley (on right with beard) and his calling partner lured this old bull within spitting distance before he drove home a broadhead from his 70-pound Predator.

crisp challenge grunts, trying to sound like a younger bull. The response from the big bull was instantaneous. He let out a challenge grunt of his own and began plowing his way through the timber, breaking over saplings as he closed the gap. With little place to hide, Pittsley crouched behind a lone stump 20 yards in front of his buddy.

For those who haven't witnessed it, there's a deep sense of awe to suddenly seeing a half-ton of bull moose appear from seemingly nowhere. The second wave of adrenaline hits when it's lumbering straight for you.

Either fate or luck had placed that lone stump there years before, and now Pittsley hugged its outline as the bull moose walked directly toward him. At 20 yards, Pittsley drew his recurve and held. The moose came onward. At 10 yards the bull paused and looked in the direction of the caller. Ron knew a frontal shot was reckless and held the 70 pounds with determination. The bull lowered his head and grunted, then resumed his approach. At 5 yards, the bull had to turn slightly broadside to get past the stump. When it did, Pittsley's arrow sliced through the bull's chest behind the shoulder and sailed down through the timber. The bull grunted and ran wildly downhill past the other hunter who sent another arrow into the bull. Seconds later, Pittsley rose on weak knees to watch the record-class bull topple over in the nearby trail.

On the surface, Pittsley's moose may sound like just another bowhunting story. But on closer inspection, it reveals the character of the man.

First, most other hunters in the party had already given up. It had been a long week filled with dashed hopes. Despite the poor odds of hunting one final morning so close to the lodge, Pittsley showed a hint of the determination that follows him in his bowmaking and bowhunting.

Secondly, when things didn't work as planned with the cow calls, Pittsley remained versatile and quickly changed tactics with his partner. From the moment he left the lodge, he never lost sight of his quest or wavered in his commitment. He does the same in his bowmaking.

Being at full draw on a grunting moose at 10 yards would have tempted many a bowhunter to release the string and hope for the best on the frontal shot. But Pittsley knew better and would rather miss the opportunity altogether than take a poor one. Few hunters could have remained so rock steady holding 70 pounds at full draw, waiting for the right window of opportunity. But years of training physically and mentally on when to shoot with all your confidence helped him hold back for the right shot.

So in the end, the story isn't about some lucky sap who just happened to sit behind the right stump and arrow a moose at 4 yards that anyone could have hit. It's a story more about the fiber of a man and how he lives his life. It's the story of a modern-day predator and the bow he builds which carries that concept into the hands and hearts of traditional archers. However, if you ask him to recount his moose hunt or the host of other big game he has taken across North America with his recurve, you'll also discover a man almost painfully shy at times, who, like his hero Fred Bear, would rather talk about your bowhunting accomplishments than try to bask in any limelight of his own.

LOOKING AHEAD

Despite the downward trends in most of the shooting sports nowadays, Ron remains optimistic about the future of old-time archery. He bases his opinions on years of working in a variety of jobs within the overall archery industry, from selling Predator recurves to Darton compounds. "In my experience in promoting archery within large and small archery companies, I never tried to let myself get pigeon holed as an archer. That's one reason I welcome all archers, including compound archers. I think it's important to gain a much broader view of how the shrinking sport of archery is functioning within our world, and the open-mindedness that it takes to promote it."

Part of Pittsley's optimism is knowing that the captivating allure of the romantic roots of archery will prevail through time — as it has for almost a hundred years since Ishi walked out of the hills of northern California and wound up in the care of Dr. Saxton Pope. "Another reason that I think traditional archery has a solid future is because it captures such a broad cross section of archers today. That's based upon the fact that there are a lot of archers moving around more within the sport of archery through interest in new challenges or boredom in what they're doing. And more and more of them are landing in traditional archery because that's the natural progression of things. It's almost ironic that traditional archery is the spot where many people end up looking for something 'new' in archery and bowhunting."

Pittsley cautions that the promising future of traditional archery doesn't rest in the hands of fate alone. Like anything worth preserving, it takes promotion and planting seeds well into the future. "For archery to continue to be strong," he says, "we need to get back into making it an all family event and make it fun for everyone with more target shooting events. That fulfills the need of a lot of families looking for more outdoor things to do as a family. This would expose more of the population to the sport and could actually make it more of a growth sport. That could result in more people eventually trying things like bowfishing for carp, which could evolve into trying for moose.

"Of course we all need to help the sport by passing it on to friends and peers by inviting them to try it. Simply invite them to try bowfishing. Man, there's nothing more fun than that. On a bigger scale there are people like Roy Grimes in Kentucky who started the National Archery in the Schools Program. That program got archery back into our schools, which is going like gangbusters now. We need to tip our hats to people like Roy because he was seeking a vision with NASP and not just personal notoriety."

In his own little corner of the world, Pittsley is passing on his archery heritage to his three sons: Myles, Trevor and Logan, who all shoot bows with zeal. Myles and Trevor, who are actually young men, have become bowhunting fanatics.

Despite the sometimes overcrowded world of traditional bowmaking, Pittsley also sees a glimmer of promise, even in his competition. "It's interesting how archery history is repeating itself on a smaller scale within the traditional bow market. You have small bowmakers continuing to perfect their products, and they're getting better year by year. Over the past fifteen years they have given fifteen years of improved products to the consumer. And that's good for traditional archery.

"It's also good to see the newer generation of bowmakers getting into the business, either through a new business or by having some older bowmaker pass on their skills and business. Naturally, there are a lot of similarities in bows, but there are also a lot of new ideas coming out at an increasing rate as bowyers try pushing the envelope — and much more so than there was ten or fifteen years ago. All of that adds up to a winning scenario for bowmakers and traditional archers.

"So really, there are two ways to look at all the new traditional bowmakers out there. If you're a bowyer who thinks that there are too many and are intimidated by the competition, you might see the glass as half empty. But if you see them as new people who will eventually help us perfect bowmak-

Fine-tuning on limb shaping and string groves plays a crucial role in maintaining perfect dynamic limb alignment. Here, Pittsley painstakingly checks dynamic alignment.

ing and promote archery as we move forward, you might see the glass as half full. It's important to remember that in any market, strong competition only serves to produce something better for the consumer and ultimately for the health of the sport."

At this point, few would disagree that Ron Pittsley is somewhat of a Renaissance man in the realm of archery. He has walked down the different paths in archery, starting as a homespun traditional bowmaker, graduating to a big archery corporation manager, then wandering back down the trail he began on decades before. Yet philosophically he finds himself on the same trail in life, the same fundamental man he has always been. And with his trademark, unabashed philosophical perspective, he offers perhaps the biggest secret of all in archery.

"The real secret to finding happiness in traditional archery," says Pittsley, "is first seeking the right gratification in an accomplishment, whether you want to bowhunt, hit a target, or just stump shoot. Then you need to be gratified in what you accomplish, and don't let ego ruin your aspirations. For instance, if you are driven by all the media hype to try and shoot a world record deer, you've set yourself up for failure because you're probably never going to get one. So if you shoot traditional archery, set goals that are meaningful to you and realistic relative to your skills within reasonable distances. It's okay to push yourself toward those goals. But don't get caught in the ego trap that is sometimes the nature of the beast. That means not getting discouraged when you can't accomplish unrealistic goals. So take a good perspective before you start. And have fun. That's what traditional archery is all about."

Predator Traditional Bows
The Hunter's Niche
 www.huntersniche.com
989-984-0838

Chapter Four

THE TRADITIONAL LONGBOW COMPANY

CONTRADICTIONS

There is a stark contradiction between the forested hills around Mahopac Falls and the rigid electric skyline of Manhattan just thirty-five miles to the south. It's a vivid contrast for those swept away from New York City in rush hour traffic like scraps of driftwood. As the current of lights and steel rushes northward, it ebbs as branching streams of cars escape into the recesses along the Hudson River Valley. Driving north quiets the spirit. Maybe it's the solitude of the rugged granite terrain or the hardwood forested hillsides. Unlike the city, the landscape here doesn't scream of human conquest. Its glacially scoured hills have served as a natural fortress through the centuries, holding back man's oppressive shaping of the land.

Narrow roads wind aimlessly between the hills like meandering game trails, often following lake contours through scattered villages. Colonial stone fences and shrouding canopies of hardwoods line many of these asphalt trails, some still whispering the ancient creaking of overloaded wagons, the heavy breathing of laboring horses, and the shuffling foot falls of Washington's troops plodding through the night.

Along one of these roads and not far from West Point, Washington's Revolutionary Headquarters, and Bear Mountain Bridge, lies the small community of Mahopac. Tucked away in the maple-covered hills east of town is a special place of interest to longbow admirers. It's the home of Frank San Marco and the birthplace of his Traditional Longbow.

Like the modern yet ancient weapon he creates, and like the land where he lives, San Marco is full of contradiction. His youthful face exudes a reserved boyish smile framed with a reddish brown beard and thick hair, but his blue-grey eyes search like an old wise man's, deciphering the person behind a face.

When greeting strangers, he shakes hands with a reserved carefulness that may be perceived as shyness. His hesitation, however, is a courtesy. His oversized muscular fingers look as though they belong on a much larger man and they stop far short of their vise-like power.

JUST PART OF IT ALL

San Marco was born and raised in New York state and has a distinctive accent to match his heritage. From boyhood he worked as a heavy duty equipment mechanic for his father's construction company and he attributes the development of his massive hands to those formative years.

Today, he shares his secluded home on the outskirts of Mahopac with his wife and two daughters. He teaches science, environmental education, and wilderness survival at the Ardsley Middle School. In his survival course, San Marco teaches more of an Indian survival rather than a modern military course. As a New York State registered Wilderness Guide he's well qualified to teach the outdoor courses, which to him represent more than just subjects of education. They're an important part of his life and represent a piece of his spirit.

At home in the woods, San Marco is keenly knowledgeable about his native surroundings. While strolling through the forest, his feet slip between delicate wonders hidden within the forest floor which most people would unknowingly crush. Stopping near the musty remains of an old log, he gently picks several varieties of woodland edibles and seems at home sitting cross-legged on a large slab of lichen-spotted granite, nibbling sprouts of sweet clover and fiddle heads. His intimate knowledge of nature's little-known plants, wild foods, spices, and medicinal plants is amazing.

San Marco incorporates his forest wisdom and strong philosophies about man's relationship with nature into his environmental education programs. Some of his philosophies were gleaned from Tom Brown, author of *The Tracker*. "Philosophically, he turned me around in life. I had always hunted and respected wildlife, but he gave me an insight into nature that was spiritual in essence. He made me look at the earth differently. For the first time, rather than feeling like a dominating creature, I really felt like a part of it. I felt like an animal, and that I was really no better than anything else. It was humbling yet also elevating, recognizing that it's okay to be part of the system and not to be in control of it. It's the system that's really important, not you per se. I've learned to value the system more than the dominance of it.

"When I go into the woods now, I legitimately feel like I'm home. But I used to feel like I stood out and I wasn't a part it, that I was an observer and a spectator. That isn't true now. I really feel like I belong there. I'm not an intruder any more."

A NEW LOOK ON LIFE

Besides being sensitive about the environment, San Marco exudes a tempered perception of life that one might expect from a wise grandfather. It partly comes from his philosophy about the environment, but even more so, it's the result of what happened to him one morning in 1975.

San Marco was participating in a midsummer motorcycle race in New Jersey. It was an off-road Enduro race with rutted trails twisting through rugged wooded terrain. San Marco was no novice to the sport. He knew about the accidents, occasional broken bones, and minor injuries that were part of pushing man and machine to the limits. It was just an acceptable hazard.

Or so he thought.

During the race, San Marco zoomed past another rider and was power sliding through a blind, water-strewn curve when it happened. His cycle spun out of control, hurling him head first into a boulder, breaking his neck. He crumpled to the ground like a rag doll and lay with his face submerged in a puddle. Although he was dazed, San Marco knew something was terribly wrong — he had no sensation from the neck down and he couldn't move.

Straining, he lifted his head and sucked in a breath before slumping back into the puddle. Determined not to drown in three inches of water, he again struggled to lift his head. This time, he tried to scream for help, but only a raspy whisper trickled from his throat before his face dropped back into the puddle. Soon, another rider came to San Marco's side and held his face out of the murky water.

At the hospital, doctors bluntly told him he would never move his body again. A part of him wanted to be back in the puddle quietly accepting the end. Yet another part of him refused to accept his hopeless future.

Total helplessness filled him with despair. To escape his dismal reality, his mind wandered to the woods and to bowhunting. He even playfully imagined someday building himself a bow and wondered what weight limbs he might be able to pull, taunting himself with the fantasy.

Although his spinal cord was severely damaged, it had not been severed. To San Marco that meant there was hope. With time, he began to get faint tinglings in his extremities, which later developed into slight movements. Filled with determination, he struggled for a year relearning how to move his body.

NEW MUSIC

After his unbelievable recovery, doctors said his recovery chances had been one in ten thousand. For San Marco, love, family, touching, feeling, and simply being able to walk in the woods again, took on new meanings. Gradually he regained most of his motor skills. However, he was unable to regain controlled, rapid hand movements.

Back then, San Marco had also hand-crafted and played custom guitars. He was an expert guitarist and music was an important part of his life. But after the accident, even his most determined efforts to once again play the guitar resulted in frustrating, feeble attempts. Shackled with childlike dexterity, playing and building custom guitars faded from his life.

His passion for the six-stringed instrument was eventually replaced by the sweet hum of a lone string. It was the music of the longbow. San Marco's bedside fantasy would come true.

CHALLENGED

San Marco's introduction to bowhunting came when he was six years old. It was a magic mixing of boyish adventure, a wooden longbow, and a bushy-tailed grey squirrel. Although the squirrel simply shrugged off a well-placed shot, an astonished but determined bowhunter was born.

In the years that followed, San Marco hunted with his father and cherished their moments together afield. After his father's death, he roamed the forests alone and plunged himself into the inner depths of hunting. He pursued the sport with zest and eventually made what he feels was a natural progression — a deep commitment to bowhunting.

As San Marco the bowhunter grew and changed, so did his equipment. He replaced his boyhood longbow with refined recurves, and he later tried a compound bow. Like many archers, he quickly discovered that the compound bow was an effective "killing" weapon, but the mechanical device prevented him from fully realizing the essence of the bowhunting challenge.

To recapture the thrill, San Marco stepped back in time, making the full circle in his gear, and readopted the simplistic longbow as his hunting weapon. "What's special about the longbow is its honesty as a weapon. By an honest weapon, I mean that the results of shooting are truly affected by the skills and ability of the archer. If you're successful with it, it's because you have the skills. It's because you have put in your time and been dedicated to its mastery. Whatever success you have earned, entitles you to the personal accolades. If you blow a shot, you can't blame it on anything — it's simply you.

"There is a sense of personal unity with the weapon. When you're drawing back you feel your life's energies being expended in the elasticity of the limbs. When the arrow is propelled forward, you know it's your life energy that's part of it. So, when it strikes and takes an animal, you feel that it's really you. There is nothing in between. Your fingers are in contact with the string and you feel your muscles stretch to their limits.

"With a compound, I'm using gadgets, pulleys, and a whole series of devices which remove my energies from the arrow. When that arrow is on its way, I don't feel the same connection between the arrow's energy and myself as I do with a longbow. The longbow is simple, direct, and a function of you. For that reason, I think it's honest."

FOREST ADVENTURES

San Marco often takes his honest bowhunting companion into the deep woods of the Catskills and Adirondacks where he enjoys blending in with these wild places. Although he prefers roaming the big woods, he consistently harvests more game hunting close to home in Westchester County. There, the ever adaptable whitetail finds refuge and even flourishes in the protection of estates and private homes.

At home in the forest, his favorite style of whitetail hunting is slipping through the brush and at times melting into the woods, but he admits that stand hunting from a tree is often more productive. Although he seldom passes a shot at a buck, San Marco doesn't consider himself a trophy hunter. "For me, the life of a small doe is as precious as a large-racked buck."

One of San Marco's most memorable whitetail hunts was his first bow-killed deer. It was a classic broadside shot at thirty-three yards from a small ground blind. As he approached the downed animal, he felt the flush of amazement in realizing that his once boyhood toy could be such an effective weapon. His bowhunting dreams lay before him in reality.

Although deer offer plenty of deep woods excitement, squirrels are his favorite longbow quarry. Wearing a pair of moccasins and cradling his yew longbow, San Marco slips through the woods in search of the little bushy-tails. He likes damp or rainy days when stalking conditions provide a hushed forest floor. With the fast-moving, sharp-eyed squirrel as the quarry and the longbow as his weapon, it's a supreme bowhunting challenge, producing shots to remember. "My best shot was right here on my property. I was stalking quietly through the woods when I spotted a large grey squirrel crossing an open field, heading towards the thick woods. If he made it into the dense cover I would lose my opportunity for a shot, so I quickly changed direction and took a few quiet steps toward him.

"There was a barrier of trees and a low rock wall between us, but he caught my movement and he ran for the trees. All I could see was this little grey body flashing through the row of trees, but there was one small opening. I drew, anchored, and shot in one fluid sweep. I watched the blunt-tipped arrow and his body converge as his air-bound chest just crossed the thicket line. It was a cleanly placed, lethal arrow, the kind of shot the late Howard Hill would make all the time. But it was perhaps a once in a lifetime shot for me."

TRADITIONAL TOOLS

To help him make those memorable shots, San Marco ventures into the woods carrying a special companion. It's his 67", 62 pound yew-cored Traditional Longbow, a simple weapon that represents an extension of San Marco as an archer and as the bow's creator.

He makes his own custom arrows from modified cedar shafts with the center drilled out in the nock end for approximately eight inches. This makes tail-light arrows, helping them recover faster from the archer's paradox. He gets his prespined, preweighed, and prestraightened hollowed shafting from arrowsmith, David Ellenbogen. San Marco stains them a natural wood color and beautifully custom crests each one. He prefers Mercury Speed nocks and fletches his arrows with three 5" long shield-cut barred feathers. He likes feather colors that are bright enough for him to easily see, but not bright enough to alert game. The colorful feathers help him see the exact location of a hit on big game, an important factor when determining his follow-up actions.

On the business end of his deer hunting shafts, he mounts Hunter's Edge broadheads, designed by John Schultz. Styled after the Howard Hill head, San Marco likes their outstanding durability, penetration, design, and flight characteristics. He mounts the heads vertically and file sharpens them, producing a sharp, serrated edge. "This filed edge cuts elastic tissue, such as arteries, more effectively than a scalpel-sharpened edge. A scalpel edge cut bleeds more profusely, but it allows more elastic tissue to slip past without being cut. I prefer the two-bladed head because complete penetration on big game is much more important than a massive bleeding hole with limited penetration."

San Marco carries his arrows in his handmade leather back quiver. Complementing his traditional gear, he wears one of his handmade leather arm guards. It's a traditional style incorporated with a small liquid-filled compass, blending functional simplicity and thoughtful design.

PERFECTING THE HILL STYLE

To make sure his custom-crafted yew and cedar function as one with the archer afield, San Marco practices his shooting year-round. He hones his running shot skills by shooting at small moving targets in his backyard. In one of his favorite practice sessions he kicks a soccer ball up or across the hill behind his house and then zeros in on the "running" target using arrows tipped with rubber blunts. When he can enlist a thrower, San Marco also enjoys arrowing disks tossed into the air. For slower paced practice, he loves roaming the woods and stump shooting at imaginary game.

Even though he practices often on moving targets, San Marco is discriminating about taking running shots on animals. He knows his effective distance on moving game and limits himself to high-confidence shots. He has taken five shots at running deer: one was a clean miss, and the others were clean kills.

San Marco patterns his instinctive shooting style after the legendary master of the longbow. "The Howard Hill style is a format of shooting that allows the hunter to react and shoot instinctively and intuitively. It's not a regimented style, but a very loose style. The body incorporates several bends. Every time you put a bend in the body there is opportunity for movement in that particular joint. That builds flexibility into your shooting style and makes it adaptable to hunting situations on the ground.

"In the field, only one out of every five or six shots might be picture book where the target is set so you can stand in a very orthodox target shooting position. So if you're hunting from the ground you have to be flexible and be able to accommodate the circumstances. With the elbow bent, a slight bend at the waist, and with a slight break in the knees, you can twist and move to make those necessary adjustments. Versatility is the essence of the Hill style. Plus, bending the joints puts certain muscle groups in opposition to each other, increasing muscular stability when shooting."

Besides bending his joints, San Marco cants his bow and leans over his arrow. "When you draw the arrow back, in effect it's to the side of your eye. But when you cant the bow, you bring the eye in longitudinal alignment with the shaft, so the estimation factor in aiming is diminished. Canting the bow simply reduces the displacement between your eye and the shaft."

With his instinctive eyes locked on target, San Marco begins aiming during his draw sequence to save time, often a valuable commodity during

SIMPLE YET EFFECTIVE IN THE FIELD — San Marco uses the Hill shooting style, bow canted, joints bent, and always fluid.

critical hunting situations. "Most of the actual aiming in traditional shooting should be done before reaching full draw. It's not necessary or even advantageous to methodically draw, anchor, and then start aiming." Practicing what he preaches, he draws and shoots in one uninterrupted motion, making it look simple and fun. The grace of his traditional form is captured for only a second before the arrow leaps almost unexpectedly from his longbow and buries into the mark.

GUITARS TO BOWS

The sleek longbow San Marco carries is a product of evolution. It represents his bowhunting transition back to a simple, honest weapon, blended with his lingering guitar crafting skills. After recovering from his motorcycle accident, San Marco wanted a longbow as a hunting companion, but he couldn't find one with the custom quality he had grown accustomed to in his guitars. So, he decided to build his own.

His engineering, guitar crafting, and woodworking skills proved to be an ideal combination for bowmaking. Even his first bow, patterned after a Hill style longbow, reflected as much quality and performance as any commercially available longbow.

One bow lead to another, and by 1979 San Marco began professionally building his longbows. He decided early on, not to limit his bowmaking methods and techniques to the established norms. Even though he was building traditional bows, he didn't want his bows or imagination confined within the traditional realm of bowmaking. Armed with a creative and inquisitive attitude, he began building bows and conducting research on materials and methods. His research, combined with his logical approach to problem solving, led to the development of several unorthodox bowmaking techniques that he now uses in creating his longbows.

"One of the things I decided when I started building the longbow, was that I wasn't going to reinvent the recurve. I know that the power of the recurve is just inherently better in its design than a longbow. Anybody who tells you different isn't telling you the whole scoop, or they know a whole lot more than I do.

"Recurves store more energy, there is no question about that. It doesn't mean you can't have a fine shooting longbow. But all things being equal, a recurve will store more energy. I was never going to rediscover that. When I started building longbows, I wanted to take the basic time-held concept of the longbow and refine it to the highest limits without violating the basic essence of the bow, and that's what I've been doing."

In refining his longbows, San Marco takes his time. He's in no hurry to crank out a product. His main goal is excellence, and that can't be rushed. "One of the things that make my bows special is that I build each bow as though I was building it for myself. I put a tremendous amount of pride into every bow I build. I know for a fact, when man starts mass producing things, he loses that vital connection between the crafting and the final product — that immersion of soul. When I sell a bow, I'm giving that person a part of my life, the most valuable possession that I have. And I want that bow to reflect the value of my life that I am giving."

The respected quality of San Marco's unhurried creations is reflected by the five to six year waiting list for one of his bows. It's a list made up of archers from around the world who believe that an exceptional longbow is worth even the exceptional wait. Although there may be ways to speed up his bowmaking and shorten the waiting list, San Marco paces himself to maintain his romance with the craft. "I decided that because longbows were so important to me, so dear to my heart, that when the joy of building a longbow ceases, I may cease building longbows."

THE BOW

San Marco's TRADITIONAL LONGBOW reflects his immersion of soul. It's an exceptional work of art and beauty, reaching back in time with its design and ancient yew core, yet its gem-like quality makes it appear almost futuristic. The rich blending of warm woods and fiberglass looks as though the bow was poured into an exquisite, flawless mold.

Its chocolate-striped shedua riser gives way to coppery laminated yew corewoods covered in dark brown fiberglass. The natural beauty of these woods is displayed by the softly flowing contours of the riser and limbs under a mirror-smooth finish. Looking beyond the sheer beauty of the bow reveals the precision craftsmanship of the limbs and their immaculate, flowing contours. It is a Weatherby among longbows.

Its distinctive visual beauty is almost overshadowed by the beauty of its performance. When grasping the bow, there's an instant sensation of grace-ful balance and lightness in the hand caused by its feather-weight limbs.

San Marco's Traditional Longbow blends ancient yew with modern materials in a classic longbow design.

Compared to many longbows, the yew-cored limbs feel unusually light. Because of its balance, the bow glides through the woods at the archer's side and effortlessly swings at full draw on moving targets.

For longbowmen who have never savored the resiliency of a yew-cored bow, there is a special surprise in the smoothness of the draw and the surge of internal life at the instant of release. This almost magical life hums a faint whisper to the hand after the shot. It's a captivating sensation.

The Traditional Longbow is offered in 67", 68", and 69" lengths. These different lengths are matched to an archer's draw length to optimize bow performance. The mass weight of a 68" Traditional Longbow is a pleasant 1 pound, 4 ounces. Its recommended brace height is 6½" from the throat of the grip to the string.

The shedua riser is 15¼" long between fadeouts, 1⅛" wide, and approximately 2" thick. The slightly dished grip is 4⅛" long and is peaked along the throat to provide a positive hand seat. The grip is wrapped with a durable, thin leather lacing. The slightly rounded sight window is cut ⁵⁄16" from center shot and the shelf-window junction is equipped with a feather-edged leather shelf and strike pad. The draw weight and creator signature are gold inked on the riser, and the owner's and the bow's name are inked on the belly of the limbs.

On the 68" length, the upper limb has a working length of 28¼" from the fadeout to the nock and the lower limb has a 27" working length. The limbs are 1³⁄16" wide at the fadeouts and narrow to ⅜" at the nocks. They exhibit a modified trapezoid, or "D" shaped cross section tapering to the belly. Unstrung, they display a slight ⅞" reflex at the time of construction. They are constructed from two solid yew tapered back laminations and one belly lamination. The three laminations are sandwiched between warm-toned, .050" thick, dark brown fiberglass.

The narrow limb tips are ornately distinctive. They have uniquely sculptured and fluted shedua tip overlays. The string nock to tip measurement is 1⅛" on the upper tip, and ¾" on the lower tip. Smoothly fashioned string grooves are handcrafted around the entire tip. The bow is protected by a glass-smooth, multilayered, hand-rubbed finish.

The following draw/force measurements were recorded on one of San Marco's 68" yew-cored, Traditional Longbows:

DRAW LENGTH	25"	26"	27"	28"	29"
DRAW WEIGHT	61#	64½#	68½#	72³⁄₁₀#	76³⁄₁₀#

Although conditions prevented actual chronograph testing of the above bow, previous chronographing of a 64 pound at 28" draw, 68" Traditional Longbow resulted in an average arrow speed of 179 fps. The bow was hand shot using cedar arrows weighing 510 grains.

THE MAGIC CORE

One of the key components of San Marco's longbow is yew, the rust colored wood used by Robin Hood, Saxton Pope, and Art Young. The extremely slow growing yew is harvested from the Cascade Mountains in Oregon and shipped to San Marco as rough-sawn boards. He stores them in his well-ventilated drying racks, where the yew waits patiently for years, aging and maturing into seasoned bow-quality wood. Every three months or so, San Marco climbs a ladder and inspects his stash of precious yew, "stirring" or rotating each piece to expose a new surface for uniform drying. Years of slow air seasoning enhance the natural qualities that make yew such an exceptional bow wood.

NATURE'S GIFT TO THE BOWMAKER, TIMELESS YEW. The bow wood legends are made from. The Old Master Crafters turn San Marco's yew boards into custom tapered laminations.

Most of San Marco's yew has been carefully aged seven to ten years. That may seem like a long time for some woods to just sit around and collect dust, but one of the sweetest shooting bows he ever made was built with yew air seasoned for over forty years. San Marco believes that two years of well circulated air drying is the minimum for properly aged yew.

Bringing down a board marked "1975," San Marco walks into the stippled sunlight near an old stone wall and examines the piece. It's one of the few that has a uniform layer of sapwood and exceptionally straight grain. Even Pope or Young would be envious of this piece. While slowly rotating the blocky piece in his stout hands, San Marco explains, "Yew's physical lightness makes an exquisitely well-balanced bow. This lightness gives it a very pleasant heft in the hand. It is extremely soft drawing. The draw/force curve for a yew bow is very smooth. From the beginning of the draw all the way back, it's got a very gentle feel. Yew tends to feel several pounds lighter for the same weight just because of its draw/force characteristics. It just glides back."

TESTING WITH ACTIONWOOD

Although San Marco uses yew corewood in his Traditional Longbow, he employs Actionwood as a corewood material when making his prototype bows. This multilaminated maple corewood is widely used by today's bow manufacturers. "Maple is a good bow wood. Its inherent tensile and compressive strengths allow it to be stressed more than the softer woods such as yew.

"Statistically, through multilaminations, Actionwood compromises the qualities of fine woods and not so fine woods. So you always get a wood that is going to be a consistent tensile strength. If you're a manufacturer, that's a real asset because you can cut a lamination to certain specifications and you will always get the same spining. The draw weight is going to be predictable.

"Plus, in Actionwood any structural flaw that may be present in any single piece of laminate is reduced to a small fraction of your total limb. If you are using a single piece of corewood and it had a structural flaw, that piece of wood would be prone to break down very easily because of the flaw. But if that piece of wood becomes only ten percent of the corewood and you have other pieces along side of it, statistically, you diminish the probability of having a limb that's going to fail.

"In terms of increased performance with Actionwood, I don't think you'll get any. I found that when I hand-spined and hand-selected the superior solid maple corewood, I would get a better bow than when using Actionwood. Actionwood will always make a good, mediocre performing bow, which is good in mass production. But if I'm looking to optimize the qualities of a shooting limb, I will hand-spine each piece to make sure that I get the liveliest of the solid maple."

When he needs custom-ground yew laminations, San Marco sends some of his select stock to the Old Master Crafters in Waukegan, Illinois. They saw and custom taper yew laminations according to San Marco's specifications.

The involved process of obtaining yew, properly aging it for years, and having it shipped out and custom-ground is many times more costly than simply buying maple laminations. But San Marco and his satisfied customers feel that the extra effort and expense in using yew are well worth it.

ATTENTION TO GRAIN

From his supply of tapered yew laminations, San Marco carefully selects three matched pairs for use in one of his bows. He takes his time patiently reading the grain qualities of each piece. With experienced eyes and hands, he searches for any structural imperfections, and then uses a micrometer to double check each lamination for proper thickness and taper.

Each pair of his laminations is consecutively cut from the same board and will be used in the same relative position on opposing limbs. This ensures uniform limb balance by providing similar internal corewood dynamics in both limbs.

When laying up a bow, San Marco arranges the three pairs of yew laminations to accentuate the optimum qualities of the complementing pieces. For example, when he uses quarter-grain laminations, he arranges them so that the stacked pieces have opposing grain angles. This provides increased stability to the overall limb composite. He also carefully positions each pair to match the adjoining butt-end grain.

For optimum bow performance, San Marco prefers edge-grain or quarter-grain laminations. He has, however, built bows with all flat-grain laminations and discovered that they performed very well. Unlike many bowyers who use uniform tapered corewood, San Marco uses differentially tapered laminations. This helps him achieve a built-in limb tiller and maximizes the performance of his limb design.

When selecting the shedua for the riser section, he prefers a piece with quarter grain. This grain alignment brings out the striking multihued internal patterns within the wood. When scribing out the riser outline, he positions the template to optimize both the wood's attractive grain patterns and internal strengths.

As San Marco band saws out the riser section, he points out that the final smoothness and sweeping curve of the fadeout portion is extremely critical because it represents a stress area in the limb. Also, the smooth flowing arc of the fadeout belly adds some preload to the belly laminations, giving his bows a little extra power.

While delicately hand sanding the riser, he emphasizes the importance of smooth and even contact surfaces between the riser and the limb laminations. This ensures thin, uniform glue lines when the bow composites are glued and pressed. And San Marco believes that the thinnest glue line is the strongest. The final finishing and shaping of the belly fadeout is patiently done with his critical eye and tactile hands showing the way. If the belly and back sides of his fadeout are not perfectly flat and in plane, it will show up as an irregular or angular edge at the end of the fadeout. He delicately fashions his fadeouts into a wispy thin, see-through layer.

San Marco's hinged, steel-framed bow press easily accepts different wooden bow forms.

UNCONVENTIONAL PRESS

Most bowyers use the air hose method of applying pressure to the bow composites. A few others use "C" clamps to squeeze them together. But San Marco's procedure for pressing his bow composites goes beyond established convention.

He wanted a press that would give him super-thin and uniform glue lines, yet would be capable of accepting different bow forms. So he designed a heavy-duty steel-framed press. It resembles alligator jaws that bite down on the enclosed wooden bow form. After the top hinged portion of the press is locked in place, pressure is applied to the enclosed form by tightening a series of bolts running the length of the upper jaws. San Marco's press enables him to laminate bow composites with significant pressure and allows him to distribute that pressure. Because the press is designed to accept different forms, he can easily experiment with making prototype bows.

PUTTING IT TOGETHER

Before gluing up his bow composites, he covers his form surfaces with plastic wrap for stray glue protection. He then cleans the riser, laminations, and fiberglass with solvent.

He applies epoxy glue to all composite contact surfaces. Before laying up each lamination, San Marco double checks his glue layers for coverage, air bubbles, or flecks of foreign material. Once the bow is glued up in the form, he closes the jawed press and begins tightening the pressure bolts along the top. It takes him approximately forty minutes working back and forth along the press to hand-tighten and evenly torque down the bolts.

The press containing the form and glued composites is then put into his preheated glue curing box. Even after the glue has cured, the bow remains in the press until it cools to room temperature. This ensures proper epoxy set on the pressure-stressed composites.

After the glued bow is removed from the press, it's rough sanded on the edges to remove the glass-like hardened glue. San Marco masking tapes the back of the bow and marks the centerline. He then positions his bow outline template made from two layers of clear fiberglass. This template has a series of small holes along its centerline. By turning the template over and reversing ends, he double checks the trueness of his centerline and then traces the bow outline. As a final check on the exactness of the centerline, San Marco sights down a taut piece of line strung from tip to tip.

He then band saws and belt sands the bow close to form. Next, he hand files and sands the limbs to final form. During this limb shaping, San Marco repeatedly checks his progress by drawing the vise-held bow, making sure there are no flat spots or stress points in the limbs. During final limb shaping, he brings the bow to the desired 3/16" positive tiller. He epoxies the sculpted tip overlays in place and heat cures the glue.

While hand shaping the rounded trapezoid belly of the limbs, he repeatedly checks to ensure that proper tiller is maintained. When completed, he makes one final check by shooting the bow to ensure that both limbs are responding in harmony and properly spitting an arrow.

NEATLY FINISHED

The last bit of wood shaping is the contouring of the grip to fit the customer's preference. San Marco shapes the handle with a pronounced peaked grip because he feels that it seats more positively into the shooter's hand. As a final step, he delicately fashions the ornate tips and then fine sands the entire bow.

The completed bow is wiped down with solvent, and sprayed with a two-part catalystic varnish. San Marco says that the finish was developed thirty or forty years ago specifically for fly fishing rods and it's one of the most durable bow finishes he's seen. The final mirror-like luster is achieved by spraying on five or six coats of the tough varnish and hand sanding between each coat. This delicate sanding removes any flecks or irregularities between coats and contributes to the ultimate gem-quality smoothness of the finish.

Between the third and fourth varnish coats, the gold lettering is meticulously inked on the riser and limbs by Mrs. San Marco. Although San Marco would like to make the entire bow with his own hands, his motorcycle injuries prevent him from producing the delicate lettering he feels belongs on his longbows.

When the final coat of varnish is dried, he hand rubs the bow to a brilliant high luster with a mildly abrasive substance he personally developed. The final immaculate glassy finish represents over four hours of tedious hand work.

San Marco then installs a piece of heavy leather next to the shelf which extends the arrow shelf 1/8" out from the grip. The sides of this shelf under-

BEEFY HANDS ON DELICATE WORK — The Traditional Longbow's fluted tip overlays add another dimension of distinction to San Marco's creation.

plate are contoured with a razor blade and the arrow strike pad is installed. The strike pad edges are nicely beveled to help obtain crisp arrow flight.

Finally, San Marco contact cements and hand wraps thin leather lacing around the grip. Although it's a time consuming method, he feels that the resulting grip is extremely durable and actually improves with usage, unlike suede grips which feel good at first and later become sweat varnished.

In caring for a custom bow, San Marco suggests occasionally using a high quality, non-abrasive automotive polish to maintain the luster of the finish. He also says that a bow should never be stored in a hot place, as the strength of the epoxy drops tremendously with increased temperatures. This means never put a bow in a hot car trunk on a sunny day. If by accident a bow does become hot, don't string it until it cools to room temperature. Don't overdraw a custom bow or let some seven-foot-tall archer shoot a bow that was specifically built for you. "Basically, treat a bow with the respect it was made with."

ONLY PERFECTION

Even Michelangelo probably had an occasional disappointment. Sometimes, San Marco discovers a minor flaw when making a bow. When that happens, the bow is put in the corner where it collects dust until he gets the courage to destroy it along with any others that may have joined its ranks. This may seem like a harsh sentence for a slightly flawed bow, but at the Traditional Longbow Company there are no seconds. Although he admits that it hurts to cut up a shootable bow, he refuses to sell any longbow with his name on it if it isn't the finest he can produce.

In bow crafting, San Marco strives for a balance of qualities. That can be a tough design problem when blazing speed and a smooth draw are bow qualities working against each other. "I try to achieve a harmony of characteristics that are most pleasing to me. The quality I cherish most in a bow is, first and foremost, stability. The bow has to shoot an arrow where you point it. If it doesn't, it's not an implement worth hunting with.

"Second, I really enjoy a bow that draws smoothly. Hunting from the ground you have to perform without any interruption in the draw, anchor, and aim sequence. So if a bow is stacking, that just robs me of all of my focus and concentration, and disarms me as an effective hunter. So I cherish the quality of a smooth drawing bow. And there is nothing like yew to achieve that. I also like the way yew balances in the hand. A bow should have high stability, be smooth drawing, and provide good balance in the hand. And of course it's got to be hard hitting."

The Traditional Longbow built by Frank San Marco isn't for everyone. The waiting list alone culls ninety-five percent of the prospective customers. But San Marco's goal is not to build longbows just to sell. He does it because he loves and respects the weapon and is personally challenged to develop it to its utmost in performance and beauty. He'll settle for nothing less. Fate has given him a second chance to use his hands for creating something he loves, and he's determined to make the most of it.

FEDORA'S ARCHERY

HAVIN' FUN

It was deer season and the sporting goods store drew a crowd of local Vermont sportsmen discussing bucks and bows. Near the back of the store, a young man from out of town passed his custom bow among a curious band of archers. "It only pulls 102 pounds," said the young man, "so I use it mostly for target shooting."

Several in the crowd gave him a suspicious glance and motioned for the bow. A heavyset hunter grabbed it first and snorted, "Humpf, it doesn't look too stiff for me." Locking his beefy hands around the bow, he grunted and pulled the string. The crowd laughed as the big man struggled, only drawing it halfway. Red-faced, he tried to hand it to one of the hecklers but everyone stepped back and laughed even harder.

"Give me that bow," groaned a tall man in the back. "I make bows around here, and I'll show you guys how to pull that thing." The laughing ebbed until the bowmaker, jaws clenched, tried twice but failed to pull the bow. As the laughing trailed off a young man standing away from the group spoke sheepishly, "Excuse me, mister, do you mind if I give it a try?"

This six-foot bowmaker from Vermont looked at the small framed man and snickered. "Save your strength sonny, you'll never begin to pull back that bow." But the owner of the bow said, "What the heck, everybody else tried, let the little guy try to pull it."

The short man awkwardly fumbled with the bow and asked, "Is there any particular way to draw it?" The crowd erupted in laughter as the owner, hiding a sly grin, replied, "Just use three fingers on the string when you pull it back."

"Like this?" asked the young man as he drew and held it to his jaw. The hunters fell silent, all except the bowmaker who blurted, "You're not pulling it a full twenty-eight inches!"

"Is this twenty-eight inches?" asked the young man as he drew the string past his ear to thirty inches. The stunned crowd watched as he switched hands and then drew the bow left-handed. Finally, he let the bow down and grinned at the local bowmaker, but only for a second. The big man wheeled and stormed red-faced out the door.

"We used to have a lot of fun like that back then," recalls the short man. "But heck, I knew I could draw that bow. It was my brother's, and I was the one who built it for him!"

Today, in his third decade of bowmaking, 5' 4" bowyer Mike Fedora still has fun with archery, and he even keeps a 150 pound bow on the rack in case any folks from the Vermont sporting goods store stop by for a visit.

A YOUNG START

Mike was born and raised in New Haven, Connecticut. Even as a young boy his life seemed guided by the bow. "Most boys have a bow when they're a kid, and I can't remember when I didn't have one in my hands. At first they were old hickory self-bows, and then I got a Ben Pearson solid fiberglass two-piece bow. That was really a big deal switching from a self-wood bow to a fiberglass take-down."

At eleven years old, Mike met his first real bowhunter, Jose Cassanova, who befriended the young archer and began taking Mike deer hunting. Mike's interest in archery grew, and when he was twelve years old he started making arrows. By the time he was sixteen he was a well established arrow maker and expanded his interest to bowmaking.

Mike became a Howard Hill sales representative when he was nineteen and soon after took the first step down his long road to bowmaking. "I made my first bow from an old junk bed. I was driving by a house and saw an old black walnut bed that someone had thrown out. I took it and used the black walnut to make my handle section and laminated it with maple corewoods and green fiberglass. There wasn't any information on bowmaking back then and I clamped directly to the bow."

STEPPING OUT

Although Mike studied offset photography and commercial advertising after high school, the lure of the bow was just too strong. He worked in advertising until his early twenties when he used his part-time bowmaking skills to land a full-time job in charge of bow production for Outdoor Sports in Connecticut. After three years in commercial bow production, Mike left the company and ventured into the new world of custom bowmaking.

"I started with longbows and then tried recurves. Then I designed what at the time were considered some unusual bows. I had my own ideas and designed a bow with a larger than conventional handle. I hadn't made ten of those bows when they started winning a lot of local championships. And those bows went on to win major championships throughout the east coast and later across the country. One was even used to shoot one of the first perfect 300 scores in the PAA round."

Even though Mike had winning bows encouraging his efforts, the long nights spent hand shaping bows were often drudgery. But a friend helped keep Mike's bow building fire lit. "Claude Herndon kept me going back then. My first 100 bows were made the hard way using big old rasps and files. When you started filing on some of the hard exotics like Brazilian rosewood, you either got strong or died. It was like filing steel. Claude used to bring down a gallon of wine, and we really used to get wild filing those bows and making dust. This of course was before I became a born again Christian. Claude was one of the first to get one of my target bows, and he really did a job with that bow. He was a natural instinctive shooter."

TO THE KEYSTONE STATE

"You've got a friend in Pennsylvania" turned out to be more than just a slogan for Mike. Rod Hoover, a top shooter in the NAA was using one of Mike's bows and invited him to Pennsylvania for a visit. Mike liked what he saw. "Back in the early seventies Pennsylvania had just incredible hunting, and I told Rod that I wouldn't mind living there. So Rod kept a look out for a place for sale, and a year later we packed up and moved there."

Mike and his family settled in the rural country north of Richland, in Pennsylvania's sprawling Lebanon Valley. Located about a half hour east of Harrisburg, the area blends rolling farmlands and pasture with scattered wood lots and forested ridges. Pheasants cackle at daybreak and whitetails frequently stroll through Mike's back yard, providing plenty of fodder for his hunting daydreams. Although the Lebanon Valley boasts fine Pennsylvania Dutch cooking and is noted for its processed meat products, the Fedora household commonly feasts on bow-harvested venison.

When Mike moved to Pennsylvania he left behind a well established archery business, and his first two years in the Keystone state were lean ones. "We lost up to eighty-five percent of our archery business, and that's when the compound bow came out. I was a recurve and longbow maker and was suddenly faced with trying to make a compound. I really didn't want to, but it got to the point that if I didn't, my family wouldn't eat."

So Mike developed a laminated wooden handled compound and continued making custom recurves and longbows. His business grew over the years as did his following of traditional customers.

The recent resurgence of traditional archery has allowed Mike to make fewer compounds, and he now looks forward to phasing them out of his line. "I don't have anything against the compound, and it's here to stay. But I have so much work building my recurves and longbows, and that's where my love is."

Today in his late forties, Mike shares his bowmaking business with his wife, Carol, and oldest son, Michael. "It's a family operation. Michael has been making bows for ten years now, and I consider him a very good bowmaker. He's twenty-four years old and already very experienced in all phases of bowmaking and bow design."

MADE FOR STALKING

When he finds time away from the bowyer's bench during the summer, Mike enjoys bass fishing with his younger son, Jason, and also spends time on the tennis courts keeping in shape. But when the first leaves of October begin to yellow, Mike brims with anticipation like a kid at Christmas, waiting for another encounter with Mr. Whitetail.

Though he enjoys tree stand hunting, Mike's favorite whitetail tactic is stalking them on the ground. Unlike many bowhunters who are easily sky-lined by keen-eyed deer, this short bowmaker always maintains a low profile in the woods, and when he bends over at the waist, he's not much taller than a yearling. If any bowhunter was ever built for stalking game, it's Mike.

Pennsylvania's bow season offers a variety of hunting conditions, and although Mike loves bowhunting, there is one time he feels it's more respon-sible to stay home. "I don't hunt in the rain. I used to when I was young, but what happens if you hit a big buck in the rain? In the areas I hunt it's very thick and in seconds that buck can run 100 yards. How do you track him in the rain? Not very easily. So I favor fair weather hunting and believe that bowhunting is a fair weather sport.

"When stalking or waiting for whitetails, Mike tries for high percentage shots. "I like about a fifteen yard shot when they're quartering away. I don't like them when they're breathing on me at five yards — my heart pounds, I get the shakes, and sometimes I still miss even easy shots."

PROGRAMMED LONG

Even though he now prefers close-range shots at deer, Mike used to loft an occasional arrow at distant game. Today's bowhunters are programmed to limit themselves to high-percentage shots, but thirty years ago archery heroes commonly arrowed game at astounding distances. "We grew up watching and reading about guys like Howard Hill, Ben Pearson, and Pope and Young. If they saw something in the field they shot at it no matter how far away it was. I didn't know anything else, that's how I was programmed. We really flung arrows back then.

"I was sneaking through the woods with this guy, and a deer came out about eighty yards away. So I just pulled back and shot it. That guy couldn't believe anybody could shoot a deer that far away. But I hunted with Jerry Smith back in Connecticut using longbows and saw him shoot a bird at a paced-off 110 yards."

No longer an arrow flinger, Mike spends most of his bowhunting hours in his resident state where he enjoys hunting with his customers and sharing the experiences of discovering new Pennsylvanian haunts. "I like hunting with a group of guys from Summerville, Pennsylvania. They're unique be-cause they consistently take the biggest bucks around and just use their bows. They really put em' down. These guys make maps, run about thirty-five different tree stands, spot their bucks, keep records, and then end up getting their big bucks."

Although Mike does get invitations to bowhunt the western states for big game such as elk, he's content staying home and chasing local deer. "I'm just a whitetail hunter. People ask why I don't go out west on trips. It's because I visualize those trips as work. If you shoot a 600-pound animal like an elk and he's four miles from camp, what do you do with him? I certainly don't know what to do with him. But when I think about it, the word WORK enters my mind. I work enough around here making bows. When I go on a vacation I don't want it to be work.

"It might be nice to shoot a big animal, but after you've shot it you have to take proper care of it. And how much can a little guy like me carry off a mountain? Heck, by the time you threw the antlers on my back that might be enough to ground me. Whitetails are plenty enough challenge for me. They generally make a fool out of me most of the time anyway."

Even the whitetails that don't make a fool out of Mike and wind up in the pot sometimes fool his perceptions. "I was sitting up in a tree stand eating an apple when this buck came by. It was a six-pointer, and I only had a head and neck shot at thirty-seven yards. It wasn't the best shot, but I knew the buck was about to catch my wind. He was feeding near a beech tree when I shot and he just kept feeding. He made absolutely no sign that he was hit. I cautiously tried to get another arrow out of my quiver but the buck walked behind the beech tree and I couldn't see him any more.

"I thought I had missed, so I decided to wait until dark to check it out. Just before dark another six-pointer came around the same tree, and I naturally thought it was the same deer I had shot at. The wind had shifted and was blowing to me, yet that buck started blowing and snorting. I couldn't figure that out. He moved out without me getting another shot.

"At dark I got down from my tree and went over to look for my arrow. I always check out each shot. I don't take anything for granted. Even if I know it was a miss I'll check out the deer's trail until I know it was absolutely a miss. I looked with my flashlight but couldn't find my arrow and decided to come back the next morning.

"When I came back, I discovered I had missed seeing my arrow in the dark by about one foot. It was covered with blood, and the buck was laying twenty-five yards away over the hill. My arrow had gone right through the neck, cutting the jugular vein. I figured out that the second buck was snorting at the blood smell from my buck. Sometimes bucks die hard and sometimes they die easy. That one died easy."

WHITETAIL EQUIPMENT

Mike bowhunts his Pennsylvanian whitetails with fifty to fifty-five pound bows. It's a weight he can handle well, yet it effectively gets the job done. "I hunt with whatever bow is laying around on the shelf. I've killed deer with recurves, longbows, and compounds — it doesn't matter to me. They're all sufficient. It's not a ninety pound bow that kills a deer, it's where you put that arrow that counts, and that broadhead better be sharp."

For maximum sharpness, Mike tips his arrows with multiple-bladed stainless steel broadheads. "I like the Razorback four when deer hunting. I like that kind of a head or even a three-bladed Wasp. If I hunted wild boar I would use a four-bladed Zwickey.

"Unfortunately, a lot of guys can't sharpen self-sharpening heads well enough to do the right job. And out here in our damp weather, self-sharpening heads have to be touched up almost morning and night, even if you coat them with Vaseline. That's one reason I like the stainless steel blades. The razor blade heads always make the best cut. It's the kind of cut that doesn't heal, whereas a serrated cut mends quicker."

Mike shoots aluminum arrows fletched with three camo feathers and carries them in his Fedora bow quiver. "I like aluminum because they're very consistent. Also, if you hit a deer with a wood arrow, he can run and break off part of the arrow, and it could remain in the deer. However, with aluminum, it usually bends and the deer will sometimes reach around and pull that arrow out. I've actually seen deer do that."

To help conceal himself in the whitetails's world, Mike covers his face with a tight fitting camouflage face sock and he wears hush-quiet clothing. "Wearing camouflage is important, but the type of camo is extremely important. When it reaches six o'clock in the woods here, at that quiet time it can sound like your breathing is loud enough for a deer to hear let alone any clothing movement. It can really sound loud. So the most important thing is quiet clothing, even if it's just a soft flannel shirt to break up your outline. But some of the sophisticated patterns like Trebark, Asat, and Skyline in Polar Fleece are great."

SHOOTING TIPS

Mike polishes his whitetail shooting skills by bowhunting local woodchucks and stump shooting. "Shooting at random objects like a corn cob or a blade of grass really sharpens your instinctive abilities." Although this form of practice may sound casual to the hardened paper-puncher, Mike knows what he's talking about. A professional archery instructor for over twenty years, he has helped top shooters develop winning form. He also serves as a certified hunter safety instructor in Pennsylvania.

One key to consistent shooting is learning proper form right from the start, yet many beginners develop bad habits because they're not matched with their equipment. "Most people are way overbowed and that causes shooting problems. In most cases a person should start with a thirty to forty pound bow and learn to shoot it properly. After they develop their form, they can work up to a heavier hunting weight. Once you learn good shooting form, it will come to you naturally when you're out in the woods shooting at game."

Mike recommends bows pulling forty-five to fifty-five pounds for whitetail hunting, especially for beginning traditionalists. "The biggest problem with guys going from a compound to a recurve is that many of them were shooting sixty-five to seventy pound compounds and think they can drop five pounds and handle a traditional bow. But the average guy can't do that. I don't want to overbow a customer because if I do, they're going to get turned off to traditional archery."

When shooting his moderate weight hunting bow, Mike grips his bow string with muscular, stubby hands that hint of his years crafting bows. He shoots instinctively, anchoring high with his index finger near the corner of his eye. "With my shooting style I can shoot a squirrel at twenty to thirty yards. With a lower anchor there is more guess work in aiming. But by anchoring higher, I reduce the gap between the arrow and the eye. The disadvantage to my style is that you have trouble handling a seventy-five to eighty pound bow because the anchor point is out of alignment with your shoulders."

Once an archer has his basic anchor, aim, and release mastered, he's ready to begin polishing the finer points — points Mike has taught for years. "You never want to grip your bow too tightly. I teach shooters to leave the hand semi-open, with just a light enough touch on the bow so they're not going to drop it. If you want to shoot accurately, you shouldn't wrap your hand around the grip. You only want to place your fingertips on the center of the back of the grip. That way it's difficult to torque or twist the bow in your hand."

A LIFETIME OF PRACTICE — Mike's high anchor, loose bow hand, and power stance all contribute to his polished shooting skills.

Although proper bow hand and anchor placement are important points stressed by most coaches, Mike believes that body position is crucial to shooting in the field. "I teach the power stance method. Many people shoot perpendicular to the target using an orthodox target stance. But with that stance you don't have much stability, especially with a heavy bow. And if you use that stance in the woods where there are hillsides and rough ground, you have even less stability.

"A boxer doesn't stand up straight with his feet perpendicular to his target. If he did, he would be out of the ring in no time. The power stance forms an imaginary "V" with your feet apart, heels pointed at right angles, and a slight bend in the knees. It provides extra movement, balance, and stability. When you start to swing on a target, your knees tend to lock up and give you more stability."

Mastering the finer points of shooting is frequently discussed among archers. But one subject that's often avoided is the conditioned shooting reflex known as snap shooting. Some call it freezing. "Within five years after getting into archery, the average guy usually develops a freezing problem. It's not that he can't hit the target. He's got the ability, but his mind and his body aren't working together.

"Freezing occurs when your eyes do the triggering of your release, not your hand. They see that you're on target and make you release before your mind is ready. Years ago I asked Fred Bear if he ever had a freezing problem and he said, 'Let's not even talk about it. Freezing is a bad word.'

"To combat freezing you have to program yourself to think about each step in the execution of the shot. If you don't, you're not going to be on target when you let that arrow go. That's one of the reasons I like shooting a lighter bow. I'm a little guy, and using a lighter bow helps me concentrate more on my shooting. It takes a lot of personal discipline to keep from eventually freezing, and the average person doesn't have that kind of discipline."

NOT LIKE IT USED TO BE

The self discipline Mike demonstrates in his shooting reflects a lifetime of mastering the bow. He remembers back to the good old days when field archery was fun and hundreds of archers flocked to local shoots. But for Mike, times have changed. With the emphasis now placed on score, performance, and professionalism, field archery has lost many of its followers. Now, even National shoots draw fewer shooters than Mike used to see at regional shoots years ago.

The changing attitudes in field archery have caused Mike to drop out of most organized archery gatherings. But he still attends one with great enthusiasm. "I don't go there to shoot, but I wouldn't miss the biannual Professional Bowhunters Society meeting. PBS is one of the best groups I've ever belonged to. Mostly its members are gentlemen who conduct themselves in a professional manner. They stand for ethical hunting and proper hunting education, and they're doing a great job. I recommend PBS to any serious bowhunter."

One of the reasons Mike enjoys PBS is because it puts him in touch with the type of bowhunter who used to roam the woods years ago — the type Mike would like to see more of. "A bowhunter used to be a guy who shot his bow all year long to become a bowhunter. But many newcomers to archery only take their bows out a week before season. Now the idea is to get a compound with a release, some kind of sight and a range-finder, and instantly someone's an archer. That's not how I remember archery."

Besides witnessing the changing types of bowhunters, Mike has painfully seen the sport of archery change from simple fun into a complicated, ever-changing mass of rules. "Archery is the only sport I know that when anybody invents something, they change the rules of the sport to accommodate that invention. In golf you have the club and the ball. They have balls that will go for miles but they're outlawed. But in archery that kind of thing is okay. I can't think of another sport that allows that to happen. Without hard and fast rules and regulations where will it end?"

With today's world of high-tech archery gadgets, sometimes it seems like there is no end. And the one Mike dislikes the most turns a bow into a gun. "If someone uses a trigger release aid, they're shooting a gun. Let's not kid ourselves. You can turn a bow in any direction but it's still a gun if it's shot with a trigger release aid. Some guns shoot arrows, some guns shoot bullets. They use guns for underwater fishing. Right? It has a trigger on it, and it doesn't shoot bullets, but it's still a spear-gun. I don't know how some people can rationalize that just because something has a string on it, it's a bow. I say if it has a trigger on it, it's a gun. Some archery companies make crossbows, and I don't know if their main interest is the love of archery anymore or if it's just the love of money."

MIKE'S POINT SYSTEM

Even though scoring systems and equipment have changed in archery over the years, Mike maintains his own unique scoring method — a method that puts dedication at the top. "When someone asks me what archery is really about, I tell them about my point system. I give 100 points to the guy who takes a deer with a basic traditional bow. If someone adds anything to that basic setup we subtract points. If he uses an elevated arrow rest or a tab we subtract a few points. If he uses a sight or a range finder, we subtract even more points. We really subtract points for using a compound and even more for using a release aid. The more aids to accuracy that you use, the more you subtract from the base score. I think that the archer who deserves the most credit is the one working the hardest."

Despite the flood of space age archery gear, a growing wave of archers is joining the longbow and recurve ranks. Mike sees it everyday, and he likes what he sees. "There are a lot of people in archery today who feel they've been gypped because they never knew about traditional archery. So now they're discovering it. Some will stay with it, but many will go back to the compound because it's a much easier way to shoot a bow. Not everyone wants to devote the time it takes to become proficient enough to shoot a recurve. But the trend is to go back to traditional archery, and it's going to continue."

FEDORA BOWS

As traditional archery grows, Mike intends for his bows to grow with it.

His ONE-PIECE 60" RECURVE has a mass weight of approximately 1 pound, 12 ounces, and a recommended brace height of 6¾" from the string to the riser face. The riser measures 21" between fadeouts, is 2¾" thick, and thins through the low-profile grip. It's 1¾" wide and narrows to ¾" through the sight window which is cut ¼" past center shot. The window is full cut for 2" above the shelf and contours back to full riser width 3¾" above the shelf. Both the shelf and the window are rounded for clean arrow flight and equipped with a synthetic fur rest and plate.

He offers the riser in standard mountain ash or a variety of domestic and exotic hardwoods. The riser wood is laminated in alignment with the string and has thumb rest and palm heel overlays of contrasting multilaminated hardwood. The back is capped with black over white fiberglass for strength and attractiveness. Other than the prominent thumb rest and heel overlays, the riser exhibits simple rounded lines and a custom-shaped grip.

Brass accessory bushings are available. Bow specs are white inked on the face below the grip and on the lower limb near the riser.

The tight radius recurve limbs have a working length of approximately 19 1/4" from the fadeout to the string nock. They are 1 1/2" wide at the fadeouts and narrow to about 1/2" at the nocks. The corewood edges are relatively flat, but the fiberglass is nicely feathered into the corewoods. The limbs are constructed from any combination of two of Mike's many corewoods. They are made from one back and one belly lamination enveloped in colored or clear fiberglass. Several of his more popular recurve corewoods are locust, bamboo, osage, red elm, and walnut.

The tip overlays are constructed from three layers of fiberglass and contain flush-cut string nocks that feather into a full-cut "Y" string groove in the belly glass. The small tips measure 3/8" from the nock to the tip. Like all of Mike's bows, his one-piece recurve is offered in gloss, satin, dull, or camo finishes.

To check the relative speed of a Fedora 60" One-Piece Recurve, Kerry Zook, a Fedora customer, chronographed his 68 pound at 28" draw, bamboo and locust cored bow. The bow was equipped with a standard Dacron string with Catwhisker silencers. Kerry shot 28 1/2", 2117 aluminum arrows fletched with three 5" feathers. The arrows had snap-on nocks and weighed 530 grains. Kerry used a shooting glove, drew a consistent 28", and had a clean pull-through release. The average arrow speed for this bow, arrow, and shooter combination was 213 fps.

The following draw/force measurements were recorded on this 60" one-piece bow:

DRAW LENGTH	25"	26"	27"	28"	29"
DRAW WEIGHT	59#	62#	65#	68#	72#

Mike also offers his three-piece take-down recurve line. Its risers vary from 16" to 24" in two-inch increments. His standard handle is made from laminated ash and displays simple rounded lines. He offers his take-down in three models varying from 52" to 70". The limbs attach to the handle with a dual alignment pin and single attachment bushing system.

For the longbow enthusiast Mike offers his 68" TRADITIONAL LONG-BOW. Its mass weight is approximately 1 pound, 8 ounces, and it has a recommended brace height of 6 3/4" from the string to the riser face.

The riser on an average 28" draw longbow measures 17 1/4" between fadeouts, is 2" thick and 1 3/8" wide. It narrows to 7/8" through the sight window which can be cut to center shot. The arrow shelf is crowned and the window rounded to enhance arrow flight. The riser is available in Mike's variety of laminated hardwoods.

The peaked grip is slightly dished and wrapped with a single 4" leather wrap. The arrow shelf and rest are equipped with synthetic fur. Bow and

Fedora one-piece (upper) and take-down (lower) recurves offer distinctive features such as tough ash handles and hardwood thumb and heel overlays.

customer information are white inked below the grip and on the belly glass near the riser.

The limbs exhibit a pronounced 1½" reflex design, and each have a 25½" working length. These relatively flat-edged limbs narrow from 1⅜" wide at the fadeouts to ½" at the string nocks. They are constructed from two tapered and one thin parallel back laminations and one parallel belly lamination. These corewoods are enveloped in clear or colored glass. In all of Mike's bows he offers a wide variety and combination of custom-ground corewoods.

The longbow's thick tip overlays are designed after traditional horn tips. They're made from riser wood over fiberglass and have deep, full cut string nocks on the back and side, feathering to the belly. The upper tip measures ¾" from the nock to the tip and the lower tip measures ¼".

To check the relative speed of a 68" traditional longbow, Kerry shot a 61 pound locust and walnut cored longbow. He used 520 grain, 28½" cedar arrows fletched with three 5" feathers and equipped with snap-on nocks. The string was Dacron without any accessories. He again drew a consistent 28". The average arrow speed for this bow, arrow, and shooter combination was 162 fps.

The following draw/force measurements suggest the smoothness of this 68" longbow:

DRAW LENGTH	25"	26"	27"	28"	29"
DRAW WEIGHT	51½#	55#	57½#	61#	64#

Mike also offers the Brushbow, a 62" flatbow.

THE CUSTOMER'S WAY

In the crafting of his traditional bows, Mike maintains the status of a true custom bowmaker. That means whenever possible, he lets the customer have the bow built their way. "A person should be able to have the color of glass, core materials, and handle section they want. A true custom bowmaker should be able to give these to his customers. But building that kind of bow takes a great deal of time. It's not like making the same bow day in and day out. Custom bowmaking is providing choices for the customer and then with those choices using your experience to make a stable-shooting, hard-hitting bow."

WHERE IT HAPPENS

To produce customer pleasing bows, Mike steps out the back door and into his bowmaking shop. It's his converted attached three-bay garage. Wearing his fleece-lined suede leather vest with glue-stained pockets, brimming with pens and rulers, Mike flits around the shop between the assemblage of work stations.

His shop looks like a small production factory instead of a family bowmaking operation. Two walls are lined with three massive industrial bow presses housed in heavy steel "I" beam frames, similar to presses the large manufacturers use. Laid out like a maze, the shop is filled with a variety of sawing and grinding stations. They include a table saw, a radial arm saw, and a band saw. For making bow dust, he has floppy belt sanders, vertical and horizontal belt sanders, various diameter cushioned sleeved spindle sanders, disk sanders, a custom lamination grinder, drill presses, and power planers and jointers. They're all connected with hoses to Mike's master dust collection system that hums away like a giant insect.

CORE VARIETY

Mike makes his own custom-tapered laminations from a variety of domestic woods. Besides using them in his bows, he also sells them to other bowyers. One his of favorite woods is black locust. It performs well, is reliable, can withstand long draw lengths, and looks good under clear fiberglass. Even though it's a straight-grained stable wood, Mike has forty percent waste when making the rough stock into quality laminations because of unusable hard spots and knots.

Osage also looks great under clear glass, but because of its grain irregularities, Mike experiences up to eighty percent waste when making it into usable laminations. A striking beauty under clear glass is coppery yew. It's not found anywhere near Pennsylvania but Mike has a good supply. "I was fortunate to buy some of Earl Ulrich's yew. Much of it was short pieces, but they're ideal for my take-down limbs. Some of that yew was cut back in the forties and fifties."

Another of his choice corewoods is local Pennsylvania black walnut. Beneath clear glass it radiates a warm rich brown. "If cut properly it can make a very nice limb. Black walnut was one of the bow woods tested by

Pope and Young, and they felt it was a satisfactory bow wood. We use walnut that we've been aging for fourteen years. We actually cut the trees down, took them to the saw mill and instructed them how to saw it."

Mike also commonly offers bamboo, maple, and red elm corewoods. But no matter what material he uses for making laminations, it's been air dried. "The difference between air-dried and kiln-dried wood is that kiln drying drives the moisture out so fast that much of the springiness leaves the wood. Bow woods should be seasoned naturally. We usually age our corewoods at least five years." Mike dries his wood slowly, away from the sunlight in his well-ventilated drying shed.

Even though his core stock is thoroughly air seasoned, Mike heat tempers his wood for about three months, reducing the moisture content to around three percent. "We temper all of our woods because we want the wood to twist before it goes into a bow, not after. Heat treating it is like aging it for twenty years."

Once it's dried, Mike band saws his boards into ¼" thick strips and restacks the pieces to maintain matched pairs of laminations. He then ties the cut strips into bundles and continues to heat temper them.

Within a week before making a bow, Mike selects the laminations and micro tapers them on his homemade grinding device. It's made from a slow-moving horizontal belt sander that feeds the laminations under a high speed vertical belt sander. When grinding the corewoods, Mike varies the taper to match the bow design, draw weight, and the customer's draw length. This helps to provide smoothness and stability in the bow.

When choosing pairs of laminations for a bow, Mike selects laminations with grain characteristics that offset grain variations in alternating laminations. For instance, when using cross grain laminations, he positions the grain at opposing angles on alternating pieces. This helps produce a more stable and true-drawing limb. To build speed into his limbs, Mike often uses edge-grain laminations.

Mike sandwiches his corewoods between clear, white, brown, black, green, or grey fiberglass — but not before drying it. "We also dry our glass because fiberglass maintains a high moisture content. Many bowyers only think about wood absorbing moisture but glass does too."

BASEBALL BAT TOUGH

Although Mike offers risers in a variety of domestic and exotic hardwoods, he commonly uses white mountain ash. "They make baseball bats out of ash because it takes the most shock. A lot of bows break not because of strength problems but because they can't take the shock. When you release the bowstring, the limbs return to their memory position, causing shock to travel down into the handle. Some woods can take more shock than others, but ash can take the most."

Mike's supply of riser ash came from a large tree that used to grow right in his front yard. It was located near some power lines and cut down by the electrical company. Although he lost some shade in the summer, Mike gained a good supply of bow handle material.

Using his handmade profiling jig, Mike grinds the riser belly and back to precisely fit his bow form.

To make the tough ash even stronger, Mike band saws it into thin boards and laminates them using Urac 185 and bar-clamps. Like his limb core-woods, Mike positions the ash pieces to best complement the grain alignment of adjoining laminations. "We want to create a plywood effect to obtain the strongest handle possible because our bows are cut past center shot. So we need an extremely strong handle, especially through the sight window."

Mike mixes the powered Urac with its resin and applies a good coat to all contact surfaces. He then heat cures the compressed block. "I think Urac was designed for use in World War II for gluing together airplanes. They needed a strong glue that would take the shock, and that's what we need in our handles."

After it's dried, Mike cuts and planes the handle block to its 1¾" width. He outlines the riser profile using a template and band saws the back and face. Mike then clamps the riser in a profile sanding jig and grinds the riser to shape on his coarse high-speed vertical sanding drum. The form-guided jig is swept against a bearing at the base of the drum, perfectly shaping the ground surface. Mike's homemade jig is shaped on both sides to allow the grinding of both the belly and back profiles on the same jig.

Even though his profiling jig produces near-perfect fadeouts, Mike backs the fadeouts with a strip of wood and feathers them by hand on the grinder. "We pay attention to our fadeouts because a lot of the stress is transferred down the limb into the fadeouts, and that's where a bow breaks. When you shoot a bow, limb stress travels down the limb to a point where it can't bend anymore. This stress starts at the fadeout and works into the handle. You might not be able to see it, but that handle is also bending."

PUTTING IT TOGETHER

Before glue-up, Mike bevels the butt ends of his laminations so he can overlap them. When handling his composites, he's careful to touch only the edges so he doesn't soil the clean gluing surfaces.

Even though some bowyers stain their laminations to make them more attractive under clear glass, Mike uses only natural-toned corewoods. "Anything you put on the surface of your laminations puts a barrier between the glue and the wood. Stain may make the woods look darker under clear glass, but it might keep the glue from achieving maximum strength."

To achieve maximum strength in his bowmaking, Mike uses and sells a popular epoxy used by many custom bowyers. "We've been using this epoxy for over twenty years. It's very stable, thick, and it works well under clear glass. One of the words people use when describing my bows is 'trusty' because they can rely on them. Our epoxy helps us achieve that reputation." Mike applies the thick epoxy to all composite contact surfaces, lays up the bow on his work table, and then puts it in his press.

BIG PRESSES

Mike lays the glued composites on his plywood bow form which represents the back shape of his one-piece recurve. This wooden form is housed in a massive steel-framed press. Once the composites are positioned, Mike hydraulically lowers the upper half of the press which is lined with a strip of rubber and an air pressure hose. This upper half is reinforced with extra layers of rubber between the hose and the form through the fadeout and recurve areas to provide extra pressure at these critical gluing areas.

Mike inflates the hose with sixty to eighty pounds of pressure and then activates heat strips lining both form surfaces. This cures the epoxy at about 135 degrees for two hours. Mike usually allows the pressed bow to cool overnight in the form before removing it. After removing the bow from the form, Mike grinds off the excess hardened glue and grinds both sides parallel. He marks the limb outlines using a fiberglass template and then saws and grinds them to shape.

SEVERAL OVERLAYS

Once the limbs are roughed in and checked for draw weight, Mike installs his overlays. He glues on his layered fiberglass recurve tip overlays using epoxy. "We use fiberglass tip overlays on our thin-limbed recurves because it's much stronger than wood. But on our longbows we use wooden overlays because the base limb tips are so much thicker."

Using a contoured form, Mike also laminates fiberglass capping on the back of his recurve risers. This is especially important when he occasionally uses a select piece of wood for a solid wood handle. "Laminating that fiberglass over the back of the riser increases the strength in the handle by at least thirty-three percent. It also adds to the beauty of the bow."

Mike also laminates an overlaid thumb rest opposite the sight window on his recurves, a distinctive trademark of a Fedora bow. "There are several

FUNCTION AND BEAUTY — Mike's front, thumb, and heel overlays are some of the trademarks of a Fedora recurve.

reasons why I build the thumb rest. In my experience as a professional coach and pretty fair tournament shot, I know the importance of getting the right grip on the bow every time. So years ago I developed my grip and thumb rest to make the shooter get the same grip every time. In fact, when you grab one of my bows, it doesn't feel comfortable unless you're holding it right. The thumb rest also adds to the classic beauty of the bow."

He also installs a multilaminated heel overlay below the belly of the grip. On all of his overlays, Mike roughens the contact surfaces, epoxies on the overlays with "C" clamps, and allows them to cure for twenty-four hours at seventy-five to eighty degrees. "Each overlay is a separate, time-consuming operation. We could take short cuts and design our bows to incorporate one piece of wood and eliminate some overlays. But we choose to build in the workmanship where it can be seen."

After the overlays are dried, Mike shapes his handles using his assortment of grinders and sanders. When shaping, he crests the shelf and rounds the window near the grip throat. "I peak them over the pivot point because it's the least critical part of the bow and makes the bow more forgiving." He also angles his shelf down into the window-shelf junction and bevels the outer shelf edge for extra feather clearance.

Mike shapes the grip, making sure the highest part is rounded and runs down the center of the throat. "I call this the pipe effect. It's the hardest type of grip to torque. A flatter surface will tend to follow your hand, but a more rounded surface won't because it pivots." He then removes any irregularities and achieves smooth riser contours by sanding the riser on his soft air-sleeved cushioned spindle sanders.

NO MORE WOOD RASPS — Unlike the "good ol' days," Mike shapes his risers on different sized spindle sanders.

MICRO-TAPER

When Mike is finished with the riser, he final shapes the limbs, grinding them into his micro-taper. "Our limb design has a sharp taper through the recurve portion. A narrower limb through the base of the recurve might twist, but if I leave it wide it won't. So I taper after the critical point at the start of the recurve. We get a limb that won't twist, yet it has high performance."

During final shaping, Mike brings both limbs into alignment by sighting down the centerline of the braced bow. He removes material from the strong side of the recurve until the string tracks true. Once it's aligned, Mike shoots the bow several times and rechecks for any minor alignment adjustments.

When the string naturally tracks down the center of the limbs, Mike finishes the nocks and files in the full "Y" string groove. Fashioning a full string groove requires extra work, but for Mike it's a must. "We could just file a single groove, but a full cut string groove makes the most accurate bow. As the limb closes, a full string groove aligns the string evenly. On a bad release that's very important. On a single groove, the string has to bounce back into the groove which varies the degree of center shot."

During the final limb sanding, Mike rounds and feathers the fiberglass where it meets the corewoods. "Any woodworker knows that a rounded edge bends more easily and is less apt to splinter than a sharp edge."

An unusual characteristic of Mike's tips is their smallness. They are barely nubs. "A limb tip is moving and vibrating. By reducing the tip's physical weight, I'm reducing tip vibration. It's also less weight for the limbs to carry when recovering. It's a small point but almost everything we do relates to the overall performance of the bow."

Finally, Mike fine sands the bow by hand and then applies a sealer to the entire bow. He then sands again and applies several more sealer coats on the open-grained ash and sands it smooth. He inks on the bow information and sprays the bow with one of his four types of finish. "We match the finish to what the customer wants. Normally we spray each bow three times with as many as seven coats of finish, sanding between each spraying."

NEVER ENOUGH

Mike's finished creations represent his three decades of bowmaking savvy. Even though he has been designing and building bows that long, he continues experimenting with new designs and production refinements. "We don't know it all, but I offer my customers a lot of experience. I've put a lot of time into developing our limb and handle designs. We feel we've refined our bows into very worthwhile products. Our single biggest problem and complaint is that we can't produce enough bows. Making custom bows takes time. We could short cut some methods, but our customers wouldn't be getting the extra workmanship."

When Mike gives his customers that extra workmanship, he's giving them more than just thumb rests, heel overlays, and delicate tips, he's giving them a piece of a special gift. "Besides the income, traditional bowmaking gives me a lot satisfaction. The Lord gave me the gift of bowmaking."

And Mike enjoys sharing it.

BEAR ARCHERY COMPANY

HE DARED TO CHASE HIS FONDEST DREAMS

Two men filtered through the murmuring crowd and out the doors of the Adams Theater. They paused under the lit marquee which was beckoning the next group of Detroit area sportsmen: "ALASKAN ADVENTURES, Featuring Arthur Young." The two walked on, filling the evening shadows with chatter about the amazing bowhunting film they had just seen.

One of them, a lanky Pennsylvanian, couldn't put the image of the buckskin clad bowhunter out of his mind. And, as he disappeared into the shadows, he carried with him a magical new spark of adventure in his glacial blue eyes. That spark would soon grow into an unquenchable flame that would guide his destiny and shape the future of bowhunting around the world. The young man was a dream chaser. His name was Fred Bear.

Fred Bear began chasing his dreams when he was a boy in Pennsylvania. "I decided when I was a kid," Fred said in the summer of 1987, "that my life was going to be hunting and trapping. I was going to wind up in Canada and be one of those big guides.

"I went to school in a little one street town in Plainfield, Pennsylvania. To go to high school, you had to take an examination, and the high school was five miles away. In the seventh grade I went with a group, just for the hell of it, to take the examination for high school, and damn if I didn't pass! So, I skipped the eighth grade.

"But I didn't want to get too deep in school because I was going to be a hunter and trapper. My freshman year was okay, and then I purposely flunked out the second year, because what the hell, you don't need to know ANYTHING to go hunting and trapping!"

Fred's father, however, was less than enthusiastic and sternly told him if he wasn't going to finish school, he had to find a trade. So with his father's guidance, Fred got a job in a local shop where he became a patternmaker. In 1923, armed with his patternmaking skills and his always adventurous spirit, twenty-one-year-old Fred Bear headed northwest for the enticing state of Michigan.

"One of the reasons I wanted to go to Detroit, Michigan, was because it was a frontier town at that time. They had great big deer in Michigan, and we had little runty deer in Pennsylvania. So I thought Michigan would be a great place to live and work. My mother left a key hanging out for two years in case I wanted to come back. But I've been gone ever since."

A START FROM YOUNG

While living in Detroit, Fred not only discovered the thrills of hunting Michigan's big deer, he also later discovered a new way to hunt them — bowhunting. Maybe it was destiny's guiding hand that led Bear and his friend, Ray Stannard, into the Adams Theater in 1927. Young's film ignited the bowhunting spark within Bear, and he later met Art Young during Young's stay in the Detroit area. The two struck up a friendship, and Young taught Fred how to craft bows and arrows.

Fred began making his own archery equipment in his basement work-shop, and continued his job managing a tire cover plant. During the Depression, the tire cover plant burned down. So Fred and his friend, Charles Piper, started a silk-screening business and Fred moved his part-time bowmaking business into a corner of the silk-screening shop. It wasn't long before his archery business grew into a full-time operation, and Fred formally created Bear Archery Company in 1939.

During those early years in Detroit, Bear Archery crafted self-wood bows under the guiding hand of Fred's most skilled bowyer. "He was Nels Grumley and he had a flair for crafting bows. He couldn't teach anybody else, but he could do it. And he was a hell of a hunter and a good shot, an instinctive snap shooter."

From the stacks of self-wood bows that Fred and Nels crafted in the Detroit shop, one stands out above the rest. "Art Young gave me a yew bow stave, a full-length stave, it was just a beautiful thing. Nels and I would look at that stave and study it, and admire it, and pet it, and then set it back in the corner. It was a nice stave but it was especially valuable because Art Young gave it to me.

"We studied it like we were going to cut a diamond. Finally we decided we would really cut into it, stick our necks out, and make a bow. It turned out to be eighty-five pounds, which was a little heavy. But when you made self-wood bows in those days, out of yew or osage, whatever weight they came out to was the weight they should be left at. When they're tillered and everything is right, they should never be changed. Well, it never was changed and it finally wound up with a fellow in AuGres.

"He went hunting with it and saw a nice buck coming that passed within fifteen yards. He waited until the buck's head was behind a tree, and then he pulled this bow back. Well, then the buck stopped and there he was, holding eighty-five pounds. He said, 'I didn't know what to do. I knew if I let it down I couldn't get it back again. But then I also knew I couldn't hold it.' So he let it down, the buck walked out, and he never got a shot at it."

Although Fred's archery business grew, he never cared for Detroit's big city atmosphere, and he moved the business north in 1947 to his favorite trout waters near the banks of the peaceful AuSable River. In the years following his move to Grayling, Michigan, Bear Archery became instrumental in establishing archery and bowhunting as popular recreational sports across the country. But growing into one of America's archery manufacturing giants didn't come easy. "We struggled through some rough times, but then things kept growing and growing, and pretty soon it got almost out of control. I never did get into the business to make money. I got into it because I liked it, and I still like what I'm doing."

BOWMAKING BREAKTHROUGHS

Bear Archery's bowmaking breakthroughs helped them grow as a company, plus they marked a new era of bow manufacturing. In 1951, Bear developed fiberglass with unidirectional fibers. Soon after, he also developed the electronic bow press. These innovations made it possible to mass produce fiberglass faced and backed bows, and for the first time sportsmen could readily purchase a durable, reliable, and affordable, high-performance hunting bow. These manufacturing developments, combined with Fred's vivid promotional hunting films, helped open the alluring doors of bowhunting and archery to thousands of sportsmen.

Although Fred made numerous innovations in the bowmaking industry, without a doubt, unidirectional fiberglass towered over the rest in significance. "You wouldn't have archery today, and you wouldn't have bowhunting today without fiberglass. Fiberglass is the thing that took bows out of the dark ages. Without fiberglass we wouldn't be sitting here talking, and the plant wouldn't be here. For the first time you could build a bow with micrometers. You really didn't have to know anything about bowmaking. Taper your pieces of wood and put glass on both sides, and anybody could do it. You could set it up on a production line and sell your bows to a sporting goods store at a price that would allow them to make some money. And it was good for the hunter too because breakage was very rare."

Even with unidirectional fiberglass and the electronic bow press, bowmaking gremlins occasionally crept into Bear's production efforts. "Back in 1960, we had about one-third of our bows break because of a gluing problem.

"I was the first to put fiberglass on bows. At that time we didn't have epoxy glues. The best glue that we had was Urac 185, but it would not glue to fiberglass — a wood to wood bond was fine, but not wood to glass. We had a friend at Chrysler in Detroit who invented 'Cycleweld' which was a cement used to glue rubber to metal for motor mounts. This Cycleweld would glue wood to fiberglass, but the curing heat was 325 degrees and we couldn't heat the wood up that much. So I got birds-eye maple veneer, about one-sixteenth of an inch thick, from the Upper Peninsula. Birds-eye maple is full of knots that are like little rivets so I figured it would hold with Cycleweld, even though it would be charred from that much heat. We would glue that birds-eye maple to the glass and cure it at 325 degrees and then sand it until there was almost nothing left. And then we could glue with Urac 185 because there was still a little bit of wood on the fiberglass.

"We took electric strip heaters for the bow presses and built housings around them. Well, two of those housings collapsed and became unparallel on their sides, or bellied, and every third bow didn't have pressure in the middle of the limb. This resulted in the veneer not gluing solidly and the limb eventually failed. That was tragic. I sent a letter out to everyone who had one of our bows and said to send it back if it broke and we would replace it. We lost a lot of money that year. My God, we just about had it."

Fred overcame the occasional production setbacks and became one of America's bowmaking giants. Still, consistently pleasing archery customers wasn't easy. "We put a compass in the handle of our bows one time, a real good compass. I ran across a fellow who supplied them to the Air Force. It was a survival compass that didn't look much different than a dime store compass. I put them in the bows and got some complaints, 'WHY DID YOU PUT THAT CHEAP COMPASS IN YOUR BOWS?' And one guy was insulted because it implied that he didn't know his way around in the woods! Here I had gone to all this trouble and it had cost a couple extra dollars to do it, so I just quit it."

Bear Archery Company continued to produce customer-pleasing bows near the quiet backwaters of the AuSable for thirty-one years until its move to Gainesville, Florida, in 1978.

BEAR'S NEW HOME

Today Bear Archery Company is located in a wooded setting similar to the one it knew for years in Grayling. It's nestled in a quiet forest of pines and oaks near I-75. The beautifully landscaped Bear factory-museum complex is located off the Archer Road exit on Fred Bear Drive. The facility even has a small well-kept field range which is attractively set in the woods near the front of the complex.

The Paynes Prairie near the present Bear factory has been a haunt for "traditional hunters" for the past 12,000 years. During this ancient past, progressive aboriginal cultures used a variety of thrown and slung weapons to bring home the bacon. But it was during the Depthford occupation of the area from 500 B.C. to 200 A.D. that the bow and arrow came into widespread use. Today it's the Gator Bowmen, a band of 150 members, who comprise the local tribe of bowbenders who share their primitive passion for the bow and arrow.

Visitors to the Bear museum-factory complex are aptly greeted near the parking area by statues of a giant Kodiak and a Polar Bear in menacing erect postures, one standing on each side of the entrance drive. Like giant guard dogs gazing down at all who enter, they make a visually pronounced statement, "THIS IS BEAR COUNTRY!"

The Bear facility incorporates the famed Fred Bear Museum and Bear Archery Company under one roof. The museum offers visitors a panorama of bowhunting, archery, animal, and historical exhibits, and provides a windowed view of ongoing bowmaking operations down in the factory work area next to the museum. This imaginative design lets visitors inspect ancient museum archery relics while keeping an eye on modern bowmaking techniques.

Youthful gasps fill the corridors of the museum as kids spy the varied life-like mounts of animals from almost every continent. Most of them are Fred's fantastic collection of personal bowhunting trophies. Each represents an exciting and interesting tale, especially when spiced with Fred's sage humor.

THE SPECIAL RAM

One of the museum's special mounts is Fred's majestic stone sheep, taken in 1957 while bowhunting in the open wilderness of British Columbia. That massive horned ram reigned for many years as the number one stone sheep in the Pope and Young records. "That sheep being first place in the Pope and Young records is not what made the hunt memorable. It was the events that led up to it.

"I was hunting with an Indian at Coldfish Lake in British Columbia. He was a real Indian, not a highway Indian, a real Indian who could live out of a tin can. Charles Quock was his name, quite a guy. He's the only Indian I ever saw that wasn't afraid of a grizzly bear. He carried a thirty-eight revolver and he was ready to take on a grizzly with it.

"We had ridden our horses up a creek and stopped there for lunch. While we were eating, we saw a white object on the mountain off in a draw. We thought it was a goat because that's the only thing that is white up there. We set the scope up and saw that it was just the flat side of a rock that was reflecting the sky. But, beside it laid this ram which we would never have seen because he was laying in the shale, and he was the same color as the shale.

"So, we tied the horses up and we did a pretty good sneak, and we had him pretty well marked down. He had been facing away when we first saw him, but he turned around and was facing to us. We came up over the ridge he was laying on and he started to run at about sixty yards. I shot an arrow at him and missed. I shot more to please the Indian than anything else."

As the ram disappeared over a series of shale ridges, Fred thought he missed his only chance at the big ram. But the Indian guide had other ideas. "Now, you don't run after sheep you know, but we did! This Indian started running after the sheep after I missed him, and I thought, 'God, he must be crazy!' But geez, you know I don't tell Indians how to hunt.

"Well, it's just the second day of hunting and it usually takes me a week to ten days to really get used to it. So the Indian was always waiting for me. We would come up over one ridge and the ram would be standing looking at us from over the next one. Then he would run off and we would run over to the next ridge. We did this three or four times, then finally I'd just about had it because you sink down in that shale when you're running. Finally, we came over a ridge and the ram didn't run, and the Indian yelled 'Shoot-shoot-shoot.

"Well, my God, all I could see was the ram's head, and that's just all horns. I wouldn't have shot except that I felt I would lose face with the Indian if I didn't. At least I had to try to shoot. But to keep from hitting the ram in the head, I had to loop the arrow over the ridge, which I did. It had a good line, but I had a feeling it had dropped too low. And then I just sat down there to get my breath back while the Indian ran over the ridge."

A few minutes later, the Indian, wearing a big smile, stuck his head up over the ridge. The Indian's smile recharged Fred's weary legs and he ran over to the ridge. "We could see some blood but we couldn't see any tracks because the shale would just roll over and cover them. Finally, we were looking down the mountain, and there about three or four hundred yards downhill the ram was lodged against a rock outcropping.

"I got him right through the jugular vein. Apparently he was standing at a little bit of an angle. I didn't know which way he was standing when I shot. The arrow cut through the jugular vein and slid under the shoulder blade and came out behind the shoulder. The arrow never got into the lung cavity. Yep, that was really somethin'! You learn somethin' every day. Runnin' after sheep!"

Fred also scored on a dall sheep but the bighorn and desert bighorn eluded his arrows. "At one time I was going for a grand slam. I had the dall sheep and the stone sheep. You know, I've been lucky in sheep hunting. I shot my dall sheep on the first day hunting them, and I shot the stone sheep on the second day of that hunt. Then I went for bighorns twice but the closest I ever got was a mountain away. Yeah, I was going to shoot the grand slam, but I got busy with other things and I finally said, 'Well, somebody else can do that.'

"I don't have a yen to shoot anything anymore. I go hunting, but I go with a gang and they think I'm an old pro. And they listen to EVERYTHING I tell them and we have a lot of fun. They think that I know everything about deer especially, but nobody knows too much about those things!"

BOWMAKING HISTORY

Besides Fred's memory-making animal mounts, Bear Museum displays a treasure chest of bow building history. Walls and glass cases display an array of ancient and modern bows from assorted cultures around the world. Many of these bows seem to faintly whisper from worn handles or scratched limbs, recalling memories of confrontations with men or beasts. Some of these historic bows, such as Art Young's 1928 DEERSLAYER, magically entrance visiting archery purists. This hand-crafted fifty-six pound yew longbow proudly hangs on the wall, beckoning softly to those who realize its significance, "Please, just one more true arrow."

The museum also displays a historic collection of Bear bows. Some, such as the all-wood laminated bows from Bear's early bowmaking days, incorporate a blend of different woods. "Bows always broke from the back before the use of glass, and hickory was the best wood that we had for backing. It broke less than any other wood. We laminated yew in the middle because it was light in weight and if a limb is light in weight it will shoot faster. And the osage orange was the toughest of the compression materials so we used that on the face."

The progressive display of Bear bows includes their line of beautiful recurves from the early 1970s. They represent the widest selection of recurves ever offered by Bear, including one of America's classic recurves. "If I had to go shopping for a bow back in time, I'd go right back to 1971 and pick up a Super Kodiak."

Downstairs from the bow displays and animal mounts, sets Bear Museum's video theater. In it, audiences accompany Fred on brief expeditions to strange lands in quest of antlered, fanged, or tusked beasts. And for many, Fred's vivid adventures kindle that same bowhunting flame Bear felt when he first saw Art Young's *Alaskan Adventures*.

For many who have seen his adventure films, the thought of Fred Bear, the bowhunting legend, conjures up the steely-eyed bowman wearing his favored Borsalino hat adorned with a feather or a small sprig. It shadows the prominent ears, bulging jaw muscles, broad nose, and friendly smile. In his right hand he holds his 60" Custom Kodiak Take-Down recurve pulling sixty-five pounds which Fred altered near the shelf to allow shooting off his knuckle. Most remember the legend facing a lumbering giant Kodiak, a ghostly Polar bear, or a menacing grizzly. And although it's true that Fred had a fondness for hunting the always unpredictable bears, some of his most memorable bowhunting adventures involved the more retiring and less intimidating herbivores.

LITTLE DELTA MAGIC

Hunting herbivores lured Fred to almost every corner of the world and he had treasured memories of many hidden places. But one magic wild patch of North America stood out above the rest. "Probably my best times were a couple of hunts on the Little Delta up in Alaska. We didn't have any guides and we planned the thing all ourselves. It was a fly-in hunt and it was the best mostly because we were on our own. You could take off and you didn't have anybody trailing you, because you didn't have a guide around. There were grizzlies in the country and you could get into trouble, but we never did. That's the hunt where I got my first Pope and Young caribou."

Fred's first book caribou still held the number four slot in the third edition of the Pope and Young record book. "I really didn't know he was that big when I shot him. I was in the open sneaking up on him uphill. I didn't know it at the time, but my buddy Judd Grindell was watching me with binoculars from a distant hillside.

"I came to a place where I just couldn't go any farther, and I was about forty yards from the animal. I shot an arrow, but it was a miserable day with sleet and the wind was blowing so hard I hit that bull through the hock. It didn't get the tendon but it did get the big artery coming down the leg. He went about a quarter of a mile. It's a crazy thing, I hit a kudu in the same exact place while hunting in Africa."

SIMPLE SHOOTING

Although fantastic shots seemed commonplace for Fred, he had his share of luckier shots like his caribou and kudu. But for Fred, luck wasn't just a fickle finger of fate — it was something he made happen. "I spend a lot of time in the woods, and I try to use my time to an advantage. I stop a lot, but I always stop where there is a runway, where I can see around, or see some new country. And by doing that, you can kinda make your own luck."

One of Fred's luckiest shots "happened" during a whitetail hunt in Nebraska with Knick Knickerbocker. "We were putting on a drive. Knick and I and another fellow were the standers in this draw. Knick was right in the middle and he made the mistake of getting himself in thick cover. It was so thick he couldn't shoot out of it. Geez, you can't do that, you know!

"I was over on the edge and this nice buck came up through the middle on the double. But Knick couldn't shoot, hell, he couldn't do anything. The buck almost ran into him and had to detour out around him. I saw Knick wasn't going to shoot, so I lofted one about sixty yards and it took the deer through the back quarters, but I got him. That was probably my luckiest shot."

Although he modestly tried to dispel some of his shots as luck, Bear's instinctive shooting style and his quick release form proved a deadly combination for game in the field. With his bow canted and his eyes locked on his target, Bear shot instinctively in one fluid motion. "Instinctive shooting is just as hard to explain as it is for a pitcher to tell you how he puts the ball over the outside corner of the plate, or the outfielder who heaves a fly ball into the catcher's mitt on the first bounce and gets the guy running to home plate. How does the carpenter hit the nail? He can't tell you! It's difficult to describe.

"Maurice Thompson said that instinctive shooting is done by push and pull, and the draw is never stopped. You never stop drawing, it just comes all at once. And when you're on the target, it's got to go right then. That's the way I shoot. I'm a snap shooter. Now there are all kinds of snap shooters. Most are never able to get back to full draw. I've got to talk to myself every time if I really want to hit something, 'Get it all the way back and follow through.' "

HUMBLE AND GENUINELY WARM

Besides instinctive shooting skills and a favorite bow, Fred agreed that one of the most important ingredients to a successful hunt is a good hunting companion. Fred shared campfires with many unique and enjoyable personalities, but there was no hesitation when he recalled his favorite hunting companion. His voice took on a tone of genuine warmth and affection. "It's Bob Munger. We've gone a lot of places, done a lot of things, been through some real tough hunts including being out six weeks on an ice pack in a tent. He's a good hard worker, he doesn't get discouraged, and he doesn't get cold. Yeah, he's a hell of a lousy shot with a bow. But he's also a hell of a hunter with eyes like an eagle."

Whether in the company of hunting companions or a crowd of admirers, Fred Bear remained a common man, who not only had a warm story to share, but who was quick to listen to others. When questioned about changing the course of bowhunting or being the "Father of Modern Bowhunting," Bear would turn on his humble charm. "Awh, go on! My timing was just good. It wasn't anything that I did. If that tire cover plant in Detroit where I worked hadn't burned down, I'd still be runnin' that damn thing, I suppose. There are a lot of people who could have done what I did under the same circumstances. Art Young had kind of set the stage. He had gone out and shot some big animals. I came at the right time, and everything was ready for something like that."

Although he tried to remain humble, it could not be denied that during his sixty-one year romance with the sport of archery, he had shaped the course of bowhunting around the world. Fred Bear helped put that magical, far-away look in the eyes of bowhunters everywhere. The timing may have been right for the emergence of a bowhunting legend, but he was the man who dared to chase his fondest dreams.

The world of archery bid a sad farewell to Fred Bear on Wednesday, April 27, 1988. And on that day, sportsmen around the world lost a great friend. He will long be remembered as bowhunter, conservationist, humorist, educator, and lifelong friend to the sport of archery. But it was common for Fred, when saying good-bye to bowhunting friends to light up his broad smile, flash his eyes and say, "Don't forget, happy hunting."

PAPA BEAR

Up until the illness that preceded his death, Fred Bear remained a commanding and active figure at Bear Archery Company. He would arrive at work in the mornings with briefcase in hand and soon find his way to his personal workshop or walk back to the R&D lab where he would check one of his ongoing projects. Most of these projects were associated with the manufacturing of his beloved recurves.

When walking through the factory, his keen eye was quick to discover a slight variation in the front overlays on a batch of Custom Kodiak Take-Down risers. It was his favorite bow, and when demanding the quality in his recurves, Fred wasn't one to mince words. During his fifty-five years of bowcrafting he remained innovative, concerned, and insistent about the creation of Bear recurves.

CLASSIC RECURVES

Although Papa Bear no longer arrives at work in the morning, manufacturing traditional bows lives on at Bear Archery Company. They still produce two of the all-time favorites of classic Bear recurves, the Fred Bear Custom Kodiak Take-Down, and the Fred Bear Kodiak Recurve. These bows remain as much of an archery legend as the man who created them. For the younger traditionalist, Bear Archery also produces a beginner's bow, the Bearcat Recurve.

The CUSTOM KODIAK TAKE-DOWN was Fred Bear's favorite, and it accompanied him around the world on many of his famous hunts. With its striking black fiberglass and laminated riser, this handsome three-piece take-down is similar to the legendary one-piece Super Kodiak.

When the Custom Kodiak T.D. was first introduced around 1970, it was offered in three limb and riser lengths. From a marketing standpoint the multiple combinations were an attractive feature. But logistically, juggling the manufacturing with optimum bow performance was difficult. Today the Custom T.D. is available in one riser and one limb size, both comparable to the older "B" riser and limbs.

Fred's early efforts to design a reliable take-down began after an Alaskan moose hunt where he discovered his one-piece bow had been lost somewhere in the shuffle between planes. After losing his bow, he was determined to make a take-down that he could keep at his side during his travels. His first design was a three-piece bow with the limbs attached to the handle with a mechanism much like the latch on a double-barreled shot gun. Fred took this prototype bow to Africa in 1965 and used it to arrow a Cape buffalo. Although it worked fine, the limb latch system proved too expensive to manufacture. So Fred went back to his workshop and eventually designed the limb attachment system used today. Fred referred to this famed take-down bow as the "ultimate recurve."

The Custom Kodiak limbs lock simply into place without any bolts or tools. Its "microgroove" limb mounting system provides positive limb alignment with a quick flick of the wrists and a snap of the thumb.

This 60" recurve is available in draw weights of five pound increments, from 45 pounds to 70 pounds. It has a mass weight of 2 pounds, 6 ounces,

TWO ARCHERY LEGENDS — Fred admiring his "ultimate recurve," his trusty companion, the Kodiak T.D. which accompanied him on many a hunt.

and a recommended brace height of 8¼" to 8½" from the throat to the string. The striking handle section is 20½" long and is composed of dark grey laminated maple accentuated with a green decorative "V" wedge. This ⅛" thick green wedge is sandwiched between thin veneers of clear maple. The northern hard-rock maple riser laminations are positioned parallel to the string for strength. The riser is capped on the back and belly with black over white over black overlay material.

The handle is 2¾" thick and narrows to 1⅝" through the throat. It is 1⅜" wide near the limb latches, and ¾" through the sight window. The slightly crested arrow shelf is 2½" across and the window is equipped with a Bear Weatherest elevated rest. The center shot sight window is slightly rounded to enhance arrow flight. It is full cut for 4½" above the shelf and contours back to full riser width at 5½" above the shelf. The medium-sized low profile grip exhibits gently flowing contours, exposing contrasting grain patterns in the laminated gray maple. This gives each handle a distinctive appearance and causes it to blend in naturally with the woods. A Converta-Accessory insert is located on the front of the handle 5" below the shelf, and brass sight mount bushings are set opposite the sight window.

The Custom Kodiak T.D. limbs are made with one parallel lamination on the belly and one tapered lamination on the back. These laminations are similar to Actionwood and are made from laminated blocks of hard-rock maple. This laminated corewood provides increased strength and uniformity over the solid edge-grain corewoods Bear Archery discontinued using around 1979.

The limbs have a slightly sharper recurve than the Kodiak one-piece and are designed to unfold later in the draw. Recent changes in the new Custom T.D. limbs are the use of laminated maple in the limb fadeout wedge instead of phenolic material, and the use of one parallel and one tapered lamination instead of two tapered laminations.

The Custom Kodiak T.D. limbs are backed and faced with black fiberglass. The fadeout wedge is made from the same grey laminated stock as the handle. The limbs have a working length of 15" from the string nock to the fadeout. They are 1⁹⁄₁₆" wide near the fadeout and narrow to ¾" at the nock. The edges are slightly rounded and smoothly finished. They have thin 1¾" long tip overlays of green laminated maple and are somewhat squared on the ends. The string grooves are cut flush on the sides and feather out to the belly which has a single string groove ground into the glass. Like the handle, the limbs are available in the standard clear gloss finish or a flat drab green camo leaf finish.

The following draw/force measurements were recorded on a stock Custom Kodiak T.D:

DRAW LENGTH	25"	26"	27"	28"	29"
DRAW WEIGHT	41#	43½#	46#	49#	52½#

To check a Custom Kodiak T.D. for relative speed, a 54 pound at 28" draw T.D. was shot using Bear's shooting machine. The test arrow weighed 486 grains and was drawn 28". It chronographed 177 fps.

BEAR ARCHERY'S CLASSIC RECURVES — The Fred Bear Custom Kodiak T.D. and the
Kodiak Recruve both display lines reminiscent of the old Super Kodiak of the 1970s.

The FRED BEAR KODIAK RECURVE is Bear's one-piece 60" recurve
reminiscent of the old Super Kodiak. It's available in the same draw weights
as the Custom T.D. and has the same brace height. Its mass weight is
2 pounds, 4 ounces.

The 26" long riser section is made from brown laminated hard-rock
maple and has a vertical ⅛" thick decorative maple wedge sandwiched with
clear maple veneer. It has a full cut 6" sight window above the shelf. Most
dimensions are similar to the Custom T. D. except the grip which is a little
bigger. The accessory and sight bushings are the same as the Custom T.D.
but there is no decorative capping on the Kodiak Recurve's riser. Like the
Custom T.D., the contoured laminated maple exhibits attractively contrasting hues.

The Kodiak Recurve limbs are constructed from one tapered back lamination and one tapered belly lamination enveloped in brown fiberglass. The
Kodiak Recurve limbs have a working length of approximately 17" from the
fadeout to the nock.

The following draw/force measurements were recorded on a stock Kodiak Recurve:

DRAW LENGTH	25"	26"	27"	28"	29"
DRAW WEIGHT	41½#	44½#	47#	50#	53#

To check for relative speed, a 48 pound at 28" draw Kodiak Recurve was
shot using Bear's shooting machine. The test arrow weighed 432 grains, was
drawn 28", and chronographed 175 fps.

BEAR BOWYERS

Today, the design and manufacturing of Bear's recurves are guided by long-time Bear bowyer, Neil Byce, and director of research and development, Gary Simonds.

Neil is Bear Archery's number one traditional bowyer. He began working at Bear Archery in 1967, and through the years has worked at most of the different jobs involved with manufacturing recurves. He knows the process inside and out. Neil learned his bowyer skills from Owen Jeffery, one of Bear's prominent bowmakers. During his years in Grayling, Neil helped develop Bear's famous take-down recurve.

When designing Bear bows, Neil strives for a balance of durability and shootability with a blend of quality and beauty that's obvious to the eye. He also points out that Bear recurves are designed for the entire bow to function as one unit with each riser and limb combination precisely matched to best achieve overall performance.

Gary notes that one of the keys to Bear recurve performance is its limb design, which attempts to maintain a relatively uniform stress distribution throughout the limb. He says that durability, stability and smoothness are strong considerations when building a bow, and that speed alone should not be an overriding factor.

Neil and Gary develop and test their design concepts in Bear Archery's comprehensive research and development lab. It's full of bow testing devices capable of awing even the most sophisticated bowmaker, and is just part of Bear Archery's state of the art bow manufacturing plant. The sprawling plant is equipped with environmental control systems regulating temperature and humidity; it also has an elaborate dust collection system that resembles some multitentacled outer space creature. The plant even features an automated electrostatic varnishing system that moves drying bows through two floors on more than 1,600 feet of elevated track.

CONSISTENT QUALITY

One of the prime ingredients in manufacturing a quality recurve is the use of quality materials. Bear recurve handle sections are made from laminated hard-rock maple. Gary points out that this popular handle material employs thin longitudinal laminations with many alternating glue lines making it uniform in strength, density, and workability. Bear discontinued using the heavier, resin impregnated solid maple for their handles in 1986.

Bear Archery uses the laminated maple stock for making risers, fadeout wedges, tip overlays, decorative wedges, and even their limb corewoods. It originates in Rice Lake, Wisconsin and comes in large blocks measuring 20" x 40", and varies from 1¾" to 2" thick, resembling oversized decks of wooden cards. Bear Archery uses both clear and dyed stock. In the dyed material, the colored dye penetrates differently into the varying densities of wood, producing contrasting patterns within the grain.

THE SAME EVERY TIME — Clamped in the profiling jig, the riser back is ground to a perfect shape on a coarse grit sander. A template on the base of the jig is run along a bearing below the sander.

FROM BLOCKS TO HANDLES

When making risers, the maple blocks are cut into handle-sized pieces which are then cut in half for the Kodiak Recurve, or in three pieces for the T.D., to accept the decorative wedge. The handle pieces and decorative wedge are epoxied together in a small handle press and heat cured. The glued riser is then band sawn following a template outline and ground to shape using a vertical belt sander. For grinding the handle to shape, it's clamped in a template-guided profiling jig which follows a bearing located below the sanding drum, producing a perfectly shaped riser.

After the T.D. riser is shaped on the back, it's pneumatically clamped in a unique machine called the "socket pocket router." This complex device automatically routs the pockets for the sockets of the limb attachment mechanism. The handle is then profile sanded to belly shape and taken back to a press tree for gluing on the decorative capping material.

The press tree is a vertical stack of short bow presses complete with air pressure hoses. It can press the capping material on up to ten handle sections at a time. The black-white-black capping material on the T.D. risers is a .050" thick compressed paper fiber which is glued in place, and pressed on the face and back of the risers. The press tree is then rolled into a preheated eight foot by twelve foot walk-in glue curing oven where it's left for one hour.

After the risers are shaped on the back and belly and then capped, they are contoured with an intriguing machine called the Richardson Duplicator. This device traces the shape of a master riser while high speed cutters whirring at 16,000 rpm precisely etch the contours on three new maple risers.

The machine etched handles are hand finished using small pin sanders. These air sleeved sanding drums are controlled for softness with air pressure, helping the operator to smooth out the flowing contours of the riser.

When the final sanding is finished on the Custom Kodiak T.D. handles, the pre-cast aluminum limb attachment sockets are epoxied onto the ends of the handle. These limb-locking mechanisms are manufactured by outside fabrication shops and cleaned up, painted, and assembled at Bear.

The final step in shaping the Kodiak Recurve risers is the grinding of the fadeouts. It's one of the more important processes in bowmaking. The fadeouts are feathered to transparent thinness by grinding the belly side of the fadeout, using a vertical drum sander, while keeping the handle flat on the working surface. Material is only ground from the belly side as the riser back has been previously ground to precisely fit the form.

ASSEMBLING THE COMPOSITES

Bear makes their own corewood laminations by band sawing 40" long laminated maple blocks into thin strips, much like cutting a slab of bacon. Consecutively cut strips are run as a matched pair through a large vertical belt sander and ground flat on one side. The pair of laminations is then turned over and placed on a tapered grinding board and then ground to a desired thickness. The finished matched pair of laminations has almost identical qualities and will be used in opposing limbs to help achieve similar limb dynamics.

TWO MADE AS ONE — Each matched pair of corewood laminations are ground side by side. Neil Byce feeds the laminations mounted on a tapered board throught the large belt sander.

Once the riser is completed and the laminations ground, the composites are ready to be laid up in the form. Bear's 2" thick maple forms are housed in heavy "I" beam steel. The steel frame ensures form straightness under the heat and pressure of repeated use. The bottom half of the form represents the bow back and is lined with an electric heat strip. The top half represents the belly and is lined with a heat strip and an inflatable fire hose running the length of the press.

Before glue-up, the press surfaces are covered with a special waxed paper to protect them from stray epoxy. Bear uses Ren Resin epoxy in all gluing processes. The two parts are mixed together in proper proportions from a hand cranked mixing pump with small hoses feeding in the resin and hardener. Epoxy is applied to all contact surfaces of the composites and they are laid up and aligned in the press. Both halves of the press are then hydraulically closed on the composites and forty-five pounds of air pressure is applied to the fire hose. The activated heat strips then cure the pressed composites at 170 degrees for forty-five minutes. Once out of the press, the dried glue is ground off the edges and the tip overlays are epoxied on and heat cured.

When making T.D. limbs, a matched pair of limbs is glued up as one unit resembling a very short recurve. This ensures uniformity of materials and construction. After this "little bow" is pressed and heat cured, the rough glue is sanded off the edges and it's shaped simultaneously on both sides with the Double-Head Reed Contour Sander. This intriguing machine sands down both sides of the bow, precisely contouring the sides to near-final shape. The sander is also used to shape the Kodiak Recurve limbs.

Once the Custom T.D. limbs are ground to shape, the "little bow" is cut in half and each limb receives several intricate machining steps to complete the limb attachment shape, slot, and alignment pin hole.

CABLING

After bows come out of the contour sander, they're ready for cabling. Cabling is the important step where limbs are brought into proper alignment and marked for final shaping. The term "cabling" is derived from a special steel cable with small notched steel wheels on each end. It's used as a steel string, with the notched steel wheels fitting over the limb tips. The bow is braced with the cable and drawn while observing the limb alignment. The cabling wheels are adjusted back and forth until the cable tracks down the center of the limbs.

Once the limbs are aligned, they are marked on both sides of the template guide on the cabling wheel and then ground to final shape near the tips. After grinding, the limbs are rechecked to ensure proper alignment. Cabling replaced the old involved procedure of scribing out limb shapes and then sanding and resanding until the limbs were brought into alignment.

Next, string grooves are cut into the limb tips with a dual cutting wheel machine that grinds the grooves at a precise angle and location, and to a specific depth. It's another one of Bear Archery's ingenious time-saving machines.

The slotted steel wheels are adjusted until the cable tracks true down the center of the bow limbs. Limb alignment is checked at both static (braced) and dynamic (drawn) positions.

Steel bow "strings" made from compound bow cable are used to string the recurves for tillering. They use steel cable because the sharp fiberglass on the limb edges cuts through standard strings in no time. Using cable reduces string breakage and the potential for bow damage and avoids the risk of employee injury. Other advantages of using cable is that unlike standard strings, it doesn't stretch and provides increased accuracy when tillering and recording draw weights.

Bear recurves are tillered to $1/4$" to $3/8$" positive tiller. This means that the measurement from the fadeout locations on the belly to the string is $1/4$" to $3/8$" greater on the top limb. To bring the bows into proper tiller, fiberglass is belt sanded off the back of one of the limbs while the bow is strung. The final check is made with a small measuring device called a tiller gauge.

After being tillered, the bows are checked for draw weight at 28" and the poundage is marked on the bows. They are then unstrung, and a single string groove is ground into the belly of the recurve with a sophisticated machine that neatly centers and cuts a shallow groove into the fiberglass.

To ensure production uniformity on the Custom T.D. limbs, the cabling, tillering, and draw weight measurements are performed using a working master handle section. The precise specifications of this working master are checked periodically with an identical non-working master handle.

FINISHING UP

Even though much of Bear's bowmaking process employs sophisticated machinery, final finishing of the nocks and final sanding is done by hand.

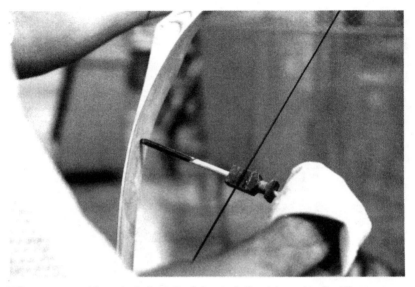

Tiller is measured from the belly at the fadeouts to the string using the tiller gauge.

The general shape of the tips and string nocks are relatively the same, but minor variations in their final shape result from the individual finisher's techniques and style using a small rat-tail file and sandpaper.

Finally the bows are ready for their finish coats. Bear recurves are first coated with two sealer coats of a sprayed acrylic varnish. These sealer coats are oven dried and then sanded smooth. Next, the Bear logo and insignia are silk-screened on the limb bellies using white ink. The bows then receive two more coats of varnish and are automatically "tracked" away on an overhead conveyor chain up into the oven for drying.

LASTING PRIDE

Although many of Bear's bowmaking devices are automatic, the quality of their bows isn't. Neil believes their sharp-eyed inspection department is important throughout the bow building process and plays a key role in the quality of the end product. Bear inspectors check the raw materials as they come into the plant and follow the bows through production. They check the risers as they come out of the duplicator and inspect the corewoods and fiberglass before lay up. Their critical eyes inspect glue lines, finish sanding, and a host of steps in between. They have pride in the products they help create, and it's evident in the quality of the traditional bows leaving the doors of Bear Archery.

The recurves built within Bear Archery represent a blend of the old and the new. Their design and materials are a reflection of fifty-five years of bow crafting experience combined with modern, state of the art production techniques. They incorporate the technology of the eighties, and the beauty and lines of the sixties, with Papa Bear's bowmaking spirit that will last forever.

Chapter Seven

BRIGHAM BOWHUNTING COMPANY

THE RIGHT DIRECTION

The boy was eight years old. Like most kids his age in the small community of Eagleville, Ohio, he spent his days chasing one adventure after another: farm pond fishing, bike riding, and just goofin' around. Then one day, his uncle stopped by and gave him a gift that would change his summers and help shape his future. It was a little Bear recurve. With the bow in one hand and a fist full of dime store arrows in the other, the boy dashed out the door, chasing after the exciting world of Robin Hood's merry men.

The boy spent hours each day shooting his new bow, and although it didn't have much cast, he soon began hitting close-range targets. Determined to improve his distance shooting, the boy practiced harder, straining his arms and the little bow to their limits. But most of his targets were just too far for the little bow.

Several weeks later, the uncle dropped in to see how the young archer was progressing. The boy was shooting the small recurve pretty well, but the uncle made a surprising discovery: the bow didn't shoot very far because it was strung backwards. After sharing a laugh about the innocent mistake, the uncle properly strung the bow and the boy was amazed at how far the little recurve could cast an arrow.

Although it happened over twenty years ago, Robert Brigham, bowmaker and bowhunter, still laughs at his introduction to the world of archery.

Robert resides in Geneva, Ohio, with his wife Diana, daughter Bridget, and son Brandon. Geneva, a small rural town not far from Eagleville, is located just south of Lake Erie about forty miles northeast of Cleveland. The area is known to sportsmen for its limit catches of jumbo walleyes from the big lake, and for the Pope and Young bucks that roam the nearby farmlands. Geneva is noted for its local grape production and even boasts an annual "Grape Jamboree" supported by local wineries. And to a growing number of archers, Geneva, Ohio, is recognized as the home of Brigham Custom Recurves.

The man behind these custom recurves is large and husky, the kind you wouldn't want to face on the scrimmage line. With his six foot, 290 pound frame, Robert usually shops for extra large in camo jackets. He has a youthful face that doesn't seem to match the stippled, premature grey around his temples, and his occasional, high-pitched boyish giggle hints of the time-lost eight-year-old somewhere within the hulk of a man.

A professional tool and die and mold maker for a local company, Robert uses his skills to help create take-down recurves in his garage and basement workshops. Besides enjoying building bows part-time, he likes designing and manufacturing new archery products and bowmaking equipment. And like most bowmakers, bowhunting is one of the driving inspirations behind his craft.

WHITETAIL LESSONS

During the fall, Robert takes time away from his bowmaking to venture afield with one of his custom recurves, usually pursuing the common but crafty whitetail. It's his favorite bowhunting quarry. Although he has yet to harvest an elusive Ohio buck, he savors the wonderful experiences associated with hunting them, even when the big ones get away. "I was watching a soybean field where I expected the deer to cross toward me when suddenly a doe busted through the brush just to my left and ran across the bean field flat out as fast as she could.

"I watched her cross the field and when I looked back over, there was the biggest buck I have ever seen in my life, standing just ten yards away. His enormous rack must have been fourteen inches over his head. He was looking under a branch with his head low, watching that doe run across the field. He had no idea I was standing there. It was a dream shot.

"I turned slowly, raised my bow, and as soon as I reached my anchor, I released the arrow. But the bow lunged uncontrollably out of my hand. Somehow a branch from a nearby tree caught my upper recurve limb and threw the shot off. That buck took off out of there like a streak. I saw him on several occasions after that but never out in the field when I was hunting."

Robert's arrows do, however, find their mark on local groundhogs whose population drops in double digits each summer from his bowhunting efforts. He has bow-bagged a Russian boar on an Ohio hunting preserve and has experienced the thrill of bowhunting black bears in Ontario's swamps. And someday, he hopes to bowhunt for the gigantic moose which holds a special place in his bowhunting dreams.

PREFERRED EQUIPMENT

Whether he's hunting bucks or ground hogs, Robert shoots his favorite seventy-six pound custom Brigham recurve. That may seem like a stiff bow for most archers, but for Robert, "It feels very comfortable." He shoots it with amazing ease.

He shoots self-made cedar arrows fletched with feathers from his treasured supply of grey-barred turkey feathers. In keeping with Pope and Young tradition, Robert even fashions his own self-nocks and makes his own broadheads. He makes solid, two-bladed broadheads from heavy steel, producing a durable design he believes is important in achieving good penetration.

Robert shoots heavy bows and tough heads to achieve more than just good penetration, he wants complete penetration. He believes it's critical when tree stand hunting because it causes an exit hole in the lower portion of the animal, resulting in a good blood trail. He's leery about using the more popular, large diameter, modular heads, because of reports from other hunters who

PRIDE IN SHOOTING HIS HOMEMADE GEAR — Robert handles his seventy-six pound recurve like a toy.

say the heads make a large entry hole but often fail to achieve pass through. This can lead to a poor blood trail and even a lost animal. Although Robert's homemade broadheads may seem a bit primitive to the "high-tech" crowd, his ideas about broadhead design are well founded and shared by many experienced traditional bowhunters.

UNPREFERRED EQUIPMENT

When carrying his homemade gear through the predawn darkness toward his favorite buck crossing, an ever-present thought haunts Robert's mind — crossbows! Sharing his Ohio bowhunting season with crossbow shooters makes him more than edgy, he's downright frightened. "Now they're even using laser sights which makes it easy for these people to shoot their 'crossguns' in the pitch dark and aim at shadows. Wherever that red dot is, that's where their bolt is going. That really scares me."

Crossbows and a never-ending array of bowhunting gadgets designed to help achieve the "success of killing" continue to creep into bowhunting. Many, including Robert, see this gadgetry encroachment as an uncontrollable virus threatening to kill its host, the sport itself. "A lot of people in the archery business say, 'Man, the future looks great, things are going well, and we are getting all kinds of business.' But I think the future of bowhunting looks grim.

"I manufacture archery products that enhance the sport of bowhunting, such as my bowhunter's camera tripod. It's a handy and useful tool that a person can use to help record a hunt. But most of today's archery gadgetry stinks! The manufacturers of these gadgets and the archery shops that sell them are trying to make a buck and in the process I think they're cheapening the sport. If all I was interested in was making a fast buck I'm sure I could come up with a product all kinds of people would be willing to purchase that would help ruin bowhunting.

"I'll admit that I have never taken a whitetail deer with a bow, but when I do take that first whitetail, it's going to be a personal victory, not a hollow victory. I would even be willing to hunt with a spear if it would eliminate all the gadgets they're letting people use. If someone invented a gadget so that a player could hit a home run every time he came to the plate, and they allowed it during a baseball game, what would be the point of having the baseball game?"

Although not everyone agrees with Robert's ideas, he has the courage to openly express them instead of passively following popular opinion. If more shared his convictions, maybe crossbows and laser sights wouldn't be such a nightmare for Ohio's true bowhunters.

NO GIMMICK TAKE-DOWNS

The mainstay of Robert's no-gadget archery business is his BRIGHAM CUSTOM RECURVE. It's a three-piece take-down that's available in two riser lengths and three limb lengths. This concept of interchangeable risers and limbs is similar to the original line of Bear Archery Company take-downs.

Robert's longer 17 1/2" riser assembles with the varying limbs producing 60", 64", and 66" bows, and the compact 15 1/2" riser yields 58", 62", and 64" bows. Like the Bear T.D. concept, his limbs are interchangeable between left and right-handed risers. Robert usually leaves the choice of a riser-limb combination up to his customers, who are generally experienced archers who know what they want. He does, however, recommend longer bows for individuals with longer draw lengths, to reduce finger pinch and bow stress.

His 58" model has a mass weight of 2 pounds, 10 ounces. The riser is 1 5/8" wide, 2 7/8" thick, and is made from multilaminated hard-rock maple. The slightly crested arrow shelf is 2 1/2" across and is equipped with a black synthetic fur rest. Its slightly rounded center shot sight window is full cut for 2" above the shelf and contours back to full riser width 3 5/8" above the shelf. It's a relatively short sight window, but Robert and his customers like it that way. "Most people shooting these bows use the instinctive method of aiming and really don't need much of a sight window. A lot of guys are looking for a compact bow because they hunt in heavy brush and from tree stands. So, I try to keep the bow a small, compact unit".

His longer 17½" riser has a full 3" sight window which contours back to full riser width 4⅝" above the shelf. Robert's bows are intended to be shot off the shelf and have a recommended brace height between 7" and 8" from the string to the throat of the grip.

His risers are constructed from brown and dark grey laminated maple separated by a curved laminated maple wedge. The curve of this vertical wedge follows the same basic shape of the riser. Black over white fiberglass capping is laminated to the back and belly of the riser accentuating its shape while adding strength. The somewhat blocky, highly contoured grip of Robert's personal bow even has custom finger grooves fashioned into the wood.

Bow information is black inked on the lower portion of the window side of the riser, and the limb specifications are inked on the edges of the fadeout wedges. Available brass quiver bushings are located near the ends of the riser on the side opposite the sight window.

The moderately recurved limbs attach to the riser with a single attachment bolt and alignment pin system, common among three-piece takedowns. The somewhat square-edged limbs have a 16" working length from the fadeout to the string nock on the 58" model. The longer limbs have working lengths of 18", and 20".

These limbs are constructed with two parallel, non-tapered, maple laminations on the back and one .002" per inch tapered lamination on the belly side of the 8" long fadeout wedge. These solid edge-grain laminations are enveloped in either clear, black, or brown fiberglass. The limbs are 1¹¹⁄₁₆" wide at the fadeouts and narrow to ¾" at the string nocks. The back glass over the fadeout wedge is covered with a reinforcing walnut overlay. The tip overlays are made from four contrasting thin layers of maple and walnut. The string nock to tip measures 1" and the tip exhibits an arrowhead shape.

To check the relative speed of his bow, Robert shot his 28¾" cedar arrows through the chronograph with his 58", 76 pound at 28" draw Custom T.D. His arrows were fletched with three standard cut feathers, had self nocks, and each weighed 530 grains. He drew the arrows to full length and had a relatively clean release. The bow was equipped with a Dacron string equipped with brush buttons and Catwhisker silencers. The average arrow speed for this shooter, arrow, string, and bow combination was 175 fps.

The following draw-force measurements were recorded on this 58" Brigham T.D:

DRAW LENGTH	25"	26"	27"	28"	29"
DRAW WEIGHT	62#	65½#	71½#	76#	80#

LITTLE ARCHERS TOO

In his bow building, Robert hasn't forgotten the younger archers. Those golden memories of his first recurve inspired him to create a youth's version of his take-down recurve. This 48" children's bow is a scale model of the bow

THE BRIGHAM CUSTOM RECURVE FAMILY — The standard model (top), 48" kid's model (middle) and miniature take-down (bottom).

the "big boys" use. And judging from Robert's son Brandon, this youth's bow can help light a fire of enthusiasm under an aspiring bowhunter.

Building this youth bow was so much fun that Robert carried the process one step further and constructed a miniature working replica, complete with bow quiver and arrows. This miniature bow is so detailed, it looks like he somehow shrunk one of his full sized take-downs. It even shoots its chopstick-sized arrows fast enough to bring down a rogue mouse.

IT ONLY SEEMED NATURAL

A natural combination of ingredients led Robert into the field of bowmaking: the challenge of making new products, working with his hands, his professional skills, and a love for bowhunting. For years he wanted to try making his own bow, but was reluctant to venture into the almost magical world of bowmaking. Then one summer, he met and talked to both Fred Bear and Don Assenheimer, and Robert came away with a determination to try his hand at bowmaking. "Don was a good inspiration because I discovered normal people build bows. I thought they were like gods or something, but when I found out they were just normal guys, I decided to give bowmaking a try." That was in 1980. Since then, Robert has not only crossed the hurdle of making his first bow, he now builds them as a part-time business.

TOUGH LESSONS

Before introducing his take-downs to the public in 1982, Robert spent over a year developing them. During that time he discovered that learning about bowmaking through trial and error can sometimes be a stern but effective teacher. Like his first experience with his little recurve, experienced advice helped point Robert in the right direction with his first bowmaking attempt.

Before building his first bow, Robert read about bow crafting from several books on the subject. Unfortunately, his reference material didn't discuss the new generation of fiberglass and its compatible glues. After gluing together his first set of limbs with Urac 185, he noticed the clear fiberglass had an odd milky appearance. Inquisitively, he picked at the edge of the limb with his thumbnail and the fiberglass flew off the limb. Not a bit of the Urac glue had stuck to it. "I didn't really expect blazing success, but I didn't exactly expect a blazing failure either. I didn't think I was that much of a klutz!"

Perplexed, he called Don Assenheimer who quickly pointed out that modern fiberglass is not compatible with Urac glues. Don recommended Robert salvage his composites by sanding off the dried Urac and regluing the limbs with epoxy. But Robert's first lesson was far from over. "I sanded the materials clean, glued them up, and put them back in the press. Well, it held and looked good. So I ground the limbs out and put them on my take-down handle.

"Those were the first limbs I had ever glued up, and they came out EXTREMELY heavy. I never got a chance to weigh the bow, but it took every bit of my strength just to string it. But they were beautiful, so I was determined to try to draw that bow back.

"As soon as I got to full draw, I saw stars! The bow broke in the center of the handle and made a sound like an explosion. I guess my handle section was too weak near the grip. The bow ended up laying ten yards behind me. My wife yelled from the house, 'What happened?'

'My bow blew up.'

'Are you all right?'

'Yeah, I think so.'

She came downstairs, looked at me, and said, 'Like hell you're all right! Come on, we are going to the hospital.'

"I thought I was all right, so I went upstairs and looked in the mirror. Then I knew we better go to the hospital. I was covered with blood from the top of my head to my waist. That bow had come back and split my nose from the tip clear up to between my eyes. While the doctor stitched me up, I had to explain what happened.

"At the time, the towns folk knew I was experimenting with bows and the razzing I later took about my bow exploding was far worse than the pain I suffered from my broken nose. Word got around and people started calling me 'Chief Broken Beak'. They told me I should next invent the bowhunter's crash helmet. But I just told them that the first time I tried riding a bicycle I didn't take off on it right away. I had to practice at it, and then after a while I learned to ride it."

After his nose and pride healed, Robert resumed his bowmaking efforts and began turning out functional bows. He admits that although his early recurves looked rough, they shot nicely. "In fact, I was proud of the first bow I built. At the time it looked beautiful to me. But when I look back at it now, it did look rather crude. I took it to a friend who is an extremely good shot. He took that bow and shot an arrow into the practice bale. He looked at the bow and then at me and said, 'It shoots beautifully! That arrow went right where I was looking.' But I thought he just said that to make me feel good because there was no target on the bale. Then he grabbed another arrow and he split the first arrow. Then I felt great!"

With that encouragement, Robert was on his way to becoming a bow-maker. Since building those first bows, he has experienced the thrills of other archers taking game with his bows and felt the pride of shooting his own handmade equipment. "When you build a bow, and then shoot it, then hit what you're aiming at, it's a special feeling that's hard to explain. It's some-thing few archers will ever know."

TAKE-DOWN MECHANICS

Although he had some early problems with glues and core thicknesses, many of the mechanical aspects of manufacturing a take-down recurve are second nature to Robert because of his professional tool and die training. It enables him to work with extremely close measurement tolerances and has provided him a broad knowledge of different industrial tools. He has even used his experience to design and build his own band saw, grinders, limb presses, riser press, precision drill fixtures, limb attachment jigs, and spe-cialized tools.

Robert begins making a take-down by building the riser section. First, he traces the riser shape on the laminated maple stock using one of his aluminum templates. He makes his templates from sturdy ½" thick alumi-

Robert's bowmaking devices include this homemade self-centering drill guide fixture for proper placement of his main limb attachment bushing.

num which ensures precision riser duplication even with repeated use. He then saws the sweeping riser wedge contact line with his homemade band saw and grinds those surfaces smooth on his homemade vertical sander. Although hand grinding the curved contact surfaces to an exact fit looks difficult, for Robert, it's almost as natural as scratching his neck.

He makes the decorative wedge from two thin strips of .040" thick maple that are epoxied between the two halves of the riser. He presses the glued riser pieces and wedge strips together using "C" clamps and then puts the riser in a glue curing heat box. Once the epoxy is cured, Robert band saws and grinds the back and belly shape, including the limb contact surfaces.

Next, he installs the main brass limb attachment bushings near the ends of the riser. For this he uses his custom-made self-centering drill jig which ensures exact placement of the bushing hole. Once the jig is clamped in place, he drills a ½" hole completely through the end of the riser and countersinks the belly side. He then epoxies a headed brass bushing in from the belly side and covers the countersunk head with a laminated maple plug. Even the maple plug is cut with Robert's own custom plug cutter. Installing this headed insert from the belly side eliminates the possibility of the insert pulling out of the riser.

He then installs his custom-made alignment pin drill fixtures on the attachment bushings and lays the riser sideways on his machinist's granite surface plate. After the flat edges of both jigs are positioned flush to this almost perfectly flat plate, he drills the brass alignment pin holes in the riser. This process ensures near-perfect bushing and pin alignment between both limbs.

Mr. Do-it-yourself sawing out a riser on his homemade band saw built from scrap steel and old bicycle wheels.

Robert epoxies the black over white fiberglass capping to the belly and back of the riser using a special clamping fixture. Like most of his bowmaking devices, Robert designed and built this aluminum and steel capping press. After placing the glued capping and riser in the press, Robert tightens bolts on the top of the fixture which compresses an internal wooden form on the riser. This presses the capping firmly against the back and belly. He then puts the fixture in the heat box to cure the glue.

Once the capping glue is cured, he installs the press-fit brass limb alignment pins. Robert then marks the final dimensions of the riser and shapes it with his band saw, wood rasps, and high-speed palm sanders. The fashioned riser is then set aside while he begins making the limbs.

THE WORKING PARTS

Like his risers, Robert's limb forms are constructed from laminated maple, which is strong, stable, and relatively easy to work with. He grinds and scrapes the form to the belly shape of the limb and glues on smooth Formica to the form surface. Robert cautions that any little flaw in the form will be duplicated in the finished limbs. Both the upper and lower limbs are glued up on the same form with the three varying lengths determined by the placement of the fadeout wedge.

The Old Master Crafters, in Waukegan, Illinois, manufacture Robert's parallel and tapered maple corewood laminations and his walnut fadeout wedges according to his specifications. To prevent them from absorbing humidity, he stores the limb composites in a box heated by a light-bulb. When handling his corewoods, Robert carefully touches only the edges to keep the gluing surfaces spotless. Although he builds limbs using either clear, brown, or black fiberglass, Robert prefers black because of its dark, natural appearance in a wooded setting.

Before gluing up a limb, Robert coats his form with plain dish soap and covers it with plastic food wrap to protect it from stray epoxy. He also masking tapes the non-gluing smooth side of the fiberglass for glue protection. He then applies a specialized bowmaking epoxy to all contact surfaces of the limb composites and lays up the glued laminates in his form. The flexed laminates are held in the curved form by a dowel stop pin at the butt end, and a small sliding aluminum plate at the limb tip.

He then places a .030" thick metal strip and an air hose on top of the composites, and locks the upper half of the form in place with two locking pins. Robert applies eighty pounds of air pressure to the hose which squeezes the limb materials together and neatly pushes in the butt end dowel pin and slides back the small tip end retaining plate. He then places the form in the glue curing oven for four to six hours.

Once the form has cooled, Robert removes the rough limb from the press and belt sands off the excess dried glue. He removes the masking tape at the tip overlay and fadeout overlay areas and roughens up these surfaces with sandpaper. He epoxies and "C" clamps the overlays in place, and the limbs are put back into the glue curing oven for a short time.

ANOTHER HOMEMADE JIG — Robert's string nock filing fixture helps provide the same nock angle and depth on every tip.

Next, using his attachment bushing drill jig, Robert drills the limb mounting holes. Through these holes he installs his custom limb alignment jig on the limb butt and places the square-edged jig on his granite surface plate. This places the horizontal limb in near-perfect plane with the granite plate and Robert marks the limb centerline with his custom-made marking surface gauge. Once the limb centerline is marked, he uses a template to outline the final limb shape and then grinds it to shape.

For making the string nocks, Robert reaches into his bag of tool and die tricks and pulls out a new little gadget. It's a string nock locating and angle positioning fixture which he clamps on the limb tip. It allows him to precisely file the nocks to a specific angle and a certain depth.

After filing the nocks, he rounds up the edges with a small rat-tail file. Robert uses the belly centerline mark as a guide and files a small shallow string groove into the fiberglass. Finally, he employs small electric palm hand-sanders to finish the limbs. This final light sanding reduces fiberglass glare and provides a good adhesion surface for the sprayed finish.

To achieve proper tiller in his bows, Robert designed a one-half degree difference in the lower limb-riser attachment angle. This gives his bottom limb a slight preload, making it a little stiffer. Although both limbs are built the same, one will usually be a bit heavier, and he places it on the lower limb to help achieve his desired 1/8" to 1/4" positive tiller. This built-in limb-riser angle difference and limb similarity usually eliminates the need for any additional work to achieve the proper tiller.

After he inks the limbs and riser with the customer's name and bow specifications, Robert sprays them with four to five coats of a satin polyurethane finish. Although this polyurethane provides a non-glare finish suitable for most hunting situations, some guys still feel the need to camo paint their bows. "It kind of makes you feel bad when you've invested a lot of time building a bow, and there are certain things that you do which add to the bow's appearance, and then the next time you see the bow, it's painted a drab green!"

Brigham Custom Recurves are designed to shoot off the shelf, and Robert usually leaves installation of a preferred strike pad and arrow shelf up to the customer.

EXTRA COMPENSATION

Besides payment for their finished products, most bowmakers receive some personal extras. "The most rewarding thing about building bows is having the opportunity to meet some of the most interesting people in archery today, especially those interested in traditional equipment. They seem to be a wholesome group of fine bowhunters. Bowmaking has also given me the opportunity to go on hunts that I may not have been able to go on otherwise.

"I've always enjoyed making different products, and I've been involved in archery since the age of eight, so building bows has always intrigued me. The personal satisfaction derived from building something and having it do what you intended it to do is very gratifying. It's also gratifying when you receive letters from people who tell you how great they feel your product is and who send you pictures of the game animals they've taken with your bow. It's a great feeling."

PARTING NOTES

Since the summer of 1987, several aspects of Robert and his products have changed. Frequent changing of bow forms and the introduction of new models is common among bowmakers. Robert has recently redesigned his bow limbs and now also offers a longbow for the more traditional enthusiast.

This one-time mountain of a man has lost sixty pounds and comments, "I'm feeling better than I ever have." He's also feeling a lightness in his step because that first whitetail finally fell to one of his homemade arrows tipped with his handmade broadheads during the 1987 Ohio bow season. It was a button buck that only made thirty yards after a pass-through shot from his seventy-seven pound take-down. It was indeed a personal victory.

Chapter Eight

ASSENHEIMER BOWS

LONE VIGIL

Assenheimer. The name sounds like it belongs on a foreign sports car or an elite automatic weapon. It has a ring of mystique. To a number of whitetail bucks who once roamed the sweeping fields of central Ohio, the name had a ring of death. It meant an end to their days of scrape lines and swollen necks. To many traditional archers across the country, the German name Assenheimer means a finely crafted, smooth shooting, three-piece, take-down recurve.

Don Assenheimer creates his bows in a quiet workshop bounded by corn and bean fields in the undulating farmland west of Bucyrus, Ohio. His sprawling shop with its spacious and well-equipped work stations is a bit atypical for most lone, part-time bowyers. In fact, it looks like there should be several men busying themselves at the varied power tools.

Throughout the shop a host of sawing, grinding, and drilling stations look like they were laid out by an efficiency expert. Each is connected with vent pipes to a master dust collection unit resembling a giant tentacled respiratory system. Overhead, profuse fluorescent lighting illuminates the light-toned ceiling, walls and floor, making it easy to see precision grinding lines, exact limb alignment, and a host of detailed bow crafting operations. The shop also contains a separate spraying and glue curing room next to an attractively decorated lodge-like office.

Don's shop is pretty impressive for a one-man show, and it only seems natural that some pretty impressive bows are created within it. Because like this expertly designed shop, Assenheimer bows are a reflection of their creator.

THE BOW

The Assenheimer T.D. recurve exudes quality, workmanship, and design. It's available in the standard 64" and 66" lengths with the risers measuring 21¾" and 23¾" long. Don also recently introduced a 62" model with a 19¾" riser. His 64" bow has an average mass weight of 2 pounds, 10 ounces. Don's recommended brace height from the string to the throat is 7⅝" on the 64" bow, and 7¾" on the 66" model.

Don handsomely crafts his risers from dyed, highly laminated, hardrock maple and commonly uses gray, green, or wine colored stock. The riser contains two vertical, multilaminated, decorative wedges. The wedge through the grip area has a sweeping contour similar to the riser shape, while the near-belly wedge is straight.

The riser is 1⅞" wide near the ends and thins to ¾" through the sight window, which is cut approximately ³⁄₁₆" past center shot. The riser is 2¾" thick near the ends and narrows to 1¾" across the throat. It is 2¼" thick across the crested arrow shelf. This shelf is 1" above the center of the bow, which is located at the low point of the grip. The slightly rounded sight window is full cut for 4" above the shelf and contours back to full riser width 5½" above the shelf.

Wood grain and glue line contrasts in the laminated maple display the riser's smoothly flowing contours which exhibit subdued decorative peaks on the back and the belly. The arrow shelf and window are equipped with a synthetic hair shelf and strike pad. Bow specifications are inked below the

The Assenheimer recurve displays craftmanship from the attractive riser to the rounded limb edges and delicate tip overlays.

grip on the window side and the limb information is inked on the side of the fadeout wedges. Brass quiver attachment and accessory bushings are available.

Don's interchangeable limbs are the same dimensions for all models and exhibit a high profile recurve with almost a fishhook appearance when unstrung. They attach to the riser with a common single attachment bushing and an alignment pin. The upper limb has a working length of 17", and the lower limb, 16¾". The limbs narrow from 1⅞" wide at the fadeout wedge to ⅞" at the string nock. They're constructed from two thin parallel laminations on the back side of the fadeout and one thin parallel lamination on the belly side. The Actionwood corewoods are enveloped in black or clear fiberglass which is nicely feathered on the edges.

The neatly fashioned tip overlays are made from three thin layers of contrasting woods and have smoothly shaped string grooves which are full cut on the back and sides, and feather out on the belly. A single string groove is etched into the recurve belly glass. The limbs are capped over the fadeout wedge on the belly and back with a wood simulated Formica and the upper limb is notched in the fadeout wedge where it blends into the sight window.

The riser section is finished with a two part catalystic varnish while the limbs are sprayed with a satin luster urethane finish.

To check the bow's relative speed, Don shot his 29", 2216 aluminum arrows through the chronograph with his 64", 59 pound at 28" draw takedown. The arrows were fletched with four standard cut feathers, and had a 145 grain field point, for a total arrow weight of 550 grains. The bow was equipped with a standard Dacron string without accessories. Don drew his arrows 28" and had a relatively clean release. The average arrow speed for this bow, arrow, and shooter combination was 182 fps.

The following draw-force measurements were recorded on this 64" Assenheimer T.D:

DRAW LENGTH	25"	26"	27"	28"	29"
DRAW WEIGHT	50#	52½#	56#	59#	62½#

The Assenheimer recurve is noted for seating comfortably in the hand while the open sight window provides a clear instinctive picture. The smooth drawing limbs unfold throughout the working recurve causing the arrows to leap crisply from the shelf. Because of the bow's length and design, finger pinch and hand shock are minimal.

FARM RAISED

Assenheimer recurves are crafted by a man whose appearance doesn't share the mystique of his name. Don looks like he could be the kindly owner of a small town flower shop or even a clerk in a little country grocery. This fifty-two year-old Ohio native has a kind face that aptly fits the man behind it. But the mere mention of big whitetails or custom recurves cracks his laid back shell, and the mild green eyes behind his glasses light up, his eyebrows begin to dance, and soon he's engrossed in a hunting tale. Other than some occasional golfing, Don's world revolves around bowmaking and bowhunting. He's a member of The Professional Bowhunters Society, Michigan Bowhunters, West Virginia Bowhunters, and Ohio Bowhunters.

Although bowhunting represents a big part of his life today, it wasn't until 1974 that Don became interested in archery. Back in the early seventies, Don's primary interest, gun hunting, was prohibited in his resident county. This protection from gunners and the archery-only seasons near his home helped create a bumper crop of huge bucks that taunted his hunting instincts. Frequent sightings of these bow accessable bucks and the archery success of his nearby friend, Roger Rothhaar, eventually inspired Don to try his hand at bowhunting. And one season was all he needed to get hooked.

During those early years around home,

LITTLE MYSTIQUE — Without his deadly recurve Don resembles just another easy going Buycrus resident. But when he unfolds his fishook recurves during November, local bucks are in trouble.

bowhunting was good. It verged on being great. But today, whitetail numbers are so low that Don hunts mostly in southeastern Ohio or travels north to Michigan. He attributes the drop in deer numbers to recent clean farming practices, where farmers clear large tracts of land, tile drain small swales, and level small wood lots. The changing of brushy swales into bean fields has dramatically altered the deer habitat near Don and the whitetail now find their necessary browse and cover along the drainage ditches and the scattered brush-filled river bottoms. The change makes the deer tougher to hunt. But like the whitetail, Don has adjusted.

WHITETAIL WISDOM

Because of their adaptability to changing environments and their almost mythical savvy, whitetail deer are Don's number one bowhunting pursuit. Some of his favored hunting spots are close to home in Crawford and Wyandot counties. Even though these areas are not necessarily crawling with deer, they still hold some real wall hangers.

When Don finds time to hunt, he usually spends his bowhunting hours perched in a tree stand downwind of a buck's travel route between scrape areas. And you can bet, no matter what the weather, he will be in that stand on November 17. That's been Don's lucky day in years past and he tries his best to keep it that way. On two separate November 17 he harvested the two record-class whitetails mounted on his office wall. "That's one of the best days to pick for a lucky day because it also happens to be the peak of the whitetail rut in our area."

During his early bowhunting years, Don was strictly a scrape hunter. But like the nearby whitetails who adapted to the changing countryside, Don has altered his hunting techniques over the years to adapt to deer patterns. "Now when I find a bunch of scrapes in one area and another bunch some-place else, I try to find where the bucks are traveling between those two scrape areas. I figure I've got a better chance intercepting the bucks between the scrapes than I do sitting over one of fifteen different scrapes."

Since he began hunting scrape travel routes, Don's buck luck has really improved. When selecting prime travel routes he looks for old fence rows or drainage ditches. Locating buck highways requires a lot of scouting and Don usually does his leg work in the early spring when the evidence of last season's whitetail activities are easier to decipher.

Once he's located a likely spot, Don unfolds his strategy. Bow bagging a buckeye buck involves a lot more than just sitting next to a rut-churned travel route. "Down here in Ohio, we don't have near the woods or the cover like Michigan has. So here you've got to find a drainage ditch with some cover because that's where the deer usually run. After you've done a lot of scouting and found where the tracks are, you must hunt downwind from where you think the bucks are going to come from. I think more people screw up by not hunting downwind from the bucks because they don't count on the buck's nose being as good as it is. I usually set my tree stand about fifteen yards from where I figure the buck is going to be and place it about ten to twelve feet high.

"I don't like close in, straight down shooting. I prefer deer fifteen yards away, angling away a little bit, and unaware of what's going on. If deer are alert, they're very hard to draw on. But if they aren't alert and don't suspect anything is wrong, they are a lot easier to get an arrow into."

When approaching his well-placed stand, Don wears rubber boots and always takes advantage of the wind. If the wind isn't perfect for it, he won't hunt a stand. That's one of the reasons he has different stand locations that can be hunted with almost any wind direction. "I figure that you're better off staying home in bed if the wind is wrong. Especially if you are hunting one particular big buck. If you spook him two or three times, he won't come back during daylight."

Besides changing his stand locations to take advantage of buck pat-terns, Don also has changed his hunting hours to match big buck activity. Most whitetailers assume dawn and dusk are the best times to bag a buck — but not Don. "I don't agree with everybody on the best time to hunt. If a guy could hunt between 10:00 AM and 4:00 PM, he would probably see a lot more bucks than in the morning or evening. I shot one record buck about 2:00 PM one season, and I shot another at 1:00 PM. I've also missed a couple of big bucks right at noon. I think hunting in the middle of the day is the way to kill big bucks. Just talk to farmers and ask them when they see big bucks. Most will say it's in the middle of the day."

Don believes that many Ohio bucks have become patterned to the ritualistic morning and evening hunting activity. So the smart hunter changes his hunting hours to accommodate sly bucks who have learned to take advantage of human patterns. He notes that some of the savvy bowhunters in his area are also beginning to hunt from ground blinds along treeless drainage ditches because the wise old bucks have learned to avoid tree-lined areas concealing waiting archers. In fact, over the years Don has witnessed bucks changing their travel patterns by a couple hundred yards just to avoid tree-lined areas.

BOSS BUCK

Using his midday tactics and his custom recurve, Don has harvested some fine bucks. But one of his record-class mounts stands out as his most memorable. "It's probably that high tined whitetail on the wall that was the best. I never saw that buck before I killed him. I was really hunting another buck in that area. I kept hunting the other buck, and one evening about sundown he came in on me. He was a bigger buck than this one on the wall. He came in about thirty yards from my tree stand when he must have caught a glint of the sun off my glasses and he just turned and went the other way. He went down over this drainage ditch toward the river so I figured that was the end of that stand because he saw me in it.

"So the next morning I hunted another stand until about 10:00 AM and then found a different place and moved my stand there at noon. It was drizzling that day, and I went back to hunt about 1:00 PM. I wasn't up there very long when this deer came by. Because it was drizzling I never heard him come underneath my stand. I looked down, and there he stood right against my tree. He was a real surprise because I had just moved my stand, and it all happened so quickly.

"It was my lucky day — the seventeenth of November! I shot straight down and hit about three inches off the spine, penetrating through the lungs and the heart and out the bottom of him. But he still went about 150 yards before he piled up."

SIMPLE GEAR

When it's time to head for his tree stand, Don doesn't bother with a varied or fancy wardrobe of camo clothing. "I guess you could say I'm not a big nut on camouflage." He just wears an old pair of green shop coveralls which he feels match tree trunks just fine and worked well when he arrowed his two book bucks and his two bears.

Like his simple coveralls, Don has also discovered a string silencer material that's tough to beat for functional simplicity. He uses the soft rubber tail replacement material for fishing lures which he says really quiets down bow noise. "Just buy a pound of that stuff and it will last a lifetime of bowhunting."

Don also prefers a simple yet effective broadhead on his arrows. He uses the Snuffer broadhead designed by Roger Rothhaar — the guy who lives just down the road. Don likes Snuffers because they're big and strong. They're also sharpened to the point and penetrate much better than the punch points found on many modular heads.

Sharpening his Snuffers to a razor edge is a task Don takes seriously. He begins by individually filing each blade to a thin knife-like edge. Then he stokes the broadhead across a sharpening stone while keeping the two opposing blades flat on the stone. This causes the stone to only sharpen a thin edge along the narrowly filed blade. He admits that this method requires a bit more work but the ultimate deadly sharpness and ease of resharpening makes it worth the effort.

Don mounts his Snuffers on 2216 aluminum shafts, fletched with four feathers. "Roger talked me into using four-fletch because he found out that on close shots he wasn't shooting through game, but on longer shots he was. He couldn't figure out why. So, he started using four-fletch which straightens the arrow out quicker. What a difference! Now everybody around here uses four-fletch. A lot of people are even going to Maxifletch for the same reason."

SHOOTING RIGHT

An ideal match for his Snuffer-tipped arrows is Don's sixty pound recurve. It's plenty heavy enough for whitetails but not too heavy to handle on frosty mornings. For Don it's a perfect weight. "Most people make the mistake of getting overbowed and therefore won't practice enough. If you get a weight you're comfortable with, and it is still an efficient hunting weight, you'll practice more with it. Therefore, you don't need a heavier weight because you will be shooting better. I always tell people that you can kill a deer with a fifty pound bow if you hit him in the right spot, but you can't kill a deer with an eighty pound bow if you hit him in the wrong place. If you practice enough to become proficient, you don't need a lot of bow weight. A sixty pound bow will kill anything in North America if you hit it in the right place."

To make sure he can hit his quarry in the right place, Don stays in top form by practicing at least once a week throughout the year. He often shoots instinctively, but when the month of August rolls around, he begins shooting every day with a single sight pin that he uses afield. During the final few months before bow season, most of his practice is done from the house top, simulating tree stand shots. Armed with his recurve and two dozen arrows, he climbs up the rungs of his sturdy television antenna to the roof. He then attempts to weed dandelions from the back yard at fifteen to twenty yards. When practicing and hunting, Don restricts his shots to high percentage angles and distances. If he has any doubts about hitting an animal, he simply doesn't shoot.

Don also attends an occasional organized shoot to stay in form, but he does it mostly to socialize with bowhunting friends. "Most shoots are set up wrong for a bowhunter. The shots are too hard and the ranges are too long. A good bowhunter wouldn't take those types of shots in the woods. But attending shoots is better than not shooting at all, that's for sure!"

A HOBBY GOTTEN OUT OF HAND

When Don first became interested in bowhunting he shopped around for a left-handed, take-down recurve but couldn't find one that he liked the appearance or price of. So after talking with his bowhunting neighbor, Roger Rothhaar, Don decided to try building his own bow. It seemed like an innocent enough project, and besides, it would give him a diversion from his long-time hobby of crafting custom furniture. His furniture crafting experience and his twenty-two years as a machine operator in Bucyrus provided an ideal combination of skills for his bow building project.

That first bowmaking diversion occurred during the winter of 1974, and Don has been side-tracked building bows ever since. "My bowmaking kinda got out of hand. My first bow came out to fifty-two pounds. It shot good and someday I'd like to kill a deer with it."

Don began selling his bows to bowhunting friends in 1976 and word soon spread about his recurves. Roger Rothhaar was the first to kill a big game animal with one of Don's bows during a spring bear hunt in 1976. Since then both Rothhaar and Assenheimer have become noted names in today's world of bowhunting.

Today, Assenheimer recurves still continue to sell mostly by word of mouth. Despite Don's scarce advertising, word spreads around the country about the performance and beauty of his bows. In fact, they're so popular that he now limits the number of new bow orders he takes each year. "Bow building can easily get out of hand. Basically I keep it to a seasonal operation from January to late July because I don't want to be sitting up in my tree stand someplace thinking about building bows."

STARTS WITH THE RISER

When he is building recurves, Don begins by making the risers. He makes them from 2" x 4" x 24" blocks of dyed and laminated hard-rock maple purchased from the Old Master Crafters. He begins by band sawing out and power sanding the contact surfaces of the straight and curved decorative wedges. Don checks the precision fit of these surfaces by placing the pieces snugly together on a light table which shines through areas requiring a little more sanding. He's careful to achieve a precision fit to ensure thin and uniform glue lines in the laminated riser.

He applies Ren resin epoxy to the contact surfaces of the curved wedge and glues together the thin veneers of bubinga and maple sandwiched between the riser pieces. He tightly "C" clamps the pieces together and puts the laminated composite into his glue curing oven. Although making the curved decorative wedge is more difficult than making a straight wedge, Don believes it makes the bow much more attractive.

TWO LONG-TIME FURNITURE MAKERS, DON AND HIS SHOP SMITH. Today Don uses his furniture crafting machines to turn out furniture-quality custom recurves.

After the curved wedge glue is hardened and before the belly wedge is laminated to the riser, Don installs the limb attachment bushings. Using a guide jig, Don drills the limb attachment bushing holes in the partially completed riser and counter-sinks the hole on the belly side. He then epoxies in headed brass inserts from the belly side. This produces a super-strong limb attachment bushing that can't pull out of the riser.

Don then glues the vertical decorative wedge and belly section of the riser which covers the countersunk headed inserts. Installing these headed insert bushings inside the laminated riser eliminates the need for detectable wooden plugs or exposed bushing heads. The glued riser goes back into the curing oven at a slightly lower temperature.

Next Don cuts the riser to rough shape with his band saw, accompanied by its high-pitched song. He grinds the flowing contours on the spindle sander attachment of his Shop Smith. The sharp angles in the sight window area require hand rasping and plenty of buckeye elbow grease.

For the final shaping Don sands the riser with a cushiony air-sleeved spindle sander which produces smooth flowing contours. It hums away at 1350 RPM on his drill press while Don skillfully sweeps the emerging riser back and forth across the soft spindle. Finally, he uses a Sand-O-Flex flapper sanding wheel with 180 grit paper to achieve a silky-smooth sanded finish.

MACHINE TOLERANCES

Once the riser is finished to shape, Don installs an alignment pin doweling jig on each of the limb attachment bolts. By placing the riser sideways on his granite surface plate, Don brings both of the flat-sided jigs into

MACHINIST'S PRECISION — Don brings the alignment pin dowling jigs on each end of the riser in near-perfect plane on his granite surface plate before drilling the pin holes.

near-perfect alignment. This machinist's plate, which is level to within one thousandth of an inch, allows Don to achieve precision alignment on his limb-to-riser attachment system. When the jigs are flat on the plate, Don tightens them to the attachment bushings and then turns the riser over to double check alignment. Once he's satisfied with the alignment, he drills the limb alignment pin holes and epoxies in the small brass alignment pins.

Don's completed riser represents an evolution of design. Over the years he has refined his riser section by making it less blocky and changing the handle to a lower profile grip. He now also generously rounds both the sight window and the arrow shelf to enhance clean arrow flight.

Making the riser section is Don's favorite part of making a bow. Fashioning the beautifully sculptured risers gives him the opportunity to experiment with different woods and to try new lamination patterns. It brings out his furniture crafting and design skills.

FISHHOOK LIMBS

After the riser is finished, Don begins building the limbs. For him they aren't much fun to work with, especially when he gets painful pieces of fiberglass in his fingers or is subjected to nasty fiberglass dust. "I may not enjoy it as much, but a pair of limbs is something you just have to make when you're building a bow."

When making typical hunting weight limbs of around 60 pounds, Don first selects .040" thick black fiberglass for the backing and facing. Because of slight variations within different pieces of fiberglass, Don uses 64" strips that he cuts in half and uses the two pieces as a matched pair on opposing limbs. This helps create uniform structural and performance characteristics in both limbs.

Most bowyers use tapered corewood laminations in their limb construction. But not Don. "With parallel corewoods I can control the bow weight a lot better because I can vary the limb thickness so much more with three parallel lamination combinations.

"Plus, the more glue lines you have, the better the limb is. The Old Master Crafters explained to me that three laminations are better than two, and the more glue lines you have, the less chance there is for warping, so the limb will perform better. In fact, if you have two laminations and one piece has a flaw in it, that flaw might show up a lot quicker than it would with three laminations. It may cost a little more to make a three lamination corewood limb, but I believe it shoots better than a two lamination limb." Also, in his particular limb design, parallel corewoods produce a limb that pushes a hunting weight arrow faster than it would if using tapered laminations.

Don selects three parallel .050" thick pieces of Actionwood for the limb core. Like the fiberglass, these are matched pairs which are used in opposing limbs to achieve similar limb performance. Don points out that this accurate matching of composite limb materials results in a bow that requires little if any tillering.

After cutting the fiberglass strips in half, he masking tapes the non-gluing surfaces to protect them from stray epoxy and to provide a marking surface for drawing out the limb shape. Like the Actionwood laminations, Don obtains his bubinga fadeout wedges from the Old Master Crafters. This exotic hardwood is custom ground into pairs of fadeouts that meet Don's specifications. Once all the composites are ready, he dry-assembles and aligns them and then drills a small hole through the butt end of the limb materials.

IN THE FORM

The precision of any bow limb is dependent on the form, and Don spent two painstaking weeks making just one pair of limb forms. These second generation forms were made from three laminated pieces of plywood which were cut and sanded to limb shape and then covered with a smooth piece of Formica. After pressing twenty-five pairs of limbs, Don carefully checks his forms for straightness and uniformity. His form is a two-piece unit with the lower half representing the belly side of his limb, while the upper half represents the back. His form also has a small wooden lip at the tip end and a small alignment pin in the butt end.

When handling the composites during glue-up, Don is careful to touch only the edges. This prevents any finger dirt or oils from getting on the gluing surfaces. Before gluing, he brushes the contact surfaces with a fine brush to remove any dust and covers his form surface with plastic wrap. Using a small Actionwood paddle, he spreads Ren epoxy on all contact surfaces and lays up the composites in the form. When positioning laminates in the form, he places the drilled butt end alignment holes on the small butt end form pin while the tip ends are held in place by the wooden lip.

When laying up the bottom limb, he positions the fadeout wedge ¼" farther into the limb composites which produces a shorter working length limb. This is how Don achieves the "built in" tiller in his bows.

Once the glued composites are laid up, Don places a metal strip on top of them and then lays on an air pressure hose. Next he locks down the upper half of the form with three bolts and inflates the hose to 65 psi to 70 psi. He prefers the simple air hose method of pressing the limb composites because it provides consistent gluing pressure throughout the limb.

The forms sandwiching the unborn limbs are then put in the glue curing oven. It's equipped with 200 watt light bulbs which produce a curing temperature of 150 degrees. A small circulating fan inside the oven helps maintain a uniform temperature throughout and prevents the build up of undesirable hot spots. After four hours of curing, the lights are turned off and the form cools for about an hour while the circulating fan continues to hum.

After Don removes a limb from the press, he trims the ends and rough sands the sides. He removes the masking tape from the tip and butt ends and roughens the fiberglass surface with a carbide file. He then epoxies and "C" clamps the wooden tip overlays and the Formica butt end overlays on the roughened surfaces. Once the glue is hardened, Don gingerly grinds down the tip overlays, blending them nicely into the fiberglass. It's a delicate task. "In bowmaking you learn to take a little bit off at a time. You don't really jump into it because once you take material off, you can't put it back!"

LIMB SHAPE

He next grinds the entire limb to a final butt end width and then drills the main limb attachment hole through the butt end. Don attaches a machined alignment jig to the drilled butt end of the limb and places the jig on his granite surface plate. He adjusts the limb until it's in plane with the granite plate, tightens the jig on the limb, and marks the centerline of the limb using his marking jig. Using a template positioned on the centerline, he outlines the limb shape and then grinds it to form.

Using a small file, he rough cuts in the string nocks and rounds them with a slightly larger file. Using sweeping motions back and forth, he feathers the limb edges on his flexible belt sander. Don attaches the limb to the same alignment pin doweling jig used on the riser, and places it on the granite surface plate. He carefully adjusts the jig so that the limb centerline is in perfect plane with the granite plate, and then marks and drills the alignment pin hole in the belly side of the limb. With his precision procedure for making limb attachments, Don notes that every riser and set of limbs he produces is interchangeable. To prevent accidental limb inversion, the top limb is contoured across the butt end to conform to the shape of the riser's sight window.

Now for the first time, Don braces the bow. He checks for limb alignment in relationship to the string. If necessary, he brings the limbs into alignment

BUILT FOR LONGEVITY — Don bevels the edges of his limbs to help prevent accidental dings from fracturing the fiberglass.

by making minor adjustments in the depth of the string nocks with a small file.

Next he checks the bow for the desired ¼" positive upper limb tiller on his 64" bow, or the ⅜" positive tiller on his 66" model. To achieve proper tiller Don feathers material off the limb edges with a block sander.

Once the limbs are aligned and tillered, Don carefully bevels and smooths the edges of the limbs. "When I first built bows I left the edges pretty squared, and if they got nicked the fiberglass would tear a little. Now, I bevel the edges pretty good. With beveled edges you will ding the wood before you ding the glass which prevents fracturing the fiberglass. I've learned a lot through trial and error."

Besides feathering his limb edges, over the years Don has also narrowed his limb tip width by ³⁄₁₆". "The narrower limbs smooth the bow out. They're a little harder to keep straight but they shoot so much better than a wide limb because they recover faster." He also notes that most mass manufacturers of recurves build a wide limb tip to reduce the possibility of limb twist. Narrow limbed bows require more care in handling to prevent twisting the limbs, but Don feels the increased performance is worth the extra care.

FINISH WORK

The finished limbs, with their matching risers, are hung from wires like sleek sleeping bats in Don's spraying room. Before spraying the porous wood handles, he rubs them with a coat of paste wood filler and sands them to a silky smoothness. Next, Don inks the bow specifications on the side of the riser.

After that, Don's son-in-law, Darin Dyer, sprays the handles with four to five coats of two-part Fullerplast finish. The risers glisten to the mist of the hissing spray gun as he sweeps the sprayer back and forth. Once it's dried, the riser is steel wooled to a low luster satin finish that is durable to the elements, attractive, and dull enough for hunting situations.

The flexing limbs are sprayed with three coats of resilient Zip Guard satin luster urethane finish. Don cautions against spraying too many coats of any finish on limbs because a thick finish may later develop small cracks along stress areas.

Don's finished product radiates a furniture-quality beauty. But no matter how much work a custom bowyer puts into creating an attractive bow, some customers still feel the need to camo paint their equipment. "The prettiest bow I ever made was painted coal black with primer paint two days after I got it to the customer. I told him sarcastically that I was really glad I had made him such a pretty bow!" Don says that it's okay to camouflage the limbs, but he feels the riser section doesn't need to be painted. He points out that during his years of intense whitetail hunting, he's never been detected by game because of his uncamouflaged bow.

TUNE FOR TRADITIONAL

Even though Don builds precision into his bows, some new recurve owners still have trouble getting their bows to shoot a clean arrow. But it's usually not the bow's fault. String stretch, improper brace height, wrong nocking point, and arrow variations can all contribute to poor arrow flight. Don suggests that his customers become familiar with recurve tuning techniques and maintain a properly tuned bow to get the most from their new recurve.

To get the most out his original bow design, Don patterned it after a one-piece Jack Howard recurve. He altered the limb configuration and also designed a more convenient three-piece take-down. Today, Don continues to refine his design and workmanship, striving for a blend of shooting and esthetic qualities. "I like to end up with a smooth shooting bow that still has enough speed to shoot a fast arrow. I also like a bow that looks nice. I want it to look streamlined because some take-down bows are so square and blocky. I want the lines to flow together so that it looks more like a one-piece bow."

Even though he occasionally gets stung by a fiberglass sliver, Don enjoys his bowmaking. "It pays for my hunting trips and my hunting equipment. Besides, if I wasn't building bows, I'd be building something else. I enjoy making a bow for somebody then seeing them go out and get a record book animal with it."

Assenheimer. To many the name may still sound like it belongs on a foreign sports car. But to traditional archers, the name means quality and craftsmanship. And for those who know the man, it means a coverall clad bowhunter perched in a leafless tree watching for the passing of rutting bucks. Especially during midday — and always on November 17.

Chapter Nine

GREAT NORTHERN LONGBOW COMPANY

ON THE ROAD

The highway runs straight for miles and you seem to be all alone on the blacktop. You try to pay attention to the road, but your mind drifts to thoughts of rut-crazed bucks and bowhunting. It's the countryside that's distracting you. It looks like it was designed by whitetails. It's a mixture of small cultivated plots and thick scattered wood lots. Rolling fields of corn, beans, and alfalfa reach out across the landscape, intertwined with willow-choked gullies and brushy fence lines.

Finally, the road swings into a wide, sweeping curve and descends into a small valley. Up ahead, you notice cars and the buildings of a small town. Old-fashioned storefronts lining the road look like a scene from the late 1800s. You cross over a lazy summertime river dotted with wispy puffs of cottonwood fuzz, odd snowflakes somehow lost in time. Everything appears so peaceful in this sleepy village that you slow to a snail's pace.

People walking down the sidewalk aren't from the city. They're too laid-back. The only activity that's not in slow motion is the crowd of jumping kids in front of the soft-serve ice cream shop. One chubby boy with freckles and a brush cut sits on the curb, engrossed in his dripping cone. The sight draws you back in time, and an inner voice makes you pull over.

You wade through the kids with your frozen treat, and pausing in front of the old hardware store, you notice monster buck mounts hanging high on the walls over the service counter. You're drawn inside. Although your mind suddenly races with whitetail questions, you fake a relaxed expression and enter the store. Even larger sets of horns decorate the other walls. You realize too late that your mouth is agape as the smiling store owner asks, "Mornin', can I help you?"

You pry your eyes off the racks and focus on his jolly, almost elfish face framed with an Abe Lincoln beard and light brown curly hair. No sense in evasion, he's seen your intent. "Well, I'm really only interested in knowing a few things about your deer heads."

His eyebrows arch as he gives you the careful once-over. "Oh, really?", he says scratching his beard.

You grin awkwardly. "I usually don't ask silly questions, but I'm a traditional bowhunter who lives to chase whopper whitetails like these."

Suddenly, his clear blue eyes twinkle and he looks you squarely in the eye as if he has just recognized you as some long-lost kinfolk. Soon you find out why.

CARRYING ON TRADITION

The sleepy village is Nashville, Michigan. It's set on the quiet banks of the Thornapple River, along Highway 66 between Battle Creek and Grand Rapids. Nearby Thornapple Lake is a past haunt of genuine "traditional" hunters: primitive Indians used the lake site as a gathering area. Although the Indians are almost forgotten, except for the occasional artifact, traditional archery lives on in Nashville. Tucked away on the north side of town is a small workshop where two men incorporate local woods into the crafting of their Indian-style flatbows. It's the home of Great Northern Longbows.

Jerry Brumm, the smiling face from the hardware store, and his partner Rick Shepard, work side by side as a team, sharing their complementary skills and creating custom traditional bows at the Great Northern Longbow Company.

The word "enthusiastic" falls short of describing the zest these men have for the sport of traditional archery. Both hold down other jobs, yet somehow make time to spend thirty to forty hours a week crafting bows. It's their labor of love. When they're not building bows, they're either shooting them, hunting with them, or attending traditional archery gatherings. They're longbow addicts.

THE QUIET BEAR

Rick Shepard is a burly man with thick brown hair. He's a big bear, at peace with the world. His full beard and wire rimmed glasses make him look like he could easily blend in with a team of Nashville lumberjacks on their way to work 100 years ago. His eyes smile as much as his mouth when he tells a humorous story or plays a practical joke, and this thirty-nine-year-old bowyer frequently enjoys doing both.

Rick was born and raised in nearby Hastings, Michigan. Living in that rural atmosphere seems appropriate for his peaceful personality. "I'm not a city person. In fact, when we go to town, I spend just about an hour there and then it's time for me to get back home!"

Even though he's not much for city crowds, Rick is an active member of The Michigan Longbow Association, Michigan Bowhunters, and the Professional Bowhunters Society. His interest in Indian culture is evident at traditional gatherings where he often spends weekends camping in his large Indian teepee. Although he doesn't like feeding the local mosquito population at night, he enjoys the romantic Indian lure of roughing it in his canvas covered shelter. The teepee's covering isn't authentic, but Rick wryly points out that an affordable supply of buffalo hides is hard to come by.

Traditional archery is a family experience at the Shepard house. Rick's wife, Chris, enjoys bowhunting and attending shoots with her forty-seven pound, Great Northern osage longbow. She is an accomplished artist who hand-crafts beautifully embossed leather back quivers. Her distinctive traditional quivers often display vivid hunting and nature scenes and have earned her high acclaim within the longbow community.

REDISCOVERED LOVE

Rick's passion for archery began when he was just a kid. By his early teens he was earnestly shooting and hunting with recurves. Later, a tour of duty in Vietnam interrupted his archery and dampened his interest. After returning from the service, his gun and bow remained locked in the closet while he let several deer seasons pass without venturing into the woods.

Eventually, Rick was talked into going deer hunting during gun season. As he waited in an old fence row, the morning air was shattered by shotgun blasts of other hunters lobbing slugs at a running deer. The next thing Rick knew, slugs were smacking the ground around him. "I hit the dirt! Then, I just took the shotgun and unloaded it into the ground and walked back to the house. I completely lost all interest in gun hunting right then. I was between mad, furious, and scared. I don't like to get shot at. I had enough close calls in Vietnam to last me a long time."

With his gun hung on the wall for good, Rick got back into archery and made the popular transition from recurves to compounds. After several years of involvement in the "compound craze" as he calls it, Rick found that even though he had become very proficient with the weapon, the thrill of archery was slipping away.

Then, one evening, he unexpectedly rediscovered the fun of old-time archery. "I was shooting on a league and Ron LaClair came in with some longbows. Jerry was also there with a longbow that he had just started shooting. He pretty much had the same experience that I did going through the compound bow craze and he said, 'You want to try this?' So, I picked up the longbow and shot three arrows out of it, put away my compound, and haven't shot a compound since. That was four years ago."

ALONE WITH HIS LONGBOW

Once again in love with bowhunting and archery, Rick enjoys escaping into Michigan's autumn-splashed forest where he savors the tranquility of nature with his favorite longbow at his side. "I'm a loner when I hunt. Once in a while I'll go up in Canada. There are places up there where I can be thirty miles from any village. I'll just pack it in and sit by a lake watching the beavers. I don't have to shoot any animals to enjoy hunting. I just like to be out in the wild."

The wary whitetail is Rick's favorite longbow quarry, and he prefers hunting haunts close to home where he knows the cover and the critters. "I really enjoy hunting deer. It's fascinating to watch their habits. In the years that I've hunted them, every season has been a little different. You think that you have the deer pinpointed and know what they're going to do, and then they do something completely different."

When alone with the whitetails, Rick blends simple hunting methods with his traditional equipment, creating a supreme bowhunting challenge. "I like to stalk and still hunt. I've tree hunted, but I don't enjoy it. I'm not one to sit still in a tree. I like being on the ground where I really have to be on the ball. I've had deer walk almost right on top of me on the ground before. Generally, I like hunting in a misty rain because then the deer are a little less attentive to what's going on around them and you can get a little closer. I don't always get my game but it's always fun."

HEAVY STUFF

For deer hunting, Rick uses equipment that could easily put down a moose. His husky frame makes shooting his favorite osage Bushbow look ridiculously easy. "I shoot heavy equipment, at least eighty pounds minimum when I hunt. I shoot a heavy arrow and, of course, I like heavy broadheads. I prefer a heavy, two-bladed head, probably 160 grains or better. I've shot Timberwolf broadheads, made by Glen Parker from Texas, which are good heavy heads. John Shephard builds a fantastic broadhead called the Mooswak that he doesn't sell commercially, but he gives them to friends and that's what I'm shooting right now. To get them shaving sharp, I file and stone hone them."

On his light brown stained shafts, Rick prefers 5¾" parabolic fletching, burned ¾" high. He feels the larger feathers provide quicker arrow recovery which is important in traditional bowhunting. He prefers a custom back quiver lined with sheepskin and padded on the bottom with thick foam to reduce arrow noise. To quiet his bow for hunting he ties wool yarn balls on his Flemish-twist bowstring.

Even though whitetail are his number one quarry, there is another Michigan critter that Rick wants to pursue with his Bushbow. "I'd like to try turkey hunting. I've never hunted turkeys, but they really intrigue me. They just started planting them in this area a year or so ago. In fact, out behind my house I heard one last year, real early in the morning. It just brought a chill in the back of my neck and I thought, boy, I'd sure like to try to shoot a turkey!"

BEAR FUN

Rick has chased a variety of animals with his longbow, but one of his most memorable hunts didn't involve any shooting. "My wife and I were bear hunting from the same platform. We sat quietly in the rain for probably four hours. Finally, we looked up and they just appeared — two cubs following a sow walked up and sat five yards from the stand. They just looked right at us with an expression like, 'Hi, what are you two doing up there?'

"They played around us for almost an hour and a half. The sow climbed up our tree about six times. She got her head above the stand and one paw was even on it. I almost had to kick her in the snoot to get her down a couple of times. One thing a lot of people don't realize is that when bears climb trees, the only way they can actually get you is to bite you and pull you down. They can't let go of the tree with their arms because if they did they would fall." Fortunately, most bear hunters don't have to test Rick's theory.

Besides giving advise on climbing bears, Rick also passes along some pointers for beginning traditional bowhunters. "First of all, don't overbow yourself. Secondly, don't try to copy other shooters. Take certain parts of what you observe and make them work for your style. Learn to concentrate and even forget that you have a bow in your hands. Picture the arrow in the animal before you shoot. And never pull that string back on anything unless you know it's going to die. Before you shoot, understand that you want to kill that animal and not wound it. Know that you want to kill it. If you don't, you'll never get him."

FUN LOVING ELF

The other half of the Great Northern Longbow team is Jerry Brumm, the hardware store owner. A mere mention of traditional archery lights up his youthful looking face and puts a genuine twinkle in his eyes. Jerry is an expressive man who doesn't hesitate to share his love of the longbow. And as you get to know him, don't be surprised if you discover a fun loving elf hiding behind his gray stippled beard and jolly face.

Jerry was born in Nashville, Michigan and has resided there all his life. He enjoys the small town flavor and is active in the community. One of the reasons he likes the area so much is the prime whitetail hunting right out his back door. During bow season you'll seldom find Jerry packing the car for an out-of-town hunting trip. He usually just grabs his bow and walks out the

THE TEAM APPROACH — Rick the bear, (left), and Jerry the elf, share both their work and play with a cherished companion, the longbow.

back door where he enjoys roaming the wood lots and brush-filled fields behind his house. Plenty of quality bucks inhabit the area, evidenced by the mounts on his walls and his stockpile of whitetail stories.

Jerry sums up all of his hobbies with just one word. "LONGBOW, plain and simple." He attributes his youthful spirit at forty-five years of age to his lifelong involvement in archery. This archery enthusiasm has spread through his family, as his wife, Sharon, and their two sons, Bob and Adam, also share a fondness for bowhunting with their longbows.

Jerry's passion for traditional archery is also reflected in his fascination with Indian artifacts and antique self-wood bows. Occasionally, he finds artifacts near old Algonquin campsites located around Thornapple Lake. While searching for these pieces of the past, he cheerfully endures biting bugs and a blazing sun just to find a few flint chips flaked by some forgotten woodlands Indian.

Decorating the rafters of his family room is his rustic collection of antique self-wood bows. It includes a youth bow crafted by one of Bear Archery's early bowyers, Nels Grumley, and an old take-down longbow with two sets of string nocks for changing bow poundage. His collection also includes a variety of finely crafted osage and yew longbows reminiscent of the classics built by Pope and Young.

LEMONWOOD SUMMERS

Jerry got his first real bow when he was twelve years old. It was a Ben Pearson lemonwood longbow which pulled thirty-five pounds. He still has it. To him it represents a special friend that led him into the exciting world of archery.

As a boy, his weekends were filled with hours of shooting his longbow, and he often traveled to archery tournaments around the state with the family of a friend. "I honestly believed a young person my age couldn't live and enjoy life without being involved in archery. Later I went through a period when I discovered girls and automobiles and I drew away from archery. But eventually I got back into it. Now I think that girls and cars were just a lull in my life, and I don't think that could happen again!"

With girls and cars behind him, Jerry became more involved in archery and later became a polished shooter under the guidance of W.G. (Bill) Pierce. Bill, who was an excellent target archer and PAA instructor, helped Jerry develop his target archery skills. Even though his target bows are now part of his past, Jerry still recalls Bill's lessons. "When I start getting sloppy and things don't go well, I go back to what Bill taught me and apply it to traditional shooting. It definitely straightens me out."

OLD-TIME ARCHERY

Jerry's involvement with old-time archery extends beyond the woods, ranges, and bow building shop. He is president of the Michigan Longbow Association and a Regular Member of the Professional Bowhunters Society. He also belongs to the Michigan Bowhunters.

The Michigan Longbow Association is a special organization to Jerry. Within its ranks he enjoys a close fellowship with members and participants at longbow gatherings; dedicated traditionalists who make an extra effort to develop their skills. Because their skills are so demanding, traditional ranks contain few slob hunters. And for Jerry, the further he can remain from slob hunters, the better. "I come unglued when I encounter slob hunters seeking the easiest and shortest path to killing something. For someone in the bow building profession, coming unglued is the unpleasant release of stress caused by an incompatible bond."

One of the high points of Jerry's involvement with the Michigan Longbow Association is their annual Great Lakes Longbow Invitational. It's by far his favorite traditional gathering. Now the nation's top longbow event, Jerry played a major role in organizing this grandest of longbow shoots which draws bowmen from coast to coast. "The first year we had that invitational it took me two weeks to get my feet back on the ground. I was on a natural high. It was the most fantastic shoot I had ever been to, an absolute highlight of my life. We were rubbing elbows with Dick Robertson, Jay Massey, and other great traditionalists. I haven't seen that much nostalgia and fellowship duplicated anywhere."

PATIENT HUNTER

Traditional shoots provide the realistic practice Jerry needs to pursue another love — bowhunting big bucks from ground blinds. It's his favorite style of hunting because he enjoys the challenge and thrills of being at pointblank range and eye level with wary whitetails. Hunting from the ground also provides him with better shooting angles and an increased depth perception for his instinctive sight picture. One of his secrets to consistently putting bucks in the freezer is patience. "At the risk of bragging, I don't miss a shot when I hunt. That's because I only take shots that I can't hardly miss. I'm in no hurry. There are a lot of deer. I don't have to get a deer tonight, I can wait until tomorrow night. I just like to be out there. I like to hunt for three months, as long as it's not cold and nasty."

Another reason Jerry enjoys such success with his backyard bucks is his concentration on that once-a-season shot. "When I hunt deer I follow a certain procedure. First, I decide whether or not I'm going to attempt to shoot that buck. Once I decide I want him, I never look back at his horns. All I do is look at the spot I want to hit. I don't care if the deer is still fifty yards away, I concentrate on that spot. By the time the buck gets close enough to shoot, I've almost got a hole burned in him, and when he presents a good shot, I go for it. There is something magic about it, because the arrow always hits that spot."

Jerry openly shares his hunting secrets with his longbow customers and offers his woods-wise opinions to bowhunting novices. "First, realize that you don't have to kill a deer to have a good hunt. Second, become a year-round bowhunter. Practice, shoot a lot, recognize the maximum yardage that you can accurately shoot, and stay within those yardage limitations."

OL' NUMBER FOUR

When Jerry heads for the woods he often takes Ol' Number Four, his favorite longbow. Unlike the beautifully crafted bows that leave the doors of the Great Northern Longbow Company, it's admittedly a poor example of their bow crafting abilities. "It's the fourth longbow Rick and I built. It's maple, it's ugly, and there is not another bow like it. But when I shoot it, it's a lucky bow. I killed a caribou with it. It draws eighty-one pounds and it shoots right where I look. It's magic! I've tried and tried but I've never been able to duplicate it. I've never shot it through a chronograph, so I have no idea how fast it is. All I know is that it shoots right where I look.

"I don't often take it to shoots because it's a poor representation of what we build. But when I do take it, I have fun with it. I wait until there are a lot of people around, and when I finish shooting, I just stick it in the ground and walk down to pull my arrows. People really look at each other, but I just tell them, 'It's okay, I know the guy who makes them.' "

When hunting with Ol' Number Four, Jerry likes the traditional appeal of a soft leather back quiver. He prefers one that conforms to his back and keeps the arrows from rattling around. Bow-mounted quivers affect his instinctive picture and can cause a stray arrow. "I keep my back quiver stuffed full of arrows, at least one for every occasion!"

OFF-BEAT ARROWS

Like Ol' Number Four, Jerry's hunting arrows are also uncommon. Most traditional archers use cedar shafts for hunting, but not Jerry. He makes his own unique arrows by rummaging through his hardware store dowels and hand selecting arrow quality shafts. He then sands the Ramin hardwood dowels from Taiwan down to a 23⁄64" diameter and stains them white. Jerry fletches his custom shafts with yellow or white feathers and burns them in a parabolic shape at least 5½" long and ¾" high.

On the business end of his arrows, Jerry installs a heavy, wide, single bladed broadhead or a three-bladed Snuffer. Mounted with a heavy broadhead these hard-hitting arrows weigh from 700 to 750 grains. "I call them 'Ramshafts', and there isn't a deer in the world that can stop 'em!"

Most bowhunters would shy away from using Jerry's high visibility arrows in the field, but he has his reasons. "I shoot a white arrow with white or yellow feathers because I want to know where I hit that deer. It makes all the difference in the world as to what you do and how you do it when recovering that animal. Shooting camouflage arrows is just a gimmick and it should never be done. I would rather have a deer see those arrows in my quiver than to ever shoot a deer and not know where I hit it."

ELEPHANTS AND LONGBOW FUN

To make sure his arrows hit home where they're supposed to, Jerry practices year round. Although he shoots paper targets and arrows 3-D foam animals, his favorite form of practice involves his imagination and sense of humor, and he has plenty of both. "I never get enough practice, and my favorite kind is 'elephant hunting'. It's simply roaming fields during the off season with my bow and quiver stuffed full of blunt arrows. It usually doesn't take long to spot the pachyderms in the disguise of old stumps, clumps of grass, and assorted dirt clods. There's no bag limit on them, and they usually remain dazed for a second arrow."

Besides bagging elephants, over the years Jerry has harvested an assortment of small game, whitetails, black bear, and caribou. Some were taken with compounds, but he now hunts exclusively with his longbow. "Hunting with a compound had lost its challenge. I killed ten whitetail bucks and a black bear with eleven arrows. But the longbow put the challenge back into bowhunting and made it fun again.

"I've summed it up many times, and no matter what you say or how long of a spiel you go into on traditional archery, the bottom line is: It's fun. Shooting a longbow is pure and simple. I spent a good many years trying to gain back the fun I had when I was a kid shooting my longbow. I never attained it until I once again picked up a longbow. I shot nine arrows out of it and it literally changed my life. I feel cheated by the years I spent hunting with a compound. I'm not taking anything away from the compound bow, I had some good hunts with it. But I wasn't having fun."

Today, Jerry has fun with his longbows seven days a week. During weekdays, he and Rick craft their quality line of custom bows. When weekends finally arrive, most professionals take a break from their business. But for Jerry and Rick, weekends are a time for stringing up their favorite longbow and heading out the door in hot pursuit of rabbits, whitetails, or elephants.

GREAT NORTHERN BOWS

Rick and Jerry offer three designs of traditional bows. For the pure traditionalist they produce their standard "Longbow" with its old English design, and thin, deep-cored limbs. Archers seeking Indian magic will appreciate their shorter "Bushbow" which blends ancient red-man flatbow styling with modern deflex-reflex limbs. And for the recurve enthusiast, the slim-lined "Ghost" represents the spirit of an early 1960s recurve.

The GHOST is Great Northern's 60" recurve. It's strikingly beautiful yet simple in its flowing lines. It represents a re-creation of one of the famous recurves that was born along the quiet banks of the AuSable River in the early sixties and somehow lost in the dust of progress. The sweeping, full-working recurve design displays the beauty of natural corewoods under clear fiberglass. The Ghost's light mass weight and delicate balance makes it a joy to carry all day long. In fact, it's so light in frame that it deceptively resembles a youth bow. But the deception ends when one discovers that this little sliver flinger zings an arrow at over 200 feet per second!

The Ghost has several design characteristics common among all Great Northern bows. All are offered in almost any combination of limb corewoods and riser woods, and they are faced and backed with a continuous layer of clear fiberglass. Great Northern bows are noted for the flowing lines of the slim riser and for the small torque-free grip. The 4¼" suede grip is 1³⁄₁₆" wide and 1½" thick. Sight windows are cut ³/₁₆" from center shot and the shelf is 1¼" above the bow center.

The recommended brace height from the string to the throat is 6¾" to 7¼" on all models. Great Northern's logo, bow specifications, and owner's name are black inked on the limb belly near the riser.

Weighing a mere 16 ounces, the Ghost is a feather-weight among re-curves. Its riser is 15" long between fadeouts and has a rounded sight window which blends smoothly back to full riser width near the upper fadeout. The upper limb measures 23" from the fadeout to the nock and the lower limb measures 22". These graceful limbs are constructed from two tapered back laminations and one belly lamination. The limbs narrow from 1³/₁₆" wide at the fadeouts, to a thin ⅝" at the nocks. Their rounded edges blend into flowing contours with the rounded riser and delicate tip overlays. Thin horn, fiberglass, or wood tip overlays display beautifully rounded edges and nicely fashioned string nocks.

The following draw-force measurements were recorded on a 60" red elm-cored Ghost:

DRAW LENGTH	25"	26"	27"	28"	29"
DRAW WEIGHT	58½#	61#	65#	68#	71½#

To check for relative speed, Rick hand shot this red elm recurve, drawing a full 28". The cedar arrows were 28" long, fletched with low-profile, 6" long goose feathers, and had open-end nocks. Total arrow weight including the field point was 535 grains. All Great Northern bows shot through the chronograph were equipped with standard Dacron strings without brush buttons or string silencers. The average arrow speed for the 68 pound at 28" draw red elm Ghost was 205 fps.

The BUSHBOW makes it easy to feel like an Indian of old or just a kid again. The flat cross-sectional limb combined with the sweeping deflex-reflex limb design results in a stable and smooth-shooting little bow. The shorter length of this 62" or 64" flatbow is a real advantage for the traditional archer perched in an old oak tree or sneaking through the brush.

The Bushbow's natural corewoods, exposed under clear fiberglass, make it melt into a wooded setting and it's a real eye catcher at traditional gather-ings. Both the romance and performance of this little beauty are evidenced by its popularity. Since it was first offered in 1986, this flatbow has taken over Great Northern's waiting list. The Bushbow offers bowhunters the beauty and grace of a traditional bow, while the shorter working length and the deflex-reflex limb design provide smoothness and cast. Jerry believes it's a great combination. "Our Bushbow is the best of both worlds. You have the length of a recurve and all the shooting characteristics of a longbow. Plus, it has a small, torque-free handle."

Like all Great Northern bows, the Bushbow varies slightly in mass weight depending on its corewood and riser materials. It weighs from 17 ounces to 23 ounces. The slim flowing riser measures 15¼" between fadeouts. The working length of the upper limb on a 64" Bushbow is 25⅛" and on the lower limb, 23½". The limbs are 1⅝" wide at the fadeouts and narrow to ⅝" at the nocks. Like the Ghost, these limbs are constructed from

Great Northern's bows are characterized by slim handles and warm woods under clear glass. Chris Shepard's handsome quivers complement these traditional beauties.

two tapered back laminations and one belly lamination. The Bushbow usually doesn't require tip overlays except on softer corewoods such as cedar where a thin layer of clear fiberglass is used.

The following draw-force relationship was measured on a 64" osage Bushbow:

DRAW LENGTH	25"	26"	27"	28"	29"
DRAW WEIGHT	54#	57#	61#	65#	70#

Rick again drew 28" and used a leather glove when shooting his arrows from this osage Bushbow through the chronograph. He used the same 535 grain, goose feathered arrows shot from the Ghost. The average relative arrow speed from this 65 pound at 28" draw Bushbow was 178 fps.

The LONGBOW has slightly reflexed limbs and a classic modified trapezoid cross-sectional shape. It is available in 66", 68", and 70" lengths. A 68" red elm Longbow weighs 20 ounces.

Its slim-throated riser measures approximately 15½" between fadeouts. This bow exhibits traditional trapezoidal "D" shaped limb cross section tapering to the belly. Through research and in-house bow tests, Rick and Jerry have discovered that this limb shape is the quickest and most efficient of the longbow limbs. The Longbow's limbs are constructed with three tapered back laminations and one belly lamination. On a 68" longbow, the working length of the upper limb is 27" and of the lower limb is 25¾". The limb width narrows gradually from 1¼" at the fadeouts to 9⁄16" at the nocks.

One of Great Northern's standard 68" red elm Longbows, had the following draw-force relationship:

DRAW LENGTH	25"	26"	27"	28"	29"
DRAW WEIGHT	61#	66#	70#	74#	79#

Jerry shot this bow using the 535 grain goose feathered arrows which he drew a full 28". He used a leather shooting glove and, like Rick, had a clean release. The average relative arrow speed from this 74 pound at 28" draw, 68", red elm Longbow was 190 fps.

IT JUST HAPPENED

Great Northern's sleek line of traditional bows evolved after Jerry and Rick began looking for a quality longbow with a special combination of feel, select natural materials, and performance. Although they shopped around, they couldn't find one that suited them, so they decided to build their own. In the process, they created bows that soon captured the interest of other longbow enthusiasts, and before they knew it, Jerry and Rick were in the bowmaking business. They began commercially making Great Northern longbows in 1983. The demand for their products is evidenced by the fact that they haven't caught up on back orders since making their first bows, and they both admit, that's a good feeling.

TEAM SPIRIT

The quiet bear and the over-sized elf are definitely a bow crafting team. Their brainstorming sessions have spawned innovative ideas about bow design and construction techniques, and they each possess individual skills that complement one another. For example, Rick's patient, searching eyes and steady hands extract the finest corewoods from the rough stock, while Jerry's artistic flair is evidenced in the logo inking, leather work, and the finish coat. A Great Northern Longbow is truly part Jerry and part Rick.

Jerry notes that the teaming up of farm boy reasoning and a logical approach to problem solving has helped them conquer many technical challenges and caused them to excel far beyond the scope of a one-man operation. Their bowmaking savvy and openness prompts frequent calls from both seasoned and novice bowyers seeking advice. Although some custom bowyers keep their craft a secret, Jerry opens the curtains of mystery and enjoys helping others. "We like to talk shop with other bowyers. We could never be where we are today if it wasn't for people like Dick Robertson. Dick has helped us immensely. We've asked thousands of questions of various bowyers.

"Also, there are other lessons we've learned through the school of hard knocks. I would do just about anything to keep a novice bowyer from losing a bow. I have talked for an hour and a half on the telephone to guys building their first bow, holding their hand so they wouldn't have to go through some of the things we went through. We have no secrets."

Each Great Northern reflects the talents of both of these skilled bowyers. Rick (left) crafts custom laminations while Jerry displays his talents during the finish work.

Jerry and Rick craft their bows in a small shop hidden in a secluded rural setting just outside of town. It's a quiet place, conducive to the patient and artful creation of bows. However, they are occasionally drawn from the work bench to watch the quiet passing of a doe and fawns, and sometimes they even get a glimpse of "Mr. Big" visiting the scrape under the old cherry tree. It's almost as if the bucks know the rules at Great Northern Longbow Company — "No shooting deer within sight of the shop!"

PRIZED STOCK

Out behind the shop rest aging stacks of bow wood. Like artists searching for the unborn beauty on a blank canvas, Rick and Jerry occasionally stroll out back and gaze at their rough sawn lumber. In some boards they see wonderfully straight-grained laminations, while in others they detect the swirling grain pattern in a future riser. On a quiet evening Jerry might cup his ear near a board and listen to the wood. Maybe it's softly whispering, "I am ready, I am worthy," but Jerry is only listening for the sound of gnawing wood grubs, sometimes a problem with exposed osage.

Their stacks of lumber represent a variety of native Michigan woods. Their favorite is the honey-hued, osage orange — a unique wood with a rich heritage in bow crafting. Tough and dependable osage self-wood bows accompanied Pope and Young on many a hunt. And some of the qualities of osage, which contribute to its performance in self-wood bows, are in part preserved in the construction of Rick and Jerry's modern composite bows.

Great Northern's osage is harvested locally and naturally aged in the shade of the old cherry tree behind the shop. Jerry believes that Michigan osage is a superior bow wood because the slower growing northern climate produces more uniform and tighter growth rings within the wood, contributing to the performance and durability of the edge grain laminations used in Great Northern bows.

Rick is admittedly the osage nut at Great Northern. He's captivated by its beauty and intrigued by its characteristics. He explains that it's a tough, dense, and very resilient or springy wood. Even after repeated bending deformation, it returns to its original shape. This resiliency accounts for the unique performance of an osage bow. It makes the bow hum and feel alive in the hand after the shot, and Rick notes it's not hand shock but a pleasant singing of the osage. Jerry believes that a unique feature of the heavier osage is its ability to shoot a wide range of different weight arrows with similar arrow flight.

For sheer beauty, osage is tough to beat. Freshly sawn, it radiates a bright honey-yellow color that intriguingly changes with age. Like a lean beachcomber, the sun's rays slowly alter an osage bow from honey-yellow to rich amber tones, and ultimately, a deep reddish brown. As if its striking color weren't enough, osage shimmers iridescently within the grain, like a tiger's eye gemstone. For Rick, this beauty adds a special dimension of excitement to his bow crafting because each osage bow is distinctive in its emerging grain patterns.

OTHER TREASURES

Michigan red elm is another local wood favored by Jerry and Rick. Like osage, it is slow growing, producing a tight, uniformly grained wood. Although it is extremely resilient like osage, it's lighter in mass weight and makes a fast shooting bow. The brown wood displays contrasting grain patterns which add natural beauty and camouflage to a bow. Red elm's fibrous grain sometimes causes it to slightly warp after it's ground into thin bow laminations. Although this makes working with it more difficult, the same fibrous grain makes it unbelievably tough and resilient. In fact, it's so resilient, it's one of the few corewood laminations that can be bent in a circle without breaking or splitting. Red elm is the toughest corewood Jerry has ever seen. "Red elm is almost indestructible. You could beat a bear to death with a red elm bow and not hurt the bow."

Michigan white cedar harvested from Seney Swamp in the Upper Peninsula is another corewood used by Great Northern. It's extremely light in weight and makes a delicately balanced, fast shooting bow. A disadvantage of cedar is its softness. Rough use in the field can cause dents on the exposed edges. To minimize this problem, Great Northern incorporates a center lamination of tough osage in their cedar bows. This center osage lamination sticks out the most on the rounded edges of the limb, and serves as a protective "bump" strip. Plus, combining the two corewoods has advantages: the osage provides stability and the lightweight cedar increases limb speed.

Although they have an affection for home-grown corewoods, Rick and Jerry also use a variety of imported exotics for making risers. One of the more popular woods is shedua. This African cherry exhibits a rich chocolate color laced with varying hues of reddish-black grain. It makes a strong and strikingly attractive riser. Rick and Jerry occasionally use shedua for limb laminations. Under clear fiberglass, it makes a stunning dark, naturally camouflaged bow called the "Shadowbow." And when shedua is combined with other corewoods, such as red elm, it produces a handsome dark-toned beauty without sacrificing bow performance.

BOARDS TO BOWS

From their stacks of treasured rough stock, Rick selects the choicest pieces for making tapered corewood laminations. He carefully reads each board for grain direction and quality before it passes as corewood material. Although flat grain laminations with exposed grain patterns usually make a prettier bow, Great Northern uses edge grain laminations to maximize limb performance as it produces a more consistent and uniform working limb.

Rick extracts quality edge grain laminations from the rough-cut stock. Accompanied by the music of the singing band saw, he cuts the slightly tapered pieces, following the most uniform qualities within the block, while avoiding splits, knots, and twisted grain. By avoiding these trouble spots, Rick's critical eye and steady hand often cull up to fifty percent of the valued corewood material. The resulting laminations are superb.

When cutting laminations, Rick pairs consecutively cut pieces as a matched set. One will be used in the upper limb while its near-twin is used

Using a 12" drum sander, Rick feeds in osage laminations on a tapering board. Bowyer's gold dust and custom tapered corewoods come out the other side.

Grinding the fadeouts to a delicate, paper-thin edge is critical because they represent major stress areas in the finished bow. When grinding, Rick is careful to keep the riser square to the grinding drum.

in the lower limb. This ensures similar visual and performance qualities in both limbs.

After laminations are cut, they are neatly stacked and air dried for several days. Each matched pair is then placed on a sandpaper covered, .002" per inch tapered board and run through a 12" drum sander which produces the desired taper. Grinding the osage produces a bitter smell like freshly broken nettle weeds, and dusts the floor by the drum sander with a dazzling yellow layer of what Jerry calls "bowyer's gold dust." The ground laminations are then tied together in bundles and stored in a light-bulb heated box to keep the lamination moisture content around six percent.

For the riser section, Rick selects a strong grained wood with visual character, and power planes it to working dimensions. He makes sure the wood grain will be in alignment with the bowstring for maximum riser strength. He then outlines the riser shape with a template and marks several critical reference points. After cutting the riser out with a band saw, he carefully grinds it to its final shape on a vertical sanding drum.

The final step in finishing a riser is a delicate one. With the utmost care, Rick supports the back side of the fadeout with a culled lamination while gently feathering out the face side of the fadeout on the sanding drum. The fadeouts are gingerly ground to a smooth flowing shape and taper to a paper-thin edge. Rick notes that properly feathering the fadeouts is important to the appearance, durability, and performance of a bow.

After the laminations and riser are completed, Jerry and Rick inspect the fiberglass for flaws and check its exact thickness using a micrometer. Great Northern bows display the attractive corewoods under clear, full-length fiberglass. Besides making the bow beautiful, clear glass shows the quality in the glue job, and will reveal any future problem in the glue joint, fiberglass, or outer lamination. Completely enveloping the riser and laminations under one full-length piece of glass also allows Jerry and Rick to fashion their sleek, slim-lined grips without jeopardizing strength through the handle section.

PUTTING IT TO FORM

Once the composites are ready to be laid up, Jerry pulls out their bow form. Trueness and design of a bow form are crucial in bow crafting as the pressed composites reflect the perfections and imperfections of the form. Great Northern's forms are built from several layers of plywood and reinforced along the base with perpendicular laminates of plywood. This "I" beam effect provides rigidity, helping to maintain the trueness of the form. A strip of fiberglass covers the flowing contour of the 2" wide form surface, providing an even, uniform, surface duplicating the exact shape of the back of the bow.

The wood and fiberglass composites in a bow are only as strong as the glue holding them together. And Rick and Jerry believe their bow glues are "superb and second to none." They use Smooth-On EA-40 epoxy on all wood-to-fiberglass bonds, and Urac 185 on all wood-to-wood bonds. Jerry says, Urac 185 provides a non-slip, positive bond, while the tough epoxy is subject to extremely minute joint slippage.

Prior to glue-up, Jerry cleans all wood and fiberglass contact surfaces with lacquer thinner to remove any dust, dirt, film, or natural wood oils. Next, he covers the bow form surface with plastic wrap to protect it from the runny glue. Even a small fleck of hardened glue on the form surface will cause a dimple in a pressed bow.

Unlike many of the bow crafting steps Jerry and Rick perform individually, gluing up a bow is a two-man operation. During the involved process, they usually work side by side in silent harmony. No directions are needed. They know each other's every move.

First, they coat all laminate-to-laminate contact surfaces with glue. This is important because it allows the glue to size or soak into the roughened contact surfaces and greatly reduces the risk of glue joint failure. They also bevel and overlap the butt ends of paired laminations so corewoods will appear as one long continuous piece.

Rick carefully positions the matched pair of laminations, precisely aligning their butt end grain to ensure similar characteristics in opposing limbs. Each pair of laminations is laid up to optimize the beauty of the grain and complement the different characteristics of the adjoining laminations.

They place a strip of rubber belt material on top of the glued composites in the form. Then they lay a length of deflated fire hose on the strip and secure the top portion of the press, sandwiching the composites and the hose. Jerry slowly inflates the adapted fire hose, which allows trapped air to escape from between the glued laminations and prevents any warped corewoods from slipping out of alignment. Finally, he inflates the hose to seventy pounds and seals off the air valve.

Both epoxy and Urac glues cure best when heated, so the entire press is placed in Great Northern's glue curing oven. It's equipped with an electronic timer and a thermostatically controlled radiant heating cable which evenly warms the press. Like many of their bow building devices, the heat box was designed and built by the two-man team.

After the glued composites have cured for four hours at 140 degrees, the timer shuts off the heat, and the bow is left in the oven to cool overnight. Jerry and Rick believe that this slow overnight cooling is very important to the ultimate alignment of the bow, and they never remove a bow from the press until it has cooled completely.

Newborn bows freshly popped from the press are covered with dangerously sharp and unsightly dried glue, which Jerry calls "bowyer's afterbirth." After rasping off the excess glue, Jerry masking tapes the bow and marks its shape using a master template.

Accompanied by the chattering whine of a dull band saw, they trim the bow to rough shape. They only use dull blades to saw through fiberglass because it quickly eats up the blade's teeth. They then grind the emerging bow to form on a belt sander and finish shaping it with files and hand sanding.

ONE OR THE OTHER

Once they remove a bow from the press, it's exclusively shaped, aligned, tillered, and sanded by either Jerry or Rick. Even though they separately craft a bow from the press to final sanding, their techniques are so similar they have difficulty telling who built a particular bow. That's one reason they ink their initials next to the bow's serial number.

During the final stages of sanding, they bring the bow into an approximate one-eighth inch positive tiller by shaping the limb edges and gently hand-sanding the fiberglass on the surface of the limbs.

They install matching riser wood or horn tip overlays before the final sanding by first roughening up the contact surfaces of the near-tip fiberglass and overlay with sandpaper. They clean the contact surfaces with thinner, coat them with epoxy, and "C" clamp the overlays in place. After the overlays are dried, Rick and Jerry delicately fashion the tips and nocks.

Before spraying on the finish coat, they apply a coat of clear wood filler on all exposed wood surfaces. This fills the little hairline grooves and grain pores, providing a smooth surface. They then lightly sand, air dust, and wipe the bow with a tack cloth. This is imperative in achieving the superb finish Great Northern bows are noted for.

Once a bow is ready for finishing, Jerry takes over. With flowing strokes of his artistic hand, Jerry inks Great Northern's swaying pines logo and bow specifications on the limb belly.

A quality bow finish should reveal a bow's natural beauty while stubbornly protecting it from the elements. It should be hard enough to provide the necessary durability, yet not so hard that it will crack along stress areas. Great Northern uses Fullerplast satin finish made by Fuller O'Brien, and Jerry admires its toughness. "It's a fast-drying clear catalyzed varnish that's superb for use on bows. It's so tough, in fact, you can stick a finished bow limb in a can of lacquer thinner overnight and not even soften the finish!" This, of course, is not a recommended test of any finish's durability.

With more artistic swaying of his hand, Jerry sprays each bow with fifteen thin coats of finish. By lightly rubbing the dried finish with .0000 steel wool, he produces the rich-looking, soft satin luster characteristic of Great Northern bows. Jerry points out that the finish can also be brought to a high-gloss sheen by hand buffing it with rubbing compound.

The final leather work is Jerry's favorite part. He contact cements on the suede strike pad and does the same to the suede grip. He then decoratively laces the front of the grip with artificial sinew. The finishing touch is the addition of a few small wooden beads on the end of the lacing — another of Great Northern's trademarks.

The finished bows reflect Jerry and Rick's preferences in design and performance, combining outstanding qualities of other traditional bows, both antique and modern, without copying any one product. Their hand crafting and varied materials make each Great Northern bow unique. "There is part of us in every one of those bows," says Jerry. "If there wasn't, they wouldn't be nearly the bows that they are."

FULL-TIME FUN

Since the summer of 1987, Jerry has sold the hardware store and with Rick at his side they now build bows full-time. Their full-time operation required a bigger shop and Great Northern is now located just down the block from the Nashville hardware store. The hardware buck mounts now grace Great Northern's office walls and still produce questions and dropped jaws from newcomers.

Even though their once innocent hobby has blossomed into bustling business, the quiet bear and the over-sized elf remain in love with their craft, and through their quality bows, help spawn similar affections in Great Northern customers across the country.

Chapter Ten

ROTHHAAR RECURVES

BOWHUNT DEER? NEVER!

The endless fields of Ohio corn were tanning into their preharvest hue and sugar maples along the roadside cast their first hint of autumn's gold. Bow season was in the air.

Sitting on his rear porch, a husky man stroked his broadhead tipped arrow with slow purrs of a file while several boys watched. With his eyes locked on the emerging blade, the man recounted one of his deer hunting tales. As he neared the part about the shot at the massive buck, he paused, gently brushed his forearm with the sharpened head, and cleanly nicked off a tuft of hair. The boy's eyes widened.

The man blew off the shaved hair with a puff and gave the boys a sly grin. When he finished his story, he put the arrow in his quiver and turned to them. "You boys ought to try this deer hunting," he said.

Open mouthed, most of them just nodded. But the man's nephew narrowed his eyes and said, "I'll never try deer hunting. I have as much fun as I want hunting rabbits and squirrels. It's silly to shoot those pretty brown-eyed deer."

The man rocked back in his chair and gave the boy a warm grin. "Just wait," he said with a chuckle, "time will change your mind."

Twenty years have passed since that autumn day on the porch. The husky man, Uncle Roger, one of the most renowned whitetail hunters in the country, was right about his nephew. Young Alan grew into an avid bow-hunter of whitetails. And because of his interest in bowhunting, he also became one of America's traditional bowyers, making and selling his Rothhaar Recurves.

THE EARLY YEARS

Alan Rothhaar grew up in the sprawling farmland just outside Oceloa, Ohio, where Uncle Roger lives. As a young man, in 1975, Alan began bowhunting the local buster bucks using a recurve made by local bowhunter and bowmaker, Don Assenheimer. "I wasn't convinced that I was going to stick with it, but all it took was that first buck at six yards. And I even missed him. One of my problems in those days was that when I had a shot it was always at one of those huge bucks that knocked my socks off. I just wasn't mentally prepared for them. I would have been much better off shooting the first spike or doe I saw to get the hang of it."

Alan's early bowhunting years were filled with lessons from more whopper bucks than many hunters see in a lifetime. "In my home county we didn't have a gun season from 1962 to 1975. Most of the bucks just died of old age or got hit by cars. That was the big reason why my uncle was very successful with big bucks during that time. Bowhunting back then was phenomenal."

With a little guidance from Uncle Roger and Don, Alan began to get the hang of the intriguing bowhunting game. But the small Ohio wood lots sometimes got crowded. "I hunted with Uncle Roger but he didn't have a lot of time for young guys getting in the way. As my friends and I became better bowhunters, we ended up hunting places that Roger had hunted for twenty years and we started bumping into him which made us kind of a nuisance. So sometimes Roger was more than happy to hunt with us just to show us some new places so we could get out of the way of his bigger bucks."

NORTHWARD

Alan discovered new and distant whitetail haunts in 1979 when he moved from the open farmlands of Ohio to Michigan. Today he lives with his wife and their three children in the rolling oak-forested hills west of Hastings, Michigan, where he works as an engineer for a local manufacturing company. His house and attached bow shop are nestled in the wilds of the 15,000 acre Yankee Springs Game Area. There, he enjoys watching and photographing his wildlife neighbors who often visit the corn patch or salt lick in his back yard, offering Alan a moment's meditation between bowmaking tasks. "Photographing game is almost as much fun as shooting them with my bow, but not quite."

In his mid thirties, Alan has light brown hair and a full rusty toned beard that hints of his German Rothhaar or "red hair" heritage. He has a warm smile which is often accompanied by a robust chuckle or an animated gesture when he recounts a hunting tale.

Alan supports the sport of bowhunting through memberships in the Professional Bowhunters Society as a Regular member, Michigan Bowhunters, and the Christian Bowhunters of America. "In the CBA it's interesting to meet bowhunters of similar faith who experience the outdoors in light of God as the creator instead of just man being an animal that is out there to kill something."

FROM FARMS, TO WOODS, TO FARMS

After moving to Michigan, it didn't take Alan long to discover the magic of frost-covered mornings in the nearby state game area. "My best shot was on the first Michigan buck I killed and it was right here in the game area. I hunted that buck all fall. He had a goofy looking rack because he carried his velvet quite late. He often came with does through this one spot, but I just couldn't get a shot at him that was within my range of confidence.

"Finally on November 6, I went to the stand where I had been seeing him and he came by at five yards. I took my time, counted to five, and plunked him through the heart. He took a couple of jumps and then stood there looking around. He didn't snort, kick, or anything. He just stood there as relaxed as could be and then just passed out dead. I like it when I can see them fall."

Alan conquered another bowhunting obstacle when arrowing that first Michigan whitetail. It was the all too common malady of buck fever. "I had to kill a few deer to break buck fever. Primarily, it involves removing your concentration from the animal and bringing it back to what you have control over, specifically your shooting. You have to think about what you are doing as if you were shooting a target. Buck fever sets in when you start concentrating on the beauty and magnificence of the animal and your nerves just go to heck.

"Some people get so shook up they don't even know if they have an arrow nocked, or their hearts pounds wildly and their arms feel like Jello and they can hardly draw their bow. I know the feeling. I wish I could go back in time and hunt those big Ohio bucks with the ability that I now have to be calm for the shot. That's critical. It took me a long time to get over buck fever, and I still have to work on it."

Although Alan bowhunted close to home during his first few years in Michigan, increased bowhunting pressure and fewer bucks in the state game area caused him to shift his efforts to private farm lands similar to his familiar Ohio whitetail haunts. "I grew up in that kind of country and it's a lot easier to learn the deer patterns there than it is in forest dominated country."

LOVES THOSE OHIO BUCKS

Alan enjoys living in and hunting the rolling country around Hastings, but the opportunities for arrowing a buster buck there are slim compared to buckeye farmlands. "Michigan's countryside is prettier than Ohio's but because of the game laws here, bucks are over-harvested. The opportunity for trophy bucks is not one-tenth of what it was in Ohio. I have hunted here for nine years and I continued to hunt Ohio. During that time, I've had two opportunities at near book bucks in Michigan and six opportunities at book bucks in Ohio.

"In fact it's harder to kill a doe here in Michigan than it was to kill a big buck in Ohio. Down there when a buck is coming in he is so confident that he swings his head side to side, scuffs his feet, and acts like he could care less. If you can pattern a buck down there, you can kill him — unless you miss."

The beginning of Michigan's firearm deer season on November 15 is Alan's cue to head south to Ohio where buckeye bucks are in the full swing of their rutting activity. He often hunts his father's farm where he's had his share of experiences with big bucks. But there was a time when the passing whitetail was a real oddity. "The first deer we saw on the farm was in 1963. They came running across the field when we were planting in the spring. We thought it was really something to see deer back then."

When he's bowhunting Ohio's flat farmlands back home, the woods, or scarcity of it, often dictates where Alan places his tree stand. "With 600 open acres around a wood lot it doesn't take long to learn the deer's travel patterns. In many of the wood lots, one bowhunter can see every deer that moves through it. So it doesn't take a genius to hunt those deer. But it does take more time because there aren't many deer traveling through those wood lots."

Long hours spent in a stand won't do much good if it's placed in the wrong spot. When Alan picks his right spot, he usually bucks tradition. Even though his uncle Roger and other noted whitetail hunters expound on the virtues of hunting scrapes, Alan prefers another approach to harvesting Ohio bucks. "Hunting over scrapes hasn't worked well for me even though it has been preached for years. I've learned that back-tracking big bucks is one of the most valuable tools any whitetail hunter can use. It's easy in Ohio because it's so open you can see them. By back-tracking bucks, I've found various little crossings that they use. So I've learned to move my stand away from the scrapes to these funnel spots where they have to cross to check out the scrapes. And that's where I get my action. I find a place that's best for the ambush instead of trying to hunt the hottest scrape areas or concentration of rubs.

"Scrape hunting was preached for years back in the late seventies. Sure, knowing where scrapes are is valuable information, but knowing where the deer travel to get to those scrapes is the information you want. Now, that's how we hunt in Ohio, but that method isn't worth beans in Michigan because there might be fifteen trails connecting scrape areas. There are so many more deer and they are all making their own trails, and that makes the big buck more difficult to pin down."

Alan has also discovered that Ohio bucks often aren't as cagey as their Michigan cousins. "I was in my Ohio tree stand when a ten-point came in. It was a crisp and snowy Christmas morning, and I was up in a tree about eighteen feet. The sun was behind me and that buck came in and looked up at me, but satisfied himself that I was something natural and he relaxed. That just wouldn't happen here in Michigan. Up here they get one glance at you and they are gone.

"But that ten-point looked at me for some time. He was following two smaller bucks that had already crossed my shooting lane. He stared at me for a while then relaxed, hopped the fence, and walked right through my shooting lane. I pulled up and thought, 'Boy, this has got to be good.' I took careful aim but in doing so I crouched just a little. I was shooting a sixty-six inch bow which was just long enough for the bottom tip to catch my knee. When I shot, I felt a little sting on my knee and saw my arrow just 'bloop' on the ground in front of the buck. I couldn't believe it. After that happened I made up my mind I would never hunt with a sixty-six inch bow again. That played a big part in my decision to try to design and build a shorter take-down recurve."

Knowing that bucks like the big ten-pointer often look up, Alan uses vertical tiger stripe or tree bark camouflage to help mask his form. "It's necessary where you have heavy hunting pressure and the deer are prone to look for you in a tree. This year I watched a group of does coming out of the corn about nine in the morning. As the big old lead doe came to within thirty yards of the edge of the woods, she stopped, raised her head, and scanned the tree line. I swear she stopped to deliberately look for any bowhunters up in the trees. Fortunately for me, I was on the back side of the tree trunk when she started looking. After several minutes, she led the entire group right by the base of my tree. Too bad a buck wasn't trailing them."

To further improve his chances on wary whitetails, Alan is careful to conceal his tell-tale human scent. When heading for the woods, he slips on his light-weight LaCross high-topped rubber boots. "I use them all year long for scouting and hunting. I like them because the high rubber gives me some scent protection, plus, if I want to walk through the swamp, I just go."

Whether he's sneaking through a swamp in Yankee Springs or perched between wood lots in Ohio, Alan enjoys the solitude of his whitetail hunting. And even though he enjoys the solitude, he also likes to see enthusiastic beginners take up the challenge of the bow. But recently he has been disturbed by a new breed of hunter walking the woods. "The biggest thing that bothers me today is the fellow who is participating in the sport but really doesn't have a genuine desire to be a good bowhunter. He's the two-season hunter type of a guy, a weekend hunter who is hunting because of the two-deer tag rather than because he would like to learn bowhunting. He's hunting because he wants to kill a deer or two or whatever he can get away with before the gun season.

"It doesn't matter to me what type of equipment he's using. But it's often the type of equipment, today's instant bowhunter stuff, that causes people to take on a casual attitude toward bowhunting."

THE BIGGEST DEER

Alan savors his yearly whitetail action but his favorite bowhunting quarry is the monarch of the mountains. "I enjoy Western elk hunting because bugling elk let you know where they are. Whitetail don't do that. So I enjoy hunting something that gives you a clue to where they are as opposed to the constant hours of just waiting for a whitetail that you aren't sure will come by."

He would also someday like to try to topple North America's largest member of the deer family. "Moose! Canadian moose. I don't know if I would ever be able to afford it, but I would love to hunt a moose with his big antlers raking the brush, him making a lot of grunting noises, and steam just rolling out his nostrils — let him come!"

PRACTICE PLENTY

To maintain tip-top shooting form for his dream moose hunt, Alan shoots whenever he gets the chance, even though his bowmaking takes up much of his practice time. "Most of the time I shoot three fingers under, with my index finger in the corner of my mouth, with a twenty-eight inch draw. My style is primarily instinctive, but I don't feel I have an inherently instinctive ability like Ron LaClair and some of these guys that are phenomenal instinctive archers. I have a high anchor and shoot three fingers under so I can look down and gun-barrel the shaft."

READY FOR THE BIGGEST OF DEER — Alan staying in tune with his three fingers under, high anchor style of shooting.

Alan not only practices plenty himself, he also preaches to beginners that they get plenty of practice before heading into the woods. "Don't go out and wound deer to get confident. Practice for two years before you go hunting.

"I wish I had done that. But I just grabbed a bow and hunted that first year and missed several deer. That's just not the way to go. It created a whole bunch of bad habits for me that never should have happened. But most people just can't bring themselves to wait two years. Unfortunately the modern attitude towards the sport is, 'Hey, it's easy. Just buy the bow, go out and practice a few hours, and you can hunt.' But that way of thinking is just not right."

MORE ADVICE

Even after beginners have years of shooting practice under their belts, they're still plenty of bowhunting lessons to be learned out in the woods. One is knowing when to trail a wounded deer and when to walk away. "Unless you hear or see him fall or know for sure that you have a heart or lung shot, you've got to go home. There is no one I know who can sit there in their tree stand and wait the proper amount of time before taking up the trail. The best thing to do is mark where the deer was hit, go home, call up your buddies, and give the deer time to die.

"On deer that you know were not hit in the heart-lung area, wait until the next morning, if it is not raining. That's not too long. Even on a heart-lung shot you should still give it several hours. There is no reason you can't track after dark. Just take one guy you can control who won't get anxious on the blood trail like a hound. You don't need a whole crew."

UNCLE ROGER'S BROADHEAD

To make blood trails he can follow even in the dark, Alan uses Snuffers on the business end of his hunting shafts. They're an effective three-bladed head and Alan would use them even if they weren't manufactured by Uncle Roger. "They've helped me get some deer that I might not have recovered with another head.

"I got a buck October 1, 1980, that I shot through the liver and stomach. That's not the best shot to make and the deer ran off without leaving much of a blood trail. I followed him by lantern finding only occasional spots of blood and finally decided to leave it until morning. The next morning I found that buck fifty yards from where I stopped trailing the night before. He was just keeping ahead of us because we were pushing him. I really believe that any other broadhead wouldn't have made a big enough hole to kill him."

To sharpen his Snuffers to a razor's edge, Alan clamps the broadhead in a vise and individually files each blade with a bastard file feathering each edge to a one-eighth inch filed surface. After he has filed the narrow edge, he runs a sharpening stone across two blades at a time. "That gives you a built-in guide so you can't go wrong. I stroke the stone straight back and forth so that I'm just honing the very tip of that thin edge into a razor sharp edge. The Snuffer's steel is just soft enough to file yet hard enough to hold an edge for quite a long time."

Alan uses Snuffers throughout most of the deer season. But during late December when extra clothes and cold muscles make it tougher to shoot his heavy bow, Alan changes to his lighter recurve and switches to a two-bladed broadhead to ensure adequate penetration.

Another reason he likes using a two-bladed broadhead is because of its accuracy. He knows how they fly. He's tested them on his homemade bow shooting machine to settle some debates over broadhead accuracy and arrow spine. "I found that the two-blade head is a little more accurate. At fifty yards I stack up the two-blade heads. With my Snuffers I usually get about a four-inch group. When I shoot them offhand they look fine, but with the machine I can tell a real difference. But with a Snuffer I'm not out there to win a target tournament. I'm out there to make a clean, quick kill. So a four-inch group at fifty yards is perfectly acceptable to me when hunting."

Alan mounts his Snuffers on swaged XX75 aluminum shafts. "I swage them myself. It's a very simple process. With the Snuffer, swaging helps reduce the tip weight. But the disadvantage is that the tip is weakened because it's softened and prone to bend. If you're hunting squirrels and hit a tree the tip may bend. But when you're shooting at deer it doesn't matter. By then it's too late. They're dead."

He fletches his own arrows from his treasured supply of barred turkey feathers. "I like a five-eighths inch high shield cut feather. I use shield cut feathers mostly because they're traditional looking. I tried four-fletch for some time but now I'm using three-fletch because they fly more consistently. And I aim to prove that someday with my shooting machine."

To carry his arrows afield, Alan uses a Delta bow quiver. "It's very lightweight, strong, and doesn't rattle when you shoot. It has two post angled brackets so it places the arrows in line with the lower limb, and adjusts where it holds the arrows so you can change the spacing between arrows and the distance between the hood and arrow griping portion. I'm even selling them with my bows because they fit so nicely. It's the best quiver I've ever used."

For driving Snuffer-tipped arrows through deer-size critters Alan recommends recurves in the sixty pound range if the shooter can handle it accurately. "I don't like my customers to shoot more than sixty-five pounds unless they absolutely have to. You don't gain that much between sixty-five and seventy pounds unless you're shooting extremely heavy arrows. A chronograph will prove that. You don't gain enough feet per second to justify pulling the extra weight."

Alan's personal favorite whitetail recurve is his custom sixty inch bow with moderate weight limbs that he can handle accurately. "I shot heavy bows around seventy pounds for years and I found that all I was doing was shooting through the deer in the wrong place. But with my fifty-eight pound bow I can hold it longer. I can take careful aim under the passion of the moment, and I have enjoyed shooting bucks and just being able to see them fall."

THE ROTHHAAR RECURVE FAMILY

Alan offers his buck-toppling recurves in three models with varying riser materials and limb fiberglass options. The SPIRIT'S riser is made from industrially laminated and impregnated walnut and has either brown or clear fiberglass on the limbs. The PIERCER has a green dyed laminated maple riser with vertically laminated stripes of clear maple veneer. Its limb corewoods are matching green laminated maple under clear fiberglass. The CAMOUFLAGE model has a laminated maple riser and brown glass limbs and is painted flat black with brown and green camouflage patterns.

He offers these three-piece take-down recurves in 60", 62", and 64" lengths. The 60" has a mass weight of 3 pounds, 1 ounce, and a recommended brace height of 7" to 7½" from the string to the throat.

On the 60" model, the riser is 18¾" long. The 62" and 64" models have a 20¾" riser. The riser is 1¾" wide and narrows to ¾" through the sight window which is cut ¼" past center shot. The sight window is full cut 2½" above the shelf, contouring back to full riser width 3½" above the shelf. The

Alan's personal favorite is the Spirit with its brown laminated riser. The limbs exhibit a tight radius recurve for top performance.

riser is 2¾" thick where the limbs attach and thins through the custom high-profile grip.

The bow is designed to shoot off the shelf which is equipped with a synthetic fur rest and strike plate. The high-profile pistol grip is designed to provide positive hand placement tight under the shelf. The riser has flat sides near the ends, is fluted on the belly near the limbs, and is rounded around the grip. The customer's name is inked on the opposite side of the sight window and the bowyer's name is inked on the belly of the upper limb. Bow specs are inked on the belly of the lower limb. Brass quiver and accessory bushings are available.

The tight radius or "fishhook" recurve limbs attach to the riser with a ⁵⁄₁₆" bolt and a single alignment pin. All limbs have a 16½" working length from the fadeout to the string nock and narrow from 1¾" wide at the fadeout to ¹³⁄₁₆" at the nock. They are constructed from a matching riser wood fadeout wedge backed with two parallel Actionwood laminations and faced with one tapered lamination. These maple corewoods are faced and backed with clear or brown fiberglass.

The striking tip overlays are made from four contrasting layers of clear and dyed laminated maple. The string groove is full cut on the sides and the back and feathers to the belly where a single groove is filed into the glass. Alan's bows are finished with a smooth satin luster sealer.

To check a Rothhaar recurve for relative speed, the author shot a 60" model pulling 63½ pounds at 28". He shot 28½", 2213 aluminum arrows fletched with three 5" standard cut feathers and equipped with snap-on nocks. The arrows were swaged behind the point and each arrow weighed 450 grains. The author used a shooting glove, drew 28", and had a slip-from-the-finger release. The bow was equipped with a standard Dacron string without accessories. The average arrow speed for this bow, arrow, and shooter combination was 199 fps.

The following draw/force measurements suggest the smoothness of this 60" recurve:

DRAW LENGTH	25"	26"	27"	28"	29"
DRAW WEIGHT	54^2/10#	57#	60½#	63½	67½

Because of a growing interest among his customers for a one-piece bow, Alan is also developing a new one-piece 64" recurve. "I don't have it named yet, but it's an unusual design and I hope to have it in production by mid 1990."

IT STARTED WITH A MISS

After missing that whopper buck in Ohio years ago, Alan was determined to shoot a shorter recurve, even if he had to build his own. He toyed with the idea of making a take-down, and after talking with bowyers Don Assenheimer and G. Fred Asbell, he decided to try his hand at bowmaking. "There weren't many short custom take-down recurves offered then so I decided to see if I could design one. I started designing in 1981 but it took me two thousand dollars and two years to get the first satisfactory bow off the press."

His experience as a machinist working with precision tolerances, his engineering degree, and his experience setting up manufacturing processes provided an ideal combination of skills for launching his bowmaking business. "Primarily, I was interested in making a little money on the side for my hunting trips. Now I can take those trips without affecting the family budget. It has even grown to the point where it has become a pretty fair business.

"Even though it's just my hobby, I would someday like it to become my boys' business. I have two boys. Timmy, the oldest, is twelve and Ricky is nine. They are just little guys now, but I can see this business someday being their full-time occupation. I'm not sure they'll want to and I won't insist on it. They sometimes try to help me sand bows but small boys and sandpaper are not a good combination."

TWO YEARS OF DESIGN

Before Alan started selling his bows in 1983, he devoted two years to developing his bow design. "When I finally had a bow to sell, I wanted it to be something that I was proud of, not something that was going to give me a bad reputation. The custom bow business is a business of reputation, and it doesn't take too many failures to change your reputation in a hurry."

When designing his bow Alan set high goals, and performance topped the list. "I wanted to develop a recurve bow that was competitive with compounds so guys who wanted to switch to recurves could have a bow that was going to perform in speed and accuracy, would be comfortable to shoot and smooth to draw, and could shoot heavy arrows. If I hadn't achieved that performance I wouldn't have continued building bows. I spent a lot of time with those goals in mind.

"I also had this idea that I would never make a bow that didn't shoot 200 feet per second. Well, I have amended that goal. Even though I get real good performance out of them, I can't say they all shoot 200 feet per second."

THE HOOK

One of the prominent characteristics of Alan's bow design is the recurve of his limbs. It's a tight radius almost fishhook-like recurve that Alan admits is one of the "magnums" of today's limb design. "You can see from my design that I have a lot of faith in the severity of my recurve. It's built for maximum performance and it actually recurves to ninety degrees."

In designing his limb configuration Alan studied a lot of today's recurves and even reached back in time and looked at some of the classics. "During my formative years I was impressed most by the Jack Howard recurve. He used to advertise, 'The World's Fastest Bow' and I was always impressed by the short, tight radius of his recurve. I also liked some of the old Bear Victor bows that had more of a hook in the recurve. Primarily I was looking for a design that would allow me to have a lot of string wrap on the recurve back at brace height. It's like an old static recurve because the last two inches of tip never really uncurl."

Besides designing a magnum recurve in his limbs for maximum performance, Alan also designed a lot of pre-stress in his limbs. "There's a lot of bend in the limbs to get them to brace height. That gives you a tight string at brace height which I felt was important for getting the performance out of the bow. But the negative side is that you get a noisier string. It has a higher frequency than most bows. I considered performance more important than just having another bow on the market that shot very quietly and was springy at brace height. That just makes a slow bow."

A STICKY LESSON

Developing his high performance recurve wasn't without its minor setbacks. Alan's first two attempts to make bows disappointed and disillusioned him. Although he used the recommended epoxy according to specifications, the limbs simply delaminated. He was almost ready to quit his bow building endeavor but decided to give it one more try. His first order of business before gluing up any more bows was to thoroughly investigate epoxy glues. "One of my reasons for being so concerned about my glue was simply economics. If I had a bunch of bows break, I couldn't recover from that. I would have been out of business before I started."

For six weeks Alan experimented with different glues to find which was the best for bowmaking. His discoveries were surprising. "I'm an engineer by trade so I had some exposure to glues and some books on epoxies that I could study. There's a lot of information about glues that isn't publicized enough.

"I spent weeks laying out little glue beads on plastic wrap, curing them, and testing their physical characteristics. I wanted to find a glue that most closely assimilated the old Urac glue which was used for making bows for a long time. I ended up with a couple of front-runners. The one that I'm now using is a slow drying epoxy that's kind of a creamy green color. It takes a full eight to ten hours to cure but slow drying glues are much harder. Another advantage in using a slow drying glue is that you can take your time in putting a bow together — a big plus for quality."

When studying epoxies, Alan even tested the glue he used on his first two bows. The results were ironic. "According to my testing the absolute worst glue to use was the recommended bowmaking epoxy at that time. And a lot of other bowyers were using it and having problems with it."

Once he had his epoxy problem solved, Alan was on his way to becoming a bowmaker. But later another problem developed that taught him a lesson about fadeout and lamination moisture. "The first year I had a major problem with the limbs cracking lengthwise down by the attachment bolts. They were just small cracks in the backing glass, and I really had to talk with a lot of people to discover what was happening.

"I was storing my laminations and fadeout wedges in a hot box heated to ninety-five degrees, and I was over-drying the wood. Testing with humidity indicators showed that it was so dry it was completely off the scale. I was getting the wood so dry that even after it was sealed with finish, the wedge wood later reabsorbed moisture, swelling and cracking the glass."

PUTTING DESIGN INTO FORM

Now with glue and moisture lessons behind him, Alan usually spends evenings and weekends out in the bow shop creating his high-performance recurves. His walls exude an old-time archery shop aura as draped deer hides, elk antlers, whitetail mounts, and deer tails help relive the thrills of past hunting adventures. Between the horns and hides, arrow racks brimming with feathered shafts and new bows quietly wait for next season's frost-covered mornings.

THE RISER

When building a bow, Alan starts by crafting the riser. His favorite riser material is an industrially laminated and resin impregnated stock made from 1/16" walnut veneer. "The beauty of walnut has always impressed me. My Spirit bow with clear glass looks like the color of an old shotgun which makes it look rustic and traditional. It's by far my most popular bow. One of the reasons I use a laminated and impregnated material is because it offers extra strength and is impervious to weather."

In his Piercer riser, Alan uses a green-dyed, maple Actionwood and incorporates vertical pinstripes of clear maple veneer. When assembling the laminated pieces of his Piercer riser, he epoxies them together and heat cures the glue.

Using templates, Alan marks the riser shape in two dimensions. He varies the heel portion of the grip to achieve a high, medium, or low profile grip. "I believe in a higher heel because I want the grip to force the hand into the throat of the bow. Even my lowest grip is considered by some to be high profile."

To get the precise angle on his riser where the limbs attach, Alan marks it using his template and double checks it using his own triangulation technique. His riser-to-limb interface angle is slightly more deflex on the top limb which produces a built-in tiller. "That gives me the exact tiller that I want. That way I can build both limbs the same and don't have to make one weaker. To me that seemed the wrong method of achieving tiller, yet it has been the most advertised method. But I do it by building tiller into the handle."

Before cutting out the riser on the band saw, Alan drills a hole through the shelf-sight window junction to achieve the desired radius. "I like to have quite a bit of radius there because I cut my window past center, and if I cut a sharp corner there I will have a stressed area. That's the first place where the riser would fracture. The hole also provides an opening to band saw into."

Once he cuts out the riser on the band saw and grinds the limb contact areas, Alan uses drill guide jigs to drill the attachment bushing and alignment pin holes. His custom-machined jigs were manufactured by Vic Berkompas of Grand Rapids, Michigan, who machined the necessary precision tolerances. Once the jigs are installed on the ends of the riser, they are brought into exact plane by placing the square-sided jigs on a machinist's surface plate. Alan locks the jigs in place and drills the holes. Each limb has its own bushing-to-alignment-pin spacing to prevent accidental limb inversion.

After the attachment bushing holes are drilled and then counter-bored on the belly side, headed brass bushings are installed from the belly to provide a positive non-pull through seat. The bushings are epoxied in and the hole is plugged with a matching riser wood plug.

Alan then shapes the riser using a spindle sander. "One of the most important parts of a custom bow is the grip, and I want it to be very comfortable to the shooter so I grind it by hand." Opposite the window Alan even grinds in a thumb groove to help provide a positive hand placement.

To enhance arrow flight he rounds the sight window and bevels the shelf edge. "I try to make it so the bow can be taken out and shot right off of the shelf. It's not really designed for elevated rests. I contour the shelf and window so the high point of the rest is brought as close as possible to right over the throat of the grip."

LIMB COMPOSITES

Alan uses Actionwood laminations from the Old Master Crafters for his limb corewood. On his Spirit model he uses a brown-dyed Actionwood and on his Piercer, he uses the green dyed. To accentuate corewood contrasts, he uses a clear Actionwood lamination in the middle which gives a pinstripe effect to the limb edge.

"I love Actionwood. I've tried making bows out of flat sawn maple or shedua, but using solid corewoods is a pain when trying to build a straight bow. With solid corewoods I have to work hard to get the limbs straight and tillered. But with Actionwood my last fifty bows have been right down the middle and have needed very little final work."

Because of his past problems with over drying, Alan now stores his Actionwood laminations and fadeout wedges in a maintained environment of seventy degrees and fifty percent humidity.

When selecting his limb composites, Alan uses combinations of tapered and parallel laminations to achieve the optimum limb characteristics for a specific draw length. "For a customer who wants a sixty inch take-down and is drawing thirty-one inches, I will make them a bow without any taper in the laminations. That way, between twenty-eight inches and thirty-one inches, the draw is still three pounds per inch, which will be smooth for them. Every limb set I make is precisely designed to match the customer's specifications. That's the most important aspect of a custom built bow."

THE FORMS

Alan's high performance limbs are a reflection of his forms. They are made from special two inch thick plywood and represent the limb belly. To make them he bolted both the upper and lower limb forms together then sawed, ground, and hand sanded them as one thick form. It was an exacting process that took six weeks. "When I got done, both were exactly the same match. It's very important to have uniform limb action, and to achieve that you need perfectly matched limb forms. Speed comes from the limbs working in unison, and you're not going to achieve that if you have varying limb shapes."

His forms are also equipped with a sliding tip plate and butt end stop which helps hold the laminations in place during lay-up.

LAY-UP

Before laying up his limb composites in the form, Alan makes sure the form is clean and covers it with plastic wrap. "The smallest imperfection on the form surfaces will show up as an imperfection in your finished limb."

Next, he masking tapes the non-gluing surface of the fiberglass and wipes all gluing surfaces with acetone to remove any dust or grime. He then applies his greenish epoxy to one side of the contact surfaces and lays up the composites in the form, making sure the fadeout is properly positioned.

Alan lays on his fire hose, clamps on the top half of the press, and then inflates the hose with one quick shot of air pressure. He inflates the hose to seventy pounds when he is using brown fiberglass and gives it an extra ten pounds when using clear glass to make sure even the tiniest air bubbles are squeezed out.

Once they're pressed, Alan places the limb forms in his light-bulb heated curing oven. He heats the composites to 100 degrees for six hours, then he increases the temperature to 150 degrees for the final two hours of curing. He regulates the temperature by varying the number of light bulbs.

After the limbs are cured, Alan squares their sides and drills the limb mounting holes. To drill alignment pin holes, Alan secures the limbs on a

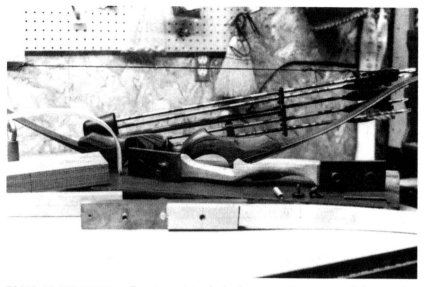

TOOLS OF THE TRADE — To get precision limb alignment, Alan uses tooled jigs and a machinist's surface plate to reference his limb alignment pins and holes.

drill guide jig and lays the jig on edge on a ½" thick alloy tooling quality plate. He then squares up both limbs, tightens the jig, marks the limb centerlines using a surface marking jig, and drills the mounting holes.

Aligning his limb template along the centerline, Alan marks the limb shape and band saws and grinds each limb leaving ⅛" of excess stock around the limb profile. He then roughens up the belly glass near the butt ends and the tip overlay areas with a thirty-six grit wheel, and uses "C" clamps to epoxy on the Formica limb belly butt overlays and wooden tip overlays. He heat cures these overlays to approximately ninety degrees. One of the reasons for the belly butt Formica overlay is to help make a silent contact surface between the limb and the riser. Fiberglass against hardwood can produce creaking noises on a cold day.

Next, he files in rough string nocks and installs the limbs on a master riser made from heavy-duty impregnated wood. He braces the bow and checks for tiller and alignment. Because of the built-in tiller in his riser-limb interface and the precision of his machined jigs, the limbs usually don't require much alignment or tillering. Minor adjustments are made by rounding the edges of the limbs.

Alan varies a bow's tiller depending on the customer's shooting style. "For standard style shooters I usually build a one-eighth inch to one-quarter inch tiller. I also have a lot of three-finger-under customers and have found that these shooters get better arrow flight with about a one-sixteenth inch tiller."

He checks a bow's tiller in two ways. "First, I measure it when roughing it in, but that's only going to tell me what exists at brace height. The second method is done on a flat surface called a tiller table. With the bow handle

TELLTALE TILLER — Alan uses his tiller table to check the dynamic tiller of his bows to be sure both limbs are working in unison.

held by a post, I pull the bow to half draw and then to full draw and mark the limb positions to be sure they are working in exact unison." Alan also uses his tiller table to reveal improper limb balance in other bows. "When I find other bows that don't have dynamic limb balance, they always chronograph relatively slow."

FINISH COATS

After his bows receive a final sanding, Alan sprays them with four coats of gloss Fullerplast and a final over-spray of low luster polyurethane. "I don't think there is a deep satin finish that's durable because the texture of the paint causes it to be easily scratched. But for the hunter it's perfect. He can carry it through the brush and if it does get scratched he can buff it up with some steel wool and bring it right back. It's a very low luster and high solids type of finish, and that's what gives you a real deep satin."

DANGERS OF LIMB TWIST

Alan's finished products are made for hard-hitting performance afield. But because of their tight radius recurve, his bows require some added customer care. "A bow stringer is a requirement when using one of my bows. Everybody gets a free stringer with their bow so they don't have an excuse for not using one. It's especially important on bows like mine with a severe recurve.

"Any bow with a wicked recurve like mine has more of a tendency to twist a limb. That's why a bow stringer is so important. I tell my customers that this bow is a magnum recurve, a wildcat cartridge you might say, and they should handle it with care. A lot of guys figure that because they're buying a custom bow it will last a lifetime. The bow may last a lifetime, but it may not always be a straight bow or may not shoot as well as it did when it was new. A bow starts out on day one shooting as well as it's ever going to shoot. As time and usage go on, deterioration occurs from constant flexing and bending. A bow may last 2000 shots or it may last 20,000 shots, but eventually it's going to weaken and change."

To help his customers with proper bow care and tuning, Alan provides detailed instructions with each bow. His instructions cover the important points of proper stringing with a bow stringer, brace height adjustments, nocking point selection, arrow spine, and bow silencing.

Alan recommends that his bows be unstrung when not in use and cautions not to store them near heat ducts or in damp basements. He also recommends avoiding the use of Kevlar or Fast Flight strings. "The most hazardous thing that can happen to a take-down bow is to have the string break during a shot. And every Kevlar string I've used broke. It's only a matter of time before it breaks in the nock. I don't want my customers using strings that can break and risk damaging their bow."

LOVES THE TRADITION

Alan cautions his customers about strings and stringers because he loves his bows. In a way they represent his traditional offspring. He also loves traditional archery, and sees it as a growing interest in bowhunting and bowmaking. Even though it's a healthy trend for the sport, Alan is concerned that the future may mirror part of the past. "One of the things that happened to recurves during the sixties is that big companies built cheap, shoddy, recurves that were poor performers because the emphasis was on mass production rather than on quality and performance. That was unfair to the recurve as a bow. With the recent emphasis on traditional archery, I hope big companies don't get involved in traditional bowmaking to the point where they sacrifice quality. It happened before, and I'm afraid it could happen again."

He's concerned about the future of recurves because he cherishes the traditional sides of bowmaking and bowhunting. "I love all of it. I support every bowmaker, and I even support the longbow guys. But I hate shooting the longbow because it hurts to draw and it hurts my hand to shoot. I like to participate in the longbow shoots and shoot a longbow then, but I really prefer my recurve. I jokingly tell Ron LaClair that longbows are on the extreme end of tradition and compounds are on the extreme end of technology, and that before long everybody is going to come smack dab on center and shoot a recurve."

When they do, Alan and his recurves will be waiting.

Chapter Eleven

ELBURG'S ARCHERY

ABOVE THE RIVER FRONT

The mighty Ohio River divided the Union and Confederate states during the Civil War and for decades provided the lifeblood to historic river towns such as Louisville, Kentucky, and smaller communities such as Madison, Indiana, upriver to the northeast. Shielded from winter winds by a river-etched limestone escarpment, Madison bustled along the banks of the Ohio during the heydays of riverboat trade. But in the early 1900s, locomotives and their boundless iron rivers replaced the stately paddle wheels, and Madison's booming economy ground to a halt like a beached riverboat.

Today this 170-year-old town remains historically rich and prides itself on its impressive and well preserved turn-of-the-century houses. Above the historic rooftops and church steeples, limestone cliffs rising to the north resemble irregular curtains stained with the tans and browns of iron-rich seeps. On top of the escarpment overlooking the Ohio River valley, sits Madison's overflow of new houses and industry that have arrived since the iron horse era.

One of the newer arrivals to the bluff area is a family that immigrated from Hamilton, Ontario. Their neighbors know them as just Harry and Eva, but the archery world knows them as the makers of Elburg's traditional bows and the popular Grizzly broadhead.

GUIDED BY FATE

Harry was born in Holland and came with his family to Hamilton, Ontario, when he was nine years old. There he grew up, married Eva, and together they raised a family. For seventeen years Harry worked for the metropolitan city as a professional fire fighter. It was a demanding and sometimes dangerous profession that was esteemed in the community. It was also a job that changed the course of his life.

One evening Harry responded to a house fire and was first on the scene with the search-and-rescue team. "Someone said there was a woman trapped on the upper floor. So I put on my self-contained breathing apparatus and ran to the upper floor. There was so much smoke I couldn't see anything and I tried to open some windows to clear out the smoke.

"As I was groping around, I put a jagged window sill through my wrist. I had no idea how badly I was hurt until I fell down the stairs and saw blood pouring out my sleeve. I had lacerated my left arm and wrist down to the bone, severing all of the nerves, tendons, and arteries. The report of the trapped woman turned out to be false.

"Later I got a staph infection and came pretty close to losing my arm. Back then they hadn't done much surgery reattaching nerves, and some of the doctors told me that I would never regain the use of my hand."

Even though the outlook appeared bleak, one doctor refused to accept Harry's fate and pushed him through a grueling recovery program. "For a long-time I didn't think that I was going to get any use out of it. But after three months of continuous exercise, I finally moved my fingers."

Harry continued to recover, but the injury made it impossible for him to continue the physically demanding job of fire fighting. "That was a bad time in my life because I had taken my fire fighting very seriously and had worked hard at it."

After some schooling he became a pipe welder for nuclear power plants and moved to California. But Harry and Eva found the pace too fast for their peaceful lifestyle so Harry followed his welding jobs around the country and finally settled in Madison around 1978. But like the river boats of Madison's past, the nuclear industry slowed to a standstill. So Harry decided to expand a lifelong love and part-time hobby into a full-time business. He became one of America's traditional bowyers.

HUNTS NEAR MADISON

Today Harry still wears his welding denims. Their small welding singes are now covered with brown patches of dried glue and wood dust from the bowmaking he does in his backyard shop. In his early fifties, Harry has glaring blue eyes and sandy hair frosted around the temples. He's a big man with chiseled features. This rugged exterior veils his sensitive side — underneath he is an accomplished artist and a thoughtful designer. He also enjoys fishing with Eva, and in the fall when he finds time to get away from the shop, he heads for the woods with his longbow.

Harry began bowhunting in Ontario and often hunted on the Bruce Peninsular near Tobermory and on scenic Manitoulin Island. "We never got that many deer, but we used to have a lot of fun. We used to have the same type of fun that people are now starting to discover with the longbow."

Later he moved out to the country near Cayuga, Ontario, about twenty miles from Hamilton. There on his twenty-five acres of forested land, deer were a common sight and Harry enjoyed vacations at home taking advantage of the deer hunting out his back door.

Today he hunts the tangled woods and rugged limestone ridges near Madison where whitetails and turkeys provide bowhunting action. He enjoys hunting close to home where he can get in plenty of preseason scouting and become familiar with individual animals.

His preferred hunting technique is to slowly stalk his prey. And when it's too dry and noisy, he mixes his sneaking with long waiting periods near runways or deer crossings. "I like to hunt in a little rain and have raindrops falling off of the branches hiding my sounds. Stalking game during a light rain is a challenge, but if you pick up the fundamentals of deer hunting it's not that hard to get close to the deer. But you have to pick the right time and weather. And with the way I shoot, sometimes I'm giving the deer more than an equal chance. My methods may not result in a high percentage of deer kills, but I get more bowhunting thrills that way."

Besides sneaking up on deer, Harry recently began rattling them in and the results were surprising. "During the last few years I've been rattling in the mornings and that seems to work real well — almost too well. I had this nice buck come in so fast that he just hand-cuffed me. By the time he got to within fifteen feet of me, he was eye-balling me and I couldn't move."

When he's not pinned down at fifteen feet and can get off an arrow, Harry is choosy about his whitetail shots and limits himself to his thirty-yard range of confidence. "My favorite shot on a deer is from the rear, quartering into the front. I aim right behind the last rib and for the far shoulder. That shot also allows you to make your move without the deer seeing you."

After his quartering shot connects and the venison is in the freezer, Harry savors the hunt throughout the winter with his spicy venison chili and other wild game dishes. "I like my venison wild game stew and I'm a good cook. First, I flour select pieces of the round steak and brown them in oil in a pressure cooker pot. Then I add seasoning and put in potatoes, carrots, onions, celery, and green pepper. Then I thicken the stew with flour and let it cook until it's tender. Sometimes I put a little wine in it too."

During the off season Harry keeps his bowhunting instincts sharp by pursuing local ground hogs. And sometimes when lofting long distance shots at the big rodents, he even surprises himself. "I once shot at a ground hog that was eighty-five yards away. I overshot him by just a hair and the arrow went in his hole. He whirled and tried to get in his hole but the shaft was blocking it and he couldn't. You should have seen the dirt fly. It was the most comical shot I have ever made. He finally got in the hole, but only after breaking my arrow into three pieces."

That same evening Harry sent another shaft at a big ground hog sitting in a hole sixty-five yards away. He remembers that arrow feeling good all the way. "I ricochetted that Bodkin-tipped arrow right off the top of his head."

Although his archery business keeps him close to home where only whitetail, turkey, and ground hogs roam, someday Harry would like to travel around the world and bowhunt more impressive species. "I would love to stalk and shoot an Asiatic buffalo, because an animal like that can fight back and get a little rowdy. I would like to hunt them in Australia because the country fascinates me. I would also like to shoot a big black bear."

INDIANA BOWHUNTING TOOLS

When sneaking up on deer with his longbow, Harry always has a fine piece of thread tied on his bowstring six inches down from his upper nock. "I can pick up any air movement with it. I can always tell which way the wind is coming from or if it's shifting near the edge of a field. And you need to know that. If you don't, you might as well stay home.

"I also like to be camouflaged for the type of area I'm hunting. My bow has to be absolutely non-reflective. I like to wear gloves to cover my hands and I use a face mask. I even practice my shooting wearing the mask because it makes shooting just a little different."

Harry usually uses a traditional back quiver but doesn't like waving his arm over his head every time he needs an arrow so he plans to try a side quiver.

Whichever quiver he uses, Harry fills it with his homemade arrows. He tapers his own Port Orford cedar shafts and dips them with orange lacquer. "I like to use an orange fletch so I can tell where I hit. I fletch them with three 5½ inch right wing parabolic cut feathers."

The main workhorse of Harry's hunting gear is his longbow. His personal favorite is his fifty-five to sixty pound Cherokee flatbow. "I like the flatbow because it's only sixty-two inches long and I can shoot it sitting on the ground if I have to. I can almost shoot it laying on the ground. Plus, it's a stable shooting bow, it doesn't get in the way, and it's light to carry."

THE GRIZZLY

Like the rest of his bowhunting gear, Harry is particular about his broadheads. He's so particular in fact, that his search for the perfect broadhead led him into the broadhead making business. "A month before hunting season I was trying to sharpen a popular two-bladed broadhead and I was having a hard time because of the ferrule. So I said to Eva, 'There has just got to be a better way to make a broadhead.' That night I sat down and made a cardboard template of a broadhead and later modified it a couple more times."

Harry didn't know it but he was on the way to making broadhead history. "The next problem was trying to get somebody to make me a die to build steel broadheads with, because the cardboard version was weak and hard to sharpen. We designed the head so the ferrule was part of the blade. That way, the ferrule would be tempered along with the blade. The heart of any broadhead is the ferrule — if it breaks, so will the broadhead."

He continued to develop his design and eventually came out with three models: a 190 grain two-bladed head with a three-to-one length to width ratio, and 160 grain and 125 grain models with similar dimensions. "A grizzly is an awe inspiring animal known for its toughness, and in a close encounter it's pretty deadly. So we decided to name our broadhead after it."

The broadhead's name later proved to be more than appropriate. Its toughness and effectiveness in the field were highlighted in a much talked about report conducted and written by Dr. Ed Ashby. Ashby tested thirty-two different broadheads on actual animal carcasses in Africa and recorded detailed observations on penetration and overall broadhead performance. Even though many of today's most popular heads were used, Harry's Grizzly proved to be tops for durability and penetration.

But Ashby's report was of little surprise to Harry. "The Grizzly flies great and has excellent penetration power. It's designed to rotate when a blade meets resistance, so it won't bind on impact and there is little shaft drag. If the head encounters a real heavy bone structure, it has a tendency to make a slashing and glancing cut across the bone or to cut right through it.

"A lot of guys say they don't need a head that will kill a bunch of African game because they're only hunting deer. Then I ask them if their compound bow and six-bladed broadhead can shoot through the scapula of a deer. They act very surprised and say 'Of course not! There's no way it can.' Then I tell them it has to be able to make it through a deer's scapula or leg bone or they don't have any business being out in the woods, especially if they hunt from a tree stand."

Harry stresses that one of the keys to recovering arrowed game is the complete penetration of a broadhead; something his Grizzly is noted for. "You want your broadhead to go in one side and out the other, especially if you are shooting out of a tree stand. Because if you don't have a bottom exit wound you will often lose game. You really need that blood trail coming out the bottom.

"Since I've come out with my broadhead I've had one common comment from bowhunters: 'Before using your broadhead I never would aim at the shoulder even though I know that's where the vitals are, because I hit a deer there once and the arrow only went in a half inch. But now I shoot deer in the shoulder with a Grizzly and it goes right through. So now I aim for the shoulder.' And that's what they should be aiming for."

Harry mounts his broadheads vertically to improve his sight picture. Plus, it provides him with a positive check when reaching full draw on game. He sharpens each broadhead in less than a minute using an 8" fine-toothed file. Harry strokes the ground side from the tip to the rear, then turns the blade over and removes the burr off the flat surface with a stroke of the file.

Although Harry designed the head, Eva helped with many of the initial production details. Today she manufactures the heads in their small broadhead shop while Harry is out in the main shop building bows.

HE STUCK WITH STICKS

Harry began building and shooting bows, mostly just sticks and strings, when he was a boy in Holland. That boyhood interest blossomed into a genuine fascination for traditional bows when he was twenty-two years old.

And it's been growing ever since. "I was a traditional archer when most guys didn't know what a long-bow was. They laughed at my longbow because they thought it was a joke, especially in Ontario."

But the comments about his bow didn't keep Harry from enjoying the sport he loved so dearly. There was little that could separate him from his bond with the bow. His love was put to the test when he slashed his left arm in his fire fighting accident. After his lengthy recovery, Harry faced giving up archery or painfully relearning to shoot left-handed. For him there was no choice. "It took me over a year and a half to get back into shooting a bow and to make the switch from right-handed to left-handed."

Today he shoots so naturally and fluidly, he looks like he's been shoot-

Now a lefty, Harry shoots with his longbow canted, taking a careful, deliberate aim.

ing left-handed all his life. But it came with practice. "I like to shoot a little every day even if it's only for fifteen minutes. Often I shoot during my lunch hour, and I don't rush my practice. I like to go through all of the right movements. But even with my practice I'm not a great target shot or any kind of great white hunter. I just enjoy shooting my bow."

Harry shoots with his middle finger in the corner of his mouth and cants his bow with a classic traditional pose. But unlike many longbow shooters, he holds solidly at full draw and takes a deliberate aim. "I like to take my time and really pick my shot. That's one reason I don't like to shoot a bow that's too heavy because it causes bad form."

Although Harry is a big man who can draw a 120 pound bow, he prefers bows half that weight. "The way I hunt deer I've got to draw my bow at least part way and then wait for the deer to make the right move. So I like to have a bow that I can control under varying hunting situations. If you can't draw your bow and hold it for several minutes, you might want to step down in poundage."

PLEASING EVERYONE

It's often said that you can't please all the people all of the time, but that doesn't keep Harry from trying by offering six traditional bow models. They are the 64" Cheetah recurve, the 62" Cherokee flatbow, the Falcon semi-reverse handle longbow, the Old Tradition longbow, the Condor Hill-Style longbow, and the Jaguar reverse handle longbow.

Even with all of these styles, Harry continues to explore the design possibilities of new recurves and longbows. "I like to suit everybody because a custom bow should be able to suit everybody's taste. If a guy has to compromise on what he wants in bow design, then he's not getting a custom bow.

"I listen to my customers, so most of my bow designs are combinations of customer requests and my own design concepts. Most of them are designed for a specific hunting situation or purpose. For example, after listening to many customers tell me about problems in making the transition from a regular recurve or compound handle to the peaked Hill-style grip, I designed the Falcon's semi-reverse handle with a dished grip. Now they can buy a traditional bow that offers them a positive hand seat.

"Our biggest concern is how our customers shoot with our bows. We worry more about the bow's overall performance. It's not unusual for us to have customers who buy four or five bows from us. I don't know what in the heck they do with all of them, but repeat customers tell you a lot about your product quality."

THE FALCON

Harry's most popular bow is his deflex-reflex designed FALCON. "I get more calls for the Falcon because it's so accurate to shoot. You get positive hand placement with the grip, and with the reflex in the limb it's a fast, smooth drawing bow."

It's available in 66" and 68" lengths and has a mass weight of one pound nine ounces. Its recommended brace height is 6⅝" from the string to the throat.

The Falcon's one-piece hardwood riser measures 16" between fadeouts and is offered in shedua, walnut, osage, and bubinga. The riser is 1⅞" thick, 1¼" wide, and narrows to ¾" through the sight window, which is cut ⅛" from center shot. The arrow shelf and window are rounded for enhanced arrow flight and equipped with a suede leather pad. The sides are rounded and feather nicely into the belly and back fiberglass. The Falcon's semi-reversed handle places the grip in a forward position, helping to reduce bow torque. The 4¼" leather wrapped grip is dished with the low point at the throat of the thumb and index finger for a positive and comfortable hand fit.

Its deflex-reflex limbs are deep cored and narrow from 1³⁄₁₆" wide at the fadeouts to ½" at the string nocks. The upper limb has a 26½" working length and the lower limb is ½" shorter. The limbs are constructed from custom-ground red elm or bamboo corewoods enveloped in either black or clear fiberglass. The back has one parallel and one tapered lamination, and the belly has one tapered lamination. The limb edges are rounded and feather nicely into the fiberglass. The tips have matching riser wood overlays with flush-cut string nocks. The upper nock measures 1" from the nock to tip and the lower nock is ½" shorter.

Like all of Harry's bows, the Falcon is available with either a low-luster satin or a gloss finish.

To check for relative speed, Harry shot a 68", 77½ pound at 27" draw, bamboo and red elm cored Falcon. He shot 28" wood arrows fletched with three 5" standard cut feathers and equipped with open nocks. The arrows weighed 550 grains and the bowstring was standard Dacron without accessories. Harry drew a consistent 27", used a finger tab, and had a pull-through release. The average arrow speed for this combination of arrow, shooter, and bow was 193 fps.

The following draw/force measurements suggest the smoothness of pull of this 68" Falcon:

DRAW LENGTH	25"	26"	27"	28"	29"
DRAW WEIGHT	70#	73#	77½#	81½#	86#

The CHEROKEE FLATBOW is Harry's favorite. "It sort of resembles an Indian bow so we decided to name it after the Cherokee Indians of South Carolina. It's compact, light, and an easy bow to shoot. It doesn't have much hand shock. Plus, I think I'm the only bowyer making a reverse handle flatbow."

The 62" Cherokee is close to the Falcon in popularity. It has a reflex design and a mass weight of 1 pound, 5 ounces. The bow's recommended brace height is 6⅞" to 7".

Its reverse-handled riser measures 16" between fadeouts. It's offered in the same hardwoods as the Falcon and has similar shelf and window features. The riser is slim-lined and narrows on the sides near the throat for non-torque comfort. It has a leather-wrapped, broomstick style grip which helps reduce handle torque. Bow information is black inked below the grip, on the opposite side of the window.

The Cherokee's limbs narrow from 1⁹∕₁₆" wide at the fadeouts to ¾" at the nocks. They're offered in osage, red elm, or combinations of red elm with bamboo, locust, and maple. The limbs are constructed from two parallel back laminations and one tapered belly lamination. These corewoods are enveloped in either clear or black fiberglass. The limb edges and tips are similar to the Falcon.

To check a 54 pound at 27" draw, red elm and bamboo cored Cherokee for relative speed, Harry shot the bow using the same arrows as noted for the Falcon. He again drew the arrows 27" and the bowstring was also standard Dacron. The average arrow speed chronographed for this bow, arrow, and shooter combination was 168 fps.

The following draw/force measurements were recorded on this 62" Cherokee:

DRAW LENGTH	25"	26"	27"	28"	29"
DRAW WEIGHT	48#	51#	54#	57#	61#

THE BRUSH-BLENDING ELBURG LINE-UP — Left to right, the Cheetah recurve, Cherokee flatbow, Condor, Old Tradition, and Falcon.

Harry also chronographed his popular Condor, Hill styled longbow. He shot his 66", 59 pound at 27" draw, bamboo-cored Condor using the same arrow and bowstring combination used with the other bows. The average arrow speed for this bow, arrow, and shooter combination was 179 fps.

The following draw/force measurements were recorded on this 66" Condor:

DRAW LENGTH	25"	26"	27"	28"	29"
DRAW WEIGHT	53#	56#	59#	63#	67#

THE START OF SOMETHING BIG

Harry made his first bow twenty years ago, and he remembers it well. "It was a sixty-eight inch longbow. I made it with Actionwood which had just come out then, and I used green fiberglass. It had a maple riser and I glued the whole thing together with Urac. I must have reworked that bow five times to get the tiller decent."

He continued his bowmaking hobby until 1983, when a slowdown in the nuclear industry presented him with an opportunity to try professional bow building. "Bowmaking was something I had always wanted to try. I was bow building part-time and when my welding job changed I decided to go into it full-time. There's some monetary value to it, but primarily bowmaking is a satisfying profession, especially when you hear nice comments about your products. It gives you pride in your work, and that's something you don't get in too many jobs today. It also gives us the opportunity to meet people nationwide with similar interests."

DESIGN STRENGTHS

Harry learned early on that bow building is a school filled with tough lessons learned over the bow bench. "If a guy wants to develop a good bow, there's no other way than to just build it. You can think up something that might work on paper, but it may turn out to be a complete flop. There's nothing like actual hard knocks. Maybe that's why a lot of bowmakers just stick with one bow design. But I get a kick out of making all of my different models. Plus, there's never a dull moment."

When designing his bows, Harry doesn't lose sight of the fact that performance is a delicate balancing of trade-offs. "There are a lot of gives and takes when building a bow. If you strive for speed you will probably pick up a little more hand shock. If you make a stable bow then you lose a little speed. So you have to judge between all of these factors when designing a bow."

One important design characteristic on each of Harry's bows is the handle. It's intended for shooting comfort and non-torque control. "I personally like the small round grip because it's hard to torque, and the reverse handle takes away some of the hand shock. It's harder to grip a small handle tightly so you have a tendency to let it move a little in the hand. That reduces bow torque and lets you shoot more accurately."

LOOKING AHEAD — Always trying to build the ultimate bow, Harry inspects a new prototype recurve fresh from the form.

Although he already offers more designs than most bowyers, Harry continues to explore new materials and designs to improve his line of bows. Some of his goals are far from modest. "I would like to build the ultimate longbow and that time may be right around the corner when I make my new fiberglass. My goal is to build bows that my customers can shoot for a lifetime, not for just a year."

Harry merges his designs and materials in the bow shop behind his house. His shop is equipped with a variety of bowmaking machinery including some specialized devices that Harry designed and made. They include his custom bow forms, his glue curing oven, a precision lamination grinder, and a special dual-bladed lamination trimmer.

GRINDING THE CORE

His lamination grinder is one of the critical machines in Harry's shop. He learned long ago the benefits of grinding his own laminations. It allows him to use a variety of combinations of core materials at a precise and sometimes varying thickness and taper. "When grinding core materials from scratch, a bowyer can really understand his materials. I can tell what a material is like just by the way it runs through my grinder.

"Also, I'm not stuck with just one bow design or limited to a few core materials. I can grind any lamination to suit a particular bow design, and I can use core materials not ground by the Old Master Crafters."

He even uses his precision lamination grinder to grind his fiberglass to exacting thicknesses. "You must have a machine that will grind laminations to within a hair's tolerance, and mine grinds to within two thousandths of an inch. I can hardly measure it with a micrometer, but you need that kind of precision in bowmaking."

After he rough grinds his laminations, he trims both sides parallel to a desired width on a dual-bladed trimming device that cuts both sides at once.

CANE IS TOPS

Of all the core materials that Harry runs through his grinder, bamboo is his top choice for performance. "I like it because it's resilient, tough, smooth, and fast." It's shipped directly from an overseas supplier. Harry carefully binds the green bamboo strips together in bundles to allow air circulation and to keep them straight. He then stores them overhead in his shop loft on racks where the bamboo dries for at least a year before he grinds it into laminations.

After it's properly dried, Harry removes the culm and hardened outer enamel on the cane using a power planer. He then grinds full bow-length laminations, tapering from a flat section in the middle to the ends. Using these solid one-piece laminations adds to the strength of the finished bow.

"Bamboo is nice to work with because it grinds to very close tolerances. I can even grind it to paper-thinness and it doesn't break. But wood will. There is a natural sugary resin in bamboo that you can sometimes smell when you're grinding it. But in wood you have starches and oils."

One of the reasons Harry likes bamboo so much is because it makes a smooth shooting bow. "When you make wood-core bows over seventy-five pounds, it's hard to get a smooth drawing bow. But I've used bamboo to build Falcons in the eighty-pound range for guys with thirty inch draws. And those bows pulled 3½ pounds per inch all the way. I couldn't do that with any other bow wood. It would stack."

Despite its advantages, there are some problems with using bamboo. "If you over-temper bamboo, it's like shooting a car spring. Also, if you use epoxy to glue bamboo, you could have tremendous headaches. It has open pores because it's a grass not a wood. And when you use a surface glue like epoxy, the outer layer can sheer off. Bamboo is really not that good in its sheer strength like many woods. You can glue a maple bow together with epoxy and it will stay together, but you can't with bamboo. So I use Urac to glue all of my corewoods together."

OTHER COREWOODS

For Harry, red elm is second to bamboo as a core material. "It's very strong, tough, resilient, and has a high sheer strength. Plus it looks great under clear glass. Red elm and bamboo make a perfect corewood combination, especially in a flatbow. But red elm is so porous the edges of the exposed corewoods are hard to seal. And it's devilishly hard to grind, it's like grinding a rope."

He also uses black walnut. "It's very light and sheer resistant. Plus, black walnut has tremendous compressive strength, looks great under clear glass, and has very little hand shock."

Harry offers the classic maple and osage but recommends them only in certain bow designs because of their heavy mass weight and tendency to produce hand shock.

He even uses red cedar from southern Kentucky. "When we use cedar, I always use it in combination with bamboo because by itself cedar is too fragile. But it's a fine bow material because it's light and makes a very fast bow."

EXACT ON THE GLASS

Harry is particular about all his limb composites, even the fiberglass. So he custom grinds it to fit the exact glass-to-core ratio for a particular bow. "It sounds very minute, but it does make a difference. There are irregularities with Gordon's glass, but after it's run through my grinder, there aren't any. It's nearly perfect."

In his search for the ultimate longbow, Harry investigated the possibility of making his own fiberglass using new materials, and recently he made a breakthrough in this often standardized material. "I've developed a new carbon 'Elite' fiberglass that we intend on using in all of our Elite model longbows. This new glass makes an exceptional longbow."

PAPER THIN

Harry crafts his riser fadeouts paper-thin with a gentle sweeping contour. He makes them so thin, in fact, that it's often tough to determine exactly where the fadeout ends and the limb begins. "A fadeout is really important because it's the transition between the riser, which is a stiff material, to the bow limb, which is flexible. And you need to have a smooth transition there. Improper taper on your fadeout can give you hot spots on your limbs where they are over-stressed. After grinding our fadeouts on machinery we still take the care to hand sand them until they're perfectly feathered. Grinding them on a vertical sander just isn't good enough."

TRUE TO FORM

The riser is shaped to precisely fit the bow form. Harry makes his forms from three layers of exterior plywood that are glued and doweled together. The doweling is important as it prevents distortion of the laminated wood. He also reinforces his forms with angle iron frames to prevent them from flexing and warping during repeated use. He covers the sweeping form surface with an Actionwood lamination to smooth out any irregularities.

HELPING HANDS

The day before gluing up a bow, Harry selects and final grinds the corewoods. This provides clean, freshly ground lamination surfaces for improved glue bonding. He then heat tempers the corewoods in his glue curing oven.

Most bowyers admit that glue-up is the one time they wish they had an extra pair of hands. In Harry's case, Eva is his wish come true. During glue-up she brightens the shop with her light-hearted humor while lending helping hands and a critical eye.

Right before glue-up, Harry masking tapes the non-gluing surface of the fiberglass and cleans the gluing surface with lacquer thinner. He also covers his bow form with plastic wrap and tapes it down to prevent it from slipping.

Once the composites are ready, he mixes powdered Urac glue for application to all wood-to-wood surfaces. It resembles a thinned chocolate-butterscotch pudding and penetrates the wood or bamboo pores, providing a super bond.

While Harry mixes the Urac, Eva mixes the thick epoxy to apply on the wood-to-fiberglass surfaces. Even though using two different glues requires extra work and special care during glue-up, Harry believes it's critical to the bow's longevity. "Our specialized gluing process and our choice of limb materials gives us a durable bow that, with proper care, can be shot throughout a lifetime."

To elevate his laminations when applying glue, Harry uses a strip of wood with two rows of headless nails. This allows him to apply glue to one side of a lamination, flip it over, and glue the other side before laying it in the form. During glue-up, Harry and Eva double check each other to be sure each lamination surface has a uniform layer of the proper glue.

When laying up the laminations, Harry uses alligator clamps as extra hands to hold the slippery, glued laminations in the form between steps. Once the composites are in the form, he lays on a galvanized metal pressure strip to prevent the laminations from cupping during pressing. He then lays on a fire hose and clamps on the upper half of the press. Using a small hand pump, he inflates the hose to sixty-five pounds, squeezing the composites into an unborn bow.

The form is placed in his glue curing oven to bake and then cool overnight. His oven is insulated, heated with a series of light bulbs, and equipped with a thermostat heat control.

FORM TO SHAPE

Once the bow is removed from the form, Harry grinds the sharp-edged excess glue off the sides using a disk sander. He marks a centerline down the bow and uses a wooden template to outline a slightly over-sized bow shape. He then band saws the emerging bow to rough dimensions.

Next, he removes the masking tape from the tips and roughens the tip overlay areas with sandpaper. He glues on the tip overlays with epoxy and heat cures them at a low temperature.

After allowing the overlays to cure for at least one day, Harry grinds the limbs to near final shape on his disk sander and files in rough string nocks. He then braces the bow and checks it on his scale to see how close it is to the desired draw weight.

He clamps the rough bow in his padded vise and begins sanding with coarse forty grit paper, rounding the fiberglass along the limb edges. Next, he smooths and rounds the exposed corewoods using a steel hand scraper, making sure to remove any grinding marks. He rounds the limb edges to enhance the bow's appearance and to make it more durable to dings and nicks in the field.

He then cuts out the sight window and shapes the handle. "By cutting my sight window to within one-eighth inch of center shot, my customers can use a wider variety of spine and weight arrows, plus it will make the bow a little more accurate."

Because of their design, Harry's bows usually don't require much work to bring both limbs into alignment. Minor limb alignment is achieved by sanding the strong side of a limb. His limb design exhibits a gradual reflex through the middle of the limb, and he avoids any reflex change in the outer third. "Limb twist can be a problem with a reflex in the outer portion of the limb. It's a poor design feature. If you want preload in your limbs it should be throughout the entire limb in a gradual curve. Another reason that my bows draw and shoot with the limbs in plane is because I build parallel laminations in the limb."

BUILT IN TILLER

Harry checks bow tiller at static or braced, and at dynamic or drawn positions. This ensures proper tiller during shooting. He adjusts limb tiller by contour sanding the limb edges along the glass, but usually not much

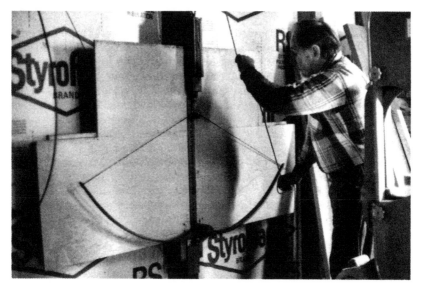

CRITICAL ON THE LIMBS — Using his tiller board and bow scale, Harry makes sure his limbs are balanced throughout every inch of the draw.

sanding is needed. "I build in tiller by cutting one-half inch off the butt end of the bottom limb lamination on paired laminations, or by shifting my one-piece bamboo lamination three-eighths inch down from center during lay-up. Building the proper tiller into a bow internally is the only way to do it."

When tillering a bow for a three fingers under shooter, he builds almost an even tiller. "If I tiller a bow for a split-fingers shooter I will tiller it from one-eighth inch to three-sixteenths inch positive tiller on the upper limb. But it depends on the bow design and whether a shooter heels the bow. I tiller most bows to one-eighth inch, but on my flatbow I usually tiller to three-sixteenths inch."

SWEEPING HARMONY

To achieve the most from a bow's design, Harry carefully crafts his limbs to work in harmony. "Every inch of those limbs should work in stages to have an efficient bow. If you have a stiff spot in the limb you can get an exaggerated build up in the last couple inches of draw. And then you're not getting every inch of that limb to work.

"I can see any stiff spots in a limb, even when it's braced. I have a tremendous eye for spotting that. I use my tiller board and I watch between both limbs to see if they are bending properly and if there are any flat areas. I also watch how the weight builds up during draw. I check that on every bow, and work on every bow until it's right. Then I hand shoot each one. If it's for a three fingers under shooter, A test shoot that bow three fingers under."

NEARLY FINISHED

Harry final sands his bows with 400 grit sandpaper and then rubs them smooth with .0000 steel wool. He alternates this process several times, removing even the smallest irregularities. He then wipes down the entire bow with lacquer thinner and inks on the bow specifications.

When Harry was looking for a quality bow finish, he investigated most of the popular finishes, finally selecting one he chooses to keep confidential. "I decided not to use Fullerplast as a bow finish because it cracks from shrinking constantly. It was meant as a car dashboard finish. I talked to the head engineer at Fuller-O'Brien in California and he said, 'Don't ever use Fullerplast as a bow finish. And please tell others not to use it for that.'

"So I called around and found a bow finish that's used by one of the largest bow manufacturers in the country. This finish is still a two-part mixture but it doesn't shrink. It's superior in durability and serviceability to any finish that I've been able to find. Plus, it doesn't crack and it's hard to mar."

Harry sprays all wood portions of a bow with one heavy coat of finish, allows it to dry for a day, and hand sands it smooth. He then sprays on two additional coats over the entire bow and sands it smooth between coats. During the spraying, Eva directs a hand-held light to help Harry obtain smooth and even coats. Spraying most bow finishes is potentially hazardous, and Harry cautions bowyers to always wear proper breathing masks and protective eye goggles.

He wraps his grips with a single piece of elk or buffalo hide. Although they're a little tougher to acquire, these thick hides conform extremely well to the archer's hand for comfortable shooting. Occasionally Harry even uses smoked or brain-tanned leathers that he gets from muzzle-loading friends.

CUSTOM CARE

Harry's completed custom bow deserves special care. He recommends using a bow stringer, especially for those not familiar with safely using the push-pull stringing method, and he recommends unstringing a traditional bow when it's not in use.

He also cautions about getting a bow too warm. "I've seen guys lean their strung bows up against a hot car on a sunny day and that's a no-no. One of the worst things you can do is to put a braced bow in a hot car, or take a bow from a hot car and then string it. On a hot day that bow core could reach 120 degrees, and at that temperature the epoxy may start to get unstable and let go."

THE RIGHT BOW

Another caution Harry passes along to new customers is not to bite off more bow than they can handle. "Very few seventy pound compound shooters can handle a seventy pound stick bow. We could lose a lot of new traditional shooters because they're overbowed. They develop bad habits, then quit after a while.

"Mastering your bow is more important than just yanking it back. There's a big difference between accurately shooting a bow and just going through the motions. The reason a lot of guys shoot better with a lighter bow is because they can master it. But when they jump up to heavy bows they lose that mastery."

To develop his controlled shooting, Harry practices with his sixty pound bow during the summer and then switches to a heavier bow for hunting. "I get a heavier arrow that shoots exactly out of my seventy pound bow like my lighter arrows do out of my sixty pound bow. When I go hunting, I just pick up my seventy pound bow and it shoots right on. That's a good system if you can develop it."

ON THE ROAD AGAIN

Each summer Harry and Eva pack up their wares and join the growing bands of archers attending traditional archery gatherings around the nation. It's an important way for them to show traditionalists who they are and what they sell. It's just part of the custom bowmaking business, but it also offers them one of things they enjoy most about their work. "We have made so many friends at those shoots," says Eva. "And Michigan's invitational is our favorite longbow gathering. We feel so much at home there because it's just a relaxed and friendly gathering."

Unlike the longbow-toting oddity he was at shoots twenty years ago, Harry now blends in with the growing bands of longbowmen at recent gatherings. He sees the popular shift back to traditional archery as a natural tendency for people escaping from the high-tech world. "At one time there were huge archery clubs all over the country. But after compounds came on the scene many of those clubs went flat because the more technical something becomes, the less people are inclined to participate in it. But when these people experience the fun of traditional archery, many of them get hooked. Shoots like Michigan's have created traditional homes for many archers. And it's that kind of shoot that is really going to help bring back traditional archery."

For the most part Harry blends in at traditional gatherings, yet many still recognize him as the customer-pleasing bowmaker from Indiana, the man who designed the Grizzly broadhead. Some even know him as the bowyer in search of the ultimate longbow — maybe an impossible search, but one that Harry's committed to.

Chapter Twelve

BRUIN CUSTOM RECURVES

GIANTS

Near the cedar swamp, the crisp air is alive, almost intoxicating with the musky aroma of frost-killed sweet fern. Growing shadows inch across the forest floor like dark creatures consuming all in their path. Besides the flicker of a nuthatch, the woods is hushed by autumn's chill.

Through the shadows and past the leafless maples, a slow movement interrupts the solitude of the setting. It's a man. Perched in a scraggly cedar, he waits like a screech owl, watching for his prey. A snapping branch jolts him to attention. Slowly, he raises his bow, and his readied arrow quivers like a bird dog on point. Even the bold jays flutter off into the shadows as a deathly silence envelops the scene.

Then a faint sound, like waves of wind pounding on a beach, grows louder from within the curtain of cedars. It's the steam-engine breathing of a large black bear sucking in the scents from the pile of pastries a scant ten paces from the bowman. Detecting only the faint smell of a single human mixed with the alluring pastries, the tank-sized creature eases forward. With confidence, the bear lumbers to the bait, swats off the covering of logs, and begins gorging himself.

For a moment, the bowman appears paralyzed. Then, as if given some silent cue, he slowly hisses the arrow back to full draw and releases the string. An ominous roar and erupting brush shatter the evening quiet. The hulk runs only fifty yards before tumbling into a ravine. He lifts his massive head and bellows a raspy growl. His death moan is quickly swallowed by the thick cedars. The hunt is over.

Sitting down on the small tree stand, the man breathes a heavy sigh. Another bear season comes to an end for bowhunter and bowmaker Mike Steliga.

Mike is more than a typical hunter of black bears. He's a master at outwitting the intimidating, huge males who roam Wisconsin's tangled swamps. Although most bears look big out in the woods, especially with a mere ten paces between the hunter and the hunted, there is a real distinction between huge bears and Mike's favorite, the almost mythical giant black bears.

Walking into the Steliga living room can be a heart stopper if you aren't forewarned. Newcomers usually speak in hushed tones when greeted by a coal black mass of fur with fiery eyes and flashing teeth. It's Mike's mammoth 536 pound bear mounted in mid-stride. A close-up of this brute is enough to cause many a bowhunter to decide that deer and rabbits are all they ever care to encounter in the wild. As if one isn't enough, another full mount looms erect in the corner, with its massive head almost touching the ceiling.

What kind of man lays these giant bears low with a single arrow? It takes a man with more than just a passing interest in bowhunting bears. It takes a man like Mike Steliga.

BLACKBIRDS TO BLACK BEARS

Born and raised in Milwaukee, Mike entered the ranks of bowbenders at the age of seven. Armed with his little recurve, young Mike hunted blackbirds and starlings, entering a world of excitement that has endured the years. Although now his quarry, equipment, and skills are more refined, he still maintains his boyish enthusiasm for the sport. "I eat, drink, and sleep bowhunting." Now in his mid-thirties, this Antigo, Wisconsin resident, also eats, drinks, and sleeps bowmaking.

Antigo is noted for its potato production in the nearby ancient lake bed flats. It's a quiet place, and Mike enjoys his rural setting just south of town where he lives with his wife and two children. There, in his small bow shop, he builds a custom line of traditional recurves that are aptly named for his fondness of big bears. It's the home of BRUIN CUSTOM RECURVES.

Before becoming a bowmaker, Mike spent a lot of time working with local wood. He was a professional logger downing big timber in northern Wisconsin where he cut mostly hardwood saw logs. Some of the trees Mike felled were giant hemlocks, growing since Columbus discovered America, and majestic maples over two hundred years old. It was a job he performed with mixed emotions. Now he works with the hard-rock maple in a different way, using it in building his handsome line of recurves.

As his company name suggests, Mike's favorite bowhunting pursuit is black bears. All of his four bow-killed bears are big enough for the book. The three recorded were shot in consecutive seasons and two of them also qualify for Boone and Crockett. His largest scored 21 2/8", and weighed an astounding 536 pounds dressed! That's a lot of bear. And when Mike refers to an animal's size, he refers specifically to dressed weights. "There is not an animal around that you're going to catch and throw on a scale and weigh him live!" As a measurer for the Pope and Young Club, Mike appreciates telling it like it is. He's also an active member of the Professional Bowhunters Society, and belongs to the Wisconsin Bowhunters.

THE MAN, HIS BOW, AND BIGGEST WISCONSIN GROWLER. This 536 pound bear made both the P&Y and B&C books.

SECRETS OF THE SWAMPS

Like any bowhunting game, hunting giant bears primarily involves planning, scouting, preparation, and patience. But even with the best laid plans, Mike warns that arrowing a giant bear doesn't happen very often because they are so few and far between. Locating a big one is a tough job, and trying to tag him is even tougher. Although there are no short cuts, this master bear hunter reveals some of his baiting tricks and bruin savvy.

Mike begins looking for likely bear areas using topographic maps. "I'll pick a good spot, because of prevailing wind direction, lay of the land, and remoteness. I always want to be on the downwind side of the prevailing winds of a swamp, a big swamp, the bigger the better. That's where BIG bears hang out. Even though northwest winds prevail during the late fall, they blow a lot from the southwest and I set up accordingly.

"After I find a good spot, I dig a hole, which is required by law in Wisconsin. I like a hole two feet wide by two feet deep and I put the bait in it. Then I cover it up with good sized pulp sticks. Most people call them logs. That keeps the little animals out. A thirty-five pound coon can roll some wood off, but if you put some heavy stuff on there, he won't. Then when a bear hits the bait you can tell."

Once his bait is set, Mike constructs a back stop next to it. "The back stop makes the bear come around and give me a quartering away shot. I use a bush or a fallen tree. A bear isn't overly aggressive and won't come in and tear it down. He will always come around and offer that quartering away shot. I have a little problem with my shooting that I think a lot of people have, a tendency to shoot high out of a tree. With that quartering away shot there's more of a margin for error. Although something that big at that range — I don't know how you could miss it!

"When I first set my bait, I use a spray bottle to scent the area with liquid smoke, vanilla, anise, or valencia. I spray up in the trees so the scent really gets blowing around. One disadvantage of being on the prevailing downwind side is your attracting scent probably isn't going to carry into the swamp very well unless you get an east wind with a storm front coming in, which is a good time to go out and scent it up. But those bears are wandering around and they'll find it. Don't worry about setting it up for the bear to smell."

Wisconsin's baiting regulations prohibit the use of meat, so Mike uses a variety of enticing pastries, grains, breads mixed with molasses, donuts, sweet rolls, cookies, and sugared Jello for soaking the baked goods. "A good variety of bait is important because a bear can get tired of one item. Cookies are an excellent choice because you don't have to worry about refrigeration. Sometimes it doesn't go over too big when your wife sees you emptying the freezer because you're filling it with bear bait."

Once Mike sets his bait, he roughens up a four foot area near the bait and places an enticing scent there. "The reason I put the scent off to the side is because when bears get on a bait it looks like something did the 'Brontosaurus Stomp' around it. You can't find a good track. But a big bear will go off to the side and inspect that scent area. Big bears aren't stupid, and they seem like they're afraid to leave their foot prints.

"But you can only trick'em maybe a couple of times. If you keep using the same scent they won't even go over there any more. I may even change scents later to some other type of cooking ingredient like anise oil or something with a sweet smell. Every time I go back to check my bait, I reclear and roughen up the scent spot with an inch of dirt so that I can get a good print. And when I see a track that I can lay a dollar bill in, boy my old heart gets going. I think I can even see my shirt moving!"

Besides tracks, droppings are another way to tell if a big bear is coming to the bait. "I had a bear coming one season and the diameter across his droppings was almost two and a half inches. I knew that bear was in the same class as these two I have mounted. He was sharp. I never saw him and could tell he was a late feeder.

"Another way to tell a bear's size is from marks where he bites trees. One day I came into a bait station and was looking around and thought I saw a bullet hole in the tree. But it was bite marks! They were almost at ceiling height. I had to shinny up the tree three feet to look at the bite spot. That's a big animal."

Usually smaller bears act edgy when they know a bigger bruin is hitting a bait, signaling the experienced hunter to wait for Mr. Big. "We had one bait station where a little bear, about 125 pounds, was coming in. We called him 'Wimpy.' My friend saw him at the bait a number of times but he never once touched a donut. He would get close to the bait and a leaf would wiggle or a little wind would come up and Wimpy would take off out of there like you wouldn't believe, just scared to death. Well, we found out later that there were two other bigger bears hitting that bait. One was over 450 pounds.

"If I have an area where a sow and cubs continue hitting, I'll just elimi-nate baiting that spot. Because usually where a sow and cubs are hitting, you won't have a big bear. The best bait station is where you have a number of bears hitting, because there's competition. If a big bear wants to get a bite of the action, he's going to want to get in there early. But if you only have one bear hitting a bait, he is going to come in when he wants."

When tending his baits, Mike doesn't bother to cover his human scent. "I don't think it's necessary because they associate my smell with the bait. But when I'm hunting, that's a different story. I shower well, and use plain Ivory soap. I normally don't worry about my boot odor because I use the same ones for baiting. But I put my hunting clothes in plastic bags with balsam boughs. I believe an animal can tell if human scent is fresh or if it's a little old. One time a bear was downwind of me for half an hour and crossed my scent stream two or three times. I can't believe he didn't run off. I think by having my human scent well taken care of, maybe he thought it was a lingering scent, like I had just finished baiting."

Mike likes to set his stand close to the bait, offering him that high-per-centage shot. "I set up ten to twelve yards away. Normally, I like to find the best set up for tree background and location, and then I get up in a tree ten to fourteen feet. I think bears are pretty much blind. They'll catch movement, but they'll look at me and I always kiddingly think, 'What are you lookin' at? You can't see anything anyway!'"

After all the planning, baiting, and preparation is through, Mike climbs in his tree stand to wait, but only during the evening. "Matter of fact, when I bait one of my better baits that I plan on hunting, I try to bait it at the same time every day within three hours of dark. And the earliest I've seen a bear on a bait is forty-five minutes to an hour before dark."

PUTTING IT TOGETHER

Seeing a black giant lumbering from the swamp toward the bait can knot a bear hunter's stomach tighter than a Flemish-twist bowstring, and etch unforgettable bowhunting memories. Mike's most rewarding hunt was for a bruin with a fondness for fresh venison and tons of bait. He recalls that hunt with a sense of pride and a tone of respect for the quarry.

"My friend told me about a big bear track he saw during deer season. He shot a deer way back in and when he returned later for it, it was devoured and big bear tracks were there. That really excited me! I went over his topographic maps and took my finger and said, 'Bang, right there, that's where I can kill that bear.'

"We went back in there during the summer and it just looked ideal. After I started baiting that spot, I had a number of bears hitting it, including one exceptional track. I hunted there three nights and was amazed that I didn't see a bear. With all of the hits, the way the bait was cleaned up, and all the different tracks, I couldn't believe that I did not see one bear. The third night, I walked in there and it was rainy, and I saw a depression right below my tree and I could make out a pad print. It was the big bear and he came in from behind me. The next day I went out there. The wind wasn't right to hunt, but I baited. I checked the whole situation out because I wanted to know what I was doing wrong."

Mike discovered trails coming to the bait from every angle like a hub of a wheel. He figured the big bear was coming in downwind and picking up his scent. "So I moved the bait station about 200 yards to a better location. Most bear hunters won't make so many changes because they're scared of over-scenting the area. But I knew I had to make changes to kill that bear.

"So, I completely changed everything. It was really rewarding when I went back the second day and his big tracks were right on the new bait spot and the bait was devoured. I just started pounding the bait to him and every day it was gone. But I couldn't hunt for almost a week because the wind wasn't right. I was antsy to hunt, and I know a lot of people who probably would have just gone up that tree and taken a chance. But I knew that I had to get him the first time, or I wouldn't.

"A friend and I baited there with two sixty-five to seventy pound feed sacks stuffed full of bait. We piled the bait on, and the big bear's tracks were there again."

The conditions the following day were perfect and Mike was sure he'd get a crack at the giant bear. When he arrived at the bait he couldn't believe the previous day's pile was gone. He dumped the fresh bait and got set. "About a half hour before dark I heard him coming. I just knew it was him. Ten minutes later, in he came. Big bears usually have a staging area where they sit and sniff it out. Once it's in their minds that it's safe, they don't hesitate, they come right in like they own the whole show.

"I never saw such an out of proportion bear in my life. His stomach stuck out from his sides from ten inches to as much as a foot. It looked like he swallowed a gigantic beach ball and someone blew it up!

"I was a little antsy at first and I had to settle myself down. Then I laced him, shooting completely through him. He jumped back from the noise of the arrow hitting on the other side of him and then he took off. He went forty-five yards and was down. He scored twenty-one inches, weighed 453 pounds dressed, and was later aged at nineteen years old."

Mike's other mammoth bear was even bigger, and arrowing that 536 pound giant represented more than just a challenge in bear savvy. "The biggest one was a challenge because I had hurt my knee in a logging accident that year. I bummed it up bad, and I started baiting bears on crutches. I then used one crutch and later went to leaning on a shovel. I set a Baker tree stand in a cedar tree I could climb quietly. But I could only climb with one leg so I didn't get very high. I felt unsafe with one leg so bummed up. After I killed that bear, he measured nine feet from nose to hind foot. If he had wanted to, he could have stood on his hind legs and swatted me out of that tree!"

What's the most important ingredient in helping Mike slay these giant, nerve-rattling, blackies? "It's CONFIDENCE. That's the number one thing to take into the woods. For years I hunted without confidence, and those were some of my most miserable years hunting because I consistently missed. But I killed these big bears because I had confidence that I wasn't going to miss.

I just knew I was going to get them. Carrying confidence into the woods will make you more successful."

Although Mike sounds like a modern day Paul Bunyan who could drag one of his 500 pound bears out of the woods by one hand, he's really just an average guy of medium height with a wiry frame. His only resemblance to Paul Bunyan is the thick, dark brown beard bracketing his youthful face. Behind black-rimmed glasses peer the smallish but penetrating eyes of a predator.

Mike not only enjoys hunting big black bears, he savors them as table fare long after the hunt is over. He actually prefers bear to venison and one of his favorite meals is bear bratwurst and sauerkraut.

TOOLS OF THE GAME

To bring down freight train-sized bears, Mike uses deadly-sharp Snuffer broadheads on the biting ends of has aluminum arrows. "On bears you should shoot a heavy arrow and a wide, sharp broadhead. You can throw most of those inserted blade heads in the garbage. They're now coming out with some modular heads that are sharp to the point, which is better. It's important to use a big head on bears because of their fat and tallow, and you need a big hole on two sides for a good blood trail."

A good hit with a sharp broadhead can put even the biggest bear down in short order. Mike's bears all gave their death moans well within hearing range. His furthest ran only sixty yards. Plus, his experience shows that an arrowed bear is usually down for the count in a very short distance or he is not going down at all.

For driving his arrows home, Mike shoots a sixty inch Bruin recurve, approximately sixty pounds draw weight, with a Delta style Bruin bow quiver mounted on the side. Mike stresses it's more important to shoot a moderate weight bow accurately, than to struggle and possibly make a poor shot with a bow that's too heavy. He uses a simple piece of masking tape on his string for his arrow nocking point because he feels that the metal nock sets dig into the fingers and can damage the string serving after several adjustments.

BUCKS, STUMPS, AND BOWS

Although bears have been Mike's biggest bowhunting love, recent restrictions in Wisconsin bear regulations have caused him to shift his concentration to the more legally accessible whitetails. Over a dozen have fallen from his well-placed arrows though he admits he has also missed a few huge mossy-horned swamp bucks. He concentrates his bowhunting in an area which produces massive bucks, some weighing over 240 pounds dressed. And Mike says that they have impressive headgear to match their bodily proportions.

To keep his shooting skills sharp for big bears or bucks, Mike stump shoots often. "It's the best form of practice because no two shots are ever the same." When stump shooting, he patiently concentrates on his shots without the distractions of score cards or other shooters. He prefers this type of practice because it simulates being alone in the woods, one-on-one with an animal. When aiming, Mike focuses his concentration on splitting that one single hair in the middle of a minute spot, an important point that helps keep his arrows bunched in the target.

Whether he's hunting, practicing, or bowmaking, Mike loves all aspects of archery, especially the simple fun of traditional archery. It's ingrained in his personal and professional life. "Traditional archery is a stick and a string. Our modern recurves and longbows are made with fiberglass, but basically they're still sticks and strings. They're not contraptions, or mechanical devices with a bunch of wheels, cables, release aids, and gimmicks. Traditional archery is simplicity and getting back to the basics of what archery is all about. It's reminiscent of our forefathers, Pope and Young.

"Traditional bowhunting is a demanding sport. People bowhunt because it's a challenge, but many of today's archery gadgets are designed to take the challenge out of bowhunting. If you're going to bowhunt for the simplicity and fun of the sport, a recurve is definitely better. It puts the human element back in bowhunting and takes the gadgets out of it. There's nothing more satisfying than pulling back that recurve, looking at a spot, and seeing your arrow plunk right in there, especially when it's behind the shoulder of a big bear or buck. That's where it's all at."

THE BEAR DEN

Creating simplistic traditional recurves requires skill, experience, perseverance, and innovation. And it doesn't hurt to receive some advice and encouragement along the way from a seasoned master bowyer. Since he began building recurves in 1982, Mike has received invaluable guidance from master bowyer and friend, Bill Pyle. With an occasional nudge from Bill, Mike's bow building has progressed to a full-time business under the name of BRUIN CUSTOM RECURVES.

Although Mike wanted a company name to exemplify the black bear image, he jokingly noted that the name "Bear" had long since been claimed. But he decided that "Bruin" was a natural for a line of bows that was in part spawned by his zest for bowhunting blackies. His logo is a round, gold and black decal, displayed on the bow's riser, depicting a bear's pad print cradled with the name BRUIN.

Mike builds bows in the peaceful rural setting of his residence. The open countryside near his shop is a mix of rolling hay fields and wood lots, dotted with glacier-carved boulders. During early summer, his garage-converted bow shop is filled with the aroma of morning dew and fresh-cut hay. Mike works to the background music of robins and meadow larks, their territorial songs cutting through the morning haze. Like an oversized flood light, the swollen sun spills its rays through the open door, casting an eerie orange glow over machinery and wood. Only the stacks of dust-covered lumber remain hidden in the overhead rafters, quietly waiting their turn to become custom recurves. During the winter, the warming rays are replaced with the crackling glow of hardwoods in the wood-burning stove. Whether it's the quiet solitude of a snow bound setting or summer's green landscape, Bruin's shop is a peaceful place for a man to carry on his labor of love.

A FAMILY OF BRUINS

Within his small shop, Mike single-handedly produces a line of recurves designed to fill the needs of the serious bowhunter. His HUNTMASTER and MASTER series are offered as one-piece bows or as similarly designed three-piece take-down models.

The HUNTMASTER is Bruin's slim-lined, 58" and 60", one-piece recurve. Like all Bruins, the Huntmaster exudes an inherent warmth from the earthy tones of natural hardwoods enveloped in brown fiberglass. Its mass weight is about 1 pound, 10 ounces, varying slightly with different density riser woods. It's available in local Wisconsin walnut and hard maple, or in shedua, bubinga, and several other exotics. The riser is 20" long between fadeouts and contains a decorative laminated wedge of maple and mahogany veneers sandwiching a 1/4" strip of striking purple heart. This wedge is typically offered in a "V" design pointing in the direction of arrow flight.

The furniture-quality riser varies from 2" to 3" thick and is 1 5/8" wide. Its slightly rounded sight window is cut 1/16" past center shot. The window is full cut 3" above the shelf and contours back to full riser width 4 1/2" above the shelf. The arrow shelf is padded with synthetic hair and is rounded to help obtain crisp arrow flight. The riser is a smooth blend of rounded contours, except for a small sculpted area on the belly below the grip where the logo is displayed. The custom-shaped grip is designed to provide a snug comfortable fit tight under the sight window for a natural instinctive sight picture. Epoxy-set brass stabilizer and quiver bushings are available.

The sweeping recurved limbs of the Huntmaster are made from one tapered maple lamination on the belly and one on the back. The limbs are backed with a full-length piece of brown fiberglass and faced with riser-interrupted fiberglass. Both limbs have a working length of 20" from the fadeout to the tip. The limbs are 1 1/2" wide at the fadeout, narrowing to 3/4" at the nock. Most of the narrowing occurs throughout the recurve. The riser wood tip overlays are 2" long and measure 3/4" from the nock to tip. The nocks are flush cut on the sides and feather into a nicely fashioned "Y" string groove filed into the belly glass. The limbs are rounded on the edges and finished with a low luster, satin epoxy finish.

Mike's recommended brace height is 9" to 10" from the shelf back to the bowstring. The recommended nocking point is 1/2" to 5/8" above perpendicular.

The MASTER recurve is similar in construction and design to the Huntmaster, but it offers more mass weight in the riser for those preferring extra heft and stability. It's available in 62" and 64" lengths. On the 64" model, the riser measures 24" between fadeouts. The Master weighs 2 pounds, 3 ounces with the lighter walnut riser. The sight window is full cut 5" above the shelf and contours back to full riser width 6 1/2" above the shelf on the 64" bow. The riser is 1 3/4" wide and the sight window is cut 1/16" past center shot. The limb construction on the Master is similar to the Huntmaster except the limb width narrows from 1 3/4" at the fadeouts to 3/4" at the nock.

Mike considers his 62" Master the "Cadillac" of his one-piece bows. And, as the chronograph results indicate, its design results in an arrow spittin' performer. Its riser measures 22" between fadeouts, and has a full cut 4" sight window which contours back to full riser width 5¼" above the shelf.

To check for relative arrow speed, Mike shot 550 grain, 2117 aluminum arrows from his 62", 60 pound at 28" draw, Master. The 29" arrows were fletched with three feathers and equipped with snap-on nocks. Mike drew the arrows 28½" and had a clean release. The bowstring was a Fast Flight string without accessories. The average arrow speed for this bow, arrow, string, and shooter combination was 194 fps.

The following draw/force measurements suggests the smoothness of draw on this 62" Master:

DRAW LENGTH	25"	26"	27"	28"	29"
DRAW WEIGHT	51#	54½#	57½#	60#	63½#

TAKE-DOWNS TOO

Mike recently introduced a line of take-down recurves that follow the basic design of his Huntmaster and Master. Although he began making his take-downs in early 1986, they weren't available until a year later. He first wanted to be sure of their performance and durability under actual hunting conditions and had them field tested by bowhunting friends.

His Huntmaster T.D. is available in a 58", 60", and 62" lengths with a 16" riser, and 60", 62", and 64" lengths with an 18" riser. This bow resembles

THE BRUIN LINE — Mike offers his one piece recurves and their three-piece take-down brothers. All incorporate solid hardwood in the risers.

its one-piece brother except for the somewhat blockier riser where it attaches to the limbs. This three-piece bow has a single alignment pin and alignment-attachment bolt limb system common among take-downs. Its mass weight is 2 pounds 4 ounces, varying slightly with the type of riser wood. Although its three-piece design prohibits using one continuous piece of backing fiberglass, Mike still incorporates fiberglass backing on the riser for handle strength and appearance.

Mike shot the noted 550 grain, 2117 aluminum arrows from his 60", 57 pound at 28" draw, Huntmaster T.D. at an average arrow speed of 186 fps. The string, shooter, and arrows were the same as noted on Master.

The following draw/force measurements were recorded on this 60" Huntmaster T.D:

DRAW LENGTH	25"	26"	27"	28"	29"
DRAW WEIGHT	49#	51½#	55#	57#	61#

THE BIRTH OF A BRUIN — HARDWOOD RISERS

Although dyed and laminated hard rock maple is becoming popular among many bowyers, Mike is committed to using select custom solid hardwoods in his risers. It's more costly and time consuming to use solid hardwoods, but he believes the warmth, natural beauty, and distinction they give his products are well worth it. "When you're making traditional bows, you can't beat the genuine beauty of solid natural woods that give every bow a unique and one-of-a-kind character."

Mike's favorite riser wood is bubinga because of the variation of its striking grain contrasts combined with the warmth of its reddish tones. He also notes that bubinga is very dense and strong, providing extra riser mass which Mike believes adds to the overall performance of his bows.

Wisconsin walnut makes a beautiful riser, resembling the cocoa colored fur of a brown bear. However, Mike warns that although it makes a pretty bow, walnut isn't as strong as some of the denser exotics. Pin knots within the walnut mark old branch locations and are potential weak spots in the wood. When selecting riser material, Mike avoids these pin knot areas and pieces with too much lighter toned, weaker sapwood. Because of its strength limitations, he does not recommend walnut risers for bows in excess of seventy pounds.

To add richness, beauty, and strength to his risers, Mike incorporates a laminated wedge. It's made from a ¼" thick strip of purple heart sandwiched with maple and mahogany veneers. Although he occasionally builds a straight vertical wedge in his risers, Mike prefers the more popular "V" style wedge as he feels it adds more character to the bow.

Mike's risers reflect characteristics that he and bowyer Bill Pyle thought would best suit a hunting recurve. Mike prefers the stability of bows that position most of the riser weight on the belly side. So he designed the peaked areas on the riser belly, providing good balance directly over the shooting hand.

When building risers, Mike usually makes four at once to economize his time. First he stencil marks and band saws a planed piece of wood to accept the riser wedge. All laminate contact surfaces of the riser wood and the purple heart wedge are then power planed to ensure precision flatness. This helps achieve strong, uniform, and paper-thin glue lines.

Mike then glues all contact surfaces of the riser pieces and wedge laminates together with Urac 185. He utilizes a ⅛" thick steel clamping plate to ensure that the riser components stay in near perfect alignment. He clamps them vertically and horizontally. Before tightening the clamps, Mike carefully aligns the grain of the pieces so that the finished riser will resemble a solid hardwood that has been magically imbedded with the laminated wedge. After it's clamped into place, the glue is cured in Mike's bow oven at 110 to 120 degrees for one and one half hours, and is left in the oven to cool slowly.

Like many bowyers, Mike constructed most of his bow building devices. His spacious, almost walk-in glue curing oven is 6' high, 6' wide, and 2' deep. It's heated with an electric dryer element and equipped with a small circulating fan. It also has a thermostat and time clock control. It's an important part of his bow building operation as the proper heat curing of glued composites is vital to a bow's longevity and strength. The oven is also used to cure the epoxy finish on his bows.

Once out of the oven, the riser is planed to width and then scribed to shape using a template that has several important reference points. One of these marks the bow center which is located slightly below the throat of the grip. "When a bow is held exactly in the center it vibrates much like a tuning fork. But when it's held a bit off center, bow vibration is significantly reduced."

To ensure uniform and strong glue lines, Mike fashions the riser to precisely fit the contour of his bow form. Next, he delicately grinds the fadeouts to wispy thinness. "The precision of the fadeouts is the most critical part of the bowmaking process because they represent the focus point of limb stress."

LAY-UP IN THE FORM

Mike's bow forms are made from sandwiched, glued layers of quality plywood that are painstakingly cut and sanded to his desired bow shape while making sure that the form surface is ninety degrees to the sides. A layer of fiberglass is glued to the sweeping bow form surface to provide a smooth, flat, and hard duplicate of the bow back.

The quality, application, and curing of a bow's glue are vital parts of the bowmaking process. Mike uses Daubond Adhesive epoxy in all glue applications except on the riser's wood-to-wood contacts. He mixes the epoxy by weight and slightly heats it during mixing to aid in a thorough blend.

Before gluing up a one-piece bow, Mike bevels and glue-splices the matched pair of back corewood laminations. The resulting single lamination eliminates the possibility of butt end separation during glue up. And when laminated with one continuous strip of fiberglass, it provides added strength through the riser section. He also measures the tapered corewood laminations and fiberglass with a micrometer to ensure proper taper and thickness. Mike applies epoxy to all contact surfaces of the composites when laying up

Mike presses his composites using "C" clamps and wrist power. Like traditional archery, it's simple yet effective.

a bow. Once the glued composites are properly aligned in the form, he lays on a rubber cushion strip, and then the contoured pieces of wood which make up the upper portion or belly side of his press. The bow composites are compressed by tightening large "C" clamps hooked into a series of holes along the bow form and screwed down on the contoured pieces of wood.

After hand-tightening the row of "C" clamps, Mike puts the form into his glue curing oven. He stresses that proper epoxy curing and cool down are crucial to the durability of the laminated joints. He heat cures his bows at 180 degrees for two hours and then allows the composite to slowly cool, in the form, to room temperature. He points out that hardened epoxy will regenerate if its temperature exceeds the original curing temperature. This is why he prefers the higher range of curing temperatures which he believes produces a superior and long lasting glue bond.

When Mike removes a freshly glued bow from the press, he first grinds off the razor sharp dried glue using his belt sander and then grinds the limb sides until the fiberglass, corewoods, and fadeouts are flush. He then trims the limbs to length and epoxies on the hardwood tip overlays using small "C" clamps. The entire bow goes back into the oven to cure the overlays at a temperature of 150 degrees.

LIMB WORK

Mike rough trims the shape of the limb edges using a belt sander and files in rough string nocks so the bow can be braced to check for limb alignment. If eyeing down the string reveals a limb that is "kicked out" to one side, he removes material from the stronger limb edge until the limb is in alignment with the string. Once the limbs are aligned, Mike files the string grooves to finished dimensions and rechecks the alignment. He points out that proper limb alignment is crucial to the ultimate performance of the bow.

After the bow is "trued up" into perfect limb alignment, he templates the tips to finished dimensions and grinds the limb edges to their final shape. During this process he double checks several reference points on each limb to ensure that both limbs have the same width dimensions.

To achieve proper limb alignment on the riser-limb match of his take-down bows, Mike has a machined jig that allows repeated precision placement of the attachment bushing, alignment pin, and limb holes. For added strength, the raised brass attachment bushings are flanged on the belly side of the riser providing a non-pull-through seat. These bushings and the alignment pins are epoxy set and heat cured for maximum strength.

When rounding off the limb edges, Mike can usually alter a bow's draw weight by several pounds. And he prides himself in being able to build his bows to the requested draw weight.

Once the limbs are finished to shape, he patiently marks and files the string nocks, blending them into the belly "Y" which flows nicely into a single string groove. For marking the exact limb center for the string groove placement, Mike uses a little self-centering scribe that etches a mark down the belly of the recurve. When fashioning the string nocks and grooves, he employs several sizes of small round files, using progressively larger ones to ensure a good string fit. When finished, it looks like he used a red-hot wire to melt a perfect string pattern into the fiberglass.

After the limbs are aligned and shaped to finished dimensions, Mike brings them into proper tiller. For a standard style shooter he strives for an approximate one-quarter inch positive tiller on the top limb and builds a one-half inch positive tiller for shooters using three fingers under the arrow. To achieve the desired tiller, Mike hand sands the belly and back glass with a piece of wet sandpaper on the limb that needs weakening, which is usually the top limb.

On his take-down models, each set of limbs is brought into alignment and tillered while assembled with the riser they will be sold with. Even though the precision and repeatability of his riser-limb attachment system is near-perfect, crafting the limbs on their matching handle assures the quality performance of each bow.

BACK TO THE RISER

Once the limbs are completed, Mike begins shaping the riser. He band saws out the sight window and arrow shelf, and makes several cuts around the grip. "One of the weakest areas is through the sight window, so this is one reason why I build a multilaminated wedge in the risers. Besides adding strength through the sight window, the "V" wedge also gives strength to the limb attachment area in the take-down risers."

When shaping the riser, Mike slightly crests the arrow shelf and rounds the sight window to enhance arrow flight. The gentle contours emerge by hand shaping with rasps, belt sanders, and finally a high-speed cushioned

Using the cushiony spindle sander, Mike blends the riser contours into soft, simple lines.

sleeve spindle sander. The adjustable air sleeve on the hand-drill mounted spindle sander enables Mike to gently blend the flowing riser contours. He finishes the job with three decreasing grit sizes of sandpaper and plenty of bruin elbow grease.

Any requested accessory bushings are then installed with heat cured epoxy. Installing these bushings before the finish coat is applied helps give the completed bow a one-piece appearance.

A SATIN FINISH

Before he begins spraying the final finish, Make thoroughly cleans his shop so that he will have a dust-free work area. "That's a nice process because it guarantees my shop gets cleaned at least once every two weeks."

First, he air dusts the bow and wipes it with the epoxy thinner to remove any residual grime. He then rubs a thick coat of the epoxy glue on the riser to serve as a filler for the porous wood. This coat is heat-hardened to 150 degrees and then sanded smooth. The bow then receives two sprayed coats of the epoxy which are also heat cured. The entire bow is then sanded with 220 grit paper and Mike installs his Bruin logo and inks the bow specifications on the riser. Finally, he sprays on another two coats of epoxy and heat-cures them.

His satin finish offers the best of both worlds in a quality hunting finish. "It's clear and smooth enough to allow the natural beauty of the wood to shine through, yet it's low enough in reflective value for hunting situations. I've tried some of the rough, low-luster finishes, but they had a tendency to hold dust and dirt, making a bow look old before its time."

Mike's last step is installing the synthetic hair shelf and strike pad. It's an appropriate launching material as his bows are specifically designed to shoot cleanly from the shelf. This feature is important to many instinctive shooters who prefer their arrow to rest almost on top of the bow hand.

Each Bruin Custom Recurve is furnished with two bowstrings and a bow stringer. Mike supplies the stringer to protect both his customers and their bow. He cautions against using the step-through or push-pull methods of stringing a bow because he has seen them damage bows and injure archers. He says that his bows incorporate a pretty significant recurve and that properly using a stringer is critical in preventing twisted limbs.

Although he has tried using Fast Flight strings on his bows, Mike doesn't recommend them. "The seven feet per second increase in speed isn't worth the trade off for the increased bow noise and vibration."

LIKE AN OLD BRUIN

Using the same innovative approach he employs in bear hunting, Mike continually searches for new ways to improve his bows. "In the last year I've refined a new limb design which I feel is superior shooting. This design has achieved a nice blend of speed and stability."

With a sense of pride and challenge he continues to explore the possibilities of limb attachment refinements, bow finishes, epoxy glues, limb composite materials, and new crafting methods. But, like an old bear circling the bait, Mike is not one to quickly change from time-proven methods or follow what seems to be any easy path trekked by the other bears in the bow building industry. With guarded caution he field tests his new concepts, discusses them with Bill Pyle, and makes sure that they truly improve his Bruin Custom Recurves.

Chapter Thirteen

HOYT/U.S.A.

THE DANCE ERA

The dance floor was crowded and already getting stuffy. Even the occasional puff of an evening breeze wafting through the open windows didn't do much to cut the humidity. But the crowd didn't seem to care. They were there for fun.

Up on the stage the band tuned their instruments, making them squeak and growl like waking wooden and brass creatures. Finally the house lights dimmed and a voice rang out above the chatter: "For your dancing enjoyment this evening, we proudly present, Eddie Lake and his Orchestra." As the announcer's voice faded, Eddie nodded and brought the twelve man band to life, playing one of the top tunes of the year.

The town was St. Louis, Missouri. The year was somewhere in the early 1930s. "Those were great years," Eddie recalls, "I think about them a lot. I started playing on the air with a local radio station, performing banjo and guitar solos. The radio guy asked, 'Would you have any objection if we used a more phonetic name?' And I said, 'No'. Then he asked, 'How about Eddie Lake?' He must have had that name in mind before he even talked to me.

"I had the name on radio, so I used it when I formed my band. In fact, even to this day there are people around who know me as Eddie Lake and don't know who I really am."

Although Eddie's band lost its leader in 1938, the sport of modern archery gained one of its most prominent forefathers. Eddie would become one of America's premier archery innovators. A few may still know him as Eddie Lake, but the world of archery knows him as Earl Hoyt, Jr.

INSPIRATION FROM POPE

Hoyt's early fascination with archery began after buying a steel arrow point from a friend at school. Prodded by the feel of the smooth point in his pocket, he was soon determined to make his own bow, and in 1925 he began a craft that would last a lifetime. "When I was fourteen, I got interested in making bows by reading the Boy Scout Manual. My first bows were made out of hickory, but hickory is not a very good bow wood. It follows the string a great deal. The first two I made were complete failures."

But Hoyt didn't give up. "I learned about an archery magazine published in Corvallis, Oregon, called *Ye Silvan Archer*. It was the only archery maga- zine published in the United States. So I subscribed to it and saw an ad for Pope's book, *Hunting With The Bow and Arrow*. I bought that book and my eyes just got bug-eyed, and I thought, 'Gee whiz, this has got to be the greatest thrill in the world — hunting with a bow and arrow.' " Hoyt wasted little time in ordering yew staves from Oregon, then followed Pope's detailed instructions and crafted his first serviceable longbows.

Young Hoyt continued to make self-wood bows, and when the great depression hit he used his bowmaking skills to help make ends meet. By 1931 he had formed a part-time arrow making business with his father and even placed an ad for his arrows in the Oregon magazine. His bows and arrows soon became popular, and after joining the St. Louis Archery Club in 1937, Hoyt's part-time bow and arrow business began to pick up.

The thirties were busy years for the young bowmaker. He attended Washington University in St. Louis, where he studied engineering. He also had a serious music career playing solos on a radio program and then organizing a twelve-piece orchestra popular during the dance band era. He also worked with his father doing architectural design for Hoyt Construction Company.

The war years of the early forties marked a time of change for both Hoyt and his father. Hoyt got a job in the engineering department of Curtis-Wright Aircraft, later McDonnell Aircraft. But those war years forced Hoyt Construc- tion Company out of business. So Hoyt employed his father to make arrows full-time, and he made bows part-time after working a sixty hour week at the aircraft plant.

A FORK IN THE TRAIL

Arrowsmithing kept Hoyt's father busy throughout the war years, but after the war he became ill. Hoyt took several weeks off from the aircraft plant to help in his budding archery business until his father recovered. His father, however, remained in poor health, and Hoyt was soon faced with the choice of leaving his engineering job or forgetting the archery business. His decision in 1946 helped change the course of modern archery.

"In the beginning I thought I had made a very bad choice when I decided to go into the archery business. I left a good job at McDonnell Aircraft and during the first three or four years, my archery business was sluggish. But in the fourth year, things started to turn around and from then on, it was a gradual upward trend. And that trend never stopped. One thing we have always made as our goal: strive for improved quality, and never let it suffer because of increased production. It's interesting that as we have steadily increased production with better applications of jigs, fixtures, methods and machinery, our quality has increased right along with it.

"Each year was better than the year before, and I started to innovate and come out with new ideas. That gave us a lot of impetus and put us in the lead over our competition. Today our bows hold most of the archery records in National, World, and Olympic competitions."

Hoyt's archery business blossomed, and he became one of the nation's top bow manufacturers. He remained owner and president of his flourishing archery company until 1978, when the business was sold to the CML Group. Hoyt stayed on as Vice president, consultant, and head of research and development, and worked in public relations. In 1983, the company was purchased by Easton, and Hoyt remained in his previous capacities.

ALWAYS ACTIVE

Besides devoting over forty years to developing and innovating archery equipment, Hoyt has been instrumental in establishing standards within the industry. He has been actively involved with the Archery Manufacturers Organization (AMO), serving one term as president, and remains on their board of governors. He was chairman of their standards committee for many years, implementing ninety-five percent of today's AMO archery equipment standards.

Hoyt's enduring romance with archery helps keep him spry and sharp. At seventy-six, his clear blue eyes and quick gestures seem like they belong to a much younger man. Only his snow-white hair hints of his age. "I believe that keeping active is very important to staying young, as is having a real interest in something. And there is never a dull moment here, believe me. There is always some problem cropping up. For instance, I was up until two o'clock this morning working on a change in the setup on our new line."

Working with bows well into the night would be enough archery involvement for most. But not Hoyt. Many evenings after work, he walks next door to his house and gets out his recurve and arrows. There in his back yard range, Hoyt and his wife, Ann, practice before dinner. In their relaxed almost effortless form, they consistently plunk arrows into the gold at seventy meters, proving that archery is truly the sport of a lifetime.

When releasing his well-aimed arrows, Hoyt reveals the polished and consistent form that helped him capture many local, regional, and state championships during the forties, fifties, and sixties. "I used to shoot very well. But today I don't have that fine edge. As you get older, you lose much of the coordination you had when you were younger. But the encouraging thing is that the best shooting of my career I did when I was fifty-eight and fifty-nine years old. I tell a lot of shooters this for encouragement. But when you reach my age, you can forget about being in the top echelon. After all, you've had your day. But I still enjoy shooting."

Over the years in the competitive circuit, Hoyt shared the shooting line with some of the finest archers in the world, so he knows what it takes to become a world-class shooter. "The most important thing for shooting well in competition is to be accomplished enough in your shooting to have confidence in your ability. This can only come through a lot of practice, developing your skills and technique so that they're consistent. Once you have good technique in executing the shot and become proficient in your ability to shoot well, you will gain a positive mental attitude that will do more for you than any other one thing. I don't know of any archer who has won a championship who hasn't been very confident in his ability to perform, and had the will to win."

Besides putting trophies on the walls and his name in the records, Hoyt's lifelong involvement with competitive archery has also helped him in developing world-class target bows. "I've

A LIFETIME BEHIND THE BOW — A premier archery innovator, Hoyt displays the form that has also made him a premier shooter for almost half a century.

always considered that my close attachment to the shooting end of the sport was one of my greatest assets in the research and development of fine shooting equipment."

ICING ON HIS CAKE

Throughout his career, Hoyt has found time away from archery competition and the demands of running a bowmaking business to help pump lifeblood back into the sport that has given him so much. He has remained actively involved in the promotion and organization of target and field archery.

Because of this involvement, he has been honored with many prestigious awards. One of the greatest was his induction into the Archery Hall of Fame. During the Hall of Fame banquet, he received the Maurice Thompson Medal of Honor as well, the highest award bestowed by the National Archery Association for contributions to archery. "To say that I am grateful for the friends, experiences, and honors that have fallen my way is an understatement. I am both humble and appreciative for all the sport has given me, especially when your vocation is your avocation. And particularly when it has brought to me my lovely wife, Ann."

In 1971, archery legend Earl Hoyt, Jr., married another archery legend, Ann Weber. She is past World Champion, six time National Champion, and National Field Barebow Champion. Plus, she is the only archer to win both the target and the barebow titles. Ann also belonged to the first group inducted into Archery's Hall of Fame in 1972. Today, she and Earl are the only husband-and-wife team in the Hall. "Ann has a distinction that no other man or woman has ever equaled. She is probably the greatest archer of all time because she was on top of the heap for twenty years. There has never been an archer on top for twenty years. Ten years is usually about the limit."

RABBITS TO DEER

Although he admittedly has spent much of his archery career facing paper bull's eyes, underneath Hoyt's peaceful exterior lurks an avid bowhunter. He has taken whitetails, mule deer, javelina, fox, and assorted small game.

His first bow trophy was a weasel. Soon after that, he began arrowing Missouri rabbits, one of his all-time favorite bowhunting pursuits. Hoyt's bowhunting challenges continued to grow and he later graduated into the ranks of deer hunters, using a homemade bow and a little beginner's luck along the way. "We all know about beginner's luck. I think beginners have that little something that gives them an edge — it's probably enthusiasm or alertness. I know it certainly applied in my case.

"We were on a hunting trip up in northern Wisconsin in Vilas County. There were a lot of deer up there in 1958, and we did a lot of deer driving which was quite successful. I found that in the northern states, deer driving is more successful than it is here in Missouri.

"We put on a drive one morning. There was a light snow on the ground, and I was at the end of the line where the guide told me I probably wouldn't have any deer come through. But he said, 'Just in case they go right on down the line of standers, you'll be here right on the spot.' I heard the drive progressing but nothing was happening.

"Then all of a sudden I heard a noise. I looked up and here were three deer coming almost directly at me on a dead run. Well, I picked the one in the lead and swung with it and hit that deer right in the neck. It almost took on the position of a toboggan. Its legs folded under it, its neck and chin stuck out, and it just slid through the snow, with the snow spraying on both sides. I was so shocked I couldn't imagine that I had actually hit this deer, because the action was so fast. It ended up within ten feet of me, and when it finally came to rest it took one long gasping breath and it was all over. I had actually severed the spinal cord. It was a quick one."

Even though it seemed like a quirk, Hoyt used his beginner's luck running spine shot two years later in Michigan to down his second deer. Over the years he has continued to be successful on his running deer shots. Nearly one-third of his deer have been taken on the flying hoof. His most recent, taken in 1986, was a bounding Missouri deer shot through the chest at thirty-five yards.

To make his running shots count, Hoyt usually uses a Black Diamond broadhead on the deadly end of his hunting arrows. He file sharpens them with a smooth mill file, stroking in the same line as the cutting edge. "There are two schools of thought on sharpening and both will argue vehemently as to which is best. I've always felt that the file was sufficient in that it leaves very minute serrations which have excellent cutting qualities. It's the same sharpening system that Fred Bear used, and he scored on as much big game as anybody, maybe more.

"The razor-edged broadhead is excellent, there is no question about it. The only question I have is, is it necessary to have that keen of an edge when a file-edge does just as well? I never lacked penetration with file sharpened heads and always had excellent blood trails. With a file I can sharpen a broadhead in less than thirty seconds. It takes considerably longer to replace a replaceable head after a shot. A broadhead choice is, of course, a personal one. All are adequate when sharp."

Blood trails and hanging venison are exciting parts of bowhunting, but Hoyt savors the fellowship and harmony with nature that the sport provides. "The camaraderie of bowhunting is certainly one of the greatest rewards for the hunter.

"I was talking with Fred Bear one time, and he told me that his great ambition was to go for trophy animals, whatever they might be. I have never had that desire. I love to hunt, but to get a trophy animal has not been an overriding desire of mine. We would all like to take trophy animals, and I certainly wouldn't turn down the opportunity to shoot one. I've had opportunities at some, but I've had bad luck with all of them. One of the biggest bucks I have ever seen was here in Missouri. That animal would have made the book. I hit it in the heavy part of the shoulder blade and later found my arrow a mile away. I recognized right away that there was very little penetration, less than half the depth of the broadhead. I have also had arrows deflect off brush or branches causing me to miss trophies."

At one time collecting African trophies was also part of Hoyt's bowhunting dreams. "But at seventy-six, I don't have that desire any more. You lose some of the enthusiasm for the chase as years go by. In fact, your whole concept of hunting changes. Today, getting the game isn't the all-important thing. It's the enjoyment of being out there hunting that's most important. I've passed up opportunities on deer simply because I didn't want that deer at the time. I let them go by because I enjoy the chase and being out in the open with wildlife."

WHISPERS FROM THE PAST

Reminding him of past chases afield, a historic collection of bows adorn Hoyt's office walls. Only some whisper of past hunts, but all have played a role in the evolution of Hoyt bows. Picking up an amber toned flatbow, Hoyt

A KNUCKLE SHELF AND OSAGE TOUGH — Before the days of working recurves, Hoyt manufactured self-wood bows with static recurves.

seemed to momentarily drift back in time. "I was a little partial to osage, particularly for a hunting bow because it's a tough wood. Yew makes a sweeter shooting bow and is better suited for target shooting. But I had a fondness for the osage simply because it's native to Missouri and it did make a good, tough hunting bow.

"It was also right at hand. However, it isn't just a matter of going out and finding an osage tree and cutting it down and making a bow out of it. You might go down a mile of hedge and not find one tree that is uniform enough and straight enough to make a bow. Because osage grows rather gnarled and crooked we seldom made bows out of a full length stave. We fishtail spliced billets together. That way we got more of the same character of wood in both limbs because the billets laid side by side in the log."

Another of his self-wood osage flatbows is backed with clarified calfskin but lacks an arrow shelf. Although this design seems odd by today's standards, years ago an archer's knuckle served as the arrow rest. Shooting off the knuckle was delicate business and required extra care when trimming the fore end of the feathers so they wouldn't dig into the flesh. Hoyt proudly displays his scarred knuckle, attesting to the years he used it as an arrow rest.

During those early self-wood bow years, Hoyt used the pure instinctive shooting method common at that time. "There was no string walking, or gap shooting, and there were no sights — it was an off-handed manner of shooting. And I still hunt that way. I can pick out random shots and feel the trajectory. It's something that you develop and almost anybody can do it if they diligently apply themselves. It's the subconscious act of aiming where you learn to feel it. You subconsciously visualize the trajectory of the arrow in flight. It's a very fascinating and rewarding way to learn to shoot."

Near the osage flatbow, Hoyt selects an old static recurve from the rack and runs his hands along the limbs. "I went from the cam or non-working static recurve to the working recurve which is smoother shooting and more efficient. It's a more recent innovation historically. The first working recurves came out in the late thirties. Bill Folberth was the first one I saw make a working recurve bow. He was an ardent archer and innovator, and probably innovated the working recurve."

The static recurve rests next to pre-fiberglass bows faced and backed with different materials. "We sort of tinkered around with all kinds of materials trying to find one that would work best under bow compressional and tensional stresses."

EVOLUTION OF HOYT BOWS

Hoyt's bow collection not only calls up nostalgic moments in archery, it also represent his many innovations in bowmaking. For example, in 1947, Hoyt developed the first step toward dynamic limb balance with equal length bow limbs. Before this, the lower limb was shorter. He also began using plastics in bow production. In 1948, he introduced a modified overdraw and semi-pistol grip on one of his bows.

During 1951, he incorporated the deflex-reflex limb design principle into his bow production. This was the first radical change from traditional limb design and is now used in all top-line recurves. "Deflexing and reflexing made a superior bow. The deflexing improved the stability of he bow and the reflexing picked up the performance. Reflexing put the stress back into the limb that was taken away by deflexing.

"I made forty experimental limbs in 1951. They were all a little different. Our basic limb today is what emerged from all of the experimenting I did then. It's a very efficient limb. I have never been able to improve upon it. It has been the most copied limb on the market."

In 1956, Hoyt introduced his true pistol grip and dynamically balanced limbs on the Pro Olympian. Both of these patented innovations were soon established as standards within the industry. "This bow was the very first bow that had a pistol grip, but it was a modified pistol grip. All bows up to this time had just vertical, broomstick type handles. But I concluded that since the hand lays in a natural sloping position, the grip should accommodate that condition. The grip wasn't extreme at first because when I introduced the concept people thought it was radical. Later, on the Pro Custom series, we made a truer pistol grip."

During the sixties Hoyt introduced the torque stabilizer, torque flight compensator, and the first adjustable arrow rest. He started stabilizing bows by drilling holes in the riser and pouring lead into them, then covering the lead-filled holes with wood and glass laminations. "I realized I was missing the boat by putting the weight in the handle. I knew if we had an extended weight it would be more effective. An example I've used in explaining the stabilizing principle is to take a broom by the end of the handle and note the resistance to movement in all directions. You can't move it very fast. But if you grab it at the middle of the handle you will be surprised how much less movement is resisted. That's the principal of the stabilizer, a simple application of physics that inhibits movement."

Hoyt first introduced his extended bow stabilizer in Hot Springs, Arkansas at the National Field Archery Association Championships in 1961. "Lon Stanton, a Missourian, shot that new bow and set records with it. He was in the barebow division, and back in those days the barebow champion was considered the true champion. Soon everybody was buzzing about the new Hoyt bow with the 'doorknobs' or 'horns' on it. And that's how the stabilizer took off. One bow at one tournament."

It was also during the sixties that Hoyt used a combination of exotic hardwoods and resin composites in the handles of his classic recurves. But over the years, exotic woods became more expensive and decreased in quality, and resin composites became cost-prohibitive. Eventually, Hoyt changed to resin impregnated maple for riser material because it was attractive, strong, affordable, and dense. But during the early 70's, metal bow handles became popular and around 1973 Hoyt stopped making impregnated maple risers. They began using magnesium sand cast risers in 1971, and changed to die cast handles several years later.

ON THE WINNING EDGE

In 1972, Hoyt introduced a new three-piece take-down recurve known as the Pro Medalist. Only two of these bows were shot in the reintroduced archery Olympics that year, and each captured a gold medal; one in the men's, and one in the women's division. Since then, Hoyt recurves have won more Olympic, World, and National Championships than all other bows combined.

Even though his innovations have helped write archery record books around the world for decades, Hoyt continues to explore new horizons in archery technology. Recently, he introduced the new syntactic foam limb core that promises to revolutionize bow limb construction. "When we first started using fiberglass, I found that the so-called bow wood cores of yew or osage didn't really add anything because they were sandwiched in between a higher modulus material. This material, fiberglass, was really doing the work, furnishing the energy to propel the arrow. Because of this, the core only becomes a glue base and a spacer. It really doesn't enter into the dynamic physical properties of the bow to a great extent beyond the sheer load imposed on it.

"Now we have a breakthrough in core material. It's a plastic with a specific gravity lighter than maple, comprised of hollow glass spheres averaging about sixty microns in diameter. The material has a high sheer loading strength. It has all the physical properties you would want, and it's completely impervious to moisture and unaffected by heat and cold. We have all of this wrapped up in our new patented syntactic foam core. We think it has the possibility of being the 'corewood' of the ages."

HOYT TRADITIONAL BOWS

Many of Hoyt's advancements in archery equipment benefit competitive shooters in World and National competitions. But he also incorporates his bowmaking savvy and design into his hunting recurves. His most popular recurve is the three-piece take-down RAM REFLEX HUNTER. This 62" recurve has a mass weight of 2 pounds 12 ounces and has a recommended brace height of 8 1/4" from the string to the throat.

Its slim-throated deflexed magnesium riser is 20 3/4" long and is painted with a three-tone camo maple leaf pattern. It is 2" wide at each end and narrows to 9/16" through the sight window. It is 2 1/2" tick and thins to 1 5/8" through the throat. Its sight window is cut 5/16" past center shot and is equipped with a Hoyt Hunter rest. The slim-lined grip contours into the simple geometric lines of the rest of the riser. It is tapped for a cushion plunger, sight, and stabilizer.

The bow's take-down limbs attach with a single hex flathead screw. Each limb is slotted at the butt end to fit over a small alignment boss in the handle and further aligned by a limb guide pin bushing engaging a slot at the end of the handle pocket.

These limbs are constructed with one back and one belly lamination of tapered maple corewood enveloped in black fiberglass. The limb fadeout riser wedge is a cloth-based phenolic material. The limbs exhibit a moderate recurve and have a 17 1/2" working length from the fadeout to the nock. They taper in width from 1 5/8" at the fadeout to 3/4" at the nock which is cut flush

THE HUNTER IN A PROUD FAMILY — Hoyt's Ram Reflex Hunter has some of the same features that help win gold around the world.

on the sides. Like the handle, the limbs are painted in a non-reflective camouflage leaf pattern.

The smoothness of Ram Reflex Hunter is indicated in the following draw/force measurements:

DRAW LENGTH	25"	26"	27"	28"	29"
DRAW WEIGHT	44¾#	47¼#	49¾#	52¾#	55½#

This bow was shot through a chronograph using Hoyt's shooting machine. The 29½", 2016 field pointed test arrow weighed 485 grains, had a snap-on nock, and three 5" feathers. It was drawn 28" and shot an average speed of 183 fps.

For the traditional bowhunter, Hoyt also offers the Huntmaster, a three-piece take-down with a laminated hardwood riser. And for the sophisticated target archer, Hoyt has the International Competition Series. These World class competition recurves have a host of technologically advanced design features. The Gold Medalist TD offers Hoyt's new Carbon Plus Syntactic Foam Limbs. These limbs boast unsurpassed stability, less susceptibility to temperature or moisture changes, and a higher storage of energy. Although these limbs are not yet available in Hoyt's hunting bows, he believes they soon will be.

DESIGN TIPS FROM THE MASTER

Whether building hard-hitting hunting recurves or gold capturing target bows, Hoyt knows what it takes to make a quality bow. He judges a bow by five main criteria. "The first is stability, which usually is synonymous with accuracy. If you have a bow that's critical to shoot, sensitive, and unforgiving, those aren't desirable traits for accuracy. So stability is foremost.

"The second criteria is speed. If you can tie in a fairly good velocity with a good stable bow, that's a desirable combination. Third, a bow should shoot smoothly without kick or jar and feel comfortable in the hand. A fourth criteria is a smooth drawing, non-stacking bow."

Hoyt learned from his early self-wood bow days that a good bow is one that lasts. "The fifth criteria is longevity. It's an important part of a bow's qualities because if it's not dependable, if it's only going to last six months or a year and then break, then it isn't what an archer wants. Certainly the manufacturer doesn't want it either. But not all manufacturers have been successful on this score. There is a possible sixth criteria which I have added more recently because of bowhunting, and that's noise. Bowhunters naturally want a bow that's quiet to minimize spooking game. All these criteria apply to both recurves and compounds."

Blending these optimum qualities into a bow is not an easy task because some qualities actually work against one another. Thoughtful bow design involves priorities and trade-offs. "Some manufacturers place different degrees of emphasis on the criteria. Many lean strongly toward velocity and sacrifice stability. In so doing, they may sacrifice longevity as well, because they build in high stress for added performance. It depends upon what degree of importance is placed on each of these criteria. In my opinion, the best is a bow that has a well balanced blend of all of these factors, with the greatest emphasis on stability.

"Stability can be affected by a recurve that's too large, a recurve that's not lined up well, and a recurve that's too narrow. Deflex designing with a forward thrust handle is one of the big factors in stabilizing a recurve bow, or a compound for that matter. If you don't put a forward thrust into the handle, you are going to increase the sensitivity of positioning your bow hand on the grip because of less torque resistance."

GLASS TOO

Recurve performance is not only affected by the limb design, but also by the components that go into it. Fiberglass is the limb component that stores the energy and provides the thrust. It's a critical component, and even its color can make a difference in performance. "We've learned that grey is one of the worst pigments that can be put in fiberglass. It adversely affects the resin or matrix that bonds the glass together. White would probably be next because it takes a lot of pigment to make it white. But on the other hand, white is desirable in a tournament bow because it keeps the limbs cooler.

"If you take a black limbed bow out in the sun, particularly in the middle of the summer when the temperatures can range way up there, you can easily reach 110 degrees of internal limb temperature. And sometimes when using black limbs, the excessive heat can cause the recurve to go out of alignment and then you have a problem. But white limbs reflect the sun and keep the temperature down. We learned years ago in tournament archery that when we used white glass we had less trouble with the recurves going out of line.

"On the other hand, black is a good pigment because it doesn't take much to make the fiberglass black. Clear, of course, means there is no pigment at all, and therefore it probably makes the best limb. But we're talking about a very small degree of difference with different glass colors. It might add up to one or two feet per second of improved performance with clear glass over pigmented glass. That's comparatively speaking and only if the glass has the same glass-to-resin ratio. If you have glass made with a higher glass content, it's going to have a higher modulus, and subsequently a better performance than glass that has a lower ratio of glass to resin. But, as in all things, there are practical limits to these ratios."

EVEN STRINGS

Bow performance is affected, not only by limb design and limb components, but even the bowstring can significantly change how a bow shoots; especially the new generation of strings. "We beefed up the limbs to give more strength in the tip section. With the Kevlar and Fast Flight material, we now have a great amount of shock on the bow tips. When we first started using Kevlar, we were making bow tips that had adequate strength for standard Dacron strings, but the Kevlar was breaking the tips off. The tips weren't beefed up enough because Kevlar doesn't have the yield or cushioning qualities of Dacron. So it's tougher on equipment. But today we build a bow to handle both Kevlar and the Fast Flight.

"In spite of what you might hear, I've found that Fast Flight will only shoot one to two feet per second faster than Kevlar. But the real plus with Fast Flight is its longevity. A Fast Flight string can last for thousands of shots where Kevlar was very limited in the number of shots it could take, usually under a thousand. But Kevlar gave us a six to eight feet per second higher velocity than Dacron. That's the equivalent of four to five pounds of bow weight when using Fast Flight, which is substantial. That's the single greatest breakthrough we've had in bowstrings, especially for recurves."

Hoyt points out that string variables affecting arrow speed go beyond the string material. Even the string's brace height is important. "Each half-inch change in brace height will change the velocity by about two and a half feet per second due to the change in the energy stored and the distance of string travel. And, for each half-inch change in the draw length, the velocity will change approximately four and a half feet per second. Also, each one pound change in bow weight is equivalent to about two feet per second in velocity.

"Analyzing briefly, a half-inch draw length change will effect bow weight by about one pound which approximates two feet per second. And, it changes energy storage and arrow acceleration distance by approximately another two and a half feet per second, totaling four and a half feet per second. These are ball-park figures but are reasonably close for most bows, especially recurves. Hypothetically, should an archer desire to increase his bow performance, he could increase bow weight one pound, draw length one half inch, and decrease brace height one half inch for a total gain in arrow velocity of nine feet per second. This assumes that such changes would be compatible — that the archer could accommodate the longer draw and heavier weight and that the arrow spine would be sufficient to accept these changes."

QUALITY STOCK FOR QUALITY LIMBS

To get the most velocity, stability, and longevity in his limbs, Hoyt is selective about limb composites. Top quality limbs deserve top quality components. Hoyt's standard limb core material is laminated maple. He prefers it because it nullifies any undesirable wood grain characteristics that could occur in the varying grain of a solid corewood. He uses matched pairs of corewood on opposing limbs to achieve similar dynamic performance.

Hoyt also uses matched pairs of fiberglass cut from the same piece because the same thickness of fiberglass can vary in its performance qualities from piece to piece due to variations in the modulus of elasticity. Using these fiberglass pairs on opposing limbs ensures similar dynamic performance characteristics in both. Hoyt cautions that although the same thickness of fiberglass in different pieces may have similar static characteristics, their dynamic characteristics can vary. And dynamic limb balance is critical to a bow's performance, especially in a recurve.

In their top of the line bows, Hoyt uses the new Carbon Plus/Syntactic foam as limb core material. Using these new limbs, Hoyt shooters have already registered new world record scores, and Hoyt believes this innovation will revolutionize bow limb construction. But like so many of his break-throughs, it didn't come easily.

The foam is manufactured in large blocks and must be cut and sanded into laminations. One of the early problems was cutting it. Because of its glass micro-sphere construction, it dulled saw blades worse than fiberglass. And fiberglass is notorious for eating up blades. So they tried every type of blade they could find and finally discovered one that would reasonably saw the foam. Using this blade, they now have their foam laminations cut and custom tapered by the Old Master Crafters.

Developing the unique limb-quality foam was a challenge complicated by trapped air bubbles. "The early stuff we were getting was just terrible. It looked like Swiss cheese. We were scrapping more than we were using. But little by little we worked that problem out. It was just a matter of technology and playing around with it."

PUTTING IT TOGETHER

To make world class limbs from quality core materials and matched fiberglass, you need world class limb presses. "We have the finest bow limb presses in the industry, no holds barred. They are beautifully controlled for temperature and uniform pressure. Everything is automated except loading them and unloading them. You hit one valve and the press takes over."

Hoyt's heavy-duty press is housed in an "I" beam frame to ensure straightness. The upper half opens and closes by a hydraulic piston and both halves are kept in perfect alignment by torsion bars with racks and pinions

DOUBLE DUTY — Hoyt's industrial presses are used to laminate two pairs of limbs at a time, side by side.

on the ends of the press. It's a wider-than-normal mold that presses two pairs of limbs at the same time.

Before laying up the composite laminations, the mold is brushed with a coat of protective wax to prevent squeezed out glue from sticking. Then all contact surfaces of the laminations are given a coat of a special bow epoxy formulated to match Hoyt's curing temperature and time. To reinforce the outer limb, Hoyt incorporates a woven nylon material into the last six inches of the limb tip. This scrim cloth is glued between the fiberglass and core to strengthen the tips for using Fast Flight strings.

Once the laminations are in place, the press is hydraulically closed, mechanically locked, and the air hose lining the upper half of the form is inflated to eighty-five pounds. Electric heat strips lining both the male and female molds reach 177 degrees, curing the glue in about thirty minutes. This temperature is electronically controlled by a probe located between the heat strips. "Our precise methods and meticulous care in laminating have given us a reputation for trouble-free, non-delaminating limbs. Remember, longevity is one of the important criteria by which a bow is judged."

Once the limbs are removed from the press, the rough glue is ground off their edges and they are machined on the butt ends to attach to the handle section. They are also ground to near finished dimensions using a limb shaping jig, and a jig-mounted high-speed pneumatic cutter grinds shallow string nocks into the tips.

STRAIGHT MAGNESIUM HANDLES

The finest limbs in the world won't perform to their potential if they're installed on a handle with the ends out of alignment. As a further example

HIGH-TECH TECHNIQUES — Hoyt's handle drilling and tapping machines resemble gear from a science fiction space thriller.

of Hoyt perfectionism, each die cast magnesium handle, as it is received from the diecaster, is checked for alignment. Although the castings come from a perfect mold, sometimes the molten metal does not easily release from the mold and must be forced out. When this happens, the hot casting can be distorted so each one needs to be checked for precision alignment.

Hoyt's handle alignment checking fixture is an intricate device that checks the handle for alignment and permits any necessary straightening. This ensures perfect limb line-up in the handle from end to end. This is critically important in recurves because even one-tenth of a degree of mis-alignment can throw the limbs out of alignment considerably at the tips.

After aligning, the handles undergo secondary tooling for the accessory mounting holes, the stabilizer hole, and the limb adjusting holes for the bushings and the limb adjustment system. This is performed in an intricate drilling and tapping machine that looks like it came from a Star Wars studio.

STRAIGHT LIMBS

Once the limbs are installed on a handle, they are braced using a steel cable string. Then the recurves are brought into proper alignment by grinding a little material off the last four inches of limb edges. This delicate hand and eye operation is repeated several times until the string tracks perfectly down the center of both recurves.

The string grooves are then ground into the belly recurve glass using a small pneumatic grinding wheel mounted on a centering alignment jig. Although the glass is tough, the same abrasive wheel has been cutting Hoyt's

TWO DECADES TOUGH — The same jig-mounted grinding wheel has cut thousands of Hoyt string grooves over the past twenty years.

string grooves for over twenty years. It whines away at 10,000 rpm while etching the string groove.

Tough phenolic tip overlays that can withstand the harsher Fast Flight strings are epoxied on then heat cured with a device that only warms the tips. The tip overlays and string nocks are dressed up by hand, and the entire limb is finish sanded.

The limbs are then hung in Hoyt's spray booth. This spraying chamber is air pressurized to prevent dust from entering. Their target limbs are first sprayed with three coats of finish and dried at 110 degrees in a drying oven for one day. They are sanded smooth and the Hoyt logo is silk-screened on the belly. They receive three more finish coats which are again heat cured and finally buffed to a high luster.

STAYING TOPS

At Hoyt/U.S.A., detailed records that resemble a family tree catalog each pair of limbs. They record every major step in limb manufacturing so they can retrace and isolate any future problem that may arise. This even includes recording the exact press that a pair of limbs was glued in.

Hoyt's production line limbs are the same ones used to win Olympic, World, and National championships. The only thing special about the limbs that win gold is the shooter behind them, because world class Hoyt quality is built into them all.

Why do so many champion archers shoot Hoyt bows? "Because they have been the most successful. We have always had a little more to offer. For instance, on the newer recurve line we have adjustable limbs, which an archer can use in several ways.

"You can tune your bow to match your arrow spine. If your arrows are flying a little stiff, you can jack up the bow weight a bit, a pound or two, and suddenly those arrows are coming out like little darts. It's simply because you tuned the bow to better match the spine of your arrow.

"Then if you go out in the spring of the year and you haven't been shooting very much, you can crank it down and have less weight. As you feel a little stronger, you can crank it up again and change the deflex angle of the limbs. Furthermore, we have developed a reputation over the years for being innovative, having good quality, and having winners."

Besides providing adjustable poundage, some of Hoyt's bows can even be adjusted for tiller. Most bowyers believe a specific limb tiller is crucial to a bow's performance. But not Hoyt. "We like to keep the lower limb just a little stiffer than the upper limb; a one-eighth inch to three-eighths inch positive tiller is fine. But it has nothing to do with the way the bow will perform. You can even reverse tiller and still group well."

His comments about limb tiller raised a few eyebrows and were seriously questioned by one of the world's top shooters, Rick McKinney. So Hoyt suggested that Rick play around with some different tiller adjustments and see what happened. Hoyt knew that Rick's pin-point accuracy would help prove his point. A bit skeptical, Rick even reversed the limb tiller and was surprised at the results. "Rick said,'You know, Earl, I couldn't believe it, but you were 100 percent right. I went as much as three-eighths inch reverse tiller, and I still shot groups just as good as I have ever shot before.' " The only difference Rick noticed was how the bow felt in the hand because the minor stiffness differences in the limbs had been reversed. "However, be this as it may, there is good reason to have the lower limb stiffer than the upper — to withstand the greater pressure imposed on it and thus prevent limb fatigue and let-down under adverse conditions of heat and humidity." But Hoyt cautions that tiller variations will have greater effects on a compound bow.

Even though most of Hoyt's greatest achievements were associated with recurves, such as his adjustable limbs, many of his innovations have applications to the compound bow. Now the company's most popular product, Hoyt once refused to produce it. "I had prejudices a number of years ago about compounds. So did all the old first line companies. Bear, Pearson, and others turned their backs on the compound. They didn't think it was here to stay or even that it was a bow. We were just prejudiced or lacked vision.

"You have to give Jennings credit. He put the compound on the market. It was developed right here in Missouri by Allen. I looked at that contraption, and they were ugly monsters then, and I thought, 'I wouldn't be caught dead with something like this much less produce it.' So I politely told him we didn't have the capacity to produce it. But then Jennings took it over and decided it had merit. He did a lot of development with it, and it started to flourish. Even then it took a while before any of us really accepted it. Well, there is no question about it now. The compound is here to stay."

BOTH BOWS — BOTH HANDS

Unlike some of the early greats in American archery, Hoyt's more deliberate style of shooting allowed him to make an easy transition to shooting a compound. Although he shoots the recurve for competitive shooting to conform with international and Olympic standards, his preference for hunting has become the compound. Over the years Hoyt learned to master the bow with both hands, and today he shoots target with sights left handed, and bowhunts instinctively right handed.

Whether it be competitive archery with recurves or hunting Missouri bucks with a compound, Hoyt shows great enthusiasm for all facets of archery — all facets except the crossbow. "Some years ago we made up a crossbow in the shop. I don't think I shot more than two dozen arrows from it and set it aside. To me the crossbow is not exciting to shoot. It never becomes an intimate part of you. You are not putting yourself into it. It's more akin to shooting a gun than shooting a bow. As a preference, I would rather shoot a gun because it has a report, a recoil, and a flat trajectory.

"To me a crossbow, although historically equal, does not have the romance of the longbow. I realize this statement is open to challenge. But I do not think the crossbow will ever become a popular weapon. Its discipline does not hold the same challenge as the hand-held, hand-draw, and hand-released bow. There is, to be sure, a hard core of crossbow enthusiasts who sincerely and understandably desire to promote their sport. I take no issue with that, and I wish them the very best."

JUST HOMEMADE STUFF

Excluding the crossbow, archery today encompasses a variety of hand-held and hand-shot bows. The high-tech crowd seems to gravitate toward the sophistication of the compound. Recurve lovers are drawn to the grace and lines of the bows that inspired a nation of bowhunters. Longbowers hang on to the simplistic yet effective appeal of the composite and self-wood longbows. But in the early years of American archery, there were mainly two types of bows — bows made by someone else and bows you made yourself. And for today's traditional bowyers of America, that's still an important distinction.

"A number of years ago at one of the Nationals a survey asked what type of equipment you used. I was well established then, so I put down, 'homemade'. It went all around the tournament site that Hoyt shoots a homemade bow!"

For some, a homemade bow might not be competitive. But for Earl Hoyt, Jr., a homemade bow means one of the finest bows in the world.

Chapter Fourteen

PEARSON ARCHERY INCORPORATED

WHO WOULD BELIEVE?

The boys huddled near the school bike rack jabbering about the weekend happenings. It was Monday morning, always the best time to talk about TV shows, movies, sports, and once in a while, girls. Each boy seemed to come up with a better story than the one before him. It was nearing class time when finally the boy with the deep brown eyes spoke up. "My dad went hunting with his bow and arrows." He paused, not knowing if he should continue.

"Big deal," groaned one of the other boys, "my Dad hunts too."

"Yeah," said the first boy, "but my Dad flew to Alaska and sneaked up on a giant grizzly bear and killed him with one arrow. And he went hunting near Siberia for polar bear and shot one of the biggest ever with his bow. Now my Dad's flying home and bringing those bears with him."

At first the other boys said nothing. They just looked at him wide-eyed and then at each other. "Go on," one boy said, twisting his face, "you don't expect us to believe that junk. Nobody hunts giant bears with arrows."

The other boys jumped in. "No way!" they said, wagging their faces, "No way with a bow. Bears? You're lying."

The class bell sounded and they broke their huddle, some still mumbling about the far-fetched story. The boy with the brown eyes remained, watching the others file through the doors. He shrugged his shoulders and sighed. They would soon see, he thought. He would bring in his dad's bear pictures, then they would see that Ben Pearson, Jr. wasn't lying.

It was on a spring day in 1965 when young Ben Jr. told his classmates at Sam Taylor elementary school about his dad's archery adventures. Soon after, everyone in town was buzzing about the two incredibly huge bears that Ol' Ben laid low with his bow and arrows.

THE SPARK OF A GIANT

The Pearsons lived in Arkansas where the official state nickname is, "The Land of Opportunity." In the town of Pine Bluff, Ben proved to the archery world that it was more than just a slogan. Because there he turned his dreams and passion for archery into one of the all-time reigning giants in archery manufacturing.

Ben became interested in archery when he was twenty-eight years old. He lived in Little Rock, and worked for Arkansas Power and Light. In 1927, he made his first bows and arrows following the instructions in a Boy Scout Magazine, in an article written by Dan Beard.

Thrilled with his new bows, Ben went to his first archery tournament, in Little Rock. Although he was filled with enthu-

A BEAR TO BELIEVE — The giant polar bear Ben bagged in the spring of 1965 dwarfs the author, left, and Ben Pearson, Jr, right.

siasm, Ben finished that tournament next to last. But he came home determined to do better the next time and began working on new bows for the next year's tournament. His determination paid off. The following year Ben captured first place.

Ben moved to Pine Bluff and continued his bow crafting hobby. In 1931, he left Arkansas Power & Light with hopes of turning his archery interest into a full-time business. During the early 1930s, Ben had a small archery shop in downtown Pine Bluff where he made and sold self-wood bows.

His business took a giant step in 1938, when with some financial backing, Ben incorporated and expanded his archery business. Quality, hickory-footed, cedar target and hunting arrows were a large part of his production during those early years. In 1939, an archer could buy a dozen of Ben's hickory-footed hunting arrows, complete with broadheads, for five dollars and seventy-five cents. One of his top bows that year was an osage longbow that sold for thirty dollars. The fancy one with the recurved ends cost thirty-five dollars.

Ben also produced self-wood bows from lemonwood and hickory, but his best were made from osage. In later years Ben would locate prized stands of osage by flying around the Arkansas countryside spotting the groves from his plane.

Overnight, Ben Pearson became America's archery manufacturing giant. He led the way in archery manufacturing during the early forties when his 600 to 800 employees turned out an astounding 3,000 to 4,000 bows and sets of arrows daily. He remained number one in the market place until the mid-sixties when he sold his interest in the company.

One of the things that helped Pearson Archery reach its prominence was Ben's promotion of archery and bowhunting. He actively promoted the sports by demonstrating archery feats across the country and by hiring some of the most famous names in archery as bowhunting advisors, including the great Howard Hill and international bowhunter Bob Swinehart.

Although Ben had men like Hill and Swinehart to help promote archery and bowhunting, he himself was an extraordinary instinctive shot in the field. Some called him amazing.

ON THE WING OR RUN

Ben was the second man in the state of Arkansas to bow kill a deer when he arrowed an eight-point buck, in 1955, in the White River Bottoms area. There weren't many deer in Arkansas back then so Ben found sport in arrowing ducks on the wing. Most shot-gunners have trouble connecting when pass shooting the fast flying fowl, but Ben enjoyed a respectable success on the high-flying targets. Using his seventy-four pound recurve, and special forked-pointed duck arrows, he neatly plucked winging mallards from the sky.

Ben also liked to pheasant hunt with his recurve. He displayed his skills on these airborne targets in a promotional film where he downed fifty percent of the flushed birds, baffling his shotgun toting film companion. Ben and his take-down Bushmaster recurve proved deadly on the fast rising fowl.

Shooting winging birds helped keep Ben's eye sharp for running game. This master of the moving target even nailed America's fastest speedster, the running pronghorn. But what made Ben's shots so amazing was not only how fast the target was moving, but also how far it was.

He commonly made seventy-five to 100 yard shots on moving targets. Although many archers couldn't hit a stationary animal with a quiver full of arrows at that range, Ben made it look easy with just one shaft. One of his spectacular shots was a deer he arrowed at a measured 104 yards. His longest shot recorded on film was made during a javelina hunt in Arizona. Ben lofted a white crested arrow that disappeared toward a group of feeding pigs. Seconds later a javelina toppled over 120 yards away.

Ben often traveled across the country on his hunting trips and developed an early fascination with the convenience of take-down bows. In 1941 he made his first take-down osage self-wood flatbow. But it wasn't until the fifties that he developed the custom take-down recurve that accompanied him on so many of his hunts. This two-piece Bushmaster locked together at the handle and was easily carried on a plane.

Another of Ben's famous bowhunting companions was developed in 1963 — his devastating Deadhead broadhead. This 1⅜" wide single blade head was Ben's all-time favorite. "Deadhead" was certainly an appropriate name, conveying the head's effectiveness. It literally dropped game in their tracks, including grizzly and cougar.

Ben used the Deadhead on his polar bear hunt. Hunting with guide Ken Oldham, Ben arrowed a 1500 pound white giant about three miles off the Siberian coast on the frozen Chukchi Sea. The first shot hit the moving bear at sixty-five yards, passing through the left leg. As the bear started to run, Ben reached into his back quiver and immediately sent another shaft on its way. His second arrow struck the bear high in the shoulder at eighty-five yards.

During that same trip, Ben flew to the Brooks range in Alaska to hunt for grizzly. After a five hour stalk, wearing snowshoes, Ben moved in on an 800 pound grizzly in a willow thicket. Jack Atkins wore a forty-four magnum revolver strapped to his hip and served as both cameraman and Ben's back-up gun. Ben crept up on the bear with Jack filming over his shoulder.

Ben's first arrow hit brush and the bear looked around in a moment of tension. Ben froze. When the bear turned, Ben aimed through a hole in the tangle of willows and drove a sharp Deadhead through both lungs of the brown giant. The stunned bear started to turn but immediately slumped in the snow. He was dead in seconds. After the ordeal, Jack discovered he had lost his forty-four magnum in the snow. Ben's only backup had been the camera lens.

Although the archery legend Ben Pearson, died in 1971 at the age of seventy-two, many of his telling shots, including his polar bear and grizzly, live on in the video, *Legendary Hunts of Ben Pearson*. During his lifetime, Ben helped put bows and arrows into the hands of a young nation of archers. His innovations in mass archery manufacturing and his bowhunting and archery promotional efforts truly marked him as one of the fathers of American archery.

CARRYING ON TRADITION

Archery manufacturing has changed dramatically since Ben's passing. Even though Pearson Archery manufactures mostly compounds today, they continue to build recurves and longbows. They haven't lost sight of their roots. And according to Tim Strickland, Pearson's Product Manager, they intend to further develop their line of traditional bows.

OL' BEN is Pearson's 70" longbow. It's available in five pound increments from 45 pounds to 70 pounds and has a mass weight of 1 pound, 11 ounces. The recommended brace height is 7⅛" from the string to the throat.

Ol' Ben's one-piece bubinga riser measures 16½" between fadeouts. It is approximately 1⁵⁄₁₆" wide and 2" thick. Its traditional longbow sight window is slightly rounded and is padded with a black, polished leather strike pad. The slightly crowned arrow shelf is 2⅛" above the center of the bow and

THE TRADITION CONTINUES — Pearson's Ol' Ben Longbow (right), Raider 285 (middle), and Legendary Classic (left), offer a variety for the traditionalist.

is covered with synthetic gray fur. The 4 1/4" suede-wrapped grip is prominently peaked on the belly and has distinct squared edges where it meets the backing glass. The one-piece suede wrap is glued on and is overlapped on the front of the grip.

Ol' Ben's slightly backset limbs have a working length of approximately 26 3/4" from the fadeout to the nock. They thin from 1 9/16" wide at the fadeouts, to 1 1/16" at the string nocks. They are constructed from one tapered and one parallel lamination on the back, and one tapered lamination on the belly. These three maple laminations are faced and backed with black fiberglass. The squared edged limbs exhibit a very slight taper narrowing to the belly. There are no tip overlays or limb tip wedges on Ol' Ben. The bow is finished in a high-gloss polyurethane.

To check the relative speed of Ol' Ben, it was shot by Pearson bowyer, Jake Mullikin. The test arrow was a 540 grain 31", 2117 aluminum shaft fletched with three 5" feathers and equipped with a snap-on type nock. The bow was equipped with a Dacron string without accessories. Jake used a shooting tab and drew the arrow 26 1/2". The average arrow speed for this 64 pound at 28" draw bow, arrow, and shooter combination was 160 fps.

The following draw/force measurements were recorded on this Ol' Ben longbow:

DRAW LENGTH	25"	26"	27"	28"	29"
DRAW WEIGHT	54#	57#	61#	64#	67 1/2#

The RAIDER 285 is Pearson's 62" metal handle three-piece take-down recurve. Its mass weight is 3 pounds, 9 ounces and it has a brace height of 7 1/8" from the string to the throat.

Its glossy black magnesium die cast riser is designed to accommodate recurve or compound limbs. The handle is 22" long and 2" to 2 5/8" wide. It is 3/4" thick through the full 6" sight window and has a replaceable black plastic grip. This is the same riser used on some of Pearson's compound bows. It has a space-age design with modern lines. It's tapped for a stabilizer, cushion plunger, and sights, and is coated with a durable epoxy powder-coat finish.

The recurve limbs have a working length of 16" from the fadeout to the string nock and have a 12 degree deflex where they attach to the handle. Pearson notes that the Raider is built for speed with the bowhunter in mind.

Its limbs narrow from 1 7/8" wide at the fadeout to 3/4" at the nock. These limbs are made of a single tapered maple lamination on the back and one on the belly. They are enveloped in black fiberglass. The limb has a 7" long bubinga fadeout wedge and matching tip overlays. Its flush string nocks feather into a "Y" string groove on the belly. They are finished in a high-gloss polyurethane. The limbs attach to the handle with a single hex-headed set screw which tightens on the limb back while two handle alignment pins seat into the belly of the fadeout wedge.

To check the relative speed of this bow, a 66 1/2 pound at 28" draw Raider was chronographed using the same arrow and shooter combination as noted for Ol' Ben. The bow was equipped with a Dacron string without accessories. The average arrow speed was 172 fps.

The following draw/force measurements were recorded on this Raider 285 recurve:

DRAW LENGTH	25"	26"	27"	28"	29"
DRAW WEIGHT	56 1/2#	60#	63#	66 1/2#	71#

The LEGENDARY CLASSIC is Pearson's 60" wooden handle three-piece take-down recurve. It has a mass weight of 2 pounds, 13 ounces and a brace height of 7 3/8" from the string to the throat.

Its striking East Indian rosewood riser is 21" long. It is 1 7/8" wide near the limbs and narrows to 5/8" through the sight window, and is 3 1/8" thick and thins to 1 7/8" through the throat. The sight window is full cut for 4" above the shelf and contours back to full riser width 6" above the shelf. The attractive laminated handle contains a vertical 3/8" thick wedge of black ebonite sandwiched in white fiberglass. The dazzling solid rosewood has contrasting grain patterns which are displayed by the handle's simple sweeping lines and rounded contours. It's equipped with brass sight and cushion plunger bushings.

The flat-edged Legendary Classic limbs are similar in composition to the Raider limbs except for the matching rosewood fadeout wedge and tip overlays, and their more subdued recurve. They attach to the handle like the Raider but have an approximate 25 degree deflex at the riser-limb contact.

This bow was checked for relative speed by shooting the noted 540 grain 2117 test arrow. The shooter, draw length, string, and arrow combination was the same as noted for Ol' Ben and the Raider. The average arrow speed for this 59 pound at 28" draw Legendary Classic was 180 fps.

The following draw/force measurements were recorded on this Legendary Classic:

DRAW LENGTH	25"	26"	27"	28"	29"
DRAW WEIGHT	50#	53#	56#	59#	63#

BOW SPEC UPDATE

Since the summer of 1987, Pearson Archery Incorporated has made some changes in their traditional line.

The Ol' Ben longbow is now offered in 66" and 68" lengths, has Micarta tip overlays, and is finished in a satin polyurethane.

Their metal handle take-down recurve is now called the Legendary Hunter 286 and is 60" long. It now has a black satin finish on the 20" long slimmer-lined and lighter-weight handle.

The Legendary Classic is now called The Traditionalist and has a solid shedua handle. Like the Legendary Hunter, its limbs contain a layer of cross-weave bias material and are finished in a non-glare satin finish.

MANUFACTURING TRADITION

Today, Pearson's traditional bows are manufactured in their steel-wall facilities near the original Ben Pearson plant. Their bows are pressed in automated bow presses similar to those of long-time companies such as Bear and Hoyt. An inflatable fire hose in the upper half of the press is used to squeeze the limb composites together. Pearson's forms are made from laminated maple and are lined with metal heating strips.

Their epoxy is mixed two parts resin to one part hardener, using an automatic crank-operated glue dispenser. Twenty-five minutes after mixing, the epoxy starts to cure and even begins generating its own heat.

Pearson's TD limbs are glued up in a form which resembles a very short bow. The limbs are made from one continuous piece of fiberglass backing and individual pieces of glass on the upper and lower limb facing. The composites are squeezed together with eighty pounds of air hose pressure and the epoxy is cured with the electric heat strips at 180 degrees for forty-five minutes.

After the limbs are glued up as one unit, they are cut in half with a radial saw. The wood tip overlays are glued on using a small heated clamping press that only heats the tips. The limbs are then shaped on vertical grinders using detailed jigs with an air lock system that holds them in place.

The limb fadeout wedge alignment holes are drilled using an air lock jig which holds the limb precisely while dual pneumatic drills make both holes at once. String nocks are filed in the tips and the limbs are then installed on a handle. The assembled bow is then braced for alignment and tillering.

Jim Kimbrell, long-time Pearson bowyer, brings the limbs into alignment. Because of their more pronounced recurve, it usually takes four grindings to remove material off the limb sides near the tips to bring a pair of Raider limbs into alignment. The less recurved Legendary Classic limbs usually require only two grindings to bring them into alignment. When checking for proper string tracking, Jim looks for both static and dynamic alignment. The bows are then tillered to a ⅛" to ¼" positive tiller in the upper limb.

After tillering, the limbs are finish sanded and sprayed with a high-gloss polyurethane finish. Raider 285 limbs are sprayed with one primer coat that is sanded smooth, followed by two finish coats. The Legendary Classic rosewood and ebonite handle receives eight coats, with sanding between each coat, followed by two finish coats. The Legendary Classic limbs receive four coats, are sanded between coats, and are then sprayed with one finish coat. Ol' Ben is sprayed with three coats that are sanded and is then given one final coat.

OLD BEHIND THE NEW

Tucked away behind the modern plant where today's bows are manufactured is the ghostly and gutted original Ben Pearson plant. Its weathered brick walls still banner a faded but proud building-length sign, partially covered by clinging ivy. Vines creep through broken windows into the littered shell of the old plant where antiquated machines, now draped in spider webs and frosted with dust, whisper of the heydays of hickory, lemonwood, and goldeny osage.

Old-time bowyer Jake Mullikin, who works in Pearson's R & D shop and started with the company in 1952, remembers those days. "When I first started to work here we were only making hickory all-wood bows. On some of the older recurves we used a vat to boil the ends in and then clamped them into a recurve. Later on, we made some that we would slot in the limb end and glue a

TWO PEARSON CLASSICS — long-time recurve bowyer Jake Mullikin and his favorite recurve, the Palomino.

wedge in, then we recurved them on a machine."

Over the years, Jake helped build Pearson's classic recurves. Many were stunning, but Jake's favorite remains the old Palomino. "It was made out of laminated walnut and white holly. It was a real classic and had a good design. It was one of the best shooting recurves we ever put on the market, and we made it for several years. It had an ornately crafted and laminated riser with distinctive peaks on the back."

In the days of the Palomino, Pearson used solid, one-piece tapered corewoods. But in 1982 they switched to the more popular laminated core-wood material. Today it's bought in large laminated blocks then band sawn in Pearson's plant into strips which are then ground on a sander using a tapered board.

TIPS FROM THE COACH

In front of the bow plant are Pearson's administrative offices. There, Product Manager and National archery coach, Tim Strickland, oversees the development of Pearson's traditional bows. He's a matter-of-fact kind of guy who knows his shooting. In 1984 he won the NFAA Indoor Nationals and the PAA Indoor Nationals. He also accumulated enough points that year to become the top point champion in the nation. In 1985 he came in second in the NFAA behind Eric Hall and then recaptured that indoor title in 1987.

Besides being active in punching the centers from paper targets, Tim uses his polished shooting skills afield in the pursuit of furry targets. He often hunts with a compound but he has shown that he also can bring home the bacon with his recurve. "Nineteen seventy-two was kind of a unique year. People had given me a bad time because that was the first year the com-pound was introduced into state competition, and I was shooting it. I shot in the bowhunter class and set all new Washington state records and sec-tional records in the field round and in the hunter round. Then people started making remarks that without a compound I couldn't hit anything. So I decided I was going to hunt that year with a recurve.

"So that year I shot a fifty-eight pound Gentleman Jim recurve and took five animals with five arrows. First I hunted one of the islands where they opened the season early, and I shot a forky buck. Then Oregon had an early season, and I shot a forky buck there too. I was then lucky enough to draw a goat permit with my first year's application, for which I got a lot of harass-ment. We went in there hunting, and I shot a real nice goat. He was actually looking at me at about twenty-five paces, and I shot right through an opening in some trees. The arrow went right in his front and exited breaking the back leg. Then I took an elk in Washington and an elk in Oregon. So it was a really neat year."

Tim has demonstrated what it takes to arrow big game when you only get one chance and has experienced the pressure of a National first place shoot-off. He's a master behind the bow whose advice helps capture gold. "Probably the simplest thing to good shooting is to be one hundred percent committed to the shot. You live with that shot. In other words, when you start to execute your shot you continue through the execution of that shot. You don't give it a meager try."

CONTRARY SHOOTING

Although Tim believes in being committed to the shot, one shooting method he uses and teaches is not being too committed to holding on the bull's eye. It's a technique contrary to much of what has been taught in archery over the years. "When I shoot, I don't practice by holding on target. I practice my motion, and I know my motion is as small as it's going to be. I'm not going to make it smaller by trying to hold on something. So I actually think about the execution of my shot as a nice fluid motion.

"With a natural motion, you have a better chance of hitting the target center if the aim is off rather than if it's on. Because if the aim is off, it's going to go back to the target center, and if it's on, it's going to move off. You're always seeking center if you're moving. If you're on the center trying to hold, you're not seeking the center. You're forcing it out. But if you just let it move around the center, you actually have a better chance of hitting it."

Tim uses his techniques in coaching some of the nation's top young shooters and has seen this dynamic shooting take over as the new shooting style. "In fact, the elite junior athletes now know a lot more in general about shooting than many of the older athletes in archery. They are starting to realize how to execute a shot — not to stand there and hold on the center, but to let it float and just execute the shot. You shoot an actual dynamic shot instead of a static shot.

"In every other sport we seek dynamic motion. In golf, you wouldn't stop your swing when the club hits the ball. But in archery, that's theoretically what we do. When you decide you are going to shoot the shot, first of all you let go, which is wrong. And you hold your arm stiff. If your draw comes through, you have shot maybe half dynamically. But the front arm is right there. It didn't go anywhere.

"Instead, you should be actually increasing your back tension, relaxing your hand while you're increasing your tension and your bow arm will follow right through. Then and only then, have you executed a dynamic shot. It's contrary to popular belief, but more shooters are now using this technique. When the orientals, with their mind control, got into dynamic shooting, they literally ate our lunch in international competition."

SUBCONSCIOUS RELEASE — SNAP SHOOTING

One shooting problem that affects both competitive shooters and bowhunters alike is the uncontrollable conditioned reflex of releasing the string — commonly known as "snap shooting." It eventually plagues most archers, but Tim knows how to avoid it. "Snap shooting is getting on the target and letting the string go because you can't hold it. You have set up an uncontrollable reflex with your mind. And it's triggering itself off of your gap system or sight system or aiming on the center of something.

"It happens when a person relates to the end result. But they get that end result wrong. The end result should be the actual feeling of the shot, not where the arrow goes. Let's say that you shoot an arrow and it's executed correctly. If it misses the center, you program your mind that the shot was wrong. Pretty soon, your mind doesn't know how to relate. Your mind doesn't want you to get hurt, it doesn't want you to feel pain, and it doesn't want you to fail. Your subconscious tries to guard against that all the time.

"So pretty soon your subconscious says, 'I'm confused here because you shot one arrow that wasn't too good and we hit the target and you said, "Hey that's okay." And then we shot one that was completely garbage and it went in the target and you said, "That's okay." And then we shot one that was executed perfectly but it missed the target and you said, "That was terrible!" Where do we go from here?'

"Then your subconscious says, 'We are going to do one of two things: When you aim on the spot you are going to turn the string loose or we're not going to ever let you aim on the spot. We are going to make it so that when you touch that spot, SNAP, the shot goes off, or we are going to freeze off target and you won't be able to get on target. So then we can't feel bad, because you can't shoot.' "

To conquer snap shooting Tim recommends that a shooter relate to the feeling of the shot for the desired end result. "When the shot is executed right, when you have executed a dynamic shot, when you've relaxed your hand properly with your draw hand behind you near your shoulder and with your bow arm straight ahead, then you've made a proper shot no matter where the arrow goes. Then you can avoid the problem of snap shooting."

Controlling snap shooting is sometimes easier when shooting a compound because of the draw weight let-off. But often it remains a tough battle for traditionalists. "The reason snap shooting was more prevalent in the days of traditional archery is because archers were holding heavyweight bows at full draw. And the mind was saying, 'We're feeling pain because your muscles are hurting. And you're more than likely going to miss because you're trying but you can't hold on the center.'

MOVE, DON'T HOLD

"But now some young stars like Jay Barrs, Denise Parker and others are shooting heavy recurves and getting off three shots in under a minute. That was unheard of. In the old days most target shooters took fifteen to twenty seconds to get one shot off. All of a sudden they are realizing holding on the center is not the thing to do."

Tim learned this principle from pistol shooting and successfully applied it to archery. "I used to pistol shoot at metal silhouettes a lot and much of it was standing off-hand shooting. And shooting a ram silhouette at 200 meters while standing with a two-hand hold on a pistol is not a real easy task. But I shot forties while standing, which not too many people in the United States have done.

"It's impossible to do if you try to hold on the center. You have a natural arc of movement and you simply work with your arc of movement and squeeze the trigger. You just squeeze and aim. And if those sights are in there and you crack it off without moving sideways, it's going to go down. That's all there is to it. You have to use the same basic principle with archery. Let it float and let it move. And when the shot goes off it's going to be there."

His technique almost sounds too simple to be true. But that's its secret; simplicity. "When you try too much you have a greater error factor than when you just let it naturally do what it's going to do. That's why the orientals work with the beginner's mind. They believe that a beginner's mind actually starts off doing something naturally. The more you get away from that natural act, the worse the end result is until you learn to do it properly. So you are going in a circle. And when you do learn to do it properly, you're back to the beginning. Then it's a natural act again.

"It's about half as complicated as we try to make it. People actually over-think the whole process. The most difficult people in archery to teach are those who analyze everything. They absolutely analyze it out of proportion. It's a very simple act, and you just do it naturally."

HOLDING ON TO THE PAST

Being natural is what instinctive traditional shooting is all about. It's one of the simplest forms of archery today. And although simple, Tim sees the trend of archers going back to the basics that Ben demonstrated so successfully. "I believe that the recurve and the traditional system idea are coming back. I thought it would return when I started shooting a compound.

"A lot of people started in archery when compounds were the only bows they knew. They knew traditional archery was there, but they didn't believe there was really anything other than the compound. And now some people are starting to feel that they missed something in archery along the way. It's a part of archery many feel, if experienced, will stay with you forever. The thought basically is that the rewards are much greater when the task is more difficult to accomplish.

"We want Pearson Archery Incorporated to always be a part of traditional archery. That's how we started. Ben Pearson himself was a leading promoter of all forms of archery and his promotion was accomplished with traditional equipment. The bottom line from Pearson Archery Incorporated's point of view is there should always be a significant place for traditional archery equipment."

Ol' Ben probably agrees.

Chapter Fifteen

ARKANSAS STICK

SOUTHERN FLAVOR

The Quapaw Indians called the land Arkansas or "South Wind." Along with neighboring Osage and Caddo tribes, the Quapaws inhabited Arkansas before the arrival of the white man. But before the Quapaws, the land was occupied by the primitive cultures of the Folsom People, The Bluff Dwellers, and the Mound Builders. Evidence of their rugged past is revealed in delicately worked stone artifacts, including fascinating arrow points which capture the interest of archeologists and the imagination of locals like Terry Hughes. In a way, Terry links with Arkansas' forgotten cultures; he too slips through the pine and oak forests pursuing game with an Arkansas Stick.

Terry lives in the small town of Gurdon in southwest Arkansas between Hot Springs National Park and Texarkana. It's a friendly place steeped in southern hospitality and spiced with fried okra, purple-hulled peas, eggs and gravy, corn bread, and cajun catfish. The mainstay of Gurdon's 2700 residents is the local timber industry.

Not far from the towering cabbage-topped pines of Gurdon is prime Arkansas whitetail country. In the fall it's an inviting blend of mixed forest and brush-filled creek bottoms. But in the heat of summer, the woods is better left alone. The underbrush is full of blistering poison ivy, gnawing ticks, burrowing chiggers, and the occasional but always threatening cottonmouth.

SPLITIN' STICKS

Despite the seasonal pests, Terry likes the area. But he avoids the summer woods by busying himself making bows. In the shade of a large woodworking shop behind his house, Terry sometimes splits cedar fence posts with a maul and wedges. With his heavy moustache and husky fore-

MAKING BIG CEDAR STICKS INTO SHOOTABLE ONES — Terry makes his corewoods by splitting, sawing, and grinding old cedar fence posts into tapered laminations.

arms he resembles a hammering blacksmith of days past. Most passers-by think he's making a split rail fence, but his bowhunting friends recognize he's just making another custom longbow that will soon bear the name Arkansas Stick.

"I've always been pretty proud of Arkansas, and this is my home, so it just seemed natural to put Arkansas on my bows. I wanted to be sure that people didn't think it was a compound bow so I added the word 'Stick.' "

Terry builds both longbows and recurves, but he calls them all his Arkansas Sticks. This part-time bowmaker is strong-willed with intense brown eyes and the deep-toned drawl of a bass fiddle. He began working as a journeyman carpenter right out of high school and over the years has done all kinds of carpentry work, including cabinet making. Now he uses his woodworking skills to shape the old countryside fence posts into sweet humming longbows.

"I've always built things. I would rather make something than go buy it. When I really got involved in archery, I got to thinking that I may as well make my own bows." It was about ten years ago when Terry decided to build his first bow. He could have ordered a kit or even found some instructions, but Terry wanted to teach himself.

"I never did string that first bow I made. It was a take-down recurve and I used a piece of bowdark — you call it osage — for a handle. I made a couple of forms and glued up a couple of limbs. Then I stuck them on the handle, but I couldn't string it. It must have been at least 250 pounds. I even tied a rope to it on each tip and still couldn't string it. That bow went in the wood heater."

Terry's first bow wasn't the only one consumed by flames during his first eight years of building bows. Many of them never loosed an arrow at game and others were used only for a short time. "Most of them went into that wood heater. I didn't want to send any out until I had a good one. Some of my buddies would say, 'Don't cut that up, let me have it,' but I'd still put it into that wood heater.

"I was amazed that something as simple as building a longbow can really be complicated. There are so many variables, so many things that you can do that will change the performance of that bow."

Over the years, through trial and error — a sometimes painful but always sure teacher — Terry developed his bowmaking skills. By 1986 he was finally satisfied with the quality and performance of his bows and began selling them to the public. "I think that I've evolved a pretty fair bow. My sticks are smooth. They're not the fastest, but they're plenty fast. I'm not real up on speed anyway. If it's there that's fine, but usually if you gain speed you give up something else. It's taken a long time to develop but I think I've found a happy medium between speed and smoothness. I could have learned more quickly if I had talked to other bowyers or if I had at least read up on it. But that just wasn't the way I wanted to do it."

BOWHUNTING IN THE STICKS

Terry is also a self-taught and strong-willed bowhunter. He has harvested assorted small game and some impressive whitetails in Arkansas. Plus, he has traveled to the aspen slopes of Colorado and taken mule deer. He doesn't care much for stump-sittin' but prefers to slip within bow range of his quarry. "Still hunting is something you've got to learn by doing it. You've got to get all your senses tuned in to what's around you. The main thing is you've got to move slow. I mean s-l-o-w. I can spend all day in two acres. That's how slow I move."

Like his hunting techniques, Terry keeps his equipment simple and effective. "I like a broadhead that I can sharpen myself. Right now I prefer a Black Diamond Delta two-blade. But I have taken deer with modular heads. The first time I ever took a thin-bladed modular head out in the woods, a fox came running along and hopped up on a log about thirty yards away. I centered him with that arrow and the broadhead just disintegrated. I didn't know where the blades went. I knew right then if it did that on a fox, it wouldn't work well on a deer. So I have more confidence in something like a Black Diamond Delta."

Terry files his broadheads to shaving sharpness by simply stroking them with a mill file. When hunting, he always carries a 6" mill bastard to touch up his heads in case he misses a shot.

For penetration Terry mounts his Black Diamonds on heavy cedar shafts. "I like to shoot at least nine grains of arrow weight per pound of bow pull. A lot of times I will have arrows that are even ten grains per pound of bow weight. If I'm shooting my fifty-six pound bow, that's 560 to 570 grains of arrow weight. With those heavy arrows, penetration is no problem at all."

He carries his arrows in a Kwikee Kwiver bow quiver that he wears on his hip attached to a customized belt loop. "It's handy, it keeps my arrows sharp, it keeps my feathers from being matted down, and I don't have any arrow rattle like with a back quiver. The arrows are completely out of the way because they're behind you, and you never know they're there until you need one, and then it's right there."

STICK STORIES

Terry doesn't have to reach too far back into his quiver of bowhunting memories to cite the effectiveness of his equipment. In a matter-of-fact slow drawl, he recalls his past Arkansas season. "I was hunting south of here on a friend's land where I had found some scrapes. I wasn't still hunting, and it was unusual for me to sit there and watch scrapes. I'd been sitting an hour or so when a squirrel came hopping along. I can't resist shooting at squirrels. So I got up and popped that squirrel, and it wasn't five minutes later when I looked over to my right and there stood an eight point buck. I thought to myself, 'If that squirrel had been a little later, or that deer a little earlier, I would have messed that up.'

"I remember not being a bit nervous. He was headed toward the scrape and I could see shooting him at the scrape would be my best opportunity. When he was a little more than quartering away from me, I drew my recurve, picked a spot on him, and shot. The arrow hit exactly in that spot. Because of the angle, it went into his flank, passed all the way through, and came out high in the shoulder cutting a rib on its way out. Something inside that deer turned that arrow and when it came out, it just shot up in the air. I thought to myself right then, 'Why would any-

MASTERING HIS STRAIGHT-END CEDAR STICK — Terry's feather-weight longbow is ideal for shooting at moving game.

body want a seventy pound bow for deer?' The deer took off and ran until it piled up."

The effectiveness of his Stick on the eight-pointer clearly supports Terry's recommendation to his whitetail hunting customers to use moderate weight stick bows. "Fifty pounds is plenty for any whitetail. I wouldn't hesitate to go elk hunting with a fifty to sixty pound recurve but probably sixty pounds and up would be better for elk."

Although Terry has enjoyed hunting with his sixty inch recurve, he plans to use his little cedar longbow in the upcoming big game seasons. Mastering a longbow takes time, and it took him several years to build up his confidence with the cedar stick. "I've used every shooting style you can imagine. I'm always trying to improve by trying something new to see if I can shoot better. I've tried everything, including every anchor point. The top of my head is about the only anchor point I haven't tried. Finally I settled on a floating anchor — I anchor in mid air. As a matter of fact, it's the same way Ben Pearson shot."

NOT BLENDING IN

Most bowhunters wouldn't think of going hunting without wearing their camouflage clothing. But Terry doesn't think it's so important. "I've worn camouflage some, but I think it's a waste. I usually wear a flannel shirt with some kind of plaid. I think that a lot of these plaids blend in as well as any camouflage, and I like soft material because I'm always moving. I can't stand it if my clothes are loud. I like to wear wool in the Rockies, but of course here in Arkansas during bow season it's pretty hot, so I wear cotton flannel."

Besides the practicality of his plaids, there is another reason Terry shies away from camouflage clothing. "Those hunters who are always in their camouflage or in their blaze orange, have a poor image. At least here they do. And I don't want to be associated with that image."

He doesn't cotton to camo, but he loves his boots. They're rubber-bottomed, leather-topped Sheboygan hunting boots with a solid rock-grabbing tread. He has plowed through the Arkansas brush with them and slogged through the wet meadows in the Rockies, and his feet have always stayed dry.

Terry also shies away from the camoed crowds when he practices. He enjoys his quite moments in the woods with his bow. Some of his best times are spent simply stump shooting with a buddy. Although he loves to shoot, he doesn't find much enjoyment at local tournaments. "I wish that there were more traditional archers. I'm by myself in this area. When I go to a shoot I tend to feel out of place. If there are a few other traditional archers there I get with them and I'm okay. But if there aren't, I'm totally uncomfortable with compound shooters. I don't fit in with them, and I don't belong in their category. As a matter of fact, I'll be blunt — two sticks and a string is archery and anything else is something else. It's not archery. If you put sights or wheels on it, it's not archery."

Discussing compounds puts a hint of tension in Terry's slow baritone drawl, but it breaks into a squeak at the mention of crossbows. "Crossbow!

That's a dirty word. That's not archery. Crossbows belong in a gun season. They have a gun stock, a trigger, and sights, and they're not bows!"

DEMANDS EFFECTIVE SIMPLICITY

Terry believes a real bow should be simple yet effective, like his Arkansas Sticks. Even though their concept is simple, he's demanding about their shooting qualities. "I want a bow that's easy to shoot. It has to draw smoothly. I don't want one that gains five pounds in one inch and three pounds the next. Also, it needs to shoot a variety of spine and weight arrows well. A good bow shouldn't be sensitive in that respect."

To ensure that his products meet his demands, Terry shoots each bow and gauges its performance before shipping it out. "When a bow leaves here, I'll tell the customer what spine and what weight arrow I'm shooting out of it, fletching and all. And that arrow will shoot well."

Terry's most popular Arkansas Stick is his 60" one-piece recurve. He also plans to introduce the more convenient take-down recurve into his line. "But it will have to perform at least as good as the one I'm making now. I'm not just going to slap one together and put it out on the market."

In making his recurves, Terry is one of the few bowmakers who use bamboo as a corewood. "I like a bamboo recurve because it has a different feel to it." He gets his tapered bamboo laminations from Howard Hill Archery in Montana. But mostly he uses solid maple laminations. "It's hard to beat maple. It's readily available and it's hard to tell the difference between maple and any other corewood unless you shoot a lot of different bows. But the average person is not going to detect a bit of difference in them."

ARKANSAS STICK RECURVES are available in 60" and 62" lengths. Terry's 62" model has a mass weight of about 1 pound, 9 ounces, and a recommended brace height of 7 ½" from the throat to the string.

He usually makes his simple lined, nicely contoured risers from shedua, but he also offers them in a variety of exotic and domestic hardwoods. The riser measures 21 ½" between fadeouts, is 1¾" wide near the fadeout, and thins to ⅞" through the rounded sight window. The window is cut to center shot and is padded with a calf hair strike pad. The riser is 2" thick and 1⅞" across the crowned arrow shelf. It has a modified dished longbow style grip wrapped with a 4 ¼" saddle leather laced in front. Epoxy-set brass accessory bushings are available.

The recurve limbs have a 19½" working length from the fadeout to the string nock, and they narrow from 1⅝" wide at the fadeout to 1" at the nock. They are constructed from two thin, parallel, standard maple Actionwood laminations on the back and one tapered lamination on the belly. These laminations are faced and backed with either clear, brown, or black fiberglass. The limbs are nicely rounded on the edges and have matching riser wood tip overlays. Full cut string nocks feather into a "Y" groove fashioned into the belly glass. This bow is finished with a low-luster polyurethane finish.

The following draw/force measurements were recorded on a 62" Stick recurve:

DRAW LENGTH	25"	26"	27"	28"	29"
DRAW WEIGHT	57½#	61#	64#	68#	71½#

To check this bow's relative speed, it was chronographed using a 29", 630 grain hunting-weight cedar arrow. It was fletched with four standard cut feathers and had an open type nock. Terry, who has a clean release, used a finger tab and drew the arrow 28". The string was standard Dacron without any accessories. The average arrow speed for this bow, arrow, and shooter combination was 183 fps.

Although he has been making recurves longer, Terry's longbows are starting to be discovered. They are a blend of old Arkansas fence posts, sweeping clean lines, and Terry's determination to craft a sweet shooting bow. These little beauties radiate a warm glow from the reddish cedar under clear glass. Their minimal hand shock and delicate, light-weight balance make them a joy to shoot.

The ARKANSAS STICK LONGBOW is available in 66" and 68" lengths. The 66" model falls in the feather-weight category, weighing only 1 pound, 2 ounces. It has a recommended brace height of 6¼" to 6½" from the string to the throat.

Its shedua riser is 15½" between fadeouts. It is 1³⁄₁₆" wide and thins to ¾" through the nicely rounded sight window which is cut ⅛" from center shot. The arrow shelf and sight window are covered with calf hair. The riser

SIMPLE ARKANSAS STICKS — Terry's bows reflect his skilled craftsmanship and functional simplicity.

is 2" thick and has a slightly dished and comfortably rounded grip. It is wrapped with a 4¼" leather grip which is laced in front. Except for the modified grip, the warm-toned riser has the simple flowing lines of a traditional longbow.

Its deflexed-reflexed limbs have a working length of 25" from the fadeout to the string nock. They have slightly rounded edges and narrow from 1" wide at the fadeouts to ⅝" at the nock. They are made from two back and one belly lamination of tapered red cedar enveloped in clear fiberglass. These solid laminations are usually used in an edge grain position and are tapered .002" per inch. The tips are reinforced with a 4" long tapered limb tip wedge between the face and back laminations. The tips are simply rounded and have flush string nocks. The bow is finished with a flat satin polyurethane finish.

The following draw/force measurements were recorded on a 66" cedar Stick Longbow:

DRAW LENGTH	25"	26"	27"	28"	29"
DRAW WEIGHT	49#	52#	55#	58½#	62#

To check for relative speed, this 58½ pound longbow was chronographed using a 510 grain, 29" cedar arrow. It was fletched with four standard cut feathers and had an open type nock. Terry drew the arrow 28" and shot with his tabs. The string was standard Dacron without any accessories. The average arrow speed for this bow, arrow, and shooter combination was 181 fps.

STEADY HANDS

Some bowmakers use a variety of sophisticated jigs and devices to help achieve a precision product, but Terry relies on his honed woodworking skills, rock steady hands, and his ever critical eye. Although some of his techniques are quite simple, he performs each step with remarkable finesse.

Terry begins crafting his stick bows by making the risers. When making a custom laminated riser for a recurve, he prefers highly contrasting grainy woods like shedua, walnut, or bubinga. He usually sandwiches the vertical laminations with a veneer of matching limb corewood material to accentuate the contrasts. Although Terry makes custom laminated risers, he likes the traditional look of his more popular, sleeker, one-piece riser.

Using a metal template, he traces the riser shape on a rough block of wood. For extra strength, Terry aligns the riser wood grain parallel with the facing and backing of the bow. Using a band saw, he precisely halves his pencil line around the riser outline. Next he shapes it freehand using a hand belt sander held sideways in a jig. Except for a rare blink, Terry looks like an animated robot executing programed precision sweeps with the hand-held piece. He occasionally breaks his staunch pose to check the fit between riser shape and the bow form and also uses a small hand square to check the alignment of the fadeouts.

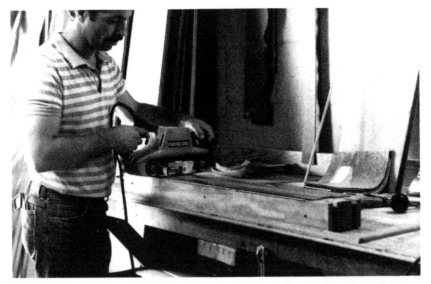

Like his bows, Terry's method of grinding cedar into laminations is simple yet effective.

FENCE POST POWER

For making longbow laminations, Terry uses local red cedar. "Right now I'm getting my cedar from a man who owns some land with a lot of cedar on it, and he has cedar posts everywhere. All of those posts are at least ten years old." After splitting them into planks small enough to handle, Terry takes them into the shop and grinds a flat surface on one side using his power jointer. He squares the piece on his table saw and cuts it into laminations, carefully extracting the desired grain. "I want edge grain because it is stronger and more resilient."

Next he runs the pieces through his power planer until they are about 3/16" thick, keeping them in matched pairs. He then places them in a simple device for grinding the taper. It's a board with two long parallel strips of steel, mounted about 1½" apart. Between these strips, Terry places an appropriate spacer strip and a tapered Actionwood lamination. He puts in one of his cedar laminations and grinds it with a hand belt sander across the grain of the exposed surface down to the steel strips bracketing it.

Terry someday wants to devise a different technique for grinding tapers, but like most of his techniques, he wants to innovate it himself. Fashioning fence posts into finished laminations is an involved process. "But compared to bowdark it's easy. I've done the same thing with bowdark, and bowdark is TOUGH. Cedar is much easier to work with."

"C" CLAMP FORM

Once his riser and laminations are made, Terry is ready to glue up one of his longbows. His forms are made of laminated plywood sandwiched on a piece of Masonite. The smoothed and sweeping form surface duplicates the bow back. The lower portion of the form is sectioned out to provide a biting surface for his "C" clamps and the edge of his form surface has little metal stops or bumpers which help to line up the laminations.

Three to four hours before glue-up, Terry places the laminations in his heat box to dry out any absorbed moisture. Right before glue-up he removes the heated corewoods and lightly sands both sides to remove any residual material and to improve the glue bonding surfaces. He also sands the gluing side of the fiberglass and cleans it with denatured alcohol and masking tapes the non-gluing side.

Now he is ready to lay up the composites. First he covers his form with plastic wrap. Terry learned early on that without the plastic wrap, he usually glued the bow to the form. Using a small paddle he applies Ciba-Geigy DA-556 epoxy to all contact surfaces of the composites. He has tried other glues but likes DA-556 best because of its bonding qualities.

He lays the glued composites and the feathered tip-strengthening wedges in the form. When positioning the laminations, Terry usually shifts the butt ends about one inch down from the center of the bow. This makes the top limb a little weaker and the bottom limb a little stronger. By building in this limb tiller, there is usually little if any tillering required to achieve his desired one-eighth inch positive tiller. On top of the composites he lays a one-quarter inch thick rubber strip and two one-eighth inch thick steel pressure strips.

Then he begins clamping twelve large "C" clamps on each side of the riser. He starts tightening them at mid-limb and works toward the ends. Terry regulates the clamp pressure by touch and often inspects the unifor-

Terry's bow press utilizes "C" clamps tightened by hand while keeping an eye on the glue lines.

mity and thinness of his glue line while tightening. He has made and used forms that utilize an air pressure hose to press the composites, but he prefers his present clamping technique.

He then places his form in his hot box and cures the glue at a 140 degrees for nine to ten hours. The box is then turned off and the bow is allowed to cool in the form.

Terry pops the bow out of the form and grinds the rough glue off the edges with his belt sander. He then lays the bow on edge on a flat work surface and uses a small surface jig to mark the centerline. He turns the bow over and repeats the marking to ensure that he has a true centerline.

STICK SHAPING

Next he uses a straight edge to mark out the limb shapes and cuts them out on his band saw. He finishes the sides with his belt sander and roughs in the string nocks with a small rat-tail file.

Then he strings the bow for the first time and checks for string alignment. The string usually tracks well, but occasionally Terry deepens one side of a string nock to bring it into alignment. Except for the slight rounding of the edges of the fiberglass, the limb edges are left squared on the sides to help protect the exposed edges of the soft cedar corewood.

Once the bow is aligned, Terry band saws out the sight window and rounds it with a rasp. He shapes it with the high point near the throat of the grip to minimize torque problems and enhance arrow flight. He contours the rounded handle and dished grip with his belt sander. Terry prefers the dished grip because it provides a more natural and more comfortable feel to the hand. He then finish sands the bow and steel wools it smooth.

Producing a silky finish on his bows is second nature to this experienced woodworker. Terry sprays them with at least five coats of Benjamin Moore satin luster polyurethane. He allows each coat to dry for two days and then rubs it smooth with steel wool. Between the third and fourth coats, he inks the Arkansas Stick logo on the face of the limbs and inks the bow specs on the riser below the grip. He lets the last coat harden for a week before using the bow. Two weeks may seem like a long time for putting a finish on a bow. "But you can't rush that part."

Finally Terry wraps the grip with premium saddle leather. It's glued on with contact cement and laced on the front. Terry doesn't like to see the sticky glue on his beautiful riser, but it's a necessary evil that keeps the leather from eventually slipping. The waterproof glue also helps prevent any moisture in the leather from getting on the bow.

LOVE AND CARE

Terry strings his finished longbows with the push-pull method, but not his recurves. "You should never string a recurve without a bow stringer. Even with a stringer you can mess up if you're not careful. You have to know how to use it. I ran across a fellow in Pine Bluff a few weeks ago who wanted me to look at his new take-down recurve. I looked at it and saw right off that the lower limb was twisted. He said that he had strung it one time without his bow stringer and he must have twisted it then. And it was a nice take-down bow."

Although Terry enjoys watching the beauty of his bows emerge when spraying on the finish, the most fun part is test shooting them. He shoots every one before it gets his stamp of approval. "Matter of fact, I have problems with that. I'll make one and get out there in the yard and start shooting it and won't know when to stop. I need to be back in here working, but instead I'll be out there shooting."

He guarantees that his Arkansas Sticks are not copies. They were developed through years of trial and error like most of his self-taught bowmaking techniques. It has been a long and sometimes rough trail from that first unstringable bow to the radiant cedar longbows that now warm the hearts of his traditional customers.

DIFFERENT STROKES

Although his longbows are attractive and fun to shoot, they do have minor drawbacks. "A longbow is long to handle in thick brush. I had a fellow call me who was upset because he was using a longbow when he got a shot at a Pope and Young whitetail. He hit his upper limb on a tree branch and missed the shot, so he was upset and wanted a short bow. But I don't make a real short longbow because they're usually unstable.

"But the Indians did fine feeding themselves with little ol' short forty to forty-five pound bows, and Howard Hill didn't have any trouble shooting heavy longbows. So the most important thing is to shoot a hunting bow you're comfortable and confident with. It just depends on whatever you like."

Down in the red cedar country of Arkansas, Terry Hughes likes doing it his way. And he does it with an Arkansas Stick.

Chapter Sixteen

BLACK WIDOW BOW COMPANY

THE SPECIAL GIFT

Many youngsters learn archery from their fathers. Others pick up the sport later in life from bowhunting friends. And ironically, some adults learn it from their children. Ken Beck was one of those.

"I was sort of a late-comer. The shop teacher got my oldest boy, Scott, building bows in shop class. And he was pretty good at it. He made one for the shop, one for himself, and made one for his brother. Then he came in one night and handed me one and said, 'Here Dad, now we can hunt together.' He was fifteen years old at the time. So we started hunting and had a great time."

With the new bows they roamed the Ozark countryside sharing their love for bowhunting. "One year later, Scott was killed in an automobile related accident. It happened during hunting season. His brother Dan and I came home that night and looked at those bows. I said, 'Dan do you think we can ever go hunting again?' and he answered, 'Well, possibly someday.' And we did. We enjoyed hunting together.

"I suppose that Scott's spirit is always there with us. He got us into archery. Usually a father gets his son into archery, but in this case it was a son getting his father and brother into archery. And it became a love and a passion. Maybe it's a greater passion because of him. We relish the good memories and the good times. And I relish the times we hunted together and the closeness that it brought to us. There is an old tree that I hunt out of occasionally that's almost sacred to me. We call it Scott's tree, on Scott's bluff. I feel close to his memory there."

A late-comer to archery, Ken is now immersed in the sport. He is owner and crafter of Black Widow bows. And he is no stranger to overcoming adversity.

FINDING A NICHE

Ken was born and raised on a farm in Iowa, and as a young man he farmed for a living. But he also had a longing for adventure in the west. He eventually bought a small ranch in Colorado and had plans to move there after harvesting his Iowa crops. However, a devastating hail storm destroyed his crops, changing his schedule. Without crops to harvest, his move to Colorado and the beginning of a new life came sooner than he had planned.

His hardships that year weren't over. When he arrived at his new Colorado ranch, he discovered that an important alfalfa crop had died from neglect. He had little choice but to leave his dreams, and his down payment, behind.

Ken headed back east and leased a ranch in Missouri. Settled at last, he looked forward to becoming a rancher. But his hopes took one final blow. "That ranch became an experimental station for veterinarians. My cattle became infected with a disease called vibriosis, which at that time nobody knew anything about." Tragically, he lost most of his cattle and was forced to look for another occupation.

He then got into sales, mostly insurance, and became quite successful. Later he worked for the Dale Carnegie courses where he became an area manager. After several years of the intense management instruction, he tired of the many evenings away from home and decided to try self-employment. He became part-owner of a sporting goods store, selling his interest when he had the chance to buy a small manufacturing operation: It was Black Widow Bow Company.

Ken knew that recurves were not enjoying much popularity then and admits buying the company was a gamble. "I decided to give it a go, but I never had any real doubts about it. I could write a book about the problems we had to solve, but I never had any doubt. I really had belief and faith that we could make it work. Sometimes we didn't know how we were going to make it work, but as Carlyle said, 'It's not for us to see what lies dimly in the future, but to do that which is clearly at hand.' There were lots of days and weeks when we kept doing what was clearly at hand and didn't dare look around the corner!"

That was in 1982. The gamble paid off. Today, Black Widow enjoys a steady growth in bow sales. To traditional archers around the world, that's little surprise. The name "Black Widow" is synonymous with speed, smoothness, quality, and craftsmanship. And Black Widow has the distinction of making recurves and only recurves, for over thirty years.

THE WILSON BOYS

The company was started in Springfield, Missouri in 1957 by the Wilson brothers, Jack, Bob, and Norman. Bob, an experienced bowyer for many years, designed the bows and was in charge of building them. Jack handled sales and helped in the shop, while Norman provided general help around the shop.

One of Bob's early models was a high-contrast, black and white recurve that needed a name as striking as the bow. Although they toyed with several, the name "Black Widow" seemed perfect.

The Wilson boys were no strangers to archery. Besides knowing how to make bows, they really knew how to shoot them. Jack won the National Championship in 1947. The three brothers with a nephew won the National Team Championship three times. The three also swept one Mid-West tournament by winning first, second, and third place. And they won many state and local tournaments. They also enjoyed bowhunting for deer and rabbits with their recurves.

Once they began making bows, their recurves remained winners. Black Widow bows won several National and World Championships, earning the slogan, "Famous Around the World."

Then in the early seventies, a new type of bow started cutting into their sales. The contraption was called a compound bow, and the Wilson Brothers had no interest in building them. By 1976, the compound had soared in popularity and Black Widow's recurve sales were down eighty percent. Near retirement age, the brothers decided it was time to get out of the recurve manufacturing business. They sold the company to one of their bowyers, who operated it until it was purchased by Ken Beck.

SNAPPING THE REIGNS

Armed with a positive attitude and his management, advertising, and sales skills, Ken headed up the new Black Widow team with the invaluable help of experienced Widow bowyer and new production manager, Bill Bonner. Helped by a renewed interest in recurves from bowhunters, Black Widow's sales grew. It's tough to page through almost any bowhunting periodical and not see one of their quality ads. Black Widow's scrap book of successful bowhunters, "our Black Widow family" as Bill calls them, looks like a "Who's Who" in the world of bowhunting personalities. And pound for pound, Black Widow recurves rival many compounds for arrow speed.

With all this notoriety, it's easy to imagine Black Widow as a sprawling operation with a large factory and plush offices next to a crowded parking lot. In Highlandville, Missouri? Not likely. Highlandville, with a population of about eighty, is just a blink along Highway 160, twenty miles south of Springfield. This Ozark hill country is a mix of rolling hay fields and old pastures bracketed by oak and walnut forested ridges, and deep brush-filled hollows.

The only prominent building in Highlandville is south of town along the highway. It's a white building with a "Dr. Pepper" sign out front next to a flagpole rippling the stars and stripes. A closer look reveals the words, BLACK WIDOW BOW CO. on the bottom part of the soda sign. It's Black Widow's headquarters. All of it. A round Black Widow logo rests under the front peak, partly shadowed by a set of 6 x 6 elk antlers.

Inside is a small shop with a well-organized, brightly-lit variety of work stations. Neatly stacked supplies and emerging bow parts fill shelves along the walls. The white ceiling and walls help illuminate the uncluttered work benches and individual sawing, grinding, and sanding work stations. Every corner of the shop reflects Ken's demand for attention to detail and organization. It's also obvious in his products.

Attached to the shop is the small bustling office where Ken and his wife Marlene quiet the ringing phones. With background music of muffled shop noises, they talk with customers in their polite Missouri drawls. "Southern hospitality" is not a cliché at Black Widow. Ken, in his soft-spoken articulate manner, unhurriedly takes the orders and inquisitive calls, treating each like it may be the only call he receives that day. But there are many. Some mornings they seem endless.

When not fielding phone calls, Ken is either giving guidance to some of his crew or shaping a batch of handle sections. Poised in front of the humming power sanders, Ken's hands sweep the emerging risers back and forth with experienced finesse.

A TEAM EFFORT

Although Ken shapes the risers, much of the bow crafting is done by the bowmaking team at Black Widow. They work together, much like a family with a common goal. They show pride in their particular skills and incorporate plenty of cross-training so that each employee knows the different phases in creating their bows.

Production manager Bill Bonner spends much of his time with the delicate task of shaping limbs when bringing them into alignment and tiller. With almost micrometer-accurate vision and machine-like movements he glides the limbs across the flexible upright sanding belt.

Ken Smith enjoys all phases of bowmaking, but he admits he likes tillering the best. Proudly extending a near-finished MA II, he points out that a lot of handcrafting goes into the creation of a Widow, about twenty man-hours per bow.

At the far end of the shop, Phil Clayman shapes handles with a spindle sander and later uses Missouri elbow grease during the final sanding.

Lanky Jim Geiger is Black Widow's glue man who takes about twenty minutes to lay up a bow in the press. It's his favorite part of the gluing operations.

Roger Fulton's artistic hand inks the bow specifications and the Widow logo on each bow. Besides inking, he also glues in accessory bushings, preps bows for shipping, and cuts out handles.

John Clayman installs inserts, helps with shipping, and assembles Black Widow's bow quivers. And Jim-Bob Clayman, who enjoys rodeoing, carefully fashions the string nocks and grooves.

This bow crafting team produces eleven different models of Black Widow recurves. With the different available limb combinations, those eleven models yield a head-spinning thirty-nine different versions. Even with the success of their present line, Black Widow doesn't forget the customers with older models. They still build replacement limbs for every Black Widow T.D. model built in the past seventeen years.

WIDOW-MAKERS — Ken Beck (left) and the local 'Missouri boys' who make up Black
Widow's bow crafting team.

PRIDE OF THE PACK

Although Black Widow offers a variety of target and hunting recurves,
two hunting models dominate their orders. They are the MA II take-down,
and the one-piece bows in their Diamond Anniversary Collection.

The MA II is Black Widow's most popular bow. It's a three-piece take-
down hunting recurve which resembles, and is often mistaken for, a one-
piece bow. It was introduced for their Silver Anniversary and was the first
bow in which Black Widow used clear fiberglass.

The MA II is available in 58", 60", 62", and 64" lengths. It has an
approximate mass weight of 2 pounds, 12 ounces, and a recommended brace
height of 8" to 9" from the string to the throat.

Its "Graybark" handle section is 18" long and is made of vertical 1/16"
laminated, gray-dyed maple. It's accentuated with a vertical trim stripe of
1/4" mahogany-dyed, laminated birch sandwiched with a total of .200" of
black and white fiberglass. The handle is faced with fiberglass for durability
and to cosmetically match the limbs. It is 4" thick near the peaks and thins
to approximately 1¾" through the throat. It's 1⅞" wide and thins to ¾"
through the sight window. The 2¼" arrow shelf is crowned directly over the
handle throat to enhance shooting. Its sight window is cut .200" past center
shot and is full cut for 4½" above the shelf, contouring back to full handle
width 5½" above the shelf.

The handle is gently contoured with prominent pointed peaks on the
back near the limb fadeouts. Its custom-shaped grip is designed to provide
positive non-torque hand placement tight under the arrow shelf for a true
instinctive picture. Brass bushings for sights, cushion, quiver mount, and

stabilizer are also available. Bow specifications and the owner's name are white inked on the limb belly near the fadeout.

The MA II limbs are constructed from a Graybark Actionwood core under clear fiberglass. One thin, tapered lamination is used on the back and a thicker lamination is used on the belly. The working length's of the limbs from the fadeout to the nock are: 16" on the 58" bow, 17" on the 60" bow, 18" on the 62" bow, and 19" on the 64" bow. These slim-lined limbs narrow from $1\,11/16$" wide at the fadeouts to $11/16$" at the nock.

Unlike most recurve limbs, these are shaped to a slightly modified trapezoidal cross section narrowing to the back. They are attached to the handle with a small hex-headed screw and utilize two brass alignment pins. The tip overlays are laminated, reddish compressed fiber-filled resin over white fiberglass, over black bias material. They exhibit nicely fashioned flush string nocks and the tip narrows above the nock. A long single groove is filed in the recurve belly glass.

The entire bow is finished with Black Widow's "Spider Webb" epoxy matte finish which produces a super low luster ideal for hunting situations, yet it shows through the woods-blending Graybark tones. Combined with the clear glass, it helps the bow melt into a wooded setting. "The MA II," Ken says, "is a beautiful bow and yet is one bowhunters don't have to camouflage and hide the beauty. So they can sort of have their cake and eat it too."

It's also available with a dull black epoxy Spider Webb finish known as the MB model.

The MA II is a smooth-shooting, arrow-spittin' demon. Its balance is superb and hand shock is minimal as the arrows leap cleanly from the fur padded shelf. Compared to many recurves, the bow exhibits excellent cast. In fact, many new Black Widow owners tend to shoot a tad high until they become accustomed to the flatter arrow trajectory.

The following draw/force measurements were recorded on a 60" MA II:

DRAW LENGTH	25"	26"	27"	28"	29"
DRAW WEIGHT	49#	$51\,7/10$#	$54\,1/2$#	$57\,1/2$#	$60\,7/10$#

To check for relative speed, Ken shot a 500 grain cedar arrow from his 58", 60 pound at 28" draw, MA II. The arrow was $28\,3/4$" long, had three standard cut feathers, and was equipped with a snap-on nock. The string was standard Dacron without accessories. Ken has a clean pull-through release and drew the arrow $26\,3/4$". At his draw, the bow pulled 56 pounds. The average arrow speed for this bow, arrow, and shooter combination was 188 fps.

ONE-PIECE POPULARITY

Black Widow stopped making one-piece recurves about seventeen years ago when the popularity of take-downs was sweeping the market. But with the resurgence of interest in traditional archery, combined with requests for a one-piece bow, Ken decided to reintroduce a one-piece recurve into the Widow line. To celebrate thirty years in bowmaking, he appropriately named the new one-piece models the Diamond Anniversary Collection. These bows have become Widow's second most popular line. Designed after one of the earlier wooden handle Widows, this limited collection includes the stunning "Crown Jewel," the soft-toned woodsy "Graybark," and the coal-black, "Black Diamond."

The CROWN JEWEL is the top of line in this collection. It has Graybark limbs under clear glass contrasting with a rich-toned mahogany-dyed birch riser. Its vertically laminated riser is approximately 24½" long between fadeouts and contains a Graybark decorative and strengthening wedge similar to the MA II. The 62" model has a mass weight of 2 pounds, 14 ounces, and an 18" working length in the limbs. Its riser is complemented with a genuine hand engraved ivory scrimshaw medallion of the Black Widow logo, located below the grip on the window side, and decorative laminated overlays on the belly near the fadeouts. The riser has prominent peaks called "horns" on the back near the fadeouts to help provide shooting stability.

The Diamond Anniversary Collection has riser and limb dimensions similar to those noted for the MA II. The Crown Jewel is offered in the matte Spider Webb, high gloss, or hand-buffed satin finish.

The collection also includes the Graybark. It has a laminated Graybark riser without the decorative scrimshaw. It's offered in the non-reflective Spider Webb finish, and is also available in a dull black finish known as the Black Diamond model.

The following draw/force measurements were recorded on a 60" one-piece Graybark:

DRAW LENGTH	25"	26"	27"	28"	29"
DRAW WEIGHT	56#	59#	62#	65½#	69#

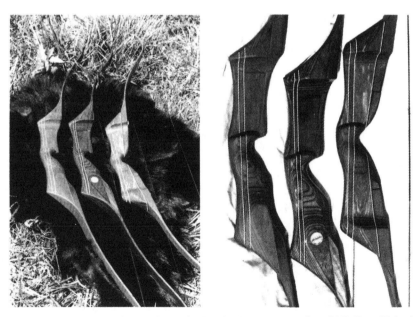

PRIDE OF THE WEB — Left to right — The Graybark, Crown Jewel, and MA II are Widow's top selling bows.

To check for relative speed, the author chronographed this 60" Gray-bark. He shot 450 grain, 28½", 2213 swaged aluminum shafts fletched with three 5" feathers and equipped with 125 grain field points and snap-on nocks. The bowstring was Black Widow's Flemish Fast Flight equipped with Spider Legs silencers. The author used a shooting glove and had a pull-through release. The average arrow speed for this bow, arrow, string, and shooter combination was 210 fps.

MAKING RISERS

When making their popular hunting recurves, the Widow team begins by crafting the handle. From blocks of laminated hard-rock maple they band saw out a patterned handle and then shape the belly and laminate surface using a profiling jig on a vertical sander. As with most of their rough sanding operations, they use a twenty-four grit sanding drum on gluing surfaces to enhance glue bond.

The wood dust is sucked away by Widow's homemade dust collection system. Bill thought up the idea for the system, which is simply a giant vacuum sweeper with a series of tubes and pipes and a dust collection box. "We hooked it up and kept our fingers crossed," Ken says, "hoping that it would in fact do the job. It worked even better than we hoped for. With this system, we re-circulate the shop air and cut down on heating and cooling expenses."

The profiled limb angle on the belly of the MA II handle is faced with two epoxied layers of fiberglass for cosmetics and durability. It's clamped in an air lock jig and all six limb mounting holes are drilled. Drilling these holes from one locked position ensures their precision repeatability. The main limb attachment bushing hole on each end is then counter drilled on the back to accept the headed insert which is epoxy glued and pressed in. The vertical trim stripe and back section of the handle are then epoxied to the belly piece, covering the countersunk brass bushing. The other two small holes on the limb attachment area accept the brass stud pins that serve for limb align-ment. Butt blocks of graybark maple are laminated to the handle belly near the grip to help give the assembled bow a one-piece appearance.

The trim stripe is preglued with .100" of black and white fiberglass on both sides. It not only makes the handle attractive, but it adds significant rigidity and strength. Ken demonstrates this by placing one end of a preglued wedge on a 2 x 4, and the other end on the floor. He then jumps on the unsupported section, barely flexing it.

For gluing handle composites together, Black Widow uses four bolt-tightened clamping jigs that press the epoxied pieces together. The handle is then heat cured at 120 degrees for a couple of hours. Widow's spacious curing oven is electrically heated and thermostatically controlled. It also contains a circulating fan. "The fan is important, so that you circulate that air and don't have hot and cold spots."

Once the handle is glued up, the sight window and grip area are rough sawn. Then profiling jigs are used to rough shape it. These jigs maintain the handle at a specific angle, while a shaped template regulates the amount and

With a fluid blur of the hands, Ken skillfully contours a handle on a spindle sander.

shape of sanding. The jig's template is moved against a bearing at the base of the vertical sander and precisely controls the ground shape.

The last bit of profiling is done using a 100 grit sanding drum. This eliminates any deep sanding marks on the near-finished surfaces. After it's profiled, the grip and remainder of the handle is hand contoured using air-sleeved spindle sanders.

This is one of the jobs where Ken shines. He seems to enjoy it and shows remarkable skill shaping the contoured grip area. It's an important step and Ken is very particular about how it's done. "I have a certain way that I think they ought to be done. Because for me, a grip should have a certain feel. That doesn't mean it will work right for you. There is no such thing as a perfect grip. But our grips have evolved considerably over the last four years in response to our customer preferences. For a small surcharge we'll also fashion a customized grip duplicating another bow's handle." After the initial shaping, Ken uses reducing grit sanding drums to achieve smooth and flowing contours. Reducing the air pressure softens the sanding spindle sleeves and helps in blending the contours.

THE POWER PARTS

To achieve consistency in materials and performance of their limbs, Black Widow uses matched corewood laminations and matching halves from single strips of fiberglass. Their corewood is graybark dyed, eastern hard-rock maple with $1/16$" laminations. They are cut and tapered to .002" per inch by the Old Master Crafters. The thinner lamination is placed on the back where it bends and bonds better to the sweeping riser contour, and the thicker lamination is placed on the flatter belly. Recently, Black Widow introduced a bias material into their limbs as a reinforcing limb core component to provide extra strength when using their new Fast Flight Flemish-twist strings.

When pairing laminations from a batch, Jimmy lightly sprays the outward facing sides with a red dye which helps to bring out the grain contrast when the laminations are glued under clear fiberglass. Although the clear fiberglass displays the beauty of the graybark corewoods, it can also show problems. "One of the disadvantages is that any little imperfections show. But that's also an advantage. Because if you are shooting those limbs and you see something starting to happen and grow, you know you're in trouble. But if it was a black or brown fiberglass limb, you might not notice a problem until it hit you in the head."

JIMMY'S JOB

Before gluing up a bow or a set of limbs, Jimmy double checks the form and steel clamping strips to be sure they are completely clean. Even a small, dried glue fleck will show up as a dent in the fiberglass of a pressed bow.

Black Widow's bow forms are made from a durable pressed epoxy resin material that is impervious to heat. The form surfaces are faced with stainless steel. Before laying up a bow, the dense form is prewarmed in the oven to accelerate glue curing and then it's coated with Johnson's "Traffic Wax" floor wax. This prevents any runny glue from adhering to the form.

When preparing to lay up a bow, Jimmy feathers the fadeouts using a thirty-six grit vertical sander. He starts with a profiling jig and finishes by holding the riser flat to the working surface and gently feathering the fadeouts to paper thinness. "It's a delicate job," says Jimmy, "that takes a long time to learn."

Just before glue up, Jimmy holds the fiberglass up to a fluorescent light and looks for any flaws or hairline cracks. Next he brushes clean all gluing surfaces of the composites.

He then mixes the epoxy by weight, five parts resin to one part hardener. Even though it doesn't look very appetizing, the fresh mixed glue emits the distinct aroma of corn chips. He applies a good coat to all contact surfaces using a foam roller.

Once the composites are laid up in the form, Jimmy begins the involved and confidential process of pressing the bow materials together. Black Widow's bow pressing technique utilizes a clamping method that is an exacting and time consuming process, one which has evolved from thirty years of building recurves. After the composites are pressed, they are heat cured at 180 degrees.

Another of Jimmy's glue tasks is laminating the tip overlays. The layers of bias material, fiberglass, and compressed fiber-filled resin, are laminated together as a strip on a curved jig that matches the limb tip contour. With its row of pressing bolts, the jig resembles the metallic backbone of a science fiction creature. Once these epoxied laminates are pressed and heat cured, they are cut into three inch pieces and feathered on both ends using a small

CURVED TIP OVERLAY FORM — Black Widow is one of the rare bowmakers that makes overlays to fit the curve of the limb tip. Jimmy hand tightens the special press.

feathering jig. They are then cut in half and each piece is glued on the limb tip back with the feathered end facing the handle.

MAKING THEM NARROW

After the take-down limbs are pressed, they are ground to riser end width. Another sophisticated air lock jig is then used to clamp them in place for drilling the mounting and stud pin holes.

To ensure optimum appearance and performance, Widow's take-down limbs are aligned, tillered, and shaped while attached to the same handle they will be sold with. To help give the finished bow a one-piece appearance, the sides of the limb fadeouts are fashioned to a flush fit with their matching handle.

Once the limbs are template outlined and ground to rough shape, Bill performs the important task of bringing them into alignment and tillering them. Although all phases of bow crafting are important, he says that proper tillering and limb alignment are the most critical. "It can be a beautiful bow," Bill says, "but it has got to shoot properly. And it has got to perform."

To bring limbs into alignment, he braces a bow using a string with tip clamping devices on each end. He uses a bench-mounted spindle to hold the handle while he stands back and pulls the string. By sighting down the string with one eye closed, he can see how the limbs track in both static and dynamic positions. Bill says that one side or the other of the limb will always be a little stronger and that experience really helps when bringing them into proper alignment. It's a difficult job that's made even tougher by Widow's narrow limb design.

He removes material off the strong side by sanding the limb edges on a horizontal belt sander until both limbs are in perfect alignment. Once the tip clamps are positioned so that both limbs are in alignment with the string, Bill marks the tip ends and grinds the edges to final shape.

Next he delicately feathers the limb edges creating a modified trapezoidal cross section narrowing to the back. He uses his experienced eye and the flexibility of the upright sander to help him achieve the desired angle of feathering. Bill explains that besides making the bow faster, feathering the limb edges to the back helps prevent limb twist by giving the limb cross-sectional stability.

When tillering, Bill strives for a five-sixteenths inch positive tiller on most bows and a three-eighths inch tiller for three-finger-under shooters. He brings the bows into tiller during limb shaping and fine tunes them by sanding a small amount of fiberglass off the backing and facing.

Producing their narrow-limbed bows requires a lot of precision workmanship. It takes time and talent. "If the string," Bill explains, "is off one eighth of an inch on a standard one and three-quarter inch to two inch wide limb like most bows, it's not off very much of the percentage of the limb. It won't hardly twist the limb. But if it's off that far on our narrow limb, it's going to come around and break the bow. Our string alignment has got to be exact."

Although it's harder to craft, Black Widow's slim limb design helps give it its speed. "If you compare a wide limb," Bill says, "to a narrow limb of the same construction, you will lose about five pounds of pull on the narrow limb. So we've got close to half as much material here in this area of our narrow limb as a two inch wide limb, with only a five pound lighter bow. With

A SPECIAL LIMB — Bill delicately feathering the limb edges to the back. Besides building their narrow limb, it's one of Widow's secrets to optimum limb performance.

our narrow limb you've got less mass recovering, so it's going to make a quicker bow. Our recurve truly uncoils during draw, providing smoothness and speed. It works as a whip rather than just a catapult like a longbow."

"Building a narrow limb," Ken adds, "takes a lot more time and expertise. Plus you've got to be able to build a glue line that's going to stand the stress because you have less surface and glue area with the same amount of pressure. So you have to have a good glue line."

NEARLY FINISHED

After Bill finishes working on the limbs, he cuts rough string nocks in the tips with Widow's nock cutting machine. The string nocks are finished by shaping them with a special round carbide saw blade and then dressing them up with small rat-tail files and sandpaper. The string grooves are filed by hand following a centerline marked on the limb bellies. This line is drawn using a block type jig which is run down both sides of the limb to ensure exact centering.

After the string nocks and grooves are fashioned, the bow is final sanded on an air sleeved spindle sander using a dull 180 grit paper. Some hand sanding is also required around the shelf and window junction. Before spraying a batch of bows, Black Widow's paint room is vacuumed and wetted down to remove any dust. The bows are wiped with Sherwin-Williams natural paste filler-sealer and then wiped clean with a special pad. This seals any porous areas in the wood and helps the finish coats go on smoothly.

Bill sprays on the two-part epoxy finish that's manufactured by Peterson Chemical. The Crown Jewel first receives two heavy coats. One week later the hardened finish is sanded smooth and the bow gets two more finish coats.

The MA II and the Graybark receive two heavy coats followed by a light stippled "Spider Webb" coat to reduce reflection. Then they get two more coats of a thinned over-spray mix of half epoxy and half thinner.

Sight and quiver bushings are optional. Their holes are drilled and tapped, and the threaded brass bushings are epoxied and screwed into the handle. This produces an extremely strong bushing.

The stud pin holes on the take-down limbs are coated with a protective sealer to prevent any moisture from being absorbed by the corewood or fadeout wood. This may sound a bit overcautious, but it's just another part of Black Widow's attention to detail.

HANDLE WITH CARE

Attention to detail is also reflected in Widow's owner's manual provided with each bow. It's a well-written and clearly illustrated booklet that explains bow assembly, proper stringing, maintaining limb alignment, bow care and storage, installing string silencers, shooting off the shelf, and proper tuning. In fact, it's such a helpful booklet that it would be an excellent reference for any recurve owner.

In the past, one of the biggest problems with Widow longevity was twisted limbs. The narrower limbs are much more susceptible to twist if strung improperly. And many new customers weren't familiar with either handling or tuning recurves. But this problem has been virtually eliminated since Widow introduced their improved stringer and the detailed owner's manual. Even with the manual, Ken gets several calls each week from new Widow owners looking for help tuning their bows — and they get it.

TESTS N' STRESS

Besides supplying manuals and stringers to ensure bow longevity, Ken designs new Widows with durability in mind. Although today the MA II enjoys the top spot on Black Widow's sales chart, it didn't come easy. When designing it, Ken trusted his strong preference for a natural wood handle and clear glass limbs. But like any new model, he wanted to be sure it deserved the Black Widow name.

"In designing the first MA, I wanted a lightweight bow. When we finished it I thought that maybe it was too light. I was concerned that it might have a lot of shock and jump in the hand. So we took it behind the building and shot it. And boy it shot nice. That was a good feeling."

But Ken's elation on how the bow shot was soon overshadowed. "After shooting that first MA, our silver anniversary bow, it developed a crack right at the shelf. That concerned me, naturally. I was in the car at the busiest intersection in the city of Springfield when the light dawned on me. It was because we had sawn that handle out with an old chrome-plated three-toothed skip blade. I remembered we had generated quite a bit of heat when sawing. Then it suddenly dawned on me that it was the HEAT that destroyed that glue line. And it was a relief to discover that.

"We were concerned about how strong that wooden handle was because Black Widow had been building metal handles for recurves. But I had a preference for the look and feel of wood. So we thought we better try to destroy one to see how strong it was.

"We had a set of old limbs, that were around ninety pounds, with a vertical crack in the glass. We modified them so we could mount them on that handle and set up outside with some pulleys and a scale. Big Bill and I got on that thing and i think that scale ran out of numbers at 230 pounds and there was another twenty pounds of space before it actually bottomed out. And we bottomed it out at 250 pounds. At that point we had those limbs pulled in the neighborhood of forty-five to forty-six inches. I thought the string was going to come off. You can only pull limbs so far, and finally they went. Man, one of them shot across and hit the building like a rocket. And it drove the handle down into the gravel. But the handle stayed together in one piece."

Early in production, Ken investigated the possibility of producing MA handle sections on a duplicating machine, the same kind used for making gun stocks. Ken asked the duplicating people if the fiberglass in the handles would pose any problem and they told him it shouldn't. So he made some specialized jigs for his handles and he went to the duplicating company. "We got set up with the first handles and turned the machine on. I asked, 'Have you got carbide cutters in there?' and they said, 'Well no, we don't think we'll need those.'

"And they tore into that handle and got down to the fiberglass and that cutter just kind of wilted. So they went and got their carbide cutters and the same thing happened. The smoke just rolled off and it got hot and broke. And after breaking a few more they decided that they had bit off more than they could chew. I remember driving home that day disillusioned and discouraged, and that's when we started developing our sanding profiler. Plus we improved on it, and now we run tolerances plus or minus five-thousandths of an inch."

BIG BILL

Ken credits much of the quality of Widow bows to his meticulous production manager, Bill Bonner. Bill, now in his mid-thirties, began working for the Wilson brothers in 1973. He's an instinctive shot who enjoys whitetail hunting with his favored 62" MA II. He likes the beauty and in-the-hand warmth of its wooden handle. "And it hits," Bill says, "right where I aim."

He hunts close to home just north of Springfield. "My bowhunting trips represent enjoyment. In my opinion, way too many people put too much emphasis on going out and killing meat. And that's what we hear from people coming back to recurves. They have gone the route of compounds and it was just KILL, KILL. They had to kill. They lost the enjoyment of bowhunting because of the continuous torment inside of them to kill a bigger one. The idea is ENJOYMENT in any sport.

"We had a guy call that had been hunting with a compound for twelve years, and had not missed a deer in seven years. But he had been hunting a buck for five years and on the third day of season, that buck walked in broadside at twelve yards. This guy drew his bow back, anchored with his release, put the peep sight on the buck, and sat there holding the bow as the deer walked off. He said that he sat there for about thirty minutes trying to figure out why he didn't shoot. Then he went home and got an old forty-five pound recurve out of the closet and went and bought some arrows. And he said, 'I'll tell you, I've missed three deer this year, but I've had more fun missing those three than all the deer I've killed in the last five years.' "

KEN'S TRAILS

Like Bill and most of Black Widow's bow crafting team, Ken Beck also enjoys the thrills of bowhunting. Now in his early fifties, this Springfield resident became interested in archery about seventeen years ago. He's a member of The Missouri Bowhunters Association, The Missouri Big Bucks Association, and The Professional Bowhunters Society.

Ken enjoys whitetail and turkey hunting, but elk is his favorite animal to bowhunt. "Hunting a bull elk is sort of like hunting an 800 pound turkey — because they respond so well to a call."

Years ago, he also enjoyed squirrel hunting. But one day outside his house, a baby squirrel hopped up to him and climbed his pant-leg. The little rascal seemed more than just friendly, he was looking for a home. So the

Beck's adopted the furry youth and named him "Rocky." Since then, Ken has put his squirrel hunting days behind.

SHOW-ME WHITETAILS

It's Missouri whitetails that bring a grin to Ken's face and make his eyebrows arch when recalling his most exciting bowhunts. "The uniqueness of these two big whitetails on the wall is that I killed them both in the same year in Missouri with my bow: one during bow season, and one during gun season.

"I had been to Colorado that year and blanked out and was feeling a little sorry for myself. So I came back here and started deer hunting. I had seen this one buck the year before, and I saw him before the season opened. On the evening of opening day I spotted him out of bow range. The third morning when I was on the stand, he went down to the spring behind me to water. I saw him coming out of the spring and was hoping he would come to my tree stand but he didn't. He jumped a fence and stood there and looked in my direction and then looked in the other direction and decided to angle my way. I promised myself that I wouldn't take over a thirty yard shot at him.

"He was going to cross an opening that I concluded was about thirty-five yards away and beyond my self-imposed limitation. But when he got to that opening, he stopped angling away, and I quickly decided that might be the best chance I'd ever have with him.

"I drew and shot, and the arrow looked good in flight. Then I heard a 'crack' and I didn't know if I had hit him in the shoulder blade or not. But when he turned from me, I could only see about ten inches of the arrow protruding. I knew then that the crack I heard was the far shoulder, not the near shoulder. And the arrow was in the right place in his body.

"So, I just got down, walked back to my jeep, went to town, had breakfast, and came back and got him afterwards. Interestingly enough, I didn't find any blood for seventy yards and he piled up at 100 yards. And it was a good hit, but he bled mostly inside. I think hitting that far shoulder caused him to run hard for a short time."

Later that year, Ken bowhunted a waterfowl refuge where only bowhunters were allowed to hunt the deer. With a gun tag on his back and his Widow at his side, Ken headed into the refuge during gun season. "This buck had a lot of fresh scrapes where I was hunting. One morning around eight o'clock, a deer came down one of the trails and instead of coming past my stand, he broke off into the brush and bedded down. I thought it was a buck and I stayed on the stand until 10:30 when I was supposed to meet Dan. So I got down and stalked toward where I thought he was bedded.

"I saw him get up. He rose and started walking about thirty yards away through the timber, unaware that I was there. I saw an opening ahead that I thought I could get an arrow through. So I drew as he was approaching it, and I was thinking, 'shoot for the shoulder blade', because he was walking and if I aimed for the shoulder blade, by the time the arrow got there I should hit behind the shoulder. I had that all figured out but unfortunately when his nose hit that window, reflex action took over and I let the arrow go. I didn't intend to, but bang, it just went off. That arrow went right under his neck and clattered. He spooked, jumped a few steps, looked around, and started walking again. So I got an arrow nocked again but he finally picked up my scent and was gone.

"I went over to retrieve my arrow and found some hair on the ground. I had just clipped him on the neck, almost accidentally cutting his throat.

"I didn't sleep too well that night. I had really been hard on myself for missing. The next morning I was back up in that stand and it was drizzling a little bit so I had my rain hood up. I was looking through this fork in this tree watching the trail where I had seen him the morning before. I checked my watch and it was about eight o'clock. Then I saw something out of the left corner of my eye on a different trail and turned my head. With my head inside the rain hood there wasn't much movement, but I moved my head a little bit, and about twenty-five yards on my left, there he was. And when I moved, he looked up at me.

"Now this deer is not very smart. After the morning before, he should have left the county, and here he was coming back the next day. Eternity seemed to pass and then he put his head down and came on down the trail. Man, I had to get my bow. I had my hands in my pockets trying to keep them dry and my bow was hanging off to the side. So I reached for the bow as he was passing some brush but he saw me. And he stopped and looked up at me again.

"In my imagination I saw this tremendous explosion that was about to take place with him leaving. But it didn't happen! He just stood there and looked at me for a long time. Then he put his head down and came on. I was petrified. I couldn't move. I didn't dare move! And I watched him walk fifteen yards right down the shooting lane, right past my stand. He was angling away and sort of in one motion, I got the bow off the hook and leaned out to my right. I drew, found a little hole through the brush, and nailed him. He went about sixty yards and I heard him go down. That deer wasn't too smart. And that was the last day of gun season."

KEEPING YOUR COOL

Memorable seasons like Ken's involve a variety of skills. But one of the most important is being able to shoot under pressure when that buster buck presents himself. "Unlike a baseball player who may get up to bat four or five times a game, and many games per season, a bowhunter, particularly if he is not the best bowhunter in the world, like me, may only get one chance. So you have spent a year preparing and choosing a bow and arrow setup. And you practice, practice, and practice. Then you scout, select tree stand locations, get in that sand and spend hours there. Then BOOM! There comes that magic moment.

"So it's like an inverted pyramid. All that preparation just comes down and focuses on that one moment of truth. Talk about excitement and pressure. I don't mean pressure that you have to kill it, but pressure from all of the preparation that's gone in to it. It's right down to that one opportunity. Then you have to be able to let it happen, because it's too late to start thinking about it. It has to just happen. But if you're well prepared and everything is grooved as a reflex, you don't have to think about it. It just happens."

Many beginning bowhunters have a tough time letting their bowhunting reflexes take over during the sudden rush of buck fever. "That first animal is always the most difficult to stay cool and under control with, and as time goes on you've been there before. And even though you're hyper and excited, you're better able to at least keep it under control. That's what makes bowhunting, bowhunting."

BOWS N' BITS

One of the things that makes Ken's bowhunting, bowhunting, is his favorite bow. It's his 58" MA II. "I like the color of it, and I appreciate a beautiful bow. You can set in a tree stand and look at it, admire it, and enjoy it. And because it is a bow that's pretty, you don't have to hide it with camouflage. It blends in real well with the woods. Matter of fact, I like to tell about the customer who called and told me about almost losing his bow in the woods because it blended in so well."

Adorning Ken's MA II, is a Black Widow bow quiver full of 28" aluminum arrows. "Our quiver is solid, quiet, and durable, and it lays in close to the bow."

To maintain that close instinctive relationship with his bow, Ken practices almost every evening, shooting with his high under-the-eye, Apache style anchor. "Years ago when I shot barebow, I shot gun-barrel or point of aim. But I've changed to a higher, split-finger anchor, probably what you would call a gun-barrel. I have evolved into what most people would call instinctive shooting in that I'm not looking at or thinking about the shaft and gap. Yet, on the other hand, I

Apache style, Ken zeros in with a new Graybark, unfolding the narrow limbs.

have a theory that any instinctive shooter sees all of these things and takes that information to the brain and computes it subconsciously."

When pulling his bunched arrows from the center of the target he jokingly distracts from his skill. "Every year my draw seems to shorten up. I don't know for sure, but if I hunt until I'm eighty, I might be shooting a twelve-inch arrow."

TIPS FOR CUSTOMERS

Many new Black Widows customers are former compound shooters, and Ken takes his time fitting them with the right recurve. "I know that whatever you shoot, you're better off to be shooting a few pounds too little than a few pounds too much. But as a rule of thumb, I suggest that a compound shooter drop down in weight at least ten to fifteen percent when switching to a recurve. If someone is shooting a seventy pound compound, I would suggest that they drop down into the low sixties. If they get a bow, and it's more than they can handle, they are going to get discouraged. On the other hand, if they get a bow that's a little lighter than they could shoot, they will develop good form and not develop bad habits. And when they get to shooting it well, if they decide they want a heavier set of limbs, they will be ready for them."

For newcomers or latecomers to the sport, Ken offers some shooting advice. "If someone wants to shoot without sights, shoot instinctively. A pretty high majority of people switching to recurves want to shoot instinctively with a simple setup. I think that's a good way to hunt, and I think that it's a challenging way. There is a certain amount of satisfaction in doing it that way.

"Start shooting close to the target and gradually move back as you develop your confidence. As you accomplish that, don't shoot at the same yardage all the time, move around and shoot. Get out in the woods and stump shoot. I heard somewhere not too long ago, another good suggestion. That is to practice after dark shooting at a candle. Because it enables you to develop an instinctive method without seeing the arrow."

Black Widow's customers are a blend of some of the most experienced recurve shooters in the country and those looking for their first recurve. Some want the famous speed while others desire smoothness and little finger pinch. And some seek a beautiful bow to hang on the wall and admire as a collector's item. Black Widow has them all. "Black Widows have always been noted for their smoothness of draw, and for having good cast. So I inherited a lot of technology and a lot of experimentation and knowledge from the Wilson Brothers. And we've tried to improve upon it. We take pride in building a bow that's fast and a bow that's smooth."

Most traditional enthusiasts who have a dozen recurves hanging on the wall always seem to have some reason for buying one more. And Ken has heard most of them. "One fellow tried to convince his wife by saying, 'I need to order a new bow.' But she asked, 'What's wrong with the old one?' He responded emphatically, 'Why I used up all its luck!' "

Chapter Seventeen

BIGHORN BOWHUNTING COMPANY

IN THE SHADOWS OF THE ROCKIES

Away from Denver's bluish haze and bustling pace, the South Platte River ambles northward through the outlying towns of Wattenburg and Platteville. It also flows through Fort Lupton, located on Highway 85 about twenty miles north of Denver. There, almost within shouting distance of the enticing Frontal Range, a handful of workers manufacture bows esteemed by discriminating bowhunters across the country. It's the home of Bighorn Bowhunting Company.

At the helm of Bighorn is G. Fred Asbell. Besides being noted for his bowmaking, Asbell is well known throughout bowhunting circles as an accomplished bowhunter, a skilled writer, and a masterful instinctive shot. With his full bristling beard, high cheek bones, and weather-etched features, he resembles a mountain man from Colorado's colorful past.

Asbell's a hard man who doesn't dabble in life — he jumps in with both feet.

HIGH COUNTRY FUN

When he jokes, he plunges in like a mischievous teenager, often making light of his own predicaments. One of his funniest occurred during an elk hunt with Bob Pitt in Colorado's high country. Asbell had arrowed a nice bull that somehow became wedged between two trees on a mountain side. "I couldn't turn him over and I didn't have a rope, saw, or anything. I wasn't really prepared for elk hunting.

"I took one side of the rack and pushed hard but the tines just dug into the ground. So finally I slipped off my belt and grabbed one leg, pulled it over and tied it to a tree. Then I took my bowstring and pulled the rack over and tied it to a tree. Then I took my spare bowstring and pulled the other hind leg over and tied it. And then I took my shirt off and tied the other leg.

"I almost had this elk around on its back. So I ended up taking off my pants and I tied the other leg off. Finally I had this elk turned completely upside down between these trees with its legs tied as far apart as I could get them so I could work on it.

"Now I'm just standing there in my underwear. I've got my knife out, and I'm squatted down behind this spread-eagle elk. Then I heard something, and I looked around and here is this couple standing there, two backpackers, just standing there looking at me with these big eyes. Before I could say a word those people just whirled and tore down a pack trail. And I'm going, 'Wa-wa-wait a minute.'

"I always wondered what kind of stories got told about that. I can just hear this guy and his wife saying, 'Do you know what bowhunters are doing now?' "

SPREADING THE WORD

Asbell not only enjoys telling his bowhunting stories, he's good at it. He's one of the country's top bowhunting writers. As hunting editor, his tag-along style narrative helps make *BOWHUNTER* America's top bowhunting periodical. His articles blend bowhunting education with humor, adventure, and vivid hoof-churning action. Asbell sprinkles his articles with just enough "Hmmm's" and plain talk to make his readers feel like they're with him on the hunt. "To me, telling a story is trying to entertain people. I have to decide what's interesting and how to tell it to make it interesting.

"When I read something that sounds good, I ask myself, 'Why is this sounding so good? What did the writer do to made that so clear?' Hopefully it's pretty simple writing, it's pretty basic and there are no big words. If I have to go to a dictionary to look up a word an author used, then he used the wrong word." Asbell's first book, *Instinctive Shooting, A Step-by-Step Guide to Better Bowhunting*, is quickly becoming a favorite among both seasoned and beginning instinctive shooters.

When he has something to say about bowhunting, Asbell doesn't limit his words to the pen. He's also a poised speaker who uses his speaking opportunities to promote and uphold the sport he loves. He maintains high personal standards and hunting ethics, and he's quick to boldly speak to those issues that threaten bowhunting. Not everyone agrees with his perspective, but most admire his convictions. "The future of all hunting, gun or bow, is totally based on non-hunter's perceptions of who we are.

"Something like seven to nine percent of the people in this country are hunters. About an equal number are anti-hunters. And everybody else in the middle are just non-hunters. They're not anti, they're not pro — they just don't have an opinion. But for most of those people it only takes thirty seconds of exposure to some jerk in camouflage for them to become an anti-hunter. I don't think bowhunters realize how critical it is how others see us."

Asbell uses his speaking opportunities to help both the quality and the future of bowhunting, even when he's up in the high country during bow season, and especially when the audience is our next generation of bow-hunters. "I was talking about ethics to these eleven to seventeen-year-old kids up at Jay Versuh's bowhunting school. I said, 'If you are going out and trying to hit on some gal your age, you are very careful about how you approach her and what you say. You just wouldn't walk up and tell her that you're a hunter, and you are going out tomorrow to try and stick sharp sticks in animals to make them bleed. You wouldn't do that at all. The same thing holds true with bowhunters talking to anyone.' It's very important how others see us because others represent our future."

When discussing hunting with non-hunters, Asbell usually makes them understand at least his perspective and the logistics of the sport. Anti-hunters, however, are often impossible to talk with. Yet he still tries. "First, I don't go out to kill an animal. What I am taking part in is a primitive need within that just hasn't been removed from me: that is to experience hunting, collecting, and furnishing meat for my family. That's a very big part of it. I don't go out there specifically to just kill something.

"I like some of the things that Aldo Leopold talked about. He said that it was very interesting that you could take a two-year-old kid and show him a golf ball, a basketball, a tennis ball, whatever, and nothing happens. But show him a deer and every hair on the back of his neck stands up. Why is that? It's true that a lot of people get excited the first time they see a deer. It isn't because at three or four years old they had been taught that they were going to be hunters. It's that little bell that's down there, that's been there since the beginning of time."

TAKING A STAND

Because of his grit, Asbell often finds himself in the middle of controversial bowhunting issues. And one of the most heated, involves preventing the use of crossbows during archery season. "People who push crossbows are as strongly on the side of the demise of hunting as any anti-hunter. The difference is that the anti-hunter just wants to see it end, but these guys with the crossbows are going to make some money and then bowhunting is going to end. Really that's the only difference.

"I think we all need to understand that the only reason anybody is talking about crossbows right now, the only reason they are even getting off first base, is because bowhunters are using so much high-tech crap. So many of the states think that today's bowhunting is not that far from using a crossbow. If they tried to put the crossbow on the market fifteen years ago, bowhunters would have gone insane.

"Manufacturers won't be able to sell crossbows if they have to be used during rifle season. That's why they're trying so hard to get them into our archery seasons."

Proponents say crossbows are similar in many ways to today's high-tech equipment. But Asbell doesn't share their views. "When you put that stock to your shoulder, and look down that barrel, and squeeze that trigger, that ain't no bow! And that's one of the things we are trying to get through to people in the Fish and Game Commissions. But the problem is that they perceive today's bowhunters as using anything that comes down the road that can be used to kill an animal, any kind of gadget. I think we all have to face the fact that if bowhunters had to take today's equipment and go to the Fish and Game Commissions and try to get the kind of seasons we've got, they would be up a creek. Our seasons today are based on what bowhunting used to be."

And what bowhunting used to be is a far cry from what it may be if crossbows infiltrate bow seasons. "I saw a write up about a guy in Florida who is making a crossbow that doesn't even use the compound concept. It uses stainless steel springs of some sort, and it's adjustable up to 800 pounds. He said that it can be used to shoot grappling hooks, and that an 800 pounder can be cocked by a child. And we know that in Europe they have repeating crossbows and automatic cocking ones. We haven't seen anything except the very tip of the iceberg here. If we let these guys get their feet in the door, we're goners."

To combat issues that threaten the sport, bowhunters need to be organized and involved. Asbell sets a shining example. He is President of the Pope and Young Club, serving his third term. He also belongs to twenty-seven bowhunting organizations. Of these, he believes that the Professional Bowhunters Society offers the best potential for strengthening bowhunting. "Across the country bowhunters are ten times more organized than any other group. That's why we are doing so well."

CATCHING THE FEVER

Asbell hasn't always been an active spokesman on behalf of bowhunting. A native of Illinois, he grew up in southern Indiana and became interested in archery after getting out of the service. "I shot a bow for a couple of years before I ever went hunting, even before I realized that there was such a thing as a deer season. I remember my brother asking me, 'When are you going to take that thing and go hunt deer?' And I said, 'What?' "

Asbell's early bowhunting years were lean ones. Indiana didn't have many deer then, and during his first year afield he saw only one. The next year he saw a buck on the last day of the season. "This guy I knew, who was a farmer and a muzzle loader, felt sorry for me and took me to his stand where he had been seeing this buck. I got in his tree stand, and the buck came down the trail at the precise time, but instead of walking under me it walked up on the hill right level with me at about fifteen yards. At that time I had probably shot two trillion arrows. I had been shooting a bow for about four years, and I was the state champ. There were very few people who could shoot a hunting bow as well as I could.

"Well, this buck came walking by and I started to pull the bow, but I had buck fever — bad — and I didn't wait until he walked past, I just drew as he came toward me. He stopped and looked straight at me. I was shooting a fifty-five pound Hoyt, and I held it while he just kept looking at me. Then he turned his head and started walking, and I shot two feet over his head. I thought I was going to throw up. I was violently sick and thinking, 'Awh God, no, bring him back, let me do it again, please.' Then I didn't want to leave the woods. I just stayed there and kept thinking, 'What can I do to change this? Is there something else I can do? Can I go find him?' Oh, that was terrible."

With that typical introduction to bowhunting behind him, Asbell was hooked and went on to enjoy his share of bowhunting successes, many in the wild frontiers of the north. "I went to Alaska for three months when I was twenty-six. I worked for IBM, and my buddy Bob Pitt owned his own business, but we took a leave of absence. We had an outfitter who said, 'You can come and stay a week for a thousand dollars or you can stay the whole season for a thousand dollars.' So we went in during August and came out the last of October. We saw the pilot about every two weeks and that was it. That was the greatest experience of my life."

It was during another wilderness trip to British Columbia a year later that Asbell made his most memorable shot. "The grizzly was my best shot only because I was young and under a tremendous amount of pressure, and because here was this big brown growler standing there. I pulled the bow back but I didn't shoot, I just let the arrow back down. I thought, 'Naw, you didn't have it.' And then I just pulled up and shot and hit him perfectly. That may have been the only time in my life that I have ever let an arrow down."

LOVES THOSE MULIES

Although he still hunts the remote corners of North America, Asbell's favorite bowhunting is chasing velvet-racked mule deer. He enjoys matching wits with whopper bucks and regards them as one of the toughest western trophies to tag. "Oh, you can take a forky with a rock, they're just everywhere and they just stand there and look at you. But when you start looking for the big ones, that's a different game."

He usually hunts in Colorado which harbors some of the best mule deer hunting in the country. For big bucks, Asbell hunts early in the season and he heads high. "It's a particularly good time for mule deer because they're in places where they're more huntable and they're still in velvet. Mule deer normally move out of the trees and the grass and into the brush as soon as their antlers get hard. Some of these big mesa tops are just covered with bucks from July until about Labor Day. But when they start losing their velvet around Labor Day they absolutely move off of those areas. It isn't specifically a migratory thing. They are particularly cautious of their antlers when they're in velvet, and they tend to avoid real heavy brush. Another reason is that the blood in the antlers attracts flies and up high, the constant wind keeps them away."

BUCKSKIN STRATEGY

Consistently arrowing trophy-size mulies is an intricate game requiring a specific plan. Asbell's is time tested. His first rule is to hunt where the big ones are. "Probably that sounds sort of foolish, but that is one of the biggest mistakes guys make. They spend nine months of the year with all their preparations, yet they still don't know where the big ones live."

Once he's in big buck country, Asbell uses his spot n' stalk technique. "Everybody thinks that in stalking you walk in one end of the woods and just walk quietly until you find a deer, then you slip up on it and kill it. That's not true at all.

"You scout just like you do when you're stand hunting. You look for activity and you hunt there — not always areas, sometimes just spots. I'm just kind of a mobile blind and happen to be on the ground. But I don't just go stumbling blindly into a big piece of woods. I know exactly where I'm going to hunt, and when I finish hunting a specific area, I go and try another area. But you don't just wander around hoping to see a deer. It's very calculated.

"The most important thing is seeing them first. If you can't see an animal before he sees you, then your chances of getting up on him are almost zero. What I do is pick a spot five or ten yards away and I move to it fairly quickly and quietly, and then I stand there. I may stand there five minutes or I may stand there twenty. But I stay there and figure out where I am going from there. And that's always when I see the deer. Then if they're moving and you are stationary, you got em'. But if you are moving, they will see you every time before you see them, believe me."

After spotting his quarry, he shifts into his "situation maximization" hunting mode. "I look at an animal and try to figure what he's doing, what he intends to do, where he's going, and what the wind situation is. To me that is so neat, it's like I'm plugged in into a 110 volt light socket all the time. And mule deer are so visible that there's never a morning or evening that I'm not into good deer."

But getting into good mule deer and tagging one don't always go hand in hand. Especially when they're really big bucks. "For almost two weeks last year I messed with a buck that would exceed the world record, there's no question about it. He looked like a big caribou. I was within twenty-five yards of him twice but I couldn't get a clean shot.

"Once I was just fifteen yards downhill from him at ten in the morning, and he was already bedded. The wind was blowing perfectly. I knew I had to get him up, so I threw my Mini-Mag flashlight at him. Nothing happened. Then I threw a powder bottle. Still nothing. I threw everything I could find. I even threw my glove, but it only went a few feet and caught on some brush. I finally ended up throwing my really nice hunting knife at him. That almost hit him, and boy did he come up then. He jumped up and was looking down at me but all I could see was about a third of his brisket, and then he turned around and started feeding. I never got a shot at him. Every time I walked away I thought, 'Gosh that was just fantastic.' Man, when I get that close to a big deer like that and don't get a shot but I don't spook him, I feel like I have won seven-eighths of the game. Plus, I get to do it again tomorrow."

That big mulie may have eluded Asbell's arrows but many others haven't. Although he's reluctant to boast, he has harvested most North American big game species with a good many making the book. "Yeah, I have been successful, but I have also spent about ten times as much time in the woods as most people. I don't think I have any more talent than anybody else. It's just that if you keep your line in the water a lot and work at it hard, eventually things work out."

SIMPLE YET EFFECTIVE

The core of Asbell's bowhunting equipment is one of his custom sixty-five to seventy pound recurves. Although he shoots them well, he warns that these heavyweight bows aren't for everyone. "We are trying to really pull people down in weight as much as possible. Most people are way overbowed. The average guy has no business shooting anything over about fifty-five pounds. I just happened to have been shooting a weight like mine for about twenty-five years, plus I weigh 220 pounds. A big portion of our business is guys changing from compounds and they all want to stay up there in the heavy weight. I try to talk them down, but invariably they ask, 'What do you shoot?' I don't really want to lie, but I wish that I could say fifty-five pounds."

On his bowstring he ties dental floss for a nocking point. "I don't like those metal things. They tear up a glove. Plus, I shoot bare-fingered a lot and, boy, are they tough on your fingers."

For arrow shafting, Asbell prefers cedar, and he fletches them with three high-profile 5½" feathers. "Just a standard five inch three-fletch doesn't stabilize an arrow quickly enough for me. And arrow flight is the key to penetration, not bow weight or anything else, but that arrow going straight into something. I can't stand to see an arrow flop around."

On the biting end of his shafts he mounts single-blade Delta broadheads and he carries his arrows in a Bighorn bow quiver.

When toting his bow during the early season, he likes wearing vertical tiger stripe cotton camouflage. During colder weather he normally wears drab wool or plaids. But no matter what season or garb, Asbell always pays attention to his face. "I really believe in face camouflage. I always put that stuff all over my face. The first thing you see on a person in the woods is their face. I may hunt in just regular grey or brown or checked patterns, but I still have my face camouflaged. I think that's super important."

To top off his bowhunting attire he wears a felt or wool hunting hat, usually sporting a good luck totem. "I always have a feather someplace. I usually stick it out of my hat band. One time I found a feather right before I killed an animal and that's always a good luck sign to me."

Another reason Asbell wears a feather in his hat is because of his fascination with American Indians. "They were exemplary human beings. They had strong feelings about moral character and all sorts of things. That fascinated me because we considered them savages. In a fashion they certainly were. They weren't very nice people to have as enemies. Plus I'm probably about a sixteenth Cherokee Indian. I doubt if that has anything to do with my fascination, but I grew up playing cowboys and Indians. And I played cowboys and Indians until I was probably sixteen!"

Asbell's Indian fascination is also reflected in his back-country accommodations. "The first time I stayed in a tepee, I loved it. So I bought one. My friend Bob Pitt couldn't believe I'd done it, and he said, 'Are you really going to take that damn tepee up there and set it up to stay in?' He just didn't care for it, and he wanted to stay in a motel. But after about a day in that tepee, from then on, if I wasn't going to take it he wanted to know, 'Why not?' It is really neat."

LOOK N' SHOOT

Asbell's Indian characteristics also show through in the way he handles a bow. He's one of today's experts on true instinctive shooting. "My form of instinctive shooting is just looking at something and shooting at it. That's what instinctive shooting is. You look at what you want to hit and then physically launch the arrow. Your instinctive memory takes care of the adjustments. But most guys don't shoot instinctively. They find it difficult to really turn themselves loose. They believe that they must have a reference point or a system. I start drawing and I look at what I'm going to hit and I just shoot. I'm not aware of the arrow's location when I'm shooting, and in fact if I am, it messes me up.

"It's like shooting a basketball or throwing a football. You must be able to go through the physical motion without a conscious effort. All of your concentration must be totally on what you want to hit, and as soon as that wavers, you've missed. But I think it's particularly good for hunting."

Asbell's method is simple and yet effective in the field, a place where excitement can sometimes foul the more sophisticated shooting techniques. "I'm always amused by the guys with their complex shooting systems with sights, compounds, releases, peeps, and all those things. These guys can shoot dimes at twenty yards and groups the size of a tea cup at sixty yards. They are almost like bench-rest rifle shooters. And yet at fifteen yards one of these guys shoots over the top of an elk. To shoot over that elk's back with a bow that shoots 250 feet per second, he misjudged that animal by about forty yards. Actually, he didn't misjudge that animal. What he really did was pull all that junk back and did just what any instinctive shooter would do: he just looked at it and shot. But he never practiced that.

"There is this movie of one of these guys missing an animal at seventeen yards. Now this guy was PAA champ for about six years in a row, shooting a bow that shoots 287 feet per second. He has all this kind of junk, he goes through this complex shooting system, and he misses it. He shoots behind it and over its back at seventeen yards! So my theory is that everybody shoots instinctively anyway."

To stay in top shooting form Asbell shoots at least twice a day, every day, from June until hunting season. Even when he's in hunting camp he shoots two to three hours every day. "I take an arrow and walk and shoot, and walk and shoot. But I enjoy shooting a bow, so I do a lot of it."

After thousands of practice shots, it all comes down to one moment of truth on the aspen dotted slopes. When that moment arrives, Asbell mentally locks in on his target like radar. "When I decide that I want to try for a particular deer, then all I do from that point on is concentrate on that deer's shoulder. I don't ever look at the antlers again. When it gets within range and turns just right, I try to shoot him as quickly as I can. And I know if I really concentrate, I can hit anything I want, out to thirty-five yards."

NEEDED A BACK-UP

Whether he's hunting alpine mulies with a recurve or mountain caribou with a longbow, the bow at Asbell's side is a Bighorn. The reputation of Bighorn bows has helped to make the man famous just as much as the reputation of the man has helped make his bows famous. It's a symbiotic relationship — a near-perfect marriage that just kind of happened. "Denny Behn and I were in Alaska just sitting on the side of a hill BS'n as guys will do, and neither of us had a backup bow with us. I was shooting a Wing take-down and he had a Bear and neither of us had a backup set of limbs. Anyway, we decided we were going to build a bow.

"So we just started piddling with the idea, one thing led to another, and next thing you know here we are making bows in his basement. Denny is a short bow nut and the very first one we made was somewhere around fifty-two inches. It looked very much like the sweep of a cape buffalo's horns. If you could look at it and not want to put it on your head I would be amazed. The second one we made was a sixty inch bow for me. I shot a couple of deer with it but it was seventy-six pounds and a little heavier than I wanted."

When designing their early bows in 1977, they adopted favorable characteristics from a variety of other bows. "We just started looking at other people's bows, and began asking, 'What is it about this bow that I like? What makes it feel good?' And then we would try that. I don't believe there is an original bow, although most bowyers won't say that. Everything is based on something that you've heard, learned, or seen. You may put ideas from ten bows together to make one bow. But in the end, the ideas, individually, aren't new. Everything I've done is based on what other people have done. And if they're honest, they'll admit the same thing."

Behn left the business around 1983 and Asbell continued to manufacture his increasingly popular recurves. Today Bighorn offers three models of recurves and a newly introduced longbow.

ONE-PIECE DESIGN

Bighorn recently redesigned their one-piece recurve by shortening the riser, changing the limb angle, and redesigning the limb. "That's probably our quickest bow right now. We began making one-piece bows and that's all we had for years. Then we decided to build take-downs and they took over the business. For years the one-piece didn't get much attention because we didn't sell many of them. So this past fall we started messing with it in an attempt to bring up its performance and built the same kind of limb that we have on the take-down. But you can never really do the exact same thing with two different designs of bows. So what we ended up with was a bow that was a little quicker. It's a real screamer."

This screamer is Bighorn's CUSTOM GRAND SLAM one-piece recurve. It's available in 60" and 64" lengths. The 60" length has a mass weight of 2 pounds, 7 ounces, and a recommended brace height of 7 1/4" from the string to the throat.

Its impregnated maple "Ramwood" riser is 23½" long between the fade-outs. It is 1¾" wide near the fadeouts and thins to ¹¹/₁₆" through the center shot sight window. The riser is 2⅞" thick across the peaks and thins through the custom-shaped grip. The nicely crested arrow shelf is 2¼" across and is padded with synthetic brown fur. The sight window is full cut for 4½" above the shelf and contours back to full riser width 5½" above the shelf. It's equipped with a brown leather strike pad.

The riser is constructed from two solid pieces of Ramwood, an impregnated maple, which is sandwiched on a "V" shaped decorative .065" thick wedge of clear maple. It is attractively peaked on the back with simple flowing lines similar to the old Bear Super Kodiak. It is capped on the back with brown over white over brown fiberglass over a maple veneer. The custom-shaped grip is designed to provide positive hand placement tight under the arrow shelf to enhance instinctive shooting. Epoxy-set brass quiver mount, sight, and stabilizer bushings are available.

The upper limb has a working length of 18" from the fadeout to the string nock, and the lower limb is one inch shorter. They are 1¾" wide at the fadeouts and narrow to ¾" at the nocks. They are constructed from one back and one belly lamination of tapered Actionwood enveloped in brown fiberglass. The limbs exhibit a low angle of deflex for increased performance. The prominent tip overlays are made from Ramwood over white fiberglass. They have full-cut string nocks and a shallow string groove etched into the belly glass. The bow is finished in a low luster splatter coat that is ideal for hunting yet displays the beauty of the bow.

The following draw/force measurements recorded on a 60" Grand Slam suggests its smoothness:

DRAW LENGTH	25"	26"	27"	28"	29"
DRAW WEIGHT	50#	52½#	55#	58#	61#

To check for relative speed, Glenn Nelson, Bighorn's shop foreman, chronographed this 58 pound at 28" draw Grand Slam. The arrows were 28¾" 2018 aluminum shafts fletched with three 5" standard feathers and had snap-on nocks. They weighed 530 grains. Glenn used a glove, drew 28", and demonstrated a clean pull-through release. The string was standard Dacron without any accessories. The average arrow speed was 185 fps.

The CUSTOM BIGHORN TD is Bighorn's top-line, three-piece, take-down recurve. It is similar in appearance and construction to the Grand Slam except for the removable limbs which attach to the handle with a single attachment bolt and dual alignment pin system.

It's available in two riser lengths and four limb lengths, yielding eight different bow lengths from 52" to 66" in two-inch increments. Unlike the Grand Slam, its riser is somewhat blockier near the ends. The center shot sight window on the 17" handle is full cut for 2" and contours back to full handle width 3½" above the shelf. The sight window is 2" fuller on the 19" handle.

The Custom TD limbs are similar to the Grand Slam's except that the working length is 17½" on both limbs. Their fadeout wedge is a sweeping piece of Ramwood matching the handle. The Bighorn name and customer

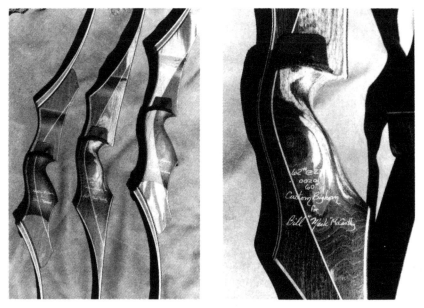

WORKHORSE RECURVES — Bighorn's Custom Grand Slam one-piece bracketed by Custom Bighorn TDs. Tone variations in the Ramwood riser and Asbell's artistic hand provide distinction to each bow.

name is artistically white inked in the handle below the grip, and the limb specs are black inked on the side of the fadeout wedge.

The following draw/force measurements were recorded on a 60" Custom Bighorn TD:

DRAW LENGTH	25"	26"	27"	28"	29"
DRAW WEIGHT	52#	54½#	57#	60#	62½#

This bow was chronographed using the same shooter and arrow combination as noted for the Grand Slam. The average arrow speed for this combination of bow, arrow, and shooter was 191 fps.

Bighorn also offers the Colorado BIGHORN TD which is similar to the Custom Bighorn except for the handle, which is fashioned from a single piece of laminated veneer Ramwood.

The combinations of handles and limbs in Bighorn's TD system are designed to accommodate different customer draw lengths and bow length preferences while maintaining maximum limb performance.

Recently, Bighorn introduced their RAM HUNTER LONGBOW. It's available in 64", 66", and 68" lengths. It has a deflex-reflex design and trapezoid cross-sectional shaped limbs that narrow to the belly. Its core is comprised of three back and one belly lamination, available in either maple or red elm, enveloped in brown glass. Its riser is Ramwood and its limbs boast bighorn sheep horn tip overlays.

MAKING IT HAPPEN

Bighorn's recurves and longbows are created in their Fort Lupton shop blending modern bow building techniques and machinery with the small-shop approach to detail and customer preference. Their office walls are strewn with pictures of successful Bighorn owners and several wooden racks cradling bows. One corner of the small office is consumed with Asbell's huge glaring elk mount posed in the full fury of a screaming bugle.

MAKING THE RISER

Outside the office where Asbell juggles a stream of phone calls, the whirring of sanders and grinders is supervised by bowyer, Glenn Nelson. When making a bow, Glenn and his crew begin with the riser. Both the laminated and the solid wood used in their handles are impregnated with a colored acrylic resin. This dense "Ramwood" is supplied by an outside source.

Pieces with distinctively contrasting tones are selected for the belly and back of their composite risers. These pieces are template outlined and then band sawn to shape. They are then ground on the wedge contact surfaces using a surface grinding jig. This jig has a Plexiglas template on the base which is swept across a bearing just below the grinder. To make efficient use of time and the jigs, both belly and back wedge contact surfaces are ground on the same jig, at the same time. The handle pieces and maple strip are then glued with Urac 185, "C" clamped together, and heat cured. Besides looking attractive, laminating the thin maple wedge between the belly and back composites makes a much stronger and durable handle.

TEMPLATE PRECISION — Using a profiling jig with interchangeable templates, Glen grinds the belly profile of a riser.

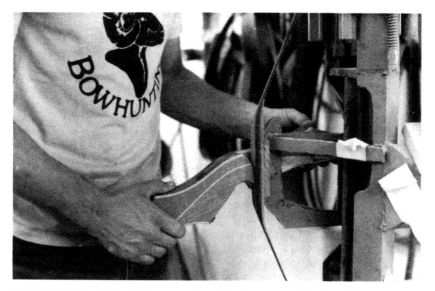

TIGHT CORNER — Bighorn's risers are shaped with a variety of power tools including the tri-corner sander that allows shaping the arrow shelf and sight window junction.

After the glue has cured, the composite block is run through a planer and ground flush on both sides. The handle shape is then traced from a clear Plexiglas template. Reference marks on this see-through template are aligned on the decorative wedge to ensure proper position. The handle is then band sawn out and ground to shape using shaping jigs. By simply changing the ⅜" thick Plexiglas templates on the base of the jig, it is quickly converted to grind different handle sizes.

Once the back and belly surfaces are ground to shape, the decorative fiberglass and maple capping are epoxied on. They are pressed on the riser in a form equipped with electric glue-curing heat strips. The form halves are tightened together with two large "C" clamps, and the heat strips are activated to cure the epoxy. Glenn points out that the jigs and capping form are so precise that even changing brands of grinding abrasives can affect the fit of the composites in the form.

The limb attachment bushing and alignment pins holes are drilled into the handle using a drill guide jig which holds it securely in place. The threaded brass limb attachment bushing is epoxied and then screwed into the handle. Before gluing and screwing in the two stainless steel locator pins, a thin black plastic spacer is installed on the handle-limb contact surface. This prevents the limbs from sticking to the riser and it absorbs compression.

Next, the sight window is cut out on a band saw and then shaped in the shelf and window area on a tri-corner sander. The handle is shaped with grinders, slack belt sanders, and hand rasps. It's finished using a pneumatic-sleeved roller sander. The roller sander's cushiony backing helps produce smooth flowing contours. Finally, the handle is completely sanded by hand.

TAKE-DOWN LIMBS

The first step in making Bighorn's take-down limbs is fashioning the fadeout wedges. The sweeping fadeouts are band sawed from matching handle material and then ground to shape on a template-guided shaping jig. The final fadeout feathering is delicately done by hand to a paper-thinness. The butt ends are cut off square and a small butt end locator hole is drilled in the fadeout.

To help achieve specific bow weight and built-in tiller, Bighorn spine-tests their fiberglass. When laying up a set of limbs, Glenn selects a bit stiffer glass for use in the lower limb to obtain built-in tiller. Depending on the bow length and weight, they use several different tapers of matched pairs of Actionwood corewoods.

Before gluing the limb composites, the laminations are cleaned and masking tape is applied to the non-gluing sides of the fiberglass. Their laminated maple form is also covered with plastic wrap to protect it from runny glue.

Next, the epoxy is carefully mixed by weight, which is crucial to achieving proper curing properties. Once it's mixed, there are only fourteen minutes to get the all composite contact surfaces glued and laid up in the steel-framed form. The locator holes in the fadeouts are placed over alignment pins in the form. The form is then closed on the limbs and the fire hose in the upper half of the press is inflated. Electric heat strips lining the form are activated and reach glue curing temperature in short order.

THREE AT ONCE — Clamped in the drill jig, all three limb mounting holes are drilled at the same time.

After the limbs are cured, they are pulled from the press and ground flat on both sides using a large machine called a Hammond flat finisher. This perfectly squares the limbs to precisely fit into the limb alignment hole drilling jig. Once they're ground to width, the tip and butt ends are trimmed to length. The limbs are then clamped into the alignment hole drill jig and all three limb-mounting holes are drilled. The upper and lower limb each have their own alignment pin spacing to prevent accidental limb inversion.

After they're drilled, the limbs are installed on a master working riser and braced using a string and devices called centering blocks. These machined steel blocks are put on the squared limb tips and are adjusted back and forth until the string tracks down the middle of the limbs. When adjusting these centering blocks, Glenn checks for both dynamic and static limb alignment. Once they're properly adjusted, the limb centers are marked, and the limb shapes are template outlined. Using a large vertical belt sander, the limbs are then ground to near final dimensions.

After roughening up both gluing surfaces, matching riser wood tip overlays are epoxied on and heat cured. String grooves are etched in the tip sides with a small masonry grinding wheel mounted on a special jig. The nocks are finished with a small rat-tail file to a gauged thickness across the tip.

Once the string nocks are cut, the bow is braced with a string and it's again checked for static and dynamic limb alignment. Any adjustments are made by grinding the recurve portion edges on the vertical belt sander. To achieve the desired bow weight, the limb edges are sanded and sometimes fiberglass is sanded off the back and belly. To bring the limbs into the desired three-sixteenths inch positive tiller, a small amount of backing glass is sanded off one of the limbs.

Glen checks each bow for dynamic limb alignment by pulling back on the string and visually surveying both limbs.

FINISHING TOUCHES

Nearly finished, the bow is dusted off and inked with Bighorn's name, bow specs, and the customer's name. Asbell's artistic hand scrolls the delicate lettering, giving each bow an extra personalized touch. Standard bow quiver bushings are drilled and epoxied in along with any other optional bushings.

A turbine spraying gun is used to apply the two-part satin Fullerplast finish. The bows are first sprayed with two sealer coats. While the sealer coat is still green or sticky, the turbine drive air gun is adjusted for spraying the three coats of Bighorn's distinctive stippled splatter finish.

Once it's dried, the synthetic fur rest and leather strike pad are installed and a waterproof lubricant is applied to the limb mounting holes.

DESIGNED TO SHOOT

The finished product is a bow that is custom made for the shooter's grip and specific draw length. "The thing that we originally stood for was to make a custom bow. We soon realized that a bow's performance is very dependent on how far it's pulled and the way the limbs bend. So to maximize performance, we decided to make a limb that would perform at its peak at a specific draw length. The old production bow manufacturers built all their bows to pull twenty-eight inches, and a good portion of them were just awful if you pulled them twenty-nine inches. But we know how to make limbs that bend more, bend less, or bend quicker to fit specific draws. We build a lot of bows for guys with a thirty-three inch draw. That's one of the things we set out to do."

BIGHORN TEAM — Headed by Asbell, right, and Glenn Nelson, second from left, the Bighorn crew produces dependable, shootable hunting bows.

Bighorns are designed and built for "shootability", consistently zinging arrows where they're pointed. "We try to find a good place between super speed and what really shoots well. We know how to build bows faster, that's no problem. But a shootable bow is the most important thing. We've steered away from trying to make the fastest bow in the world because that doesn't solve anything. It's like owning a race car that will run one thousand miles per hour but you can't keep it on the road. Our philosophy is to make a super quality bow that lasts, is dependable, and shootable."

Even though Bighorn enjoys widespread popularity among traditionalists, Asbell doesn't rest on his laurels. "We're always piddling with things. We will play around trying to see if some things are a little more stable or if something is a little quicker. We are always doing that sort of thing and changing stuff. For example, recently we built fifteen experimental bows in developing our new high-performance Grand Slam."

PLEASING CUSTOMERS

Bighorn's customers, a strong following across the country, are a blend of seasoned traditionalists and the new wave of compound shooters discovering the thrills of traditional archery. "Suddenly lots of guys are trying traditional archery just because other people are enjoying it. One thing we hear consistently from guys who used to shoot a compound and now shoot our bow is, 'This is so much more fun. I had forgotten how much fun archery was.' They don't say that it kills better; they just say that it's more fun. A lot of them say, 'I didn't realize that I had reached a point where I just didn't enjoy shooting anymore.' And many say they have shot more arrows out of their new recurve than they shot out of their compound in the last five years."

Bighorn's bows help fuel the growing blaze of traditional archery, and consistently put game on the meat poles and in the record book. They enjoy widespread, well-deserved popularity. But it wasn't always that way.

In his fledgling bowmaking days, Asbell's bows were unknown, and sometimes he went to great lengths to impress prospective customers. But despite his efforts, some failed. "I was shooting indoors with an archery shop owner and a guy I had met. I was explaining to them why this new bow we were building worked so well. I started to pull the bow, and I was having this guy watch the recurve. I said, 'Now watch how this recurve works, and you will see why this bow pulls so smooth.' Well, this guy was standing right there with his nose six inches from the bow looking at the limb, and the bow broke when I pulled it back. No parts of the wood hit him, but the string slapped across his face. He looked like Lash Laroo got a hold of him.

"I never did sell that guy a bow. I wonder why not? Hmmm."

WAPITI RECURVES, LONGBOWS

ELK ADDICT

Wapiti. To the Shawnee it meant "white rump", the eye-catching distinction of the great deer whose bugle echoed into the night. Today's bowhunters call it the elk. And for many, this majestic creature of the mountains represents the pinnacle of bowhunting excitement. At close range, its shrieking bugle can raise the hackles of even the most hardened hunter. An elk's size and splendor are breath-taking — the high country it inhabits is alluring. It's little surprise that most bowhunters who taste the thrill of hunting wapiti find it addictive.

One such elk addict is bowhunter and bowmaker, Keith Chastain of Denver, Colorado. "I love them. They are just absolutely superb to bowhunt." In fact, Keith believes wapiti are so superb, he has named his line of custom traditional bows after them.

THE WAPITI HERD

Keith offers six Wapiti models: a one-piece hunting recurve, its three-piece take-down counterpart, a slide-lock take-down recurve, a standard longbow, a three-piece take-down longbow, and a two-piece take-down longbow.

The WAPITI TD is Keith's most popular bow. This three-piece take-down recurve has a standard length of 64". It's also available, in two-inch increments, from 58" to 70". The 64" model has an approximate mass weight of 3 pounds, 4 ounces which varies with handle materials. Its brace height is 6⅞" from the string to the throat.

A STRIPED EFFECT — Keith's Kamo wood risers accentuate the flowing contours of his recurve handles.

The TD handle section on his 62" bow is 19½" long, 1¾" wide, and thins to ⅝" through the center shot sight window. The riser is 3¼" thick near the ends and narrows to approximately 1¾" through the throat. The amply rounded sight window is full cut for 1¾" above the shelf and contours to full handle width 3½" above the shelf.

The handle is constructed from a variety of laminated, domestic or exotic hardwoods, depending on each customer's preference. It is also available in "Kamo" wood — a resin impregnated compressed laminated maple. The handle displays soft merging ridges above and below the contoured grip blending into a sculpted belly near the limbs. These sweeping handle contours expose the contrasting striped patterns within the wood.

The shelf and window are equipped with a synthetic rug and calf-hair plate. Bow and customer names are inked on the window side of the handle below the grip, and the limb specs are inked on the edges of the fadeout wedges. Brass quiver and sight bushings are available.

On his standard TD, the limbs attach with two ⁵⁄₁₆" Allen flat-head screws. Keith also offers a machined "Slide-lok" dove-tail limb assembly system. The working length of the limbs is 15½" from the fadeout to the string nock. They narrow from 1 ¹¹⁄₁₆" wide at the fadeouts to 1" at the nock.

His recurve limbs exhibit a tight radius or pronounced "fishhook" appearance. They are constructed from a sweeping 11" fadeout wedge with single belly and back Actionwood laminations that taper .002" per inch. The corewoods are enveloped in black fiberglass.

Unlike most recurve limbs, the tips narrow from 1" wide at the nock to a ½" squared tip, much like Ishi's flatbow. They are strengthened with thin hardwood tip overlays. The limbs are finished in a low-luster splatter coat varnish.

The smoothness of draw is suggested from the following draw/force measurements recorded on a 62" Wapiti "TD":

DRAW LENGTH	25"	26"	27"	28"	29"
DRAW WEIGHT	49#	52#	54½#	58#	61#

Keith also offers a one-piece "SR" recurve. It's almost identical to the "TD" except for the limbs which are permanently glued on.

For traditionalists seeking the challenge of the longbow, Keith offers standard and take-down longbow models.

The WAPITI "LB" is offered in 69" and 71" lengths and has a mass weight of 1 pound, 8 ounces. Its laminated hardwood riser is 15¼" long, 1¼" wide, and thins to ¾" through the sight window. The riser is 2⅜" thick and has the simple lines of a standard longbow design. The riser is accentuated with a vertical maple wedge and a maple backing that makes up part of the fadeout. The custom grip can be either slightly dished or traditionally flat. It's wrapped with a single piece of suede, laced in front.

The LB's slightly reflexed limbs have a working length of 23½" and narrow from 1⅛" wide at the fadeouts to 9/16" at the nocks. These relatively flat-edged limbs are constructed with two back and one belly tapered Action-wood laminations enveloped in black fiberglass. The thin tip overlays are made from maple laminated to riser hardwood, and have full cut string nocks. The bow is finished in a low-luster satin finish.

To check the relative speed of the LB, Keith shot 28½" 530 grain wooden arrows through the chronograph with his standard 69", 66 pound

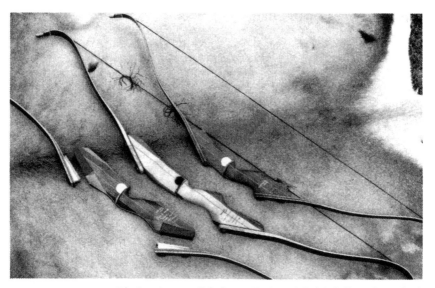

WAPITI OVER WAPITI — Displayed on an elk hide, are Keith's "Slide-lok"(left), and standard three-piece TDs — complete with fishhook style recurves.

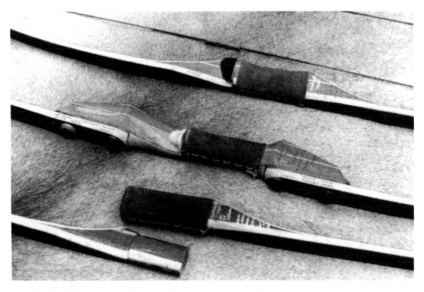

WAPITI LONGBOWS TOO — Keith offers his sleeve fit two-piece longbow (left), his three-piece longbow (middle), and his standard one-piece longbow.

at 28" draw longbow. The arrows were fletched with three 5" standard cut feathers and had snap-on nocks. The string was standard without any accessories. Keith shot using a glove and had a pull-through release. He drew the arrow approximately 27". The average arrow speed for this bow, arrow, and shooter combination was 168 fps.

The smoothness of the LB is suggested from the following draw/force measurements recorded on this standard 69" one-piece longbow:

DRAW LENGTH	25"	26"	27"	28"	29"
DRAW WEIGHT	55#	58½#	62#	66#	69½#

Keith also offers his unique three-piece take-down longbow. Its laminated hardwood handle is heftier than his standard longbow handle and provides more stabilizing weight. It has 20½" working length limbs that attach to the handle with two Allen cap screws. Keith has also recently introduced a two-piece longbow that has a sleeve fit at the handle. Field testing this new two-piece longbow provided plenty of excitement for Keith when he used it to arrow a Pope and Young whitetail on the eastern Colorado plains.

STAYING IN COLORADO

Even though his bows all wear the Wapiti name, Keith hunts more than just elk with them. Recently, Colorado's buster whitetails have become Keith's second favorite bowhunting challenge. "I'm an avid elk hunter, but whitetails are just superb. There's always an argument as to which is the hardest to get; big mulies or big whitetails. And there is no question about it — it's big whitetails. Big mulies are tough, don't get me wrong. But they're tough simply because of where they live, not because they are the smartest. If you want to go after them you can get them. But a big whitetail is a different story."

Keith's respect for the whitetail can be traced back to his home state of Indiana. There at the age of fourteen, he bought his first bow. "There were two reasons for that: archery was becoming very popular in southern Indiana back then, and I had a bird dog that was gun-shy. But he would go hunting with me if I used my bow, and I've had a bow in my hand ever since."

Working as an engineer for the Ball Corporation, Keith transferred to Colorado in 1974. Four years later he was asked to transfer back to Indiana, but the lure of the Rockies had a firm grip on the Chastain family. They decided to stay. They stayed mostly because of the community and western climate, but local bowhunting opportunities also played a role. "Colorado is a bowhunter's paradise. There are nine big game species to bowhunt here. It's a big gun-hunting state but a very small bowhunting state. You can bowhunt almost all year long if you want to."

Keith is a member of Colorado Bowhunters and a regular member of the Pope and Young Club. He also belongs to the American Bowmen, a local group of archers, and regularly shoots their outdoor and indoor ranges. "We have one hundred members in our club, and we are probably the premier bowhunting club in the United States. There may be clubs that take more animals than we do, but nobody takes a greater variety of animals from so many places. We normally take animals from ten to twelve states, provinces, and other countries. We usually take around sixty animals of fifteen different species, and fifteen to twenty of them will make Pope and Young. And we are all 'local Joes'. We don't have the big-name bowhunters you see in the magazines. One of our members just completed his grand slam by taking his dall sheep. He's Tom Tietz, and he's the fifth person to make the grand slam. And he got the last two sheep using one of my bows."

Keith is one of the club members who has harvested most of Colorado's big game species. He hopes to someday try for Colorado's bighorn sheep and mountain goat. If he scores on these elusive mountain dwellers, he will have taken all of Colorado's "big eight."

ALASKAN ADVENTURE

Besides hunting the Rocky Mountain states, Keith bowhunts wild places such as the last frontier. Recently, his bowhunting itch drew him to the remoteness of Alaska. He arranged the entire drop-camp and self-guided hunt where timing and circumstance set the stage for his meeting with some of Alaska's most impressive bowhunting trophies — moose and barren ground caribou. "Three of us flew in to the south edge of the Brooks Range and started hunting the next day.

"Caribou normally don't bed down, but it was warm. When they were full, after eating, they would lay down at about four o'clock in the afternoon.

Suddenly all of these caribou were just laying down, and the three of us spotted this big bull caribou.

"The other two guys picked spots in the alders about forty yards away from him, and I sneaked around to the other side of him. I crawled up on him straight across this park where he was dozing. At about fifteen yards he finally realized something was wrong, and when he came to his feet I came to my knees and shot him. He went about thirty yards and fell in the alders. Then he got up and went another fifteen yards and fell right in front of one of the other guys." Keith's high-racked bull made the book, sweetening the hunt of a lifetime that was steeped in the vastness of the land, marked by the solitude of a twelve day drop-camp, and spiced with the excitement of a marauding grizzly who ate over 200 pounds of their cached meat.

The caribou mount proudly gracing Keith's wall is visually his most impressive trophy, but his most memorable shot was made on an antlerless quarry. "The best shot I ever made on an animal was the coyote I shot last fall. I shot him at eleven yards and I hit him absolutely perfect, and he only went ten feet. That was the first shot I ever got at a coyote. They are one of the toughest animals to get with a bow."

BOWHUNTING GEAR

To put bulls on the wall or stop coyotes in their tracks, Keith uses one of his custom sixty pound recurves or longbows equipped with a Wapiti bow quiver manufactured by Delta. He is an instinctive shot who uses self-made cedar arrows fletched with three 5½" feathers exhibiting a strong helical twist. "I haven't bought or shot an aluminum arrow in twenty-six years. Aluminum arrows are noisy. Every time you hit a little twig they rattle, and they're noisy to shoot. Animals hear that. I'm convinced they do. So I shoot wooden arrows."

On his cedar shafts Keith mounts broadheads that he can sharpen himself. "I'm a three-blade broadhead fan. I like Snuffers, MA-3's, Hill's Hornets, or Bodkins. The best are Snuffers and MA-3's because they can be easily sharpened and they cut a superb hole."

Although Keith cuts his hunting arrows to his draw length, he practices with full length shafts. "I shoot with about three inches sticking out in front of the bow, which is not the norm, and I wouldn't recommend that for other people. But I guess I'm too cheap — if I break off the tip I can install another one and use the arrow again."

Keith fletches his arrows with bright yellow and white fletching because he is partially color-blind and these colors stand out in nature. "Camouflage arrows are absolutely ridiculous. Guys find that out after they shoot one out in the brush and can't find it. Yellow and white feathers may be one of the worst combinations to hunt with, but I use them because I can see them. I want to know where I hit an animal or where I missed. I don't like not knowing where you hit an animal with camouflaged arrows."

Like the rest of his bowhunting equipment, Keith keeps his garb simple. "I usually hunt in blue jeans and a camo shirt, but that's it. I also wear my old gray cowboy hat. There's no doubt that you can conceal yourself more with camo, but if those animals know you're there or they have already spotted you, they have spotted you no matter what you've got on. I don't have any trouble with elk just staring at me at fifteen yards, if they haven't smelled me or if I haven't moved."

Elk hunting requires footgear that can handle the terrain and dampness of alpine parks. Keith's favorite wapiti country boots are rubber-bottomed Bean boots. "They tend to wear out in about two years, but they're absolutely superb. Wearing my Beans is just like walking barefoot. I go on the rocks and everywhere with them."

Keith is not about to change his favorite brand of boots, but he recently retired his favorite bowhunting hat. "I had a hat that I used for almost ten years, and it was worn

DRESSED TO KILL — Decked in his cowboy hat and brush-tattered coveralls, Keith draws back one of his full-length practice arrows.

until it wasn't much more than a rag. I hunted over in Nebraska one day and I was way up high — about thirty feet up in a big cottonwood. I hung that old hat on a limb and then I took my tree stand down. As far as I know my hat's still up there in that tree."

MAKES EVERYTHING

Intense and full of energy, this silver-haired bowmaker immerses himself in his hunting and his bowmaking. "Archery is all I do. I make bows and go hunting. And I probably make more different types of equipment than anybody else. I can make anything. I make six different bow models and if somebody wants them, I can even make certain discontinued limbs."

Keith's confidence in being able to make "anything" is a product of his background. He has a bachelor's degree in mechanical engineering, a master's degree in physics, and he has worked as a design engineer at Ball

Corporation setting up their research and development labs. Using these engineering and designing skills, he set up his custom bowmaking shop in the garage behind his house.

Power bow crafting machines are expensive, specialized items. Most bowmakers purchase industrial saws and grinders, but Keith's are hand-made and he's proud of his array of custom-built equipment. One of his belt sanders is over twenty years old and has helped him shape most of his bows. He has two workhorse sanders, the "big one" which is a horizontal belt sander, and the flexible torn-edge belt sander. To cut materials, Keith built a heavy-duty band saw and a tilt-arbor table saw. A skilled tooling engineer, Keith even built his machined drill guide jigs. All of this machinery is snugly fit around his work benches and crowded supply shelves.

Most bowmakers chew through fiberglass with a dull band saw blade because the tough fiberglass eats the teeth off good blades. Bowyers just accept this as one of the problems of working with glass. But Keith efficiently cuts his with an abrasive tungsten-carbide band saw blade, made by Remington, that's unaffected by fiberglass.

YOUNG LESSONS

Although today Keith brims with confidence about his bowmaking skills, his first few attempts at bow building were cast in doubt. He tried making his first bows when he was a young man studying for his engineering degree. "I built my first bows when I was in college in Flint, Michigan. But they just didn't hold up. I got the materials from Old Master Crafters and made a bow. It blew up. So did the next two. But the fourth one was good and it still is good to this day. One of the problems with those early bows was that they were glued together with Urac, and it's just not as good as the epoxy glues we have now."

He treats those first bows as lessons. "Bow breakage happens. It's part of bowmaking. What we are shooting is just a very highly stressed leaf spring and unfortunately it's going to break. They are all going to break eventually. But you hope that they don't for a good while. Now I have a very low percentage of breakage."

Keith began building bows part-time in 1960 and expanded his one-man operation into full-time production in 1984. Unlike most bowyers who work exclusively with their own line of bows, Keith also repairs other brands. "I do an awful lot of specialty work. For example, I'm working on a sixty-six inch slide-lock limb system to fit a Groves handle. Everything is so special about that bow, and nobody else in the world would build it. In fact, the customer couldn't even get anybody to build him a Groves handle. As long as it is safe to build, I can essentially tailor to what someone wants."

Tailoring to what a customer wants also applies to Keith's Wapiti line. He offers a variety of riser materials and often lets his customers design their own bows. "Almost all of my bows are very special in length and wood type. They're true custom bows."

RADICAL RECURVE

Keith's take-down recurve system utilizes a single limb design and length, and he achieves varied bow lengths with different length handles. "I can get by with a single limb design because the limb is so smooth. I can make a longer or a shorter bow and still give a guy a smooth bow. This gives me great versatility. I have twenty-five sets of limbs here, and I can make probably two hundred different bows out of those limbs. Nobody has a system as versatile as mine."

His universal limb incorporates a pronounced tight-radius recurve similar to the old Louthan. Some call it radical. "It actually approaches the old Turk bows. And it is similar to Frank Eicholtz's hook limb. In theory what I'm trying to do is to get the limb to lengthen as it's pulled back. The Turk bows were recurve but they broke over. The outer portion of their limb or long arm actually breaks over just like a compound. When it breaks over it goes from a seventy-five pound bow to a thirty pound bow. But their materials were horn and sinew, and their tensile strengths were so much less than our modern fiberglass that we can't build a Turk bow. Now if I wanted to build a two hundred pound bow like that I could probably do it.

"The whole principle is to try to get a limb smoother by breaking the recurve over. You can do that by making a longer limb with a tight-radius recurve. If my limbs fail, they fail in the recurve because it's highly stressed. My recurve doesn't start to open up until about twenty-seven to twenty-eight inches of draw, and for a guy with a short draw it probably isn't as good as a bow they might get in a different style. But for guys with longer draws my limb is just fabulous. Guys with thirty-one to thirty-three inch draws can't get any other recurve like I can give them. Because twenty-six to twenty-seven inches is about the point that almost all large-radius recurves start stacking. A stacking bow with a large-radius recurve shoots fast. Making a fast bow is not a problem. You can make a fast bow, and you can make a smooth bow, but getting a fast and smooth bow is a real design problem."

KAMO RISERS

When building his tight-radius recurves, Keith often varies his tasks to suit his mood, so it rarely gets boring. He begins most of his days by gluing up a set of limbs then starts working on a riser. Like a bee gathering pollen, Keith busily flits from machine to machine, rarely pausing between tasks.

In making a riser, he first selects the custom materials. One of his popular riser materials is his "Kamo" wood. It's a resin impregnated, dyed, compressed, and highly-laminated product that's strong, heavy, durable, and striking in appearance. "The three that I carry are the gray Zebra, the green Kamo, and the brown Desert Kamo. The big advantage to the Kamo compressed riser is its camouflaging, but it also has more strength and weight. Now, that may be an advantage depending on an archer's desires. For consistent shooting it will help, but for carrying around in the mountains, it won't."

His Kamo woods offer advantages, but Keith's favorite risers are made from combinations of natural hardwoods. "I'm a walnut fan. I just love

PRIME CUT — Like a skilled butcher trimming fat, Keith uses his band saw to free-hand trim a riser's shape and rough contours.

walnut and maple." One of his most popular hardwood combinations is bubinga and walnut, a blend that displays subtle contrasts and exudes warm tones.

After cutting out and power planing the riser composites, Keith uses a small clamping fixture to vertically laminate the pieces together. He epoxies all contact surfaces and tightens them together in two directions with "C" clamps. The epoxy is then either heat cured in Keith's hot box or baked in Colorado's summer sun.

Next he glues a piece of fiberglass to the riser on the limb mounting surfaces. With the riser still in block form, he drills the limb mounting holes using a drill guide jig, and he installs the epoxied and threaded bushings from the belly side so they can't pull out.

Keith then traces the riser shape around a template, and cuts it out with a band saw. Most bowyers use profilers and grinders to shape their risers. But Keith uses his band saw to free-hand cut the sight window, shelf, sides, and major contours. It's one of his most versatile tools.

Once the riser is sawn to rough shape, Keith finishes shaping it by hand with a sure-form file. When shaping, he crowns the arrow shelf, bevels its outer edge, and rounds the sight window — all to enhance arrow flight.

Because of the variation of materials and Keith's hand shaping, each riser is distinctive and unique. "I have a basic standard shape, but I alter that just unbelievably. I have gone to a more square-look. I'm not doing nearly the rounding that I prefer because the guys don't like it as well. So basically I leave it flatter and just hit it with the sander. But that will change in five years because everything changes and goes through cycles."

WAPITI LIMBS

Although he occasionally changes the contours of his risers, Keith maintains strict specifications when building his limbs. "The key to limb performance is optimizing the limb design. It's selecting the best fiberglass and corewood combinations. You could use infinite combinations to make a sixty pound set of limbs but there is an optimum for each particular design. My limb is much thinner than anybody else's even though it's wider. And it has less mass. That's because I use .030 and .040 inch thick fiberglass."

Keith primarily uses black fiberglass, but he also uses brown and green. "Black has been 'in' for seven or eight years and now brown is becoming popular. But buying fiberglass is a real problem for small bowyers because there is only one source for the glass, and that's Gordon. They won't sell to us unless we order a minimum quantity, which is more than most of us could use. So Gordon has forced us to go to distributors such as Old Master Crafters and Bingham."

Keith takes the time to hand mike all of his fiberglass when he receives it. To ensure matched fiberglass on opposing limbs, he cuts one strip in half and uses the pieces on opposite limbs. This, and his matching of paired corewoods, helps achieve balanced limb characteristics. Keith warns that a bow can be thrown out of tiller by using different pieces of fiberglass on opposing limbs, even if the fiberglass thicknesses are the same, because the tensile strength of the fiberglass can vary, plus or minus ten percent.

Another important part of Keith's limb design is his sweeping fadeout wedges. He makes them from maple, and the more-popular bubinga, paying special attention to his selection of the wood and its grain alignment.

GLUE-UP

Once Keith selects his limb composites, he prepares them, and his forms, for glue up. His single-limb forms are made from laminated plywood and tempered hardboard. They are equipped with a fadeout butt stop for accurately positioning the laminates.

Keith waxes his form and specially prepares his composite gluing surfaces. He then applies epoxy to all contact surfaces and lays up the limb composites in the form. Next he lays a fire hose on top of the composites, clamps down the upper half of the press, and inflates the hose to fifty pounds.

The pressed limbs then go into his curing oven which is equipped with heat lamps and a circulating fan. It cures the glue at 150 degrees for six hours.

SHAPED TO SHOOT

After curing, Keith lets the forms cool for about three hours before removing the limbs. Once out of the form, he removes the masking tape from the fiberglass while it's still warm because once it cools completely, it's tough to get off. He then grinds the edges on his belt sander until they are nearly parallel and again masking tapes the fiberglass for marking the centerline and outlining the limb shape.

Keith marks the limb centerline and adjusts the limb in his drill jig until its centerline aligns with the center of the jig's guide holes. Then he drills both holes with his drill press. Using a template, he marks the limb's form and then grinds it to shape.

After roughing in string nocks Keith is ready to assemble and brace the bow. He installs the limbs on their matched handle to ensure proper limb alignment and to later achieve a flush fit on the sides near the limb-riser interface. Also, when he makes additional limbs for a riser, Keith requests the original riser back from the customer so that he can shape the new limbs to an exact fit. "I primarily do not build interchangeability in my bows. They are custom-built, one-of-a-kind. The majority of my risers and limbs are interchangeable, but they are not meant to be."

Keith's one-piece recurves are almost identical to his TD except that the limbs are pegged and permanently glued on instead of bolted on. "The first thing that most people think about gluing the limbs on, is that it won't work. But it most certainly does. That glue is rated to 5000 psi tensile strength."

When assembling his TD recurve, Keith installs a thin cork gasket between the limb and riser to ensure a snug fit and help improve the bow's appearance. He then tightens the two limb attachment bolts. "In the market today, my bow is overkill. It is safer, stronger, and sturdier than any of the others on the market. However, it takes more time and more expense to build. I use a two-bolt per limb system and nobody left in the market today does that. But there used to be a lot of them. The reason I use this system is basically because if you break a string, the limb cannot go forward. It's essentially a one-piece bow. But with other bolt-pin systems, when you break a string, sometimes that limb will go forward and break. That's quite typical with compounds."

Besides using more bolts, Keith also uses heavier ones. "I use two, five-sixteenths inch bolts. Almost all the other systems on the market are using one-quarter inch bolts. If they would do the strength calculations on their bolts and take a maximum bow weight of 100 pounds with the leverages involved, and take in a safety factor, and four-to-one is not unreasonable for a sporting piece of equipment, they would find that one-quarter inch bolts aren't heavy enough."

Using a steel cable which won't be cut by the rough fiberglass, Keith braces the bow and adjusts the limb alignment. "There are several ways to correct limb alignment. Number one is to deepen the string grooves. If it's a standard recurve the only other way is to remove material from the limb edge until the string centers in the groove. But if it's a take-down there are two other ways. You can move the bolt holes slightly, or on a flat limb mounting surface, you can change the mounting surface of the riser. But the most common way I do it is to move the bolt holes. I rarely grind material off the limbs to bring them into alignment because my recurve is so critical that anything I take off of the outer portion starts giving me recurve problems. So I try not to do anything to the recurve."

Once the limbs are aligned, Keith installs the matching riser wood tip overlays and finishes the narrow limb tips, which aren't much wider than the string nocks. "The traditional heart-shaped tip doesn't do anything. In fact, it's detrimental in two ways: one, it makes the bow a little harder to string; two it adds mass to the limb which is dead weight." He also files in a shallow single string groove which leaves more strengthening fiberglass on the belly tip.

Keith builds a three-sixteenths inch positive tiller in the upper limbs of his bows by removing a slight amount of material off the sides of the limbs. "The only reason tiller is in favor of the upper limb is to reduce finger pinch because the arrow is above center, and tiller gives a little more bend to the upper limb. But you can tune any bow to shoot correct arrow flight regardless of what the tiller is. Even if it's an inch in favor of the lower limb. So tiller really means nothing. The majority of arrow flight problems are related to release. And hardly any of us can do much about our release."

Once the fadeout wedges are sanded flush with the finished riser, Keith wipes a tinted wood filler on the open grained wood of the riser and fadeouts. This helps to achieve a smoother final finish. It's then wiped down, and the bow specs and names are inked on.

AN IDEAL FINISH

When Keith has finished a batch of limbs and risers, he hangs them from wires over the open deck in his back yard for spraying. Glistening in the sun, they slowly rotate on their wires like massive archery mobiles. He first sprays on four primer coats of the two-part catalystic varnish. "Actually the additive

ARCHERY MOBILES — Weather permitting, Keith sprays completed bow parts on his backyard deck. Each bow receives six coats of finish.

in Fullerplast is sulfuric acid and it just changes the pH so it will harden. It's an ideal finish. It's usually a problem finding a material that sticks well to the fiberglass, but Fullerplast sticks great. Some epoxies may, but a lot of the commercial finishes won't."

After spraying the four coats of Fullerplast, he adjusts his spray gun for applying two coats of the final satin splatter finish. "I use a commercially available Sherwin-Williams satin finish. I have used that for twenty-five years and it just works great. The textured finish we use now I couldn't give away ten years ago. But now it's the 'in' thing, and it's an ideal finish to spray. It's better for the hunter, and it's better for the manufacturer."

The final step is sticking on the synthetic fur strike plate and arrow rest. "Even though I use a synthetic hair plate and rest on the bows I make, I use Texas whitetail hide with the hair on it on my personal bow. It's absolutely superb. It's slick and it wears well as a strike plate, but that deer would freeze to death in Colorado."

With every one of his completed bows, Keith supplies one of his home-made bowstrings and a bow stringer. "The bow stringer is the best way for today's archer to string a bow because he can't step through and string it, especially with my recurve. The push pull method is safer on the bow but it's not safer for the archer, and it's not recommended."

Many of his customers are new traditionalists looking for their first recurve or longbow. Keith doesn't have much trouble matching these new stick shooters with specific handle woods, but matching archers with the proper draw weight can be tricky. "Draw weight is usually a problem for a guy who is just getting into shooting a recurve. I want to get him a heavy enough bow that he can go hunting with, but I don't want him to have to buy another set of limbs in two months. Plus, I don't want to overbow him either." So if new customers are unsure of what they want in a custom bow, Keith suggests they purchase an inexpensive production recurve to discover what weight and features they like before spending the money on one of his custom products.

Keith sees the new wave of traditional customers as a growing trend in the popularity of recurves and longbows. "Traditional archery is apparently on the rebound. Everything is cyclical and we're approaching a twenty-year cycle with compounds. People are just wanting to go back to a little simpler life. They are finding out that they have been fed a big story over the years, that compounds are the best, and that just isn't true. There are many recurves that will shoot just as good as many compounds. Sure the compound and cam are here to stay, but there are a lot of people who want to go back to traditional archery. People have finally realized that although the compound has advantages, the recurve also has its advantages. And the recurve is not the bad weapon they have been led to believe."

CLOSER TO THE WAPITI

Despite the growing list of new customers and his healthy list of Wapiti back orders, Keith enjoys being, and staying, a one-man operation. "I make only a very limited number of high-performance bows. I'm by myself and I won't hire anybody. I'm not about to put out several thousand bows a year like some other companies."

Content to stay the lone tender of the Wapiti herd, Keith plans on building traditional bows well into his retirement. But he would like to someday change his bowmaking location from the bustle of Denver to a quieter location closer to his company namesake, the wapiti, possibly somewhere on the western slopes.

There the dry mountain air would still be good for sun-baking his glued risers or drying his outdoor sprayed finishes. It does occasionally rain in the dry mountain climate of Colorado, but it seldom interrupts Keith's bow building. "Oh, once in a while we'll get a five or a ten incher. That's where the drops are five inches or ten inches apart. And we even get a three incher now and then."

It would take more than a "one incher" to keep this determined bowmaker from getting his herd to market.

Chapter Nineteen

SCORPION LONGBOW

THE BLOOD OF CHRIST

There are few hidden corners of the nation that match the rugged beauty of Colorado's Sangre de Cristo mountains. Jutting sharply from the eastern edge of the vast San Luis Valley, they soar upward to a head-spinning 14,000 feet, their rocky crags scraping the bottoms of passing clouds. Sometimes the setting sun burning its rays through forty miles of San Luis haze splashes an eerie red across the jagged peaks, proclaiming their Spanish name, "The Blood of Christ."

The gnarled expanse of the Sangre de Cristos provides a fortress home for high-country mule deer, elk, mountain goat, and majestic bighorn sheep. Above timberline, alpine basins filled with lush cover serve as lofty summer homes for these retiring mountain dwellers. But each winter, piling snows drive the herds to the lower elevations where they hole up in the pinyon pine and oak brush near the valley floor.

For nearly seventy miles along the western flank of the Sangre de Cristos, the herds roam freely among the hills. Only one town shares their lonely winter home. It's the isolated community of Crestone, Colorado. A booming mining town of forgotten days, Crestone now sports a population of thirty-six. Hunting is prohibited in this end-of-the-road town where deer roam freely like pets, grazing in front yards and lingering along road sides.

Hidden south of town in the pinion pines and rock-strewn hills, a young man greets each day by surveying the game around his house. With his eye pressed to his spotting scope, he scans the blue-shadowed peaks looking for bighorns. As the morning sun frees his rooftop from the cool mountain shadows, the man settles into his daily routine — handcrafting longbows reminiscent of the primitives who once hunted these hills. This is the birthplace of Scorpion Longbows, and home of their maker, M.R. Hamilton.

DESTINED A MOUNTAIN MAN

Barely a stone's throw from the immense Rio Grande National Forest, M.R. lives a quiet life with his wildlife neighbors. Besides the herbivores, summertime swarms of hummingbirds flit around M.R.'s deck-side feeder like oversized insects. His nearest human neighbors live over a mile away, and the distant growl of a passing jet is sometimes his only reminder that somewhere, a modern world lies beyond the jagged peaks.

"Even when I was a kid all I ever wanted was to live in the mountains in Colorado. I used to watch all of the mountain man movies, some thirty times. I saved my pennies and I came out here hunting with Ed Wiseman in 1978 and even bought my first Colorado hunting license in Crestone."

Although most kids have adventurous dreams, few turn them into reality. But M.R. did. After serving four years in the Marines, he made his boyhood fantasies come true, purchasing mountain side land and building his own mountain man home.

Other than his shooting-style glasses, M.R. even resembles one of Colorado's historic mountain men with his long, flowing hair and full beard. Behind his beard booms an almost innocent flashing smile that intensifies his sharp features. And M.R. adds to his mountain man character when spinning hunting tales in his banjo twanging, down-home Kentucky jargon.

FROM THE BANKS OF THE OHIO

M.R. was born in Paducah, Kentucky, near the junction of the Mississippi and Ohio Rivers. There he grew up hunting, trapping, and fishing along the Ohio River, nurturing his wilderness dreams. When he was fourteen, M.R. became interested in bowhunting and after his first bow season he plunged into the sport.

With his bowhunting feet barely wet, he dropped a dandy eight-point whitetail during his second bow season. "Boy, from then on, bowhunting just caught me on fire. After I got my driver's license, my interest in small game hunting with a gun faded, and I started going after everything I could with my bow."

M.R. began bowhunting with an old Allen compound and soon followed the high-tech archery craze. "I was convinced that the only way to get a deer with a bow was to buy all the gizmos and gadgets. By the time I was sixteen, I had release aids, peep sights, stabilizers, wrist grips, range finders, lighted sights, and the whole routine."

It didn't take M.R. long to discover that his equipment was effective in dropping game. But he also felt something was missing in his approach to this ancient sport. Thirsting for more of a bowhunting challenge, M.R. drifted to the recurve and then to the lure of the longbow. "I decided I had to have a longbow, but there were none to be found. But I met Chuck Jones who ran Oka Valley Longbows in Vandalia, Illinois. He built a few longbows, and he told me to come on up and he would help me build my own longbow. Well, of course, I just went crazy. I was eighteen when I went up there and I built that longbow, and I've been building longbows every spare minute since."

His first longbow duplicated a Howard Hill style bow and blended a black walnut handle with maple corewoods and green glass. But it didn't last long — neither did the next ten. Even so, M.R. stuck with his new love and eventually he began producing longbows that performed well and lasted. "I kept building them at my house and soon friends wanted them, and the next thing I knew, I was building them continuously."

IT JUST HAPPENED

M.R. continued to build longbows in his spare time. He also studied electronics and mining technology, and later worked as an electrician in an underground coal mine. But he longed for sunshine and open spaces. Upon the recommendation of a supervisor at work, he enlisted in the Marine Corps. Eventually M.R. was stationed at Twentynine Palms in the southern California desert. "When I arrived at Twentynine Palms it was 132 degrees and during my three years there I never saw a drop of rain."

M.R. taught aviation electronics at the base for three years. His off duty recreation was limited, but M.R. and his longbow itch found their way into the base's special services wood shop. "Fred Pullen, who ran the shop, set up a bow building program. So I organized a bowmaking shop, built long-bows, and taught other Marines how to build bows.

"We tried every bow design we could think of. Then I developed a new loaded limb with a trapezoidal cross section. In April of 1984, I produced the first Scorpion longbow. And since then, I've been refining and improving that original design."

M.R. was prohibited from selling his popular bows during those years in the Marines, but once he left the service and moved to his mountain retreat, he became one of America's traditional bowyers. "I never planned on being a bowmaker. It just happened!"

MR. GUNG-HO

Since he started bowmaking full-time in February of 1987, M.R.'s bows have been on the winning edge of traditional shoots across the country. Although this newcomer's bows have raised eyebrows in some older archery circles, their performance and fast-growing reputation is of little surprise to M.R.. "Mediocrity has never been part of my lifestyle. I'm a gung-ho type of individual. I believe that if you're going to do something, do it the very best you can or don't bother doing it at all."

Armed with his gung-ho attitude, M.R. scurries around his downstairs shop with the energy of a five-year-old who's been eating too much candy. But that kind of energy is just fine for a man who devotes so much tedious handcrafting to the creation of his longbows.

M.R.'s SCORPION LONGBOW is offered in 66", 68" and 69" lengths. It has an approximate mass weight of 1 pound, 6 ounces, depending on the riser wood and corewoods. It has a recommended brace height of 6⅛" from the string to the throat.

Its hardwood riser measures 17" between fadeouts, is 2" thick, and is 1³⁄₁₆" wide, narrowing to ¾" through the sight window. The rounded sight window is cut ⅛" from center shot and the arrow shelf is crowned near the belly side for enhanced arrow flight.

M.R.'s standard riser is black walnut, but he also offers a variety of hardwoods such as shedua, osage, rosewood, bocote, and ebony. The riser is laminated with a thin contrasting decorative vertical wedge. The 4" grip is moderately peaked and slightly dished on the back and belly. The front of the grip has a thin 4½" long buffalo horn overlay. The grip is wrapped with thin leather lacing for positive hand placement. Bow specifications are inked in contrasting black or white above and below the grip on the opposite side of the window.

The Scorpion's limbs exhibit a slight ⅛" deflex from the riser and sweep into a 1" reflex through the outer one-third of the limbs. On the 69" bow, the working length of the upper limb is 26½" and on the lower limb it's 25". The deep-cored limbs taper uniquely to the back, exhibiting a modified trapezoidal cross section. They narrow from 1⅛" wide at the fadeout to ⁷⁄₁₆" at the string nocks.

The limbs are constructed from three back laminations and one belly lamination enveloped in fiberglass. The tapered corewoods are available in solid maple, purple heart, osage, red elm, or stained Actionwood. Fiberglass options are clear, brown, and black.

The beautifully rounded tips are overlaid with a thin layer of water buffalo horn. The nock to tip measurement is 1". Full cut string nocks are smoothly fashioned around the tips.

SCORPIONS WITH A STING — M.R.'s longbows incorporate a deflex-reflex design with a deep-cored limb tapering to the back. His hand-rubbed finish makes them a real show piece.

The Scorpion's high-luster finish highlights the smooth flowing contours of the limbs and riser while displaying the natural beauty of the woods.

To check a Scorpion longbow for relative speed, Terry Henry, World Champion longbower from Michigan, chronographed his 69", 67 pound at 28" draw, red elm-cored longbow. The bow was equipped with a standard Dacron string without accessories. Terry used a shooting glove, drew 28", and had a smooth, pull-through release. His arrows were 28" cedar shafts fletched with three 5" high-profile feathers. They were equipped with Mercury speed nocks, and weighed 530 grains. The average arrow speed for this bow, arrow, and shooter combination was 188 fps.

The following draw/force measurements suggest the smoothness of a 69" maple-cored Scorpion longbow:

DRAW LENGTH	25"	26"	27"	28"	29"
DRAW WEIGHT	50#	53#	56#	59#	62½#

M.R. hasn't forgotten the younger generation of longbow hunters. He offers the 60" Cub, an exact reproduction of his Scorpion.

HIGH COUNTRY LOVE

When he's not building his longbows, M.R. spends much of his time enjoying the great outdoors just out his back door. He's an avid fisherman who designs and ties his own flies for plucking trout from cascading streams or emerald mountain lakes. "I'm strictly a purist with my fly fishing, just like my longbow hunting. Above the house there are thirty-seven high country lakes and almost every one of them has a stream coming out of it. Plus, along the canyon here there are lots of streams loaded with trout. It's simple to catch plenty of fish because we are so far away from everybody, few tourists come here. I make my own fly pattern similar to the Rio Grande King, which is a popular large Colorado fly. But my creation works better in the white water rushing off the mountains here."

When he's not fishing, M.R. enjoys outdoor photography, mountain climbing, and backpacking. Despite the cold, one of his preferred times for savoring the outdoors is when winter hushes the landscape. "My favorite time of the year is when the remote areas become even more desolate. You can hike back into the lakes and not see anyone. Winter in the Rockies is so beautiful and it's not cold like most people would think. Plus, much of the game is down low here and you can see and photograph it."

FIRST LOVE

Most of M.R.'s outdoor pursuits revolve around his first love — bowhunting. For him the sport has special meaning. "Too many bowhunters think like gun hunters. They believe the reason you go hunting is to kill something, and that's their idea of success. That's not my philosophy at all. During the most memorable hunts of my life I never killed a thing."

In support of his love for bowhunting, M.R. belongs to the Colorado Bowhunters Association, The Illinois Traditional Bowhunters, and The Professional Bowhunters Society. "I'm a strong follower of the PBS. They have an anti-crossbow committee, and they take a stand on equipment issues that are important, like lighted sights. They're good people."

Although some of M.R.'s bowhunting friends shoot compounds, he doesn't mind. He's tolerant of most bowhunting weapons, as long as it's not a crossbow. "It's not what you shoot that counts, but how you shoot it. But the crossbow just sends me. If I see one in the field it upsets me so bad that I just go home."

Over the years, M.R. has taken whitetail, wild boar, mule deer, black bear, javelina, and mountain lion with his bow. Since moving to the mountains his quarry has become big-antlered elk and deer in the nearby national forest. When M.R. changed his bowhunting quarry he also changed his bowhunting methods. "I learned from and always hunted from tree stands in the Midwest, but I fell in love with western spot and stalk hunting. Now, I love to hunt high, spot my game, and sneak in on them.

"The wind always blows up the mountains during the day and by midday it's really blowing uphill. So before dawn I try to get on top where I can spot game. Then I watch the animals and see where they bed. From 10:00 A.M. to noon the wind and the animals have set in for the day and you can plan your stalk from above. But you've got to spot all of the animals in a group because if you don't, the one you didn't see might send the rest of them running. And if you spook one, all the critters in the whole basin clear out and you may as well move on to another. The key to hunting this high country is to get high fast and always stay above your quarry."

Even though M.R. climbs high and hunts hard for Colorado's antlered trophies, his favorite lacks headgear. "Bears! They've always been my number one animal to bowhunt. I'm fascinated by their power, the way they move, and the difficulty of finding them. But recently my thoughts are starting to shift toward the antelope that live here in the San Luis Valley. I frequently photograph all the animals around here but I've never taken a picture of a good buck antelope. I've tried and tried, but they're tough to get close to."

BAD TIME BEAR

Possibly one of the reasons M.R.'s thoughts are shifting more to the antelope is because of his terrifying bowhunting encounter with an enraged black bear. For many hunters it probably would have been their last bear hunt.

M.R. traveled to Ontario, Canada, for a June black bear hunt with noted Toronto outfitter, Jack Leggo. One of Jack's bear baits was located far from the road in a big alder swamp on a small island of high ground. Most of his hunters weren't interested in trudging that far back into the stand, but to M.R. it sounded like a great setup for a big bear.

He sat over the remote bait for three evenings without seeing a bear, yet the bait was being hit each night. "I knew there was a big bear there. So I told Jack not to come for me until well after dark because I wanted to see how big this bear was.

"I got up in my tree stand about 5:00 P.M. and around 8:00 P.M. I heard this crashing coming through the woods. I thought it was a moose because

I'd been seeing a lot them and it sounded much too noisy for a bear. Then sixty yards in front of me the biggest bear I ever saw stood up and he immediately started growling, snapping his teeth, and really getting belligerent. He even started tearing up small trees by the roots. I'd heard of big dominant bears scaring other bears off, and I thought he was just making sure no other bears were around.

"But then he stood up at fifty yards, looked directly at me, dropped to all fours, and charged. Before I even realized what was happening, he charged up my tree. He grabbed on to my tree stand and then grabbed my quiver. Arrows went flying all over the place. Then he slammed the bottom of my tree stand and knocked me backwards against the tree. It was a good thing I was tied to that tree. I started thrashing as his head came over the edge of the tree stand and my boot caught him square in the face. He screamed like a pig, fell backwards on his shoulders, and started spinning in circles.

"He was furious. Then he bashed into the tree and almost knocked me out of my stand. Enraged, he started digging at the tree roots. I tried to lean out over the stand for a shot but he was thrashing around too much. Suddenly he just took off like a dart back to where he came from."

Stunned and bewildered, M.R. wondered what he should do. But the bear gave him no time to react — in moment he was back. "He circled around me until he got about seventy yards out, he stood up, dropped to all fours, and charged again. But this time he stopped thirty-five yards out, stood up, and started snapping his jaws. I thought he was coming for me again so I pulled up and shot but hit him too low. The arrow went right through him but the back of the shaft broke off under his hide. Then he walked up slowly and laid down right under my tree.

"Every thirty minutes he would get up, walk around the tree a couple of times, and sit back down to watch me. All this time I was wondering how I was going to get another arrow because I knew he was eventually going to get tired of waiting and come up after me again. I tried to lean over and hook one of the arrows on the ground with my bow tip, but every time I tried he ran back over to the tree. They were just too far. And, the more I tried to get an arrow, the madder he got. So I climbed the tree as high as I could and strapped myself in.

"That big bear wasn't afraid of me at all. He kept me up in that tree for three hours until Jack finally showed up about 11:00 PM. It was quiet and dark, and that bear heard the truck coming. Then I heard the bear move off to the side and I figured that was my chance. I hit the ground running like hell. There were two creeks to cross on the way out and when I crossed the first one I heard that bear splashing through it coming after me. I was flying. I jumped into the truck and yelled, 'Man, that bear is right behind me.' "

Both M.R. and the bear ended that hunt with stories about, "You should have seen the one that got away!" Ten days later another hunter killed M.R.'s belligerent bear several miles from the alder swamp. The 500 pound boar was still carrying the piece of M.R.'s arrow under his hide. "I plan on hunting bears again in the next few weeks, and I wonder now what I'll do when I see a big one coming in."

M.R.'s bear hunt may have been his most memorable, but his most memorable shot occurred during a javelina hunt in southern Arizona. "Another bowhunter and I were on a big cliff with a two hundred foot deep canyon separating us from these javelina. One javelina was standing broadside about forty yards away at the same level we were. The guy behind me whispered, 'Try for him,' so I shot across the canyon. That arrow arced and hit that pig perfectly right behind the shoulder. He started sliding down the canyon and slid right to the bottom. And the guy behind me even got it on film."

TOUGH GEAR

Whether he's hunting the big boars of Ontario or the little boars of Arizona, M.R. uses the toughest of bears on the biting end of his hunting shafts. "I use Elburg's 160 grain Grizzly broadhead for practice and for hunting. There's no way I can break that head. I shoot them into the rocks and sand until the ferrule is worn through on the sides. They penetrate so well that I shot right through a bear's shoulder blade and the arrow exited out the other side, and I'm only shooting a sixty-two pound bow. It's the toughest broadhead I've ever seen."

M.R. vertically mounts his Grizzlies which helps his aiming. "When I feel that broadhead touch my finger, that's my cue to shoot. It helps my shooting because I have a tendency to creep, and with a vertically mounted broadhead I can force myself to draw until I feel the broadhead."

He mounts them on sixty-five pound to seventy pound spined $23/_{64}$" parallel cedar shafts. He fletches them with three, high-profile, $5\frac{1}{2}$" feathers with a strong helical twist to minimize wind planing and increase arrow stability.

Conforming with the rest of his traditional gear, M.R. carries his arrows in a standard Howard Hill style back quiver. "It's extremely productive for me because I can slip it up under my arm if I'm going through brush and then just slip it back up. It's the only quiver I know of that you can use with the quick draw method. If more people learned to speed shoot they would get more game. A lot of bowhunters miss their first shot, and sometimes the animal just stands there for a second, especially small game. I've killed more rabbits on my second shot than I ever have on the first."

"The second I let go of my first arrow, I reload immediately. I'm not real fast, but I shoot seven arrows in about twenty seconds. I'd like to be able to shoot ten arrows in fifteen seconds. I don't execute my shot that fast, I just reload fast. It's important when you're able to get another shot at your game. My last bear I shot three times."

M.R.'s speed shooting companion is his 69", 62 pound, maple-cored Scorpion with a large grip to match his spindly hands. That may not seem like a heavy longbow for high country critters such as elk, but M.R. thinks it's plenty. "Most longbow shooters are overbowed. Just because you can draw a bow back doesn't mean you can shoot it. The most important part of shooting a bow is being relaxed. If you can't relax your grip and your body, you're not going to shoot tight groups."

To make his high-gloss longbow compatible for sneaking in on keen-eyed antelope, this lanky bowman cuts down the reflection by waxing the limbs with string wax. "That gives it a satin finish that won't reflect light. And when you're done hunting you can polish it up in five minutes and make the bow look brand new again."

BEING PREPARED

Whether zeroing in on big game or fleeting rabbits, M.R. shoots with the fluid Howard Hill style. "I bring both arms up at the same time. I don't hesitate very long before I shoot, although I lock in for just a second and release with a twist of my hand. I don't really let go of the string, I just twist my hand free from it. I don't look at my arrow but I see it in my peripheral vision."

M.R. practices almost every day for at least an hour, sometimes two. During the winter he shoots inside his shop. When the snows begin to melt in the spring, he shoots his small field range laid out in the pinions behind his house. "I practice out to sixty yards all the time, but I like to contain my shooting at animals to thirty yards or less. I shoot at small game on the run but not at big game because there is no guarantee where you're going to hit them. I prefer to rely more on my hunting skill than my shooting."

Bowhunting the thin-aired high country not only requires fine-tuned shooting skills, it demands that the hunter be in top physical shape. For many seasonal bowhunters, preparing for the high country represents a grueling summer of training. But for M.R. it's just part of his daily routine. "I go for a hike every day, regardless of what goes on. It may even be at midnight.

INSPIRED BY THE MOUNTAINS AND THE GAME THEY HOLD—M.R. practices in his back yard using rock-tough Grizzly broadheads and employing the Howard Hill style of shooting.

"Our low elevations here are 10,000 feet, and from there everything goes almost straight up. It's not going up these mountains that gets you, it's coming back down. That's when you can develop severe knee problems if you're not prepared. You have to get used to it and then you have to stay in shape. I do a lot of quadricep exercises to build up my knees. It's important because your quadriceps support the knee when you're going downhill. I also ride my bike a lot and that helps my legs."

THE DESERT STINGER

M.R. learned how keep his knees and legs in shape during his desert training in the Marines. The desert also taught him to check his boots before putting them on. "When I was in the middle of the Mohave desert, I had to shake my boots out every morning to make sure there were no scorpions in them. We had lots of them in the field and they always impressed me, so I decided to name my bows after them."

Besides helping M.R. select a name for his longbow, his Marine years helped in developing his longbow design concepts. "The Marine Corps has massive computer systems for computing things like missile trajectories. I used to sit down with the computer programmer, and we programmed in my limb design and taper and then had the computer determine the best place to put the load in the limb. I was building load in the center of my limb, but I discovered that the best place was in the outer one-third. It's much more efficient and one of the important features of my bows."

A UNIQUE CROSS SECTION

Another feature of M.R.'s longbow design is his unique modified trapezoidal limb tapering to the back. Most bowmakers taper their limbs to the belly or leave them relatively square-edged. But not M.R. "When I was experimenting with corewoods, I built three identical bows at a time. I fashioned one square limbed, the second tapered to the belly, and the third trapezoidal to the back. In the Marines electronics program we had a lot of good systems for testing my bows. I discovered that the taper to the belly had the least cast, the one with the square limbs was second, and the one trapezoidal to the back had the farthest.

"I shape my limb to trapezoid tapering to the back because in physics you learn that the only force that moves something is a force from behind, a push. The force that moves a limb forward is the push from the behind, the compressed belly material. By slightly tapering a limb to the back you increase the compressional portion and decrease the stretchable portion, improving limb performance. I've even shown this on recurves and compounds. The reason most people build longbows tapering to the belly is because that's the way the old English used to build self-wood bows. But with today's glues and fiberglass we can taper a limb to a trapezoid in either direction. However, my trapezoidal shape is very slight. If you shape a trapezoid limb too much, you start developing problems with limb twist and breakage."

M.R.'s design blends the performance qualities he demands as a bow-hunter. "My bows are built for smoothness and stability. Because if that cotton pickin' bow isn't smooth then you've got some real problems. My bows are plenty fast, but they're not the fastest around. But in fast bows small mistakes are amplified."

PUTTING DESIGN TO FORM

When making his smooth drawing Scorpion, M.R. begins by crafting the riser section. He usually uses black walnut because of its light mass weight and its availability.

He begins by band sawing a riser-size piece of walnut down the middle and planing the vertical wedge contact surfaces. He then epoxies the thin contrasting vertical wedge between the two riser pieces, and "C" clamps them together and wraps them in opposing directions with inner tube strips. When gluing his risers or laminations, M.R. applies Ciba-Geigy epoxy to all contact surfaces.

After the glued riser has dried for twenty-four hours, he traces the riser's shape using a template and then band saws the shape out. Using a curved sanding jig held in a vise, M.R. vigorously hand sands the sweeping contour of his belly fadeouts in about thirty minutes.

His sanding jig is made from laminated plywood and is the same radius as his fadeout contour. It's padded with rubber-backed carpet and covered with replaceable sandpaper. "Everybody thinks there was some scientific way I figured the exact sweep of my fadeout. But the curve is just the outline of a toilet lid from the Marine base at Twentynine Palms. It was the best sized circle I could find, and it's been the design of my riser fadeout ever since."

HAND-SANDED FADEOUTS — Using his curved sanding jig and plenty of gung-ho energy, M.R. hand fashions his fadeouts to perfection.

When sanding, M.R. checks the alignment of his vertical wedge and the ends of the fadeouts to be sure he's sanding the surfaces perpendicular to the sides. "If I'm not perfectly square when I'm sanding, the fadeout end will run at a little angle. I may huff and puff for fifteen minutes when I'm sanding, but that finished fadeout is perfect. You can hold that hummer up and see light through it without seeing a ripple. If I glue a bow together and can see the end of my fadeout, then the fadeout was too thick."

By hand sanding his paper-thin fadeouts, M.R. achieves a gradual sep-aration between the face and back laminations without a break or interrup-tion in his thin glue line. "I've been building my fadeouts this way since 1984, and I've never had a bow break. That's because I make my fadeouts so thin and long, and by hand."

THE LIMB CORES

M.R. receives his custom-tapered laminations from Old Master Crafters and double checks each matched pair with a micrometer. He regularly matches brown fiberglass with maple corewoods, black glass with purple heart, and clear glass with red elm, or with gray and red Actionwood.

Although M.R. offers a choice of corewoods, he believes that the impor-tance of using different corewoods is exaggerated. "Most bowmakers will tell you that their special corewood is best. Their bow is simply designed to handle that particular corewood. My all-around favorite is maple. It's not the fastest, but it's the most consistent shooting of all the corewoods. The most consistent shooting of the faster corewoods is red elm. It's smooth, quiet, lighter than maple, pretty under clear glass, and it's the fastest."

M.R. stores his corewood in the rafters of his shop and doesn't worry about them absorbing moisture. "The San Luis Valley here is the sun capital of the world. We have 330 days of sunshine a year and it's actually classified as a desert because we get less than ten inches of rain a year."

When selecting his pairs of laminations, M.R. checks his composite thickness chart for specific bow weights. He always uses .050" thick fiber-glass in a continuous 72" strip for the back and two 36" strips for the belly.

IDENTICALLY SHAPED LIMBS

Once his riser is completed and the limb composites selected, they are ready to go into the press. M.R.'s 1¾" wide press is constructed from three layers of plywood laminated with glue and nails. The form portion of his press was made from a thick fir board fashioned in the shape of one limb and then sawed lengthwise, producing two identical halves. M.R. attached the twin halves to his plywood press, making a full-length bow form with identical upper and lower limbs. He installed a ⅛" thick strip of aluminum on top of the wooden form surface to protect it from wear and tear. The mirrored upper half of his press is cut into two pieces for ease of handling. During his Marine days, M.R. experimented with several press systems and discovered a nice blend of two popular methods. "I took the best of the clamp system by putting

BEST OF BOTH WORLDS — M.R.'s press utilizes eight clamps and an air hose to squeeze the glued composites together.

the press clamps close together. Then I used the fire hose method under the upper half of my form to even out the pressure."

LAY-UP

Before lay-up, M.R. bevels the butt ends of his laminations so they will overlap and add strength through the handle section.

Next to his main shop is his isolated, dust-free, glue-up and spraying room. Here he covers his form surface with wax paper to protect it from stray glue. To improve bonding, he lightly hand sands the gluing surface of his fiberglass and wipes it with a clean rag.

M.R. applies epoxy to all composite contact surfaces and lays up the bow on his work table. He places the glued bow in his form and lays a small block of wood on the center of the handle. After positioning the composites to match the form reference marks, he lays the fire hose on top and attaches the upper half of his press.

Once he tightens the eight clamps on each side of the press, he pressures up the fire hose to forty pounds using a small foot-pump. He double checks the alignment of his composites and pumps the hose up to sixty pounds.

M.R. places the press in his preheated glue curing oven. His homemade oven is equipped with four heat lamps, a heat deflector, a small circulating fan, and a thermostat control. A one-eighth inch thick steel heat deflector suspended between the lamps and the bow form prevents hot spots and helps retain heat in the oven. M.R. cures the pressed composites at 160 degrees for four hours.

FROM FORM TO SHAPE

M.R. allows the cured bow to cool overnight before removing it from the form. Using a string drawn tight between both ends, he marks the centerline on the back of the bow. He then uses a straight edge to mark the limb outlines and band saws them to rough shape.

Next, he epoxies on the buffalo horn grip overlay and tip overlays. M.R. prefers using the water buffalo horn because it's strong and extremely light-weight. Both overlays add beauty and function. "Without the grip overlay you feel the squared fiberglass on the grip. The grip overlay also allows me to concave the back to give a more positive grip."

After the overlays dry at room temperature for a day, M.R. power sands the limb edges smooth and begins shaping the entire bow using files and sandpaper. "I concave both the backing overlay and the grip throat. I have my customers give me their hand measurements, and I make the grip to fit their hand so their hand won't walk up and down the grip. I also narrow the handle slightly on the sides to fit their grip."

During the final shaping of the trapezoidal limb back, M.R. crafts a one-eighth inch positive tiller into the upper limb. Even though it takes longer than using a power sander, he patiently hand sands his bows into a smooth melting of riser and limb contours. "I like shaping my bows by hand because it's an art, like sculpturing."

A REVEALING FINISH

After inking the bow specifications and customer's name on the riser, M.R. sprays the bow with Fullerplast. He applies up to twelve coats on the handle and just a few on the glass. Once it's dried, he wet sands the finish with 400 and 600 grit sandpaper. He then rubs the finish with coarse polishing compound and finishes it with fine polishing compound. Finally, he brings it to a radiant luster with paste wax. "Including spraying, sanding, and polishing, I have about eleven hours in the finish on a bow. That's probably more time than anybody spends on their finish."

Why does M.R. devote so much time to hand-rubbing his mirror-like finish? "I want that glassy finish so the customer can see exactly what kind of quality he has. You can't hide mistakes under that kind of finish. I put a lot of work into the cosmetics of my bow. I use ebony, water buffalo horn, hardwoods, dyed laminations, and just about anything I can think of to make that bow more pleasant to look at. I get as much enjoyment from looking at my bows as I do from shooting them. I know a lot of my customers feel the same way because they often buy two or three of my bows. I have customers who don't even shoot longbows who own my bows just to hang on their wall for show."

GOAT LACING

Nearly finished, M.R. epoxies on the cushiony soft-backed leather strike pad and arrow shelf. He also epoxies and wraps the grip with a thin rounded-face goat lacing. "Goat seems softer and has more texture than calf lacing.

Calf lacing is just too slick. I've had people request a solid leather grip but I just refer them to another bow builder. My grip is by far superior to a one-piece leather. It's rough and each layer of lacing is rounded. Once you get used to it you will never grip it in the wrong place. If you're one lace off when holding that grip you'll feel it immediately. Plus, it looks so much more attractive than simply a one-piece leather grip. I don't polish my bows for all those hours just to put a one-piece grip on them."

Before sending them out, M.R. tunes his longbows and even installs a nocking point on the string. "I use a number four nylon serving for the nocking point and I tie above the nocking point down to the nock and then back up which gives it a double thickness. Some people change it to a metal nock but I like it because it's more traditional."

THE SWEET PART

After the long hours of shaping, sanding, and polishing, M.R. gets to savor his favorite part of the bowmaking profession. "I love to hand a guy his bow and see the look on his face. That's what it's all about. I draw my satisfaction from other people enjoying my bows. That's one of the reasons they are reasonably priced. I'm not in this to become rich. I like making someone's day."

It's M.R.'s policy to call his customers about a week after they've received their bow and then two months later, to be sure the bow is shooting like it should. "Most of my sales are from word of mouth. If I sell a man a bow, I honestly expect to sell him at least three and sometimes up to six."

Besides having repeat customers, many of M.R.'s customers are first-time longbowers. When they are, he's careful to try to match them with a bow they can comfortably handle. "A guy coming from a compound to a longbow can get overbowed real quick. Many of them think a longbow won't perform and therefore they need a heavy one. But that's not the case. Sure, longbows are slower, but you can use a heavier arrow and get the job done. For deer hunting a sixty pound longbow is plenty efficient. If you get a bow that's too heavy when you're first starting, you'll develop bad form. So I recommend that first time traditional shooters start with a lightweight bow and practice until their form is flawless, then they can work up to a heavier bow. Form is the key to shooting any bow, especially the longbow."

DO IT RIGHT

While many traditional bowyers offer a variety of models, M.R. is content to craft only his Scorpion. "I'm hard on myself. When I develop this model to the point where I can't improve it any more, then maybe I'll start working on a new model. But I've been building this design since April of 1984, and I don't think I have it completely refined yet. I'm going to continue to improve it with new technology and materials. My design is a good one. I've shown that in my research. But my bows could be better, and one at a time I hope to make them that way."

In the morning shadows of the Sangre de Cristos, a young bowmaker from Kentucky returns from a sunrise hike among the pinyon pines. He settles into his workshop and begins another day of bowmaking, hoping to make someone else's day. "The longbow is my life. It's what I do from morning until I go to bed at night. I'm like Kentucky Fried Chicken, I only do one thing, but I do it right!"

Chapter Twenty

HERITAGE ARCHERY

A RUGGED LAND

Montana's Gallatin Valley lies between the wild peaks of the Madison and Bridger Ranges. Like the early pioneers who settled there, pathfinders Lewis and Clark saw it as a promising land of rugged beauty harshened by bitter winters and sometimes haunted by the terror of hostile Indians and marauding grizzlies.

An early pioneer to the area was the adventurous John Bozeman who led wagon trains into the Gallatin Valley during the 1860s. But Bozeman's pioneering days were cut short in the spring of 1867 when he was killed by renegade Blackfeet Indians disguised as friendly Crow braves.

Although the man perished, his pioneering efforts gave birth to the town that bears his name, and today Bozeman is a bustling center for year-round recreation and home to Montana State University. Located ninety miles north of Yellowstone Park, the town soon gives way to the surrounding hay-covered valleys speckled with livestock and ranches. To the north, the fields rise into brush-covered slopes that reach upward to the jagged peaks of the Bridger Mountains.

Up in the Bridger's wind-swept meadows, spring grasses reach for the warming sun. It's a time of alpine rebirth. Black bears emerging from their dens graze on the open slopes, filling their delicate stomachs with spring greens.

But the bears are not alone.

Drifting through the pines like a silent breeze, a lone man slips through the brush with the deliberate movements of a predator, his sleek bow often parting the way. His bushy salt and peppered beard brackets a stern face dominated by piercing eyes.

Down slope, two bears paw in the brush, unaware of the readied arrow and the deadly approach. Within striking distance, the bowman carefully checks his target, making sure it's the older sow and not the juvenile almost her size. He sidesteps a bush for a better look. Suddenly the brush erupts in a bawling fury of commotion as an unseen juvenile scurries up a nearby tree.

The stunned archer whirls at the sound of pounding feet and faces the enraged sow. Instinct grips their actions: the sow advances hackled and ready, the bowman draws and shoots without thought. At twelve paces the arrow slices through the bear. She wheels, lunging headlong down the slope. On her third bound, she plows lifelessly through the grass, coming to rest near a lingering patch of snow. The Bridger Mountains again surrender one of their trophies to their neighbor, bowhunter and bowmaker, Rocky Miller.

INTENSITY PLUS

Rocky Miller, owner of Heritage Archery, is an intense man who plunges into his bowhunting and bowmaking with a zeal he can't hold back. Whether he's closing in on game or crafting traditional bows, he attacks the task, his intensity honed to a razor's edge. It shows in his brow, in the tilt of his head, and in the dagger-like stare of his icy eyes. Misjudged by some as stern, Rocky's intensity simply reflects the depth of his passion for the sport that guides his life — traditional archery.

An outgrowth of his zest for traditional archery, Rocky enjoys part-time guiding and outdoor writing. He belongs to the Montana Bowhunters, The Professional Bowhunters Society, Bowhunters of Wyoming, and the local Gallatin Bare Bow Hunters. Their fourteen-target animal range, tucked away in the shadowed slopes south of town, is a challenging course where Rocky polishes his skills with the longbow.

His fascination with the longbow began early in life. Like so many youngsters during archery's golden years, Rocky was inspired by the grand master of the longbow. "Movies at the local theater were a Saturday morning affair for me when I was a kid. Most of the time they showed a Howard Hill short. I watched every one of those probably 100 times. And during the late fifties and early sixties, Fred Bear was certainly an archery hero. But today we don't have the heroes we had back then, and that was part of the romance of the sport."

A BLEND OF STYLE AND MIND

Even though heroes such as Hill and Bear are gone, their inspirational shooting styles live on. Displaying fluid Hill-style movements on the range, Rocky empties his back quiver with impressive accuracy. Like Hill, Rocky leans into the shot with bent knees, cants his longbow, leans over his arrow, and pauses only a split second before releasing the shaft. It leaps from the bow with a life of its own, kerthumping into the target next to its feathered mates.

He's a talented, instinctive shot who enjoys teaching his skills to traditional newcomers. "Instinctive shooting is about ninety-nine percent mental. An important part of it is how you feel when you step up to a target or walk into a situation where an animal is presenting a shot. If you attack that situation with confidence, you're going to make that shot."

Before an archer can employ a positive mental approach, he must first master basic shooting skills to help create confidence. "It's important to learn and practice sound fundamentals. I try to get people not to even think about accuracy until they develop the fundamentals. But in half an hour I can teach a guy who has natural hand-eye coordination and who has never picked up a bow in his life, to shoot six-inch groups at fifteen yards."

The first point Rocky teaches, is an open shooting stance, which shortens most archer's draw length by two or three inches. "A typical target stance is to stand at a right angle to the target with your head back and draw the bow as far as you can. I could shoot a thirty inch arrow if I shot that way, but I actually shoot a twenty-six inch arrow. I open up to the target a bit with my body and bend my bow arm a little. I don't like to move my bow shoulder in. If you can't keep your shoulder out, you're shooting a bow that's too heavy."

His second fundamental focuses on drawing the bow. There are two main styles: the push-pull style, and Rocky's method. "I come up with my bow arm, and then begin pulling my bow. I have my spot picked out, and I'm aiming before that arrow ever comes back. I try to maintain that bow position all the way through the shot until that arrow strikes the target.

"I normally anchor right up in the front of my face, but regardless of where you anchor, just make sure that it's consistent. Occasionally, if I want to impress somebody on the target range, I will shoot three fingers under and anchor right under my eye. That way I can shoot tight groups at twenty yards all day long. But gun-barreling like that is a whole different kind of shooting and I can't hunt that way. Once you get past the point of trajectory, you have to mentally make some yardage decisions, and I don't like to do that. I like to be able to hunt without thinking about anything except the spot that I want to hit."

When he's concentrating on that spot and reaches his anchor point, Rocky continues his release in one fluid motion. "Now if I'm concentrating exceptionally hard, I may hold a bit longer, I won't snap shoot quite as much. In snap shooting there is a flow of instinctive shooting that is all rhythm. You can't achieve that rhythm with a compound bow because with the break over you can't even start aiming until you are at full draw. And that's what you want to avoid when you shoot instinctively, because the minute you come to full draw and then pick your spot you have to think about yardage. The whole idea behind instinctive shooting is not having to think, it's being able to shoot automatically with an uninterrupted flow of movement."

Besides teaching the solid basics of instinctive shooting, Rocky teaches a method of picking a spot that helps his students zero in on the mark. "I call it a concentration marker. I start you out on a bull's eye target that has concentric rings. This helps focus your attention.

"Then I take a three-quarter inch stick-on fluorescent dot and put it right in the center of the bull's eye. That makes those concentric rings focus down to a fine point. Using this concentration marker, I have you start shooting at ten yards until you are automatically shooting one to two-inch groups. If the arrow goes high or low it doesn't matter. Too many people try to adjust and aim. But you don't want to aim or see the arrow or anything.

You just want to be able to see and concentrate on that marker. Your hand is your front sight, your eye is your rear sight, and what sits on your shoulders is your trajectory computer. It's all hand-eye coordination."

Once he has his students grouping arrows around the fluorescent dot at ten yards, Rocky takes them to the next phase. "Then you can start increasing the yardages, but you should continue to use that fluorescent dot. Once you become confident at fifteen yards, I replace the bull's eye target with an animal target, and I put that dot in the kill zone.

"When you're not shooting and just sitting in your office or watching television, you can pick out any object and visually project that fluorescent dot on the spot that you want to hit. It's an inner mind visualization projection. When you start varying your yardages as you're projecting, you will never think about yardages again while shooting."

MOUNTAIN SIDE PRACTICE — With his ever-intent stare, Rocky takes aim using one of his Predator T/D recurves.

Besides enjoying teaching instinctive shooting to newcomers, Rocky enjoys spreading the contagious thrills of traditional archery. "I used to shoot with some of these target guys, and they were absolutely amazed that I could hit a three inch bull's eye at twenty yards without anything on my bow. They couldn't believe it or understand it. They didn't know anything except compounds, sights, and releases. And now many of those guys are getting interested in traditional archery. It excites me showing someone who started with a compound how much fun they can have with traditional equipment. And each person who changes over is excited about it."

PRACTICE PAYOFF

When he's not teaching shooting or promoting traditional archery during his off hours, Rocky prepares for the upcoming season on the practice range, honing the fundamentals he teaches. His long hours of shooting pay off when he heads for the high country. It's there that stealth and chance bring this dedicated bowman within range of his quarry. Sometimes it's only twelve paces, sometimes it's more. "My longest killing shot was probably sixty yards, and I don't even know for sure why I shot at the animal, because I normally don't shoot that far. It was that instant in time that made it work. But ninety-five percent of my shots are inside of twenty-five yards."

Even though most of his shots are within reasonable range, in the animated world of big game hunting the critters are often standing at odd angles and moving. When they are, this versatile bowhunter just makes the most of the opportunity. "I've killed animals on a dead run, but I don't advocate shooting animals on the run. But on antelope, I think it's the safest way to shoot at them because then they can't duck your arrow!

"Shooting at running or moving game is different than shooting at stationary targets. It's just one of those instinctive reactions. It's all reflex, like throwing something up in the air and shooting at it. The shooting mechanics are still there but you don't have time to think."

Rocky had little time to think when he was faced with the advancing sow bear which now graces his den. The reflex shot was one of his most exciting. Another memorable shot was made on a huge bull elk whose mount dominates his west den wall. "This old guy here had a lot of scars and old antler wounds. When I caped him out, I took out a three-quarter inch long piece of antler tine that was imbedded in the middle of his forehead. It had gristle growing around it."

BONUS BUCKS

Rocky tagged the bull during a high country hunt with his friend Jim Diercks. They packed their camp into a remote mountain canyon using Honda 90 trail bikes, hoping to find a few elk. They found more than they bargained for. "We had so many elk back in there, we even had them bugling thirty yards from camp during the night. We camped at the bottom of the canyon and it was a long climb in the morning to get up to the level that we wanted to hunt. So we decided to grab our sleeping bags and spend the night on top where we wanted to be at daylight.

"On our way up to the top that evening, we were looking for a tree to bed down under, when this huge buck deer jumped up, ran out, and stood broadside at forty yards. We had deer tags and he was tremendous with wide, heavy beams. I was standing behind Jim, and as he slid his sleeping bag down and got an arrow out, I did the same thing. Jim shot, but he missed and that monster buck took off.

"When the huge buck took off, another buck walked down and stood right where the huge one had been, and I let him have it. So we ended up taking care of my three point and getting him hung up in a tree. By the time we were finished, it was dark and we couldn't find a very good place to bed down."

After spending a miserable night on the mountain side in a mix of rain and snow, Rocky and Jim positioned themselves near a game crossing. "We hadn't been sitting there five minutes, when I heard this 'clomp-clomp-clomp', and here came a giant buck. He had to weigh 300 pounds. He was coming right at me but he spotted me, turned, and ran right over to Jim. As he ran by, Jim plugged him.

"So that was the end of our 'elk' hunting. Jim's buck only scored 166 inches but his body size was just incredible. After dressing him out, the two of us could not dead-lift that monster off the ground. So we cut him up and packed him down to camp. It was snowing and raining and we were soaked and miserable, and spent the next day in our tent. It never let up and the only extra clothes we had were hanging outside covered with three inches of snow. We left the camp there but packed the deer up the next morning and got out of there."

A few days later Rocky and Jim went back up the mountain to break camp and decided to take their bows. Maybe some luck still lingered on the mountain side. "We got camp all loaded up, and were about halfway out and stopped to bugle along the trail. And by gosh we heard an elk bugle back.

"So we jumped off the bikes and took off. About halfway up the mountain we bugled again and he immediately answered. We started working in on him and got in front of the spot we figured he was coming to. I got set up and saw him raking some trees on his way in. He walked out broadside thirty yards in front of me, and I nailed him. I hit him high in the back of both lungs, and he took off and went 120 yards without much of a blood trail. I finally spotted him still alive eighty yards below us. It was getting dark, so I sneaked down to within fifteen yards of him and let him have it again. He died on the edge of this steep slope, and we had to tie him to a tree to keep him from sliding on down the hill. Then we really had some packing out to do."

Whether he's hunting bonus bucks or last minute bulls, Rocky prefers stalking his prey. It's the ultimate way to bowhunt all of Montana's trophies, especially the keen-eyed prairie goat. "Antelope are exciting because they're so much fun. They're hard to stalk, and they're a real challenge in that respect. To stalk antelope you need the right terrain. It also helps to get between a herd buck and a smaller buck — they tend to pay more attention to each other than they do to you. By using real slow, straight ahead movements, I have sneaked into a whole herd of antelope, and much of it was across barren ground.

"Using a decoy is probably the most effective way to hunt herd bucks. I've watched herd bucks come on a dead run for a mile to pick up a single doe, and they will always go after a smaller buck away from the herd. Every good herd buck will have at least one and up to three smaller bucks around his herd, and they just drive him nuts. If you can imitate one of those small bucks, you will definitely get your shot."

High on Rocky's list of bowhunting favorites are trophy-class mule deer. For tagging big bucks, he uses the spot n' stalk technique, catching them right in their beds. It's a tricky game requiring plenty of patience. "When I'm hunting bedded bucks, I'm moving so slow that it's almost like I'm not moving at all. I'm effectively standing still. I have to be able to spot those deer before they spot me.

"I don't care how close you are to big bucks, if they spot you first your chances of getting them are slim to none. So to spot them first you must move incredibly slow with no sideways motion. They don't seem to be able to relate to distance real well, but if you move sideways they spot you right away."

As he slowly drifts through the brush searching for buckskins, Rocky often scans ahead with field glasses, even at fifty yards. "Once I've spotted that out of place antler tip or ear, I use terrain features and whatever vegetation is available to get close enough for a shot. My biggest problem is having enough patience after getting in on them. It doesn't bother me to spend all afternoon sneaking up on one deer, but once I get into position and can see him ten yards away blinking his eyes, I tend to get impatient. And that's when I need patience the most. I guess that's my Achilles heel."

A LONGBOWMAN'S TOOLS

When stalking bedded mulies, Rocky usually totes his 62" longbow and carries a half dozen cedar arrows in his Catquiver II. The quiver's pouch also holds the extra gear he needs for a day's hunting in the mountains.

Rocky fletches his wooden shafts in a strong helical twist with three 5½" shield-cut feathers. He installs Mercury speed nocks on the back ends and mounts file-sharpened four-bladed Delta broadheads on the business ends. In the mountain man tradition, he silences his bowstring with Beaver Balls, beaver hair string silencers.

Another hunting accessory customized for his traditional style is his hat. It's a baseball style camouflage cap with the outer two inches of brim trimmed off and the fabric covering resewn. Unlike the full brim, the shortened version doesn't interfere with his longbow string at full draw.

For bowhunting Montana's alpine terrain, Rocky also customizes his footgear. The wet mountain meadows require a boot that's dry and grips well. By improvising, he takes a good pair of boots and makes them better. "The problem with rubber-bottomed Maine hunting boots is that they don't grip very well on wet surfaces, so I put Air Bob soles on them."

THE HERITAGE

The core of Rocky's customized gear is his handcrafted longbow. It also represents his livelihood and a Miller family tradition. "My dad was into archery and used to build bows, and 'Heritage' just seemed to fit what I was doing. I was carrying on what he had started."

Today, Rocky's Heritage longbows and recurves enjoy a reputation throughout the country and overseas as hard hitting hunting bows. They're also known for their simple, clean lines and effectiveness in the field.

The PREDATOR T/D, a three-piece take-down recurve, is Rocky's most popular model. It's available in 60", 62", and 64" lengths. The 62" model has an approximate mass weight of 2 pounds, 6 ounces, and a brace height of 7¼" from the string to the throat.

The 17" or 19" riser is constructed from highly laminated green, brown, or gray dyed maple and incorporates a sweeping vertical decorative wedge sandwiched with maple veneer. The riser also has a thin vertical lamination on the back which accentuates the contours near the shelf.

The riser is 1⅝" wide and narrows to ¾" through the rounded sight window, which is cut ⅛" from center shot. The window is full cut for 2½" above the shelf and contours back to full riser width 4½" above the shelf. The riser is 2½" thick and thins to approximately 1¾" through the custom throat. The arrow shelf is crowned and the outer edge is beveled for clean arrow flight. The entire riser is softly contoured with simple flowing lines which expose the contrasting tones of the laminated maple. The custom grip has a low to medium profile. Bow information is black inked on the opposite side of the window. The bow is equipped with a leather strike pad and synthetic fur shelf.

The large radius recurve limbs have a working length of 18¾" from the fadeout to the nock. They narrow from 1⅝" wide at the fadeout to ⅝" at the nock. They attach to the riser with a single Allen head bolt with a brass bezel and a single alignment pin. They're constructed from one belly lamination tapered .002" per inch and two parallel back laminations. The maple or red elm corewoods are enveloped in either clear, brown, or black fiberglass. The thin tip overlays are made from laminated maple. The flush string nocks fade to the belly where a single string groove is filed into the glass. Heritage bows are available in low-luster satin or lightly textured finishes, radiating their earthy colors, yet ideal for hunting.

To check for relative speed, Rocky chronographed his 64 pound at 26" draw, 62" Predator T/D recurve. Rocky's 26¾" wooden arrows weighed 460 grains, were fletched with three 5" shield-cut feathers, and had open nocks. The bow was equipped with a standard Dacron string without accessories. Rocky used a shooting glove, drew a consistent 26", and had a crisp pull-through release. The average arrow speed for this combination of arrow, bow, and shooter was 205 fps.

The following draw/force measurements were recorded on this 62" Predator T/D:

DRAW LENGTH	25"	26"	27"	28"	29"
DRAW WEIGHT	61#	64#	67#	70#	74#

The BRIDGER MOUNTAIN LONGBOW is Rocky's preferred traditional weapon. It's available in the 64" Hunter, the 62" Magnum, and the 60" Brushmaster. The 64" model has a mass weight of approximately 1 pound, 6 ounces, and a brace height of 6¾" from the string to the throat.

Its solid hardwood riser is 16½" long between fadeouts, is 1" wide, and narrows to ⅝" through the sight window. It is 1⅞" thick and thins through the straight traditional or custom semi-dished grip. The grip is wrapped with a 4½" leather wrap and laced down the front. The bow's information is exquisitely black inked on the belly below the grip and on the limb edge above the window.

The reflexed limbs exhibit rounded edges that taper to the belly. The working length of the upper limb is 24¾" and the lower limb is one inch shorter. The limbs narrow from 1 1/16" wide at the fadeouts to ½" at the flush-cut string nocks. They incorporate the unique "Heritage Tri-Flex" core.

MADE FOR HUNTING — The Predator T/D and Bridger Mountain Longbow are designed for shooting heavy arrows and putting down game. The T/D riser (right) incorporates a sweeping decorative wedge and pocket cuts where the limbs attach for a one-piece appearance.

It's constructed from one tapered corewood belly lamination and three back corewood laminations sandwiching a layer of fiberglass. This unusual fiberglass and multi-laminated core is faced and backed with fiberglass and is one of the secrets to the Bridger Mountain longbow's performance.

Rocky commonly uses brown fiberglass in his longbows but also offers clear glass over a thin veneer of attractive hardwood with the striking Sacajawea model. The maple and riser wood laminated tip overlays are somewhat elongated and delicately fashioned. The bow is finished in a low-luster matte finish ideal for hunting, yet it displays the beauty of the woods and multi-laminated core.

Rocky chronographed his 62" longbow which pulled 66 pounds at his 26" draw. He used the same arrows and string type as noted with the Predator T/D and obtained an average arrow speed of 185 fps.

The following draw/force measurements suggest the smoothness of his 64" longbow:

DRAW LENGTH	25"	26"	27"	28"	29"
DRAW WEIGHT	52#	55½#	59#	62#	66#

IN THE SHADOWS OF THE BRIDGERS

Rocky crafts his bows in the back room of a downtown shop just north of Main Street in Bozeman, the town he proudly calls home. But it hasn't always been.

Born in Nebraska, Rocky moved to Minnesota when he was twelve and later to California as a young man. After two hitches in the army, he returned to California and worked with his father doing carpentry and cabinet work. Carpentry agreed with Rocky, but California didn't. He decided he needed a place with more open skies and less cluttered countryside. "I wanted to move to Alaska or Canada, but I couldn't get my wife, Pat, to move that far. So I said, 'Let's go to Montana and look around.' I knew about Bozeman because I was a pretty serious fly fisherman back then. And when we came out and looked it over we said, 'This is it.' " Six weeks later, Rocky was living there.

He worked as a finish carpenter for ten years and then started building bows as a hobby. As his interest grew, he began visiting with Bob Savage, originator of the Savage Deathmaster recurve. "Every time I would come up with an idea, Bob would say, 'If you want to know if something works, you've got to build it and find out.' That's basically how I learned to build bows."

Mostly self-taught, Rocky started building bows in 1981 and began crafting them full-time in 1983. "I don't know that I'm the best bowyer around, but I have learned fast, and I feel like a quality craftsman who builds a quality hunting bow for a reasonable price."

Late summer usually finds Rocky working late into the evening, committed to fulfilling as many new orders as possible so his customers won't have to shoot compounds in the upcoming season. He also works extra hard then so he can take some time off to enjoy his own bowhunting pursuits.

With Willie Nelson grinding out a tune over the radio, Rocky shapes a riser with the same fluid movements he shows on the practice range. His years as a cabinet maker show. Despite Willie's foot-stompin' cadence, he

TRI-FLEX CORE — The Bridger Mountain Longbow's unique limb core is one of the secrets to its performance.

can't keep up with Rocky's energetic rasping; the rhythmic growls of his file staying one step ahead of, "Can't wait to get back on the road again..."

His shop is spacious and well lit. Over a dozen machine work stations and several work benches make it appear that more than one bowyer works there. But it's just Rocky, sometimes putting in the time and energy of two men. Downstairs houses his office and a shooting area for testing bows.

Although customer demand requires that Rocky spend most of his time crafting his popular take-down recurves, he favors making longbows. "I enjoy the gracefulness of my longbows. I think they're more classically elegant."

His longbows are classical to a point, but not in their unique Tri-Flex fiberglass core. Laminating a strip of fiberglass into the core was such an unheard of concept that even other bowyers said it wouldn't work. But their opinions didn't stop Rocky from developing his design into one of the fastest shooting longbows on the market. "The basic idea behind my longbow was to make a shorter longbow suited for hunting that shot well. I never really knew what it was going to do when I started playing around with it. You can get an idea, but the only way you are going to know is to build it and shoot it. And that's the bottom line — how the bow shoots."

CRAFTING A HERITAGE

Rocky begins crafting a bow by building the riser. For his composite T/D handle he first uses a template to draw the sweeping decorative wedge line on a block of laminated maple. With hair-splitting precision he band saws the wedge line and then trims the contact surfaces smooth using a template guide on his 3" flush-trimming table-mounted router.

He then epoxies and sandwiches the maple wedge components between the riser pieces and "C" clamps them together. The riser is then put in the glue curing oven to dry. Once it's dried, the riser composite is ground flush on the belt sander and then both sides are sanded parallel on a thickness drum sander. Rocky runs it through the humming machine until it is precisely 1⅝" thick. It's squared on the ends with a table saw and he uses another template to outline the belly and back profiles, including the limb notches.

Rocky's recent notched "pocket cut" design on his T/D gives the assembled bow more of a one-piece look. Using shallow set screws, he attaches a ½" thick template guide to the riser block, cuts it to shape, and then trims the pocket notches and riser outline smooth on his table router. Rocky drills the limb mounting bushing hole and alignment pin hole using a guide jig, and he taps the bushing hole. He then screws the threaded steel attachment bushing into the tapped and epoxied hole. He also epoxies in the alignment pin.

Whether he's crafting T/D fadeout wedges or the fadeouts on a longbow riser, Rocky takes his time delicately fashioning these critical areas. "The fadeouts are the most important part. Most people probably come up short by not having good, long, quality fadeouts. They are the highest stress points in a bow, and making the proper limb to riser junction is very important. But

CRITICAL SANDING — Rocky hand sands the final feathering on the belly side of his fadeouts. It's one of the most important steps in bow crafting.

everything you do in bowmaking is going to affect something else, and it's all inter-related to the bow's performance."

After band sawing a longbow riser or T/D fadeout wedge to shape, Rocky supports the back of the fadeout with a piece of wood while gingerly grinding it to almost paper thinness on a vertical sander. Then he lays the back down on a flat surface and block sands the feathered portion of the belly by hand to see-through thinness, making sure that the ends of the fadeouts remain square to the sides

CAREFUL COMPOSITES

Once his fadeouts are completed, he prepares his limb composites for glue up. Besides using a micrometer to check his limb components, Rocky performs an extra step when checking the fiberglas. "The main problem that bowyers are having today is Gordon's quality control. I spine every piece of glass that comes in the door. It's the only way I can even get close to poundage. Otherwise I'm just building bows by guess or by golly. I can take two pieces of .050 inch glass and one of them will spine test differently enough to make a ten pound difference in a bow. I spine test a one foot section of glass using a plumb bob and a deflection chart and measure its deflection to within one-sixteenth of an inch. You can't assume anything in this business."

When preparing the center lamination of fiberglass for his longbow core, he sands both sides to ensure a good glue bond. He also bevels and glues together the butt ends of the matched corewoods into one piece and sands the joint smooth before lay-up. Rocky buys his maple laminations from the

ASSUME NOTHING — To help him achieve desired draw weight, Rocky spine checks each piece of fiberglass using his own deflection chart.

Old Master Crafters, but he custom grinds his red elm, yew, and osage laminations on his drum sander.

Before glue-up Rocky covers his forms with Visquine. The forms are made of laminated birch plywood and the form surface is covered with Formica. His T/D forms are single limb forms mirroring the belly, and his longbow form mirrors the bow back and is mounted on a square steel beam to prevent warping.

BIRTH OF A BRIDGER

Rocky first wipes all gluing surfaces clean with acetone and then applies epoxy to all contact surfaces with a putty knife. Using nylon strapping tape as an extra pair of hands, Rocky lays and positions the composites in the form. He then lays a metal pressure strip and an air hose on top of the composites and installs the upper half of the press. When pressing a long-bow, he also installs wooden wedges under the hose near the fadeouts before inflating the hose to ensure sufficient pressure at these important areas. Rocky then inflates the hose with enough pressure to snug up the compos-ites, and checks their alignment. He then inflates the hose to eighty pounds and sticks the form in his curing oven.

He cures the glue at 190 degrees for three to four hours and then allows it to cool overnight. "One problem people have is leaving bows in hot cars. A lot of epoxies start to break down at 125 to 130 degrees. That's one of the reasons I cure mine at 190 degrees."

After he pulls the cured T/D limbs from the form, Rocky grinds one side flat on a belt sander and then grinds both sides parallel on the drum sander until the limbs are 1 5/8" wide. Using a jig, he drills the limb mounting hole, and he marks the centerline on the back. Next, he carefully marks the limb shape using a template, band saws it out, and grinds its form on a belt sander. He center punches and pilot-hole drills the alignment pin hole on the centerline.

Now Rocky installs the T/D limbs on their matching but still square-sided handle, and he checks limb alignment by visually lining up the center-lines of both limbs. Occasionally he removes a small amount of material off the edges of the limb to bring them into alignment.

He mostly uses hand rasps and a 1 1/2" spindle sander to contour the riser. But like Montana's Indians who used obsidian scrapers to carve their bows, Rocky also uses steel wood scrapers when hand-smoothing the gentle contours. He carefully fashions the sides where the limbs attach to the riser, helping to give the T/D a one-piece appearance.

Rocky epoxies on thin tip overlays using "C" clamps and fashions them to a sleek profile. "I think it helps the lines of the bow, and it helps the speed. With the fiberglass and corewoods you really don't even need the overlays. A lot of guys will even put material on the belly side and decorate the tips with excess material which I think just slows a bow down."

He files in shallow string grooves making sure that they are each cut the same distance from the centerline and that they feather out on the belly with identical angles. They're not filed much deeper than what is needed to hold the string flush. "I don't see a whole lot of point in going any deeper. I have made some nocks pretty narrow, but I had one blow up that was using a Fast Flight string and that changed my ideas about how narrow I wanted them."

FUTURE T/D LIMB — Rocky holds the glued composites in the form with tape before securing the upper half of his press.

When laying up a longbow or T/D limbs, Rocky offsets the tapered corewoods a bit toward the lower limb which makes the lower limb a little stiffer, providing a built in tiller. He strives for a ³⁄16" to ¼" positive tiller and sometimes sands the belly fiberglass to adjust it.

During the final hand sanding Rocky can alter the bow's draw weight by a few pounds but rarely makes more than a three pound adjustment. To make a bow draw lighter he lightly sands the belly glass of the limbs.

Once a bow is ready to be finished, Rocky brushes a coat of wood sealer on all wood surfaces and wet sands them with 320 grit paper. He then sprays on one smooth coat of finish. When it's dried he inks on the bow's specs and names with an artistic flair. He then sprays on four coats of either his matte smooth finish or the textured finish.

After a bow is finished Rocky takes a moment to admire his labor of love. "It's just like when I built cabinets or a fancy stair rail. It's being able to stand back and look at it and appreciate it. Bows are different in that they have both art form and function, and that's neat."

For Rocky, part of admiring a new bow is test shooting it, and sometimes he discovers one with almost magical qualities. "Every once in a while I'll produce a bow better than anything else I have ever made. I don't understand it, because I can check everything and can't find or measure any difference. Yet there will still be that rare bow that I absolutely cannot miss with. That has happened to me three times and I didn't want to let those bows go. I did, but I know where they all are."

MADE FOR HUNTING

Rocky tries to build a little magic into all his bows. They're designed and crafted to be effective hunting weapons — hard hitting bows that can throw a hunting shaft to the mark. They're also custom made, which means Rocky does his best to fit the customer with the right bow. "The materials in all bows are pretty much the same, so it's the design that mostly determines performance. I build a fairly heavy and massive limb. And I like a long working limb with a recurve that opens up properly to provide a smooth draw. I feel this combination provides the best performance for heavy hunting arrows. I try to find out what characteristics are important to a customer, and then I try to build a bow to match their desires and shooting style."

When matching a customer with a bow, Rocky selects the optimum bow length design for a specific draw length. "I don't like bows that are too short or too long. I like them sixty to sixty-four inches. With my shorter draw length, I get more performance with a shorter bow. But I also like the stability of a longer bow so I designed my limb to compensate for that. An optimum bow for a twenty-eight inch draw is sixty inches in my recurve design. That bow is designed to perform best between twenty-eight and thirty inches. And if a guy is shooting over thirty inches, I recommend the sixty-two inch or possibly the sixty-four inch bow.

"Even sixty-eight and seventy inch longbows are too long. My longest is just sixty-four inches, but I came up with a relatively good design that makes it a smooth drawing bow. Most longbows are not made to shoot over twenty-eight inches but I have guys shooting my sixty-four inch bow who have thirty-one inch draws. And at thirty-one inches, those arrows have to be coming out of that bow like rockets."

EITHER/OR

Although his healthy list of customers suggests that traditional archery is on a strong upward swing, bowhunting's future is not without its dark clouds. "I think we have some problems facing us in the upcoming years. The crossbow is definitely one threat, but I'm also in favor of either/or hunting seasons. I know a lot of people will argue that point, but I think we need to get rid of the instant bowhunters who are bad for our image. Bowhunting is a lot worse now than it was twenty years ago. Back then if you were a bowhunter you were really respected but that's not as true today.

"Obviously, the increased number of hunters is affecting the kill numbers, and that's a problem. I think that an either/or season would put fewer but more serious bowhunters in the field. But our Fish and Wildlife Department isn't for it, and many bowhunters aren't for it. A lot of people enjoy hunting both bow and gun season. But many of them may be taking the easiest route with their equipment and amount of practice. With an either/or season those people would be rifle hunters instead of bowhunters. And I would prefer they were. But the problem then becomes a smaller number of bowhunters trying to protect their season. There aren't any easy answers."

Regulating hunting seasons may be complex issues, but when it comes to an either/or choice of hunting bows, Rocky casts his vote without question — it's the versatile longbow. For Rocky, it elevates his challenge and lightens his spirit. "There is something special about the longbow. It just makes you feel a little bit different. It's hard to describe. For quick shots you can't beat it because it comes up so much quicker. My hunting longbow only weighs seventeen ounces. Plus I always figured if I ever got lost with it I could also use it for a fishing pole or a spear. And if I had a long hike out, it would make a good walking stick."

It's not every bow that has an either/or use, but then again, not every bow is crafted in the shadows of Montana's Bridger Mountains.

Chapter Twenty-One

MONARCH LONGBOWS

CHASING MONARCHS

"Two years ago," says Byron Schurg with a soft grin, "my friend George and I literally chased an elk down. We bugled and this bull answered, but he sounded like he was going away from us. Normally when they do that, they're pushing out their cows and they don't want to fight. But we discovered that if you run after them, sometimes you can catch up. So we bugled and then ran to where he answered from. After a mile and a half of chasing him, all of a sudden there he was. But we weren't ready for him and he was only ten yards from me and only fifteen yards from George. We could see the tips of his tines through these thick fir trees, but it was too late. There just isn't anything else like elk hunting."

Chasing after Montana's alpine bulls was the core of Byron's bowhunting. He wanted nothing more than to down a Royal bull with his custom-made longbow. It was a vision that inspired his bowhunting dreams.

But a year later his high country dreams and hopes of a royal bull took a heavy blow. The rigorous exercise that had made Byron a man who could chase elk through the mountains eventually sentenced this avid bowhunter and bowmaker to a world seldom traveled by elk — the flat lands.

"I jogged for twelve years and the position of my bones is such that I'm bow-legged. I didn't realize it but when I jogged I was wearing the outside of my knees out and it wore the cartilage off." Byron underwent knee surgery to remove the worn cartilage, but the damage was extensive. "Now I just have bone against bone, and the doctor said not to go out in the woods anymore. I told him that I may as well crawl into a hole. Then he said just to be as easy on my knees as I could and avoid rough country. So I may be doing a lot of whitetail hunting from tree stands in the future. But I would first love to get a big royal bull elk — then sitting in a tree wouldn't matter so much."

NORTH OF THE BITTERROOT

Today in his late forties, Byron lives with his wife, Diane, and their two sons in the eastern hills overlooking Missoula, Montana, where he teaches the sixth grade. This soft-spoken longbow builder was born in San Francisco and grew up in San Jose, California, where he worked in a machine shop. But his love for the outdoors lured him eastward to the mountain states, and in 1969 he moved to Montana's big sky country and became a teacher.

He used to enjoy gun hunting and fishing in western Montana, but after discovering the thrill of the longbow it became his full-time hobby and part-time business. "Since taking up the longbow I don't feel the need to kill an animal any more, and that has made me a much better bowhunter."

Byron is a member of the Professional Bowhunters Society, the Montana Bowhunters Association, the Traditional Bowhunters of Montana, and the local Five Valley Archery Club. "The lobbying that the MBA does is really important to us. We have a tremendous bow season here, probably the best season anywhere in the country. We start bowhunting September 5 and we can hunt through January 17. Then we can start April 15 for bear and hunt until June 1."

Autumn turns the mountains near Missoula into a contrasting patchwork of golden aspens and emerald conifers. It's a time when buckskins start loosing their velvet and elk ring out echoing challenges. It's a time for bowhunters. But for Byron, it's also a time to teach. "My trouble with bowhunting is that being a teacher I only get to hunt weekends. I can't take seven to ten days off to go hunting. If I could, I would have a better chance of getting my royal elk. But school starts September 2 and bow season starts September 5. When I reach fifty-five, I can retire from twenty-five years of teaching. That's in eight years and if my bow business is going pretty well, I may retire then. Hopefully I will still have these knees holding me together enough so that I can get out hunting."

ELK EXCITEMENT

There's little doubt that Byron will still be charged with his zest for elk hunting when he reaches those retirement years. "There is nothing like elk hunting and bugling one in and having the hair stand up on the back of your neck. One year, my boys and I bugled in ten bulls within fifty yards and some within twenty. We never got a shot, but it was a fantastic hunting season just because we were so close to so many animals."

Byron became hooked on elk hunting ten years ago when, for the first time, his bugles produced a mix of charging tines and shrieking elk talk. "My brother and I bugled in fifteen bulls that day. We were just novices and didn't really know what we were doing. Several times we had bulls within forty yards of us but couldn't get them in any closer. But to just see them rip trees apart and come charging in gave us a feeling that only elk hunters know. That sold me on elk hunting. We didn't even get any shots, but that was the start of my elk hunting education which I keep building on every year."

Byron has harvested a couple of elk, and each year his dream of downing that first ivory-crowned bull seems to come closer to fulfillment. "Last year we bugled in a six by seven bull that was all by himself. I was bugling and my son and a friend were off to the side of me. That bull came out broadside forty-five yards from them but they couldn't shoot because of the glaring sun. He stopped twenty yards from me but I didn't shoot because he was facing me and that's just not a good shot. You're taking too much of a chance crippling that animal with a head-on shot. Maybe if he had been five yards from me I would have taken a shot, but that's pretty point blank. But at twenty yards you don't have a very big hole to shoot through. The wind finally shifted and he took off."

When bowhunting bulls, Byron usually works with his sons or a friend, bugling until they locate a responsive bull. After closing the gap, they split up, the caller hanging back twenty to forty yards while the shooter conceals himself near a likely spot. When the bull comes in, his attention is usually directed toward the caller, sometimes offering a chance for the waiting shooter.

To imitate his realistic elk dialog, Byron uses several techniques. "For cow mews I use one of the Cow Talk brand plastic calls with a rubber band in it. Before that, I always used a diaphragm call. I can also bugle through a grunt tube with just my voice. But that's not quite as good as a diaphragm because with a diaphragm I can switch to a cow call or a bugle without taking the call out of my mouth."

Using his orchestra of calls, Byron mixes up his elk talk. "When calling elk, I recommend bugling twenty percent of the time and cow calling eighty percent of the time. This is because the bulls are more interested in the cows, and if they think you are a cow, they're more apt to come in."

BEYOND THE BULLS

Besides harvesting elk, Byron and his longbow have taken bear, mule deer, bighorn ewe, and one of his newer bowhunting challenges — whitetail. "I have a hard time sitting in a tree stand, although I have done it. I'm starting to get into rattling in whitetails and I imagine they are going to take over some of my bowhunting."

Seemingly undaunted by his bad knees, Byron's bowhunting dreams also reach for the lofty peaks of Montana's rugged ranges. Two animals he would like to try for are a bighorn ram and a mountain goat. "I just love sheep and goats, and part of the thrill of hunting them is the high country where they live."

Another of Byron's back country challenges is bowhunting black bears. Montana's rules for fair chase prohibits the use of baits or hounds when hunting bears, putting the archer in a one-on-one stalking situation with his prospective prey. With a bear, that makes for a tough and often exciting game.

During the spring bear season, Byron saves his limited mileage knees by using a mountain bicycle to travel old logging roads while scanning the mountain sides for feeding bears. Riding roads that are closed to vehicle traffic, he can cover a lot of distance and often stops to glass clear-cut areas where bears forage on plush grasses.

Once he locates a bear, he usually prefers sneaking uphill where the cooling evening thermals and an occasional gurgling creek help hide his approach. "I saw this big bear in one area, and I got within 150 yards of it. The bear didn't see me, so I went back the next evening hoping to find it. I was moving slowly through this clear-cut area with some big standing timber when here came this bear. I watched him for twenty minutes while he worked below me, but for some reason he didn't pick up my scent. I was using some cover scent which I think helped. After he worked around me, he dropped down into the creek and by then it was getting pretty dark.

"Down along the creek was real dense undergrowth, and I couldn't sneak in on him there. I figured maybe I should just try for him the next day when all of a sudden he just walked out from the creek bed fifteen yards away and slightly downhill from me. As I drew back he heard the arrow going across the rest and he turned toward me. I was just partly drawn and I froze. When he turned away, I drew back the rest of the way, released, and made a good shot on him. Most people in Montana hunt a long time before they get a bear that way."

Although you can't hunt with hounds in Montana, a few hunters have discovered that sometimes just sounding like them is good enough to tree a bear. This offbeat bear hunting method requires good legs, a realistic hound's howl, and plenty of nerve. "The fellow who told me about running bears up trees, said that if you scare them first, the chances of them going up a tree are a lot greater than if they scent you first. Then they take off running and you don't have a chance.

"Barking like dogs, we ran at this bear and he went right up a tree. We did the same thing the year before on one about the same size. I tried it on a big bear but he caught my scent. Then I got to thinking about what might happen if I ran at him barking and he stood up, looked at me, and decided that he wasn't going to run or climb. Maybe then I could get a close-up shot while he was chewing on my leg!"

Bears and bulls may stir the memories of his most exciting hunts, but Byron's most memorable shot was on lesser game. He was hunting along a mountain side with a friend when they spotted a grouse partially hidden in a tree thirty yards away. "If I missed, my arrow would be gone off the side of a ridge. My friend, John, had a compound and I said, 'Why don't you shoot it, John?' But he said, 'No, I'm not going to waste an arrow.' So I shot and the arrow went right there. It hit the grouse and the bird fell down at the base of the tree. John couldn't believe it."

LONGBOW SHOOTING SECRETS

Byron became interested in archery when he was eighteen and in college. He took an archery class and learned to shoot using a Bear recurve. "I went from a recurve to a compound, and then to a longbow five years ago. Even though I shot with a compound and sights for six years, I never hit anything out in the woods because I wasn't good at estimating distances."

However, since switching to the simplistic longbow, Byron's effectiveness in the field has proven the value of instinctive shooting and the longbow's versatility. Now, even running game consistently fall to his arrows. But he knows the limits of his skills and equipment, and restricts himself to high confidence shots. "It depends on the person and the situation and how you feel at the time. I shot a running doe and hit her in the heart and she only went forty yards. But I've also passed up other shots on running deer. One time I passed up a broadside shot on a seven foot bear at forty yards. I just didn't feel comfortable about that forty yard shot. I've done that on other animals too. There are times I've shot forty yards, but I felt comfortable with the shot and I never hesitated. If you hesitate at all, then you're not comfortable with the shot and you shouldn't take it."

Byron's confidence is built on hunting with a longbow that's heavy enough to tackle big game, and on his ability to shoot accurately. But mastering a longbow doesn't come easy. It requires building up shooting muscles and proper practice. "You should shoot a longbow that you can handle comfortably. The mistake most people make is to shoot a longbow that's too heavy. Then it's not fun and they don't learn to shoot properly. If you're struggling with something, you can't enjoy it. I had one customer who bought three bows from me and his first was seventy-five pounds. I told him I thought it was too much for him, but he wanted to try it. Now he's shooting a sixty pound longbow and just loving it."

To help strengthen his shooting muscles, Byron exercises with a three-spring chest puller. "It helps tremendously. Last year at a Utah shoot, I met the fellow who holds the world record for shooting a 176 pound bow. He doesn't look that big, and he said that a chest puller is all he uses to exercise. He went into a body building shop with his 125 pound bow and asked some weight lifters if they could pull his bow but they couldn't. He determined that they weren't lifting for bow pulling muscles and that the spring chest puller is the only thing that exercises those muscles. I was having trouble shooting my sixty-nine pound bow at that time, and after two weeks of using a chest puller, I had improved my shooting by thirty percent. I just worked myself into the bow. Inside of six weeks I could shoot an eighty-five pound bow. I couldn't have done that two months earlier."

With his bow muscles toned, Byron keeps his shooting form sharp by practicing often at home, attending 3-D shoots, and stump shooting. And sometimes he even shoots in the dark. "If I'm having trouble with my shooting I go out at night and shoot just for form. I get ten yards from the target so I can only see the outline of the bale. I draw back, anchor solidly, and make sure my bow arm is steady. Sometimes in the dark I shoot really tight groups. It's a good technique for working on your form."

His style is not the traditional push-and-pull method but is more like Asbell's point-and-pull technique. Byron, however, anchors and aims. "You can establish your own style, but you still have to use the basics behind good shooting.

"For someone just starting to shoot instinctively, the hardest part is not having any idea where the arrow is going to hit." So Byron suggests using a point-of-aim technique with the tip of your arrow until your subconscious instinctively learns the arrow's flight path and trajectory.

PART OF THE HUNTER

Whether he's practicing in front of the bales at night or drawing on an elk in the morning shadows of high country, Byron prefers shooting one of his Monarch longbows. His favorite is his 60" longbow pulling 73 pounds. It's shorter than most longbows, but Byron likes its maneuverability in the brush-filled world of actual hunting conditions. To give his short stick added zip, he recently started using a Fast Flight string to see if it improves the bow's shooting qualities without damaging it. Byron notes that the new Fast Flight strings are however, a bit noisier, and require string silencers.

When hunting with his Monarch, Byron carries his arrows in a Catquiver II. It keeps his feathers dry and holds up to eight arrows. He fletches his cedar arrows with three 5" die cut feathers and waterproofs them with Scotchguard. "I like to use brightly colored feathers like fluorescent pink and yellow because I can see my arrow going through shade and in the evening. Once I shot a mule deer standing in the shade, and I had brown and green fletching on my arrow. It struck in the ground like it hadn't hit the deer. I didn't see it hit, but I dis-covered rich-colored blood on the shaft. From then on I've been using brightly colored fletching. Also, the Catquiver hides my fletch-ing so the animals can't see those bright colors."

Byron mounts three-bladed Snuffers on his brightly fletched shafts, and sharpens them with a file and a Gerber ridged ceramic stone. "I shot my last three animals using Snuffers, and the last elk was dead in less than five seconds. It ran thirty yards as hard as it could and then just fell over. I shot my bear this spring through the lungs and part of the heart, and it was dead in six seconds. Snuffers don't get as much penetration as some broadheads, but I've had such success with them I just can't see using an-other head. I used a Hunter's Edge which is

MUSCLING HIS MONARCH — A big advantage of Byron's 60" longbow is its maneuverability in heavy brush.

similar to a Howard Hill head, and I shot a buck through the lungs with it. But he went 120 yards before I found him, and he didn't bleed for eighty yards. So I'm an advocate of a multiple blade head. There's a lot of cutting surface on a Snuffer. I'm sold on them."

To help get within Snuffer-biting distance of his prey, Byron uses camouflage. He's not too particular about his clothing, but he pays special attention to his face. "I think camouflaging your face is critical. I used to camo my face with cream, but I got tired of trying to wipe it off all of the time so now I use a face net as much as possible."

SLEEK MONARCHS

Between his elk hunts and bear adventures, Byron finds time after school in the evenings and during the summer to build custom longbows. He retires to his basement workshop where he crafts his line of sleek Monarchs that reflect his love for bugling bulls. "My bows are named after elk. The Raghorn is named for a small bull, five-point or less, and is my standard longbow. The Royal is named for a six or seven-point and is my top line bow. My younger son and I were returning from a longbow shoot and discussing different names when he mentioned 'Monarch', which is a bull with seven points on each side and is considered a royal head. The name fit right in and sounded good for a company name."

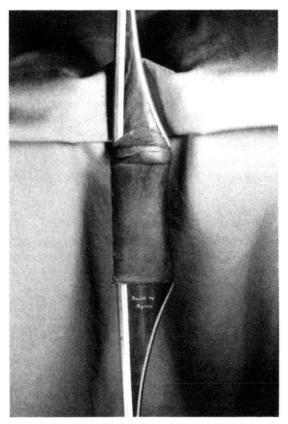

Although the company name represents one of North America's largest deer, Byron's bows are some of the smallest longbows on the market. One of the lightest and most maneuverable is his short, 60" longbow. His Monarchs are also available in lenghts up to 68" in two-inch increments. They have an approximate mass weight of 1 pound, 4 ounces, and a recommended brace height of 6¼" to 6½" from the string to the throat.

COMPLETE WITH MONARCH HIDE — Byron's longbows exhibit a crested arrow shelf and rounded window for enhanced arrow flight. (Photo by Byron Schurg)

The solid hardwood riser measures 15" between the fadeouts, is 1¾" thick, and is 1¼" wide near the fadeouts and narrows to 13/16" through the sight window. The slightly-rounded sight window is cut 3/8" from center shot. Standard riser woods are ash or myrtlewood on the Raghorn and exotics on the Royal. The slightly dished grip narrows around the throat and rounds nicely to the back. It's wrapped for 3¾" with deer or elk skin and laced down the front. Matching grip leather covers the entire shelf and is used for a strike pad. Bow information is inked on the sides of the riser.

The limbs exhibit deflex from the handle and sweep into a gentle reflex. On the 60" model, the working length of the upper limb is 23½" and the lower limb's is 1½" shorter. Both limbs narrow from 1¼" wide at the fadeout to ½" at the string nock. They have relatively flat edges that feather slightly into the fiberglass facing and backing. The limbs are constructed from three tapered back laminations and one tapered belly lamination enveloped in fiberglass. Byron offers his Raghorn model with maple cored limbs covered with brown fiberglass or his coppery toned Royal model with yew or yew-maple core under clear fiberglass.

Distinctive elk antler tip overlays exhibit the natural rough antler texture in the center of the overlay and feather into smooth ivory white around the edges. String nocks are flush cut on the side and shallow on the back. The bow is finished in a low luster polyurethane suited for hunting situations.

To check both a 60" Royal and a 64" Raghorn for relative speed, Byron shot 27½" cedar arrows that weighed 520 grains. The arrows were fletched with three 5" die cut feathers and equipped with Mercury speed nocks. Byron used a shooting glove, drew a consistent 26½", and had a clean release.

His 60" yew-and-maple-cored Royal pulling 65 pounds at 26½" was equipped with a Fast Flight string without accessories. This bow, shooter, and arrow combination produced an average arrow speed of 182 fps.

The following draw/force measurements suggest the smoothness of this 60" Royal:

DRAW LENGTH	25"	26"	27"	28"	29"
DRAW WEIGHT	55#	59½#	63#	67#	71½#

Byron also chronographed his 64" maple-cored Raghorn that pulled 60 pounds at 26½". Byron shot the same arrows, and the bowstring was standard Dacron without accessories. The average arrow speed for this bow, arrow, and shooter combination was 174 fps.

The following draw/force measurements suggest the smoothness of this 64" Raghorn:

DRAW LENGTH	25"	26"	27"	28"	29"
DRAW WEIGHT	55#	58½#	62#	66#	70#

HE COULDN'T WAIT

Necessity may be the mother of invention, but for Byron it was impatience brought on by longbow fever. He ordered his first longbow from Dick Robertson in 1982, and as is often the case when ordering from busy custom bowyers, Byron had a lengthy wait. But he couldn't. Deeply bitten by the longbow bug, he decided to build his own. "I also wanted a different style longbow and I also thought my boys would be interested in them. Since there was no way I could afford to buy them custom longbows, I went ahead and built my own."

Before attempting to build his first bow, Byron visited with long-time bowyer and Missoula resident, Dale Jasperson. Dale shared his forty years of bowmaking savvy with Byron and gave him plenty of pointers to get him started. "Dale developed the deflex-reflex design that you see in my bows. But my degree of limb curve is a little different than his because I didn't want to make the exact same bow. My limb curve is more gentle, but I don't think I lost any speed or smoothness of draw with it."

After experimenting with different handle designs and limb curvatures, Byron built his form and glued up his first bow. His first lesson in becoming an experienced bowyer was not long in coming. Maybe there was some truth to the old adage 'too many cooks spoil the broth' — or the glue. "My Dad, who was visiting, mixed the epoxy for me and he didn't mix it right. It took me over thirty hours to build that first longbow and it literally fell apart when I started to string it. The second longbow I made was rather club-like but it gave me a lot of satisfaction. I even killed two deer with it that first year."

With both his first bowmaking disappointment and bowmaking success behind him, and encouraged with a field-proven design, Byron went on to build and refine his longbows. By April of 1986 he was professionally making and selling them.

Although he started building his longbows in conventional lengths, he soon discovered the advantages of a shorter longbow. "I made the short longbow as an answer to shooting out of a tree stand. I had maneuvering problems shooting from a tree stand with my sixty-six inch longbow. So I made a sixty inch bow and took it to a shoot to show someone. But when I got there, I dropped the tailgate of my station wagon on my regular bow and knocked the tip off it. So I had to shoot the sixty inch longbow, and I shot pretty well with it. I kept shooting it and I haven't gone back to anything longer. It's easier out in the woods because I don't get hung up in brush like I would with a longer bow. It also seems as smooth as longer bows."

Even though he offers one of the shortest longbows in the country, breaking into the established longbow market proved difficult for Byron. "Last April I even told ten prospective customers I would give them a free trial period — if they didn't like my bow after ten days they could call me collect and ask for a refund. I told them I didn't care what their reasons were, if they didn't like it they could return it and I would refund their money. Only one person took me up on my offer, and that was rather frustrating. Then I got a three-page letter from that customer saying how great the bow was and that pepped me up. It just takes time. Now I'm starting to get a lot of sales by word-of-mouth."

THE BIRTH OF A MONARCH

Byron begins making his maneuverable Monarchs by crafting the riser. His standard one-piece risers are made from ash or myrtlewood, and he also offers them in exotics such as cocobolo, and his favorite, gongola alves. The orange-hued cocobolo is attractive, but Byron notes it's a tricky wood to build bows with because of its high natural wood-oil content. When working with cocobolo, he heats it in his curing oven to drive the oil out. He buys his riser hardwoods from Southern Lumber Company in San Jose, California.

When building a riser, Byron cuts and squares the hardwood so the grain will be parallel with the string and bow for maximum strength. After outlining the riser shape using a template, he band saws and grinds the back side to fit his form. During grinding, he occasionally lays the riser on the form and shines a light from behind it to reveal any areas that need more sanding to produce a flush fit.

Once the back fits the form precisely, Byron marks and band saws the belly shape and sands it on the end of his horizontal belt sander. He freehand grinds and feathers the belly fadeouts, checking them to be sure they are square to the sides.

LIMB COMPOSITES

Byron offers limb cores built from any combination of custom-ground maple, yew, and "featherwood" laminations. "Most of my bow limbs are made from yew. It's a very smooth drawing wood and has good cast. I use four laminations and put the edge grain in the middle and the flat grain on the outside. A flat grain under clear glass is more beautiful, and the edge grain in the middle provides strength.

"Dale Dye of Trails End Recurves introduced me to a new wood that when dyed a walnut color looks beautiful under clear fiberglass. It has excellent shooting qualities and I call it featherwood."

Byron tapers his laminations to .015" per inch, and varies their butt end thickness to help him achieve specific bow weights. Using a wood moisture meter, he checks each lamination before glue-up to be sure that it has dried to a moisture content of six percent or less. When selecting laminations for a bow, he flex tests each one to check for uniformity of bend and for straightness. He then positions the laminations to best complement the characteristics of the adjacent corewoods.

Byron uses the same form to make all of his different length bows. It's the end product of developing a half dozen experimental forms. His form is made from laminated plywood with a one-eighth inch thick strip of steel formed and welded to steel bracing to fit the form surface.

Before laying up his composites in the form, Byron masking tapes the non-gluing surfaces of his fiberglass and cleans all composite surfaces with acetone to remove any residue. He also checks his form to make sure it's clean and free from dried glue, then covers it with plastic wrap.

He mixes two-part Smooth-On epoxy and applies it to all composite contact surfaces. Byron then lays up the glued laminates, puts another layer of plastic wrap over them, and secures the riser and limb tips with large rubber bands. Next, he lays on a fire hose and attaches the top half of the form. After making sure the reference marks on his composites and hose are lined up properly with the form, he inflates the fire hose to sixty pounds. He double checks the alignment of the laminations once more before putting it in his glue curing oven. He cures the glue at 130 degrees for five hours, then lets the form cool until the next day. To control the curing temperature, he places a thermometer on the form and adjusts the door opening.

SHAPING UP

After removing the glued bow from the form, he grinds off the rough edges and draws the limb shape using a straight-edge and a limb template. He then uses his table saw sander and horizontal sander to grind the limbs into shape. This saves ruining costly band saw blades.

Next, he rough sands the tip overlay areas on the backing fiberglass and cleans the limb tip and the elk antler overlay with acetone. He epoxies the tip overlays in place, secures them with inner tube rubber bands, and places small light bulb heated curing units over the tips for five hours.

Once the cured overlays have cooled overnight, Byron rough shapes the tips and files in the string nocks. He then braces the bow to check for tiller and alignment. Checking for tiller and alignment aren't unusual, but the way Byron braces a bow is. "A lot of people can't string a longbow with the conventional push-pull method. But with my technique I can string a bow pulling over one hundred pounds. I lean back against a wall and place the lower tip on the floor next to the wall. You should use some sort of lower tip protector or a soft surface. Then I put my knee above the handle on the belly, pull the upper limb toward me while holding the string in one hand, and simply slip the string over the tip. Then I always check the lower tip to be sure the string is properly seated. By stringing my roughed bows this way, I don't destroy my strings on the sharp edges of the fiberglass."

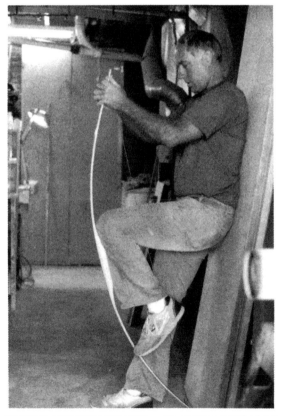

UNUSUAL BUT EASY BRACING — To string a roughed out bow, Byron uses his knee and the floor to bend the bow enough to slip the string over the tip.

Byron brings the limbs into alignment and tiller by grinding a little off the limb sides with his horizontal belt sander. Although his bows rarely need fine tuning, he sometimes makes minor alignment adjustments by filing one side of the string nock until the string tracks down the center of the bow. To check for alignment, he lays the bow sideways on his flat work table and sights down it. Once he gets the limbs aligned and tillered, he shapes them to their final dimensions and sands them smooth with an air sleeved spindle sander, making sure to feather the fiberglass edges.

Although Byron tillers his bows to a one-eighth inch positive tiller, much of it is already built into the bow. He achieves this by making the top limb 1½" longer than the lower limb and by slightly offsetting the butt ends of his laminations below the center of the bow.

Next he band saws out the sight window and shapes it with his table saw disk sander. Then he files the riser to its finished shape, making sure to crest the arrow shelf and round the sight window for enhanced arrow flight. When shaping the grip, Byron slightly dishes the belly and narrows the sides around the throat area to provide a firm hand seat in close alignment with the arrow. "I developed the depression on the sides of the grip because I feel it gives a more positive grip and you won't get as much hand torque."

FINISH WORK

Using a file with a smooth edge, Byron files open the nock throats on the belly to allow the string to cleanly seat and to prevent string damage. He uses a small rat-tail file to fashion the back of the nock and then finishes the nocks using an abrasive cord material. By working this cord back and forth in the nock, it removes any grooves or uneven spots caused by the files. To test the smoothness of his finished string nocks, Byron wraps a piece of

THE STRING TEST — Byron checks the smoothness of his nocks using a soft cotton string drawn back and forth over the nocks.

cotton string around the nock and pulls it back and forth for sixty strokes, maintaining the same angle as the bowstring. If the string shows any sign of fraying, he smooths the nocks more with the abrasive cord.

He uses files and sandpaper to fashion his tips. Byron generally makes the upper tip about 1" above the nock and the lower tip ⅝". This provides a little more tip on the upper limb for safety during stringing and makes the blunter lower tip less susceptible to wear and damage.

After he's finished shaping a bow, Byron shoots it to check for smoothness and hand shock. If it shoots fine, which most do, he hand sands the bow, starting with 80 grit sandpaper. He is so precise in the sanding that he actually counts his sanding strokes to be sure he removes the same amount of material from each limb. Then he uses 180 grit paper and repeats the process. Before sanding with the fine 320 grit paper, he carefully inspects the bow under a large shop magnifying lens, looking for any file or sanding marks that may have been missed. After it's sanded with the 320 grit sandpaper, he rubs the bow smooth with fine steel wool.

On his Raghorn model, he stains the exposed edges of the maple corewoods with an oak or cherry stain to match the riser wood. With an air brush, he then sprays on four coats of satin polyurethane, steel wooling between the dried coats. He inks on the bow information after the first coat. "I put a satin finish on my bows because they are built for hunting and it lets their beauty show through. So they don't need to be camouflaged."

Finally, he glues on his deer or elk leather shelf, strike pad, and grip, then laces down the front of the grip with artificial sinew. When sending the new Monarch to a customer, Byron supplies a bow case and two self-made Flemish-twist Dacron strings.

"THREE-FOUR-FIVE..." — During finish sanding, Byron counts his sanding strokes to help maintain balanced limb dynamics.

COMING AROUND

Byron notes that his Monarch customers are a blend of seasoned traditionalists and past compound shooters discovering a simpler and more challenging form of archery. Whichever camp they come from, he welcomes them to his world of the longbow. "I know that a lot of people who make primitive bows don't like compounds or compound shooters. But as far as I'm concerned, it's still archery. I may not like a lot of the gadgets they have, but the compound bow has done an awful lot for archery. If you look at many of the people in primitive archery now, you'll discover they came through the compound ranks. And I think traditional archery will benefit from those people."

Byron knows. He was one of the converts who was bitten by the alluring longbow bug, and because he couldn't wait, he joined the ranks of Traditional Bowyers of America. "Longbows are just so much more fun. Everyone I have talked to who has come from a compound says the same thing; 'The longbow brought the fun back to archery.' "

Chapter Twenty-Two

KRAMER ARCHERY

ON THE WING

The draped tarpaulin gently billows and ebbs like an incoming tide. In front of it, a lean bowman nocks another rubber-tipped arrow and locks his gaze on the clay pigeon clutched by an older man near the backstop. The archer seems oblivious to the chattering onlookers, the flapping tarpaulin, and even his poised partner. Detached from his surroundings, he sees only the center of the four-inch disk.

As the partner lowers the target for the throw, the bowman's eyes narrow and his waiting longbow springs to life. The clay bird soars across the blue backdrop in a lazy arc, its maiden flight shattered by a blur of feathers, its broken remains showering to earth.

The crowd howls and claps in admiration, but they are not part of the bowman's world. He remains detached, distant. His body is gripped by the trance-like rhythm of nocking, drawing, and shooting; his conscious thoughts quietly hover like a curious spectator.

His next arrow smacks a silver dollar-sized disk into pieces. As the targets become smaller, the archer intensifies his hawkish pose, neck twisted, eyes seizing each airborne prey. A quarter-sized target flattens against the backstop with the resounding slap of an arrow. Pausing for effect, the thrower slowly reveals the final target — a white marble. A heavyset man near the front scoffs, "No way!" The bowman doesn't hear him. He is alone with the marble. The audience sees the tiny white sphere tossed into the air, but the bowman perceives only a motionless target in perfect harmony with his fluid body, the blue backstop slowly floating past them. A "twang-swish" is followed with a sharp "click" as the marble ricochets over the backstop.

The sound seems to snap the archer from his trance. He briefly acknowledges the spectators with a humble grin before trading places with his seasoned partner who proceeds to astonish the crowd by plucking a new

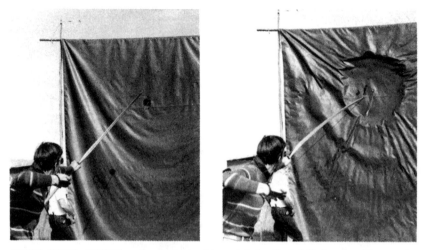

GOING, GOING, GONE! Lee demonstrates his aerial shooting skills by smashing soaring clay pigeons. It's a trick he says most longbowers can learn.

assortment of targets from the air. The new shooter has silvery hair and deeply etched features, yet he handles the stout longbow with the grace of the younger man. The thrower and shooter exchange places several times until all their targets have been tossed, smashed, popped, and rattled into the tarpaulin, clattering to the pile of aerial debris.

When the final clapping trails off, the bowmen conclude their show by encouraging the audience to discover the thrills and simple fun of shooting a longbow. For many, the pull of the string and the arcing limbs means a form of recreation, but for the two bowmen, it truly represents their way of life. Ted and Lee Kramer, father and son, not only dazzle crowds with their archery exhibitions — their lives are immersed in shooting, promoting, and building longbows.

AMONG THE INDIANS

The Kramers live in the remote town of St. Ignatius, Montana. It's within the Flathead Indian reservation in northwestern Montana between Flathead Lake and Missoula. The town's scenic neighbors are the National Bison Range to the west and the serrated Mission Range to the east. Wave-carved escarpments on the hillsides around the Flathead Valley show evidence of water levels during ice-age times when a glacier-dammed lake filled the valley.

Today the valley supports an Indian and tourist-based community. It's a difficult place for most outsiders to make a living, but for Ted and Lee it's the perfect place to live their peaceful life-style and build longbows. "Montana," says Ted, "is one of the least populated states in the country. We don't have to crowd behind cars on turnpikes losing half of our lives sitting behind the wheel of an automobile. Out here you can sit back, relax, and think about

The Old Ponderosa cabin now serves as Ted and Lee's bowmaking shop, adding a bit of
Indian heritage to their longbows.

those things that are important in life instead of worrying about all the
details of living."

Just outside their homes sets the Kramers' bowmaking shop. They call
it the Old Ponderosa Ranch House. It's a hand-hewn 100 year-old log cabin
they purchased from an Indian family on the reservation. Ted numbered
each log, dismantled the cabin, moved it home, and reconstructed it stick by
stick like an oversized Lincoln Log set. Its sun-bleached pine logs, etched by
winds and pocked with old bullet holes around the windows and door, speak
of the cabin's long and somewhat colorful heritage. Although its walls once
witnessed the births and deaths of native inhabitants, today it's the quiet
birthplace of Kramer's Autumn Longbows.

SIMPLE AND SWEET

Within the cabin's low but cozy walls, Ted and Lee make a standard
longbow, its take-down counterpart, a pistol grip model, and a reverse handle longbow. Their recently introduced two-piece take-down is quickly gaining popularity among Kramer customers, but their standard longbow
remains their number one product.

The standard AUTUMN LONGBOW is available in 66", 68", and 70"
lengths. It has a mass weight of 1 pound, 5 ounces, and a recommended
brace height of about 6⅜" from the string to the throat.

Its riser measures 15" between fadeouts, is 1⅛" wide, and narrows to
¾" through the sight window. The window is cut ³⁄₁₆" from center shot and
is equipped with a leather strike plate which also covers the shelf. The handle
is 2⅛" thick and has a prominently peaked grip wrapped with a piece of 4"

leather. The riser is made from a single piece of bubinga or osage and exhibits simple longbow lines.

The moderately backset limbs have a deep core tapering to the belly. On the 70" bow, the upper limb has a working length of 28⅛" from the fadeout to the nock and the lower limb has a working length of 27⅜". The limbs narrow from 1³⁄₁₆" wide at the fadeouts to ½" at the string nocks.

The limbs are constructed from two back and one belly lamination enveloped in fiberglass. These tapered laminations are offered in bamboo, osage, and yew. Although clear fiberglass is the bowyer's choice as it displays the natural beauty of the core materials, they also offer black, brown, or white. The limb tips are reinforced with a 4" fiberglass tip wedge in front of the belly corewood. The tips have flush-cut string nocks and the bow is coated in a gloss finish.

The following draw/force measurements recorded on a 68" bamboo-cored Autumn Longbow suggest its smoothness of draw:

DRAW LENGTH	25"	26"	27"	28"	29"
DRAW WEIGHT	58½#	62#	65#	68½#	72½#

To check for relative speed, this bow was shot by Ted Kramer using 28¼", 520 grain wooden arrows. They were fletched with three 5¼" high-profile feathers and had Mercury speed nocks. Ted drew the arrows 28", used a glove, and had a clean pull-through release. The string was standard Dacron without accessories. The average arrow speed for this arrow, bow, and shooter combination was 184 fps.

Kramer's classical styled Autumn longbow is available in a quiver-toting two-piece take-down. Lee's artistic lettering adds flair to each custom bow.

The Kramers also offer their Autumn Longbow with a take-down handle section. The two halves of its sleeve-fit handle go together like a finger in a glove and are held in place with a small set screw. The bow offers compact convenience for travel or storage, and its steel-sleeved handle adds stabilizing mass to the riser. This take-down has a mass weight of 1 pound, 9 ounces, and other than the handle, it's almost identical to the one-piece model.

BONDED BY THE BOW

Although the moderate climate and small-town pace make St. Ignatius appealing to the Kramers, hunting is strictly prohibited on reservation lands, and the bowmen must drive at least twenty miles before they can test their longbow skills on fur-bearing targets. One of their favored bowhunting retreats is the Little Belt Mountains where the mix of beautiful scenery and a sprinkling of mule deer, elk, bear, and even whitetail make for memorable longbow adventures. Ted's wife, Cindy, and Lee's wife, Patty, also participate in the longbow outings and help in the bowmaking business. They share a strong family bond strengthened by deep spiritual ties linked by their common affection for the longbow.

Ted is the head of the Kramer clan and responsible for spreading the longbow magic among the family. With more salt than pepper in his moustache and hair, he has weather-checked wrinkles that hint of his years spent in the outdoors. Now in his early sixties, he retired in 1976 from a varied career with the Fish and Wildlife Service.

Ted began working for the Fish and Wildlife Service in his home state of Oklahoma as a professional trapper involved in predator control. He later worked for the Forest Service in Oregon as biologist for the Bull Run Watershed area studying the interrelationships of wildlife, logging, and recreation. Once an avid skier, Ted also worked for six years in mountain rescue and in public skiing safety. He then transferred back into the Fish and Wildlife Service in predator control for southwestern Oregon, curbing troublesome coyotes, cougars, and bears. Later, he transferred to Montana's Bison Range and then retired to build longbows.

Ted became interested in archery long before commercial bows were available. At seventeen he fashioned his first bow from a lemonwood stave in hopes of achieving a Boy Scout merit badge. But to earn the badge he had to shoot a qualifying archery round with his new bow. Even though no other scout in his entire council had passed the stringent archery requirements, Ted and his twin brother, Ace, were determined to earn their archery merits. During his first day on the range, Ted not only learned to shoot his new bow — by noon he had shot a qualifying round and earned his badge.

Armed with his natural instinctive ability and his new bow, Ted took to the field and was soon captured by the lure of bowhunting, a romance he still courts today. Although Ted was exposed to firearms during his years with the Fish and Wildlife Service, the longbow remained his chosen hunting weapon. "Guns never impressed me much. Even a five-year-old could go out and aim the sights in on a 30-06 and shoot a deer with it. When you do that you're just collecting meat. My main interest in hunting is to take my family out and have a good time in the outdoors. That's the part we enjoy, and if I collect an animal that will fill my freezer and help us through the winter then that's just icing on the cake. But by going out there I already have my cake."

Over the years Ted has had plenty of icing. He has taken bear, elk, whitetail, blacktail, and mule deer with his longbows. He lost count of his deer harvests somewhere around forty. And small game, especially rabbits, have always stirred his bowhunting instincts. "Back in Oklahoma and Oregon rabbits provided plenty of shooting action. Small game hunting produces the greatest fun of actually shooting the bow and arrow, and it's a real challenge."

Although rabbits have challenged his shooting skills, one particular animal who chose not to flee forced Ted to the ultimate longbow challenge. "With all of the wildlife work I have done, I have never gotten into trouble with an animal. But I have to admit, I got into trouble with this one."

LONGBOW BACKUP

Ted was bowhunting with Cindy on a Montana mountain side, slipping through shadows in big timber. Armed with their longbows, they spotted a large bear feeding on elk remains. After a few tense whispers they began sneaking uphill toward the bear. "I told Cindy she might have to climb a tree, but she was my only backup if something happened."

Ted hadn't crept far from Cindy when the bear lifted its ominous head and spotted them. In a flash, it laid back its ears and plunged both archers into a bowhunter's worst nightmare. "Boy, I want to tell you, that bear was mean. He charged out of there straight for me. I shot three arrows faster than I have ever drawn and shot in my life. The first arrow went through the fur on his neck and hit a tree. He spun in mid-air at the sound, and as he came back around to resume his charge, the second arrow caught him right through the chest. He had already covered half of the forty-five yards separating us. The second arrow turned him and I shot my third arrow as he was running off. The adrenaline was flowing and we were excited, to say the least. Afterwards, I asked Cindy, 'What were you going to do, climb that tree or shoot that bear?' 'I wasn't going to climb the tree,' she replied, 'But I was worried about shooting at the bear for fear of hitting you.' "

Besides his hard-hitting seventy pound bamboo longbow and his shooting skill on moving targets, Ted credits his arrow quiver as instrumental in helping turn the charging bruin. "I don't think I would have gotten that bear if I had been using any quiver other than my back quiver because I can draw and shoot so fast with it. Without it, I might not even be here."

IN THE RHYTHM

"A back quiver helps you establish a shooting rhythm. A runner who breaks his stride is going to lose the race. When you shoot with rhythm, you are maintaining your stride in shooting. When I was shooting at that bear, all of those arrows came out of that quiver in a rhythm, and that's the only reason I was able to hit him when he charged. When using a back quiver it's very important to grab an arrow by the nock every time, catch the nock index, and roll the cock feather up. If you can't, you're going to lose precious loading time and become awkward in your shooting. You should be able to load with your eyes closed, without thinking. It should be an automatic reflex and part of your shooting rhythm."

Because of his polished quick-shooting technique, Ted seldom pauses to admire his first arrow. In the field he likes to maintain his natural rhythm, shooting and reloading, often catching fast-reflexed game off guard. "It was late in the evening on the last day of hunting season. I had been sitting in a tree stand, but this whitetail buck wasn't coming in so I got down and stalked him. I sneaked around a haystack, and then every time he put his head down I moved forward until I got within forty yards of him. Then his head came up and he spotted me. I knew he was alerted and I also knew that a whitetail can jump an arrow, but I didn't think he could out-jump my rhythmic shooting. I shot fast three times, and by the third shot he didn't know where to jump. I hit him in the hind quarter and it came out his chest. That's one benefit of rhythmic shooting and not quitting after the first shot."

Besides mastering his moving target and quick loading skills, Ted spent years honing his long-range shooting. Some of those lofted arrows fly forever in his mind's eye. "I hate to admit my best shot because most people shouldn't shoot that far. But that year I had practiced a lot of long-range shooting. One morning at the crack of dawn I spotted this elk running eighty-five yards away. I came back automatically and knew the arrow was going to hit when I released. I put that arrow through its shoulder and heart. But that's probably a shot that most archers shouldn't take."

Even though Ted has harvested game on the run and at considerable distances, he hunts with a keen knowledge of his abilities and limitations. "Whether someone uses a spear, a bow and arrow, or a high powered rifle, the important thing is for a hunter to know the accuracy of his weapon and to only shoot within that range of accuracy. If a hunter does that, he's hunting right, no matter what he uses. Whatever his choice of weapon, hunting should include good sportsmanship, personal integrity, and respect for the animals being taken."

Part of knowing your hunting limitations is recognizing the effectiveness of your equipment, right down to the killing end of your arrow. "To achieve maximum penetration with a longbow, you should never shoot a broadhead with more than two blades. They are putting broadheads on the market now that have multiple modular blades, and no longbow shooter should ever put something like that on his arrow."

A YOUTHFUL REFLECTION

The younger half of the Kramer bowmaking and shooting team is Lee. In his late twenties, he is tall and lean, and when he's shooting, he closely resembles his father's pose. He is quick to smile and has a warm easy-going manner.

Lee was raised shooting a longbow and for him it's the only hunting weapon he knows. His astonishing skill hitting marbles in the air, which he has done for the last ten years, is the product of fatherly advice and years of practice.

Although he's a crack shot, Lee limits bowhunting shots to his range of high confidence. For most archers that would be less than thirty yards, but for Lee it's farther. "I don't like to shoot at game much over fifty yards because then I'm getting into yardages where I'm not certain about a good hit. Generally most of my shots are under thirty yards."

Lee's skill on moving targets and his ability to confidently reach out to fifty yards, proved to be a great combination for one of his more memorable shots. "I had already shot this buck through the chest and I pursued him, but he was still running on adrenaline. I caught up to him in the middle of an opening, and I raised up and shot at thirty yards. He jumped up and took off. I shot again when he was fifty-five yards out, and the arrow hit him in the back of the head and he dropped right in his tracks."

TRICKS OF THE TRADE

Shooting charging bears, fleeing elk, or bucks on the run may seem like gifted shots, but knowing the tricks of trick shooting certainly improves the odds. The Kramers' shooting exhibition includes smashing an assortment of aerial targets. Soda cans, tennis balls, clay pigeons, frisbees, and coin-sized disks all fall victim to their hissing arrows. As if shooting these flying targets isn't impressive enough, they add spice to the game by shooting while lying on their backs and jumping on a trampoline. Lee even shoots behind his back and between his legs. The two also team up to execute their "wounded bowman shot" where Ted holds the bow and Lee draws the string and releases the arrow which magically finds the mark.

Even though their shooting feats seem to be beyond the limits of most shooters, the Kramers admit it only takes practice and knowing a few tricks for zeroing in on the sailing targets. Some of the important facets of trick shooting include rhythm, being in sync with the thrower, focusing your concentration, reducing the aiming point, and knowing when to begin and when to make the shot.

A typical shot at a disk is immediately made easier if the shooter has a small dot in the center to aim at. This helps the shooter's concentration and reduces the aiming point from the entire disk to the small dot. A thrower with a smooth consistent toss helps the shooter establish a rhythm and makes it easier to anticipate the arc of the target. As the disk is lowered in the hand before the toss, the shooter should begin his aiming and drawing. Once the disk is airborne, the shooter is already "locked in" to its flight and follows his aim upward until the target reaches the apex of its arc. As it hovers for a split second and then begins to drop, the shooter simply pops it in the center.

But being able to see only the small center of the disk requires complete yet relaxed concentration. "When we are shooting in front of large crowds," says Lee, "there is nobody there except me and the target. The crowd is totally ignored and when my target is up there I'm burning a hole in it. I may be tense in front of the audience before the show gets started, but when I draw that first arrow there are no distractions. I don't hear the clapping or the talking. Matter of fact, the audience might even think that we are a bit rude because we don't acknowledge their clapping, but we're concentrating on the next shot."

NOT TOO MUCH

During the summer, Lee and Ted practice their trick shooting once a week. That may not seem like much to pluck coins out of the air, but Ted believes that too much shooting is worse than not enough. "If you shoot too much, your muscles don't have time to rebuild, and you can actually tear them down. So you don't want to overdo it, especially with heavy longbows. Twice a week would be enough for a heavy bow. By limiting your practice you don't have all those stiff muscles and you actually shoot better. When you shoot too much your muscles don't perform and you start developing bad habits."

Shooting too much can not only tear down the muscles, it can painfully damage the joints. "A few years back," Lee admits, "when we first started putting on our aerial shoots, we were practicing almost every day. I developed tendonitis in my shoulder, and I had to quit shooting for three months. Now I only shoot once a week, and I haven't noticed any difference in my accuracy. The main thing I like to maintain is a consistent anchor on my cheek, because without it I won't shoot consistently."

When they're exhibition shooting, the Kramers use fiberglass arrows helically fletched with three 5 1/4" high profile feathers. The glass arrows shoot as soft as wood yet provide the consistency they need for pinpoint shooting.

Ted installs his arrow nocking point 1/8" above perpendicular and nocks his arrow over it. "When you are speed loading for that quick second shot,

DONNING BUCKSKINS AND BOWS — For the dazzling Kramer duo, Ted (right) and Lee (left), the sweet hum of the longbow is a way of life.

which sometimes really counts, the arrow nock will slide down into place much quicker by nocking on top. It only requires one downward motion and is by far faster than nocking under."

Ted wraps his nocking point with serving thread and then coats it with glue. "The brass ones will cut up your finger tabs, and they develop nasty edges. Our wrapped and glued thread nock becomes part of the serving, and it isn't going to move. If your nocking point slips, it could cost you a shot. When you get used to putting on a self-nocking point with serving thread, you can replace it right out in the field."

Being experienced trick shooters comes in handy when bowhunting, but it also creates a stir at archery shoots. "We quit competing," says Ted. "If we go to a shoot now, I ask if it's all right to just shoot for fun. Competition seems to bring out something bad in people. If you are a bowyer and you don't win then it's thumbs down. And if you do win, you shouldn't have been shooting because you had an unfair advantage. You just can't win. The most fun is simply going to a shoot, being relaxed, and enjoying shooting. Who cares who wins? We do it for the fun of it, and we don't want to ever get to the point where the competition and winning are the end results."

LEMONWOOD TO FIBERGLASS

For Ted, shooting the longbow remains as much fun as it was over forty years ago when he made his first longbow. Back then, he glued a wooden riser to a lemonwood stave and bound them together with cord. He painted his finished bow with some "Indian colors" and made a bowstring out of shoestring linen. He cut self-nocks in dowels for arrows and bound them near the ends so they wouldn't split. For arrow points he used copper tubing that he pinched and riveted shut on the end.

Since those early days, Ted has seen some major innovations in bow-making; the most significant were improved facing and backing materials. "I actually worked with Toxhorn first. It didn't increase the speed of my bows, but it sure did make them last. Then they started putting rawhide on the back of bows and that increased their life. Then Eicholtz and Gordon got together and invented fiberglass, and I started using it on my bows when I lived in Oregon."

During his years in Oregon, Ted finished bows for noted self-wood bow-yer, Earl Ulrich. For payment Ted received yew wood laminations which he later used to build longbows of his own design. He later began selling those longbows in Roseburg, Oregon in 1966. Although Ted made some semi-recurves, the longbow has always remained his favorite.

Today Ted shares his time-gathered bow building secrets with his son Lee. Together they produce their own Autumn Longbows and stock longbows for Howard Hill Archery, all of which receive Ted's stamp of approval. "I like doing whatever I do well. When building longbows it's important to me that we build them the very best we can."

Despite his personal standards, Ted's bow building has sometimes held unforeseen disappointments. Ever since bowyers began laminating bows, their success has depended largely on the reliability of glues. "You can be the best craftsman in the world, but if you get a hold of some bad glue, your bows will blow up. Actually it's not the bowyer's fault, but he gets stuck with it. I know guys who built bows and had to quit because one batch of bad glue absolutely tore them up financially. Unfortunately, with bad glue you find out too late what the problem is. I don't like to have myself and all my bows hanging in the balance because of bad glue. But today, we have an epoxy glue that is the best that has ever come out, and I have real confidence in it. It's Smooth On epoxy."

TRADITIONAL WITH A HINT OF BACKSET

With tough Smooth-On bonding the composites together, Ted's bow design incorporates traditional longbow features. It has a deep-cored limb with a modified trapezoidal cross section tapering to the belly and a peaked standard longbow handle. Its only deviation from a traditional design is the slight backset to the limbs "The difference between a straight and a backset bow isn't all that great. Backset bows just have more pounds of tension at their brace height because there is more stress built into the bow. The more stress you put into a bow, the more speed you are going to get out of it. But with that increased speed, you also get more hand shock. If you leave out the backset, you increase stability but lose speed. It depends on what a guy likes. There are sacrifices either way."

In achieving his blend of design features, Ted also considers the limb cross section. "We like a nice core depth because it makes our longbow shoot sweet and stable, and makes it easy to draw. Fiberglass is a complement to the core and it increases bow speed. When we use different thicknesses of glass on a bow, we put the thickest piece on the belly because that surface is going to be rounded more to form our "D" shaped limb. Consequently, we need more glass strength in the belly to help hold the limbs in alignment. Compression is more severe on the belly than stress is on the back so we want thicker belly glass to handle those compressional forces. We also like to roll our limb edges over so there are no sharp edges, and so a blow from a rock isn't going to make a big nick in your bow."

PUTTING IT TOGETHER

Inside the Kramers' cabin shop is where Ted and Lee put their design concepts to the test. Their shop is equipped with an array of homemade bow building devices which include a spindle sander, vertical belt sander, fadeout grinder, and lamination grinder. All of these dust generating machines are hooked up to their dust collection system which is made from an assemblage of old clothes dryer parts. "Most of our machinery," Lee says, "is designed to waste away material that's in the way, and once it's removed we have more time to put hand work into the areas where it's needed."

The Kramers' bowmaking workhorse is their custom lamination and limb tapering device. This moveable sander mounted on a run, designed by Ted, is also used to prepare laminations for splicing.

Another of Ted's inventions is his movable fadeout grinder. After a piece of bubinga or osage is marked and sawn to riser shape, it is ground on this

RESEMBLING STEEL VERTEBRAE — Kramers' laminated steel form uses welder's clamps to squeeze the glued composites together.

movable device which produces consistent and uniform tapers on both ends of the riser belly. Final fadeout feathering is delicately done by hand on the vertical sander.

The Kramers custom plane and grind their own tapered bamboo, osage, and yew laminations on their tapering device. To provide a freshly ground surface for gluing, the laminations receive their final tapering right before glue up.

In preparation for glue up, Lee tapes the non-gluing fiberglass surfaces and covers the bow form with plastic wrap. The form is made from three, ¼" layers of steel that were clamped to a wooden form and welded together. This produced a laminated steel bow mirroring the back shape of their longbow.

They apply Smooth-On epoxy to all contact surfaces and lay up the composites, being sure to position the riser and laminations to the marked reference points on the form. A steel pressure strip is placed of top of the composites, and the limb areas are compressed with welders clamps. The riser area is compressed by tightening a series of bolts fastened from the form to the edge of the steel pressure strip.

The formed composites are then put into the glue curing oven and baked at 150 degrees overnight. The oven is heated with five 100 watt light bulbs, and a thermometer is placed in the oven for monitoring the temperature. After the oven is turned off, the bow is allowed to cool before removing it from the form.

Using a string, the bow centerline is marked from a center point on the handle to the limb tips. The limb edges are then ground to form using Ted's tapering device. Most of the limb and riser shaping is then done on the vertical belt sander. When roughing in bows, Lee wears welder's gloves to protect his hands from the biting and splintering fiberglass.

After the bow is rough shaped, the nocks are filed in and the bow is braced to check for alignment and tiller. Material is removed from the edges to bring the limbs into alignment, and the fine tuning of both alignment and tiller is done by rounding the belly of the limbs. They tiller their longbows to a one-eighth inch positive tiller. "After building thousands of bows," says Ted, "working the limbs into alignment and tiller is almost an instinctive sense that comes to you. A beginning bowmaker may spend two weeks working a bow down to a point that we can achieve in ten minutes."

Ted and Lee make limb shaping look as easy as scratching the back of their necks. But it's not. "Anybody who wants to build a bow," Ted says, "can usually count on losing the first one. Chances are you are going to do something bad enough to where you are just going to throw the bow over in the corner and start all over again. Only if you are very fortunate will you ever shoot the first bow that you make."

The string nocks and limb tips are finished by hand and the angles are a product of experience. "My dad," Lee says, "showed me the angle and had me build several nocks in an old bow limb before he would let me make them. Basically, you just imagine the natural curve of the string going around the nock. The only mark I have is a certain distance from the tip."

The pointed upper tip is 1 1/8" from the nock and the rounded lower tip is 1/2" from the nock. This makes the lower limb less susceptible to damage during stringing and general use. The tip belly is shaped so that the fiberglass wedge will help support string pressure exerted on the sides of the corewoods. When finishing the belly side of the nock, Lee files open the throat to provide plenty of room for the string to follow into the belly when the bow is shot.

The bow is final sanded with a small electric orbital sander. Wood sealer is then wiped on the exposed wood surfaces and the bow is rubbed smooth with steel wool. Lee then uses his pen and artistic hand to ink on the bow's distinctive lettering.

Although most bowyers spray on their bow finish, the Kramers use an arrowsmithing technique. They dip their bows, one half at a time, in a tube filled with finish. This vertical tube is uniquely installed in the floor of the shop which makes dipping possible in the low-ceilinged cabin. After a bow receives its one dip of finish, it's hung in a light-bulb heated drying closet on the wall. When it has dried, the leather shelf-strike pad and grip are glued in place and the grip is laced down the front.

THE TAKE-DOWN DIFFERENCE

To make their two-piece longbow, the Kramers glue up and rough out a one-piece bow and saw it in half. That may seem to be an easy way to make a two-piece longbow, but the trick is then fashioning the two halves into a functional take-down bow.

First, they have a special steel handle fabricated on a twelve-ton press using an inside-outside mold. The top half of the bow is fashioned to tightly fit into the steel handle, and it is permanently epoxied into place. The lower half of the bow is ground, then pressed with auto body filler into the steel handle that has been coated with a non-stick material. When the filler has dried, the finished fit is so snug that a small air hole must be drilled in the handle to break the air suction between the handle and lower half of the bow. The front of the grip is tapped with a small set screw to hold the two halves together. The bow is then finished like a one-piece bow. Even though the two-piece riser is sure-fitting, Ted continues to refine and modify his take-down assembly.

To brace the finished product, Ted recommends stringing the longbow with the push-pull technique. "If you put all of your weight on one foot and use your other leg as a fulcrum to help, you can brace very heavy bows. But you should use your whole thigh and put it up in the handle so you don't damage the lower limb."

FINDING A HOME

Most of his customers are bowhunters, and although Ted admits that a forty-five pound bow at the right distance could kill most animals in North America, he recommends heavier weights. "Most archers should be able to work up to sixty pounds, and that's a good hunting weight. If you can shoot accurately with more then you should do so, but not to the extent that you sacrifice accuracy. A good rule is to draw the heaviest bow that you can, and drop twenty pounds in bow weight. Man's ego says that 'more is better'. But don't get caught up with more is better in bow weight, because it's not better if you can't handle it accurately. Don't let ego get in the way of what you draw and shoot."

Even though the Kramers live in a remote part of the country, their longbows seem to find their way across the nation. Some of their sales come from magazine adds, but Ted notes that most are generated through the traditional grapevine. "If you get enough bows out there the bows will sell themselves. The people who like our bows are our salesmen. We advertise some, but it's very expensive and advertising is part of the product cost. So we advertise as little as possible to hold our bow prices down."

SOMETHING NEW

Most bowmakers also make or offer quivers, arrows, arm guards, and standard archery fare with their bows. But Ted has thought about offering some unique traditional items. "I was thinking about putting the atlatl on the market. The public would have fun with it because it preceded the bow and is very primitive. It's an extension of the arm throwing stick that's used to cast a spear. It's fun and can be quite accurate.

"I would someday also like to market whistling arrows. Matter of fact, fifty years ago the National Field Archery Association wanted to start their events with everybody shooting whistling arrows, but they weren't successful in developing one. But I have developed a couple types of whistling arrows, and people could have a lot of fun with them."

BACK TO THE FUTURE

Having a lot of fun is what many feel archery is all about. Even though compound bows dominate the archery industry today, there's a growing trend of archers looking to an earlier time when the challenge and fun of archery meant a stick n' string. "The real surge in traditional archery," says Ted, "took off when the compound bow became common. And people began wanting to go back to a simpler form of archery. I think the longbow is going to become a standard in archery that everything will relate back to. People who really love archery won't be satisfied until they own a longbow."

For the Kramers, people who own longbows are often a pretty special group. "I love longbowmen," says Ted, "because they are generally good hunters and good sportsmen, and they don't care about winning that much. They just like getting together."

AUTUMN DREAMS

Now in the autumn years of his bowhunting career, Ted finds the mountains a little steeper each season. But despite his age, he still looks forward to new and grand bowhunting adventures. "Sheep and goat are supposed to be prized trophies, but I have always wanted to take a moose. I know they are easier to take, but there is something about them. I would like to see one of these biggest animals if North America fall from my bow and arrows. And, there is a sense of danger in hunting moose because they can, and sometimes do, charge."

It seems that a charging bear would be enough for most bowhunters to face in a lifetime without wanting to add a three-quarter ton bull moose to the list. But then not everyone shoots like Ted Kramer or has a backup nearby who's not afraid to stand her ground with a readied Autumn Longbow by her side.

Chapter Twenty-Three

ROBERTSON STYKBOW

LESSONS IN THE BITTERROOTS

In the morning shadows of the Bitterroots, two rust-colored forms bob oversized racks as they feed near the logging road. They lift their regal heads to the sound of an approaching car and stare curiously as it rolls to a stop. Mixed whispers and a clicking shutter from the open window draw only a brief gaze from the deer who casually resume feeding, seemingly aware that hunting season is still a week away.

"Dad," a young voice hisses, "you could get out and shoot that big one with your bow."

The reply is quick and firm. "No, Yote, it's not season yet. Besides that's not the way to hunt deer." Twenty yards away, the larger buck directs his ears toward the car as if listening to the conversation. "You can't shoot deer from the road son," the man says, now raising his voice. "It's not right — it's not hunting."

The boy looks back at the deer for a moment, then with a quizzical arch of his eyebrows he says, "But, Dad, you could step off the road a little in the grass and then shoot him."

Without taking his gaze off the bucks, the father replies, "The way to hunt those bucks, son, is to sneak up on them in the woods without using cars or roads. People that shoot deer from the road aren't hunters, they're just killers, and that's not right."

The largest buck browses nearer, and father and son share in the wonderment of the big mulie. Then the boy narrows his eyes and says, "Yeah, people that shoot deer from the road are stupid!"

"That's right Yote," the man says, "and bucks that hang around the road aren't too smart either." He steps from the car and tosses a stick in the direction of the deer and yells, "Beat it you stupid deer. Bow season starts next week."

The stick smacks a nearby tree startling the deer who lay back their ears, whirl, and pogo-stick down the hillside into the thick timber. Exchanging grins with his son, the man gets back into the car and begins to drive away. Hugging the window sill, the boy spouts, "Yeah, quit hanging around the roads. Just beat it you stupid deer!"

Unlike many of today's bowhunters who thirst for gadgets, gimmicks, and short cuts to easier kills, Dick Robertson, Yote's father, slips into the woods carrying what can't be purchased from the archery shop: strong bowhunting ethics and a deep pride in honest hunting, both of which are reflected in his methods and his choice of equipment.

Dick hunts with a longbow, a simple weapon that challenges and elevates both his shooting and his hunting skills. Even though he has taken a host of trophy animals, their numbers or impressive size are not important to him. "Pope and Young scores don't mean anything to me. I have one elk in the book because someone else sent in the score sheet, but I haven't bothered to enter any of my other trophies. And I never will. I don't consider myself a trophy hunter. I only have a certain amount of time to hunt and I like to harvest animals."

HOMESTEADING UNDER THE BIG SKY

For a guy who likes to harvest animals, Dick lives in the right place. His log home is in the big sky country of Montana's Bitterroot Valley just south of Hamilton. It sits on land homesteaded by his grandparents who came to the Bitterroot as children in the back of covered wagons. He shares his home and bowmaking business with his wife Vikki, aspiring bowhunter son, Yote, and younger daughters, Yana, and Yavon.

Besides occasionally wetting a line for local trout and spending time with his family, Dick immerses himself in building and shooting his traditional bows. "My whole life revolves around bowhunting."

Dick belongs to the Professional Bowhunters Society, an organization he believes is the nation's strongest in supporting the sport. He was one of the first members of the Montana Bowhunters Association, and in 1985 was selected as Montana's Bowhunter Of The Year because of his long-standing commitment to promoting the sport. He was also instrumental in recently creating the Traditional Bowhunters of Montana, serving as president. "We are trying to promote traditional equipment, and we hold a fun shoot where we don't even keep score. We float a section of the Blackfoot River and shoot at animal targets. It's like a mini Moose John River float trip like Jay Massey runs up in Alaska. We get about 100 people and have a lot of fun." On the local scene, Dick belongs to the Bitterroot Archers and roams their rocky and pine shrouded range in the hills west of town.

THE NATURAL WAY

When he can't make it to the range, Dick enjoys free roving shooting at sticks, pine cones, or whatever catches his eye. He shoots in a classic longbow style, making each shot look as natural as blinking his eyes. With effortless movements, he draws his canted bow, focuses his eyes as muscles bunch at full draw, and executes a clean pull-through release, his arrow hissing away in a gray blur. "Some people call it instinctive, but I say it's more of a conditioned reflex. You've done it enough to where it just happens. It's rare to find someone who just picks up a bow and pumps them in there. Reflex is where it is an unconscious effort. Most good bowhunters shoot a bow unconsciously just like you would swat a fly or cast a fishing rod."

CREATING MYSTICAL MAGIC — Dick enjoys shooting at imaginary sagebrush critters near his shop.

Dick only pauses for a split second at full draw before releasing the arrow to its mark. "I just mentally burn a hole in the spot I want to hit, and by the time I get it back I just let my body shoot the bow. Any time I start thinking about it, I shoot like beans. All of the good hunters have a quick release — Fred Bear and Howard Hill shot that way."

BIRDS TO ELK

Dick began bowhunting at an age long before most archers pick up their first bow. "When I was four years old, I was playing cowboys and Indians, I always wanted to be the Indian. I bugged my Dad until he cut off a green limb from the cottonwood tree in the back yard. He shaved it down and put a string on it for me. Then he cut some square arrows on a table saw, cut in nocks with a hacksaw blade, and turned me loose. The arrows didn't even have fletching. When I was five, I killed a bird with one of those square arrows."

Dick's next bow was a genuine hunting bow, a Shakespear Wonderbow. Although he was still just a boy, that bow catapulted him to new heights. "When I was twelve they opened up the Missouri River Breaks area to bowhunting, and I went after elk with my bow and arrow. Those elk hadn't been hunted and it was open prairie country. When the season opened, they were in large herds of 150 animals but some guys on motor bikes scattered the herds into small groups. After a few weeks of bowhunting without much success, most guys quit hunting and it was fairly easy to find groups of six to twelve animals and stalk them. I messed up three or four stalks but then I just happened to get lucky and got a fifteen yard shot on some elk bedded in the shade of a coolie. The whole herd stood up and I got an arrow in the right spot on this cow. My bow only pulled forty pounds at twenty-eight inches, but I was anchoring about three inches behind my ear."

A blossoming bowhunter in a rifle hunting family, Dick hunted both bow and rifle seasons until he was sixteen. "Then I put the rifle away and I haven't used one since."

SEPTEMBER MAGIC

September is Dick's favorite month because he leaves the bow shop behind and heads for the woods to get "hammered." For many, getting hammered means having a few too many drinks at the local pub. But not Dick. He has his own special bowhunting vocabulary. For him, it means the spiritual and emotional intoxication caused when sneaking within bow-range of big game animals. And to Dick, "zork" is not some computer game. It's what he intends to do to his bowhunting quarry.

Since he was sixteen, Dick has spent Septembers bowhunting. He often starts his season trying to sneak within range of an antelope, then heads to higher ground looking for mule deer. By mid-September the elk are bugling and Dick grabs his bow and bugle and heads for the alpine forests. And recently, he has started hunting later in the year when Montana's boss whitetails start thinking about the rut. "I enjoy them all, but I get the most pleasure out of hunting mule deer, because I'm on the ground in semi-open country where I can spot bucks, watch them bed, and then make my stalk on them. I've had more success on elk, but you hunt them in forested terrain and only get a brief opportunity to see them. And when that opportunity presents itself you better be ready."

Most of Dick's September bowhunting involves stalking. He loves the thrills of sneaking within eye-blinking distance of his prey. He even uses his stalking techniques on keen-eyed antelope and retiring black bear. But recently Dick started hunting from trees in Eastern Montana. "Lately, the whitetail has captivated my interest, and I plan on devoting quite a bit of time to hunting them. I only take 110 to 120 inchers now, but I'm new to it and just learning. I ignored them during my earlier years, but I've hung around with Gene Wensel so long that whitetails finally have my interest peaked. When Gene moved here he was the first real bowhunter I had any contact with. It was nice to have someone to share a common interest, and we shot and hunted together."

MORE CHALLENGE

Arrowing that first elk when he was just twelve plunged Dick into a bowhunting challenge that grew with each season. When he was sixteen, Dick took a record-class mule deer with his recurve; when he was eighteen he tagged his first bull elk. And in the years that followed, Dick and his sixty-one pound Browning Safari recurve put a dent in the local game populations. "I really went on a rampage and killed an elk and a mule deer about every year, and it got to the point that shooting them with the recurve wasn't as challenging as it used to be. That's when I decided to change to a longbow."

Dick's first step in converting to a longbow was to find out more about them, so he visited Ted Ekin of Howard Hill Archery in Hamilton, who gave him advice on shooting a longbow and developing an anchor point. Soon after, Dick met John Schultz who had been a custom bowyer for Howard Hill. "We struck it off good and I ordered a longbow from him. But in the meantime I borrowed one from another guy and went out and killed a bear with it. It was about a sixty yard shot which is longer than I shoot now. After shooting that bear with that longbow, I was hooked. There was something magical about the longbow and it was definitely more challenging. I went hunting with it and missed elk that I was sure I could hit with a recurve. I struggled with the longbow for three years before I killed an elk with it."

ELK BUSTING GEAR

Dick no longer struggles shooting his longbow. Today he hunts with one of his custom Mystical styks. "My favorite has gone just about everywhere with me. I took it to Alaska, and it has taken antelope, mule deer, whitetail, black bear, elk, and moose. I decided to retire it because I don't want anything to happen to it. It's sixty-four inches long, pulls seventy-two pounds, and made from black locust with a shedua handle. I'm replacing it with a little sixty-two inch all black locust longbow pulling seventy-five pounds at twenty-eight inches."

Dick equips his bowstring with Beaver Balls string silencers and ties and glues on a dental floss string nocking point so the bottom of his nock is 1/8" to 3/16" above perpendicular to the string. He hunts with Kustom King arrows made from fir shafting that he turned himself. His arrows, including the broadheads, weigh 600 grains and are fletched with three 5 3/4" high-profile feathers. "A mistake a lot of people make when shooting a big broadhead, is that they use five inch die-cut feathers. If you have a poor release, those small feathers won't stabilize the arrow very well." He carries his hunting arrows in a small strap-on bow quiver.

THE CUTTING END

For years Dick used Zwickey Delta broadheads, but recently he switched to a three-bladed head after Roger Rothhaar gave him some Snuffers during one of Jay Massey's Alaskan float trips. "I was reluctant to shoot them because of their size, but I tried them on whitetails in eastern Montana. I was amazed by how well they performed on a marginal hit. Any broadhead will work great when you put them where you are supposed to. But if the animal moves or jumps the string and you get a marginal hit with a Snuffer, your likelihood of hitting a major vessel or artery is tripled over a two-bladed head. And with the big hole the Snuffer makes, you have a trail to follow."

Dick gets his Snuffers deadly sharp by using a homemade wooden jig with two twelve inch mill bastard files mounted on angled surfaces. With the broadheads mounted on his arrows, Dick simply pushes the broadheads down the file-surfaced jig, rotating the head after every few strokes. When sharpening them, he purposely files off about twenty-five grains of blade weight to make his Snuffers lighter.

Even though Dick knew how Snuffers worked on deer, he was still hesitant to use them on larger game. But after talking to a friend who had successfully used them on elk, he decided to try them on something bigger. "After twenty years of applying for moose, sheep, and goat in Montana, I finally got lucky and drew a moose permit.

"I was hunting with my sixty-seven pound longbow and had seen thirteen different bulls but none that I wanted. Finally I saw this good one coming, and I thought I was going to get a fifteen yard shot. But I was in his terrain. He was walking down this trail that he had probably been using all of his life, and he looked over at me like, 'Hey! You don't belong here.' He was thirty-five yards away and quartering to me, which is a bad position for a shot. Finally, he got tired of looking at me and as he turned broadside to leave, I shot. My timing was off and I hit him in the second to the last rib, going through the diaphragm, the liver, and eight inches of meat on the far ham, and it poked out the hide on the far side about eight inches. He went less than seventy-five yards and just toppled over. That moose was a forty-three incher, which is a good one."

CLOSE RANGE EXCITEMENT

Whether he's stalking mulies or moose, Dick likes to work his way in for close-range high-percentage shots. "Typically, most of my shots are twenty yards or less, and my maximum range is around thirty. The reasons are twofold. I'm not as good of a shot as I was, plus I get more satisfaction the closer I get to the animal. When I do better stalking in close and make that fifteen-yard shot, I have done a better job as a hunter. Besides, I don't feel personal with an animal until I get within thirty yards and can see the glint in their eyes."

One of Dick's most memorable stalks was played out like an actor on a stage, complete with an audience. "I watched this buck for three days during some cold weather, but instead of going to an area that was conducive to stalking, he would lay in an open spot where it was almost impossible to stalk. Finally we got some warm weather and this buck moved into the shade to bed with some other bucks. I was hunting with my friend, Duane Garner, and we flipped to see who was going to stalk the buck.

"I won and Duane watched through his spotting scope while I stalked up this ridge. I got to within about twenty yards, and the buck got up and started running. I made a good shot on him right through the chest where you're supposed to, and he ran out into the open and died. It was special to have a good friend to share the experience with. And we even repeated the experience a couple of years later when I got to watch Duane shoot a bear."

DICK'S STYKS

Stalking bucks and bulls in the rugged west calls for a bow that's lightweight, dependable, true-shooting, and hard-hitting. For Dick and his large following of satisfied customers, this means a Stykbow. The name says it all. "I always thought when people started calling real bows 'sticks' that it was somewhat of a slam. So when I started building bows I didn't want any question about what type I was making. And I stuck the letter 'Y' in there to be different."

The MYSTICAL LONGBOW is Dick's favorite Stykbow to build and shoot. It's also his most popular. The Mystical enjoys widespread popularity across the country as a premier traditional hunting weapon. It incorporates a deflexed handle and reflexed limb design for reduced hand shock, smoothness, and speed. It's available from 62" to 70" in two-inch increments. The 62" length has a mass weight of 1 pound, 3 ounces and a brace height of 6 ½" from the string to the throat.

The one-piece hardwood riser is available in a variety of striking exotic and domestic woods. It measures 14 ½" between fadeouts, is 1 3⁄16" wide, and narrows to 3⁄4" through the sight window which is cut ⅛" from center shot. The riser is 1 7⁄8" thick and thins through the slightly dished grip. This custom grip is dished just above bow center for positive and consistent hand seat. It's wrapped with a piece of 4" suede leather, laced down the front. The window and shelf are padded with leather. Bow and customer information are black inked above and below the grip on the side opposite the window.

The deep-cored limbs exhibit a deflex-reflex design and are rounded to the belly in a modified trapezoidal cross section. On the 62" bow, the working length of the upper limb is 24 3⁄8" and on the lower limb it is 24". The limbs narrow from 1 ¼" wide at the fadeouts to 3⁄8" at the nock.

They are constructed from three tapered back laminations and one tapered belly lamination, all enveloped in clear fiberglass. Dick uses a variety of custom-ground solid corewoods. His most popular are red elm, osage, and black locust. The slim-lined tip overlays are crafted from animal horn over riser wood and have full cut string nocks that wrap around to the belly. Like all Stykbows, it's finished in a matte low-luster Fullerplast finish.

The following draw/force measurements suggest the draw smoothness of a 62" Mystical Longbow:

DRAW LENGTH	25"	26"	27"	28"	29"
DRAW WEIGHT	59#	62#	66#	70#	74#

To check for relative speed, Dick shot this bow using 520 grain 28¾" wooden arrows which he drew to 28". The arrows had three standard 5" feathers and snap-on nocks. Dick used a shooting tab and had a clean pull-though release. The bowstring was standard Dacron without any accessories. The average arrow speed for this bow, arrow, and shooter combination was 195 fps.

The BUFFALO BOW is offered for traditionalists interested in the romance of the Indian flatbow. This 62" flatbow is similar in overall design to the Mystical except that its limbs are wide and flat. This evolved after Jay Massey built a flatbow using Dick's longbow form. A friend saw the new flatbow and wanted one, and in no time, Dick was receiving orders for the little bows from as far away as Michigan.

GAME GETTING STYKS — The Buffalo bow (left in photos) and the Mystical combine select custom ground corewoods under clear glass. Their deflex-reflex design is a proven winner.

Both the upper and lower limbs have working lengths of 24" from the fadeout to the nock and they narrow from 1 5/8" wide at the fadeout to 13/16" at the nock. They are constructed from two back and one belly lamination of .002" per inch tapered corewood. The limbs have rounded edges and no tip overlays. The draw/force characteristics and arrow speeds are similar to the Mystical.

The PEREGRINE represents a step between the Buffalo bow and a standard recurve. This 60" recurve is a fast-shooting lightweight bow that Dick originally called his Quick-Styk. It has a slim-lined simple riser which measures 20" between fadeouts. It only weighs 1 pound, 7 ounces, and has a brace height of 6 3/8" from the string to the throat.

Its solid hardwood riser is 1 1/2" wide and narrows to 11/16" through the center shot sight window. It is 2 1/8" thick and thins through the modified longbow grip. The rounded sight window is full cut for 3 1/2" above the crowned shelf and contours back to full riser width 4 3/4" above the shelf. Like the longbows, the grip and shelf-window junction are covered with leather.

The Peregrine's limbs have a working length of 20" and narrow from 1 1/2" wide at the fadeouts to 13/16" at the nocks. They are constructed from one back and one belly lamination tapered .015" per inch, enveloped in clear glass. The tip overlays are made from laminated matching corewood and animal horn. The limbs also have a thin veneer of riser wood laminated to the outer several inches of the limb belly. The string nocks are full cut on the back and sides and feather into a groove filed into the belly overlay.

The following draw/force measurements suggest the smoothness of draw on the 60" Peregrine:

DRAW LENGTH	25"	26"	27"	28"	29"
DRAW WEIGHT	48#	51#	53#	56#	59#

To check for relative speed, this Peregrine was chronographed using the same arrow and shooter combination as the Mystical Longbow. The average arrow speed was 184 fps.

The PRAIRIE FALCON TD is a three-piece bow offered for archers desiring a more conventional recurve. "I'm interested if falconry, and I named this bow the Prairie Falcon because we have them here in Montana and they're kick-ass little birds."

The Prairie Falcon is available in 60", 62", and 64" lengths and weighs approximately 2 pounds, 6 ounces, depending on the riser wood. It has a recommended brace height of 7" to 7 1/4" from the string to the throat. The composite hardwood riser is 18" long, 1 3/4" wide near the limbs, and narrows to 5/8" through the center shot sight window. It is 2 5/8" thick and thins through the custom medium-profile grip. The rounded sight window is full cut for 3 3/4" above the crowned arrow shelf and contours back to full width 5" above the shelf.

The riser's hardwoods sandwich a sweeping vertical wedge of multi-laminated veneers. It's flat on the sides near the limbs and blends into soft contours around the grip.

BIRDS OF PREY — The Peregrine (left in photos) offers a modified longbow handle. The Prairie Falcon TD has a heavier and more striking handle with a decorative wedge and a standard recurve grip.

The 17½" working length limbs attach to the riser with an attachment bolt and single alignment pin system. The limbs narrow from 1¾" wide at the fadeout to ⅞" at the nock. Each limb is constructed from an 8" long fadeout wedge with one back and one belly lamination enveloped in clear fiberglass. The limbs have slightly rounded edges and tip and belly overlays similar to the Peregrine.

The following draw/force measurements were recorded on a 62" Prairie Falcon TD:

DRAW LENGTH	25"	26"	27"	28"	29"
DRAW WEIGHT	57½#	60#	63#	67#	71½#

This 62" Falcon TD was chronographed using the same arrow, string, and shooter combination as the other bows. The average arrow speed was 194 fps.

A CHALLENGE IN THE MAKING

Dick creates his line of Stykbows in the shop behind his house. The view out the window is a post card scene, the light greens of Bitterroot Valley merging with the emerald tones of the imposing mountains to the west. It's a peaceful place to create his popular styks. Although today Dick enjoys noted distinction among America's traditional bowyers, it was a long road to notoriety.

Now in his mid-thirties, Dick got into the archery business when he was fifteen by making and selling arrows. He later opened one of the first archery pro shops in Montana in 1970 but sold his interest in the Missoula-based shop when compounds took over the bow market.

In the late seventies Dick wanted the ultimate challenge of making and harvesting game with a homemade self-wood bow. But his efforts met with disappointment. So he decided to build a laminated bow, hoping the experience would help him learn how to craft a serviceable self-wood bow. Little did Dick know that his bowmaking lesson would sprout into an occupation.

Dick sought the help of friend and long-time bowyer Dale Jasperson. With one of Dale's forms and guidance from the seasoned bow crafter, Dick used his carpentry skills in making his first longbow. "When Dale was teaching me how to build bows, he would be very meticulous. I had never been much of a perfectionist, but he kept stressing that everything had to be perfect down to one-thousandth of an inch then rechecked, and that rubbed off on me."

Even though his first bow was barely cooled from the oven, it didn't take Dick long to establish a clientele. "When I went out to test shoot my new bow, my friend, Scott Leibenguth, came over and saw the new bow and asked me to make him one. So I made him one. Then I showed both of the new bows to Gene Wensel, and he started passing the word around that I was building bows."

SUCCESS BREEDS SUCCESS

Dick and Scott took the new bows out hunting, and proof of Dick's success as a maker of "game getting" bows was not long in coming. Coincidentally, Dick killed a dandy mule deer buck with his new longbow on the same day that Scott killed a bull elk with his.

Dick was encouraged by the success of his first bows, but his early bow building years were also sprinkled with occasional setbacks. "I think Murphy was a bowyer because anything that could go wrong, would. Even though Dale tutored me, initially I had all different kinds of disappointments. Bowmaking captivated my interest so much that I didn't know when to quit. I would be out working in the shop late at night and would cut the sight window on the wrong side or make other 'little' mistakes."

Although Dick made a few mistakes in the beginning, using a deflex-reflex longbow design was not one of them. Today it remains one of the most popular and widely used designs throughout the country. Dick's deflexed handle and reflexed limb design was patterned after the first bow he made on Dale Jasperson's form. "That first bow came out sixty-six pounds and my favorite reflexed longbow was seventy-two pounds. To compare the two I went out and flight shot them and discovered that the sixty-six pounder shot an arrow slightly farther than the seventy-two pounder."

With the performance of the deflex-reflex design behind him and some help from Gene spreading the word about his bows, Dick soon had orders for over fifty of his fast-shooting longbows. "I attribute my longbow's performance more to the design than anything else. The deflexed handle seems to help absorb the hand shock that longbows are notorious for. By deflexing the handle slightly, I can put more reflex into the limb, so I gain speed without increasing hand shock. With this design I gain from five to twenty feet per second arrow velocity over a straight or a slightly reflexed longbow."

Even though his longbow design was a winner among his growing customers, it didn't take Dick long to follow it up with a recurve. "I couldn't get my friend, Duane Garner, to try a longbow, and I wanted to experiment with recurves, so I made him one of my first take-downs. Then people saw his and they wanted some. It started snowballing to where I was spending all my evenings building bows. Then it got to the point where I was working construction four days a week and building bows three days a week. I was just driven. I couldn't wait to wake up in the morning to make bows, and I would work past midnight." Dick's bowmaking skills grew, and by 1979 his bow crafting mushroomed into a full-time business.

COREWOODS

Even during his early years as a bowmaker, Dick wasn't content with the common maple core and colored fiberglass that most bowyers used. "Gordon was experimenting with clear fiberglass, and I wanted a wood that showed more color through the clear glass and would be strong.

"Dale Jasperson was again an inspiration because he shot ninety and 100 pound bows and had one break, so he was always looking for the ultimate bow wood. The American Hardwoods Association puts out a list of the physical and mechanical properties of different hardwoods. By reviewing it we found which woods were superior in bending, shock resistance, and stiffness. We decided that osage was the strongest and a good handle material, and that black locust had the highest bending strength and was the best limb core. Also, through clear glass it looked great."

Dick's first 700 to 800 longbows were built from a select supply of black locust. "I cut all the trees myself, dried the wood, cut them into laminations, and ground my own tapers. By doing it all myself I control the moisture content, which is an important aspect. I want my handle wood to have a maximum of eleven to twelve percent moisture, and I want my limb corewoods to have about six to seven percent moisture. If you get more than that it can cause gluing problems."

Dick also uses other corewoods such as red elm, which is cut in the Midwest and sawn into 2" boards with the desired grain alignment. The ends are coated with paraffin to prevent cracking and the wood is air-dried in the moister Midwest climate for six months to two years before being shipped to Montana. Hamilton's climate is so dry that unseasoned boards crack and warp.

Using his select stock of aged woods, Dick makes all of his custom corewood laminations. He first rips the 2" boards into .150" strips on a band saw, then stacks and dries them until the moisture content reaches six to eight percent. Keeping consecutively cut strips as a matched pair, he grinds them parallel to about .130" thickness and then puts them on a tapered

CUSTOM LAMINATIONS — Using a drum sander and a taper board, Dick grinds his own corewoods from rough stock.

board which he runs through a dimension drum sander, tapering the pair of laminations to within .010" of their desired thickness.

Red elm is one of Dick's more popular corewoods because of its strength and contrasting striped grain. It makes an excellent shooting, naturally camouflaged bow. Red elm is also one of the few corewoods that can be used cross grain or flat grain yet still retains its natural stress characteristics. But to be sure, Dick tests all his laminations by flexing each and checking for trueness, cracks, and uniformity of flex. Unlike some softer corewoods that can dent and fracture easier, red elm has good side hardness.

To enhance the grain contrast and match the color of the riser wood, Dick stains his red elm laminations with an alcohol base stain. When selecting the limb composites, he tries to use an attractive flat grain under the clear glass to maximize the natural beauty of the wood.

RISER MAKING

When making a bow with a solid hardwood riser, Dick begins by inspecting the wood for integrity and proper grain alignment. For heavyweight bows he always uses a grain that is parallel to the string, as it makes the strongest handle. On standard weight bows he selects an attractive grain alignment and pattern that still provides sufficient strength.

He then planes two sides flat and squares the ends on his table saw. Using a template he marks the riser outline, making sure to align the straightest grain in the fadeout sections. He then band saws the back shape and grinds it on a vertical drum sander and block sands it until the deflexed riser back fits flush to the template. Dick then marks the belly outline and shapes the sweeping fadeouts. While grinding them on the vertical drum sander, he supports the back with a piece of wood and gently feathers the belly side of the fadeouts. Dick gives special attention to this delicate task because proper feathering is the key to a tight glue line at the highly stressed fadeout areas.

When making his take-down risers, Dick begins with a planed 2" thick hardwood block. Using a template, he marks the curved decorative wedge line and cuts and grinds the wedge contact surfaces to a precision fit. He then glues the wedge laminations between the riser pieces with Resourcenol wood glue and "C" clamps the composites together.

When the riser is dried, Dick uses another template to outline the limb attachment surfaces and grinds them on a vertical sander. He drills the limb attachment bushing and alignment pin holes using a drill-guide jig system. Dick taps the bushing holes then screws the threaded bushings into the epoxied holes. Dick's limb attachment system uses a different riser-to-pin spacing on each limb to prevent accidental limb inversion.

GLUE-UP

An hour before gluing up a one-piece bow, Dick selects and prepares his limb composites. First he grinds the corewoods to final thickness to provide fresh, clean gluing surfaces. He then uses a table saw to cut scarf joints on the butt ends of the matching corewoods and glues these overlapping butts together with Resourcenol. This produces continuous laminations which add strength to the center of the bow.

He masking tapes the non-gluing surfaces of the fiberglass to protect them from stray glue, then wipes all composite gluing surfaces with acetone. This ensures residue-free bonding surfaces. But Dick cautions that it's important to wear rubber gloves when working with toxic acetone as it can be absorbed through the skin.

Dick mixes his thick butterscotch-looking epoxy by weight in a plastic cup. Using waxed paper cups can result in small fragments of wax getting into the glue which can reduce the epoxy's bonding qualities. Next Dick lays his laminates on elevated gluing boards which allow excess glue to run off the sides. He then spreads an even coat of epoxy on all contact surfaces and lays the composites in his form. Coating each contact surface is important as it allows the glue to penetrate into the fibers of the laminations, which is crucial to achieving a strong bond.

Dick makes his forms from laminated Douglas fir and they mirror the back of his bows. He covers the sweeping form surface with a strip of fiberglass to help make it smooth. Before glue-up he cleans the form surface to remove any hardened glue or wood chips which could dimple a pressed bow. He then covers the form with cellophane to protect it from runny glue. Dick positions his laminations to achieve a built-in tiller. He lays on a galvanized metal pressure strip and his air hose, securing the upper half of the press. He applies seventy-five pounds of air pressure to the hose, squeezing the glued composites together.

HATCHING A BOW

Next, the pressed composites in the form are placed in Dick's bow oven which heats and expands the air hose even more, adding ten to fifteen pounds more pressure. His oven is heated with a thermostat-controlled space heater which cures the glue at 140 degrees for five hours. After the heat is turned off, the pressed bow is allowed to completely cool in the form overnight.

Using a string, Dick marks the bow's centerline on the back near the tips and fadeouts. He then positions a limb template on his reference points and marks the shape of both limbs. On his longbows, Dick uses the whining table saw to cut the limb's rough shape, and he uses his band saw on recurves. He grinds them to the template lines with a belt sander and band saws out the sight window.

He rasps the handle down to its general shape, then smooths and rounds the limb edges with belt and hand sanders. Dick files in rough string nocks and braces the bow to check for limb alignment, tiller, and bow weight.

Dick aligns his longbow limbs by sighting down the string and removing material from the side of the limbs. He strives for a 1/8" to 1/4" positive tiller in his longbows and makes minor adjustments by sanding the edges of the belly fiberglass. He adjusts poundage by rounding the belly and slightly rounding the edges on the back. The rounded limbs are finish shaped using a pneumatic-sleeved spindle sander.

When crafting a take-down recurve, Dick aligns and tillers the limbs on their matching handle. And when building new limbs for returning customers, he has them ship their original handle so he can shape the fadeout edges and adjust the limbs to specifically fit.

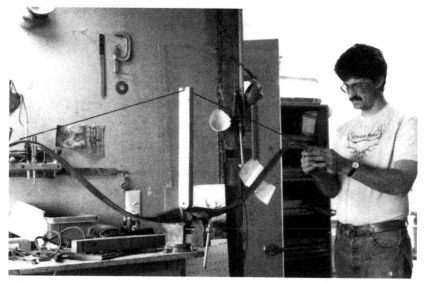

CHECKING HIS STYK WITH A STICK — Dick sights down the braced bow to ensure proper dynamic limb alignment.

To check alignment he strings the recurve, then braces the string with a stick to about 18" of draw. He makes minor adjustments in the string nock depth until the string tracks true and both limbs are aligned. Then he grinds material off the limb edge until the nocks are an even depth.

TIP WORK

After filing the nocks, Dick marks where the string naturally tracks on the recurve belly, then he shoots the bow several times. If the string returns to its marked position, Dick files in the belly string groove. But if tracks slightly off the mark after being shot, he slightly files one of the string nocks until it tracks true.

For his tip overlays, Dick uses a thin piece of riser wood overlain with a piece of buffalo, bighorn sheep, or antelope horn. He roughens up the tip fiberglass with sandpaper and epoxies on the tip overlays using clamps. The overlay glue is heat cured with special little tip curing ovens made from coffee cans equipped with fifteen watt light bulbs. The rims of the cans are notched and one is set over each tip heating them to 100 degrees.

Dick also laminates belly overlays on his recurves. These thin pieces of riser wood are installed the same way as the tip overlays, adding more strength and providing extra material for filing in the string groove. These belly overlays also make the limbs a little easier to line-up and help keep them from twisting.

Once they are dried, the overlays are feathered into the limb using a small drill-operated drum sander. To prevent scratching the limb fiberglass, Dick clamps on a thin strip of wood next to the overlay.

Dick likes to cut deep string nocks on his recurves, close to the center of the limb, because it helps keep the limbs in alignment and prevents limb twist. When feathering the nocks to the belly, Dick stops short of making a full shaped "Y" string groove because different strings have varying "Y" configurations.

NO NEED TO CAMO

Dick finish sands the bow with 220 grit paper and then wipes it down with lacquer thinner to remove dust and residue. Dick then sprays on four to five coats of undiluted Fullerplast as a main filler coat. After it dries for a day, he sands the finish with 320 grit paper and inks on the bow information. The bow is wiped down with a tack cloth and mist sprayed with a thinned Fullerplast, producing a slightly textured satin finish and cutting reflective glare, yet displaying the natural woods under clear glass. "I do a lot of work finishing my bows, and if anybody camo-paints one of them, I get extremely upset."

A PROPER MARRIAGE

Dick's completed styks are custom products, which means he matches the customer with the right bow to help produce that special relationship between the traditional hunter and his weapon. "I like to find out someone's height and shooting form. That way I have a good correlation on how long his draw length should be, especially if he is shooting a longbow.

"Then I try to match the archer's draw length with the optimum bow length. If it's a customer's first longbow I recommend a longer bow because it will pull a little smoother. But if it's someone's second bow, I will try to talk them into a shorter bow for increased maneuverability. Plus, a guy will get better performance out of a shorter bow, especially if he has a shorter draw length."

Besides matching his customers with the right length and style bow, Dick is careful not to overbow his clients. "Most people peak out with bows they can shoot accurately and comfortably in the sixty to seventy pound range. Unless they are very dedicated, there are very few archers that can comfortably handle more than seventy pounds. Without a doubt, the most popular weight is sixty-five pounds."

No matter what poundage or length, Robertson Stykbows are a blend of natural beauty, high performance design, and custom crafting by a man driven to build bows. They characterize the essence of traditional bowhunting by offering the adventurous archer an elevated challenge in the bow-hunting game — a game that's not just measured by winning or losing, but by the way it's played — especially in the morning shadows of the Bitterroots.

Chapter Twenty-Four

TRAILS END CUSTOM RECURVES

BITTERROOT

To Flathead Indians of old, bitterroot was a large starchy root used for thickening food and for medicinal purposes. It supplemented their staff of life, the mighty buffalo, which provided them with food, tools, and shelter.

To botanists, bitterroot is a low-growing plant. Its pink sunburst flower hugs Western alpine soils. Introduced to science in 1807 by Meriwether Lewis, bitterroot blossoms profusely in Montana's rocky terrain. In fact, it's their state flower.

To geologists, Bitterroot is a diverse area of glacially-sculptured mountains surrounding a broad valley filled with over 3,000 feet of sediment. Much of the sediment is lacustrine, ancient lake bed clays deposited 10,000 years ago when glacial Lake Missoula filled Bitterroot Valley.

To trout fishermen, Bitterroot is a rock-strewn river meandering through willow thickets and past gravel bars, hiding lunker trout in shadowed riffles. It means spring evening hatches and grasshopper fly patterns of late summer.

To hunters, Bitterroot is a vast wilderness bordering Idaho, its rugged mountains harboring elk and mule deer. It means climbing through the morning mist up heart-pounding ridges to catch a glimpse of flashing antlers at first light.

And to traditional archery buffs, Bitterroot is the custom bowmaking capital of the nation, spawning more varieties of longbows and recurves than any corner of the country. It's home to Robertson Stykbows, Howard Hill Archery, Monarch Longbows, and Trails End Custom Recurves.

Finally, to residents of Ravalli County, Bitterroot is their home, their heritage, and the intertwined ecosystem of industry and people encompassing the expanse between the Bitterroot and Sapphire Ranges. The county seat is the small town of Hamilton sitting along Highway 93 and the Bitterroot River. It's a friendly place where people say "Howdy" on the street and still call a rusty-haired bowmaker, Sheriff.

BAD GUYS TO BOWS

Now the crafter of Trails End Custom Recurves, Dale Dye spent twenty-seven years enforcing the laws of the Bitterroot. Serving as Ravalli County Sheriff for twenty years, he caught his share of bad guys, with many captures involving intriguing and blood-chilling man hunts. But today Dale leads a peaceful life. "I didn't retire, I quit. I had all of the crooks, bad guys, and soft justice I could stand. So I pulled the plug. And I have never regretted it for a minute." For Dale the future now promises the silent thrills of bows, bulls, and buckskins.

Since leaving his duties as sheriff in January 1987, Dale has devoted himself full-time to the quiet world of custom bowmaking which he discovered in 1981. He supports his new love by belonging to the Montana Bowhunters Association and the Professional Bowhunters Society. He also belongs to the local band of bowmen, the Bitterroot Archers.

This wry-humored bowmaker was born in the Bitterroot and loves it. It's a sportsmen's paradise surrounded by immense tracts of US Forest Service land. "It's the only place in the world to live. Up until ten years ago you had to really look to find a no trespassing sign. You were welcome to hunt and fish just about anywhere. The hunting and fishing was tremendous. But we will never see it like it was twenty years ago."

Besides the sportsmen's opportunities, Dale likes the friendly small-town atmosphere of Hamilton where walking downtown usually generates a warm chorus of, "Mornin' Sheriff". "I noticed in big cities that nobody ever looks in your eyes when you're walking down the street, they all look at their feet. I came to the conclusion that if those people met a friend at the street corner and he wore a new pair of shoes, they would never spot him."

Dale lives on the east side of town where trout waters rush past his back door. Next to the house is Dale's converted barn bowmaking shop. The brightly lit main work room resembles an art studio and offers a serene view of the Bitterroot Mountains. He shares it with his ever faithful shadow and archery range sidekick, Con. "I was just getting out of the law enforcement business when I got that dog, and Con kind of sounded like a good name for him." Con's favorite rough-and-tumble playmate is Pee Wee, an albino ferret and the family house pet.

In addition to creating bows, Dale expresses himself artistically with oil paintings and soapstone sculptures. He also enjoys cabinetmaking and woodworking. These talents blended with his blacksmithing experience make a unique combination of skills that are revealed in his bow crafting. They're expressed in his attractively contoured risers, delicate logo inking, and specialized bowmaking equipment.

LOVE AT FIRST SIGHT

Dale became interested in bowhunting around 1977 when an archery acquaintance encouraged him to try the bow and arrow. Although it sounded fun, Dale didn't care for the looks of compounds, but he found an old recurve with a twisted limb. He heated the damaged limb, straightened it, and went bowhunting. After that first bow season, Dale oiled his lifelong hunting companions, his rifles, and retired them to the gun rack. "And I haven't hunted with a rifle since. Bowhunting was like love at first sight."

He may have been in love with archery, but like a teenager of his first date, Dale didn't have anyone to show him the right moves. "When I started shooting, I was trying to get plastic veins to fly off the shelf, and I had no idea whether there were cock or hen feathers on the arrow. I didn't even know that there was a big loop and a little loop on the bowstring."

Even though it was rough at first, Dale taught himself to shoot instinctively. Today, he's deadly accurate. "I generally shoot with my bow straight up and use a Mediterranean release, anchoring in the corner of my mouth. But I can also shoot effectively with the bow held canted or horizontally. I can even shoot on my back with the bow over my head, but not as accurately.

"Fred Bear and Howard Hill shot with a canted bow because when they started shooting, bows weren't center shot and they had small sight windows. The archer's paradox was real prevalent in those bows. By canting them, the archer's paradox was reduced and it gave the arrow more of an elevation boost. Also, without a sight window, it's hard to see the target unless you cant the bow. But today's bows are center shot with big sight windows, and I like to shoot mine straight up and down. If you read a ruler from the side, you are going to be off on your measurement, but if you look straight down on it, you'll get an accurate mark. The same principle holds true with my shooting."

Dale practices at least one day a week throughout the year and increases to several times per week as bow season approaches. "The best practice is both at targets and stump shooting. A lot of archers fool themselves when they go stump shooting by saying that they made a better shot than they really did. They say they can't hit a target because they're not paper shooters but claim they can knock the tassel off a blade of grass when stump shooting. But when I went stump shooting with them they didn't shoot that well. Targets keep you honest, the stumps help you judge distance."

To keep his shooting honed, Dale also attends as many organized shoots as he can. "The pressure that shoots put you under helps simulate the pressure that game animals put you under, and it helps strengthen your concentration. It also gives you a comparison on how you stand with the people you're shooting against."

THE ALPINE GAME

After a long summer of practice, Dale is ready for the real thing. Even though he spends much of his time bowhunting whitetails in Eastern Montana, his most exciting quarry is the monarch of the Bitterroots. "Elk are my favorite because they make noise and will come into your call. They're as sharp as a whitetail but more difficult to hunt. Elk are larger so they make a bigger target. And the country they inhabit makes hunting them enjoyable. Most of it is on Forest Service property, and I don't see many, if any, other bowhunters. But if you spook an elk you can't go back a couple of days later and expect him to come by. He will probably go two or three miles before he slows down and makes camp again. All of that makes him a more interesting target."

Dale's elk-stopping recurve pulls sixty-five pounds and he usually recommends at least sixty pounds for bowhunting elk. But it can be done with less. "A fifty to fifty-five pound bow will kill any elk in the country if you are sure of your target and limit yourself to the range you can accurately shoot. And you must have good arrow flight and good sharp broadheads. I have seen a moose shot completely through with a fifty-five pound bow shooting Black Diamond broadheads. And you can't get them any deader than dead."

When going after the masters of the meadows, Dale combines his calling skills, scouting techniques, and elk savvy. "Try to out-think them. Don't just go out in the woods bugling, hoping that one is going to stumble into you. You have to figure out where they are traveling and how they are going to react when you bugle. You have to learn where and when not to bugle, when to run and when to sit still. You may try your best to call in a bull, but if he's wearing a six-point rack, he has spent some years in the hills and has seen a few hunters and he's going to know pretty well how to react to keep from getting taken. And sometimes it all depends on luck."

During one elk hunt, Dale mixed in some luck with a bowhunter's prank and added a touch of Indian medicine. He was elk hunting with his brother-in-law on Medicine Point and was using his seventy-four pound Big Medicine recurve. "We hunted awhile, but didn't find any elk sign so I bugled in my brother-in-law just for kicks. He thought that I was an elk and we had a good laugh over it. We sat there eating lunch, laughing, talking, and not being quiet at all because we hadn't seen any game.

"After lunch, we split up to hunt back to the truck, and I bugled right after my brother-in-law disappeared. Then I heard this thumping coming up the hill, and I thought it was my brother-in-law getting even with me. But then I saw antler tines coming over the crest of the hill so I crouched down. I held up my bow and that bull walked up to within twenty-nine steps, stopped, and looked right at me. He watched me for so long that the bow got too heavy to hold up any longer. I realized that I either had to shoot or move. So I shot and caught him right behind the shoulder. He went down over the hill about fifty yards and laid down. I took my boots off and stalked him while keeping a big fir tree between us. It took me three hours to get within thirty yards, and then I put another arrow in him. That finished him."

Occasionally, Dale shares his elk hunting and bugling skills with beginning bowhunters, guiding them into the mysterious world of this regal deer. Despite his best efforts, sometimes his lessons in elk talk leave Dale dumbfounded. "This young fella, Greg, who bought one of my bows, had never hunted elk and I decided to take him hunting. He had never bugled and didn't even know what elk sounded like so I bugled for him and played a bugling tape. 'Now that,' I said, 'is a typical challenging call for a bull, but elk make a lot of different sounds. They are individualists just like people.'

"We went out in the hills that first day, and I met him for lunch and asked, 'How was your day?' Greg said, 'Well, I had a rotten day.' 'What do you mean?' I asked. 'Aw,' he said, 'I had some guy with one of those flute-bu-gles following me all over.' I asked, 'What do you mean a flute-bugle?' Greg said, 'Aw, it sounds just like he's playing a flute.'

"Now I thought this was unusual because we were way back up in the hills. And while we were sitting there eating lunch, a bull bugled down over the hill. 'See,' Greg said, 'there he is again. Ain't that a silly soundin' bugle? Why don't you fake him out Dale, and bugle him in.'

"Well, my hearing is not all that good, and I thought maybe it was some guy in camouflage. So I bulged and that bull answered, and I thought, 'Boy, that sure sounds real to me.' So I bugled again and that bull let out a roar, and I said, 'Hell, Greg, that ain't no man, that's an elk!' So we tore off over the hill and never did get a shot at him. That night in camp I explained again to Greg that elk make a lot of sounds that are not typical.

"The next morning we went hunting, and I was on a bald ridge not far from where Greg had heard this flute-bugle elk. I heard an elk down in the valley calling a cow with a long serenade whistle, not really a challenge. I got a fix on him and took off after him and soon ran into Greg. 'Where are you going?' he asked. I told him, 'I'm goin' after that bull elk down there.' 'I didn't hear any bull elk,' he said. 'Well it couldn't have been more than 100 yards from you,' I said. 'Gee,' he said, 'All I heard was some guy down in the bottom making some kind of half-coyote call.' Well, I explained to him that the sound was really a courting bull. By the time we got down there the elk had winded us and took off. We didn't get any game, but that was some hunt."

Besides tagging elk, Dale and his custom recurve have harvested Mon-tana whitetail and black bear. Dale also has his sights set on some of Montana's rarer species. "I want to take a moose in the worst way. I don't know why, because they aren't that difficult to hunt. But I just have this thing about getting a bull moose. Also, I've killed three mountain goats with a rifle. The first one I killed with a 30-06, the second one with a 30-30, and the third one with a muzzle-loader. Now it would be nice to get one with my bow."

BITTERROOT GEAR

When Dale slips into the Bitterroots, he tries to blend in with the sounds and sights of the forest. If the footing is noisy, he takes off his boots. To help hide, he wears camouflage. But Dale's camo is different and somewhat fitting for this western-humored clown. "I always felt that the most effective camo would be like a jester's suit with one blue leg and one red leg and opposite tones on each half. When you look at them they almost present an optical illusion. Duane Jessop's wife makes camo clothes, so I had her make me an outfit with one green leg and one brown leg, and the jacket with a reversed pattern. I've had hunting partners tell me, 'You are just about invisible out in the woods.' That color combination really helps break up your silhouette. But it looks terrible walking down the street."

To conceal his impish face, Dale uses a tight-knit camouflaged face sock with holes cut out for his eyes, nose, and mouth. "It clings to your face so that when you turn, it turns comfortably with you."

For arrowing elk or deer, Dale prefers a three-bladed fixed broadhead. His favorite, the Talon Copperhead, is manufactured by Bohning. "They are fairly lightweight, but strong. They weigh 145 grains and cut a three-point star in the hide. They're slim-lined enough that you get good penetration and good arrow flight. I've hunted with Snuffers, but they weigh about 200 grains and I had a little trouble with arrow flight. Plus, I'm an advocate of shooting a light arrow."

Dale prefers using Graphflex arrows because they're durable, as quiet as wood, and have a wide spine range. He fletches his own with colorful 5" feathers and uses snap-on nocks so they don't fall off the bowstring when he's up in a tree waiting for whitetails. "I also like a color on my shafts, so that when I'm out in the

ARMED FOR ELK — Dale's orthodox shooting style and his finely tuned gear, make a deadly combination on Bitterroot bulls.

woods shooting under marginal light conditions I can see the flight of my arrow." He carries his arrows in a Delta bowquiver.

Although he uses yarn ball string silencers, Dale doesn't care for brush buttons. "It's just another weight to put on your string that saps arrow speed."

The workhorse of Dale's traditional gear is his recently introduced sixty-two inch take-down recurve pulling sixty-five pounds. "I believe that the TD is a little smoother drawing and a bit more stable than my one-piece. I think it's because of the deflex in the limbs coming off of the handle. Also, I put a little more recurve in it to offset the deflex. I plan on redesigning my one-piece bow to put some of these features into it."

HANDCRAFTED BOWS

Dale's TRAILS END TD is a three-piece recurve. It's currently offered in a 62" length, and Dale plans to introduce limbs to also make 60" and 64" lengths. The bow has a mass weight of 2 pounds, 6 ounces, varying with the riser wood. It has a recommended brace height of 7¾" from the string to the throat.

Its handle section is 20" long, 1¾" wide, and narrows to 1¹⁄₁₆" through the rounded sight window. The window is cut ⅛" past center shot for clean arrow flight and is full cut for 3½" above the shelf and contours back to full width 6" above the shelf. The handle is approximately 3" thick and thins through the high-profile grip. The crowned arrow shelf is beveled on the edge and crested directly over the grip throat to enhance arrow flight.

This beautifully crafted handle section is commonly made from shedua which sandwiches a series of vertical African vermilion wedges. It's delicately sculptured with flowing contours and two ridges below the grip similar to an old Damon Howatt. The custom-shaped grip has a high profile that causes the hand to seat tightly under the shelf to improve the shooter's instinctive sight picture. The back is capped with clear fiberglass over matching core-wood veneer for strength and to help create a one-piece appearance.

The window-shelf area is equipped with a pony hair pad. The bow name is artfully black inked in the sight window and the bow specs are inked below the grip. Brass sight and quiver bushings are available.

The large-radius recurve limbs attach to the handle with a single bolt and one alignment pin. Both limbs have a working length of 17" from the fadeout to the string nock. Assembled, the bow measures 27" between the fadeouts. The limbs narrow from 1¹¹⁄₁₆" wide at the fadeouts to 1¹⁄₁₆" at the string nocks. They are constructed from 7¾" fadeout wedges with one flat

ART FORM AND FUNCTION — Dale's striking recurves offer beauty and top performance. His grip forces the hand tight under the shelf for an optimum instinctive picture.

grain back lamination and one edge-grain belly lamination.

These tapered laminations are commonly red elm enveloped in clear fiberglass, but they are also offered in maple with black or brown fiberglass. The 3" long tip overlays are made from three contrasting layers of hardwood. The belly tip also has a 4" long overlay of matching riser wood which contains a full cut "Y" string groove. Both the handle and limbs are coated with a satin-luster finish.

The following draw/force measurements suggest the smoothness of Dales's 62" red elm TD:

DRAW LENGTH	25"	26"	27"	28"	29"
DRAW WEIGHT	52½#	56#	59#	62#	65½#

To check for relative speed, Dale shot this 62" take-down using 29", 2117 aluminum arrows. These 535 grain arrows had three 5" feathers, and snap-on nocks. Dale drew the arrows 28⅜", used a shooting glove, and had a clean release. The bowstring was standard Dacron without accessories. The average arrow speed for this bow, arrow, and shooter combination was 191 fps.

Trails End also offers a one-piece bow in a 60" Swift Medicine, a 62" Good Medicine, and a 64" Big Medicine. Their construction, dimensions, and performance are similar to Dale's take-down.

FUN AND A GOOD TIME

Dale became interested in recurves before the resurgence of traditional archery when there weren't many recurves on the market to choose. "I always liked the style and grace of the recurve, but I couldn't find a new custom recurve that I could afford. So I told my wife that I was going to build my own. And that's how I got started building bows. She thought I was crazy then. Probably still does."

He made his first bow in 1981. It was a one-piece recurve with an African vermilion handle that copied an old Damon Howatt. It shot well and Dale even killed a couple of deer with it. "I thought it was a work of art, the most beautiful thing that had come down the pike. But it's really pretty crude compared with what I am making now."

Shortly after making that first bow, Dale started making and selling more of his recurves, and in no time expanded it into a full-time job. "I really enjoy making bows more than I ever anticipated. It's something I can do by myself, and I enjoy talking to archers from around the country. Bowmaking is the complete opposite of law enforcement. This is all fun, and everybody is looking for a good time."

To stay competitive in the market, Dale eventually introduced his take-down model. "I really didn't want to build a take-down because there are so many problems associated with making them. But I had so many requests that I finally decided that I should design one. And it took a year and a half to develop."

When searching for a name for his new bowmaking business, Dale called upon his fondness for western art. "One of my idols is Charlie Russell, the western painter. I probably have every piece of literature published on him. Just prior to his death he was going to retire in California. He was going to call the place Trails End because for him it was. I have some similarities to him because this is probably going to be the last job I will ever have. So I figured Trails End would be a good name for my company, and as it says in my brochure, my bow will bring your trophy to the end of the trail."

DISTINCTIVE QUALITY

One of the noted features of a Trails End recurve is the striking furniture-quality riser. It exudes warm tones from the exotic hardwoods with attractive grain patterns exposed by finely sculptured contours. Below the grip, small ridges on the handle give it distinction and provide extra strength. The riser resembles one of the west's most famous recurves. "The first one I built was a copy of a Damon Howatt, and although I have changed its design some, try as I will, I can't get away from it. Whoever designed that bow put a good deal of thought into it."

Dale's risers blend solid exotics with contrasting vertical wedges. He likes to use at least three wedges, to make the handle esthetically pleasing and to add strength by providing different grain characteristics in the alternating pieces. "A traditional bow should be a thing of beauty and have some class to it. You might be able to turn out a little better consistency and quality with a laminated maple handle, but that isn't traditional. There's nothing like the look and feel of exotic wood."

His handle incorporates a grip designed to give a positive hand seat tight under the shelf. "You get quicker bow alignment if the handle forces your hand into an exact position. And to keep the shelf close to the hand, I've curved the shelf to conform with the natural curvature of your hand. I also bevel the outer shelf edge to give better feather clearance and improve arrow flight."

AN EYE-CATCHING CORE

Dale's most popular corewood, and by far the most attractive, is Michigan red elm. Under clear glass, it makes the limbs naturally camouflaged and traditionally beautiful. He uses edge grain on the belly for strength and the more contrasting flat grain on the back for eye-catching distinction.

Although it is cheaper to buy pretapered laminations, Dale cuts, grinds, and tapers his own to maintain strict specifications and quality control. First he rips them from a two inch plank using his band saw. When sawing, he inspects the uniformity and alignment of the grain, cutting only the laminations that he believes will pass his bend test. After he cuts and tapers them, Dale flexes each lamination into a half circle, checking for uniformity of arc and to see if both ends stay in plane. "With red elm you have to watch for variations in grain density. When you find tighter growth rings on one side of a lamination and give it the bend test, it squirrels off to one side like a corkscrew."

When making laminations, Dale carefully maintains consecutively cut pieces as a matched pair. "Because of the varying bending characteristics of the wood you have to pair them. If you don't, it will throw the tiller out and cause the action of the limbs to be off."

After sawing a batch of laminations, Dale runs them through his thickness drum sander using a coarse thirty-six grit paper to grind rough grooves into the laminations. The rough surface improves glue bonding. Once they are ground smooth, he puts a pair of laminations on a taper board and runs them through again, producing tapered corewoods. Each pair receives one final grinding to a precise thickness within six hours before bow glue up to remove the outer oxidized layer. "Wood oxidizes and that oxidation can effect the strength of your glue bond."

His grinding and sawing generates plenty of wood dust, but Dale's shop doesn't show it. The dust is sucked away in his homemade dust collection system constructed from a series of hoses and pipes going into a large collection box equipped with eighteen nylon cloth filters. "I copied it from the wood shop at the high school. Their system cost 6,000 dollars. But I looked it over and went home and duplicated it for twenty-five dollars."

Before glue up, Dale checks his laminations with a moisture meter, and if necessary, dries them until their moisture content is below eight percent. Even though the Bitterroot's climate is relatively dry, Dale has his shop "wood widgit" keep an eye on changing humidity conditions. His widgit is a homemade humidity device using a needle to balance a piece of end-grain shedua. It's so sensitive that Dale can tell when storm fronts or hot spells are approaching.

Special homemade jigs allow Dale to firmly clamp his glued riser composites in two directions.

A BLEND OF EXOTICS

To make a riser, Dale first cuts and planes the exotic hardwood components, varying their overall thickness to accommodate a customer's hand size. Using homemade square clamping jigs, Dale glues the woods together with a special adhesive that withstands excessive heat and is absolutely waterproof. "I used to glue my handle composites together with epoxy. But epoxy is heat sensitive, and my bowmaking process subjects the handle to two heatings which could weaken its glue joints."

Once it's dried, Dale runs the riser composite through a jointer, making it flat and parallel on both sides. He then marks the riser shape using a template, and band saws and grinds it to precisely fit the form. His take-down risers are shaped to fit a small form for gluing on the back capping, and his one-piece riser is shaped to fit the belly of the bow form.

On his one-piece riser and take-down fadeout wedges, Dale checks the exact taper of his fadeouts with a micrometer and ruler, making sure both fadeout tapers are identical. "I grind them on the drum sander until the paper-thin ends begin to serrate all the way across which will make them fade right into the limb composites. If you don't grind them paper-thin, they will have little air pockets where the riser connects to the limbs, and those will always be weak spots in the bow."

IT'S IN THE FORM

Dale's bow form reflects his blacksmith and woodworking skills. The bottom belly half of his form is made from three pieces of plywood glued together and reinforced with lengths of angle iron bolted to each side to keep

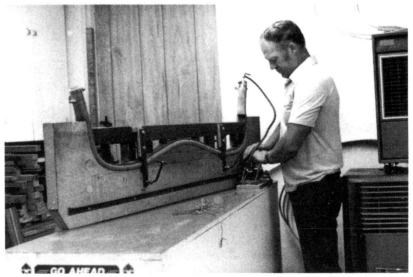

WOOD N' IRON — Dale uses a hand pump to pressure up the air hose in his steel reinforced press.

it true. "When you subject the form to sixty pounds of air hose pressure plus 130 degrees of temperature, the form will bend to one side if the laminations and hose aren't perfectly lined up. And if the form takes a set, it's ruined. It's a common problem with wood forms." Dale's form surface is covered with a strip of Formica which provides a smooth and strong surface for the fiberglass to slide on during pressing. The form center has a small locator pin which fits into positioning holes drilled into the composites. This prevents them from sliding during glue up.

The top half of Dale's press is homemade from heavy reinforced steel. It can't warp and helps keep the bottom wooden half in alignment.

Before glue up, Dale masking tapes the non-gluing surface of the fiberglass and cleans the gluing side with acetone. He also waxes and covers his form with plastic wrap.

Using a one inch high board to elevate the laminations, Dale spreads epoxy on all contact surfaces and lays the composites up in the form. He positions them over the alignment pin and laces them in place with a waxed string. He then puts on a metal strip and the air hose, and bolts on the top steel half of the press.

Although Dale has a large electric air compressor, he slowly inflates the air hose with a small hand pump to prevent trapping any air bubbles between the laminations. He pumps in ten pounds of air to squeeze the laminations snug, aligns them, and then pumps the hose up to sixty pounds.

Dale puts the form into his thermostat-regulated and timer-controlled curing oven. It's heated with four heat lamps and equipped with a metal heat shield to prevent the lamps from directly heating the form. The glued composites are cured at 120 to 130 degrees for six hours and then allowed to cool in the oven for twenty-four hours.

TRIMMING THE ROUGH

After the bow has cooled, Dale grinds the ragged epoxy off the edges and cuts the limb tips to proper length. Dale uses a template to trace the limb shapes and band saws and grinds them to rough dimensions.

Next he epoxies on the tip and belly limb overlays with "C" clamps and cures them with his "Maxwell House" can heaters equipped with fifteen watt light bulbs and a timer. These heaters are set over the limb tips, reach 110 degrees, and automatically shut off in four hours.

After the tip overlays have dried for twenty-four hours, Dale shapes them to template dimensions, ensuring consistent nock placement, angle, and depth. He then braces the bow and sights down the string to check for limb alignment. Using a small rat-tail file, he makes small adjustments in the string nock depth until the string tracks down the center of the bow. He then grinds the outside edge of the tip until both nocks are equal in depth.

By staggering the position of his laminations, Dale normally builds a 3/16" positive tiller into his limbs. But he also varies the tiller for shooters who string walk or shoot three fingers under. Minor tiller adjustments are made by removing material from the sides of the limbs.

Resembling a bow doctor, Dale uses his specialized bow cradle and high-speed tools to help him shape the delicate contours of his risers.

Dale marks the handle design with a template and band saws the sight window and general shape. Next he uses a vertical belt sander for rough shaping then attaches the bow to his bow cradle. It's an adjustable dual-arm holding device that acts like extra hands, allowing Dale to work on the bow at different angles. Illuminated by an overhead light and sitting in a roller-bottomed chair, Dale fashions the handle with his high-speed rotary rasp and air-sleeved drum sander. In the tight corners he uses cabinet makers' files and an old sheriff's elbow grease.

Once the riser is shaped, he shoots the bow and makes a final check on tip alignment and tiller. If the string tracks true, Dale marks the belly grooves and files them in the wood overlay down to the fiberglass. "I strongly believe that a hunting bow's string groove should retain the string in the center of the limb when going through brush, and it should help bring the string into the center during stringing."

Dales makes final poundage adjustments by rounding the limb edges and then finishes shaping the tips with a small drum sander and file. He final sands the bow with decreasing grit sizes from fifty to 220 grit sandpaper.

After final sanding, Dale sprays the bow's wood surfaces with eight coats of finish which is later sanded with a rubber sleeve drum sander using 220 grit paper. He repeats the process with four more coats, and after sanding inks on the delicate lettering. The bow then gets four more coats, is hand sanded with 320 grit paper, and final sprayed with three more coats. When using his spray gun, Dale is careful to only spray the fiberglass with a few coats to prevent a heavy buildup that might cause stress-cracking in the finish.

TAKE-DOWN STEPS

Dale caps his take-down handle back with a hardwood veneer and fiberglass. After it's taken out of the small handle press, it's installed in a drill guide jig and the bushing and alignment pin holes are drilled. The bushing hole is also tapped, threaded, and epoxied, and the threaded steel bushing is screwed in. The knurled alignment pin is forced into its epoxied hole. The limbs have different alignment pin spacing to prevent accidental limb inversion.

When making his take-down limbs, Dale glues them up as a one-piece unit resembling a short bow. He uses continuous pieces of fiberglass to help balance limb dynamics. After it's cured and cooled, he squares the sides and saws it in half. He then uses the guide jig to drill the main bushing and alignment pin holes. The holes are waxed for moisture protection and lubrication.

The rough handle and limbs are assembled and the bow is finished as a one-piece unit. This ensures that limb alignment, tiller, and shaping are precise with the matching handle. When returning customers want extra limbs, they must send their handle back to Dale so he can fashion a perfect match.

AN EYE FOR DETAIL

One of the trademarks of Dale's bows is his attention to detail. It shows from the contours of the handle to the way he dots the "i" in Trails End. It also shows on the order form where he even asks the customer to outline his hand. "I try to fit the handle with the customer's hand. By placing my hand over the top of their drawing, I can determine the approximate length and width of their hand, and judge how their bow should fit. You would be surprised at the different hand shapes and sizes. I have to vary the throat where the thumb and index finger meet by quite a bit according to the heft of the hand."

Even though Dale has a "bowyer's choice" of woods on his order form, he encourages customers to order a truly custom traditional bow. "Buying a custom bow means being able to request different riser materials, fiberglass, limb cores, and grip shapes. I will use anything that the customer requests as long as it's sound for the bow design. The buying public should be aware when they're buying a custom bow that they can expect more from a bowyer because they are paying an extra price for custom work. Otherwise, why not walk into some archery store and buy an over-the-counter bow."

Like the word Bitterroot, Trails End has many meanings. It means a custom bow. It means craftsmanship and quality materials. It means skilled bowmaking techniques with an eye for detail. It means fast shooting recurves that perform as good as they look. And for a rusty-haired sheriff, it means happy trails ahead.

Chapter Twenty-Five

HOWARD HILL ARCHERY

THE LEGEND

Many recognized Howard Hill as the genuine Robin Hood, splitting arrows and outshooting the King's finest bowmen while making Errol Flynn appear so amazing with the longbow. Theater goers across the country also marveled during his movie shorts when he topped each stunning shot with the next arrow. He was a man who made his living with a longbow, and in doing so, earned the distinction, "The Greatest Name in Archery."

Although the legendary Howard Hill died in his home state of Alabama in 1975, his vivid archery career and uncanny skill with a longbow helped inspire a nation of archery enthusiasts. Today, Howard's spirit of hunting the hard way lives on with the growing wave of traditional bowmen, many who emulate his fluid, effortless style.

During his flamboyant career, Hill made twenty-three archery movie shorts for Warner Brothers and starred in his own African adventure film, *Tembo*. Hill performed archery feats in seven motion pictures, including his most famous, *Robin Hood*.

Hill was a premier showman with bow and arrows. He astounded audiences at world's fairs, wild west shows, and sportsmen's shows throughout the United States where he displayed crowd-gasping feats with his longbow.

Although he enjoyed the limelight in front of the targets, Hill considered himself primarily a bowhunter. He was a man of the forests. During a lifetime of bowhunting in North America and Africa, Hill arrowed over 4,000 animals including over 130 different species. He was the first white man reported to down an African elephant with a bow and arrow.

Hill's adventure-filled exploits and amazing archery career are portrayed in the book, *Howard Hill; The Man and the Legend*. Its author, Craig Ekin, has shot Howard Hill longbows most of his life. He also spends his life building them.

PASSING THE TORCH

Years ago, Craig's uncle, Dick Garver, was a traffic control board member who tried to prevent a proposed freeway from going through Howard's California home. Howard and Dick struck up a friendship and later entered into a business relationship in which Dick and Ted Ekin, who were in the sporting goods business, made and sold Howard's archery products while Howard promoted them. Ted later sold his interest in the sporting goods store and moved Howard Hill Archery to Montana's Bitterroot Valley in 1968. Ted died in 1979, and his son Craig took up the reins of the traditional archery business.

Craig was born and raised in Los Angeles, California. There, his father introduced him to the thrills of archery when Craig was just four years old. That boyhood interest flourished with encouragement and instruction from "Mr. Archery" himself. "Howard was around a lot when I was a youngster. To me he was just Howard Hill. He wasn't 'Howard Hill the Greatest Archer' or the famous personality, he was just Howard, our family friend. He took me hunting when I was young, and I didn't realize then how special that was. But now I look back on it as quite an adventure."

Today, in his late thirties, Craig shares the bow business and the splendid view of the Bitterroot Valley from his hillside home, with wife, Evie, and their three children. Just a stone's throw from his house and bow shop is Craig's trout pound which boils at fish feeding time with four varieties of arm-size trout. He enjoys rearing fish and even has time between building bows and fletching arrows to catch an occasional "volunteer" for dinner.

A LITTLE TIME FOR WHITETAILS

Although Craig also loves bowhunting the Bitterroot, slipping away for a hunting trip is not as easy as wetting a line. His bowhunting opportunities are often overshadowed by other bowhunters; anxious archers awaiting their new Howard Hill longbows. "Our biggest sales are from back east where the seasons open in October. By the time our orders have slacked off, our September bow season is almost over. So I have to work my hunting in around fulfilling customer orders. I have a hard time telling customers they won't get their orders because I want to go hunting."

The pressure to fill bow orders usually lets up late in the Montana rifle season, and when it does, Craig grabs his longbow and sneaks down to the willow thickets near the house. Hunting pressure down in the bottoms area along the Bitterroot River, often drives whitetail bucks up to the higher brushy areas. And some of these bucks make the mistake of hanging around Howard Hill Archery.

A heavy ten point rack that most Easterners would drool over, sits on top of Craig's bow curing oven next to another dandy set of antlers. They're evidence of lingering bucks near the shop. "These bucks were coming out between ten and eleven in the morning. I didn't see them the first thing in the morning. They seem to have learned that the hunters are out there early and they wait until midday before they travel. These bucks here are okay, but they're not really big for Montana whitetails."

Craig knows what big is. At 6' 2", and 230 pounds, he's a big man who shoots big bows. His hunting longbow pulls seventy-two pounds. Although it's a stiff bow for most men, it pulls easily compared to his practice bow. To stay in shape, this ex-karate buff lifts weights and practices shooting his 125 pound longbow, twice the bow that most archers shoot. "After you're used to shooting 125 pounds, you don't even have to think when pulling a seventy-two pounder. All of your attention and concentration can be focused on aiming at the animal." Shooting a 125 pound longbow may seem like a exceptional feat, but Craig has shot a 160 pound longbow and drawn one that pulled 172 pounds.

When toting his heavyweight longbow in the woods, Craig often heads for the east side of the Bitterroot Valley where he hunts his favorite Montana game, the mule deer. His preferred method is stalking, and when sneaking through the brush, he carries a blend of Howard Hill's best. "My favorite bow is one that I made not too long ago. It has thin layers of yew under clear fiberglass and four laminations of bamboo. It gives me the performance of the bamboo and yet the appearance of yew."

ARROWS AND ARROWS

Most traditionalists get a thrill out of making their own hunting arrows. But for Craig the task is far from novel — he started making arrows when he was eight years old. Now his arrowsmithing takes a big bite out of both his days and nights. When he "stays with it for a day," he can turn out ten to twelve dozen custom arrows that have been spine tested, grain weighed, double dipped, crested, fletched, and the feathers burned and ground. His personal hunting arrows have the same quality that he builds into all Hill arrows. Craig prefers a stained shaft fletched with three red 5½" offset feathers and equipped with Mercury speed nocks. He doesn't care for a helical fletch as they make excessive feather noise in flight.

Although he carefully separates his cedar shafting by grain weight and spine, Craig believes most longbow shooters wouldn't notice a 100 grain weight change in their arrows because of the longbow's unique quality of casting both heavy and light shafts about the same. "With the longbow it's surprising how it takes extra arrow weight and throws it out there, with the exception of real long shots. I made up a prototype of the elephant broadhead Howard took to Africa. It weighed 320 grains which is twice what our regular broadhead weighs. I shot it at sixty yards with my seventy-two pound longbow, and I didn't have any change in elevation.

"Howard proved that there were more variables with the archer than there were with arrows. He would be at a tournament with a group of people watching him shoot, and he would take a couple of arrows from each person. They could be shafts for bows pulling forty to 100 pounds. He would then take his bow and shoot everyone's arrows into a box."

On his hunting shafts, Craig mounts Howard Hill broadheads vertically to reduce windplaning. He points out that horizontally mounted heads can cause the arrow to rise before the feathers can stabilize it. Craig sharpens his broadheads with an eight inch mill bastard file by stroking it parallel to the blade.

Besides having a reputation for taking and holding a keen edge, the two-bladed Hill broadheads are famous for penetration. "My arrows have passed completely through every deer that I have shot. Three years ago I went hunting with a guy and we were together when we saw these three deer. I let him shoot first and the buck heard his release and lifted its head up, looked for a second, and then went back to feeding. The arrow went completely through the chest cavity and stuck in the ground on the other side of the deer. He went ten feet and that was it.

"Two years ago another guy shot a whitetail through both shoulder blades before the arrow stopped. That was with one of our sixty-four pound longbows. Howard Hill broadheads are designed to cut through bone like that."

THE HILL STYLE

To keep his shooting eye sharp for bucks, Craig practices by roving around, stump shooting at varying distances and elevations. "Most people fall short by not practicing field shooting situations. They go out to a bale with a target on it and shoot until they can hit the bull's eye or relatively close to it. Then they figure they are ready for hunting, but that's not what they encounter when hunting. Bowhunting is going out in the woods and seeing an animal and letting your mind automatically judge the distance as you are pulling the bow up and shooting. The only way you can achieve that is by practicing it. After a while, you will be surprised by how fast your mind will relate to your hands and tell you where you should be aiming."

When he's shooting, Craig uses the natural fluid technique he learned as a boy. It's the Hill style. "I cant my bow, lean into the shot, and slightly bend my left elbow. Instead of being withdrawn from the sight picture, this style of shooting puts you into it. Holding the bow straight up and down covers some of your target, but by canting the bow, it exposes more of your target so you see it better."

Craig enjoys shooting his longbow but usually doesn't get the chance when attending traditional shoots. He's too busy showing his products. His favorite gathering is Michigan's Great Lakes Longbow Invitational sponsored by the Michigan Longbow Association. It's a fun-packed three days where he gets to match faces with the customers he has talked to by telephone, and he has the opportunity to show interested traditionalists what he and his products are like.

Hill's BIG FIVE longbow is one of the bows he proudly shows. It's Craig's favorite and Howard Hill Archery's top of the line longbow. This four lamination bow is designed after Hill's Sweetheart three lamination safari bow. Like all of Hill's longbows, it's available in lengths from 66" to 70", in two-inch increments. The bow has an approximate mass weight of 1 pound, 7 ounces, and an approximate brace height of 6½" from the string to the throat.

On the 66" bow, the one-piece bubinga or shedua riser measures 14½" between fadeouts, and is 2" thick. The riser and limb dimensions vary according to bow length and draw weight. The riser is approximately 1¼" wide and narrows to ⅞" through the sight window which is cut approximately ⅜" from center shot. The arrow shelf is extended with a thick piece of leather under the grip wrap, and the window-shelf junction is covered with suede leather. The Big Five has a traditional high-peaked grip which is slightly dished and covered with a single 4½" suede leather wrap. The peaked grip is designed to seat into the hand. Bow specs are inked below the grip, and the bow name and "Howard Hill" are inked on the limb bellies.

The slightly backset limbs exhibit a deep-cored design with a modified trapezoidal cross section tapering to the belly. The working length of the upper limb is 28¾" from the fadeout to the nock, and on the lower limb it is 27". The limbs narrow from 1¼" wide at the fadeouts to ½" at the string nocks.

They are constructed from four full-length back laminations of tapered and heat-tempered bamboo. They are bonded to the back of the riser and are faced and backed with brown, white, black, or clear fiberglass.

Instead of using tip overlays, the limb tips are strengthened with fiberglass tip wedges. These 2½" to 3" long wedges are used on all Hill longbows and are placed in front of the belly lamination. The fiberglass is slightly rounded on the edges of the limbs. Simple string nocks are cut flush into the sides and feather to the belly and the back. The bow is finished with a gloss Fullerplast.

The following draw/force measurements suggest the smoothness of draw on a Big Five 70" bamboo longbow:

DRAW LENGTH	25"	26"	27"	28"	29"
DRAW WEIGHT	53#	56#	59#	62#	66#

To check the relative speed, the author chronographed this 70" Big Five using 28¾", 520 grain cedar arrows. They were fletched with three 5" feathers and equipped with snap-on nocks. The author drew 28", used a glove, and had a slip-from-the finger release. The bowstring was a Flemish-twist Dacron without any accessories. The average arrow speed for this bow, arrow, and shooter combination was 176 fps.

The REDMAN is Hill's yew-cored longbow. It's distinctive butterscotch tones and fine grain are displayed under clear fiberglass. The historic yew wood core made of two back laminations and one belly lamination, gives this longbow a liveliness in the hand and makes it an eye-catcher. Its dimensions and appearance are similar to the Big Five.

The smoothness of draw is suggested from the following draw/force measurements taken on a 70" Redman longbow:

DRAW LENGTH	25"	26"	27"	28"	29"
DRAW WEIGHT	48#	51½#	55#	58#	61#

To check this 70" Redman for relative speed, the author chronographed this longbow using the same arrow and string combination noted for the Big Five. The average arrow speed for this bow, arrow, and shooter combination was 180 fps.

TREND SETTERS — Hill's Big Five (left in photos) remains one of the most copied longbow designs. The Redman (right in photos) blends classic Hill styling with west coast yew.

The TEMBO is Hill's standard longbow. Tembo is the African name for rogue elephant. Inspired by Hill's Grandma longbow, which Howard used to down three African elephants, the Tembo is similar to the Big Five except the riser is made from shedua or myrtlewood, and the limbs are constructed from three bamboo laminations.

Howard Hill Archery also offers the Half Breed, which has a recurve style handle, slightly reflexed limbs, and a combination bamboo-yew core.

For the longbow hobbyist, Craig offers specific draw weight glued longbow blanks that have been trimmed, tillered, and aligned. This gives the do-it-yourselfer a chance to shape and finish his own Hill longbow.

WEST SIDE OF THE BITTERROOT

Hill's line of longbows are created in the peaceful hills west of Hamilton, Montana. During the summer, the lazy mix of hissing sprinklers and buzzing hummingbirds drifts through the open shop doors, blending with similar sounds of emerging bows and arrows. The arrow shop has its own unique aroma of burnt feathers and glues while the bow room smells of corn chip-epoxy and pungent lacquers.

The shop resembles an overstocked greenhouse sprouting colorful clusters of arrows rooted in boxes, back-dropped with a grove of glistening longbows. Within this forest of archery flora, Craig juggles phone calls and paperwork at his desk, often flitting to the circular arrow fletching table or broadhead aligning station. He learned arrow making skills from his father and bow building talents from past Hill bowyer, Dan Schultz.

Helping to run the archery business is Craig's wife, Evie. Lending a hand with product manufacturing is arrowsmith and bowyer, Tom Hardy. Craig also gets bow building help from Lee and Ted Kramer in St. Ignatius, Montana and Tim Meigs in Carson City, Nevada. These experienced longbow makers have their own lines but also build stock bows for Howard Hill Archery.

TREASURE FROM THE ORIENT

One of the key components and trademarks of Hill longbows is their prized core material, Japanese bamboo. It's lightweight, tough, resilient, hard, and grinds and glues beautifully. All this and it's not even wood. Bamboo is a cane, the segmented stem of a tropical grass. "Because of bamboo's fiber content and alignment it's conducive for throwing out an arrow. You can actually put a string on a piece of bamboo and shoot it. It doesn't have to be laminated with fiberglass. Howard tried everything he could when trying to find the best possible core material because he made his living shooting the bow, and he had to have the best."

Craig gets his exclusive shipments of bow-quality bamboo through suppliers that Howard discovered in Japan. "When Howard selected this bamboo, he went to Japan and made an arrangement with the growers not to sell it to anyone else in the United States, and they still abide by that today. We've had individuals who worked for Howard Hill Archery try to buy our bamboo but the suppliers wouldn't sell."

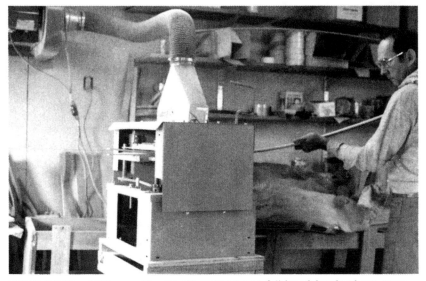

PRIZED GRASS — Hill bowyer, Tom Hardy, custom tapers full-length bamboo laminations— a trademark of Hill longbows.

As a longbow maker and avid archer, Craig has a variety of reasons for treasuring his oriental core material. "If a bowyer knows what he's doing and puts craftsmanship into all of his bows, the main performance difference in his bows will be the result of the limb core. Bamboo is by far the easiest core material to work with. It's easy to see when you have good glue coverage because the color of the bamboo changes. The laminations are one continuous piece so there is no jointing of tapers. It's also an extremely straight material and doesn't warp like wood. Bamboo grows in seasonal sections connected by a joint called a node. Even though these nodes are a bit denser, they bend the same as the rest of the lamination."

Once a year Craig receives his prized shipment of bamboo. The crates contain select bamboo strips cut from 10" diameter cane and trimmed into 2" wide strips that are 73" long. These strips still have some of the natural curvature of the cane. They are first run through an industrial planer and ground parallel on both sides. Then they are placed on tapered laminations with a reverse taper and run through a dimensional drum sander. This produces a continuous bow lamination which tapers from the middle. Besides making and using their own bamboo laminations, Howard Hill Archery also sells them to other bowyers.

IRON AND CLAMPS

Once a bowyer has good core materials, he needs a form to laminate them in. It's one of the most important items in any bowmaking operation. Hill's longbow form is made from a piece of channel iron that Craig had specially rolled and bent into their longbow shape. "When you start using

BOWMAKER'S SAUNA — Craig checks on two curing bows in the oven. The oven also warms composites before glue-up, making the thick epoxy easier to work with.

wood to make forms, you better figure that you will be replacing them pretty soon. Because the curing heat will warp and distort them, and just through normal wear and tear they are going to break down. But with a metal form you don't have to worry about replacing it as often."

His steel form mirrors the bow back and has a slight backset. "Our longbows have a five-eighths inch to three-quarter inch backset. This design makes an extremely smooth shooting bow, and because of the bamboo core you still get good cast out of it."

Before gluing up the composites, the form is covered with a strip of plastic which is later folded over on the sides of the glued compsites to capture all extruded glue. The continuous strip of backing fiberglass is masking taped on the non-gluing surface, and the composites are marked in the center for proper positioning in the form. Craig then preheats his composites in the bow oven to help the epoxy penetrate the porous laminations and the riser wood.

He also preheats his epoxy which helps when mixing and applying the thick glue. Craig even heats the gluing room between seventy-five and eighty degrees to make the epoxy easier to work with. At standard room temperature, the resin is so thick that it must be scraped from the can. "But when it's heated, it's more like runny honey and it's easy to spread." Since he started using this epoxy, Craig has not had a single bow delaminate.

During glue up, Craig and Tom usually work side-by-side, making the operation go faster and easier. It helps to have an extra pair of hands for lining up the laminations and another set of eyes for making sure all the composites are properly positioned.

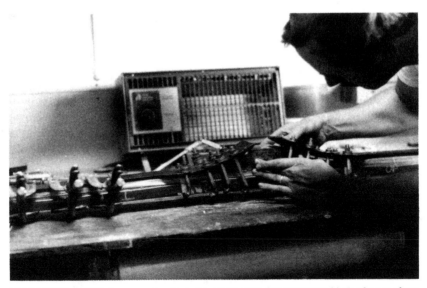

WON'T WARP — Hill's bows are laminated in their steel form using welder's clamps along the limbs and "J" bolts along the riser.

Craig applies epoxy to all of the contact surfaces and smears an extra glob on the fadeout. "Any place there is a joint, such as at the fadeouts, there is the possibility of having air pockets. I do the same thing on the tip wedges." The feathered fiberglass tip wedges are glued between the belly and the second lamination to provide limb tip strength and add contrast between the corewoods.

While Tom holds the glued composites in the form, Craig masking tapes them in place so he can begin clamping them together. Once they're taped in place, Craig puts a rubber gluing strip on top of the belly fiberglass and then lays on the steel pressure strip. Craig then begins squeezing the composites together using welder's clamps.

Starting at the tips, Craig clamps his way toward the riser. The adjustable clamps are set to take a firm bite, and he uses his big hands to snap them closed on the form and composites. After securing the clamps, Craig and Tom tighten a series of "J" bolts along the fadeout area. These bolts are attached to the pressure strip and hook onto the bottom of the form, providing the pressure along the curved portion of the fadeout and riser.

Once they're pressed, the glued composites are cured in Craig's oven for four hours. It's an insulated box, heated to 185 to 200 degrees with light bulbs. "Epoxy is strange stuff. It holds up well to the temperature that it's cured at. That's why bows that are cured at room temperature will have more delamination problems."

FROM FORM TO SHAPE

After it's cured, the emerging bow is unclamped from the form and the centerline and limb shapes are marked on the back. Then Tom saws the limbs to shape on the screaming table saw with a carbide-toothed blade. Tom has a good eye and a steady hand. He actually splits the pencil line with the whining blade.

Next, he grinds the limb's shape with belt and disk sanders. When rounding the limbs with the belt sander, Tom also rough shapes the riser. Once the tips have been shaped into rough form, he cuts in the string nocks so the bow can be braced to check for limb alignment, tiller, and weight.

Craig sights down the string and checks if it's tracking down the center of the bow and then checks the bow on a flat surface to be sure both limbs are in the same plane. Although his longbows are designed with a built in 1/8" and 3/16" positive tiller, Craig checks them, removing material from the limb belly if they need adjustment. Weight reduction is accomplished by sanding the limb edges and belly fiberglass.

After sanding, the lettering is inked and the bow sprayed with four to five coats of gloss Fullerplast. The suede grip, leather strike plate, and leather arrow shelf extension are trimmed by hand and glued in place.

Although their gloss finish lets the beauty of the bow shine through, some bowhunters opt to dull the limb glare. "If someone wants to dull up their bow we recommend waxing it with paste wax, and just leaving it on. When they want to remove it, they can just rub it down and have a nicely polished bow. It does the same thing as covering up the shine with camo paint. We also sell camouflaged longbow limb socks for those who want them."

ENJOYS THE CHALLENGE

Building custom longbows requires determining what combinations of corewoods and fiberglass will produce a specific bow weight. Craig enjoys the task, and is always anxious to find out how close he came to matching the expected weight. "There are so many variables. When making a certain weight bow, the bamboo, yew, and maple all require different core thickness. So hitting the exact bow weight is a challenge."

Sometimes Craig receives a special longbow order that really challenges his skills. One avid Hill customer repeatedly put Craig to the test. The longbowman is a burly lumberjack from Minnesota who has purchased six Hill longbows, all pulling over 110 pounds. "The last bow I made for him, he could draw twelve times within one minute, and that bow pulls 180 pounds at twenty-eight inches. I made up another one for him that pulls 207 pounds, but I think that one is strictly for trying to set a bow-drawing record."

Not all of Craig's customers can shoot bows heavy enough to penetrate several animals at once, so he helps them select a weight they can handle that will still drive home a heavy hunting arrow. If a customer discovers he bit off more bow than he can pull, Craig encourages him to return the bow, and he tries to fit the customer with a more comfortable weight. "A fifty to fifty-five pound longbow is sufficient to take deer, but if you are going for elk, I recommend no less than sixty and sixty-five pounds if a person can handle it. It's not that the lighter weight bow wouldn't kill an elk. But with bigger animals there is more chance of hitting bones that may stop an arrow. You want a bow with enough power to push an arrow through those bones. So I recommend a heavier bow for someone hunting elk and bear."

Each year more archers accept Howard's challenge of hunting the hard way by picking up a longbow and discovering the thrills and rewards that go with it. And Craig sees the longbow market as healthy and growing. "When we moved to Montana in 1968, there were only two main manufacturers of longbows in the United States. Now, twenty years later, there are over thirty manufacturers of longbows, yet our sales continue to increase every year. I think that says something about our products and the popularity of traditional archery."

A PROUD NAME

Even though the upswing in traditional archery has caused a proliferation of new bowmakers on the longbow scene, Craig warns that it's not easy breaking into the business. "It's an awful tough market to get into because there are so many bowyers out there now, and a lot of them are good craftsmen. Coming up with a better bow is very tough to do. All of the corewoods have been tried, and there is not much you can do to change the basic longbow designs that are out there today. Some people try getting into the longbow business because they want to do something they enjoy, but they end up getting out of it because the competition is so tough."

Tough competition requires quality products, bows that not only have a name, but stand up to it. "Initially it helps to have Howard Hill's name on our bows, but we have to produce the quality people keep coming back for. Our biggest form of advertising is the people out there with our bows telling others how our equipment performs. The quality has to be there."

Besides putting quality into their established line of bows, Craig looks ahead to designing longbows that will continue to capture the imagination and spirit of Hill customers. "We're thinking about putting out a commemorative elephant longbow. In 1950, Howard was the first white man to shoot an elephant with a longbow. So we have been checking into getting materials from Africa to make fifty commemorative bows.

"They would probably include some ivory overlays. The handle section would be made of African tamboti which we already have. But before I start building the first one, I want to be sure that I have enough of the special materials to make all fifty. It will be made after our Big Five design because that was the bow that Howard used in Africa. And it might incorporate both yew and bamboo in the core. Although Howard preferred bamboo, he liked the performance of yew and he especially liked its color."

Whatever materials Craig employs in his longbows, whether it's ivory, tamboti, yew, or bamboo, they represent bits of the man who many revere as the world's greatest archer — the man some knew as just Howard, the family friend.

Chapter Twenty-Six

MARTIN/HOWATT

THE TRADITIONAL FLOW

In the high desert country of south-central Washington, the Yakima river flows southeast through the broad Yakima Valley, past the sprawling fruit orchards, eventually merging with the mighty Columbia River. The Yakima's waters barely mingle with the torrent before they're joined by the waters of the Snake River, tumbling headlong on their journey down the Columbia's gnarled gorge.

Just as the Yakima's peaceful waters contribute to the force of the Columbia, a thirty-year flow of traditional bows from Yakima, Washington, has swelled the current of traditional archers sweeping across America. For Yakima is the birthplace of Damon Howatt bows.

MARTIN/HOWATT

Today, Damon Howatt, a prominent name in classic recurves, is owned and operated by Martin Archery. Martin's main facility is located in Walla Walla, Washington, and their Howatt recurve and longbow plant remains near its original site in Yakima. The Howatt operation, with its constant flow of traditional bows, is managed by long-time Howatt bowyer, Larry Hatfield.

Larry, a lifelong resident and cattle rancher of the Yakima Valley, became interested in archery in the early 1950s after a group of local archers asked him if they could use his range land to play archery golf. The sport looked so fun, that Larry soon visited Yakima bowyer, Damon Howatt, and got his first bow. Little did Larry suspect his new fascination would help shape his future. "My first Damon Howatt bow was yew wood with some kind of early facing and backing. I became good friends with some of the people working with Damon, and I would go over to the shop and watch them make bows.

"I was fascinated with bowmaking, and I was envious of the way they could shape out a bow. So I started making bows, and after building a couple I went to work for Damon in 1961. My first bow was made from a rosewood and partridge wood riser with maple laminations and early Gordon fiberglass."

Shortly after, Damon sold the company and retired. Not long into his retirement, Damon Howatt, one of the early pioneers in American archery, was killed in an automobile accident on his way to a fishing trip.

THE GOOD OL' DAYS

Back in the early sixties, Larry used his large ranch-tough hands and hand tools to muscle four to five bows a day into shape. "When I went to work for Damon we used a converted chicken house for our bowmaking shop. We had a crew to glue the bows up, but we hand-shaped them from a rough composite to finish sanding and then carried them over to the bow finish spraying building. We had no sales representatives back then. We just got a letter from a customer asking for a bow. They almost always enclosed a drawing of their hand and a sketch of how they liked to hold a bow. We just read their letter and then built their bow. It was a very personal way of making bows."

During the good ol' days of the fifties and sixties, a new wave of working recurves was the archery craze, and although all the major archery companies were making them, none claimed to have invented it: the recurve had been around for centuries. But U.S. patents hadn't. "The guy who patented the recurve was a postman who was delivering his mail and noticed that the design of bows had changed. He did a patent search and found that no one had patented the recurve, so he did. Damon thought that was really funny and admired the guy even though all the bow companies had to pay him a royalty.

"Back then, the pioneers in archery shared their ideas and improvements with the industry because it made the entire industry better and helped it grow. Damon used to talk with Fred Bear and Earl Hoyt and other manufacturers, exchanging ideas."

YAKIMA HUNTING

Today, Larry and three other early Howatt bowyers still work for the company. Larry oversees Howatt's bow production and also maintains his cattle ranching business. Even though both jobs are demanding and often tax his time during bow season, he loves to escape to the rugged hills with his longbow when he gets a chance. Not far from his home, the rocky canyons offer good deer and elk hunting and predators roam close by — evidenced by the bobcat he arrowed in his yard and by his biggest black bear, killed within a half mile of his house.

A large and rugged-framed predator himself, Larry is strictly a loner when he bowhunts. He likes to hunt out-of-the-way and isolated places overlooked by most hunters; places where cagey animals find refuge.

Although Larry occasionally arrows fur-bearing critters that growl and snarl, he's mostly a deer and elk hunter. He enjoys roaming the country they inhabit and the bowhunting challenges they offer. Larry has been around wild and domestic animals all of his life and for him, sneaking up to spittin' range of herd animals such as elk is almost as easy as falling off a log. "Elk are very predictable and to go kill one isn't that big of a deal. I turn my cattle loose in the woods and have to find them, and locating elk is pretty similar. I've got elk all over my range land so I know them well, and they're mostly just a nuisance. I've taken a lot of them over the years, but killing a big herd bull is a tremendous accomplishment. I've only taken three really big bulls, and I've never been able to call one in. I'd like to someday, and I really respect someone who has that ability."

Larry often blends his hunting with field testing new Howatt bows, and the Yakima's nasty fall weather, rough country, and big elk make a good combination for trying out a new stick. "Two years ago I went hunting with a new longbow we built. I left at ten in the morning and ended up in the middle of a really violent storm.

"I got into some brush and spotted elk. They were just holed up in the brush because the wind was blowing hard and sheets of rain were coming down. It wasn't that hard of a hunt because the elk were where they wanted to be, and all I had to do was not trip and fall into one of them. Before I moved in on them I laid down and strung my longbow. I spotted a nice fat cow that wasn't packing a calf so I shot her. Then it took me about six hours to get back home and get my horses, and I didn't get her packed out until about one the next morning."

HALF MULIE, HALF BLACKTAIL

Larry enjoys elk hunting, but local deer are his favorite bowhunting quarry. Most that inhabit his area are a cross between a mule deer and a blacktail and every bit as wary as both. Successfully stalking any deer is a tough job for most bowhunters, but as with elk hunting, Larry uses his common "animal sense" to close the gap to within paces. Recent evidence of his uncanny stalking ability graces his office wall. It's a set of heavy antlers from a buck Larry arrowed in its bed at eight yards. "To me, getting in really close like that and putting the arrow exactly where I want to hit the deer is what bowhunting is all about."

Larry's secret to getting within good bow range of deer isn't all sleuth and sneak. It's more in subtleties of body language, a common language animals understand. "The only thing I've ever found that scares an animal is a predator. If you don't move like a predator, animals aren't very concerned with you. Animals just have a way of moving, and if you get into their pattern of movement, it's no big deal to sneak up on them.

"I was raised around animals and there are certain ways to approach them. For instance, I like to go hunting when it's crunchy and icy. Everything makes noise on crunchy snow so I just make the same noises the deer make. Deer take several steps and then stop and listen because they can't hear very well when they're walking. So if you move the same way, they don't pay much attention to you. If a deer is watching me, I'll bend over at the waist and never look directly at him. If you move just like they do, you'll find that you're moving right along with them. Then you just get a little angle on them and when you get close enough, you shoot. I've never had to crawl on my stomach for hours choking rattlesnakes to death to get close to animals."

Even though getting within bow range seems natural for Larry, he admits that some animals are tougher to approach than others. "The older a deer gets, the smarter he gets, and the closer to people he lives, the smarter he is. Those are the deer that are hard to get up on. I can tell from their tracks that I have deer living on my ranch that I've seen once in my life. I've also found that the further a deer lives from people the easier it is to hunt. I used to pack goat hunters up into the Cascades at 7,500 to 9,000 feet. There are deer up there that have never seen people, and again, if you don't move like a predator you can walk within five feet of them. They're curious but they're not frightened."

MEMORABLE DEER

Although Larry has harvested many deer over the years, two stand out above the rest in his album of hunting memories. "When I shot my first deer with a bow I was using an old Howatt Mamba pulling seventy-five pounds. The deer was trying to sneak by me, and I'd been watching him for about a half hour. I had my bow on my lap and I just stayed still. He was stretched out and really sneaking and when he got parallel with me I picked up my bow and shot. I was using an old Ace express head and it went right through both shoulder blades and the arrow stuck in a tree. I've never killed a deer quicker."

His other memorable buck is the only deer mount to grace his wall at home. It's an old deer with spindly horns, but for Larry it's special. Unlike most hunters who hunt for horns, meat, or recognition, Larry hunts for the personal challenge, sometimes sneaking to within easy range, only to walk away without shooting. He knows who won the game. He sometimes also hunts with a rifle to spare an old friend from a crueler side of death. "I knew that deer for seventeen years. He was a straight mule deer but he was pinto colored and came from a white doe. He lived in our pasture, and I could have shot him a hundred times but I really liked that deer. There were about four years of his life when he had a tremendous rack and would have been a real trophy if you were horn hunting. But I don't horn hunt.

"During rifle hunting season he would hole up under a big pine tree that had fallen over. He would crawl up under that tree, and that's where he'd stay all day long. I've seen rifle hunters sitting on that fallen tree swinging their legs and looking around, and that old buck was just laying right under that tangle of limbs.

"Finally one year we saw he was going downhill. He was just skin and bones and didn't grow hardly any horn. He only had two points that were just as big around as my index finger. They were each twenty-seven inches long and he had a twenty-two inch spread. His teeth were worn off, and he didn't have anything left to exist on. He would have died that winter. I hated to think of him laying down for the last time and having the coyotes start eating on him. So my brother and I flipped a coin and whoever lost had to shoot him.

"I lost.

"I waited until rifle season and I got uphill from him. I knew him all his life and knew exactly where he'd run. My brother went down and heaved rocks under that fallen pine and he jumped out and started running right to me. I let him get up to full speed before I shot him right between the eyes. He was still running when he died, and he'll run forever in my memories."

BACK TO THE LONGBOW

Larry has hunted mostly with a recurve since he began bowhunting some thirty years ago, but in the last six years he has been drawn to the longbow. "I wanted to build a longbow that didn't kick because I never enjoyed the hand shock longbows were noted for, plus that was the main thing that turned a lot of people off about longbows. So I started playing with longbow designs and started shooting them. I was really having fun with the longbow, and then I went to The North American Longbow Safari. That was the most fun I've ever had in any type of competitive archery. It was very realistic. You only get one arrow per target. The targets are life-size animals, and they're difficult shooting conditions — you either hit or miss. We also shoot moving targets. It's two days of total enjoyment and as much fun as hunting.

"For four years I shot target archery heavily. That was about the time they were dividing the sport up into all these classes. They had a trophy for almost everybody that was there, tables just full of trophies. It just got disgusting. That's not what archery is all about. But at most of these longbow shoots they don't even have trophies. Usually it's something that someone made and not some piece of metal with standard engraving. It's a different attitude and nobody cares who wins. They're not there to win, they're there to share the joy of the sport."

Between longbow shoots, Larry practices frequently at home and around the shop. As hunting season approaches, he tries to shoot at home every evening. "I don't shoot at targets. I use something with a really small point of aim. I like to put three or four bottle caps on different bales and shoot at them from varying distances. I also like to get someone to throw or roll something for me to shoot at.

"To get ready for bowhunting, I stump shoot with my broadheads in the type of country I hunt in. I shoot out of canyons and across gullies. I like to shoot at deceptive angles and distances because shooting on level ground with ideal conditions won't help you much for hunting."

When hunting with his recurve, Larry limits his shots to fifty yards. With his longbow, he limits himself to twenty yards. "I've shot the same model recurve for so many years. I have a certain sight picture at forty yards and with the longbow that same picture is shorter. But at twenty yards shooting the longbow is like pointing my finger. I'm really confident at that range. The difference between shooting a recurve and a longbow is kind of like the difference between shooting a compound and a recurve. Longbows simply don't shoot as flat, and they're not as efficient as recurves which are quicker, a lot more stable, and more forgiving. The recurve may be my favorite hunting bow, but the longbow is definitely more fun, and it helped revive my interest in archery."

OPTIMUM BOW WEIGHT

When Larry first became interested in archery, he shot heavy bows. Most pulled somewhere around seventy-five pounds. For him that seemed like a reasonable draw weight because most of the guys who worked for Howatt in the early sixties shot heavy bows. "Damon just chuckled about me getting a seventy-five pound bow. Later he told me that the most efficient bow was about sixty pounds. You can pull a bow fifteen pounds heavier but you're not gaining much speed and you're losing efficiency."

Besides not being as efficient, heavy bows are often a frustrating struggle for new traditionalists. "Most people coming from a compound and buying their first longbow or recurve buy a bow that's twenty to thirty pounds too heavy. They're not capable of stringing, drawing, or shooting it properly."

Larry recommends that new traditional archers visit an archery shop where they can shoot stick bows in the forty pound range and discover what weight they're comfortable with. As their shooting muscles and form improve, they can later work up to an effective big game hunting weight. "There's no advantage in hunting with any composite fiberglass bow made today that pulls over sixty-five pounds. I know I can shoot through elk with a sixty pound longbow, and a fifty-five pound recurve will kill any North American big game animal very efficiently."

Larry also advises that new longbow shooters accept the limitations and challenges of the straight-limbed stick bow. "Most people can shoot a recurve much better than they can shoot a longbow because a recurve shoots from dead center of the sight window. You can get perfect arrow flight with no effort. But with a longbow, you're shooting off the side of the bow and the reaction of your wooden arrow is a lot different. The longbow is more erratic, and your arrows have to be really good to get consistent flight. I don't care who you are, if you shoot four arrows from a longbow you're going to hit four different places because the arrows simply aren't going to react the same."

HOMEMADE GEAR

Even though longbows are not as consistent, Larry enjoys hunting with one of his new longbow designs and has always hunted with wooden arrows. His favorite hunting arrows are made from the old compressed Forgewood shafting. They're heavy, for excellent penetration, and they fly great. Larry still tips them with old Ace express two-bladed broadheads.

He carries his arrows in the homemade quiver he built in 1956. "It resembles a Catquiver, and I made it from aluminum sprinkler pipe. I like it because I don't make much motion when I get an arrow, and I never carry more than four or five arrows in it."

Larry enjoys the lightness and versatility of his longbow when hunting. Besides shooting critters with it, he finds it helpful in bringing them out. "You can even use your longbow to drag a deer out. You just tie the front legs under the chin, slip your longbow through there, and start dragging. That way you don't have much deer on the ground."

MARTIN/HOWATT LINE-UP

Two of Martin/Howatt's most popular deer draggers are their ML-10 and ML-14 longbows. Although both bows are made from the same form and have similar dimensions, the ML-10 has a bubinga riser, maple corewoods, and brown fiberglass.

THE ML-14 boasts all zebra wood construction under clear fiberglass. "The ML-14 has a live feeling that we think is desirable and is the closest to a pure traditional bow that we have been able to come. It's like shooting a comparable yew wood bow because you can feel the reaction of the limbs bending and recovering. We're also coming out with a new longbow that will actually shoot a little quicker than the ML-14, and I think it's a much more comfortable bow to shoot.

The ML-14 is 68" long and has an approximate mass weight of 1 pound, 1 ounce. Its highly contrasting zebra wood riser is 15½" long, 1¼" wide, and narrows to 1¹⁄₁₆" through the sight window which is cut approximately ³⁄₁₆" from center shot. The riser is 1¾" thick and exhibits simple traditional lines. The flat grip is rounded on the belly and somewhat squared where it blends into the backing glass. The grip is covered with a 4" light brown leather wrap. The shelf-window junction is not equipped with a shelf or strike pad.

The limbs exhibit a 1½" sweeping reflex and are 1¼" wide at the fadeouts, narrowing to ⁹⁄₁₆" at the nocks. The upper limb has a working length of 27½" and the working length of the lower limb is 24¾". The limbs are constructed from two back laminations and one belly lamination of tapered zebra wood enveloped in clear fiberglass. The limb edges are rounded. String nocks are flush cut on the sides and the tips do not have overlays. Like all Howatt bows, the ML-14 is finished in a semi-gloss Fuller-plast finish.

The SUPER DIABLO is one of the classic recurve stars from Howatt's early line. "My favorite Howatt of all time is the old Super Diablo. It really hasn't changed much. It's exactly the same limb design, and we've changed the handle slightly for appearance. It's an extremely fast and stable bow, and sometimes when I get disgusted practicing with my longbow, I'm tempted to pick up my Super Diablo because I know right where it shoots."

The Super Diablo is 60" long and has a mass weight of 1 pound, 14 ounces. Its recommended brace height is about 8¼" from the string to the throat.

The Diablo's riser is 23¼" long between fadeouts, 1⅝" wide, and narrows to ¾" through the center shot sight window. The flat sight window is full cut for 4½" above the shelf and contours back to full riser width 6⅝" above the shelf. The riser is 3⅛" thick and thins through the moderately high-profiled grip. The riser belly is decoratively overlaid with four layers of white and black fiberglass.

The riser is constructed from zebra wood sandwiching a vertical decorative wedge of grey-dyed laminated maple bracketed by thin veneers. The butterscotch-toned zebra wood exhibits darker brown grain patterns and dark stippled wood pores. An accessory bushing is mounted on the back 5¼" below the shelf, and the window is equipped with an elevated plastic rest. The riser displays simple flowing lines and a sculptured ridge on the sides near the accessory bushing.

The recurve limbs each have a working length of 18" from the fadeout to the nock, and narrow from 1¾" wide at the fadeouts to ⅝" at the nocks. They are constructed from one back lamination and one belly lamination of zebra wood enveloped in clear fiberglass. The limbs have belly and back tip overlays made from zebra wood over laminated maple. The tips have flush cut nocks which grade into a nicely crafted string "Y" in the 4½" long belly overlay.

The following force/draw measurements were recorded on a stock Super Diablo:

DRAW LENGTH	25"	26"	27"	28"	29"	30"
DRAW WEIGHT	38#	41#	43#	46#	48 ½#	51 ½#

The HUNTER is another long-standing workhorse in the Howatt recurve line-up. This 62" recurve has a mass weight of 2 pounds, 1 ounce, and a brace height similar to the Super Diablo.

"We've fiddled with our Hunter handle a little but we don't mess with the limbs. They've been proven over thousands of bows and a lot of years. It's an excellent limb design and we have no reason to change it. We sell more Hunters by far than any of our other models. The closest to it is our Lynx take-down which will shoot right along with the Hunter. The Lynx is a quick one, and we sell a lot of them in Europe for competition because they're so fast and stable."

The Hunter's riser is 26" long between fadeouts, 1¾" wide, and narrows to ¾" through the center shot sight window. The riser is about 3" thick and thins through the grip. It's made from solid brown hardwood with five contrasting veneers making up the ¼" vertical decorative riser wedge. The overall riser shape is similar to the Super Diablo.

The limb working length, dimensions and overlays are similar to the Super Diablo except that the corewood is solid maple enveloped in black fiberglass.

The following draw/force measurements were recorded on a stock Hunter:

DRAW LENGTH	25"	26"	27"	28"	29"	30"
DRAW WEIGHT	49#	52#	55#	58#	61#	65#

Martin/Howatt also offers the MTD three-piece take-down recurve, their white glass Ventura, and the 58" Mamba. "We used to build the Mamba back in the late fifties and early sixties and I later revived it. We even built 130

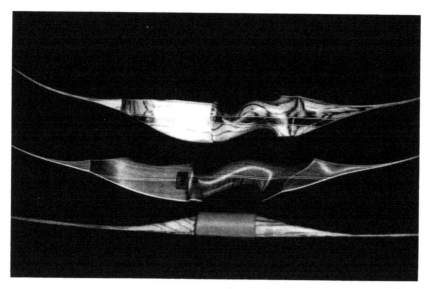

THE MARTIN/HOWATT TRADITIONAL LINE. The famous Super Diablo (top) and ML-14 longbow (bottom) boast zebra wood construction. The Hunter recurve (middle) remains a long-standing Howatt performer.

Mambas in the early sixties for the Army for use in Vietnam. It doesn't stack and even people with a long draw have very little finger pinch. It's light, extremely stable, and it's very quick. It shoots about as fast as our Hunter. Around sixty pounds it should shoot a hunting weight arrow at or above 200 feet per second. And that's with a standard twenty-strand string."

IMPORTANT DIFFERENCES

Although many bowmakers across the country use unique combinations of corewoods, glass, and riser components, only Martin/Howatt makes an all zebra wood bow. Securing a quality supply of the rare wood and then extracting bow-quality laminations is an involved process, but Larry thinks it's worth the effort. "Zebra wood produces a bow that really feels alive in your hands. We don't just use it for its looks. It's superior to maple in quickness of recovery, and is probably closer to yew wood in its characteristics than any wood available today. Yew wood is almost impossible to obtain on a reliable, commercial basis. In the entire Pacific Northwest I only know of one firm that cuts yew wood and they produce veneer only."

Larry's treasured supply of zebra wood comes from the Cameroons of western Africa. "It's strictly a rain forest species, and it's disappearing quite rapidly. All rain forest species of hardwoods are disappearing at the rate of up to 500 acres per hour every day around the world. In a short time there will be no more rain forest woods available. That's one reason why we're experimenting with other woods such as dyed laminated maple. Within a few years some of these exotic woods are going to be impossible to obtain."

Larry is picky about his woods and demands the best for Howatt bows. "We don't buy our zebra wood from suppliers in the United States because none have a quality grade. I get it from firms in Germany or Switzerland that cut it for the European furniture industry. Their quality grading standards are more than twice as stringent as American standards. I buy only clear, defect free zebra wood. I go to Seattle when it comes in, and I inspect it before it ever comes out of the container. They know I'm not a bit bashful about turning down a container load of wood."

Even though Larry is demanding in quality, much of the prized stock is culled when producing bow-quality laminations and risers. "We saw through a lot of zebra wood to get a bow because it's extremely difficult to produce no-defect laminations. Even with all our quality demand we still end up with less than sixty percent that we think is suitable for our product."

Martin/Howatt faces and backs their striking zebra wood bows with clear fiberglass. It not only displays the zebra-like contrast of the wood, but it's functionally superior. "Clear fiberglass is stronger than colored glass because it has no coloring additives. The materials they use to color other glass reduces the strength properties of the resin. White glass has been a troublesome glass because it's brittle from the resin coloring, and it really became noticeable in manufacturing compounds."

Besides using zebra wood for laminations, Martin/Howatt is one of the few bow manufacturers who use full-length back laminations in bow construction. "We use full-length laminations because we want to have grain continuity, which is important in a recurve and a must in a longbow. You need a minimum of two full-length laminations in a longbow because the bow bends in your hand, even though it's not visible. Full-length laminations add 150 percent more strength through the handle than butting two short laminations. For a longbow to be really efficient it must bend evenly from tip to tip, including through the handle section, and you can't achieve that without continuous laminations."

MAKING LAMS

To make laminations, they saw and grind full-length strips then taper them from the middle toward each tip. They have a sophisticated tapering machine that uses a thirty-six grit abrasive to taper both the thickness and grind the desired width.

On their recurves they use laminations with a dual taper. They taper from the riser toward the recurve, then get thicker again through the recurve. "Our dual taper is to control how the recurve opens during the draw. We want the recurve to completely open during the draw, and after release it should regain its original form in one motion without any reaction that would cause kick in the arrow. And we want it to recover as quickly as the materials can react."

Even though the ground laminations look perfect, Martin/Howatt gives each one a flex test, and if it twists or turns, they break it and throw it away. "We also do destructive testing on our limbs. We take a limb, put it in a vise, and smash it. Then we take a hammer and a chisel and go through it lamination by lamination and destroy it. We've found by producing our own quality laminations that we have a much stronger product."

THE RISER

When making their laminated risers, they epoxy glue, clamp, and heat cure several at the same time. The riser blocks are then band sawn and ground to shape. The belly and back shapes are ground on a horizontal grinder using profiling jigs that grind the riser to a template controlled shape. After grinding, the back of the fadeout is supported with a piece of wood, and the belly side of the fadeout is hand feathered on the grinder.

IN THE FORM

After the riser is finished, the composites are ready to be laid up in the form. Unlike most industrial bow presses where the entire top half of the press moves up and down, Howatt's are hinged in the middle over the riser area and both halves swing up at the ends during lay-up and then swing back down on the composites and are locked into place for pressing. Their forms are made from solid maple and reinforced with steel on all sides. The upper half of the press is equipped with an air hose that is inflated to eighty pounds for pressing the composites. Electric heat strips line both the top and bottom forms for curing the epoxy.

During lamination lay-up, they are careful not to use laminations consecutively cut from the same board. Mixing the laminations nullifies any grain characteristics in one piece and makes stronger limbs that are less prone to twisting.

GLUE CREEP

Epoxy is applied to all contact surfaces of the composites, then they are pressed and heat cured in the form for about a half hour. Despite the strength of bow components and the epoxies holding them together, glue creep continues to be a problem in today's bows. "Back in the early days, 3-M also built fiberglass and you could glue it with Urac. It's a tight glue that's very rigid and it doesn't creep. Now, everyone in the industry is forced to use a two-part epoxy that has glue creep which contributes to twisted limbs.

"Epoxy stretches, and anybody in today's industry who says you can't twist their bow limbs is telling you a story. You can just take their limb and bend it off to the side and it will stay there, but you can straighten it back out again if you know how. That's one of the biggest problems with recurves today. A bowmaker works hard to get a bow just perfect, and someone can string that bow improperly and twist it in a second."

Howatt uses sophisticated temperature sensing units in their presses that control the optimum glue curing temperature of 190 to 196 degrees for six minutes. That's a relatively high curing temperature, but it's designed to minimize glue creep. "Almost everybody in the industry uses Ren epoxy and Gordon glass recommends we work with Ren. There are two types of Ren

Using a drum sander, a Howatt bow builder brings the limbs into tiller by grinding off backing glass.

available. One is less temperature critical, but it's not as strong and it's a little more subject to glue creep. We use the other one because it's stronger even though it's more temperature critical. But there is a danger if you cure too warm. You can drive moisture out of the wood into your glue lines which causes the glue to chalk."

TIP-OUT

Once the bow is out of the form, the edges are ground clean and the tips are trimmed to length. The bow is then braced using cabling blocks strung on a steel cable. The metal cabling blocks are moved back and forth on the tips until the cable tracks true down both limbs. Because of glue creep and the tendency for limbs to stray when they're twisted, they carefully cable the limbs to determine their natural alignment, avoiding any sideways limb stress. The limb tips are marked on each side of the cabling blocks then ground to the marked width.

Next, string nocks are cut in the tips and the bow is braced to check tiller. They strive for about ¼" positive tiller on the upper limb, and they make any tillering adjustments by grinding off some of the backing glass on a limb. The tip overlays are epoxied on, and after they're cured, the tips are finished by hand. Most Howatt bows are custom orders and they bring a bow down to a desired weight by removing material from the edges of the limbs.

HAND SHAPING

After the limbs are aligned true and tillered, the riser is contoured by hand. First it's given a couple of rough cuts on the band saw and then it's

It takes a good eye and experience to fashion Howatt handles using wood eaters such as this large floppy belt sander.

freehand ground to shape using different size sanding drums, spindle sanders, and a floppy belt sander. It's a job that requires a good touch and plenty of skill, one that Larry performed for many years.

TOUGH FINISH

After final sanding, the bow is sprayed with a minimum of four coats of semi-gloss Fullerplast which is sanded between coats.

Larry and the crew at Howatt take pride producing proven traditional performers, and Larry suggests using common sense bow care to make them last. "You don't want to leave a strung bow in a warm place such as your closed car or in the back window of a pickup because most bows are glued at temperatures of 175 to 185 degrees. They could delaminate. Store your bow in a cool, dry environment. A damp basement is not a good place and neither is a dry warm closet.

"You should periodically inspect your bow for nicks where you may have hit it on a rock. If you spot a nick along the edge, you can take a piece of sandpaper and sand the nick out. That may keep your bow from delaminating or splintering the fiberglass."

THE WALLA WALLA CONNECTION

In close contact with the Howatt bow manufacturing operation is Martin/Howatt Sales Manager and Director of Research and Development, Terry Martin. Over the last several years Terry has seen their recurve production triple, a growing trend that gets stronger every year. "People are getting back into shooting recurves," says Terry, "primarily for fun. Sometimes people

PLENTY OF HAND WORK — Even though they use a variety of power sanders, each Howatt bow receives hand sanding and a critical eye.

who shoot compounds get too serious, and nobody is having any fun because they're all so intense trying to figure out every angle so they can be the winner.

"But if you go to a longbow tournament, those people are out there to have fun. They're not out there to shoot a real great score. No matter what kind of equipment you're using, you shouldn't just be out there to win, you should be shooting to have a good time in archery. But too often that's missed."

At Martin's main facility in Walla Walla, they produce the Martin line of compound bows and accessories. Although much of it isn't totally compatible with old-time archery and relaxed fun, one product they don't produce is crossbows. While several of the larger archery manufacturers were expanding into crossbow production, Terry and the crew at Martin were taking a hard look at what it could mean to the sport. "There was a movement by some crossbow manufacturers," Terry says, "to legalize crossbows during archery seasons. That would be a real disaster because you would eventually be shortening archery seasons.

"We had a compound crossbow developed, but in the long run we felt it would hurt the archery industry to promote the use of crossbows during archery season, so we didn't produce it. We're the only major company that helped fund the Professional Bowhunters Society study to help game commissions understand the difference between crossbows and compounds. The movement was so strong against crossbows that a lot of archery dealers wouldn't carry a company's products if they manufactured crossbows. We even discontinued selling the crossbow arrows that we carried for twenty years."

LOOKING AHEAD

Even though Larry relies on the decades of proven performance in some of their Howatt models, he also continues to design and build new traditional bows for the future. "Right now we're building bows for three years into the future because we like to get our new designs into people's hands, get back comments, and see how they hold up out in the field."

Besides getting comments from other hunters, Larry will no doubt do some intense field testing himself, especially if he can find some time during bow season. His longbow adventures may find him ambling like a deer through the crusted snow, or clinging to his longbow on a rain-swept ridge. His arrows may find their mark on an elusive bear or a bugling bull elk, but there's one animal that can pass within his bow range safely. It's the coyote.

Although they have a bad reputation among some ranchers, Larry admires these wild western dogs. He has even been known to save them from harm's way and give them a home. Larry has studied them intently, admiring their tenacity for life. The tough little dogs always adapt and hang on despite fluctuating cycles in an ever-changing environment. In some ways, they're like old-time bowyers.

Chapter Twenty-Seven

TIM MEIGS CUSTOM ARCHERY

GAMES OF CHANCE

In the afternoon shadows of the Sierras, just east of Lake Tahoe, sets Carson City, the capital of Nevada. Like Reno to the north, its casinos flicker non-stop, their dings, clangs, and clinkings of chance clattering through the night. Just a stone's throw from the flashing neon and high rollers, another Carson City establishment provides implements of intrigue and uncertainty for those daring enough to try for big stakes and a jackpot of personal rewards. It's the small shop of Tim Meigs, Carson City's traditional bowyer.

Tim's shop door is a corridor to the past. A small brass ship's bell hanging over the door chimes visitors into a world of old-time archery somewhere back in the 1950s. The shop is dimly lit, its high rough-sawn timber walls strewn with forty years of memories. Gazing down from the walls, aging deer and sheep mounts stare through the dust of a thousand crafted bows. The dust hangs heavy on their delicate eyelashes and decorates their horns with fuzzy cobweb drapes. Behind the old oak glass-topped counter, assorted longbows and recurves adorn rows of pegs. Above them, elderly and retired recurves rest quietly on higher racks between the patchwork of old animal hides, rattlesnake skins, flight-weary arrows, and comic strip archery cartoons.

Near the counter, another doorway sheds beams of light from between floor length chains of Budweiser pop tabs. Tim's baritone hum and file purrs drift through the doorway, both keeping tune with the country western cadence from a small radio. In his back room workshop, Tim leans over an emerging bow locked in the padded vise on his worn bench.

Although he's no casino gambler, Tim's bowyer's bench represents a poker table where he held on to his traditional bowmaking hand and gambled on the survival of the true spirit of archery, a spirit he has believed in for over forty years. "The interest in recurve bows had fallen to the point where we weren't selling many except to a few real die-hard archers. But then about eleven years ago the longbow became popular again and now the recurve is popular again, and that makes it worthwhile being a traditional bowmaker. The upswing in old-time archery has helped turn my business around."

Now Tim's cards are coming up aces.

ACCIDENTAL APPRECIATION

Tim grew up in Oakland, California, where as a teenager, he accidently gained a deep appreciation for a bow. "It was the day after Pearl Harbor, and I borrowed my brother's lemonwood bow. I was riding down a hill on my bicycle and somehow got the bow stuck in the spokes of the front wheel. I went flying end over tea kettle and broke the bow, so my parents made me replace it. I had my paper route, and I saved for about two months until I had the seven and a half dollars to buy a new bow. I replaced that bow and I've been shooting one ever since."

During the war years, Tim's interest in archery bloomed and he was introduced to bowmaking by engineer and part-time bowmaker, Bill Childs. "He was instrumental in establishing the California bowhunting season, and he was also an accomplished bowhunter and a good competitor in the early days of archery. Bill took me under his wing and taught me how to build a bow."

With Bill's guidance, Tim made his first bow around 1943. It was a modified lemonwood longbow with rawhide backing, and Tim still has this maiden bow in his collection at home. "Bill could take a piece of lemonwood, cut it out on a band saw, and be shooting the rough bow in fifteen minutes. We made a lot of bamboo-backed yew wood and osage bows, and we also backed them with sinew and whale bone or baleen. Most bows back then were static recurves and if you had good materials you had a good bow, but if your materials were bad, you had a lot of broken bows."

The bowyer's dilemma of broken bows took a giant step forward around 1945 when San Diego bowmaker, Frank Eicholtz, developed a fiberglass backing material. Tim began using the new miracle backing, but his bow-making was still fraught with disappointments. "When they first developed fiberglass and compatible glues, we had problems. I can remember gluing up bows and having them fall apart when I took them out of the form. Sometimes they lasted until I was applying the finish and then fell apart. For a lot of years, six out of every ten bows I built would break. Finally, Gordon came out with fiberglass and since then the bowmaking industry has stabilized."

After high school, Tim was drafted into the service and later worked at a bakery supply company and continued his bowmaking part-time. But he soon left the cake mixes behind to become a full-time bowmaker, joining the ranks of the fifty or so bowyers in California during the early 1950s.

CLOSER TO HUNTING CAMP

Tim built bows professionally in the San Francisco Bay area from 1954 until 1972 when he and his wife, Fern, moved to Nevada. "The main reason we moved was to get out of the metropolitan rat-race. We were returning from one of our annual Nevada hunting and fishing trips and stopped in Carson City to visit my son. It was so nice we decided to look around town. We found a house for sale and two weeks later moved here."

Now just stepping into his sixties, Tim continues his bowmaking with the zest of a man half his age and with undampered enthusiasm, despite his thirty-five years at the bowmaking bench. He tosses his lanky, six-foot-plus frame into his work, pausing only long enough to retrieve or replace a template or file before jumping back to his task. There's nothing casual about his bowmaking. Engrossed in each exacting step like a surgeon, white dust mask in place, Tim peers from behind his horn-rimmed glasses, eyes locked on the band saw incision and his over-sized ears listening for the right hum on the feathering sander. His bowmaking intensity changes him into a high-energy salesman when he answers the phone — his booming voice spilling past his curled lower lip, his eyebrows dancing at the prospect of making another custom bow.

GREAT NAMES AFIELD

Even though Tim enjoys making bows, he loves shooting them even more. He's shot at tournaments and bowhunted all over the United States, and during the past forty years this low-key bowman has shared the field with many of the greats in archery history. "I've hunted and shot with Hugh Rich and Glen St. Charles. I shot with Ben Pearson, and I hunted with Fred Bear for deer down in Kentucky in 1952. Howard Hill and I even hunted pack rats with our bows. Most people don't think of kicking a pack rat nest, getting them to run up oak trees and then shooting at them. But that can be a lot of fun, especially if you get one running up your leg!

"In 1956, Roy Hoff, Bill Childs, and I went to Alaska after caribou. Most people would think that back then Alaska had big game running all over the place and trout in every stream. But we spent three weeks up there, and I never shot an arrow at a caribou and never saw a trout. It's the same old story: you've got to be in the right spot at the right time. But we did get a lot of ptarmigan and it was an enjoyable trip. If I killed something or caught my limit of fish every time I went out, pretty soon it would be very boring. I have as much fun watching another archer shooting at an animal, even if he misses, as I would if I shot at it myself."

CALIFORNIA ACTION

Tim's introduction to the realm of big game bowhunting happened in 1943 when he and a friend were hunting California river bottoms for wild hogs. His friend's Doberman pinscher brought a wild hog to bay, and young Tim made quick work of the pig with his homemade bow.

Even though he has hunted a host of big game animals across America since that first pig, California's wild hogs remain one of Tim's favorite bow-hunting challenges. "Wild hogs are unique animals. They're tough to kill and they're very smart. Hogs can't see well so you can stalk them pretty good, but you have to watch their nose because it's every bit as sharp as a deer's. You usually find them feeding early in the morning and in the evening.

"You have to hit them in the right spot and you must use the right equipment or you aren't even going to hurt them. You should never use a multiple-bladed broadhead or ever shoot a hog in the shoulder because you won't get any penetration. I use a Black Diamond Eskimo, and I really try for a quartering away shot on them. I also use my seventy pound bow because of the hog's shoulder shield. On one pig we dressed, that shield was over two and a half inches thick and it was very tough cartilage. The local rancher told us about a black powder hunter who shot a big hog at fifty yards and knocked it down. But the pig got up and took off, and when they got over there, they found the flattened black powder ball laying on the ground. It didn't even penetrate the shield. But a sharp single-blade arrow from a heavy bow will penetrate it."

Another of Tim's bowhunting firsts happened during leave from the army after basic training. He flew home and decided to go deer hunting with a friend in Glenn County, north of Oakland. Tim's adventure started off on the wrong foot and ended with his first close encounter with a bear. "Before my buddy Burt Johnson and I could go hunting, we had to trim a palm tree for his mother in front of the house. In the process of trimming the tree I sprained my ankle, but we went hunting anyway.

"My only problem was that I had to walk with my right leg uphill or I would fall. We were working up this canyon and jumped a couple bucks. So Burt and I split up and he went down the hill and I continued working along the ridge. Soon I spotted a brown patch moving in some thick brush and I thought it was one of the bucks. I sneaked up there quietly and when I got within ten yards, I saw it was a brown-phase black bear tearing a log apart.

"Back then you could shoot bear during the deer season, and I was brash enough that I knew I could hit that bear in the eye if I wanted to. But I was scared because I could barely walk, let alone run. I drew back on that bear a couple times at close range but I didn't release the arrow. Finally, he started moving uphill and when he got out about sixty yards, I took a shot, but missed."

Even though he missed that first bear, Tim has taken his fair share of blacktail and mule deer during the last forty years of bowhunting. Like his first encounter with a bear, Tim's first arrowed buck stands out as a shining memory. "I was just a young fellow fresh out of high school back in 1947, and I went with a bunch of archers to hunt Crocker Mountain, which was a very good deer area. The mountain bordered a game refuge, and the deer would come out of the refuge during the evening and go up on Crocker Mountain. At daybreak, half the archers would line-up along the game refuge and the others would string out for about a mile up on the mountain and start moving the deer down the mountain toward the refuge.

"That morning I was one of the sitters along the refuge. I spotted this fork horn coming down the mountain and I got set. He was moving pretty fast and I shot right in front of him. My arrow turned him around and he started going back up the mountain so I shot again. This time I hit him, cutting the femoral artery."

SKINNY DIP DEER

Tim has made other running shots over the years, but he prefers his quarry standing still. He doesn't even like to shoot when they're walking. His ideal shot is about thirty yards, which is his "dead on" point of aim. Nowadays Tim limits his big game shots to within his range of confidence, but years ago it was common for archery greats to make telling shots at phenomenal distances. Tim was no exception. "I was hunting the Kiabab Forest and it was an extremely dry year. We hadn't seen any deer in several days and one morning we found this canyon with a water hole that had quite a few deer tracks around it.

"I was working down this ridge toward the water hole when I spotted two bucks drinking. They only looked about eighty yards away, so I though I'd shoot at one of those critters. But my arrow only made it about halfway across the meadow. So I shot another arrow and that one went a little farther, but the deer still didn't spook. I shot my third arrow and it hit in the water, spooked the deer, and they ran off.

"Then another buck came down to the water at the same spot as the first two bucks, so I figured I'd give it another try. That arrow arced out across the meadow and came down right into the buck. The deer stumbled in the water so I started running down there and slipped in a fresh cow pie, falling, and somehow breaking my bowstring. I finally got down there and this deer was swimming across the pond, so I put another string on my bow and shot it through the chest.

"Then it started to sink. So I quickly yanked off my pants and started into the water. Well, this was October and there was snow on the ground but I went out in that freezing water, got my deer, and dragged it out. About that time, my buddy arrived and wondered what I was doing out in the water. He thought I'd gone crazy.

"He paced off from where the deer was standing to where I shot from and it was 166 paces. Then I paced it at 160. I don't think that bow I had back in 1958 would have shot that arrow another foot farther. I had to get the soaked deer validated, and the game warden told me, 'Next time, we want you to shoot the deer, not drown it!' "

Today, Tim still enjoys his deer hunting, and each year he and archery shop and sagebrush companion, wife Fern, take their vacation near the little gold-mining ghost town of Jarbidge, Nevada. "It's one of my favorite fly-fishing trout spots. I catch mostly rainbow, and we combine our fishing with mule deer hunting. But we usually end up doing more fishing than we do hunting."

When he does grab his bow, Tim prefers to sit and glass during the mornings and then stalk the deer after they've bedded. "That gives me the thrill of a one-on-one situation. I'm not a trophy hunter, I just like getting out in the woods. But we do enjoy the meat, and we use all I harvest."

NOT TOO MUCH BOW

For deer hunting, Tim recommends that traditionalists use bows drawing at least forty pounds for women, and a bit more for men. But he cautions archers about getting overbowed. "Most people today shoot too heavy of a longbow. A well-shot arrow is the answer in bowhunting, not how much weight you're pulling. I've shot completely through a deer at twenty yards using a thirty-five pound bow.

"Four years ago I was selling mostly seventy-five to eighty pound bows back in the Michigan area. But in the last several years I've been selling a lot of sixty to sixty-five pound bows. Now archers are learning what bow weights they can handle accurately."

A majority of Tim's longbows are sixty-eight inches long and designed for an archer with a twenty-eight inch draw. But often the shooter short-changes himself. "Most people shooting a longbow don't get the efficiency out of the limbs because they don't draw the bow to the draw length it was made for. Too many people order a heavy sixty-eight inch bow and then only draw it twenty-six inches because they're overbowed. They would be a lot better off getting a shorter bow specifically made for a twenty-six inch draw, or better yet, a weight they could handle at twenty-eight inches."

Tim's preferred bow weight for deer hunting and general field shooting is sixty pounds, and he keeps his longbow muscles and instinctive eye tuned by shooting with Fern at the local Clear Creek Bowmen's range. Besides belonging to the local band of bowmen, Tim is also a member of the National Field Archery Association and the Nevada Bowhunters.

REALISTIC PRACTICE

Unmarked 3-D targets and stump shooting are Tim's favored forms of practice for polishing his bowhunting shooting skills. Although almost any target will do for general archery practice, Tim recommends that bowhunters practice on realistic targets. "Too many of the paper animal face targets and some of the 3-D targets are not life-size, and that can throw your distance estimation out of perspective. When you're hunting and you get a shot at an elk standing six-foot at the shoulders, but you've been practicing at a paper elk that's only three feet high, it's no wonder you miss."

Tim's favorite realistic traditional shoot is the yearly North American Longbow Safari held at different locales in the northwestern United States or southwestern Canada. "It's so realistic because you shoot at full-size 3-D animal targets set up in true hunting conditions. For example, one shot is at a full-size elephant down in a stream bed and you have to shoot though some willows. And the people there come to have fun and see everybody else's equipment. It's just a great all around shoot."

Although Tim practices methodically on the range, he lets his time-ingrained instincts take over when he gets a shot at game. Tim jokes, "Being a bowmaker all these years I know I've got something wrong with my mental condition, so I just let my instincts do the shooting instead of trying to second guess the shot. If I don't have much time to think about it, nine times out of ten I'll make a better shot. The majority of my first guesses about distance and trajectory are the best."

SIDE BY SIDE

Tim's first impression about instinctive arrow placement is often good, so good in fact that he usually places high in the final standings at traditional shoots. But even when Tim is shooting well, one familiar archer frequently betters him — even when he wins first place in the men's division. This high-scoring archer is Mrs. Tim Meigs.

Fern recently left her lengthy career in medical administration to join Tim in the shop where she now makes arrows and Flemish-twist bowstrings. Like Tim, she has been active in archery for forty years and is an intense longbow shooter. In 1987, she captured first place women's honors at the North American Longbow Safari, and at one time she was the number three woman archer in California.

Fern bought her first bow in 1947. It was yew wood with a plastic belly and baleen backing, but it lasted only a month before it broke. She bought her next bow from noted California bowyer, Frank Eicholtz. "Frank was a good personal friend," says Fern, "and one of the people in archery whom I admired most. He taught me a lot about shooting, especially about shooting from feeling."

Today Fern shoots a Meigs custom longbow. It's a fifty pound, sixty-four inch standard longbow with a bamboo core and a Papa Gene grip. As her score suggests, she shoots it well, using a relaxed form polished over the years. "To me," she says, "archery and fencing are the fine arts of sports. They are as old as man. Since they are truly creative processes, it's hard to tie them down to an exact set of rules.

"When I shoot, I hold the bow loosely. As I draw and concentrate on the target, my bow arm will settle and when it stops, it's usually in the right spot.

THE MEIGS TEAM — Fern puts Tim through the paces on the range but lends a helping hand around their archery shop.

If I say, 'No, that's not the right place,' that's the logical side of my brain interfering. When the logical side interferes I try to ignore it. I may even let the arrow down, take a deep breath to relax, and then do it again. We make shooting a bow much more difficult than it really is. It's really a very simple thing if we can be relaxed about it."

Besides shooting from feeling and working on mental relaxation, Fern uses visualization to help her shooting. "Before I shoot," she says, "I visualize my arrow in the spot I want to hit. Since I've been using visualization it's been amazing what I've been able to do with a longbow."

New longbow owners looking for shooting pointers get plenty of understanding and patience from Fern. She's the shooting instructor at the shop and she professionally guides beginning traditionalists through shooting mechanics.

Fern even takes her archery instruction skills outside the shop where she enthusiastically helps spread the joy of archery. "Teaching people about archery is delightful," she says. "One of my favorite things is working with the Girl Scouts every year. Last year in two days my friend and I taught over 300 Girl Scouts how to shoot, and every one of them had hands-on bow experience. I've also worked with the Boy Scouts helping them earn their merit badges by teaching them how to make arrows and bowstrings. I helped the scouts put up a shooting booth at the Boy Scout exposition and they won first place — everyone there wanted to shoot a bow and arrow. I've also applied to become the archery counselor in this area for the Boy Scouts."

Fern would also like to devote her skills to the introduction of archery in the special Olympics in her area. She's a wonderful example of giving back a bit of herself to the sport that has meant so much to her. "I do it," she says, "because you always get back more than you give. I get a great deal of satisfaction and a tremendous amount of pleasure seeing other people learn to enjoy archery."

TIM'S GEAR

Whether he's after tough hogs or sleek deer, Tim prefers the penetration and flight characteristics of a two-bladed Eskimo. "I sharpen them with a twelve inch mill bastard file then use a small carbide sharpener. After that they're plenty sharp. Many of these modular heads have so called razor-sharp blades, but they're not very sharp when you take them out of the package. They're a lazy man's way of bowhunting. Years ago, we used to glue injector razor blades on the Black Diamond and you really had a razor-sharp head. Matter of fact, I think there was more blood spilled from archers putting razor blades on their broadheads than there was from the deer they were shooting at."

Tim mounts his Eskimos on 30 1/4" wooden or aluminum shafts. He fletches his arrows with three 5" white feathers and uses white Nirk nocks. "The deer might be able to see the white, but I want to be able to see my arrows fly early in the morning or at dusk so I can see where I hit."

He carries his arrows in an old snap-on Bear bow quiver that he installs about a month before deer season so he can get used to the extra weight. He mounts the quiver on his favorite sixty pound, sixty-six inch Du-o-flex bow. "It has all the stability of a straight-end longbow and the shooting qualities of a recurve. I also have a matching one pulling seventy pounds that I use for elk hunting."

THE MEIGS LINE-UP

Tim's Du-o-flex is popular among his traditional customers. It fills the Meigs line along with his popular standard longbow, his three-piece take-down Du-o-flex, and his 62" flatbow. For small women and youth long-bowers, Tim builds his Little Stick 60" Longbow and his smaller Mity Stick 48" longbow. Tim even offers a semi-finished bow blank that requires final shaping, sanding, and finishing for the do-it-yourselfer who wants to try a hand at bowmaking.

The MEIGS LONGBOW is Tim's classical longbow with gently reflexed limbs and a deep core slightly trapezoided to the belly. It's offered in standard lengths of 66", 68", 69" and 70". Tim's custom 64" bow with an ebony riser and bamboo core has a mass weight of 1 pound, 3 ounces. It has a recommended brace height of 9" to 9½" from the front of the shelf to the string.

The hardwood riser measures 16" between fadeouts, is 2" thick, 1⅛" wide, and narrows to ¾" through the sight window. The crested arrow shelf is equipped with a small leather shelf extension and is padded with a suede leather pad and strike plate. The riser is available in standard shedua and bubinga or custom hardwoods. The 4¼" suede-wrapped grip is available in the classic high-peaked Hill style grip or Tim's special "Papa Gene" low-profile recurve grip.

The gentle sweeping limbs of Tim's unbraced longbow exhibit about one inch of reflex. Following the classic longbow design, the upper limb is one inch longer to provide a built-in tiller. On his 64" length, the upper limb has a working length of 24½" from the fadeout to the string nock. On his longer models the extra length occurs in the working limb length.

The limb cross section exhibits a slight trapezoid to the belly, and the edges of the fiberglass feather into the corewoods. The limbs narrow from 1⅛" wide at the fadeouts to ½" at the nocks. The limbs are usually constructed from two full-length tapered laminations on the back and one tapered lamination on the belly. Tim offers bamboo, maple, osage, and yew corewoods enveloped in green, brown, black, white, or clear fiberglass.

The tips are stiffened in the outer several inches with a fiberglass tip wedge inserted between the corewoods. Tip overlays are made from three layers of hardwoods feathered on the edges to expose the contrasting woods. Simple string nocks are cut flush on the sides and slightly grooved into the overlay. The bow is sprayed with a standard high-gloss Fullerplast finish which can be hand buffed to a high luster or steel wooled to a satin sheen.

For shooters who prefer the grip throat forward of the limbs, Tim offers his longbow with a reverse style handle where the riser extends away from the belly laminations.

To check his personal 64" bamboo-cored longbow for relative speed, Tim chronographed it using 30¼", 2216 aluminum arrows fletched with three 5" feathers and equipped with open-end nocks. The arrows each weighed 540 grains. Tim's bow pulled 63 pounds at his 30" draw, and the bowstring was Flemish-twist Dacron equipped with small rubber tab string silencers. Tim used a leather glove, drew the arrows 30", and had a fairly clean release. The average arrow speed for this bow, arrow, and shooter combination was 188 fps.

The following draw/force measurements were recorded on Tim's 64" bamboo longbow:

DRAW LENGTH	25"	26"	27"	28"	29"	30"
DRAW WEIGHT	47#	50#	53#	56#	59½#	63#

The DU-O-FLEX offers archers the smooth pulling and fast shooting qualities of a recurve blended with the lightness and simple lines of a reflexed longbow. The slim-throated handle is set forward of the fadeouts which makes the bow less susceptible to torquing and has contributed to its popularity. The Du-o-flex turned out to be so popular, in fact, that Tim also developed the travel-convenient take-down model with interchangeable limbs that attach to the laminated hardwood riser with a single bolt and alignment pin system.

The standard length of the one-piece Du-o-flex is 65" and of the take-down it is 66". The one-piece bow has a mass weight of 1 pound, 9 ounces, and a recommended brace height of 8½" from the string to the throat. The limbs exhibit a deflex coming off the 24" long riser then sweep into a pronounced reflex that stops short of being a true recurve as the braced string doesn't touch the belly of the limbs. It's the uniform unfolding of these heavily reflexed limbs that gives the Du-o-flex its smoothness and cast.

The solid hardwood riser is a slim 1¼" wide and narrows to ⅝" through the sight window which is cut near center shot. The riser is 2½" thick and thins to 1¾" across the grip's throat. The arrow shelf is crested and the sight window rounded for clean arrow flight. The sight window is full cut for 4½" above the shelf and contours back to full riser width 5½" above the shelf. The low-profile pistol grip thins through the riser to provide positive hand seat and a comfortable grip for almost any hand size.

The sweeping limbs have a 20½" working length and narrow from 1¼" wide at the fadeouts to ½" at the nocks. They have relatively square edges and are constructed from a single belly and a single back lamination of tapered solid maple enveloped in brown fiberglass. A single layer of matching riser wood is used for the 1½" long tip overlays. The string nocks and finish are similar to the longbow.

To check his Du-o-flex for relative speed, Tim shot the same 2216 aluminum arrows using his 59 pound, at 30" draw bow. The bow was equipped with a Flemish Dacron string without accessories. The average chronographed arrow speed was an impressive 198 fps.

The following draw/force measurements suggest the smoothness of Tim's 65" one-piece Du-o-flex:

DRAW LENGTH	25"	26"	27"	28"	29"	30"
DRAW WEIGHT	45#	47#	50#	53#	56#	59#

OLD-TIME ARCHERY IN CARSON CITY. Tim's longbow (left of bull's eye) offers a custom "Papa Gene" modified recurve grip. His one-piece and take-down Du-o-flex bows blend the performance of a recurve with the lines and weight of a longbow.

AN EVOLUTION OF BOWS

Tim's bows represent a forty year evolutionary process involving proven design, modern materials, and input from his customers. The current design of his traditional longbow was introduced in 1977 when Tim was building longbows for the Howard Hill Company. "I followed their basic design and made a few of my own alterations. The bow is slightly tapered to the belly like Hill used to do. Their reason for tapering the bow to the belly was to reduce the draw weight by taking some of the stress off the belly. But trapezoiding to the belly doesn't always make a better shooting bow. I've made some bows with a reverse trapezoid, and I believe you get a more efficient bow. But I also think it puts more stress on the materials and the bow may not last."

A recent feature of Tim's longbows has gained popularity among his west coast customers. It's his Papa Gene grip. A cross between a low-profile recurve grip and a dished longbow grip, it indexes the throat of the hand tight under the shelf for an enhanced instinctive sight picture. "Papa Gene is a gentleman I've known for over thirty years, and he's getting back into shooting a longbow after many years of not being able to shoot at all. Several years ago he had a cancer operation that removed the muscles around his left shoulder and neck area. Now he can't raise his left arm up or use a traditional longbow grip.

"So he brought me a piece of roughed out pine in the shape of a grip that he could hold and that would allow him to move his arm. I reworked one of his longbow handles to match that grip and named that grip style after him. With the Papa Gene grip, your hand stays where you put it and it's much more comfortable to shoot."

Fern has the Papa Gene grip on her longbow and she swears by it. "I want a grip that my hand fits into the same way every time I shoot," she says, "so I don't have to worry about where my hand is positioned. By moving the hand from one side to the other on a grip you can throw your groups off target. But with the Papa Gene grip I don't have that problem."

Tim's Du-o-flex is another star in his traditional line-up that was influenced by a customer's wishes. The Du-o-flex and its take-down counterpart are truly a blend of the old and the new. "I initially started building the Du-o-flex about twenty-five years ago. Back then, I built flat-limbed longbows and recurves, but I wanted a combination of the two. So I came out with the Du-o-flex, and it was a very popular bow in the San Francisco Bay area for several years. But then I got heavy into recurves and stopped making it.

"About three years ago a customer saw my old Du-o-flex hanging on the rack and he wanted to shoot it. He really liked it and wanted me to build him one but I told him I didn't think I had the old form. Besides, I was more than busy enough building my longbows.

"But he was very persistent so I dug around, found the old form, and put the bow together for him. He thought it shot great and soon I started building them for a few people, and the word got out and lots of people stated wanting them. Then I developed the take-down version so that with three sets of limbs you can hunt anything from moose to rabbits."

Tim's Du-o-flex has a deflexed handle with a reverse attitude riser that puts the hand in front of the limbs and prevents bow torque. "It's a very forgiving bow to shoot, and it's almost impossible to affect the arrow flight by torquing it. You get the smoothness of the deflex and the action of the reflex to give it cast. But it's not classified as a true longbow at some of the traditional shoots, so I don't push it if someone also wants it for shoots. But it's a real efficient hunting bow."

CREATING OLD-TIME ARCHERY

To create his Du-o-flex or a longbow, Tim begins by crafting the riser section. He buys exotic hardwoods from MacBeth Hardwoods in Berkley, California, and insists on quality straight-grain wood.

Using a template, Tim draws the riser outline on a squared hardwood block and band saws its shape. Then, using an oscillating spindle sander, he grinds it to precisely fit both halves of his bow form. Tim has used this patternmaker's grinding device for thirty-five years. Its rotating sanding spindle hums at high-speed and rhythmically oscillates up and down several inches. The oscillation prevents sanding drum wear and allows precision sanding. During grinding, Tim backs the riser with a block of wood to keep it square to the spindle. "That's especially important on the fadeouts where it's narrow so there's no tendency to lean it one way or the other."

When the riser fits the bow form so precisely that no light shines between the contact, Tim feathers the fadeouts to an edge thin enough to see light through the wood fibers. "I'm exacting on my form-to-riser fit because it gives me a better glue bond, and it's very important to get the fadeouts as paper-thin as possible so you don't have exceptional stress areas at the ends of the riser."

DIFFERENT CORES FOR DIFFERENT BOWS

Although Tim offers maple, yew, bamboo, and osage corewoods, he likes working with maple the best because of its straight grain and uniform characteristics. "Yew is also pretty consistent, but bamboo can vary in density and springiness from one piece to another. Occasionally a bamboo bow comes out a bit heavy even though it has been built to exact tolerances. As far as speed, yew, maple, and bamboo are all about the same."

Because of their characteristics, different corewoods perform better in different bows. In the Du-o-flex Tim prefers maple, and in his longbows he favors bamboo or yew. He especially prefers bamboo in heavyweight long-bows because of its durability.

Tim gets rough bamboo strips from Craig Ekin at Howard Hill Archery in Montana. A friend supplies him with Oregon yew wood and Tim ages it at least six months to a year before making it into laminations. He also buys hard rock maple boards to make his own laminations, and sometimes buys parallel laminations from the Old Master Crafters and tapers them himself.

MAKING BLACK EBONY DUST — Using his patternmaker's spindle sander, Tim backs an emerging riser with a block of wood and gently feathers the fadeouts.

FULL-LENGTH LAMINATIONS

Tim prefers making and using full-length laminations because of their consistency and because they don't require butt end splicing. Plus, full-length laminations add extra strength through the handle. When working with maple, he trims off a full-length ⅛" thick strip on the band saw and grinds it to a desired butt end thickness. Many bowmakers use a thickness sanding drum to grind laminations, but Tim uses a table saw equipped with a special carbide grinding blade. By backing the lamination on his table saw fence with a tapered board, he tapers each end of the lamination until it measures his desired thickness. Tim's process requires repeated grinding runs and micrometer checks before he's satisfied with the exact thickness. "I've pushed so many thousands of laminations through this grinding blade on my table saw that I know how to keep the proper tension on it to get the lamination within a couple of thousandths of an inch from one end to the other."

When tapering laminations Tim refers to his "bow recipe book" to be sure he hits the desired bow weight. Detailed records show the composites, thickness, and tapers of every bow he has built in the last thirty-plus years. These records also reveal that black fiberglass will produce a bow heavier than other colors of glass.

Tim also selects and precisely measures the fiberglass before tapering his final lamination. "A lot of times the glass is not exact, and on my longbows a thickness of just three thousandths of an inch will add a pound of draw weight. So I check the glass thickness and then alter my core thickness to achieve the overall composite thickness for an exact draw weight."

Although the dry Carson City climate usually doesn't pose any moisture absorption problems for his laminations, Tim stores his bamboo in his curing oven which helps temper it and dry out any residual moisture.

GLUE-UP

Before gluing up the composites, Tim vacuums the dust from the laminations with his big shop vac. He lays a strip of fiberglass on the form surface to provide a smooth gluing surface and covers it with wax paper. His form is made from laminated alder boards, and the bottom one-piece female form represents the bow back and the top segmented pieces represent the belly.

Tim arranges his laminations with opposing grain direction in alternating laminations to help neutralize any internal tendencies in the corewoods. Using Bohning's commercial bow epoxy mixed by weight, Tim applies glue to all contact surfaces and lays up the composites in the form. When working with bamboo, he applies a heavy coat of epoxy and watches it to be sure the glue isn't absorbed into the porous cane. When all of the composites are properly positioned, Tim lays on another strip of wax paper and fiberglass and begins clamping down the upper sections of the form using "C" clamps, starting at the riser and working toward the tips.

Tim places the pressed composites in his glue-curing oven for a minimum of three and a half hours. His heavy-duty timer-equipped oven is

ALWAYS IN ACTION — Tim tapers his full-length laminations using his carbide table saw blade.

electrically heated to 160 degrees and circulates the heat with an internal blower.

After the glued bow has cooled all night, Tim pops it from the form and grinds the edges down using a horizontal belt sander until all the composites are flush.

TAKING SHAPE

Next he puts masking tape on the back of the bow blank and traces the bow shape from a full-length fiberglass template. To cut down on later sanding, Tim adjusts his band saw table to an angle and trims the bow to its shape, producing the rough trapezoidal limb cross section. He grinds the handle to its rough shape then grinds out the saw marks along the limb edges using his belt sander. Once the bow is roughed out, Tim epoxies and "C" clamps on the tip overlays and cures them in the oven for about an hour.

After filing in rough string nocks, Tim braces the bow and checks the limb alignment, removing material off the sides of the limbs until the string tracks true down the center. If the bow draws too heavily, Tim grinds a small amount of equal material off both sides of each limb. He builds his maple and yew bows to within a pound of a desired weight and the more temperamental bamboo to within two or three pounds.

Tim builds in bow tiller by making a longer upper limb on his longbow. In his Du-o-flex, he positions the butt ends of the laminations down from center, producing a stiffer lower limb. To make any minor adjustments to achieve his desired ¼" tiller, he removes material from the sides of the limbs.

OLD-TIME BOWMAKING — Tim has tried many methods of laminating his bows but prefers the old-time technique, using wooden forms compressed with "C" clamps.

FINISHING TOUCHES

When the bow is tuned true, Tim final sands the entire bow smooth and coats the riser and limb edges with a paste wood filler. He then white inks on the bow specs and sprays on the gloss Fullerplast finish. Tim sprays a minimum of three coats on the handle and limb edges, waiting fifteen minutes between coats. He sprays one heavy coat on the fiberglass. If a customer wants a dull finish, Tim rubs it down with steel wool. If they want a high-gloss luster finish, he wet sands it and buffs it with polishing compound. After the finish, Fern steps in and installs the leather shelf extension, strike plate, and grip using leather contact cement.

HANGING ON TO HIS CARDS

Tim has stuck with his bowmaking over the years despite hard times through the compound era. One thing that helped keep him going was customers dedicated to the magic of traditional archery. For Tim they're special people. "Traditional customers are generally a lot easier to please. They aren't buying scores and they aren't buying a trophy. They're buying a piece of equipment to shoot and enjoy, even if they don't hit the target with every arrow. That's something traditional archers have over the compound shooters. It's hard for compound shooters to understand how someone can have fun when they aren't hitting the target very well."

Besides helping support his business, Tim's customers give him a deep sense of pride in his work. "One of the greatest feelings is to make a bow for an individual, and then they pick it up and say, 'This bow is beautiful.' I recently got a letter from a gentleman back east who bought one of my bows, used. He told me it was the finest bow he had ever owned. You don't always hear about your equipment if it's good, but if there is a problem with it you'll hear about it immediately. But I guess that's just human nature."

It also seems to be human nature for many archers to drift back to their roots in archery, joining the wave of bowmen rediscovering the challenging thrills of the stick bow. Following in their wake, many compound shooters are experiencing the first-time excitement of shooting traditional gear. "People are finally getting tired of all the competition, and they don't like the physical weight of packing around a compound that isn't very pretty. A lot of people nowadays just want to go back to the good old days of archery, whether they were there or not."

Tim and Fern Meigs were there, and they are making the good old days of archery last a lifetime.

Chapter Twenty-Eight

MOUNTAINMAN LONGBOWS

MODERN-DAY MOUNTAIN MAN

For the ambling blackie, the rancid odor of the elk carcass smelled better than a Saturday morning breakfast special. Its pungent aroma drew him up the lodgepole slopes toward the thicket holding his prize. The bruin approached downwind of the thicket, his flaring nostrils searching for any intruders needing to be run off. But the carcass remained his sole claim.

Morning shafts of sunlight lanced through shadows as the bear finished gorging himself and settled near the elk to forewarn any would-be scavengers. The lengthening rays warmed his glistening coat and, sleepy-eyed, the bear curled up in a patch of sunlight. Soon his heavy sighs of contentment ebbed into raspy snores.

Downslope from the bear, another omnivore slipped quietly between the trees and lingered in the shadows. This one carried a longbow. He peered upslope, sky-blue eyes framed by rugged, weather-checked features, his bushy beard and long wavy hair streaked with silvery wisps. Cat-like, the bowman crept nearer to the bear, blending each footfall in rhythm with the heavy groans of the sleeping bruin. His leather-patched pants brushed quietly past the branches, his drab shirt blending with the shadows.

The bowman cast an image of a rough-hewn, bear-wrestlin' mountain man from frontier days — an image John Watson is known for, but one he prayed he wouldn't have to prove.

"I took one final step around a tree to get a clear shot, and I thought, 'This is the ultimate stalk. I've snuck right up on this sleeping bear in his bed.' But just as I put my foot down to take the shot, I snapped a twig. That bear jumped up on his hind legs and looked me right in the eye at three yards. He didn't look that big when he was curled up sleeping, but when he stood up he was taller than me.

"All I could think was, 'This bear thinks I'm going to steal his dinner and I've got to nail him — now!' It was a split-second shot. I pulled back and shot at the white patch on his chest. The arrow hit him in the neck and the bear let out a roar. Then he spun around and took off."

Shaken, John heaved a sigh of relief and hiked back to camp. There he enlisted the help of his buddies and they returned to track the bear. But John's chance to wrestle that bear wasn't over.

"The blood trail was easy to follow, and we soon spotted the bear with his head on a log watching us come up the slope. He knew we were coming for him, so I snuck around behind him. When I got close enough for a shot, he stood up, giving me a perfect quartering away shot. I just pulled back and let 'er go. The arrow caught him in the third rib back and came out the same hole in the neck that my first arrow had made. He just fell over dead.

"Later an old-timer told me, 'If that bear thought for a second you were threatening his food, you would have been in a world of instant trouble.' I know now that I'll never again sneak up that close on a sleeping bear."

John shot his face-to-face bear north of his home in Klamath Falls, Oregon. There, his rugged appearance has earned him the title, "The Mountain Man" — a nickname he carries to local archery shoots and the name he has given to the longbows he builds.

CALIFORNIA DAYS

John's fascination with archery started in his home state of California. He grew up in the Los Angles area where he spent Saturday afternoons watching Mr. Archery on the big screen. "When I was a kid, I couldn't wait to go to the movies on weekends because of the Howard Hill shorts. They just fascinated me to no end. Howard was my idol, and he helped start the Verdurgo Hills Archery Club in California which I belonged to for years."

John's first bow was a lemonwood self-wood longbow that his grandfather gave him. Over the years John replaced his longbow with recurves and later with a compound. "I shot the compound for a few years but I got burned out on it. There was just too much emphasis on winning. I still see that today. But the only person you should really be in competition with is yourself."

Besides getting burned out on the wheeled bow, John also grew tired of the Los Angles compound life-style. "When I discovered they had put a hunting season on jack rabbits in L.A. County, I decided the rat-race wasn't for me anymore, and around 1974 I moved up here to Klamath Falls."

KLAMATH COUNTRY

Now in his early fifties, John lives on the south side of town with his wife, Romaine. He works days at a local woodworking shop and builds longbows during the evenings and on Saturdays.

John's adopted town of Klamath Falls is in southern Oregon just north of the California border. It's bounded on the north by Upper Klamath Lake and on the south by Lake Ewauna. The town, originally called Linkville, was a frontier settlement established on the banks of the Link River. Before the infiltration of white settlers during the mid 1800s, the Klamath Basin was inhabited by Klamath Indians and their ancestors who occupied the area for over 5,000 years.

The vast pine forests surrounding town represent the mainstay of the community. Weyerhaeuser's Klamath Falls plant is one of the largest pine sawmills in the world. The saw logs are harvested from Weyerhaeuser's Klamath Tree Farm which covers over 650,000 acres. Besides its timber processing and wood products industry, Klamath Falls is also the home of Oregon Institute of Technology.

North of town in the basin flats, over 150,000 acres of marsh lands provide seasonal nesting and wintering ground for flocks of Pacific Flyway waterfowl. During the fall, migrating flocks peak to approximately one million birds, one of the largest migratory concentrations in the world. The Klamath Basin also boasts one of the lower 48's largest wintertime populations of bald eagles.

The vast country surrounding Klamath Falls is rich in natural beauty, offering sportsmen such as John the opportunity to bowhunt in the big timber for deer, elk, and bear, or to fish for trout in pristine mountain lakes. It's the kind of country to make a mountain man feel right at home.

MOSTLY A DEER HUNTER

Although John has had chance encounters with bears and loves chasing elk, his number one bowhunting quarry is local mule deer. He pursues them in southern Oregon where the open expanse of high country desert and the close quarters of the dark timber offer a variety of bowhunting action.

One of his favorite mule deer spots is Yellowjacket Springs. There, he locates a remote area without too many logging roads where he can roam with his longbow and free spirit. "I usually still hunt or spot and stalk for deer. I'm just not much for sitting on a stand very long. I always have to see what's on the other side of the next ridge. When I get there, I imagine that next ridge must look even better. So I keep going. I cover quiet a bit of country that way. But I do stop periodically and glass for game, and if I spot a buck, I try to make a decent stalk on him."

When sneaking in for the shot, John likes to get within thirty-five yards where he can confidently "punch both tanks" through the lung area. But sometimes the open high desert areas contain only sparse cover, and John and his longbow are occasionally summoned to reach out past his usual fifty-five yard limit. "I snuck to within seventy yards of this buck deer and I just couldn't sneak any closer. Finally, he knew I was there and after all that stalking he decided to just walk off. So I stood up behind a sagebrush and said to myself, 'I'm gonna nail that dude.' Normally I don't shoot that far, but some days my shooting feels good. I let it fly and the arrow knocked him right off his feet.

"But making a shot like that hinges on your self-confidence. When I was shooting all the time, I feared nothing in North America as long as I had my longbow. It's about as efficient as any weapon I've used for hunting."

When John's high confidence arrows strike home, Romaine adds to his savoring of the of the hunt by fixing John's favorite — mule deer enchiladas. "I cook a deer roast in a pressure cooker," says Romaine, "until the meat falls apart. Deer ribs also work great and they make good tacos too. Then I shred it up and make regular style enchiladas and put in a Mexican hot sauce called El Podo. I've also made enchiladas with bear and about every kind of wild meat John has brought home."

John boasts that Romaine's enchiladas are not only good, they've become too good among his hunting buddies. "All the guys used to give me their deer ribs because they didn't care to cook them. Then we had the guys over for enchilada dinner. After dinner, Romaine said, 'Thanks, guys, for giving us those enchilada deer ribs.' They haven't given me any ribs in the past five years!"

Even though it probably wouldn't fit in the pressure cooker, John dreams of someday traveling north to bowhunt the largest of the deer family in the Alaskan or Yukon wilderness. "I would love to go moose hunting like in Jay Massey's book where they float down remote rivers on rafts. Bowhunting in wild moose country where the big bears also live would be exciting."

OREGON STYLE PRACTICE

To keep his instinctive longbow eye sharp for distant bucks or his dream moose, John often stump shoots at unmarked yardages. It's his favorite style of practice. "Roaming around stump shooting really helps you shoot automatically without thinking about the distance, and that's important when hunting."

Besides whacking stumps with blunts, John takes his longbow to local 3-D shoots. Today, he blends in with the growing crowd of fun-loving longbowers, but years ago he was an oddity. "When I came up here fourteen years ago, I was the only guy around shooting a longbow. They just looked at me like I was weird and asked, 'What does he think he going to do with that stick?' But in the last few years I've seen more traditionalists, and most shoots now even have a traditional category. For us, winning isn't all that important, we just go out to have a good time. At many shoots they place too much emphasis on who is the best shot. I think the increase in traditional shooters is because a lot of guys got tired of the gadgetry and having to carry a tool box around when they shot their contraption. It's much easier to just carry an extra bowstring."

Local shoots may offer challenging practice, but none compare in fun to John's west coast favorite, The International Longbow Safari. "It's the ultimate gathering of guys using traditional gear. I love going and talking to all of the people, especially a lot of the old-timers like me. Plus, their traditional shoot is more realistic in distances and target placement than most of the compound shoots where they stick targets out in the open at 120 yards. I don't take shots at deer standing in the road at 120 yards!"

Although John stump shoots and attends 3-D shoots to help develop his instinctive eye, most of his practice hours are spent in his back yard where he polishes his form. "The important part of shooting a longbow is developing your rhythm. It's like walking; you get pretty good and don't stumble much after you've done it a lot. I try to shoot an arrow in one smooth motion. I fix my concentration on the target while I'm pulling up and drawing the bow at the same time. And when I'm on target, I let go. I don't hold my bow very long. I just let my brain tell my hands automatically what to do."

John not only practices year round for those one or two shots each bow season, but he also makes sure his shooting is on the mark during every hunt. "I always carry blunts with me. If I'm taking a break or not seeing any game, I'll take some warm-up shots to get my muscles toned up. I don't think anyone should go out bowhunting cold turkey. A bowhunter is just like any other athlete. You should warm up a bit before you start your game. It's not only fair to you, it's also fair to the game for you to be able to place that arrow where you're supposed to."

When a year's worth of practice focuses down to the final moment of truth, John gives his self-confidence one final edge through visualization. "Before I draw down on a deer, I always foresee the shot and see my arrow striking home. You must picture that shot in your mind."

MOUNTAIN MAN GEAR

Living up to his mountain man image, John often hunts in an old pair

of soft jeans patched with buckskin. He also wears one of his good-luck plaid shirts that matches the tone of his hunting terrain. It's simple garb, but it's effective. "The Indians didn't wear fancy camouflage and they got quite close to their game. The main things that give you away are smell and movement.

"For instance, once I was hunting and could hear this guy coming for fifteen minutes. He was fully camoed with his compound and all his junk clinking and clanging. I just stood with my back against some brush, and I stepped out from behind a tree and said, 'Good morning!' I scared the pants right off him. He said, 'Where in the devil did you come from?'"

Sticking with tradition, John shoots wooden arrows. He's particular

MOUNTAIN MEN IN ACTION — Executing a blend of rhythm and power, mountain man-looking John Watson confidently handles his MountainMan longbow.

about arrow flight and he makes his own arrows from tapered Port Orford cedar shafting. "I've been shooting tapered shafts for many years, and I really like how the arrow corrects itself faster at close range. The back ten and a half inches of the shaft is tapered.

"I stain my shafts, dip them in bow varnish, and then crest them. I fletch them with five and a half inch long Pope and Young cut feathers because they stabilize the arrow. I also like using five-sixteenths inch Arizona nocks. They're strong and don't grip my eighteen-strand string too tight like most nocks."

Even though John loves his cedar arrows with the same traditional romance he has with his longbow, he knows only too well that a damaged wooden arrow can unexpectedly turn on the shooter. A nasty scar on his bow hand reminds him daily. "I was rabbit hunting and had shot about four rabbits when another cottontail jumped up, so I drew back. I didn't realize it, but that arrow had been fractured on a previous shot.

"I let it fly, but the arrow broke in two, driving the back half right through my bow hand. At first I couldn't figure out what happened because I felt no pain, my bow just flew out of my hand. Then I moved my hand and saw the arrow sticking halfway through it. I put my hand between my legs and I tried to pull the arrow out but it wouldn't come. It isn't like in the movies — you can't just pull it out. So I broke the other end off, packed up my gear, and drove into town to the emergency hospital. I walked in, held up my hand and said, 'I'd like to have this thing removed.' "

When hunting big game John tips his arrows with Mountain Man broadheads made by Dale Phillips. "It's a replica of the Howard Hill head but Dale makes the ferrule smaller so you can sharpen the head more easily. I like a single-bladed head because they're easier to get out of your back quiver and they're easier to sharpen.

"I use a bastard file and put a serrated edge on my heads. I believe that edge cuts better, especially if you nick a vein that is pretty tough. The serrated edge cuts like a fine band saw blade when it goes through. Plus, you can use a good single-bladed broadhead again and again. But you're lucky if you can shoot an insert-bladed head a second time. The blades just pop right out. We have a lot of rocks in this country, and you're fortunate if you can shoot between the rocks every time you miss."

For years John carried his hunting arrows in a traditional Hill style back quiver, but recently he tried using a small strap-on bow quiver. "I used it last year and found it was really nice when crawling on my hands and knees, and I could still carry six arrows with me. I've been in situations where I've taken off my back quiver and only taken one arrow. I've missed and had to sit there with egg on my face because I didn't have any more arrows. Having a quiver on my longbow took some getting used to but it's very convenient. And during our early season hunt, I found it pretty comfortable not having that hot quiver on my back."

Since John's longbow is inherently quiet he doesn't use string silencers. "To me silencers slow the string down a little. Besides, if you're in the right position to the animal when you shoot, that arrow is through him before he realizes what's going on."

John used to shoot heavy longbows pulling eighty-five to ninety pounds. But now that he's building them more and shooting them less, he shoots more comfortable weights pulling between seventy-two and seventy-eight pounds.

Unlike most bowmakers, his favorite bow was made by someone else. "I have a bow that Don Burdett made for me twenty years ago and it still shoots great. I've shot that bow for so many years I just pick it up and it feels super good to me. I've tried to duplicate it, and now I have two that I made which I think are really close.

"My bows are still pretty heavy but they're really comfortable for me to shoot. In a hunting situation it's not like shooting in a tournament where you have to shoot 120 arrows a day. In hunting you only need to make one shot plus you have more adrenaline in your system so you really don't notice the draw weight."

Even though John shoots heavy longbows, he tries to talk most of his customers into shooting moderate weight bows. "I tell my customers it's immaterial what I shoot. They put too much emphasis on what they read about Howard Hill shooting heavy bows. Most people don't realize how extremely strong Howard was. Also, he shot heavy bows every day. A fifty-five to sixty pound longbow will kill anything in North America and probably half the game in Africa too."

Besides matching his customers with the right weight bows, John tries to fit them with the right length bow. He has them place the end of a yardstick on their sternum and hold the other end with outstretched arms. While keeping their shoulders straight, they note the draw length measurement at the end of their fingertips. "Using this true draw length I can determine what length bow a customer should be shooting. There is no reason for somebody with a twenty-six inch draw to be shooting a seventy inch longbow. The limbs won't function properly for them."

Most compound shooters switching to one of John's longbows soon discover a whole new style of shooting, usually resulting in a shorter draw. "Many archers were taught the military stance with their bow arm extended straight out and their head back. Some of these guys who are five foot, six inches tell me they're shooting a thrity-one inch arrow. I explain to them if they are, they're shooting wrong. I generally take a bow and show them that you shoot a longbow like a shotgun; you lean into it and keep your bow arm bent a little. Testing has shown that a twenty-seven inch arrow gives you perfect arrow flight and if you're shooting a longer arrow you're not gaining much."

THE MOUNTAINMAN LONGBOW

To match his customers with the right bow length, John offers MountainMan longbows in 62" to 70" lengths in two-inch increments. The 68" length weighs 1 pound, 6 ounces, and has a recommended brace height of about 6¼".

The hardwood riser is 14½" long between fadeouts. His standard riser is made from local Oregon myrtlewood, and it's also available in walnut, bubinga, shedua, and winewood. The riser is 1" wide and narrows slightly to ¾" through the sight window which is cut ¼" to ⅜" from center shot. The riser is 2⅛" thick. Its high peaked Howard Hill style grip is slightly dished and wrapped with a 4¼" suede leather grip. The shelf-window junction is equipped with a suede strike plate and shelf pad. The bow specs are black inked below the grip opposite the window.

On the 68" bow, the working length of the upper limb is 28" from the nock to fadeout, and the lower limb's working length is 25¾". The limbs exhibit 1" of straight backset and narrow from 1 1/16" wide at the fadeouts to ½" at the string nocks. They are constructed from three back laminations and one belly lamination of solid maple corewood. The maple laminations are enveloped in either clear, black, brown, green, white, or blue fiberglass. The limbs are feathered on the edges of the glass and are slightly tapered to the belly. The bow is dip-finished in a semi-gloss luster varnish.

BUILT FOR ACTION — Styled after the Hill longbow, John's bows are made to take rough use in the field — whatever a mountain man can dish out.

To check the relative speed of one of his MountainMan longbows, John shot his 68" longbow which pulled 69 pounds at his 26¼" draw. He shot 26¼" cedar arrows fletched with three 5½" feathers and equipped with open end nocks. The arrows each weighed 525 grains. The bow was equipped with a Dacron Flemish string without accessories. John used a shooting glove, drew a consistent 26¼", and had a clean release. The average arrow speed for this bow, arrow, and shooter combination was 186 fps.

The following draw/force measurements were recorded on this 68" MountainMan Longbow:

DRAW LENGTH	24"	25"	26"	27"	28"
DRAW WEIGHT	60#	64#	68#	72#	76#

INTERLUDE WITH YEW

John began his bowmaking efforts by carving out self-wood yew long-bows. But his attempts proved disappointing. "I got some yew wood from Mr. Ulrich who was a fabulous old guy. I started making self-wood bows, but I wasn't really impressed with them. Most of them broke. I know they're beautiful, but there's a reason why most bowmakers went to fiberglass. It makes the bow stronger and depending on how you build your bow, fiber-glass can make a flatter shooting bow."

John shifted his attention to composite bowmaking and enlisted the help of some other longbow makers. "I contacted Dale Phillips and Don Burdett and they helped me. Don, who now lives in Arizona, used to work for Hill Manufacturing, and he showed me how to build longbows. I designed my bow after the Howard Hill longbow. I used the same thickness and the same laminations Hill preferred."

After getting some pointers from Don and Dale, John built his first longbow around 1980. Unlike the self-wood bows, it was durable and shot with authority. "Matter of fact, I took a nice little buck with that bow, but I lost the bow in a recent fire that gutted my home."

John continued his bowmaking hobby and by 1982 so many of his friends wanted his bows that he decided to expand his hobby into a part-time business. When John and his longbows were later featured in a traditional archery magazine orders began to pile up.

Today, he works hard to maintain his remarkable thirty-day delivery time on new orders. John's bowmaking has its rewards, but not without sacrifice. "My bowmaking keeps me busier than I want to be. It's not enough work to keep my family going financially, yet it's enough to keep me from doing the things I enjoy, like stringing up my bow and shooting in the back yard. I won't stop building them, but I may slack off so I can have time for the things I really enjoy doing."

THE MAKING OF A MOUNTAINMAN

John begins making a longbow by building the riser. Although he offers exotic hardwoods, local Oregon myrtlewood is his favorite because it blends well with the maple core and absorbs hand shock more than other woods. It's also readily available and holds up well in the heavier draw weight bows.

When a customer selects a certain color fiberglass John tries to match it with complementing natural tones within the riser wood. "If a customer wants black fiberglass, for instance, I like to use bubinga with its red tint. Green glass goes well with shedua because of its natural green tint. With clear glass I suggest my myrtlewood riser. I also use thicker glass on the belly and thinner glass on the back because it makes my bow recover a little faster."

After cutting the riser wood to rough shape, John uses a special machine for grinding the belly contour of the fadeout. This device was designed and made by Curt Phillips and incorporates a jig that is run against a belt sander to grind the belly curve through the fadeout.

John uses maple as his standard corewood, but he also offers a custom yew core. "I prefer maple. Yew wood stiffens up in cold weather. Because of maple's consistency in any weather it is used in the finest musical instruments. I want that consistency in my bows." John gets his solid tapered maple laminations from the Old Master Crafters and yew laminations from fellow Oregon bowmaker John Strunk.

Although John usually orders tapered laminations, he sometimes needs to taper his own so he uses a machine designed by Dale Phillips. "Most bowmakers use a sander of some kind, but my tapering machine is a cutter and with it I can taper super-hard woods to within two thousandths of an inch. It uses a floating bladed head, and when I cut laminations with it they have a nice rough surface for good glue bonding. If I use clear glass, I sand the cutting marks off the exposed side of the lamination."

PUTTING IT TOGETHER

Before gluing up his composites, John masking tapes the non-gluing side of the fiberglass and covers his form with wax paper. His bow forms are made from solid wood and reinforced along the bottom with steel to prevent twisting.

John spreads Gordon's recommended bow epoxy on the fiberglass and lays a dry lamination on top of it. He applies glue on the top of the dry lamination and lays on another lamination, repeating this process until all the composites are in place in the form. During glue-up John staggers the butt ends of alternating laminations like brick-work to provide extra strength through the handle.

Once the composites are laid up in the form, John lays on a metal strip and begins "C" clamping every three inches. The metal strip is intended to prevent prominent "C" clamp dimples in the belly glass. John tightens the clamps by hand and applies a little more clamping pressure through the fadeout area to try to achieve a uniform glue line.

John then places the form in his plywood hot box which is heated to 120 degrees with a series of light bulbs. The epoxy cures for eight hours, until an electric timer turns the lights off. The bow usually sets in the form, cooling overnight and John removes it the next day. Before shaping the bow, John lets the rough bow cure for another thirty-six hours at room temperature.

TAKING SHAPE

Next, John trims off the excess glue with the band saw to remove the dangerously sharp glue edges. He clamps the bow in the vise and draws the bow outline on the back by tracing a metal template. He band saws it to rough shape and uses a belt sander to grind off the saw marks.

Using a micrometer to occasionally check his limb dimensions, John files the limb's shape and then files in rough string nocks. He strings the bow with a low brace height and checks the tiller. The longer upper limb is designed to provide a built-in tiller, and John strives for a 1/8" positive tiller.

Once the limbs are near tiller, John places the bow on his wall-mounted tiller board. "I use the tiller board to see if I have any rough spots in the limbs

John shapes his bows by hand and checks each bow on his tiller board to be sure both limbs are bending in harmony.

and to see if both limbs are working properly. You can't have one limb working more than the other or the bow won't cast properly. I don't see how anybody can build a bow without a tiller board. I check the contour of the bow to be sure I'm getting full working limbs."

When John has the limbs bending in harmony, he begins sanding the sides and rounding the belly to reduce the limbs to the desired draw weight. Finally, he shapes the handle, grip, and finish sands the bow. "I shape the handle the way the customer wants it, and I try make sure there are no sanding marks in the bow."

Before applying the finish, John checks each bow's performance by shooting it a few times. Similar to an arrowsmith finishing arrows, he dips his bows one half at a time up to the handle, in spar varnish. He dips on six coats, inking the bow specs between the first and second coat. "I try to give my bows plenty of finish protection because the weather is a bow's worst enemy."

MADE FOR HARD HUNTING

John's finished longbow is a rugged hunting weapon that's intended to live up to its mountain man image — to keep going when the back country gets tough. He doesn't want his customers to be shy about taking his bow on a rough hunting trip, and he doesn't claim that his bows are a work of art. "I've found over the years that a pretty bow isn't everything. I'm not much into the cosmetics of trying to make them look so pretty that you only want to hang them on a wall. I try to make the MountainMan longbow a good-performing hunting weapon, a functional piece of equipment that someone can take hunting, and if they drop it or ding it, it's not going to hurt the bow much. It's got to withstand some hard use."

Beside putting tough MountainMan longbows in the hands of his customers, John's bowmaking gives him the satisfaction of helping archers rediscover the true meaning of archery. "My customers come from all walks of life: old-timers and new compound converts who are tired of all the gadgetry. It's people wanting to get back into the romantic aspects of archery. And I get the enjoyment of helping those people go back to the basics of traditional archery — shooting old wooden arrows with feathers out of a stick. That's really true archery."

Especially if you're a mountain man.

Chapter Twenty-Nine

DON MCCANN CUSTOM ARCHERY

THE BOWMAN'S GIFT

Taxus brevifolia, commonly know as yew, has been regarded throughout the ages as the finest bowmaking wood known to man. Highly coveted by warring countries during the Middle Ages, yew longbows hummed sweet victory in countless battles, conquering kingdoms and saving nations. In some cultures, illegal possession of the prized yew was even punishable by death.

Remarkably lightweight and resilient, yew was hand-crafted into sleek longbows by America's forefathers of modern bowhunting, Saxton Pope and Art Young. Their hard hitting yew longbows laid low many a beast. In his book, *Hunting with the Bow and Arrow*, Pope explained in detail how to harvest and fashion yew into a worthy bowhunting weapon — helping ignite a nation of bowhunters.

Even though the innovations of composite bows and fiberglass toppled yew from its throne as king of bowmaking materials, it remains irreplaceable among discriminating self-wood bowyers. Yew also holds a special place in the hearts of a few composite bowmakers who use it as a limb core, blending its timeless qualities with modern materials and innovative design.

TREKKING THE SHADOWED SLOPES

Don McCann of Auburn, Washington, is one bowmaker who still clutches to the romantic ties of using yew. He designs and sells traditional bows that incorporate the coppery hued wood into classical longbow designs reminiscent of Pope and Young's stave yew bows.

Within the shadows of stately Mount Ranier, Don climbs the steep slopes of the White River drainage and wades through snow drifts and over deadfalls in his time-honored search for bow-quality yew. He represents the lingering shadows of generations of bowyers before him. "I'm fortunate to live near some of the finest yew wood country in the world. Cutting a yew tree is like opening the archives of the Cascade Mountains and seeing the past several hundred years. The yew's growth rings tell of good growing seasons and hard winters. Harvesting yew puts me in touch with the pioneers of archery. It's a privilege I'll never take for granted."

With a forester's permit for "yew billets or staves" in his pocket, Don scales the hills on his calculated search. "It's imperative that bow-quality yew come from 2,000 feet or higher because there the growth rings are much smaller. It makes a tremendous difference. I get most of my yew from around 3,000 feet, and I've taken some from 5,000 feet."

To prevent excessive splitting and warping during aging, Don only cuts yew during the late fall or winter when the sap is down. He selects his yew from north facing slopes where the trees grow slower and produce tighter growth rings. When searching under the canopy of tall firs, he looks for male yew trees because of their tighter grain and darker reddish brown wood. Female trees display a light reddish-orange wood and have small berries hanging from their branches. Many of these ten inch to fifteen inch diameter yew trees are an amazing 300 to 500 years old.

When Don fells one of these ancient but diminutive trees, he shares a somber moment with the stillness of the forest. "I have a lot of respect for yew. It's a special creation. But for yew to realize its potential, it has to be harvested and put into the hands of a competent bowyer, where it can be designed and crafted into what it was meant to be."

SLOW AGING

After felling the trees, Don cuts them into forty-eight inch lengths and muscles them down the mountain to his truck. Before storing the logs in a cool, covered drying area, he waxes their ends with paraffin to prevent cracking. Leaving its shaggy bark in place, Don slowly dries the yew for two to five years before it's made into laminations.

One of the tricks to using yew as a corewood is knowing how to extract the best laminations from a log. Don prefers using edge grain yew laminations because they create a stiffer limb than flat grain corewoods of the same thickness. "By using edge grain you lighten the limb mass and create more speed. It's also a more predictable wood when tillering and aligning the limbs."

Occasionally Don produces extremely fine-grained yew laminations and has to be careful using these extra resilient woods. "Some of these trees have growth rings finer than a frog's hair split four ways. These super-fine grained woods produce a bow with up to thirty percent heavier draw weight than standard yew of the same core thickness.

"Yew is the Cadillac of woods, the very finest you can use in a longbow. It's lighter than all the other bow woods and it takes less to create a stiff limb because it's so resilient. That's why it's so fast."

BACK TO THE CASCADES

Don was born in Portland, Oregon near the Cascades and its fabled yew, but he was raised on the flat lands of Wichita, Kansas. There, his grandfather, Archie Cox, professionally crafted bows from 1926 until 1960. Archie also crafted a small lemonwood bow for his toddling grandson, introducing Don to the thrill of archery. "I was just four years old when my grandfather gave me my first bow. Then he built me another when I was seven. Grandpa used to baby-sit me and I would spend the better part of the day seeing how many arrows I could lose or break. I've had a romance going with archery ever since."

Now in his late thirties, Don again lives near the fir-shrouded Cascades. Living on the outskirts of Seattle, he works at Boeing Corporation in engineering and also distributes his custom bows. He's a family man who shares outdoor and bowhunting adventures with his twin teenage boys. These adventures include steelhead and salmon fishing on Washington rivers, where Don once worked as a fishing guide, and wing shooting over their bird dogs.

Besides the fishing and upland birds, Don enjoys the variety of local bowhunting species. Although Washington's forest harbor and impressive list of big game, Don remains concerned about the future of bow seasons in his home state. "Out here bowhunters have a primitive weapons status that helped establish our special seasons. But in reality our primitive status is gone because bowhunters aren't shooting primitive weapons anymore. There's a bow in Oregon that shoots a hunting weight arrow over 300 feet per second. I shot a bow with 95 percent let off that I could hold at full draw with one finger. There has got to be a ceiling on equipment or where will things end?

"Muzzle-loaders had the common sense to be self-limiting. They decided they didn't want high-performance powder and telescopic sights. They wanted to maintain their primitive status, but not today's bowhunters. They are looked upon as not being so primitive so maybe they don't need special seasons. Here in Washington, bowhunters have been loosing ground with their seasons and have had to share seasons with muzzle-loaders."

ST. CHARLES INFLUENCE

An early pioneer in establishing Washington's archery seasons, is Pope and Young Club founder, and owner of Northwest Archery Company, Glenn St. Charles. For Don and many others, Glenn is a nearby idol whose sage stories sprinkled with wry humor help stir their bowhunting embers.

In one story, Glenn recalls the painstaking process of making early hunting arrows. He almost seems to amaze himself as he recounts the two hours spent crafting a single footed arrow from raw materials and then building an early broadhead from an old saw blade and a cartridge casing. "If you lost one of those arrows," Glenn tells Don with a lurch of his eyebrows, "you spent two hours looking for it!"

When visiting Northwest Archery, Don likes to linger in their archery museum where a special corridor leads bowhunters into archery's golden past. Their show room, where the Pope and Young Club was created, glows with a sacred aura from stunning archery relics collected by Glenn's son, Joe. A large display case back-dropped with the creamy white Polar bear hide taken by Art Young, contrasts with rows of time-stained arrows which whisper of their singing flights over toughened knuckles.

One of these shafts is an ornately crafted Indian arrow found in Ishi's hut at Deer Creek in 1911. Near Ishi's shaft hangs Art Young's fang-damaged lion arrows and his deadly Polar bear arrow. With stark contradiction, Saxton Pope's savage-looking rhinoceros arrow hangs near his delicately crafted flight arrows.

Below the arrows rest some of Pope and Young's self-wood bows. Young's "Ole Grizzly" and Pope's "Robin", battle scarred and limb weary, proudly rest with strings forever limp.

ARCHERY TREASURES —Glenn and Don(left) admire some of Pope and Young's self-wood bows displayed in Northwest Archery's museum. The museum has a wealth of archery relics such as the leg bone of Young's African lion, complete with imbedded broadhead.

BOWHUNTING TRAILS

Over the years Don has arrowed winging ducks and geese, and has harvested "gobs" of blacktail and mule deer. He has also taken bear and recently began bowhunting Washington's Roosevelt and Yellowstone elk. "I've gotten to where I don't feel like I have to get an animal anymore. I'm not pressured to get one, I just enjoy bowhunting — being out there in the wilds and matching wits with the animals."

His number one quarry is mule deer. They usually offer plenty of close-range stalks, and when things work out right, he even gets an occasional shot. One of his favorite times to chase mulies is during the late season when piling snows and frigid temperatures cause the deer to congregate into roaming herds. "We make a nice winter camp using a big army tent with a wood stove. We hunt there for a week and see lots of big migratory bucks.

"Three years ago it got down to twenty-eight degrees below zero during our deer hunt. That was mercilessly cold. But when it's that cold the deer feed constantly and bunch up. We just looked for feeding animals with spotting scopes and then mapped out a stalking route. We also located some well-used travel routes and ambushed them."

BEARS TOO

Besides bowhunting local deer and elk, Don baits black bears. He hunts them relatively close to home, baiting with meat scraps, fruits, and pastries. "Our bear population is just outstanding. It's hard to believe we have so many bears around a residential area. In some areas they are even more plentiful than coyotes. The bears in eastern Washington tend to get a little larger but we still get some whoppers around here."

During a recent hunt for these black recluses of the underbrush, Don and his custom yew-cored recurve reacted as one. "I climbed in my tree stand about three hours before dark, and a bear really surprised me by popping out of the brush a half hour after I got there. She caught me with my guard down — I didn't even have my bow in my hands.

"The bear came in right under my stand, but every time I started to draw she whirled. I would freeze half-drawn and begin shaking but she would resume eating. I repeated this two or three times then finally decided to draw all the way back. As I started to draw, she whirled around and looked right up at me. I just held because she was facing me head on.

"After a moment she started feeding again so I let down my draw. But the arrow made a noise and she whirled and then just high-tailed it. She headed for a tunnel in the thick Oregon grape and I shot. It all came down to that instinctive split second reflex. She was fifteen yards away, and the arrow went in behind the rib cage and exited out her brisket. She only went twenty-five yards, and it was a very humane kill. I never could have made that shot with a compound bow. It was automatic."

Although Don made that running shot on his bear, he's reluctant to take shots on moving game unless they feel perfect. "I've been pretty successful at the ones I have taken. But arrow placement is critical on big game animals and you should be sure of your shot."

NEAR THE EDGE

Besides being sure of your shooting, bowhunting the Cascades requires being sure of your footing. It's a land of rugged beauty and alluring bowhunting trophies, but it can also be dangerous and unforgiving. Don has bow-hunted the rocky crags of the High Cascades — a desolate place where he narrowly cheated death by using his longbow.

For years Don applied for a mountain goat permit in Washington, and his persistence paid off. He drew a tag. Immediately he began contacting friends who had hunted goats, and he followed up leads with several scouting trips into a remote wilderness area. Hiking above 6,000 feet along the

Cascade Crest Trail, Don discovered plenty of goats and the treacherously rugged country they inhabit.

By the time the season opened, Don was ready. Loaded with heavy packs, he and photographer friend Bret Smith, trudged the seven miles into his hunting area and struck camp at nightfall. "We had to carry our own water because there wasn't any in there. Our packs weighed over eighty pounds. About halfway back in I shot a forty-pound porcupine for camp meat. It was a pain to carry, but we needed the meat and it was pretty tasty.

"The next day we had some trouble locating goats and decided to check out a dust bowl on the other side of the mountain. Bret is an experienced climber, and I asked him if he thought we could inch our way up the side of this mountain. He thought we could so we started climbing almost straight up. Halfway up I knew we couldn't come back down that way — it was just too dangerous.

"We scaled the mountain face using hand holds and inching our way up. We finally made it over the top and started down toward the dust bowl. I was sure I was going to get a shot at a goat but we came over the bowl edge and found it empty.

"Our only way out of there was on a small ledge that I had spotted earlier. It was a narrow shale slide right below a steep rock face. I asked Bret if he thought it was safe and he replied, 'Well, there's one way to find out.' I told him to be careful, but when he got halfway across he started losing his footing and then began leaping like a deer. Somehow he made it. He said, 'There's solid footing underneath the shale. Just hop across it, you'll make it.'

" 'But I've had knee surgery,' I said, 'and I'm not much of a hopper!' I was really nervous because right below the shale slide was a sheer drop-off for hundreds of feet, with jagged rocks at the bottom. It looked like a bad way to turn into a grease spot on the rocks.

"I took a deep breath and started across — but when I got halfway, I started losing it. My feet began sliding downhill in the shale and I knew I wasn't going to make it. I figured I was dead.

"Suddenly Bret yelled, 'Stick out your longbow,' and he reached out as far as he could. Somehow he managed to grab my longbow. Fortunately, Bret is real strong and he kept me from sliding off the edge. Using my upper body strength, I pulled myself up. I'm sure glad I wasn't using a short recurve — I wouldn't be here now."

Later during his hunt, Don passed up a perfect broadside shot on a huge nanny because he thought she may have kids. "I wasn't fortunate enough to get a goat, but at least I lived through it."

NOT TOO MUCH

One reason Don survived the High Cascades is because of his upper body strength. A serious weight lifter since high school, he has a fireplug build and large muscular arms. They come in handy for pulling him over rocks or yanking back heavy longbows.

CASCADE PRACTICE — Don hunts with both his take-down recurve and his longbow, but he admits he's a longbower at heart.

Even though Don shot bows in the eighty to ninety pound range for years, he has recently dropped down fifteen to twenty pounds in draw weight, and he's noticed fewer shoulder problems. "Getting overbowed used to be a bad trend in traditional archery. Everybody was trying to shoot heavy bows.

"There's no sense in buying a bow you can't shoot comfortably. Traditional archery is a fun shooting sport. But if you can't handle your bow it's no fun. If your bow is too heavy, you're not going to practice, get proficient with it, or use it. So I try to screen my customers and get them into a bow that will fit them well. I recommend to most of my longbow customers that they use bows sixty pounds and up. A recurve shoots so fast and smooth that a guy can use a lighter weight, but I like them to use fifty-five pounds and up for hunting."

Since his early archery instruction from Grandpa Cox, Don has continued to refine his form. "I've studied Howard Hill's style and other shooting styles and I use certain points to help polish my style. My form is a lot like Howard Hill's. I cant my bow, shoot instinctively, and anchor with my index finger in the corner of my mouth.

"Many traditional archers just touch their anchor briefly or snap shoot. I had a heck of a bout with target panic and snap shooting. I quit shooting my heavy bows because I was developing those bad habits. Then I deliberately started anchoring longer, and my form changed quite a bit. Now I anchor solidly for a second or two, open my fingers, and wipe the side of my face with my release. But I have a hard time getting a clean release because I cut the end of my ring finger off a long-time ago. They sewed it back on but there's a little nerve and a knob that sticks out. One reason I like shooting heavier bows is because they come off my string fingers easier."

INSTINCTIVE PRACTICE

To develop basic instinctive form, Don recommends that beginners start shooting at ten yards and get the feel of the bow. "Many people learning to shoot a longbow try to hold it straight up and down with a stiff arm and then yank the string back to thirty inches. But by the second shot when it tears their arm guard off, they realize they have to bend their bow arm a little and lean into the shot. The longbow dictates the way you have to shoot it.

"After you become consistent bunching your arrows together at ten yards, start moving back until you become proficient at a reasonable hunting range and just keep practicing. The best practice is stump shooting at varying distances, uphill, downhill, and across gullies. It's my favorite type of practice, and I usually stump shoot a couple of times each week. It will help make you a good traditional bowhunter."

When shooting at game, Don prefers shots from fifteen to thirty yards, but he sometimes shoots farther. "I like to get in close with my longbow and make it a hunting sport instead of a shooting sport. I'm a responsible bowhunter, and I only take shots I feel good about. Most of my personal bows shoot 200-plus feet per second and have a very flat trajectory, and I feel very confident out to forty-five yards."

One reason Don feels so confident out to forty-five yards is because he frequents local shoots where the targets are set up for technical shooters. "I shoot a lot of 3-D shoots, and unfortunately the average distance at our shoots is forty-seven yards. That's ridiculously long. But they're geared for all these guys with overdraws and sights. I don't encourage anybody to shoot at game that far unless they're really confident in their ability."

Whether he's on the 3-D range or within striking distance of a feeding buck, Don hones his concentration right before the shot. "I always try to tell myself to pick a spot or even pick a hair. That was something I had a lot of trouble doing when I began bowhunting. I just looked at the whole deer and would likely put one through his antlers. I think everybody goes through that at first. Now I try to keep my cool, not rush my shot, be calculated, and wait for the right moment. If it doesn't present itself, I don't take a shot."

TRADITIONAL GEAR

When Don slips into Washington's west coast rain forests in search of bowhunting action, it's often wet and chilly, so he dresses for the occasion. "I wear mostly earth-tone wool because most rain garments are too noisy. When you're sneaking in on an animal you can't wear a noisy Goretex material. Polar fleece works well, but I just wear my wool, get wet, and stay warm. And I always wear my Pendelton tweed wool hat."

Don usually hunts with aluminum arrows when shooting his recurves and cedar shafts when toting his longbow. "When I shoot aluminum arrows, I like using Satellite II broadheads. They cut on entry instead of puncturing. I've taken six animals with them and they work really well. I like a cutting-on-entry head because they get better penetration. Plus, I like sharpening my own heads and reusing them. Half the fun of bowhunting is preparing your own equipment. Recently I've been trying multibladed heads such as the Snuffer and the Magnum II."

Many bowhunters look for a broadhead that flies true, is durable, and doesn't cost much. That's a tough combination to find, but Don has discovered an older style head that has it all. "The Bodkin is a relatively inexpensive head that works great. I developed a sharpening system for them, and I can sharpen them super-sharp and faster than any other head. I use a ceramic True Angle hone covered with varying grits of wet-and-dry sandpaper. When I get it to a keen edge using sandpaper I sharpen it on the ceramic hone and then they're shaving sharp."

Don fletches his recurve arrows with three feathers and uses four on his longbow shafts. "The four-fletch shafts pull my longbow arrows into control faster. I shoot a lot of tournaments and I'm fanatical about tuning my equipment. I don't care what kind of bow that arrow is coming out of, all I want to see is that nock going to the target, and the four-fletch ensures me perfect longbow arrow flight."

For carrying his longbow arrows, Don uses a hip quiver developed by his friend, Jack Bowers. "It's just excellent. It's a side quiver that can be worn on a strap around your chest like a creel, or on your belt. It holds eight to ten arrows and has a waterproof hood on it. It's so lightweight you hardly know you're wearing it. It's easy to stalk with even when you're going through the brush. It has many of the advantages of a Catquiver without the bulk, and you can still wear a pack with it."

When toting his recurve, Don carries his arrows in a Delta bow quiver. "It's super quiet, durable, and adjustable, and I recommend it to anybody looking for a recurve bow quiver."

Don spends a lot of hunting time sneaking through Washington's brushy jungles and needs a bow that will follow him without hanging up. "Brush buttons are mandatory on recurves out here because you wouldn't believe some of the places you can get into. It's really thick and it's easy to get branches stuck between your string and limb. You lose a little arrow speed using brush buttons, but they're worth it."

BACKWOODS BUDDIES

Don's favorite recurve is his own 62" Black Diamond TD. Its yew-cored limbs draw 71 pounds and contrast with his darker cocobolo riser. But his treasured sidekick on the bowhunting trail is his High Cascade life-saver. "I'm primarily a longbow archer. That's where my heart is. My first personal yew longbow I named 'Me and Yew,' and my second one I named 'Me and Yew Two.' "

The ART & SAXTON COMMEMORATIVE LONGBOW is Don's most popular longbow and recaptures the classic yew longbow look of Pope and Young self-wood bows. They're available in lengths of 63" to 70" in one-inch increments. The mass weight of Don's 65" bow is 1 pound, 6 ounces. It has a recommended brace height of approximately 7⅝".

These longbows are available in the slim-lined reverse attitude handle or the slim conventional handle. The risers are available in several hardwoods and resemble the old straight-handle design of stave self-wood longbows. Its riser measures 16¼" between fadeouts, is 1¼" wide, and is 1¼" thick. The rounded handle is designed to provide a torque-free grip even in a small hand. The leather-padded sight window is cut ¼" from center shot, and the thin arrow shelf is extended with a leather extension pad. The 4½" grip is wrapped with a moose, elk, or deer hide and laced down the front.

The Commemorative Longbow incorporates traditional deep-cored limbs that reflex 1¼" from mid-limb to the tips. On the 65" length, the upper limb has a working length of approximately 25⅝" from the fadeout to the nock and the lower limb has a working length of 23⅜". The limbs narrow from 1³⁄₁₆" wide at the fadeouts to ⁹⁄₁₆" at the nocks.

Although yew is the classical favorite, maple and osage corewoods are also available. The limbs are constructed from one back and three belly corewood laminations. Full-length fiberglass envelopes the corewoods and riser on both the back and the belly providing extra strength through the thin handle. The limb edges are extremely rounded and feather gently into the fiberglass. A 4" corewood wedge is incorporated into the tips to provide stiffness and the tips have thin riser wood overlays. String nocks are flush cut on the sides and shallow on the back. The bow is finished in a high gloss, to display its natural beauty, or a flat matte for hunting.

To check his 65", 80 pound at 28" draw, yew-cored longbow for relative speed, Don shot 29", 2216 aluminum arrows through the chronograph. His 550 grain arrows were fletched with three 5" feathers, had snap-on nocks, and 150 grain field points. Don used a leather shooting glove and drew a consistent 28". The bow was equipped with a Flemish Dacron string without accessories. The average arrow speed for this bow, arrow, and shooter combination was 191 fps.

The following draw/force measurements were recorded on this 65" yew-cored High Cascade longbow:

DRAW LENGTH	24"	25"	26"	27"	28"
DRAW WEIGHT	63#	67#	72#	76#	80#

The BLACK DIAMOND TD is Don's most popular recurve. It's offered in 60", 62", and 64" lengths. Don's personal 62" bow with the heavy cocobolo riser has a mass weight of 3 pounds, 5 ounces. Its handle section is 19" long, 1¾" wide, and narrows to ¾" through the sight window which is cut ¹⁄₃₂" from center shot. The handle is 2½" thick near the limbs and thins to 2" through the grip. The nicely rounded sight window is full cut for 3" above the crested shelf and tapers back to full riser width 4½" above the shelf.

The hardwood handle incorporates several thin vertical maple wedges sandwiching thin strips of riser wood. Contrasting riser wood over white fiberglass capping accentuates the front of the handle. It has a low-profile grip similar to the classic grip of the old Bear Super Kodiak. Above the grip the riser flows into simple rounded contours while slightly peaked ridges accentuate the sides near the accessory bushing.

The Black Diamond's moderately recurved limbs each have a 16½" working length on the 62" bow. They narrow from 1⅝" wide at the fadeout wedges to 13/16" at the nocks. The limbs are offered in the longbow corewoods and are constructed from a single tapered lamination on the back and one parallel lamination on the belly of the fadeout wedge. These corewoods are enveloped in clear or black fiberglass.

The limb tips are overlaid on the belly with a thin veneer of riser wood in the outer six inches. This recurve overlay provides extra stiffness and gives stability throughout the recurve and allows for a deep string groove which helps achieve positive string alignment. The back tip overlays are made from riser wood over white fiberglass.

The TD limbs are also capped with riser wood over the limb attachment area to provide strength. They attach to the riser

YEW IN THE FOREST — A prominent feature in Don's take-down recurve (left) and his slim lined longbow is their radiant yew wood limb cores. For Don it's the ultimate corewood.

with a single bolt and single alignment pin system.

To check his 62" maple-cored TD for relative speed, Don shot the same 550 grain arrows used to chronograph his longbow. His bow pulled 75 pounds at 28" and had a Flemish-twist Dacron string equipped with brush buttons and Catwhisker string silencers. He again drew a consistent 28". The average arrow speed for this bow, arrow, and shooter combination was 201 fps.

The following draw/force measurements were recorded on this 62" maple-cored Black Diamond TD recurve:

DRAW LENGTH	25"	26"	27"	28"	29"
DRAW WEIGHT	64#	68#	71½#	75#	80#

Don also offers his one-piece Castle Mountain Recurve which is reminiscent of the classic sixties recurves. This 60" recurve has features similar to the TD. Its warm-toned woods under clear glass and matte finish make it a practical hunting bow and an eye-catcher on the range.

A BOWMAKING START

Don began making bows when he was a boy. Guided by his grandfather in Wichita, he learned how to make self-wood bows in the fifties. Later as a young man backed with carpentry and cabinet making skills, Don tried his hand at building a composite longbow. His interest in bowmaking soon grew into a hobby, and before long his friends began asking him to build them longbows. Word spread about his longbows, and by 1979 Don's hobby had grown into a part-time business and he was three months behind in bow orders.

STAVE HANDLE

During his first two years of hobby bow building, Don experimented with almost every conceivable limb and handle design and even looked back in time to come up with new ideas. "I dug into the history of my grandfather's bows and discovered that many of his old self-wood bows had small round risers. I also studied the early days of American archery and looked at the bows Howard Hill used to accomplished his greatest archery feats. Most of those bows had smaller and rounder handles. So I made a few prototypes back in the seventies and discovered they were superior for reducing torque and were very comfortable to shoot. My small, round handles were actually similar in feel and appearance to an old stave bow."

Don refined his thin handle design, then incorporated it with a reverse handle concept in his longbow. "When you shoot a longbow with a stacked riser on the belly, you're pushing the heart of the bow further away from your grip, and that can increase the effects of torquing. But a reverse handle bow puts the majority of the laminations right in the web of your hand and gives you leverage for controlling the bow, plus there isn't a peaked riser for your hand to teeter on."

Don's small torque-free handle was introduced into the custom bow market in the early eighties and later became a popular grip style among other bowyers. "There are lots of small-handled bows available now, and I suppose that's one of the highest forms of compliment."

SUCCESSFUL DESIGN

Following the similarities of the old stave bows, Don designed his limbs with a deep core and a rounded cross section. He also blended in a sweeping reflex for performance. "I experimented with different trapezoid designs and with some of the extreme ones I actually lost speed. I extensively chronograph tested different limb cross-sectional designs and found that the rounded limb was the fastest. Rounding the edges and feathering the glass removes fiberglass mass, giving you a faster limb.

"We also incorporate a wooden tip wedge in the outer four inches of our longbow limb. The limb has reflex from mid-limb out to the tip to get the shock away from the handle, yet it still produces a lot of speed. The tip wedge stiffens the tip and forces the limb to work about four inches down from the wedge in the heaviest part of the limb reflex."

With his bow design refined, Don continued to experiment with varying corewoods, but age-old yew best suited his stave-styled composite longbow. Then he took this magical corewood one step further. "We started offering longbows with bamboo, yew, maple and osage cores. Recurve bows were primarily made with maple cores so we started dabbling with yew wood, and produced some fast and smooth shooting recurves."

HELP

During the early eighties, Don's bows grew in popularity, and after advertising nationally, his business blossomed. He increased production, but the longer hours spent grinding and sawing aggravated a lingering respiratory problem. Finally, failing health forced Don to make a major decision about his bowmaking — quit or get help. "I had very severe health problems. I thought I had emphysema. I was so sensitive to bow dust that I couldn't even finish speaking a sentence and still breathe. I was constantly taking bronchial dilators and fighting respiratory infections."

Faced with a backlog of orders for a bow design that he had put so much of himself into, Don decided to look for help. His search for a bowmaker led him north across the border where he discovered Checkmate Archery Manufacturing Limited in Abbotsford, British Columbia. One of Checkmate's owners, Larry Courchaine, is an avid longbow archer, and Don hoped they could reproduce his longbow with the quality he demanded.

Don took his bow forms to Checkmate and showed them his bowmaking techniques and specifications. They then built several of Don's bows, and he heaved a sigh of relief when he saw the results. "Fortunately, Checkmate produced the quality I was looking for. They are probably the number one bowmaker in Canada, and maybe the only company in the world capable of producing my bows."

Checkmate began manufacturing McCann bows in 1984, using Don's stock of Oregon harvested yew. But as that supply dwindled, they found a new source. "I showed Larry how to find, harvest, and season yew in British Columbia. And their mountains contain some of the finest yew wood on the face of the earth."

Even though Don doesn't glue and grind bows any longer, he still devotes much of his time to his bow business. "I continue to design and build prototype bows, and I help put them into production in Canada. I also monitor all of the quality control. I set standards that my bows have to stay within. I don't allow file or sanding marks, and the finish has to be flawless. The fadeouts have to be perfect in the risers and in the TD limb wedges. I check every bow for alignment, tiller, and limb arc. On the longbows I also do the leather work."

BOW BUILDING SPECIFICATIONS

Don makes sure that his bows are tillered with a ⅛" to ¼" positive tiller on the upper limb. This tiller is designed and built into the limbs so they usually don't require much tiller adjustment during manufacturing.

His bows also incorporate solid, edge or quarter grain laminations in the core. "We always use a matched pair of laminations that are cut side by side from the same board. We also use a variety of grain alignment in alternating laminations in a limb so we don't get a stiff side in the limb."

RISERS

Don's standard riser wood is bubinga, but he also offers osage and cocobolo. "The most popular riser wood by far is cocobolo. It's quite heavy, strong, very pretty, and makes a sweet shooting bow. When we make a riser we try to align the riser's wood grain in line with the string for strength and rigidity."

On Don's recurves, the riser is laminated vertically with maple strips to add visual contrast and provide extra strength. "We cut our recurve risers in half and sandwich maple laminations with alternating strips of cocobolo. This breaks up the grain of the wood and tends to nullify any inherent weakness in a particular piece of wood and gives us a sturdier handle."

FADEOUTS

Fadeouts are critical areas which Don watches closely when inspecting his bows. "If a limb is going to come apart, it's going to break in the fadeout. We need the fadeout taper absolutely paper-thin. It's critical on all bows but especially on a longbow. First, we grind them down on a grinding jig, then we block sand them and feather them out until you can literally see daylight through them."

TD LIMBS

During TD limb construction, much of the rough work is performed while the limbs are attached to a master riser. But the final tillering and limb alignment is completed when the limbs are attached to their matching riser.

"We build a custom bow for the individual. Recurves in the past didn't perform like today's bows because they were designed to have a uni-draw. But building a universal limb takes the speed out of it. We build our limb to be stressed at a given draw length, and we have two limb lengths with different working lengths. We also use different shaped fadeout wedges to create varying preload in the limb."

One of the prominent features of Don's recurve limbs is the overlay of riser wood on the last six inches of the recurve belly. "That lamination makes the limb more durable and less inclined to twist. Twisted limbs have plagued recurves because of improper stringing and abuse. But our overlay produces a stiffer limb making it more twist resistant.

"It also enables us to fashion a deeper string groove in the recurve belly. During rugged field use, a deep string groove helps keep the string aligned. Plus, the overlay allows us to make the deeper groove without compromising the strength of the fiberglass. We keep the overlay wood thin so it doesn't add much mass weight to the tips or inhibit the unfolding of the recurve. The chronograph speeds show it's right up there where it's supposed to be."

HEAT-CURED GLUES

Don's risers are glued using Urac 185, and limb composites are glued together with Ren epoxy. The bows are pressed using the fire hose method with electric heat strips curing the epoxy at 200 to 220 degrees for one hour. "In the beginning I atmospherically heat cured my limbs. But I learned at Boeing and by talking to adhesive chemists that epoxy is much stronger if it's cured at a higher temperature for a shorter time. You can get two to four times the strength with a high temperature epoxy cure."

Don also learned that corewood moisture content was critical in achieving a reliable glue bond. "A common story with some bowmakers is they got a bad batch of glue. That's an overused excuse. The real problem is they just don't understand the importance of moisture content in their corewoods.

"When heating corewoods during glue curing, moisture is driven out and it rises through the adhesive creating a moisture barrier between the glass and the adhesive. It also gets between the laminations. That bow might only stay glued together long enough to complete. So it's imperative to use corewoods that are absolutely moisture free — down to six percent. We heat-temper all our laminations in a heat box for a couple of weeks so they will be moisture free and absorb the epoxy better. You can maintain wood at 120 to 125 degrees for extended periods without damaging it."

PREVENTING LIMB TWIST

Even though Don has designed twist resistant recurve limbs, he cautions his customers to be extremely careful and always use a bow stringer when bracing their bow. "Using a stringer not only protects your bow, it protects you. My friend was unstringing his bow with the push-pull method and it got away from him. Fortunately, he was wearing safety glasses because it just about drove the lens into his face. I used to have a fine shooting recurve that I sold to a friend. He never used a stringer and he ended up twisting the bow's lower limb."

Besides cautioning about improper stringing, Don warns customers to keep their bows away from heat and moisture. They should also be stored with care. "You shouldn't stand a bow in the corner on its limb, especially some of the finer limbed bows. It should be laid flat, preferably in a large elk or deer rack."

TRADITIONAL TRENDS

Like most traditional bowmakers across the country, Don has seen a growing interest in stick bows within the last ten years. "The trend towards traditional archery is healthy because it represents many archers who have come through the compound ranks and have taken archery seriously enough to look for more satisfaction and variety in the sport. A big part of this transition started out as a fad, but it's not anymore. It represents a good cross section of archers. About ninety percent of the people who try traditional archery stay with it.

"The reason they stick with it is the satisfaction they derive from the sport is directly proportional to how much they put into it. If you can just pick up a compound bow, bolt a bunch of stuff on it, then go out and shoot pie-plate groups at forty yards in a weekend, I don't think you gain much appreciation for the sport. But if it takes you months to learn to shoot a recurve well using instinctive skills, you have a lot more appreciation for archery."

HANGING IN THERE

Like the beginning traditionalist who appreciates the sport because of the extra challenge, Don now appreciates bowmaking more than ever. Because of his health problems, crafting custom bows is like harvesting yew — it's something he doesn't take for granted. Despite his setback, Don looks forward to conquering his respiratory problem and hopes to once again fully enjoy the craft he learned from his grandfather in Wichita.

Until then, Don will continue to head for the high country when winter snows blanket Mt. Ranier's northern slopes. There, he will reopen the ringed archives of the Cascades. And when he's able to resume bowmaking, his aged yew will be silently waiting as it has been for centuries, for a bowyer's hand to shape it into its destiny.

JIM BRACKENBURY BOWS

MADE FOR ACTION

Life is a game involving players and spectators — some people make life happen while others watch it happen.

One of the players who makes things happen in today's world of bow-making is matter-of-fact, cut-to-the-chase, Jim Brackenbury. At work or play, he attacks tasks with the single-mindedness and intensity of a bulldog going for the leg of a prowler.

As a production manager at Tektronix Corporation in Portland, Oregon, Jim designs the most efficient and effective methods of achieving production. He's a fat trimmer, a time saver, and a guy who gets results.

During his part-time bow building he dives into his work with his sleeves rolled up and forehead furrowed with concentration. He plunges into each step, never wasting a movement as he flits from one work station to another, the bow continually emerging with every fluid move.

His intensity peaks during hunting season. It's then that Jim transforms from a weekday production manager and evening bowmaker into an elk's or a chukar's nightmare. In the field he focuses his dogged approach to the job at hand, sinking his teeth deep into the hunt and letting the quarry know the chase is on.

For Jim Brackenbury life is not for the timid.

ROUND TRIP HOME

Jim was born in Portland and raised on a farm in nearby Gresham, Oregon. When he was eight years old, his father bought him a thirty pound lemonwood self-wood bow and a handful of little arrows, opening the gates to a lifetime of adventure. "I ran around shooting those arrows at everything, and I ended up skewering one of my mom's chickens. I sure got my butt beat for that, but that night we had chicken dinner."

During his junior high school years, Jim replaced his lemonwood bow with a solid fiberglass forty-five pound recurve and made himself a set of cedar arrows. Armed with his new bowhunting arsenal, he often headed out into the evening shadows to hunt for small game and test his budding bowhunting skills.

After high school, Jim received a two-year electronics degree from the Oregon Institute of Technology in Klamath Falls, then enlisted in the Air Force where he spent four years as an electronics technician.

Jim bought a new Bear Grizzly recurve while stationed in Las Vegas, and he practiced with his recurve around the base. Later he had it shipped overseas, when reassigned to duty in Vietnam, where he arrowed some local jungle reptiles.

Jim finished his Air Force term in Alamogordo, New Mexico, and after being discharged he decided to stick around long enough to enjoy the archery mule deer season. Finally, with time to seriously bowhunt, it didn't take Jim long to bag his first deer.

Back in Oregon, Jim became caught up in the thrills of elk hunting, and the following year he killed his first bull elk with a bow. It was sweet to be home.

HOME TO STAY

Now in his mid forties, Jim still lives in the rural countryside outside Gresham where he grew up. There, he enjoys the moderate climate of the Willamette Valley, the nearby steelhead rivers, and the lush green landscape of northwestern Oregon.

Besides his love for bowhunting, Jim shares a zest for shotgunning chukars with his two bird dogs Brandy and Char. Guided by Jim's methodical approach to getting any job done, this hunting threesome make the wary upland birds plenty nervous. "Hunting chukars is similar to back country bowhunting. They inhabit steep and rocky country and are a tough game. I often average ten miles a day, and half of that is up and down steep slopes. Because of the rugged country there aren't many avid chukar hunters. Besides, most people aren't crazy enough to go after a bird that runs uphill and flies downhill."

SMALL GAME ACTION

To sharpen his bowhunting eye, Jim has spent many a long night arrowing small game along nearby rivers where an abundance of possum, raccoon, beaver, and nutria offer a variety of nighttime action. "A nutria is an aquatic rodent that lives along the water like a muskrat and averages about twelve pounds. But they're like a beaver — they never quit growing. I've killed them up to twenty-five pounds, and I've had other people tell me they've killed them over forty pounds.

"Lots of people up and down the valley here once raised them for their pelts. But the bottom fell out of the market and instead of destroying them, some people just let them go in the creek. The nutria have up to seven or eight litters a year with eight to ten in a litter. The only thing that keeps them in check is our cold weather, some trappers, and a few hunters.

"To hunt them we get in a boat at night with a spotlight and cruise along the rivers, ease up on them, and do our best. But when you're shooting under artificial light late at night you don't always shoot your best. And after midnight your shot-to-hit ratio usually goes to hell."

Over the years Jim's interest in small game bowhunting has been replaced mostly with bow building, chukar hunting, and bowhunting for Oregon's big game species. He has taken deer, coyote, antelope, and his longtime favorite, the majestic elk.

ELK MYSTIQUE

Jim has been bugling and chasing elk for the past fifteen years and the game never gets boring. "I don't know of anything that's more conducive to keeping man's adrenaline at a high level for such a long-time. The excitement is in the combination of getting a bugling response and then anticipating that bull coming in. But every elk is different and I often have the uncanny ability of being in the wrong place just in time to screw up."

When Jim heads for elk country he usually concentrates on the north facing slopes where elk find more shade, damper conditions, and the heavier cover they prefer. Jim has also discovered a correlation between concentrations of bulls and the remoteness of the country. "Bulls generally stay away from man. For years I hunted the Eagle Cap Wilderness Area in northeastern Oregon. We packed way back into the center of that area and found two square miles of the best elk hunting in the country. I took seven elk out of there in nine years. But it's steep, rugged country with 3,000 feet of elevation between the valley floors and the ridge tops. Hunting that big country requires getting up before daylight and back after dark."

Even though Jim located a super elk hideout in the Eagle Caps, it didn't last. "The elk were pressured by another group of hunters for three days in a row on two consecutive seasons. They just ran all the elk out of the area and the elk haven't come back. That's how sensitive they are. Elk are extremely intelligent and have good memories. They'll just pack up and leave."

Once he's located remote elk country, Jim attempts to pinpoint bulls by using long-range bugles. Weather conditions, bull-to-cow ratio, time of the rut, and time of day can all affect a bull's response. But one of the most important factors affecting a cagey bull, even in desolate country, is encounters with two-legged predators. "If a bull gets bugled in during a season and determines that it was a human that bugled him in, either by smell, sight, or getting shot at, he may answer a bugle and even come in to within 100 yards, but the odds of ever getting him within bow range that season are pretty damn slim."

THE SETUP

After Jim locates a responsive bull, he maps his final approach and setup. His first consideration is the wind. "Your scent is the one thing that will give you away in elk hunting. So you must determine the wind direction and what it's going to be by the time you get set up for that elk, because thermals change throughout the day. Always plot your approach from the downwind side of the elk."

With his approach plotted, Jim prefers to work with another bowhunter as a two-man team. One hunter bugles from thick cover while the shooter positions himself in front of the caller on the downwind side of an opening the bull is likely to come from. "Bulls tend to come in head-on toward the bugler and a shooter setting off to the side and slightly in front of the bugler will often get a better shooting opportunity. Most shots at elk are a lot closer than the average mule deer shot.

"Bugling is more of a verbal joust, like people shouting profanities at each other. Usually a bull elk isn't going to travel too much out of his way to come to your call, so I try to get within a quarter of a mile of the elk for my setup.

"I prefer to set up near more open cover because a big bull doesn't like to wallow through heavy brush. If he's responding well then all of a sudden he shuts up, that's a pretty good indication he's coming in or leaving. Then you have to wait and continue bugling. Sometimes they come in silently, but being able to judge if he's coming in quietly or leaving is nearly impossible."

Whether he's the caller or the shooter, Jim usually kneels to conceal his form from the elk's keen eyesight. "Unlike deer, elk will see you even if you're motionless. A mule deer will just bumble along and won't spot you if you don't move. But even on a dead run an elk will spot you if you're in the open. Once he spots you, camouflage is useless, and much of today's camouflage clothing is polished cotton which is fairly noisy at close range."

ELK ADVENTURES

Although the well executed two-man bugling setup often works, Jim sometimes changes his tactics to elude the elk's acute defenses. To get above those sharp eyes and sensitive noses, Jim and his hunting buddy once put up tree stands along a heavily used elk trail. The hunters were confident the elk would fall victim to the plan, but the elk had other ideas. "Opening day passed without an elk coming by our stands, and there were hardly any fresh elk tracks in the area. We hunted there for a couple more days and still nothing happened. On the third day another elk hunter tried hard to drive those elk downhill past our tree stands, which was their natural escape route. But they finally found a way around him and went up over the ridge. Somehow our tree stands had bothered the elk enough for them to change their patterns."

Jim knows that even the slightest human pressure can make elk mighty scarce, and it's a rare hunt indeed when too many bugling bulls leave him baffled. But he recalls one special season when a combination of perfect weather, ideal hunting country, and an overabundance of elk caused his adrenaline to run wild for several days.

"I was hunting in a place where hunting isn't usually allowed, but my friend, John, had permission for a few of his friends to hunt there. It was a relatively flat area with some rolling country covered with good timber and laced with old logging roads. It was a neat place. It even frosted a little at night and got up to seventy degrees during the day.

"During my first couple of days in there I went absolutely crazy. I'd never heard so many elk bugle. I couldn't get any of them to come in, yet they were everywhere. Every two or three minutes a different elk would bugle. Then I would pick out which one was best for the wind direction and work in on him. But I could never see the bull.

"I had just run off this one small herd and was going up a logging road when I spotted a spike bull elk about seventy-five yards away. He had about six cows with him, and he would bugle then run over and mount a cow. He repeated this bugling and mounting routine about every ten minutes. Finally it clicked what was happening in this area.

"There were a lot of elk but not a very good mature bull population carry-over from the rifle season. In this whole bunch of elk there were just a lot of spikes and small three points, and they each had five or six cows. They were all happy running around, breeding, and bugling, but none were mature enough to come in to my bugle."

Near the final day of season, Jim decided to fill his tag and freezer if the finicky elk would cooperate. "I was after this herd and for some reason they doubled back. The lead cow was the biggest, longest, leanest, and ugliest elk I'd ever seen. She was walking downhill at a good pace and I swung and shot. The arrow caught her in the loins and broke her back. She took one step, piled up, and rolled down the hill. Another arrow finished her in seconds."

ELK SHOOTING TIPS

Although Jim now enjoys consistent success arrowing elk and other big game, his early bowhunting years were often frustrating. Back then, it seemed like most of the deer and elk were protected from his arrows by some magical invisible barrier. "I think it takes most people years to bag that first head of big game, but after that they score more frequently. Usually that early lack of success doesn't have anything to do with a bowhunter's ability to shoot a bow.

"One fellow told me he was switching to a compound because he was missing game with his recurve. I asked him if he could hit my truck tire nine out of ten times and he said, 'Of course!' So I said, 'That tire is about the size of an elk's chest, so why can't you hit an elk at the same distance?' He didn't know why. I told him it probably had nothing to do with his shooting ability. It was his lack of ability to pick a spot on the animal and to control the adrenaline flowing through his veins. That's why champion target shooters go for years missing big game animals."

With his adrenaline mostly under control, Jim employs a specific method for shooting at game. It's a technique that improves the odds. "I wait until the animal has its head behind a bush or tree. Then I raise up, get my bow in position, and come to one-third draw. That movement is what many animals see when you're bowhunting. When I complete my draw, my string-hand movement is hidden by the limbs and the riser. As the animal starts to move, I draw back and concentrate on the spot I want to hit."

At the moment of truth, many bowhunters shoot for the crease behind the front leg and others pick a particular tuft of hair. But when Jim focuses on his quarry, he looks beyond the side he can see. "A friend of mine asked his father where to shoot a big game animal and his father replied, 'Shoot at the farthest leg.' If you think about that, no matter how an animal is standing that arrow or bullet has to go through something awfully vital to get to that far leg. However with a bow, head-on shots on big game with a bow are extremely marginal and should never be taken. Even most shots on game quartering toward you are questionable."

With broadside shots on big game most bowhunters try to place their arrow behind the shoulder. But that's dangerously close to the back edge of the lungs. If the animal is moving, the hit may well be too far back for a clean, killing shot. "I shoot for the middle of the front shoulder. Most people think the leg bone goes straight up like a table leg, but it actually turns forward about forty degrees at the elbow. So really there are only a couple inches of meat to punch through to hit the vitals.

"Some guys are afraid of hitting the leg bone. But if you shoot a two-bladed head with the tip rounded off and you do hit the leg bone, it will slide past the bone and still enter the vitals. I just round mine off a little bit with a file. But three-bladed heads and sharp-pointed heads don't slide worth a hoot."

Even though picking a precise spot on the animal is usually important, sometimes the hunter is faced with aiming at something other than the game. Some call it threading the eye of the needle. "The first few elk I killed I wasn't shooting specifically at those animals. I was aiming for openings in the trees.

"My first big bull was standing at thirty yards and about five yards this side of him were two tree limbs six inches apart. So I concentrated on shooting my arrow between those two limbs. If it made it, I had to hit that elk. I wasn't aiming at the elk, but that arrow went between that six-inch gap in the branches and got him. My second elk was behind a small fir tree and I had to shoot within an inch or two of the tree trunk near some limbs. Well, that's where I put the arrow and killed the elk on the other side of that tree."

SHOOTING STYLE

Jim's purposeful and direct nature is also reflected in his shooting. He's an instinctive archer who executes shots with confident fluid moves polished over the years. He cants his bow slightly, anchors his middle finger in the corner of his mouth for a split second, then pulls cleanly through with a sweep of the hand. "Great archers such as Ben Pearson, Howard Hill, and Fred Bear all had one thing in common: they shot fast and didn't hold at full draw. They also shot as well or better than we do today, and we use better equipment. Many of today's good shooters also shoot fast."

Like some of the archery legends, Jim leans into his shot and narrows his eyes in concentration. "The style target archers teach is to keep both feet parallel to the target face. But that's unstable for hunting because you can sway back and forth. I put my left foot forward and place over half of my weight on that foot. That gives me more stability in the plane of the bow and it prevents swaying."

To help sharpen his shooting, Jim attends an occasional 3-D animal shoot. His favorite is the spring Klickatat shoot held in Washington. Although 3-D shoots can provide good practice, many don't represent realistic hunting conditions. "Sometimes the targets are set up to encourage shots that a bowhunter wouldn't take. They have too much brush between the archer and the target, and they make the shots too far. Everybody likes to watch arrows fly, but I don't believe the average distance at these shoots should be

SOLID FORM — Jim leans into his shot for stability, pausing only a second before burying the shaft in the mark.

forty-five yards. I would like to see most of them between twenty and thirty-five yards which are more realistic shooting distances in the woods."

When practicing on the range, Jim tries to simulate his field form, right down to the way he nocks his arrows. "The first thing I learned hunting at night was never to take your eye off the animal, and there's no way you can look at your string and stab the nock on while you're watching an animal. So I lay the arrow on the rest while I'm looking at the game and then I slide my hand back to the nock and slip it on the string under the nocking point."

ELK BUSTING EQUIPMENT

For targets or elk, Jim shoots orange XX75 aluminum arrows fletched with pink feathers. "In a black and white picture, which is what animals see, my arrows are a dark gray. But with that autumn orange arrow with pink feathers sticking in an animal there is little doubt where I hit it, even at a hundred yards. Also, I don't lose nearly as many arrows as I would with camo shafts."

Jim fletches his arrows with four 4¼" feathers at seventy-five and 105 degree angles then burns them into a parabolic shape. "Back when I first started shooting, my role models all made their own arrows and they all used four-fletch. With four feathers you get better arrow steering because you have more surface area at the back of the arrow where the maximum leverage point is. You can literally lose one feather and the arrow will still stabilize a broadhead. You also get better clearance because the arrows travel another inch before they engage the bow. And with my method of nocking without looking, the four-fletch always goes on right."

Jim prefers using open-throated speed nocks because they work best with his nocking technique. Although he has tried snap-on nocks, he swears, "Never again! A snap-on nock cost me a nice bull elk.

"I packed a couple of miles into Anthony Lakes to hunt elk. It rained on our bows that night then froze before dawn. We hit the trail early and I was sneaking along a creek when I spotted two bull elk drinking. I whipped an arrow out of my bow quiver and flipped it up on the arrow shelf and tried to nock it on the string but it wouldn't go. I kept twisting that arrow and trying to get it on the string. Then the elk started moving and I looked down and discovered that a drop of water had run down the shaft, settled in the nock, and frozen solid. I lined up the nock on the string and really pushed until I snapped that ice out, but by the time I got the bow up the elk were disappearing into the brush. That wouldn't have happened with my speed nocks."

On the elk-biting end of his shafts Jim prefers the superior penetration of two-bladed self-sharpening broadheads that sharpen all the way to the point, such as the old-style Bear Razorhead and the Zwickey Eskimo.

Jim carries his arrows in a Delta Products bow quiver which he offers with his bows. He's not completely happy with any quiver, but for him it's the best way to tote arrows. "I prefer not to even use a quiver, but unfortunately I need to carry extra arrows. I don't think there is a good quiver. Back quivers are noisy and they're tough to get multibladed broadheads out of. Catquivers are okay but you can't wear a pack with them. So a bow quiver is simply the most convenient."

Wool plaid is usually Jim's choice for bowhunting attire and he complements his outfit with one of his favorite elk hunting companions, a homemade leather fanny pack. "I use it to carry fire starting material, a butane lighter, aluminum foil, my lunch, extra broadheads, a flashlight, a camera, elk meat bags, tracking tape, my folding knife, and thirty feet of eighth-inch nylon rope for either hanging or holding animals in position while I'm working on them.

"For fire starter I use fiberboard cut into one inch squares and soaked in melted paraffin. They will burn for almost twenty minutes. Also to help start a fire, I use the aluminum foil as a moisture barrier between the damp ground and the fire. I carry fire starter because lots of times I get wet from rain or snow, and it's nice to get a fire going during the middle of the day to dry out my weary bones."

Most recurve shooters use brush buttons and string silencers. Jim uses them too, except he gets twice the mileage out of his bow string accessories. "I only use one small brush button on my lower limb. I could never figure why anybody would need one on the top limb because that's not the limb that gets hung in the brush. I also use half of a set of Catwhiskers, and they don't seem to affect my bow's performance much. But those big brush buttons do so I use the small ones. If you have too much stuff hanging on your string it starts making your bow not shoot as well."

During his younger years, Jim shot recurves pulling over seventy pounds, but arthritis problems in his neck and finger have caused him to drop down to bows pulling sixty-three to sixty-seven pounds. "There aren't many people who can shoot bows over seventy pounds and shoot them well. After you get over sixty pounds you only pick up about one foot per second per pound of bow weight which is fairly insignificant. A heavy bow causes many guys to shorten their draw length and they don't even get any extra speed out of it.

"A sixty pound bow shooting a broadhead is adequate for hunting anything in North America. Broadhead and arrow dynamics have a lot more effect on penetration than bow weight. Bows are all made to be close-range weapons so there's not a big difference between a longbow that shoots 180 feet per second and a cam compound that shoots the same arrow 220 feet per second. With either one at twenty yards, an elk or a deer have the time to give you their autograph and leave before your arrow gets there."

BRACKENBURY'S BOWS

For the serious close-range hunter, Jim offers three different risers in his three-piece take-down recurve. The LEGEND is his top-line riser made from bubinga with a vertical wedge of shedua sandwiched with maple veneer. His TRADITION is made from solid bubinga and the DRIFTER is constructed from one piece of highly laminated hard-rock maple.

Jim's personal favorite is the exotic looking Legend. Although the riser incorporates imported hardwoods, Jim used some local help in coming up with its name. "Dwight Schuh wrote an elk hunting article about Billy Cruise and Larry Jones roaming through the hills of eastern Oregon like two 'living legends.' For awhile people ribbed Jones about being a legend. He shoots one of my bows and one day he said, 'You ought to name that bow after me, The Legend.' I laughed about it and then got to thinking that was a hell of a name for a product to live up to."

Larry Jones is one of the country's top name bowhunters specializing in bugling elk and chasing open country mule deer. He was one of the first archers to shoot Jim's bows. "Larry had his body shop back then, and he traded some body work on my truck for two of my early bows. He shot quite a bit and had a fairly long draw, and he would break a bow every three or four years. I told him, 'Well, I don't think you're going to live long enough to break my bow.' That was seven years ago and he's still shooting that first prototype bow."

Jim's bows are available in 60" to 68" lengths in two-inch increments and have a mass weight of 2¾ to 3 pounds depending on length and riser materials. He recommends a brace height of 7½" to 8" from the string to the throat.

All three riser models exhibit the same design and contours. The riser is 18¾" long, 1⅞" wide near the ends, and narrows to ¹³⁄₁₆" through the sight window which is cut ³⁄₁₆" past center shot. The riser is 2½" thick near the ends and thins to 1¾" through the throat. The rounded sight window is full cut for 3" above the shelf and gradually contours to full riser width 5" above the shelf. The arrow shelf is nicely crested with the high point over the throat for clean and forgiving arrow flight. The shelf is covered with black leather, and the window is equipped with a matching strike pad.

The riser exhibits simple flowing contours except for a sweeping ridge below the grip on the window side. Jim fashions his grips with a low to medium profile and a medium throat. The grip is shaped to make the bow hand seat tightly under the shelf for an optimum instinctive picture.

The bow specs are inked on the riser below the grip opposite the window and on the limb belly near the riser. The belly side of the limb attachment bushings are threaded and serve as the quiver attachment bushings.

The take-down limbs attach to the riser with a single ⁵⁄₁₆" flathead bolt and single alignment pin system. On the 64" model, both limbs have a working length of 17¾" from the fadeout to the nock The limbs narrow from 1⅞" wide at the fadeouts to ⅝" at the string nocks, and exhibit a sweeping, large-radius recurve.

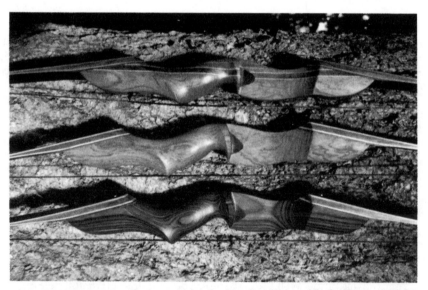

BRACKENBURY'S BOWS — The Legend (top), Tradition (middle), and Drifter (bottom) exhibit simple sweeping contours and blend with the limb fadeout wedges for a one-piece appearance. (Photo by Jim Brackenbury)

The limbs are constructed from one belly and one back lamination of Actionwood tapered .015" per inch and enveloped in brown fiberglass. The edges of the exposed corewoods are relatively flat and the fiberglass is feathered along the limb edges. On the 64" length, the corewoods are bonded to a gently sweeping 10½" long shedua fadeout wedge which is nicely contoured on the sides and back to conform to the riser, giving the bow a one-piece appearance. The limb tips are overlaid on the belly with a 3" hardwood recurve overlay and on the back with a matching short tip overlay. String grooves are cut flush on the sides and feather into a full cut "Y" in the belly overlay.

The entire bow is finished in a low-luster polyurethane designed for hunting and easy care.

To check his bows for relative speed Jim shot 29", 2117 aluminum arrows fletched with four 4¼" parabolic cut feathers. The arrows were equipped with speed nocks and had a total arrow weight of 535 grains. Jim shot with a glove, drew a consistent 28½", and had a crisp pull-though release. The bows were equipped with Flemish Dacron strings without accessories.

Using his 64", 65 pound at 28" draw take-down, Jim shot a relative arrow speed of 199 fps.

The following draw/force measurements suggest the smoothness of this 64" bow:

DRAW LENGTH	25"	26"	27"	28"	29"	30"
DRAW WEIGHT	56#	59½#	63#	67#	71#	74#

Shooting his shorter 62" model which pulled 61 pounds at 28", Jim shot an average relative arrow speed of 192 fps.

The following draw/force measurements were recorded on this 62" model:

DRAW LENGTH	25"	26"	27"	28"	29"	30"
DRAW WEIGHT	51#	54#	58#	61#	65#	68#

Jim's recurves are noted for their clean arrow flight off the shelf and for full working limbs which completely unfold providing both smoothness of draw and good arrow cast.

PRODDED BY PAIN

The Brackenbury recurve evolved from Jim's original challenge to make a lighter bow that he could shoot after he developed painful arthritis in his string finger when he was thirty-four. Before making that first bow, Jim spent a year studying bow designs and corewoods. In designing his recurve, he wanted a sixty-five pound bow that would perform better than his old seventy-five pound recurve. That was a tall order to fill, but Mr. Can Do was determined to try.

Jim designed his bows to provide a blend of durability, stability, speed, smoothness, and quietness. "One of the most important qualities in a hunting bow is dependability. With my design, bow failure is almost non-existent.

Shooting stability is also very important. Arrows have to go where they're pointed.

"I chose a limb design that would bend well for the full length and recover uniformly to get better performance. My long limb is also thicker and heavier which adds to the stability. It's less sensitive to torquing to one side or the other, and it helps gain a little more speed with heavier arrows.

"Limb speed also comes from the wood-to-glass ratio. My bows are designed to hurl nine grains of arrow weight per pound of bow weight, at 190 fps. But speed isn't nearly as important as many people try to make it. The animal doesn't give a hoot if the arrow is going 180 or 220 feet per second. When he's dead, he's dead. I've contended for years that it makes little difference how fast your arrow MISSES an animal."

A long-time do-it-yourselfer, Jim blended his design concepts, making his first try at bowmaking a surprising success. His first bow, built early in 1979, came within two pounds of the desired draw weight and shot great.

FINDING THE BEST CORE

Originally Jim decided to use locally available yew wood for his limb core. "I heard yew was the greatest thing since popcorn. But I learned real quick that yew is soft. If you don't build your fadeout with the right taper it will compress the yew."

Jim designed a long tapered fadeout that would work well with his yew core, but after his first fifty bows, he decided to switch to a different core-wood. "Yew is noted for not being as dependable or having as long of a life span as maple, so I built a bow with Actionwood and discovered there wasn't much difference in performance. The bows made with yew felt a little softer and seemed to have a bit less recoil. But out of ten yew bows, five would shoot good and the other five wouldn't perform as well. However, with Actionwood, all ten bows would shoot alike. Yew just doesn't have the average stability and good shooting characteristics that Actionwood has."

GETTING BIG

The popularity of Jim's bows grew and by 1984 he began professionally making bows part-time. "I had made enough bows using sandpaper, rasps, and files and decided if I was going to continue to make bows it was time to get big or stay home."

Using his production efficiency skills, Jim spent over a year designing and building a sophisticated bowmaking shop with specialized power tools. Today, his spacious shop looks like there should be at least half a dozen bowmakers working there. It has a well-planned arrangement of grinding, sawing, sanding, and drilling workstations to accommodate almost any bow-making task.

Jim's shop looks like overkill for a one-man bowmaking operation, until he springs into action like a beaver after first frost. Unwavering, he attacks his work, briskly flitting from one work station to the next, pausing only long enough for his constantly moving hands to grind, drill, or sand the emerging bow. "Being a manufacturing manager by trade, I learned that repeatability and consistency is important. I set up my shop for the best process flow for bowmaking, and it's a small enough shop so my time to get from one machine to another is just seconds."

MAKING IT HAPPEN

To save time, Jim saws and glues together his laminated Legend risers in batches. He glues the riser composites with Ren epoxy and "C" clamps them together. When working with hardwoods for the Legend and Traditional risers, Jim positions the wood grain in alignment with the bowstring for maximum strength.

After the glued riser has dried, Jim sands the block flat on both sides and traces the riser outline using an aluminum template. He band saws out its shape then grinds the limb contact surfaces by holding the block firmly on the grinding table and actually splitting the pencil line in half using a disk sander. This ground surface represents the critical limb-to-riser contact angle, and Jim says, "There isn't any room for error in this part of take-down bowmaking."

He then clamps the riser into a drill guide fixture. Jim machined all the components of his riser and limb drill guide fixtures, which are mounted on a small steel bench and placed at the appropriate location in his bowmaking process. He drills the bushing holes through the riser and counter sinks the belly side to later accept the stemmed bushing. "I wanted a secure spot to mount the quiver, so I decided to use headed bushings that go all the way through the riser. The hole going through the riser is seven-sixteenths of an

MR. EFFICIENCY — Jim's limb attachment drill guide jigs for his riser and limbs are mounted on a specialized bench. Like all of his work stations, it's even set up at the optimum working height.

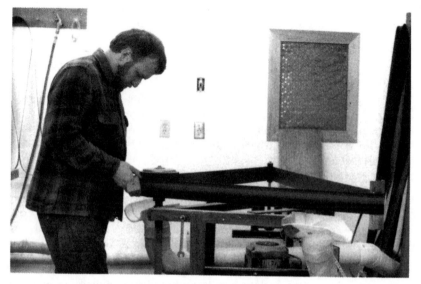

THREE IN ONE — Jim's three-station sanding machine makes short work of shaping risers. It can also make short work of fingernails if he's not careful.

inch and the head on the back of the bushing is three-quarter inch. I refuse to install standard sight bushings unless a customer intends to put sights on them, and I request they don't use them for attaching a bow quiver because brass press-fit bushings in the side of the riser aren't designed for bow quiver durability."

Next Jim uses his band saw to cut out the shelf area and sight window. "I cut the window past center shot so the centerline of the arrow is in true alignment with the string. That provides the maximum versatility in arrow spine that will shoot well. When you get away from center shot, as in a longbow, you have a narrower spectrum of arrow spine that will shoot well."

Jim carves the riser's rough shape on the band saw by gingerly slicing off contoured sections. Guided by his trained eye and experience, he skillfully, free-hand trims the rough shape in seconds without wasting a motion.

For grinding the riser's shape, Jim uses his custom-made "big sander." This long vertical sander uses twenty-four grit belts. Jim discovered an economical supply of these large belts, then specifically designed his sander to accommodate them. The big sander uses two sizes of replaceable spindles for grinding the different contours. The large spindle as used for general contouring, and the smaller post is used to shape the grip area.

Although Jim makes the shaping look like a carefree job, he keeps a trained eye on his progress and uses a micrometer to check the throat thickness during his shaping flurry. "When I shape the throat I mike it to within ten thousandths of an inch. I fashion a saddle in the grip so the hand fits every time and feels comfortable. Also to minimize torque, I make the high point of the throat directly in the center of the bow."

To eliminate hours of drudgery hand-sanding his risers, Jim designed and built an intriguing tri-drum sander. It's a large vertical belt sander using three sizes of air-cushioned sleeve drum sanders. Like all of his machines, it's hooked up with 4" PVC pipe to his dust collection system. Quickly moving from drum to drum, Jim works the riser on the drums until it's sanded to its finished shape. "Part of me goes into every bow — sometimes that's not just philosophical, as the twenty-four grit belt sanders can eat up my skin quickly."

THE POWER PARTS

Jim begins making his limbs by crafting the fadeouts. He uses solid shedua in board form and rough saws the fadeout taper on the band saw. He then clamps it into his fadeout tapering guide jig and sands its shape using his big vertical sander. Jim finishes feathering his delicate fadeouts by grinding them free-hand. "Even one and a half inches into the fadeout, it's still very flexible. It actually bends four to five inches into the fadeout on the completed bow which increases the working limb length and distributes the stress over a longer section."

Besides using matched pairs of Actionwood laminations, Jim cuts 60" strips of fiberglass in half and uses each half on opposing limbs to ensure balanced component properties. To reduce limb sanding time later, Jim orders his fiberglass roughly sanded on the gluing side and smoothly sanded on the exposed side. "The glass and the wood are sanded as well as humanly possible, but they still can vary slightly in thickness. Also, if you use varying pieces your bow may be out of tiller."

Depending on draw weight, draw length, and limb length, Jim varies his wood-to-glass ratio to achieve maximum performance in his limbs. "Some people say there is something magical about their bows because of the way they change the formula of their limb components. I really don't find anything magical about building bows, it's just flat-ass hard work."

Jim is one of the few bowyers who installs belly overlays. Like his tip overlays, they are cut from a thin strip of shedua, feathered on the grinder before glue-up, then laminated in the limb form with the rest of the composites. This saves the extra step of later gluing and clamping on the overlays. "Besides looking nice, my belly overlay functions as a protective cushion for the limb belly.

"Fiberglass is brittle, and if you chip the belly glass near the tip there is no way to stop that sliver from working up the limb. The wood overlay protects it from rocks and other things the tip might get jammed into. I had a friend slam his limb tip in the door of a truck, and I figured it was destroyed. It had a big dent in the belly overlay so I sanded it off and found the integrity of the glass underneath was still good. Without that belly overlay the glass would have been crushed."

GLUE UP

Always economizing on time and procedures, Jim glues up two pairs of limbs at a time. His two sets of limb forms are made from laminated 1" plywood and represent the limb back. When he made them, Jim dowel pinned both the upper and lower limb forms together then sawed and sanded both forms as one wide form so both limbs would be exactly the same. "A bowyer friend once told me, 'The best bowyer in the world can't make a good bow on a bad set of forms.'"

All of Jim's limbs are glued up in the same forms, and the different limb lengths are achieved by varying the placement of the fadeout wedge and/or by trimming the butt end of the fadeout wedge.

Prior to glue-up Jim covers his form surfaces with plastic wrap. He doesn't bother covering the non-gluing fiberglass surfaces with masking tape because the glue curing heat also dries out the tape and makes it devilishly hard to remove.

Jim applies Ren epoxy to all contact surfaces of his composites, including the overlays, and lays them up in his forms. "If you don't apply epoxy to all gluing surfaces, I think you're going to have some dry spots and you may have glue-joint failure. I've seen people who glued only one contact surface and couldn't understand why their bows were blowing up."

When laying up the limbs, Jim also laminates a thin strip of riser wood over the belly fiberglass where the limb attaches to the riser. This butt overlay provides extra cushion between the limb and riser and is later sanded to ensure that both limbs are in plane.

Once the limb composites are laid up and aligned, Jim lays on a fire hose and bolts on the upper half of the press, then inflates the fire hose to 100 psi. He cures his glued limbs for six to eight hours at 140 degrees in his thermostat and timer-controlled hot box. "The strength properties of epoxy get better the longer you leave it at curing temperature. But with most glues, the temperature jumps up about forty degrees when the resins catalyze. If you're curing too hot, it drives the moisture out of the corewoods and it combines with the glue between the laminations and causes a failure."

LIMB SHAPING

Jim removes the cured limbs from the forms and trims the tips and butts to proper length. He then sands the limb edges flat, installs the limbs in his drill jig, and drills the bushing and alignment pin holes. Jim bolts the pair of limbs to their matching riser where they will stay together during the rest of the bowmaking operation.

Next, Jim braces the bow using tillering blocks attached to a steel cable. The notched blocks which slip over the rough tips are moved back and forth until both limbs are in alignment. Jim then scribes the limb width and string nock location and unbraces the bow. He cuts in rough string nocks using a masonry grinding wheel. Then he grinds the limbs to width and rounds up the string nocks with a rat-tail file.

Jim braces the bow with a string, checks tiller and alignment, and makes any adjustments by grinding the limb edges on his big vertical sander. He commonly tillers his limbs from ⅛" to 3/16" positive tiller on the upper limb and tillers the limbs almost even for three fingers under shooters.

Using his whining band saw, Jim trims the butt ends and fadeout edges to conform with the riser contours. He then sands them until they blend in nicely with the riser, giving the three-piece bow a one-piece look.

Jim prides himself on being able to usually come within one pound of draw weight. He reduces from one to four pounds of draw weight by feathering the edges of the limbs. While feathering, he counts each pass on the sander and repeats it on the opposing limb to maintain tiller and limb dynamics.

He finishes the tips by filing in a "Y" string groove through the belly overlay and just scoring the belly glass. After sanding the nocks and groove smooth, Jim hand-sands the tips into their rounded and low-profile shape.

FINISHING TOUCHES

For quick and effective finish sanding, Jim uses a power floppy sander that whirs away and flap-sands the entire bow smooth.

Next he gets out his spray gun and savors the moment when his polyurethane finish brings the bow to life. "The wood grain in the riser is always subdued and dull until that first coat of finish hits it, then it just jumps out at you. It blossoms from this dead piece of wood with suppressed character to the beauty of the true grain patterns."

Jim sprays his bows with four coats of Deft polyurethane number two satin finish and flap-sands the bow smooth between coats. "Urethane, which is slower drying, is tough and flexible whereas a catalyzed finish such as Fullerplast dries quicker but tends to get harder with time and crack."

Besides its flexibility, Jim prefers a polyurethane finish because it can be easily touched up by the customer. "I recommend that customers don't use any wax over the finish because it prevents any touch-up finish from adhering. If the limb edges get beat up, a customer can rough up the edges using 320 grit sandpaper or steel wool and then spray it with the same finish I use."

Jim supplies a Flemish-twist bowstring with each bow and has his reasons for not using any others. "Flemish strings are more traditional, they're quieter shooting, and I believe they last longer than endless strings. Fast Flight strings are bow breakers. To use one I would have to beef up the tips or it would tear them off. You only gain five to seven feet per second of arrow speed with Fast Flight but you pick up a lot of hand shock and bow vibration. By beefing up the tips to handle Fast Flight you're adding weight to the end of the limb which will reduce your speed, so your net gain isn't worth it."

Before Jim ships out a bow he installs a string nocking pointing set 5/8" over absolute square and shoots each bow about fifteen times to be sure the bow is shooting true — just the finishing touches by a man who assumes nothing in his methodical approach to bowmaking.

LOOKING AHEAD

Besides looking forward to the day when he can build his bows full-time, Jim is always dreaming about that bigger elk next season. It's not that he's so intent on downing another several hundred pounds of elk steaks; he's just helplessly in love with the lure of traditional bowhunting.

"Archery dates back thousands of years and is as much a tradition as it is a sport. If a person just wants to harvest game they're far better off using a rifle, traps, or snares. The real definition of hunting may be the acquisition of game, but that's not what's important. It's the camaraderie with your fellow man, the enjoyment of nature, and the relaxation from our everyday lives that makes bowhunting special."

UPDATE

In June of 1988 Jim left his job at Tektronix to sink his teeth full-time into his bowmaking business. And according to Jim, his bowmaking is booming. He also says traditional archery has never looked healthier. One reason it's healthier than ever is because of the quality traditional bows that custom bowyers put into the hands of America's archers — bowyers such as Jim Brackenbury, a guy who makes things happen.

Chapter Thirty-One

CASCADE MOUNTAIN ARCHERY

THE FIRE RING

As the evening shadows hushed the forest, two Indians kindled a fire near the creek. The fir sticks popped and sparked, casting a glow on the moss-covered trunks of nearby trees. Soon the other braves would be returning to camp with their day's bounty. Maybe the spirits would bless their fire ring with fresh elk or deer. Surely the young braves would bring back belts hanging heavy with rabbits and grouse.

At the ebbing side of the fire one of the Indians heaped a mound of wet seaweed mixed with shellfish gathered from the nearby salty inlet. When the tide was low a fireside meal was always at hand. The aroma of steaming shellfish mixed with the simmering smell of salal, the carpeting edible leaf that fed man and beast. Busying themselves near the fire, the Indians paused to listen to their brotherly gray owl echoing his waking hello through the mist. As the owl's call faded, a thundering splash downstream signaled an early arrival to the season's salmon run. The braves grinned at each other and agreed it would be a skookum harvest season and the fire ring would witness an endless feast.

Today the fire ring of the Squaxin braves is cold and covered with a heavy blanket of moss. Their fireside tales of past hunts only echo in the distant spirit world, their long ago passing reclaimed by the forest.

But one man knows of their campsite, its fire ring, and the scattered stone tools they left behind. This white man with stream-blue eyes who now lives next to the fire ring also knows the trails of their footsteps, their thrills during the hunt, and their pride in crafting a bow to harvest nature's bounty.

UNDER THE QUIET CANOPY

This lanky white man is long-time traditional bowyer, Fred Anderson. His secluded home sets in the fir-shrouded Pacific Coast forest near the shoreline community of Grapeview, Washington. He lives a quiet life in these southern reaches of Puget Sound up Case Inlet and near the backwaters of Pickering Passage. It's a mystical place of solitude where Fred creates his Skookum, Chinook, and Diamondback longbows.

The surrounding forests of the Olympic Peninsula represent the lifeblood of the area. The mild, wet, and lengthy growing seasons cause the conifers to crowd and reach skyward, providing a healthy timber and Christmas tree industry.

Much of this Pacific rain forest is so dense that local blacktail deer, Roosevelt elk, and black bear travel through winding tunnels within the underbrush. Umbrella-like ferns rise up from the mossy and shadowed slopes to compete with the sprawling patches of salal. It's a unique plant that Fred shares mixed emotions over. "We couldn't die of starvation if we wanted to eat it. You just boil some up and it's edible. It's a primary food for both deer and elk. In some areas elk eat it right down to the bare ground. But if you're a bowhunter you learn to hate it. You get tangled up in it plus it gets you all wet. You can't see game in it, and it's almost impossible to sneak through. It's awful stuff. But a lot of people around here make a living picking it for commercial greenery."

Although the dark forests draped with spider-like gobs of moss appear dreary, Fred enjoys the solitude of the lush canopy around his home. Despite the often damp and sometimes gloomy surroundings, Fred brings sunshine into his world with his off-the-cuff humor and bright outlook on life. He's man at peace with himself and the world around him. "My biggest interest in life is my family. Outside of my family I like to bowhunt and fish. We fish for salmon and steelhead, and I really enjoy catching sea-run trout here in the sound. Our Dolly Varden is a sea-run trout and it's the best eating fish around these parts."

CALIFORNIA INFLUENCE

Fred was born and raised in San Diego, California, and like many teen-age boys during the early fifties he was inspired by the movie adventures of Howard Hill. "I lived near two golf courses that had some brushy areas loaded with rabbits. I'd been shooting at those rabbits with my slingshot, but after I saw Howard Hill's movie, *Tembo*, I knew there was a better way to shoot those rabbits. So I saved my allowance and bought a little Ben Pearson hickory bow. Within a week I shot my first rabbit and from then on I was hooked on archery."

It wasn't long before Fred made his first rabbit bow. It was a six-foot yew longbow and, although it was a little sluggish, the budding fifteen-year-old bowmaker used it to shoot nearby bunnies. He continued his bowmaking hobby and a year later his brother gave him two dozen Oregon yew staves. Fred threw himself into his bowmaking and even made his first composite bow when he was sixteen. "It was about sixty pounds and was a straight-limbed bow with a maple core and a small simple handle. Like my yew longbows it was a dog too, but I had a lot of fun with it."

Fred not only had fun with his homemade composite longbow, he made the most memorable shot of his life with it. "I had this friend who always was bugging me about my bows and arrows so I invited him to come out one evening and try for some rabbits. The golf course was closed in the evening and the rabbits would come out onto the fairways to eat the grass.

"We came over this hill where the golfers teed off and there was a rabbit sixty-five yards away feeding on the fairway. I told my friend, 'Watch this.' I pulled back my bow but the rabbit started running up the hill toward the brush so I led him and shot. The arrow and the rabbit magically came together, and that rabbit rolled back down the hill deader than a doornail. I was really excited but I tried to act like I made that kind of shot all the time, and even to this day my friend thinks I'm the greatest shot there is."

Fred's interest in all aspects of archery continued to grow and he soon discovered that his home town was a prime place to feed his archery appetite. "Back then, San Diego was a hub of archery and we had beautiful target and field ranges. Some of the best bowmakers and shooters in the country lived there. There was a lot of glamor in archery then because of the noted trick shooters and archery heroes.

"I was really influenced by our local archery champion, Rube Powell. He was my hero when I was fifteen. You have heroes at that age, but I don't tend to have heroes much anymore. He was a tremendous athlete and won the Nationals at least five times."

Besides tournament shooting heroes, San Diego also had its share of bowmaking idols, and Fred learned bowyer's skills from some of the best. "Frank Eicholtz was one bowyer who helped me a lot and taught me bowmaking. He was the first bowmaker to ever put fiberglass on a bow and many consider him the father of the modern composite bow. He even made Howard Hill's bows for his African trips. Frank made an oriental-handled bow back then that was just the cat's meow. I also met up with Harry Drake when he was making target and hunting bows and I got a lot of bowmaking ideas from him."

HEADED NORTH

Fred later went into the Air Force but continued his bowmaking hobby in the service. After he was out of the Air Force, Fred married and moved north to work for Seattle Archery Company in Washington making Fasco bows. For eight years he built bows and attended college part-time. Eventually, Fred earned his degree and left the bow presses to pursue a career in teaching.

Although he taught full-time, evenings and summers still left time for bowmaking so Fred built bows for himself and friends. Years later his bowmaking zest again blossomed, and he began making and selling longbows under the name of Cascade Mountain Archery. "During the eighties I became thoroughly disenchanted with compound shooting and the direction of archery. I started making longbows again and they started really catching on.

Now the longbow has become so popular I'm almost a slave to my bowmaking."

When he's not making longbows or spending time with his wife and three children, Fred teaches the sixth through eighth grades at Grapeview school. "I'm really interested in how people learn and the pedagogical sciences. I really enjoy teaching and the interpersonal relationships that go with it."

THE HUNTER'S ROLE

Besides being a family man, teacher, and bowmaker, Fred is also an enthusiastic bowhunter. Like many facets of his life, bowhunting has deep personal meaning. "I'm not a great trophy hunter. For me hunting is an intrinsic experience composed of many different things. One part is just being out in the woods, and that's a joy in itself. Another part is pitting myself in a natural way against an animal. If I really wanted to kill a deer, I have a 30-06 that would do the number on one real quick, but that takes the human element out of it. To me hunting is involving that human element, and that's why I love traditional archery."

Much of Fred's bowhunting is similar to his life-style: he keeps it simple. "I'm just a plain bowhunter, not one of those real fancy bowhunters. I like hunting anything. Matter of fact, carp shooting is one of my most pleasurable forms of bowhunting. I hunt them in the desert area of eastern Washington where it's usually nice and warm and there are lots of carp. There is plenty of action yet it's a relaxed, enjoyable hunt. Rabbit hunting can also be tremendous bowhunting fun. With big game bowhunting you can hunt a whole season and get maybe only one shot, but with small game you're out there shooting all the time."

Even though he may only get that one shot, each fall Fred heads for the nearby mountains in quest of Washington's biggest game. "I think elk are great to bowhunt because they're so big and majestic. I'm pretty good at bowhunting deer, but elk always leave me bamboozled. I rarely can get in on them, then when I do, they go the other way or something goes wrong. Being a teacher I can never take the time off to go elk hunting like I should. My weekend elk hunting trips are always like reaching for the carrot in front of your nose — you never quite get it."

DEER ADVENTURES

Elk may be an elusive bowhunting quarry for Fred, but he enjoys regular success on local blacktail deer. He prefers stalking them in semi-open hill country without much timber where he can spot deer and then sneak in for a shot. One of his favorite deer haunts is only twenty miles away, and it always presents him with a thrill. "I deer hunt in a canyon located in the foothills of the Olympic Mountains. It's one of my favorite places, and hardly anybody knows about it. Every time I go down that canyon I have an adventure. It might just be a grey owl making a swoop at me or I may shoot a deer or just see some. This year I shot a deer in that canyon and later on I called in a big black bear, but I wasn't able to get a shot at him."

Fred also finds deer hunting adventures in eastern Washington. He sometimes travels there for a late season mule deer hunt, and once in while he gets more excitement than he bargained for. "I drove over there right after Thanksgiving, and it was snowing when I got there. It was early afternoon, and I started quietly walking up a canyon I was familiar with. The way that light snow was coming down it was like being in a different world.

"I was following some tracks in the snow up this one trail when a big old mule deer doe came out of nowhere. She stepped out on a little ridge about fifty-five yards away. The whole scene was kind of eerie. I pulled back and shot an arrow between her ribs and she went bounding down the hill and across a field.

"I immediately followed her because of the falling snow and it was easy tracking. I found her without much trouble, but the roads back in there were real treacherous and it took me a long time to get her out. I even got involved in a little scuffle. I was putting on my tire chains when some town toughs came up and saw the deer in the back of my car. They started giving me a hard time about shooting a poor animal, and as they approached I stood up with that tire iron in my hand and chased them off. Then I had some more adventures getting home on those icy roads."

STAYING IN TUNE

Now in his early fifties, Fred stays in shape for chasing off ruffians or chasing after elk by walking on a treadmill during the winter and hiking during nicer weather. "I try to keep up my endurance because it's no fun hunting when you're out of shape."

Besides keeping his body tuned to enjoy the rigors of bowhunting, Fred also pays attention to the mental aspects of the sport. "I think you have to be right with the world and at peace with yourself to enjoy bowhunting. You can't be too far off course on your goals, and you can't have too much personal turmoil in your life. If you're worrying about debts, your job, your marriage, or where you stand in relationship with your Maker, it's hard to enjoy hunting. It's also hard to enjoy if you take yourself too seriously and are out there to prove that you're the world's greatest hunter."

Even though he has nothing to prove, Fred takes shooting practice seriously. For him, it's just part of being a responsible bowhunter. "I start really practicing in the spring when it starts to warm up. I begin by retraining myself, and I even keeps notes on what works well and refer to them. I usually start off by just standing in front of a bale and working on my form. Sometimes it takes two or three weeks of working on my form before I can start practicing at hitting something.

Fred's shooting form has changed over the years from a deliberate California aiming style to an instinctive reflex style. "I try not to think too much about my shooting when I'm hunting, because when I do I usually blow it. But if a shot just presents itself and if I can rely on my instincts more than my brain, I usually shoot better.

"Traditional shooting is an athletic endeavor, and the more you practice the easier it becomes. I use a high anchor with my middle finger near the corner of my mouth. But no one person has the best way of shooting a bow and arrow. I think it's crazy when people think they have to shoot like someone else. Just shoot with a style that fits your body and stick with it."

After he has his form polished, Fred jams his quiver full of arrows and heads for the stump fields. "The greatest practice is going stump shooting. We have great places to stump shoot because logging operations have been going on for the last hundred years — we have stumps upon stumps. Stump shooting is fun, it gets you outdoors, and it really tunes you up for shooting at game."

When stump shooting, Fred doesn't hold back with concern about losing his arrows. He just lets them fly. "I like to shoot arrows just to watch them fly. Most tra-

EACH TO HIS OWN STYLE — Fred settles into his high anchor, maintaining the consistent form he polishes each spring.

ditional archers have that childish instinct of loving to watch their arrows fly through the air — if they don't, they won't last too long in traditional archery. Real archers like to go out and fling arrows. It's addicting."

Besides flinging arrows, Fred attends a number of big-name traditional gatherings. "Humans are social animals, and we get our social releases from different places. I like to go to shoots during the summer and see my old friends. I go to one shoot where I see this friend who I only see once a year. We're the best of friends and for us the shoot is mainly social. I don't go there to tear up the targets. But I sure like to go down there and brag and carry on like a jack-ass."

When his summer of practice and carrying on is over, Fred is ready for the Washington deer season. He likes his shots at buckskins to be in the open without much obstructing brush and under sixty yards. Most close-range Easterners would squeak, "Sixty yards!" but for Fred it's a confident range. "I got my deer this year through the heart at sixty yards. I've gotten a lot of them that far. It's not that I'm good, you just get accustomed to shooting that far. There's east-coast and a west-coast shooting. On the east coast most people practice at short ranges, but out here we practice at longer ranges. I prefer my shots at deer between thirty and thirty-five yards because if they're too close I get too excited or the animal gets too spooky. And that distance gives me a better sight picture."

NATURAL ATTIRE

To match his equipment and personality, Fred's hunting attire is simple, neat, and rarely camouflaged. "Camo tends to identify me as a modern style compound shooting archer. Also, I don't want to look like a jungle commando when I'm out hunting. I typically wear a light pair of wool pants and a flannel shirt. A plaid flannel shirt offers plenty of camouflage, plus it's softer and more comfortable. I like what Howard Hill said, 'A person ought to be a gentleman when they're out hunting and not some wild looking creature.'

"If it's mild I like to wear the lightweight leather hunting shirt my wife made for me. It's not practical at times, but it gives me a feeling of being more of a natural person."

When Fred heads for the remote mountains he often carries a day pack stuffed with essential survival gear. This makes a back quiver impractical so he uses an Idaho Ranger hip quiver. "I really like the hip quiver but it doesn't carry enough arrows. If it's raining I like to use a Catquiver because it covers my fletching. If the weather is nice and I'm out in an area where I don't have to carry a lot of stuff, I'll use my homemade Howard Hill style back quiver."

Although Fred uses several quivers to fit his hunting, he never uses a bow quiver. "They're a no-no for me because they throw my bow out of balance and flag animals every time I raise my bow. Plus they add too much weight to the bow, and they're usually noisy. To me traditional archery is also an esthetic sport and a bow quiver takes away some of the esthetics."

No matter what quiver he's carrying, it holds heavy cedar arrows weighing from 525 grains to 600 grains. Fred fletches his shafts with either four 4" or three 5" feathers and burns his own parabolic style. He also uses Mercury nocks because of their index and deep seating.

Fred collects broadheads and has tried many styles over the past thirty years. But few come close to the quality of the Hummer designed by a bowhunting friend. Fred recently began distributing this head for discriminating bowhunters demanding the very best on the business end of their arrow. "I also like Zwickey Eskimos and Deltas that have been cut down a little. On deer-sized animals Bodkins and MA-3's are nice. But for elk you need a three-to-one length-to-width ratio two-bladed head.

"A broadhead has to fly well because it has to hit where you're aiming. Then it has to maintain its integrity once it hits an animal. It can't fly apart, it has to be structurally strong. But it shouldn't be too heavy or it will nose down or cause too much archer's paradox in your arrow. It must have quality steel that will take and hold a razor edge."

Fred sharpens his broadheads with an eight inch mill bastard file. "I've used razor blades and I've honed them, but I've found that if you pay attention, a regular file works fine. No matter what sharpening method you use, you must keep them sharp and pay attention to their sharpness all the time."

THE MAIN INGREDIENT

The final item on Fred's bowhunting checklist is the most important — his longbow. When this sage bowman enters the forest he wants a bow that looks great and shoots even greater. His favorite hunting companion is his sleek-lined Skookum longbow. " 'Skookum' is a northwest Indian term meaning strong or great, and people around hear use it when referring to something as great. But people from the east usually don't know what it means or how to pronounce it. My Skookum longbow is more skookum — a bit hotter and faster. It looks really classical when it's strung and it's an accurate shooter with a real crisp action."

Fred's hunting bow pulls around sixty pounds, a comfortable weight that's enough to down North America's toughest game. "I had a customer kill a Grizzly with my sixty pound longbow and his arrow plunked right through the bear. The most efficient bow weight is between fifty-five and sixty pounds. Anything beyond that and you're getting diminishing returns. With heavier bows it's hard to get an arrow heavy enough to be efficient with the limbs. If you're shooting a 500 to 600 grain arrow out of an eighty-five pound bow, you're wasting your time and energy. You need a much heavier arrow to be efficient."

The DIAMONDBACK is Fred's presentation grade Skookum and one of America's premier longbows. It's a stunning blend of thoughtful design, intricate craftsmanship, and breath-taking beauty. This snakeskin backed creation is a work of art. "When you see one of my Diamondback longbows, you're looking at the best bow I can make. I put everything I can into them without getting silly. But even with their price I put way too much time into making one."

The Diamondback is 68" long and with a dense cocobolo riser it has a mass weight of 1 pound, 8 ounces. Bow weight varies by several ounces depending on riser and corewood combinations. The approximate brace height is 6½" from the string to the belly of the shelf.

The slightly deflexed hardwood riser measures 16" between fadeouts and is intricately laminated with an artful assortment of wood and phenolic underlays. These contrasting layers of riser composites are delicately feathered into wispy thinness and disappear in the fadeouts. To add even more distinction to the riser section, contrasting layers of thin overlays are capped on the riser face and back.

This striking slim-lined riser is 1⅛" wide and narrows to ⅝" through the sight window. The slightly crested shelf is 1¾" across and equipped with a pigskin shelf and a strike pad which covers a small raised shock pad. The gently rounded sight window is generally cut ¼" from center shot. The slim grip is nicely rounded and moderately dished at the thumb index finger junction for a positive and comfortable grip. The grip is wrapped with a single 4¼" piece of suede leather.

PREMIUM SKOOKUM — Stunning riser underlays and overlays blended with a combination of corewoods under its reptilian backing make the Diamondback one of the country's most impressive longbows.

The Diamondback's deep-cored limbs exhibit a gentle reflex through the outer portion of the limb. Both limbs have a working length of 26" from the fadeout to the nock. They are usually trapezoid shaped tapering to the belly. The thin-lined limbs narrow from 1 ¼" wide at the fadeouts to a delicate ⅜" at the string nocks. They are constructed from one thin belly lamination and three thicker back laminations.

Fred uses a variety of corewoods and commonly uses a blend of maple, yew, and longui. These corewoods are backed with brown fiberglass and faced with clear glass. The brown fiberglass is covered from the tip overlays to the leather grip with genuine diamondback rattlesnake skin producing a lifelike, naturally camouflaged backing.

The limb tips are reinforced with a 4" tip wedge. A delicately feathered piece of riser wood is used for the back tip overlay and a thin layer of phenolic is overlaid on the tip face. The string nock to tip measures ⅞" on the upper limb and ½" on the lower limb. Finely fashioned string grooves are flush cut on the sides and the back.

Before the snakeskin is applied, the bow is finished to a high-gloss glassy polish which makes it look as though the composites were melted together. Beside of its outstanding beauty, the Diamondback is noted for its delicate balance, minimal hand shock, and true-shooting qualities.

To check a standard Skookum longbow for relative arrow speed, Cecil McConnell, a Washington traditionalist, chronographed his 68" Skookum which pulled 61 pounds at his 28" draw length. The bow was equipped with a Flemish-twist Dacron string without accessories. His 28" cedar arrows were fletched with three 5" feathers and each weighed 530 grains. Cecil drew a full 28" and shot with a tab. The average arrow speed for this bow, arrow and shooter combination was 186 fps.

The following draw/force measurements were recorded on Fred's personal 68" Skookum:

DRAW LENGTH	25"	26"	27"	28"	29"
DRAW WEIGHT	52#	54½#	57½	61#	63½#

The CHINOOK is Fred's second most popular longbow. Chinook is Indian jargon for King; it also means a hot western wind. "My Chinook has more of a modern look because of its forward riser. It's a little more forgiving than the Skookum because the handle is placed slightly in front of the fulcrum point of the riser. Plus, the forward thrust handle makes it point real nice. But that design also makes it lose a little draw length and speed."

The Chinook is a field-grade 67" longbow and has an approximate mass weight of 1 pound, 4 ounces. Its brace height is similar to the Skookum.

The Chinook's one-piece hardwood riser is 18" long between fade-outs. This deflexed riser is 1¼" wide and narrows to ⅝" through the rounded sight window which is cut almost to center shot. The riser is 2" thick and has a custom-dished grip. The window, shelf, and grip are similar to the Skookum.

The Chinook's deep-cored limbs have a working length of 25". These reflexed limbs are similar to the Skookum's in dimensions and construction. Brown glass typically envelopes the edge-grain corewoods. The combination of the forward handle and the deeply dished grip gives the shooter a sense of control and helps make instinctive shooting more natural. The chronograph and draw/force measure-

NEAR THE FIRE RING — The forward thrust riser on Fred's Chinook (right) is designed to minimize the effects of handle torque and improve its pointing characteristics.

ments on the Chinook are similar to the Skookum.

Fred also offers a short 56" flat-limbed ambush bow called the Siwash.

A SKOOKUM DESIGN

When Fred decided to get back into professional bow crafting he wanted to build a premium quality longbow with smooth-shooting performance. Using his lifetime of bowmaking savvy, he spent two years refining his Skookum design. "I didn't like a standard backset longbow because it kicked and was slow. So I designed a slight eighth-inch deflex into the handle and reflexed the outer limb. I don't like the tips to bend back too much because they lose energy, so I maintained a fairly straight end section in the working limb. My deep-core limb style gives my bows a lot of snap and they handle heavy arrows very well."

Fred blended his Skookum design with his meticulous craftsmanship and his artful eye for combining materials in overlays, risers, and limb cores. After his bows hit the market, their popularity was almost more than Fred could handle. "The bows started selling and in no time I was two years behind in orders and running in every direction. But I enjoy building my Skookums because I try not to build any two alike in the handle and overlay materials. Each has its own distinction. It gets boring building bows — anyone who says it's fun hasn't built enough bows. It's hard work, and I add a little spice to it by using different materials."

Even though Fred spent two years in developing his Skookum, he continues to explore the potential of new bow materials to keep it a true Skookum among longbows. "In the future I'm probably going to be using more exotic material in the core such as carbon, carbon/graphite, and bias ply fiberglass. But those materials have to be placed in the most effective position in the limb core."

THE INGREDIENTS

When building a Skookum, Fred begins by selecting a combination of corewoods to best fit the customer's wishes and the bow's design. "I like to use yew wood down the middle of the core because it's light and strong. I use longui on the belly side because it holds compression very well. For color I sometimes use a thin lamination of bubinga, which is also a good compression wood.

"In a laminated bow I want corewoods that are lightweight, structurally strong, and have a high modulus of elasticity — in other words, the corewoods should bend and return to their original shape without snapping. They have to glue well, be consistent in their qualities, and come from a reliable source."

One of the key corewoods Fred uses in his Skookum is a drab creamy wood that some bowyers consider mediocre at best. "Maple is an outstanding corewood. Many bowmakers, especially longbow builders, don't understand the mechanical properties of maple and how wonderful it really is.

"Maple is a plain looking, light-colored wood used to make compound bows and some cheap traditional bows, so it has a bad reputation. But you can pre-stress maple and use it edge grain or flat grain. It's wonderfully light and strong, and it has a high modulus of elasticity. Plus it's tough and it glues well. It lasts longer than most woods so you can plan on getting a lot of shots out of it. It has a few minor drawbacks, but there isn't a wood that doesn't.

"A lot of people write off maple as a bow core. But what corewoods have they used to set all the flight records? And what corewoods have won the Olympics? They're all maple-cored bows, and there's a reason for it. When I hear someone downgrading maple as a core, I know they haven't made too many bows, and they sure didn't make any high-stress recurves that had to stay together."

Fred buys solid, edge-grain maple laminations from the Old Master Crafters and occasionally he grinds them himself. His yew is cut locally and air dried for several years before he cuts it and personally custom grinds it into laminations.

Besides using common corewoods such as yew and maple, Fred also incorporates African longui into his limb core. "Longui is a long-grained brown wood with a nice springy feel. It has mechanical properties similar to maple and its characteristics are almost a cross between maple and yew."

CUSTOM-TAPERED FIBERGLASS

For strength, Fred envelopes his corewoods with one long strip of fiberglass on the back and one on the belly. Like his corewoods, he knows the qualities of fiberglass and blends his composites to achieve optimum bow performance. "Gordon uses different hardeners in the resins of different colored fiberglass. Black pigmentation sets up the hardest and makes a real stiff glass. But black glass stores up heat when it's in the sun which isn't good.

"White is the next best glass and it's very hard. It makes an excellent bow for hunting in the snow, but you don't see too many of them around.

"Clear is one of the softest glasses. If I make one bow with brown glass and another with the same specifications using clear glass, the bow with clear glass will come out almost ten pounds lighter."

Besides selecting the right color of fiberglass, Fred pays special attention to matching the glass thickness with the corewoods. "Most bowyers don't use a thick enough glass with maple and as a result they get a harsh shooting bow. But with yew wood you should use a thinner glass to make the core work nicer. If a guy wants a real snappy bow I use less glass and if they want a softer shooting bow I use a little more glass."

Fred is one of the rare bowyers who also custom tapers his fiberglass. Using his lamination grinding device, he grinds the gluing surface from the middle and tapers the glass to the ends. "I taper my fiberglass because I like to keep the glass ratio about the same throughout the limb length. My overall core taper is about .0045" per inch and my glass taper varies with the customer's needs.

"I've made bows with and without tapered glass, and the tapered glass bow is about three to five feet per second faster. That might not sound like much but it's one more thing that adds up to the bow's overall performance. Also, glass is heavier than wood and when you have more glass moving forward in the tips you develop more hand shock."

A PRE-STRESSED CORE

After Fred selects and measures each composite with a micrometer, he places the corewoods in his curing oven for a few hours to drive out any moisture. He then epoxies and presses the corewoods together in his special pre-stress form. "My bow form is different than my core form which causes the finished bow to be under tension even when it's unstrung. This gets the most out of the maple core and the bow starts storing more energy earlier in the draw, so when you're drawing those last few inches it's very smooth."

Fred uses progressively quicker or lower temperature curing epoxies throughout his gluing and heat-curing procedures. This ensures that the previously glued components will maintain their integrity. "You have to learn how to use epoxies and know their properties. My philosophy is once you have a good glue, don't change just because some other guy is using a quicker-drying glue. Gordon's epoxy works very well on my overlays because it's quick-drying and putting it in the oven for a short time doesn't loosen up the other glues."

After the laminated corewoods are cured, Fred grinds the sides flush and precisely grinds the tip faces to accept the wedges. He often uses Micarta as a tip wedge and varies the wedge length to make the limb work best for the customer's draw length.

THE RISER

To save time, Fred usually makes several risers at a time. Using a template, he traces the riser outline on a solid piece of hardwood. He saws out the riser and then gently feathers its fadeouts. "This job might get tedious if I didn't put some variety into it, so I use all kinds of hardwoods. There is beauty in almost all wood, and this is where my artistic side comes out. I blend the riser wood and underlays to bring out their beauty. On some bows I work with harmony, on others I use contrast."

Fred also prepares the tapered and feathered riser underlays that will be laminated between the riser and the facing. He uses a variety of woods and phenolics for his underlays and overlays.

IN THE FORM

Fred's Skookum form is made from laminated indoor/outdoor plywood and the form surface is covered with layers of fiberglass. This male form represents the contour of the bow's back and although it looks relatively simple, it involved a lot of work. "When I come out with a new bow I often spend sixty to seventy hours designing and making my bow form. It has to be perfect."

Rubber and sectioned pieces of wood make up the top of Fred's bow form. The "C" clamp method allows him to apply extra pressure at critical areas.

Before glue-up, Fred covers his form with plastic tape, brushes the composites with a clean brush, and checks for any grime marks. "If I see any little dirt spots I wipe them off with acetone. But you have to be careful with solvents because some can dissolve your glass."

He applies epoxy to all contact surfaces of his composites and lays them up in the form. Fred then lays on his cap form made from a strip of rubber with pieces of wood glued on top. He lines up his composites and begins "C" clamping down the cap form starting at mid-riser and working towards the tips. Fred has used the air hose method of pressing his composites, but he prefers the "C" clamps because they allow him to apply extra pressure in critical areas.

Fred places the clamped form in his oven and cures the epoxy at a slightly lower temperature than he used to cure the core.

TAKING SHAPE

After the bow has cured, Fred removes it from the form and grinds off the sharp dried glue from the edges. He lays on his limb shape template, traces one limb, then lines the template up by eye on the other limb and traces it. Most bowyers use a detailed centerline system but Fred simply relies on his experienced and critical eye.

He then band saws the limb's shape and grinds the edges to the scribed outline. Next he files in rough string nocks and braces the bow to check for rough weight and tiller. Unlike most bowyers, at this point Fred doesn't have a predetermined upper limb. He simply checks which limb is stiffer and marks it as the lower limb.

Fred scribes the overlay areas on the fiberglass and roughens them with sandpaper. He epoxies on the delicate overlays and "C" clamps them in place, again heat-curing the epoxy for a shorter time at a lower temperature. "When you use so many overlay materials, it's like gluing up two bows and it takes a lot of time. I use different tip and handle overlays on each bow. I figure my customers don't want a custom bow like every Tom, Dick, and Harry has. So I make every one of mine a little unique."

Once the overlays are cured, Fred begins aligning and tillering the limbs. "Aligning the limbs makes the bow straight and tillering affects how much the limbs bend. There are two ways to align a bow — you can take material off the strong side of the limb edge, or you can deepen the strong side of the string nock, or you can use a combination of both. We used to have on old saying back at Fasco's bow shop, 'Do you know how long it takes to learn how to align a bow? About 100 bows before a guy really learns it right.' That's a lot of bows for an amateur." Fred usually sands material off the sides to bring the limbs into alignment.

TRAPPING THE LIMBS

When it's aligned, Fred begins shaping the belly of the limbs and making minor adjustments in alignment and tiller. He usually tillers his longbows to ⅛" to ⅜" positive tiller for standard shooters. "Shaping the limb in a trapezoid makes a geometric figure which makes the limb stable and more forgiving when you're shooting. A trapezoidal limb has a tendency to jump forward instead of off to the side. But you can also overtrap it and weaken the belly, and then you start losing shooting qualities."

Many of Fred's customers are seasoned longbowers who sometimes even request a specific limb shape. "If they want a lot of trapezoid I'll put it in. Some customers want a reverse trapezoid, trapped to the back, and I'll put that in. Matter of fact, that's a real good way to make a bow if you're using the right kind of corewood. If I'm using maple I can trap to the back.

"Most people call trapping to the back a reverse trapezoid but that's a misnomer because it's really the correct way to trapezoid a limb. You actually want more material compressing and less material stretching. The back of the bow is the stretching side or the tensile side, so when you trap to the back of the bow you're causing it to stretch less material and compress more material on the belly side. But most corewoods can't take that kind of trapezoid and will crack. I usually trapezoid to the belly and it makes a pleasing bow."

Fred cuts out the arrow rest and window on the band saw and then shapes and sands the bow by hand. "From that point on it's artistic. It's like a dentist who fills your teeth — he can just make it serviceable or he can make it smooth and perfect. I love working with wood, and this is the part where a lot of us bowmakers get the creative, esthetic experience of working on a bow."

FINISH WORK

Fred final sands his bow with 400 grit or 600 grit sandpaper and wipes it clean with acetone. He then inks on the bow information. Fred mixes his Fullerplast with a special solvent which makes the dried finish a little more pliable. He sprays three coats over the glass and heavier coats over the handle.

After it dries for at least several days, Fred sands the bow with 600 grit paper and rubs it with steel wool until it's smooth. Using a polishing compound, he then buffs the bow to a high-gloss luster. For customers wanting a low-luster finish, Fred uses a different Fullerplast additive and rubs the dried finish with super-fine steel wool.

Nearly finished, Fred contact cements a small piece of cushion leather to the strike plate and glues on the strike pad and shelf leather. "That gives your arrow a high point on the rest so it doesn't ride all the way across the shelf. I find that it gives you a little more accuracy." Last, Fred glues on the leather wrap grip.

BOWMAKING SAFETY

Over the past thirty years Fred has been nipped by sharp glue and glass and has acquired a keen respect for power machinery. He offers a few safety tips to budding bowmakers. "To prevent a lot of fiberglass infections I use lightweight latex gloves. I also wear dust masks when grinding glass and wood, and I use a vacuum at each grinding station to suck away dust. I also recommend that amateur bowyers wear eye protection. It's more important to have good eyes than a homemade bow. You should also respect any kind of tool that's grinding or whirring away. They can really bite you. I've been fortunate over the years and have only been really bitten once by a saw. Latex gloves help if you're nipped because they take the place of your outer layers of skin."

DELICATE YET TOUGH

Fred's sleek longbows are so delicate looking they almost appear frail. But a few bowhunters have proven the Skookum's grit. "One customer from the Midwest went hunting up in Alaska for caribou. He was walking across a rocky hillside and slipped. He fell and his longbow skidded down the rock face, crashed into a river, and was swept away at least 300 yards downstream. He was hurt and had to stay in camp for several days. When he finally could get around he went back and fished out his bow, and there wasn't a square inch on it that wasn't dinged up with pits and scratches. He sent it back to me. I fixed the broken nock overlay and refinished the bow. I made it look brand new, and he's been using it ever since.

"Another fellow from Salt Lake City bought a Skookum for a hunting trip in Canada. After the hunt he called to say how pleased he was with the bow. Someone had shot a moose and he discovered a bear feeding on the gut pile. As he was crossing a river to get to the bear, he dropped the bow in the river and it was carried away downstream. He figured it was lost.

"With his bow gone he was devastated, so he went back to camp and got someone with a rifle and they shot the bear. They didn't think they would have much of a chance, but the next day they went looking for the bow and somehow spotted just the nock end sticking out of the river on a branch. They pulled the bow out and it was still strung. He dried it off and went out hunting later that day and shot another nice black bear with it. He said it was sand-blasted from being in that raging river for a day but he wanted to keep it that way as a memento of his trip."

ONLY THE BEST

When Cascade Mountain Archery customers draw their field-tough long-bows they're pulling back more than just wood, glue, and glass. They're drawing on thirty years of bowmaking experience from a craftsman who demands only the very best in his materials and workmanship. "I'm not out to make a lot of bows. That would take the enjoyment out of it. Because of my other interests in life, I make bow crafting enjoyable by building a very high quality bow and devoting a lot of time and workmanship to it. The quality and expense of my bows weed out a lot of potential customers who wouldn't appreciate them. I'm only looking for a high quality market of people who want the very best."

If the Indians who once tended the fire ring could see and shoot Fred's bows, there's little doubt what they would say — "Hmmm, Skookum!"

Chapter Thirty-Two

DON ADAMS ARCHERY

A SILTY GRAVE

It was a clear summer day on July 19, 1545. But the peaceful calm of that sunny morning was to end in tragedy.

Poised in the English channel off the Isle of Wight, the English navy lay ready, waiting for the oncoming French Armada. The pride of the English fleet was the thirty-five year old Mary Rose. A heavily armed battleship, she carried 700 fighting men and upper decks loaded with cannon and munitions. Her ranks of stout longbowmen readied their yew longbows and quivers full of deadly missiles. Each bowman could shoot a dozen arrows per minute up to 300 yards. This deadly force, combined with the fire power of her newly-mounted bronze cannons, made the Mary Rose an ominous defender.

But fate and the murky channel would cheat her from the sting of battle.

Preparing to engage the French fleet, the Mary Rose swung tightly with sails full of a fickle shore breeze. Top-heavy, she unexpectedly heeled on her side, the chilling sea flooding in through her lower gun ports. As King Henry VIII watched from the Southsea Castle in horror, the sea swallowed the Mary Rose in less than a minute, forever muffling the screams of her men trapped under the anti-boarding nets. The waters of The Solent entombed 650 of England's finest men in a salty grave.

The outnumbered English force ultimately turned back the French invasion, but that ghostly day marked one of the worst naval disasters in English history.

For 437 years the Mary Rose lay in the silt of The Solent until her remains and 17,000 artifacts were recovered by archeologists from the Mary Rose Trust. Among the sunken finds, they discovered over 2,500 arrows and 139 yew wood longbows.

Some of these bows were in such remarkable condition that they were later strung and drawn — a testimony to their amazing longevity. The archeologists meticulously examined each bow and were puzzled by the diversity of limb dimensions and overall shapes. They wondered why the King's finest bowmen carried such a hodgepodge of bows all made from the same wood. Surely they must have had a standard.

IN TOUCH WITH THE PAST

While the team pondered their questions, a silvery-haired man on the other side of the world in Elmira, Oregon, rhythmically pulled his draw knife down the bronze belly of an emerging yew bow. Don Adams, master bowyer of self-wood yew longbows, knew the answers to the puzzling questions about the ancient bows from the Mary Rose and eventually helped solve their archeological mystery.

"The Mary Rose Society sent me a number of letters asking me questions about the longbows they had recovered from their sunken ship. The bows weren't standardized like the society thought they should be. I told them yew bows can't have standard dimensions because each one's shape is relative to the grain and fiber texture of the yew stave and to the natural shape of the stave, including bumps and hollows. The shape of the belly alone can vary several times in a self-wood yew bow, and understanding that is one of the big secrets in crafting them."

Like the longbows recovered from the Mary Rose, each one of Don's yew wood creations is unique. "When they sent me letters telling me what they had found, it warmed my heart because I realized I was building my longbows like they did 500 years ago. When I'm making my bows, I feel like I'm holding hands with my dead ancestors. I'm using exactly the same materials, making exactly the same product, and experiencing exactly the same problems and thrills they had. The only thing that has changed is the finish."

AN EARLY START

Don was born in Eugene, Oregon, and has seen his share of self-wood bow bumps and hollows over the years. When he was four, Don got a small wooden bow set, complete with suction cup-tipped arrows, for Christmas. That was over forth-five years ago and Don has been shooting bows ever since.

It didn't take Don long to wear out his first bow and he soon learned to use the bow materials nature offered. "I came from a poor family and couldn't buy more bows, but I had a Boy Scout pocketknife and I began whittling my own. My first bow was made from a piece of a sweet cherry limb and some of the cherry shoots were the right size for arrows. I got my string from an old feed sack.

"My first bows weren't real fancy but they did shoot arrows until they dried out and broke, so I had to shoot them while they were still green. My brother and I whittled out those bows by the hundreds. We used willow, cherry, maple, and just about whatever we could get our hands on. The imagination that went on while I was whittling those bows was worth way more than the bows were."

Later, Don received sage advice from an old-timer who lived down by the river where Don and his brother used to shoot their cherry bows. The old man told Don to make a bow out of yew and to use Indian arrow wood for arrows. Although Don didn't know what a yew tree was, he found the Indian arrow wood and made both bows and arrows from it and found that it worked great.

In the early fifties Don's mother moved to Elmira, Oregon, where Don and his bowmaking zest soon met yew bowmaker Leonard Daily. "Old Reverend Daily was a minister, a bowyer, a logger, and even did a little boxing in his day. He was the flight champion in 1930, shooting a 100 pound yew longbow. He even beat Howard Hill who was shooting a much heavier osage bow then.

"Leonard Daily was a tremendous influence in my life during my teens. When I knew him he was near retirement from logging, but he was always making arrow shafts or bows. He tutored me in bowmaking from 1952 to 1957. Back then most of the bows we made were self-wood billet yew wood recurves. We boiled the ends and then formed the recurve. Years later when Daily died, he left me most of his yew wood stock and tools."

Don made arrows to help pay his way through aircraft mechanic school. After receiving his aircraft mechanic's license, Don moved to California, worked for United, and continued building bows during his spare time. He later moved back to Oregon as an aviation mechanic, but the lure of archery proved to be too much and Don quit his mechanic job and opened Adams Archery.

FULL-TIME BUSINESS

From the mid sixties until 1980 Don operated his archery pro shop near Eugene, and it even contained forty-yard, indoor shooting lanes. Besides selling top-name bows, Don manufactured and sold his own line of composite recurves. Some of those classic recurves he still regards as tops, even by today's standards. "There is no question about which bow was best, it was the old pre-AMF Wing 62 inch Thunderbird. There was never a better recurve built. That's not opinion, that's fact. On a force/draw curve that's the smoothest bow you'll ever pull — all the way to thirty-two inches.

"One time I flight shot with a guy who had a four-wheel sixty-seven pound Jennings compound. We marked half the arrows from a matched set and we each took four. I shot four arrows with my sixty pound Thunderbird. After he shot we started walking down there and saw there were four arrows in one group and the other four were twenty-eight yards farther. 'Boy,' he said, 'that recurve of yours did a lot better than I thought it would.' I didn't say anything at first and kept walking. Finally I said, 'By the way Ron, these first arrows are yours, those farther ones are mine.' That really blew his theory on compounds."

Don was so impressed with Wing's Thunderbird that he manufactured a copy which he called the Model 1000. "It was a fantastic recurve. I've had people call me by the dozens wanting me to make those again, but I'm two years behind with what I'm doing now. Besides, I'd much rather work with yew wood than fiberglass. But I'm tempted to turn out a batch because the used ones are selling for three times what I sold them for new."

Don sold compounds during the mid to late seventies because of their popularity among his customers, but they were a far cry from the archery he had known for over thirty years. "In my mind, compound bows did not represent archery and I didn't like selling them. The sport became too sophisticated. I ended up with a lot of employees and spent most of my time sitting behind a desk. I may as well have been selling pots and pans because it was all just merchandising. It took me totally away from the grass roots of archery."

THE BOY RETURNS

To recapture his boyish love for archery Don sold his business and once again began whittling old-English yew self-wood longbows, giving the world a stunning new look at one of the oldest of weapons. "Now I get more thrills looking at just one quality piece of yew wood than I ever got from looking at every compound bow I ever sold. Running around with a six-foot bow and a quiver strapped on your back may not be the best way to go hunting, but it was my way. Now I'm again doing something with archery that I love."

Today, his sleek and glistening yew wood creations rival any yew longbow ever built. "The most common complaint I get about my bows is that they are too beautiful to shoot. One guy even told me his bow was so pretty he thought it should be put in a museum. Robert Hardy, the British film actor, is an authority on longbows and said, 'Everybody in the know, knows that you make the finest yew longbows in the world. I have a collection of longbows that dates back into the 1800s, and there's not a one of them that compares to yours.' "

Besides Mr. Hardy, Don has many satisfied and distinguished customers around the world. His bows have found homes throughout England and Scotland — lands where yew longbows once decided the fate of nations. Even The Royal Company of Archers in Edinburgh, Scotland, the oldest archery organization in the world, shoots Don's longbows.

Don's two year waiting list doesn't seem to dissuade his long line of new customers, or keep the satisfied ones from coming back for more. "I have a customer from Massachusetts who has almost a dozen of my bows. He has shot one of his bows 250,000 times, and he says it shoots like it always has. I have a tremendous following in some areas. I even have one customer who has twenty-six of my bows."

CLOSE TO THE SOURCE

Don crafts his customer pleasing bows in his quiet workshop next to his house in Elmira. He enjoys the temperate climate of this old lumber community and likes being close to his prized source of yew, the Cascade Mountains.

In addition to bowmaking, Don enjoys sailing, model railroads, and playing the guitar, which he has strummed for the past thirty-five years. He also likes building both scale-model and full-sized airplanes. The quarter-scale plane hanging in his bow shop flies on remote control, uses a converted chain saw engine, and has over 300 flights under its wings.

In the outer part of his shop next to stacks of aging yew sets the shell of a full-sized airplane under construction. "This is my own design — a biplane that's a two-seater with an open cockpit — a helmet and goggle special. This is the sixth airplane I've built. It's kind of funny that building airplanes, which used to be my profession, is now my hobby and building bows, which used to be my hobby, is now my profession."

A FAMILY AFFAIR

Crafting traditional archery products runs in the Adams family. Don's wife, Vivian, makes beautifully crested Port Orford cedar arrows. She also administers the bow business and makes the strings for Don's bows. Their son Dave also helps in the family craft. He provides the youthful vigor for scaling the steep slopes of the Cascades and the muscles for felling and hauling out their precious cargo of bow-quality yew logs.

For making shafts, Don uses cedar over twenty years old which was cut by old-time arrowsmiths. He cuts the wood into 7/16" square lengths, cutting a dozen square shafts from the same 4" x 8" x 34" bolt of cedar to ensure similar shaft qualities. He then runs them through his special doweling machine which rounds each shaft and tapers the last ten inches. "Tapering the last thirty-five percent of the shaft reduces the archer's paradox and makes the arrow recover more quickly after the shot."

COMPLEMENTING TALENTS — Using nature's gifts to the bowman, Don and Vivian craft their exquisite bows and arrows from Oregon conifers.

After doweling, Vivian's delicate touch takes over. She spine tests and grain weighs each shaft for perfect matching. Then she clear dips and hand rubs each arrow before crown dipping and custom cresting. Her cresting is so precise that some customers insist she must be using printed decals. Vivian fletches her distinctive shafts with three 5" standard die-cut barred turkey feathers. "The mark of a good feather," she says, "is the heavy oil line. Burning the feathers is bad because it burns the natural oils from the feather, and they get prematurely fuzzy around the edges."

Her finished arrows rival Don's bows for delicate beauty and they shoot as great as they look. Don says, "She has her heart in her arrow making 1000 percent. I've never seen any pair of hands do a finer job of cresting arrows, and I've been looking at arrows for a long-time."

FIT FOR A KING

Vivian's delicate arrows complement the old-time aura of Don's longbows. Although each of his yew wood creations is unique and distinctive, they also exhibit similarities.

Self-wood yew bows have two separate colored layers of wood: the ivory colored sapwood covering the back and the bronze-toned heartwood of the core and belly. The creamy sapwood layer varies from ⅛" to ½" thick depending on the tree it came from and how much it has been worked down. After it's smoothed and finished, the sapwood radiates a pearlescent sheen from its silky fibers. This outer backing layer abruptly changes to the cop-

SHADES OF SHERWOOD FOREST — Don's sleek longbows look like they belong in the hands of Robin Hood. Variations in the creamy sapwood (right) and grain make each unique.

pery hued heartwood which displays fifty to 100 growth rings per inch and speaks of its centuries in the mountains.

Even though Don makes an American style longbow, his most popular bow by far is his traditional English style longbow with its deep-cored "D" shaped limbs rounded to the belly. The immaculately contoured belly softly blends into finely rounded sides, sweeping around to the flatter sapwood back.

The delicate bow is covered with a glossy hand-rubbed finish and fitted on the tips with ornately carved horn nocks. The slim grip is wrapped diagonally with a fine-textured 1" wide leather strip skived on the edges to provide a positive grip. The upper portion of the grip covers a small leather arrow shelf covered with fine animal fur. The broomstick sized handle portion tapers gradually to approximately ½" at the horn nocks.

One of Don's 42 pound English longbows weighs a mere 15 ounces and his heavier drawing 65 pounder has a mass weight of 1 pound, 7 ounces. He recommends a brace height of about 6½" which can vary on any bow, especially a self-wood bow.

To check Don's 71", 65 pound English style yew longbow for relative speed, the author shot 28" Port Orford cedar arrows which weighed 500 grains. The arrows were fletched with three 5" feathers and equipped with snap-on nocks. The author used a shooting glove, drew the arrows 26¾", and had a slip-from-the-fingers release. The average arrow speed for this bow, arrow, and shooter combination was 168 fps.

Because Don's personal yew longbows had been shot for years at his specific draw length, and because of a yew bow's somewhat delicate nature, draw/force measurements were not recorded.

THANKS TO THE COMPOUND

Over the years Don has experienced a growing demand for his longbows. Much of this demand reflects the quality of his product, but he also feels some of the thanks should go to the weapon that caused him to revert back to old-time archery. "Compounds have gone too far for their own good. Actually the compound bow and the horribly gadgetized sport that archery has become have helped the interest in the longbow. It has taken people and turned them around. Now their interests are going the other way. That's why we have such a tremendous demand for longbows. Now people are appreciating more and more what real archery is all about.

"I've been making bows for thirty years, and I see more of a demand for the longbow now than I've ever seen. I think people are wanting to go back to what is fun about archery. They're backing away from the twentieth century archery of compounds and saying, 'Hey, let's go have some fun again, let's fire up these old wooden longbows and strap on our back quivers.'"

LONGBOW FUN

When Don fires up his longbow it's just for fun. His thirst for bowhunting thrills was quenched years ago. He used to enjoy hunting the west coast blacktail deer in the Cascades, but now his favorite form of archery is stump shooting with a friend where he can savor the relaxed simplicity of his longbow. "My killer instinct has long been satisfied, but I used to be hot and heavy into bowhunting. I might get back into bowhunting with my longbow, but I just hate to gut out animals. I've never killed a deer in my life that wasn't an absolute chore to gut out. I just don't like cutting animals up."

Although he doesn't hunt much any more, there was a time when almost any animated target deserved a well-placed arrow. One of Don's most telling shots was a phenomenal distance but the results proved embarrassing. Of all times, it was Thanksgiving day, and Don was innocently shooting with his brothers in a field near his mother's house. "We were coming back to the house when one of Mom's chickens ran out into the nearby school yard. It was probably 200 yards away and I thought, 'Well now, look at that target!' I pulled back, anchored, and let it fly.

"Well that arrow looked pretty good arcing in toward that ol' chicken. Matter of fact, it looked damned good, and then it finally looked too good.

That arrow stuck right in that chicken's brisket and the chicken took off and ran back into our yard and right under the kitchen window where my mother was standing fixing Thanksgiving dinner. She saw her chicken go running by with my arrow sticking in it. Then I had to explain that I honestly didn't mean to shoot her chicken and that really it was a very BAD shot."

Years later Don and his yew longbow teamed up to impress a group of boy scouts who were touring his shop to see how Don built yew longbows. What they witnessed that night would have impressed Robin Hood. "The boys were looking at my bows and some of them asked, 'Well, can we see how they shoot?' So I said, 'Why sure!'

"It was getting pretty dark out, and we couldn't

JUST FOR FUN — Don no longer hunts with his longbow. He's content to savor the arc of the limbs and feel the singing resiliency of the yew in his hand.

see the target very well. I grabbed three arrows and my sixty-seven pound English longbow. I shot those three arrows at the target but didn't have any idea where they were hitting because it was too dark. Then we walked down to the target about twenty-five yards away and I discovered that all three arrows were sticking so close together they looked like one arrow. Those kids were quite impressed, but not nearly as impressed as I was. I could never do that again in a thousand years."

ENOUGH WEIGHT

Whether it's chickens, targets, or deer, Don feels that it's important for an archer to shoot a bow weight that he can handle comfortably. "One of the problems in the longbow world is that a lot of people have what I call the 'Howard Hill syndrome.' They think they should shoot 100 pound longbows because Howard did. But Howard Hill was one in a million men who was exceptional, and he was also a professional archer. He shot the longbow for a living. Someone trying to emulate Howard Hill on a sporting level isn't going to make it. So just shoot a bow weight you can handle.

"A fifty pound bow, if properly handled, will take any game in North America. A good hit with a sharp broadhead is the name of the bowhunting game. It's that well-placed shot that gets the game, not the arrow out of the 100 pound bow that barely misses."

TIMELESS QUALITIES

Since he was a youngster whittling cherry-branch bows, Don has seen and shot almost every kind of bow, from the efficient killing compound machines to the durable composite recurves. But for Don there is only one that captures his heart and boyhood imagination — the self-wood yew long-bow. It's not so much the bow itself as it is the mystical material it's made from. "Yew is a fantastic wood and makes the greatest longbows in the world, without exception. It has always been the king of bow woods."

Don creates his exquisite longbows by artful liberation of God's gift to the archer, Taxus brevifolia. "Yew is the perfect blend of two bow woods and fortunately it grows in the same tree. The sapwood on the outside of the tree just melts into the heartwood on the inside of the tree. If you could cut down two different trees and glue pieces from each together you couldn't make it any better than what grows naturally in a yew wood tree. It's an absolutely perfect marriage of two totally different woods.

"The sapwood is soft, stringy, stretchy, and fibrous. It holds the bow together. The heartwood is springy, takes the compressional strains, and delivers the power. And the lightness of both adds to yew wood's cast."

Don knows yew wood inside and out. He's been harvesting and whittling on it for thirty-eight years. He learned its properties from old-timers such as Leonard Daily, Gilman Keasey, and Chet Stevenson, and even though more yew has passed through his hands than most bowyers could imagine, he's still learning about this special bow wood.

SWEET HARVEST

Besides requiring dedication, there are many secrets to becoming the world's finest self-wood yew bowyer. One of the most important is first selecting that one tree in every 500 that contains a hidden bow-quality stave.

Don begins his search with permit in hand, in the shadowed undergrowth beneath looming virgin stands of Douglas fir in the recesses of the High Cascades. He even has an airplane altimeter mounted in his pickup to keep track of the elevation where select trees are harvested. "We cut our yew wood above 2,500 feet and some of it comes from 4,000 to 5,000 feet. In those high elevations yew trees have a sharper definition between the sapwood and the heartwood. And the higher elevation wood is a lot tougher.

"It has to come from under the old growth fir where the yew had to reach up for sunlight. There it grows straight and is clear of branches. If yew grows in the sun it looks like a Christmas tree with a hundred limbs. Growing slowly in the shade also makes the yew fine-grained."

Even though the quiet mountains seem like a peaceful place for a tree to grow for hundreds of years, Don points out that it's a tough environment. "Yew is the gnarliest, crookedest, most cantankerous little tree you'll ever see in your life. It's had to survive right under all those old growth firs where limbs fall on it, lightening hits, trees fall across it, sap suckers chew on it, bears claw on it, and heart rot and ring shank scar it. Those little trees endure almost every kind of natural problem you could imagine."

Under Don's guiding eye, son Dave climbs the steep slopes passing over hundreds of yew trees before finding one that has the special combination of qualities Don demands. "We look for straight yew trees that aren't leaning too much. If they lean, one side contains compression wood and the other side contains tension wood. Some people claim that the male yew tree has darker heartwood than the female tree, but I can't tell any difference and they both work fine for me. I believe the color of the wood is more indicative of the soil it's growing in."

Don doesn't concentrate his search on any particular facing slope, and he doesn't put much credence in old folklore about when to cut yew. "I cut yew any time I can get to it, every year from spring until fall. I can't tell any difference in the finished bow if the sap was in the log, but I can sure tell the difference in getting them off the mountain when the ground is covered with waist-deep snow.

"There are all these books, with formulas for finding yew, that were written by people who have never cut a stick of yew wood. They write things like, 'It has to be cut in the winter or it contains the seeds of death.' If you try to get up there in four feet of snow during the winter you'll think about seeds of death. It's so steep and high where we cut our yew, we could never make it up there in the winter."

Once they select a near-perfect tree, they either cut it into forty inch lengths for making billets or into a seventy-four inch section for making a stave bow. Don prefers making a full-length stave bow, but long sections of quality yew are a rare find. After they're cut, the logs are muscled down the mountain to the nearest trail road where Don and Dave load them into the pickup for the ride home. "For me, cutting one of the those little old yew trees is almost a religious experience. It's God's gift to the bowyer and it's been there forever. The fact that yew wood grew in conjunction with those old firs to make it a beautiful bow wood has to be by God's master plan and design."

THREATENING YEW

Even though yew has been God's gift to the bowmaker for countless generations, Don fears that its years are numbered. Today the ancient little tree is threatened on several fronts.

A recent cure for cancer was discovered in a derivative of yew bark. It's a noble cause for the little tree to serve, but the only way to harvest the bark is to kill the tree. "They bought 60,000 pounds of yew bark around here this year. That's a lot of yew trees. They contract people to cut the trees and strip the bark, and sometimes they just strip the bark from the standing trees."

Another threat to the American yew is a growing foreign market. Shiploads of yew are shipped overseas to Japan for making religious figures and to Germany for making furniture.

The debarkers and the foreign market threaten the irreplaceable yew trees, but their biggest threat lies in the clear-cutting policies of the Forest Service. "The loggers go up in there and cut the old growth harvest timber and level everything else. The yew just gets pushed into piles with the other slash and is then burned. They don't even try to save it. It's very wasteful and is going to be the inevitable end of our yew wood."

Even though Don loves his bowmaking, if bow-quality yew becomes too scarce, he will no longer make self-wood bows. Other woods may be acceptable for some self-wood bowyers, but not for Don.

FROM LOGS TO BILLETS

After Don brings the yew logs down from the mountains, he band saws them into billets and staves as soon as possible. But before slabbing them on a saw, Don peels off the shaggy bark so he can see any small imperfections or knots in the wood. When peeling the bark, he is careful not to damage the delicate sapwood which is critical for holding together the finished bow.

Once the bark is removed, Don extracts the best quality billets or staves from a log by avoiding trouble spots. "I cut a straight line down two sides of the billet so I can later see if it takes a crooked set. When I'm sawing yew into billets I'm like a kid in a candy store. I sometimes appreciate a quality stave more than the finished bow. I have a terrible love for those roughed-out staves, but when I make it into a bow the rough wood becomes just a memory."

Don saws his billets into matched pairs, as they grew next to each other in the tree, to help provide similar characteristics in both limbs. He then grades and marks the wood, and stacks it for aging.

One of his key secrets to successful self-wood bow crafting is understanding the complexities of yew grain quality and texture. It's a secret Don has learned over the years and keeps close to his vest. "You learn what quality wood does the best job in certain bows. You wouldn't want to take a stave that would be good for a 100 pound bow and make a forty pound bow out of it. It would be too tough and dense for that weight bow. So depending on the poundage, I match the right wood with the bow. It's all different and that's where experience comes in.

"I'm not trying to weave any mystery into it, but after so many years of handling yew I can cut it up and feel from the grain and fibers what kind of bow a particular stave will make. It's not mystical, I make very calculated tests on every piece of yew before I make it into a bow. Yew can vary all the way from 'cheese to chalk' as the saying goes. Just because you have a beautiful fine-grained piece of yew doesn't mean you have a good piece of bow wood. It might be a piece of garbage because it's a brittle and brash piece of compression wood. But it may look gorgeous to the untrained eye and even to many trained eyes."

Covered from the sun and rain, Don's yew ages for at least three summers. Although the wood dries within six months, it won't make a good bow until it has properly aged, and according to Don, sixty years isn't too long. "In England where they have a wetter climate, they let bow yew age six or seven years. I made one batch of bows from yew that was cut back in the twenties. I don't think it ever gets bad. The yew longbows from the Mary Rose were still good after over 400 years on the bottom of the ocean."

BEGINS WITH A FISHTAIL

After the wood is properly aged, Don selects a pair of billets and planes them flat on the sides. Using a special jig, he then cuts a fishtail splice in the butt ends and glues them together with Weldwood plastic resin glue. He drives a small nail through the splice so it won't slip and then "C" clamps it firm.

Once the splice has dried, Don marks out the profile and length of the bow. These dimensions vary depending on the desired draw weight, draw length, and wood characteristics. For a standard 28" draw, he builds the bow 72" between nocks. For a 60 pound bow he profiles the limb width from about 1³⁄₁₆" inches at the handle and narrows it to approximately ½" at the nocks.

Using spokeshaves, rasps, files, block planes, and lots of sandpaper, Don trims the wood to the rough bow dimensions and files in temporary string nocks. He doesn't have a specific procedure when whittling a bow to shape — it depends on the emerging grain and swirls within the yew.

SHAPING THE LIMBS

When working down the bow back, Don carefully follows the sapwood grain and usually doesn't take much off, other than feathering the edges into the sides. The sapwood backing is left in relatively the same shape as the natural curve of the tree.

Don fashions the belly into a "D" cross-sectional shape. "There isn't a standard "D" shape because it varies according to the wood. Knowing how to shape and vary that "D" is one of the big secrets to making an English longbow. I try to get the minimum amount of wood to do the maximum amount of work, and there's a real fine line between success and failure."

ALIGNMENT

Don also balances the limbs vertically so they will stay in line. "A lot of the vertical balancing depends on the piece of wood. If you have a piece with stressed fiber content then chances are you'll end up with a crooked bow. So having non-stressed wood in your billets is number one. That's why I cut them straight and mark them so I can watch to see if they bend. If a bow takes a stress set when I'm working on it, that bow goes in the fire. The finest bowyer in the world will never straighten it because that stress is actually within the limb."

Releasing its timeless qualities with a spokeshave, Don carefully shapes the rounded belly — one of the secrets in crafting a yew longbow.

TILLERING

Once Don shapes the limbs into rough balance, he strings the bow and puts it on his tiller board. This wall-mounted board is a non-glare gray board where Don places the bow handle in a notched block of wood and then draws the bow using a rope and pulley system. By standing away from the bow and gently drawing it, Don can evaluate the symmetry of the bending limbs. His tiller board is mounted near a large window providing plenty of light for him to see any inconsistencies.

Don is gentle with his new yew creations and only draws them a little their first time on the tiller board. "A bow may go on the tiller board a hundred times. I stand back and look at the arc of each limb and compare

AN ARTIST AT WORK — Using his tiller board and a critical eye, Don fashions each limb to bend in perfect arc and harmony.

both limbs. It's more of an artist's eye than it is mechanical. That's one reason I don't tiller bows at night. I have to have the light just right.

"When I'm shaping the limbs, I don't just try to get them to bend the same amount, I must also make both limbs have the same style. You can have everything from a hinged limb to a whip-ended limb, and even though both limbs bend the same amount they might have different styles. A lot of newcomers to self-wood bowmaking end up with two totally different limb styles on the same bow and don't even realize it.

"You don't want a hinged limb that bends right off the riser where the limbs stay practically straight. A lot of the old-time bowyers used to make them that way and they wondered why their bows didn't have good cast and why they followed the string prematurely. Proper limb styling and the quality of the wood will keep the limbs from following the string."

When tillering and styling his limbs, Don strings and unstrings the bow repeatedly between sandings. "Sometimes it takes so long to work it down that my shoulders are killing me by the end of the day. Tillering can take a lot of extra time if you're working with a contrary piece of wood."

Don fashions both limbs to bend uniformly throughout the entire limb without any flat spots, which cause overly stressed areas. "Flat spots cause bad cast and premature breakdown of the bow which shows up in the form of a chrysal, being out of tiller, or simply by blowing up. A chrysal is a little line that runs ninety degrees to the grain, a minute compressional fracture of the fibrous grains in the belly of the bow. It's so fine you can hardly see it, but all of the fibers on the belly across that line have been fractured. A chrysal is caused by not properly tillering the bow and by having spots that bend too much, or from trying to get too many pounds out of a poor piece of wood, or from trying to make the limb arc too high, or any combination of these factors."

When shaping his limb, Don strives for a full-working limb with a slight bit of whip in the tips for cast. Using sandpaper and his experienced touch, Don usually hits the desired bow weight without much trouble. "I have great flexibility with weight because I can simply sand material off, whereas with a composite bow you're pretty much stuck with what you have. I make my bows a little heavy at first, then just keep working them down to the right poundage."

Don fashions his handle down to broomstick-sized proportions to follow the same lines as the limbs. The handle is delicately small compared to most longbows, but his customers like it. "Big handles are one of the complaints about longbows today. Some shapes on longbow handles don't even come close to fitting my hand. The human hand is curved and you should be able to grab the bow and have it be comfortable without searching for a way to hold it. Most of my customers are very happy with my smaller handles."

COW-HORN NOCKS

After Don shapes and sands the limbs to their final form, he installs his classical cow-horn string nocks. It's a task he dives into with mixed emotions. "Grinding those cow-horn nocks is one of the parts of bowmaking I like the least because they stink like burnt fingernails. But then I polish them on the buffer and they're so pretty and have such a beautiful luster that it doesn't seem so bad after all."

Vivian points out that working with the cow-horn is like polishing an agate because you never know what intriguing patterns will be exposed during the shaping. Although their shine makes the cow-horn tips look heavy, they're remarkably lightweight yet durable.

To produce the exact male taper on the wood and the female taper in the nock, Don uses a special cutter which makes matching tapers. The base of the horn tip is feathered down to a knife edge and when it's epoxied on to the limb tip, it looks like there is a magical transformation from yew to cow-horn. Don usually fashions the upper nock a bit longer and thinner.

FINISH WORK

To protect the soft sapwood from the rigors of hunting, Don frequently backs his hunting-weight bows with clarified calfskin. He applies the calf-skin with glue and then burnishes it. "The calfskin doesn't make the bow any stronger in draw weight but it sure makes the back tougher. It's so thin and clear you can actually see the fine sapwood grain through it."

One of the finishing touches on the bow is Vivian's artistic hand inking the fine lettering on the creamy sapwood above and below the handle. Her delicate lettering style fits the bow perfectly.

The final finish coat on any bow is important, but especially on a self-wood bow. Don sprays on four to six coats of clear finish, sanding and rubbing with steel wool between each coat. Don's special two-part finish is a polyurethane enamel and is the toughest and most pliable bow finish he has ever seen.

After the finish is dry, Don installs a leather shelf wedge and then diagonally wraps and glues the handle section with a skived 1" leather strip. The knife-edged skive on the back of the strip produces a slightly ribbed handle for a positive grip. Don glues on the leather strike plate which is also skived to improve arrow clearance. Finally, he covers the arrow shelf with distinctive seal hair, mink, or sable fur.

The leather shelf wedge is optional for those archers not wishing to shoot directly off their knuckle and it helps to achieve consistent arrow flight. One of the unique features of Don's bows is that they can be shot either right or left handed. There is no sight window side. "I won't cut in an arrow shelf because it weakens the bow. Plus it spoils the esthetic lines of the bow. Those esthetic lines are pure — they haven't been prostituted by any twentieth century styling."

CARING FOR THE BEST

Yew is a naturally soft wood and even with a protective finish it's not designed to take abuse. "A yew wood bow is like a good friend — if you treat it well it will last a long-time, but if you don't, it won't. There have been people over the years who I simply refuse to make any more bows for because they didn't treat them right. I don't want to make a bow for someone who is going to beat it up. I put too much effort into crafting them, and they deserve better than that. They're like my children. I wouldn't want my children going out into the world with somebody who would mistreat them."

To help protect his children, Vivian makes standard endless bowstrings instead of the traditional Flemish strings. Don explains, "Modern Dacron is the wrong material to make a Flemish string with. It doesn't have enough abrasion resistance. I've seen many good bows go down the tubes because of Flemish strings breaking in the loops without warning. I won't ever put a Flemish string on one of my bows because I've seen too many bows broken from broken strings."

NO MATCH FOR YEW

Over the years Don has tried other woods for making self-wood long-bows, but he feels there's little sense in using anything else when he has the world's best bow wood beckoning him from the nearby Cascades. He recalls one instance where his west-coast yew outshined the Eastern competition. "I bought my brother a Ben Pearson fifty-five pound hickory recurve bow and some arrows. At the same time I had just made a self-wood fifty pound yew wood bow at Daily's. We were out shooting in this field and we decided to see whose bow shot the farthest. We lined up and got ready to shoot, and my brother shot before I did. As his arrow arced up I shot mine and it passed his arrow as if it was standing still and went almost twice as far."

YEW TIPS FOR NOVICES

Devoting the time and skills required in making a self-wood yew longbow is not for everybody. But Don believes the rewards are worth the efforts, and he passes along some pointers to those romantics who want to try their hand at whittling out yew longbows.

"First, try to find a quality stave or quality billets — something worth working with. If a yew tree isn't standing straight, don't bother cutting it because it contains too much compression wood. Cut only what looks perfect in the woods because once you get it home it always looks worse. If you look hard and long enough you will find some perfect wood.

"Second, don't start by trying to make yourself a seventy pound English longbow. Their deep-cored stacked limbs are much harder to make than a flattened limb because they have a greater tendency to wander out of line. So start off by making yourself a twenty-five pound rectangular cross sectional target bow. When you learn to fly an airplane you use a trainer, you don't jump in a top gun jet.

"Finally, don't get into self-wood bowmaking thinking you're going to make an English longbow the first time you try, and don't think that you're going to get into it just to save money. Get into it with the idea that you're learning something new and challenging and because you enjoy it."

MORE THAN MONEY

Some might think that building the Stradivarius of longbows would bring fame and fortune, but like most bowyers who operate one-man bow crafting operations, Don doesn't build his bow just for money. "This is my labor of love. I spend so much time on each bow that it comes out to very poor wages. But there's no way to mass produce self-wood bows. I take my time making each one, one at a time."

Although he's not getting rich, Don reaps personal rewards both while he's making a bow and long after it leaves his shop. "I enjoy doing a specialty job and doing it well. I may not be paid well for all the time and effort that goes into building an Old English longbow but I love what I'm doing. I quickly spend the money I am paid for a bow, but when a customer gets his bow and he calls me up to tell me how much he appreciates it, that's my true payment and it lasts for a long time. And that happens with almost every bow I sell."

Besides receiving a payment of pride, Don's craft allows him to transcend the barriers of time and space and puts him mystically in touch with Old England's finest bowmen and the forefathers of American archery. "I'm very moved by working with such a beautiful natural material as yew. And there's nothing more beautiful on this entire earth than nature itself. I'm lucky I was turned on by bows and have been able to work with yew. Even though I've spent most of my life doing it, the longer I work with yew, the more I appreciate it. It's a fondness that just grows and grows.

"I have God's gift to the bowman to work with and the God-given skill to make it into Old English longbows. So God knows where all the credit goes."

Don's featherweight longbows and their humming limbs intensify that special feeling of the bow seeming like an animated extension of the archer.

Bunched shoulder muscles sweep the bow back into its graceful arc, and as the bowstring slips from the fingers, the ancient yew springs forward with centuries of resiliency. Although its wind-brushed branches are forever silent, Don's yew sings on in the hand and the heart of traditional bowmen.

Chapter Thirty-Three

THE SPIRIT LONGBOW COMPANY

FEELING THE SPIRIT

The challenge of traditional archery draws many bowmen back to a laminated recurve, the bow that led them into archery years ago. Others reach for the simplistic lines of a laminated longbow, the weapon Howard Hill used to spark a nation of longbow followers. And some traditionalists step even further back in time, testing their skills with self-wood longbows like Pope and Young used to kindle America's early bowhunting flame.

Within this troop of self-wood bowmen, a few thirst for the ultimate traditional challenge. They link with primitive man by harvesting bow-quality trees and craft their own longbows. But the rarest breed of all is the traditionalist who makes his own primitive equipment, professionally crafts it for others, and finds time to warmly share time-hushed self-wood bowyer's secrets with all who will listen. John Strunk, of Tillamook, Oregon, belongs to this rare breed. He's one of America's traditional bowyers dedicated to spreading the true pioneer spirit of American archery.

LAND OF PLENTY

John lives seventy-five miles west of Portland in the oceanside community of Tillamook perched along Oregon's west coast. The lifeblood of the town flows from the natural bounty of the surrounding countryside. The emerald Pacific coast forests support the local logging and lumber products industry, and lush dairy pastures in the lowlands near town represent the beginning of the cow-to-milk-to-curd-to-cheese process. The town's nationally famous cheddar cheese is produced at the Tillamook County Creamery Association where they make thirty million pounds of cheese a year. The ever restless waters of the nearby Pacific provide commercial fishermen a variety of shellfish and assorted finned fare. In Tillamook the seafood lover's plate is never empty.

Nature's offerings also entice local sportsmen. Tillamook, the Indian name for "Land Of Many Waters," speaks of the cascading waters of the Trask, Wilson, Kilchis, Miami, and Tillamook rivers that tumble headlong from the mountains of the Tillamook State Forest and embrace the Pacific in quiet Tillamook Bay. Within these rushing streams lurk cutthroat trout, brilliant salmon, and silvery steelhead. Not far from town, where rolling meadows reach up into forested mountains, Roosevelt elk, blacktail deer, and black bear offer hunters challenges aplenty.

Once a native of Eugene, Oregon, John is now one of the local sportsmen who couldn't resist Tillamook's lure. "I came to Tillamook primarily because of the fantastic steelhead fishing. And the bowhunting is great. The last elk I shot was just two miles from home. A year after shooting that elk I took a blacktail buck on the same mountain using an English self-wood yew longbow. I can even see that mountain right from my house."

John lives with his wife, Pat, son, Morgan, and daughter, Kristin, on the quiet outskirts east of town, just several arrow shots from dark timber. An industrial education graduate of Oregon State University, John is Tillamook's junior high school shop teacher. He teaches drafting, woodworking, and plastics, metal and leather crafting. After John's students complete their normal shop assignments, they're free to make whatever they want, and John always seems to have a few students eager to make their first bow. Whether their choice is a modern laminated composite bow or a self-wood yew longbow, John is the perfect shop teacher for the task. He knows how to build both. Bow crafting is John's part-time business and full-time love.

LURED TO THE LONGBOW

John's romance with archery began in the late fifties after a little coaching and inspiration from his brother-in-law. "We shot at a few cardboard boxes with our lemonwood bows and handfuls of arrows and thought we were ready to go bowhunting. But we were about as green and ridiculous as you could be. We had a few shots at deer, but I think the most we got that year was one chipmunk."

John continued to dabble in archery until the early seventies when he became engrossed with bowhunting and made his own recurve. But in 1975 a new concept in archery caused John to waver from his bowmaking. "I was elk hunting with a friend and we were using our homemade recurves when we met a fellow who was shooting a compound. We were so impressed with his bow that we each bought one.

"Without even practicing much, the new compound was so easy to master that I shot an elk with it a few days later. I hunted with it for four seasons and took deer and elk every year with it. The compound was an effective hunting tool, but it didn't look or feel like a bow, and I knew it wasn't what I wanted from bowhunting."

So John returned to bowmaking and began building take-down recurves. He also became interested in longbows and ordered one from a custom bowyer. But he grew tired of the lengthy wait for the new bow and decided to try his hand at longbow building. "My first longbow came out too heavy. It pulled eighty-two pounds, but I was determined to shoot it anyway. My first day hunting with it I missed an elk at close range. I just didn't have any confidence in the longbow then so I took my compound out the next weekend and killed an elk at twelve feet. I knew there was no reason why I couldn't have shot that elk with my longbow except I didn't have the faith to stick with it. But from that day on I stuck with it and have only shot the longbow."

John's early longbows were laminated fiberglass and corewood composites, but he was soon drawn to the mystique and challenge of self-wood bows. "They're not as smooth as laminated bows, but I can go find a tree in the woods and carve a bow out of it. Now I look at a tree and wonder what kind of bow is in it. I also have a greater love for a self-wood bow than if I had bought the materials and put it together. I want to go back as far as I can making primitive equipment including arrows, as long as they're effective weapons."

HIS OWN "ALASKAN ADVENTURES"

Now in his late forties, this soft-smiling bowman has taken a giant step back in time by tracing the footsteps of Art Young. John ventured north to Alaska in 1986 where he spent eleven days in the wilderness bowhunting with his homemade gear. His memorable caribou hunt was spiced with the excitement of being stalked by a grizzly and being serenaded by howling wolves near his tent at night.

One of John's companions on the trip was a special longbow made from a piece of yew purchased from long-time self-wood bowyer, Earl Ulrich. "Earl was about ninety-five when I met him. I showed him a couple of my self-wood bows because I wanted him to see that the yew he cherished so much would be used to make a bow he appreciated. When I was looking over his supply of yew wood I noticed a piece he had marked 'Good Stuff'. I bought that piece, made it into a bow, and named it 'Good Stuff.'

"In addition to taking 'Good Stuff', I made a set of broadheads from an old lumber mill band saw blade. It was excellent high-carbon steel. I made a simple Christmas-tree blade pattern one and a half inches wide and two inches long. I sawed a slit into the end of my arrow shaft, and mounted the broadhead until it spun true, glued it with a Locktite glue, and bound it with dental floss. For my arrow shafts I used Ramin wood dowels and fletched them with trimmed turkey feathers."

Armed with his homemade equipment, John flew from Anchorage into Jay Massey's remote caribou camp. After being intimidated by grizzlies his first few days in camp, John finally settled into· some serious hunting with noted Alaskan bowhunter, Doug Borland. It wasn't long before John discovered some of the complexities of hunting with his simple equipment. "On my first day out with Doug we spotted six small caribou and started stalking them.

"Suddenly two bulls came from nowhere and they knew something was up. With one of the biggest bull caribou Doug had ever seen standing broadside at twenty-five yards, he said, 'Take him, John.' I'm trying to put my arrow on my string, and for some reason I couldn't figure out why my bowstring was limp. To prevent my self-wood bow from taking a set, I had it unstrung and hadn't remembered to string it. So I quickly strung the bow and took the shot. My homemade broadhead struck the caribou high in the neck and severed the windpipe. He went about 150 yards and went down.

"It was great to be able to set back on a warm day and enjoy the beautiful Alaskan mountains and know you were able to pack out your share of caribou meat when you're over forty."

OREGON BOWHUNTING

Whether he's in Alaska or Oregon, John savors the transition from late summer to winter. It's then that he heads for the big timber near home in quest of Roosevelt elk and blacktail deer. Even though he has bowhunted for nearly twenty years, each season represents new adventures that bring him physically and spiritually closer to nature. "The fall is the peak of our hunting season, and the salmon are returning to the streams. The autumn air has a quickness to it. I'll be up on a hillside in the morning and the wind will bring tears to my eyes because it's so cool, yet by evening it's calm and the fog and haze put a glow in the air. Sometimes when I'm hunting and setting up on a hill, it's like I'm the last person in existence alone there with God. It's then that I really feel close to Him and the land."

Even though fall is his favorite season, John often begins his hunting season during the spring when he scouts new elk or deer areas while stump shooting. He prides himself on locating areas overlooked by other hunters, then getting to know the resident elk herd or occasional blacktail. By the time he returns in the fall, he knows the game patterns and his quiver is loaded with deadly broadheads. But he still carries a few blunts. "As I sneak along I still shoot stumps, but in fact I'm still hunting, and I've taken several deer and elk that way."

SECOND CHANCE ELK

Sneaking along and plunking stumps may be an enjoyable method of hunting, but John's most effective and favorite technique is taking to the trees. He enjoys the methodical planning of stand hunting and spending long hours perched undetected among the pines where he watches the often comical actions of the undisturbed game. During one hunt in eastern Oregon, a combination of second chance luck and persistence provided John with his first longbow kill. "Elk came into the clearing near my stand that morning but I missed the shot and spooked the elk.

"I climbed out of my tree stand about 8:30 to meet my hunting partner. I hadn't walked fifty feet when I heard elk coming, so I hid in a little depression and waited. The elk walked within ten feet of me, and when the lead cow's head went behind some small jack pines I started to draw. The second her eye came past the trees she spotted me and shifted into high gear. I swung my aim with her and shot, but I hit the tree that my stand was in."

Remaining optimistic, John returned to his stand later that afternoon. "I got there in time for my scent to dissipate from the ground before the elk came in. Later, a cow elk came into the clearing and stood broadside offering a good shot. But I shot over her shoulder and the arrow stuck in the ground. She looked at it, ran twenty feet, and then stopped. She turned and walked back to where she had been standing. When she finally relaxed and looked away, I carefully aimed and shot, hitting her right where I wanted, in the shoulder. I heard her run for about eight seconds and then it got quiet. I knew she was down. She only went eighty yards."

STEAK AND MUSHROOMS

Not all of John's hot spots for elk produce several shots a day. Even though he hunts hard and long, elk can sometimes remain as elusive as the fabled Sasquatch. One season John hunted elk for an entire month without even seeing one, yet their bugles and feeding noises taunted him daily. Finally, he had been beaten enough at the game of hide and seek so he took a day off from hunting to go mushroom picking. It was just the change his luck needed. "As I drove up to my mushroom spot the road was full of elk!

"I had my bow so I tried for them but again the elk won the game. They went over a steep hillside, so the next evening I snuck down in there, and after sneaking around for an hour I finally heard them talking to each other. It took me another hour and a half to cautiously sneak in on them. Finally I got so close I could hear them feeding and I saw the bushes moving twenty-five yards away, but I couldn't see them.

"As I waited next to an old snag tree, this wiggling bush materialized into an elk, and she fed to within ten yards of me. She was close but didn't present a good shot. Finally another elk stepped in front of me offering a shot. I shot through a small opening in the brush, and even though I couldn't see my arrow, I knew I hit the elk.

"She just walked twenty-five yards away, her front legs buckled, and she fell over. That was the first elk I ever shot that didn't bolt and run. The other elk walked back to within five yards of me and looked around as if to say, 'Where did my friend go?' Finally she spotted me and left. Normally I wait quite a while after shooting an elk, but I knew she was down so I just walked over to her. Somehow the arrow had entered near the sternum and traveled lengthwise through that elk."

CALIFORNIA THRILLS

Besides pursuing local elk and deer, John has recently expanded his bowhunting quarry list to include the unpredictable wild hogs that inhabit northern California. The wild pig's eyesight isn't as keen as Oregon's elk but the pigs have remarkable noses, good hearing, and flavor the hunt with an element of danger.

As John was planning for a recent hog hunting trip, he wondered if his sixty-two pound self-wood yew longbow would drive an arrow through the tough gristly plate that protects the hog's vitals. He also planned to take his son Morgan along to share the experience. But one thing John didn't plan was the near-tragic start to his California adventure. "We were turning around on this back road when our Jeep rolled off the edge.

"It began rolling over and over and the next thing I knew I was sitting in the middle of the road dazed. Then I heard my son yell, 'Dad!' I thought he was still in the Jeep which I could see rolling end over end down this hill. But luckily he had already been thrown out, and he was actually uphill from me, and was just concerned about me.

"We all survived the wreck but some of our equipment was broken. Somehow my English longbow, which had been sticking out both sides of the Jeep, hadn't been broken. I had a cut over one eye and a buggered up knee so I hobbled around for a couple of days hunting with my son.

"One evening we worked down into a canyon and spotted three pigs feeding in a small meadow. I checked the wind and we stalked into a small ravine. When we got close I asked Morgan to stay put.

"I stalked to within fifteen yards of one pig and shot, but I hit the pig directly below the ear. The arrow hit hard with a 'crack' and went all the way to the bone. As the pig turned to leave, the blood flow was so strong that it pushed the arrow out of the wound. I was using a Timberwolf broadhead and it made a terrible gash. Because I severed the jugular vein, blood was gushing out of him. I called for Morgan and by the time he got there the pig had gone forty yards and toppled over."

TRAILING ADVICE

Animals shot in the jugular vein leave a profuse and short blood trail. But more often the hit is in the main part of the body and the bowhunter is faced with a tracking job. John has helped unravel many a blood trail over the past twenty years, and he offers some sage advice on how to go about it. "Most people are too anxious to find the animal and don't wait long enough. Wait the traditional half hour and longer if possible before taking up the trail. If you think you've made a bad hit it's best to leave the area and come back later with some help. I've seen too many animals lost by people being impatient. If they just relax and let the arrow do its job they would be more successful."

During a recent mule deer hunt John proved that trailing patience pays. "Two bucks came by and I shot the closest one at fifteen yards. Even though the arrow penetrated all the way to the fletching, I thought the hit was too far back. As the buck ran I kept my eye on it for about 150 yards before I lost sight of it. Before I left my tree stand I visually marked the spot where I saw the deer last.

"Morgan was in the tree stand with me and we snuck out to the road. We took our shoes off and continued sneaking along the road. Pretty soon I saw the buck's tail flicker. I also saw the other buck quite some distance away and figured that if my deer was able he'd be with that other buck. I could see that my deer was down, but as it got darker I couldn't tell for sure what he was doing. Knowing where he was hit, I decided to mark the spot and leave.

"We went back the next morning and as soon as I looked through my binoculars to where I had last seen the buck, there he laid. If we had gone over there in the evening and spooked him, I may never have seen him again."

TRADITIONAL GEAR

To create a telling blood trail John prefers a large two-bladed broadhead he can sharpen himself. "Of the manufactured broadheads, the Timberwolf, is my favorite. It was made by my friend Glen Parker in Texas. He's also a good customer. He's bought eleven of my bows over the years. Timberwolf broadheads look like the old Bear Razorhead except they're much larger. They weigh about 205 grains unsharpened. I sharpen them with a real shallow bevel using a twelve inch file, and I get an edge that's so sharp I'm sure if I forgot my hunting knife I could skin an elk with one of my broadheads."

John mounts his broadheads on Douglas fir shafts. He likes fir because it's heavy and durable. "I can shoot fir arrows all day long in rotten stumps and not break an arrow. A good fir shaft weighs 450 to 500 grains." John plans to soon make his own shafting and to complement his homemade arrows with homemade broadheads and self-nocks.

For toting his homemade arrows it's only fitting that John uses a homemade hip quiver. It's made from soft deer hide with the hair on the outside for quietly slipping through the forest. "I made it a small diameter and only carry a half dozen broadheads and maybe a couple of blunts. It's easy to maneuver, and it's quiet when I pull the arrows out. And it doesn't distract from the beauty of my longbow. It's just one more step back to the way our forefathers bowhunted."

Light but steady rains often accompany bowhunting in Oregon and John opts for the quiet and warmth of wool or polyester clothing. To keep from interfering with his bowstring he tops off his attire with a simple stocking cap that covers most of his brown curly hair.

The pride of John's hunting gear are his self-wood longbows. He has five that pull from fifty-eight to sixty-four pounds, and although some of his yew bows are sweet shooters, his favorite is his sixty-six inch osage flatbow.

GOOD FOR THE SPIRIT

John shoots his self-wood bows almost every evening. Most of the time he practices his form in the backyard. When he can sneak away for a little longer, he heads for the rolling beach dunes or the mountains to stump shoot and get some exercise. "I'd rather not even be in the woods if I can't have my bow with me. It may be eleven o'clock at night and freezing outside, and I'll prop up a flashlight on the back fence and start shooting. That may sound odd, but for me shooting my bow is a form of relaxation. All of the trials and tribulations of daily life disappear when I start shooting."

Over the years John has developed a shooting style that is comfortable for him, but he advises archers to discover what works best for them and not to copy another shooter. "I draw the bow smoothly and hold my bow arm as steady as possible while concentrating on the spot I want to hit. When my index finger touches the corner of my mouth, I release in one motion. It's a comfortable fluid method, and I can shoot for hours without getting tired because I'm not holding a long time."

During January John spends extra time at the beaches lofting arrows into the mist. Most Easterners might mistake his lofty shooting for a loony attempt to lose all his arrows. But he's really just warming up for the yearly Traditional Archers of Oregon golf shoot held each February. Golf

DEDICATED TO THE SPIRIT OF TRADITIONAL ARCHERY — John loves roaming the mist shrouded dunes near Tillamook, lofting arrows at distant clumps of grass.

archery may be a foreign sport back east, but in Oregon it's big time fun. "Golf shooting is probably more fun than hunting. You don't get to shoot the bow very often when you're seriously hunting, maybe one shot a season. But in golf shooting you get to shoot the bow a lot. It's an event where you can shoot the full cast of your bow and watch your arrows fly. It's also an activity I can be very good at, and I can compete with any type of bowmen. We shoot at unknown distances, and it involves some strategy on how to play a certain shot."

John also eagerly attends Oregon's Pope-Young shoot. "This shoot started in 1936 for testing bows to see if they could shoot a broadhead arrow 180 yards, which was required for hunting big game in Oregon. We shoot the English clout at a flag 180 yards away. We shoot thirty-six arrows in six flights and every arrow within thirty feet of the flag scores. The closer to the flag, the more points you get. Another part of this event is the wand. It's a one and a half inch wide strip, six feet tall, that we shoot at from 100 yards.

You're not there to be the winner. If you win, that's great. But if you don't, you're going to have a good time anyway."

SHOOTING WITH SPIRIT

Whether John is lofting arrows at distant flags or shooting at point blank elk, he shoots with traditional spirit in his heart and one of his Spirit longbows in his hands.

The SPIRIT LONGBOW is John's 68" laminated slightly reflexed longbow. It has a mass weight of 1 pound, 3 ounces, and a recommended brace height of 6" to 6¼" from the string to the throat.

Its solid hardwood riser is approximately 17" long, 1⅛" wide and narrows to ¾" through the rounded sight window which is cut ⅜" from center shot. The riser is 1⅞" thick and has a slightly crested arrow shelf. John offers risers in bubinga, angico, walnut, maple, osage, yew, rosewood, and shedua. The riser displays simple rounded traditional lines and has a slightly dished, peaked grip. The 4¼" grip is covered with suede leather and wrapped with a crisscross diagonal lacing for positive hand indexing.

The 1" reflexed limbs are constructed from two back laminations and one belly lamination of .002" per inch tapered corewoods enveloped in clear or brown fiberglass. John offers yew, maple, ash, osage, black locust, bamboo, and cascara corewoods. The upper limb has a working length of 26¾" from the fadeout to the nock and the lower limb has a working length of 24¾". The limbs narrow from 1⅛" wide at the fadeouts to ½" at the nocks.

The thin tip overlays are made from riser wood over fiberglass and form a spear-shaped point. String nocks are cut flush on the sides and about half of the string depth on the back. Bow information is ornately black inked on the belly of the limbs. The Spirit is available in the standard satin finish or a hand-rubbed gloss finish.

To check his 65 pound at 26" draw, 68" laminated yew and fiberglass Spirit longbow for relative speed, John shot his 26½" cedar arrows. They were fletched with three 5" feathers, equipped with Mercury speed nocks, and weighed 560 grains. The bow was equipped with a Dacron Flemish-twist string without accessories. John used a shooting glove, drew 26", and had a smooth pull-through release. The average relative arrow speed for this bow, arrow, and shooter combination was 172 fps.

The following draw/force measurements were recorded on this 68" Spirit Longbow:

DRAW LENGTH	25"	26"	27"	28"	29"
DRAW WEIGHT	61#	65#	68#	72#	76#

The TRADITIONAL SPIRIT is John's spliced billet self-wood yew longbow. His 68" English style longbow has a mass weight of 1 pound 3 ounces and an approximate brace height of 6".

This bow is approximately 1 1/16" wide near the lace-wrapped grip and narrows gradually to the horn nocks. The archer can traditionally shoot off his knuckle, or request a small leather shelf extension under the grip.

FROM YEW BOARDS TO BOWS — John's oval gripped Spirit Stick (upper) can be shot from either side of the handle. His laminated Spirit (lower) blends modern glass and glues with ancient yew.

A thin layer of creamy sapwood quickly grades into the coppery heartwood. The bow's deep-cored limbs exhibit a "D" cross section rounded to the belly, and reflect any slight undulations in the inherent grain of the yew. The delicate string nocks are fashioned from elk horn. The upper nock is slightly hooked and 1½" long and the lower nock is 1⅛" long and more rounded. John also offers the Traditional Spirit in a flatbow design in osage or black locust.

John checked his 63½ pound at 26" draw, 68" self-wood yew longbow backed with rawhide and snakeskin for relative speed. He shot 560 grain, 26½" cedar arrows. This bow was also equipped with a Dacron Flemish-twist string without accessories. The average arrow speed for this bow, arrow, and shooter combination was 166 fps.

The following draw/force measurements were recorded on this self-wood yew longbow:

DRAW LENGTH	23"	24"	25"	26"
DRAW WEIGHT	52#	56#	60#	63 ½#

John also offers the American Spirit which is a cross between his laminated Spirit and the self-wood longbow. The American Spirit is a flat self-wood longbow with fiberglass backing for longevity and cast.

One of John's favorites is his Spirit Stick. It's a fiberglass laminated longbow with a small English-style oval riser grip without a window. Because it doesn't have a window side, the Spirit Stick can be shot either left or right handed.

BIRTH OF THE SPIRIT

Even though John's first longbow came out too heavy and he missed his first shot at an elk with it, he was fascinated by the weapon. He also knew he could build a better longbow and immediately began designing another. That second bow, built around 1980, was constructed from five tapered maple laminations and came out to John's intended draw weight. He continued making more longbows, refining each one. Soon, bowhunting friends began ordering bows from John, and by late 1981 his hobby had grown into a part-time business.

Throughout his bowmaking, John has learned his share of lessons through trial and error, a method of learning he believes is healthy. "There were people available who offered commercial bowmaking classes, but they were discouraging the trial and error process of learning, which is an excellent teacher. If you're taught by someone else you're limited more in the way you think than if you experience the trial and error process. By having determination in trial and error, you develop a bank of knowledge far greater than if you had someone else simply plant ideas in your head."

As John became more proficient at making his laminated bows, he was drawn to the mystique of the dying craft of making self-wood longbows. He tried his hand at carving these delicate bows and soon became hooked. Their primitive popularity has recently swelled, and today John's self-wood creations represent almost half of his orders. "I think self-wood bows are another trend in traditional archery where people are looking further back in archery for a greater challenge. Self-wood bows require more skill to build and to hunt with."

UNDER THE FIR

To fill his increasing yew longbow orders, John relies on his treasured supply of aged yew logs. He harvests them from the western slopes of the High Cascades east of Oregon's Willamette Valley. John hunts for the ancient but diminutive trees in elevations of 2,500 to 3,000 feet under the towering stands of virgin Douglas fir. "Most of those fir trees are four to six feet in diameter, and there isn't any undergrowth except yew wood. Much of the yew is six to ten inches in diameter and is unblemished up to seven feet. Some of those yew trees are over 300 years old."

To aid in curing, John harvests his yew from November to early May when the sap is down. With a yew permit in hand, he sometimes fells standing trees or searches through clear-cut areas for fallen yew. "Because loggers clear-cut everything and then burn the slash, the yew tree is just going to be lost in the future."

When he's lucky enough to find a long clear section, John cuts the log into a seven-foot length for making a stave bow. More often he cuts it into four-foot sections for making billets or laminations. After he brings the logs home, he uses a wedge and maul to split them into quarters. He then paints the ends and stacks the yew under a covered drying area to season for at least a year before using it in a bow.

NOT JUST YEW

Besides crafting historic yew, John also uses tough osage and black locust. Much of Oregon's osage was planted as fence rows a century ago by early settlers. Near Eugene, John discovered a good supply of osage trees which keeps his drying rack full. He locally harvests black locust, an excellent wood for making laminated or self-wood longbows. "Black locust has such a thick bark if you don't remove it right after the tree is cut, it will retain so much moisture in the cambium layer under the bark that the sapwood will rot — And that would break the backing layer on a self-wood bow."

John has also discovered an unconventional bow wood that grows near Tillamook. "Cascara is one of the best woods I've found for making laminated bows. Locally it's called chitum, and its bark is used in the production of laxatives. After they strip the bark off, they cut the tree down and a new crop of trees grows back rapidly from the stump. Cascara casts about the same as yew wood but it's smoother. It has a pleasant grain pattern and looks good under clear glass."

THE SELF-WOOD SPIRIT

When making a Traditional Spirit, John begins by selecting a quality piece of yew wood that will be worthy of his efforts. "It should have relatively straight grain from end to end without any large knots or flaws in the wood. I split my billets and pair them as they grew side by side in the tree. By splitting them I can see if the natural grain is straight, and if it shows evidence of an internal twist, I won't use it."

Once John has selected a pair of suitable, aged billets, he uses a special jig and a band saw to cut out the fishtail splice in the center of the handle. He then epoxies and dowels the billets together.

After the splice has dried, John removes the bark from the back of yew wood bows, being careful not to damage the underlying sapwood. For locust or osage bows he removes all of the backing sapwood down to the darker heartwood.

Referencing a thread strung from tip to tip and taped at the handle, John marks the bow centerline on the back and traces the limb shape using a metal template aligned on the centerline. He positions the upper limb template one inch above center which produces a built-in tiller in the longer upper limb.

Next, he bands saws the bow to its rough dimensions and begins hand planing the bow to its shape. Using files, scrapers, and sandpaper, he rough shapes the limbs. Although osage and locust allow shaping the bow across grain layers, John must follow the natural contour of the grain when crafting a yew bow.

When John reduces the bow enough so he can flex it in his arms, he files rough string nocks near the tips and braces the bow to an approximate three inch brace height. By drawing it gradually, John checks the arc of both limbs and scrapes stiff areas, slowly refining the belly shape until he achieves symmetrical bending in both limbs without weak or stiff spots. Once John

FROM THE DESERT AND SEA — John's unusual self-wood bow backings include spotted sturgeon skin (upper) and diamondback hide (lower).

has sanded the self-wood bow to its final shape, tiller, and draw weight, he's ready to apply the backing.

UNUSUAL BACKINGS

When building laminated bows, John follows conventional techniques using standard materials such as fiberglass and wood laminations. But when he begins crafting his self-wood bows, John pulls out some unusual backing materials from his bowyer's grab bag. Besides using rawhide, John backs his self-wood bows with whale baleen, deer sinew, diamondback snakeskin, and even sturgeon skin. "I'm using the skin of a sturgeon I caught this spring in Tillamook Bay, and with a little fisherman's luck, I plan on catching some more. I also plan on contacting other fishermen to establish a fish skin source. I get my snakeskins from friends who live in the southwest and Montana. I'm not the least bit interested in going out and catching live snakes, but if they're dried and stretched I'll put them on the back of a bow."

John prepares his rawhide backing by drum sanding it to a .030" thickness and soaking it until it's pliable. He applies his soft-soaked backing skin with Elmer's carpenter's glue and then wraps the skin in place with an Ace bandage. After it dries for several days, John scrapes the backing edges smooth with a cabinet scraper.

When applying fiberglass, wood, or baleen backing on his all-wood bows, John uses epoxy and presses the backing to the bow with his air hose and bow form. He heat cures the backing epoxy at about 100 degrees in his hot box. John applies the baleen, wood, or fiberglass backing on self-wood bows

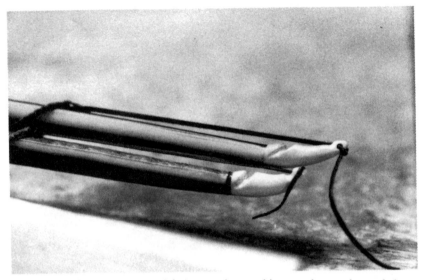

SHADES OF POPE AND YOUNG — John's ornately carved horn nocks even have a hole in the upper nock for tying on a leather string keeper.

before trimming them to their rough shape as these materials affect the bow's draw weight.

John usually equips his self-wood bows with ornately fashioned horn nocks that he glues on about an inch over the wooden tips.

LAMINATED SPIRITS

John begins building his composite Spirit by making the corewood laminations. Using seasoned quarter-split logs, he uses his band saw, jointer, and table saw to cut ¼" thick , 1½" wide, and 37" long laminations.

Next he hand scrapes one side of the lamination, removing any saw marks that may show under the clear fiberglass. He then tapes the rough lamination to a tapered lamination and rips the rough side, producing a .002" per inch taper. John has discovered that this lamination taper combined with an equal thickness of belly and back glass produces the best performance in his longbow design.

John stress tests his laminations by bending them in his hands and checking for any grain twist or cracking. He prefers using flat grain on the back and belly to provide an attractive grain pattern under clear glass and he uses edge grain in the center lamination. He cuts an overlapping skive joint on the butt ends of paired laminations to provide greater strength where they join in the middle of the riser.

RISER SHAPING

After marking the riser outline on a select piece of hardwood, John band saws its shape and grinds the belly shape using a drum sander. He feathers his fadeouts by backing them with a strip of wood and gently brushing them across his sanding drum until the ends become tissue paper thin. "The fadeout is an important area in the bow where it flexes. If the fadeout and lamination junction is filled with glue and air pockets instead of thin riser wood, it's going to break down and fail."

Once his composites are ready for glue-up, John wipes them down with acetone to remove any oil or grime from the gluing surfaces to ensure good glue adhesion. He also covers his sandwiched plywood form with plastic wrap and masking tapes the non-gluing fiberglass surfaces.

NEW GLUE

He then mixes a Vaseline-consistency epoxy and applies a coat to all contact surfaces. It's a relatively new glue for John and he loves it. "I've used other epoxies that were very harmful. Their vapors were so strong that I wore a heavy filtered mask and they were harmful enough to burn my skin. I wore rubber gloves but the epoxy went right through them. At one time I considered quitting bowmaking because the epoxy poisoning was so bad. But since I changed to this thicker epoxy, I haven't had any delaminations and my epoxy reaction has cleared up."

John secures the glued laminations in his form with filament strapping tape and then lays on a fire hose. He bolts on the top half of the form and slowly inflates the hose, checking the alignment of his composites. When they're all lined up, he inflates the hose to sixty pounds and places the form in his hot box.

His plywood curing box is heated with five 150 watt light bulbs that cure the glue at 130 degrees for five hours. After the form cools overnight, John removes the bow from the form. "One thing to remember about epoxy glue is it loses strength when it's heated. If you take a bow out of the press when it's hot, you could have slippage in the heavily stressed areas."

John trims the limb tips and attaches his centerline thread to both ends and marks out his limb shapes with the same method he uses for his self-wood bows. "Marking that centerline as perfectly as possible is really important in bowmaking, and it's sometimes difficult because of the reflexed limb design. If your centerline is crooked, chances are your bow will always be crooked."

TAKING SHAPE

With his band saw screaming at the fiberglass, John trims the limbs to their rough shape and grinds them to the marked outline using his disk sander. He again checks for bow straightness and makes any minor adjustments by grinding the limb edges. Using rasps and files, John shapes the limbs to a trapezoidal cross section narrowing to belly.

He then files in string nocks with a small rat-tail file, braces the bow, and checks the limbs for straightness. John files material off the strong side until the string tracks true down the center of the bow.

John sands the edges of the limbs to make minor tiller adjustments and to bring them down to a desired draw weight. He strives for a ¼" positive tiller in the upper limb measured from the fadeout to the string at brace height.

When the limbs are completed, John contours the riser with rasps, files, and sandpaper. He finish sands the entire bow with fifty grit sandpaper and works his way down to 180 grit. He glues on any tip or handle overlays with fast-drying Locktite glue and sands the overlays and string nocks to their final shape.

FINISH WORK

After John shoots each bow to be sure it's spitting arrows where it's supposed to, he sprays on the finish. He sprays both his laminated and self-wood bows with six coats of Varathane gloss aerosol finish that he cures in his heat box at eighty-five degrees. Between the second and third coat, John's wife, Pat, uses her calligraphy pen and talented hand to artfully ink on the bow specs and customer's name.

After the final coat is dried, John sands smooth any finish imperfections with 400 grit paper then rubs the bow with .0000 steel wool. To smooth out the finish even further, he polishes the bow with a pumice powder mixed with vegetable oil. He then rubs it to its final luster with rotten-stone mixed with vegetable oil.

One of the distinguishing features of John's bows is their grip. He glues on a suede leather grip and laces over it with goat skin lacing in a crisscross pattern. It's become a recognized characteristic of his Spirit longbows. Finally, John polishes his bows to a silky luster with Trewax paste wax.

SERVICE AND CARE

Besides selling craftsmanship and quality, John also offers his customers a highly valued commodity — service. "I don't have much control over a bow once it's out of my hands, but if it breaks, in most cases I replace it. I pride myself on the type of service I provide, and that's one of the things that has people coming back for more bows over the years. They like to know they're going to be treated fairly and get their money's worth."

To be sure each self-wood bow customer gets his money's worth, John devotes time to explaining the use and care of the new traditional weapon. "I tell them that when they're just moving through the woods and not really hunting or shooting, they should unstring the bow to preserve it. I also tell them not to overdraw their bow or give it to someone else to draw. Also, if a customer lives where it's very cold or hot, I recommend osage or black locust because yew has a natural resin in the wood which becomes solid when it's cold and fluid when it's hot. During cold weather, a yew bow will actually draw heavier and during hot weather it will lose some of its cast."

Even though his slim self-wood creations appear fragile, John firmly says, "My bows are designed for as much bowhunting as the customer wants to give them."

THE FUN SIDE

Although John makes his own Flemish-twist bowstrings for his bows, it's not one of his favorite jobs. He makes them in just minutes, his nimble hands moving like busy spiders spinning their intricate Dacron web.

There are, however, plenty of gratifying moments in John's bowmaking. "I don't make bows for a livelihood. The real payment in bow building is meeting my customers and listening to their comments about my bow's performance and appearance. Most of my customers come back for a second or a third bow, and some up to seven or eight. Customers like that are my main form of advertising.

"Another real reward in bowmaking is being able to get another person interested in making his own bow by sharing the knowledge I've learned and helping him reach a higher level of enjoyment in archery. Some of the people I've met through bowmaking have become good friends, and some I feel as close to as a brother. That's the big reward in bowmaking.

"But the main reason I build bows is because I get a deep satisfaction learning how to build something that has been with man for centuries, yet so many secrets about bowmaking have been lost."

SPREADING THE SPIRIT

Even so, John is determined to spread his bowmaking knowledge to the ranks of traditionalists searching for a deeper and purer meaning to the word archery. "There are people out there who share a feeling for Robin Hood and the Old English longbow that slew knights and ruled the world for hundreds of years. A self-wood longbow enthusiast is probably one of the most fanatical archers there is, and eventually, most want to try building their own longbow.

"But some bowmakers — who are looked up to by the general traditional archery community — are telling the average archer that they must be 'God chosen' to be a bowmaker and that the average guy shouldn't attempt bowmaking because it wasn't in the 'big plan.' Some bowyers have this attitude to discourage others from trying bowmaking and therefore forcing them to buy a bow from a bowmaker so they can make a few dollars.

"God gave us all the ability to be creative. Sure, he gave us different talents, but he gave us all the ability to learn, to be curious, and to make choices. I want people to fall in love with archery by making their own bows. I may not always have my ability to build a bow, but if I can help someone else discover the enjoyment of bowmaking, then I have used what God gave me — the ability to pass my talents on to someone else."

For John Strunk, teacher, bowmaker, and bowmaking teacher, bow crafting is a personal passion, a vehicle for reaching into the inner depths of traditional archery, and an avenue for passing on the true spirit of the longbow.

Epilogue

During the peaceful days when the clover blossomed, the two boys lingered near the fireside of Chu-no-wa-yahi, learning the sacred craft of fashioning man-nee. With each passing moon the old bowmaker watched the boys grow too quickly into young men, their visits becoming less frequent as they neared manhood.

Before the annual acorn harvest, the day came when the boys were ceremoniously presented with their tribal bows. The sleek bows were immaculate — the ultimate reflection of the old warrior's bowmaking skills and his deep love for the boys, now men. He knew their days would now be spent on the trail as hunters and warriors. He also knew his fireside would be hushed with gnawing worry for their safety. Although none would speak of it, a recent hunting party had not returned after venturing into the lowlands near the dreaded white men. Most knew they had probably been slaughtered by Saltu and his fire-spitting sticks that thundered of death.

In the chill of a leafless night, Chu-no-wa-yahi wrestled with the horror of a terrible dream. Tightly clutching his bow, he shuddered, embarking on his final journey to the land of shadows where he would hunt forever with the thousands of warriors silenced before him.

Chu-no-wa-yahi escaped the suffering his people endured. In the years that followed his passing, the raw wind howled a deathly moan at the base of the great cliff. It mingled with the mournful cries for the ever growing number of Yana killed by the invading whites.

The white men purposefully massacred the Yana of Northern California, reducing the once-proud race from several thousand to less than a dozen. Battered, hunted, and clinging to life, the remnants clamored into the desolate canyons of Deer and Mill Creeks. There, under the cover of the shadowed cliffs and dense brush, the survivors slipped into their secretive existence, disappearing from the white man's conquered world.

People mostly forgot about the staunch survivors until 1908 when a survey party surprised three of the primitives near Deer Creek. After shooting warning arrows at the party, two Indians abandoned an old crippled woman and disappeared into the brush. The survey party approached the trembling old woman, her withered legs wrapped in willow bark. Nearby they discovered two brush huts hidden in dense foliage. In typical white man fashion, they ransacked the huts, confiscating bows, arrows, and primitive utensils, and left. Returning the next day they hoped to find the Indians, but the huts were abandoned. The primitives had disappeared forever. Except for one.

For nearly three years the tales about the wild Indians of Deer Creek lingered — until one morning a half-starved, ragged Indian was discovered in the small town of Oroville, over thirty miles from Deer Creek. Brought to bay in a corral by a barking dog, the wild Indian was captured and locked in the local jail for safekeeping.

Hearing of the Indian's capture, Professor T.T. Waterman, from the Department of Anthropology at the University of California, visited the jail and established broken communication with the primitive. The Indian was Ishi, lone survivor of the Yana Indians.

Waterman befriended the fearful Indian and took Ishi to San Francisco and to the Museum of Anthropology where he became a subject of study. During his years at the museum, Ishi had little immunity to the white man's infectious world and was often sick. He was treated by Dr. Saxton Pope, instructor of surgery at the University Medical school.

Pope became friends with Ishi and admired him for his kindness, honesty, and high moral standards. In turn, Ishi admired Pope for his ability to learn the Yana tongue and for his deep interest in Ishi's most prized possessions — his bow and arrows.

Ignoring the barriers of race and culture, Ishi and Pope grew to love each other as brothers and became bonded by their common affection for the bow. Ishi taught Pope how to make, shoot, and hunt with Indian style bows and arrows. The two friends took many outings together, bows in hand, sharing a fragment of Ishi's lost world. Ishi showed Pope how to call game and how to understand the language of the birds and animals. He taught Pope how to still hunt for deer, while using the forest sounds, the wind, and the rising sun to the hunter's advantage. And when their arrows missed game, Ishi would tell Pope the shot could easily have been made by the great Yana hunter, Chu-no-wa-yahi.

After three years in civilization, Ishi returned with Pope and company to the Yana homeland along Deer Creek. It was a brief and flickering bright spot in a life clouded with so much terror and loneliness. Pope wrote: "We swam the streams together, hunted deer and small game, and at night sat under the stars by the campfire, where in a simple way we talked of old heroes, the worlds above us, and his theories of the life to come in the land of plenty, where the bounding deer and the mighty bear met the hunter with his strong bow and swift arrows."

Pope planned a return trip in the fall when he and Ishi could devote more time to hunting deer with their bows and arrows. But circumstance would cheat these brothers of the bow from their autumn hunt.

Ishi fell into ill health and later contracted tuberculosis. He quickly wilted before Pope's eyes like a wild flower plucked by the roots. With Pope by his side, Ishi faded from the white man's world in the spring of 1916 when hills along Deer Creek once again bloomed with clover and the creek thundered with the splashes of mighty salmon.

With some acorn meal, dried venison, and his treasured bow and arrows by his side, Ishi was sent on his final long journey to the land of shadows. Pope wrote: "His soul was that of a child, his mind that of a philosopher. With him there was no word for good-by. He said: 'You stay, I go.' He has gone, and he hunts with his people. We stay, and he has left us the heritage of the bow."

From the last of the Yana to the unnamed bowmakers of generations to come — the heritage lives on.

A SNAPSHOT IN TIME—TWO DECADES LATER

Obviously, the one constant throughout life is change. Our paths can take some dramatic twists and turns over two decades. We grow wiser, older, life's priorities shift, some of us move on to other professions, others to different places. A few have found their final place in recorded history.

It's been twenty years now since the traditional bowyers were interviewed in 1987. So it only seems right that the archery world should know in part what they're up to these days and what changes are noteworthy in their lives.

One thing worth mentioning is a general observation about the traditional bowyers as a group. Studies show that most people change jobs every seven years. In today's volatile job market, it may be shorter. That's why it's a little surprising that so many of these bowyers are still immersed in their craft of turning wood and fiberglass into someone else's traditional archery dreams. Should we be surprised when a few pursue other things in life? Or should we more surprised that so many of them still make bows for a living? No, not if we truly understood what made them do it in the first place.

Like the original chapters in this book, the following updated paragraphs offer but a brief snapshot in time that give us a glimpse of the bowyers today. Unlike the first edition, you'll find some Web site addresses here for the bowyers who have them and are still in business. Others have offered phone numbers for new business or contact information for past customers.

As you read about where they are now in life compared to their chapter from twenty years ago, you might ponder a great many things about changes in their lives. Perhaps the most enlightening thing of all might be to imagen even deeper—about where you might be today if you had walked in their shoes.

The Traditional Longbow Company—Frank San Marco—Still living in Mahopac, New York, Frank is retired from formal teaching and now teaches a special course about Native American values and their connection with the earth. He still builds longbows but on a much smaller scale, and the wait-time can be considerable. Over the past ten years, Frank's bowmaking became too overwhelming to fit in with his family life and teaching. So he cut way back on building them. Though he will always love the graceful lines of the longbow, Frank is also developing a new recurve that handles like a longbow, yet stores more energy and throws an arrow like a recurve. During the past dozen years he has also modified his longbow limb and handle design to increase performance and feel. 845-628-5717.

Fedora's Archery—Mike Fedora is still making custom bows full-time from his shop in Richland, Pennsylvania. Over the years, he has maintained the trademark of his bow designs with refinements in the specialty grips with their handcrafted thumb-rests and expanded a line of takedown longbows. And in an age of mass production and machine-assisted shortcuts, Mike still maintains his true custom bowmaking business with son Jason by offering bows built one-at-time with classic rarities such as true Brazilian rosewood. In fact, he laughs at people collecting his bows for their "classic art value," which customers point out will jump up when Mike dies. But for now, Mike still leans into the joy of this work and plans on building custom bows for as long as traditional shooters want them. www.fedorabows.com. 717-933-8862.

Bear Archery—Fred Bear—After nearly seven decades of making bows and shooting arrows heard by sportsmen around the world, the father of modern bowhunting, Fred Bear, died at the age of eighty-six in April 1988. His contributions to bowmaking and bowhunting will live on as long as we shoot bows and arrows. He inspired the thrill of traditional bowhunting in more of our souls than anyone in modern history. A lineup of Fred Bear Archery traditional bows are still produced today. The company is now a division of Escalade Sports that was acquired in 2003. www.fredbearoutdoors.com.

Brigham Bowhunting—Robert Brigham—Because of other obligations in life with family and work, Robert Brigham stopped making bows professionally about five years ago. He still makes a few bows however, for previous customers, friends, and family. And he's still bowhunts with family for those big Buckeye whitetails back where the magic all began. Because now, he lives back in the house where he grew up in Eagleville, Ohio. 440-563-5209.

Assenheimer Bows — Don Assenheimer—Don still resides in Bucyrus, Ohio, where he continues to handcraft his famous recurves in his backyard shop. He's retired now and has scaled back his bowmaking to more of a part-time hobby. Nonetheless, Don still cranks out about fifty bows a year. He notes that over the years his bow designs have become slimmer in the riser and limbs, plus he uses mostly exotic woods in the risers and laminated bamboo corewoods. In 2001 Don fulfilled his quest of tagging a bragging-sized record book caribou with this recurve. www.assemheimer-bows.com

Great Northern Longbow Company — Jerry Brumm and Rick Shepard—Jerry and Rick at Great Northern continue to craft some of the sweetest longbows and sleekest recurves to ever make a string sing. Oh sure, they've made some tweaks here and there to improve performance and also developed some new designs such as a hybrid bow that's well . . . a hybrid. Perhaps the biggest change over the years has been in their arrow quiver business, which has grown from a concept of featherweight bow quivers into a solid cornerstone of their business. Jerry and Rick are still great guys making great bows. www.gnbco.com. 517-852-0820.

Rothhaar Recurves — Alan Rothhaar—Alan stopped making his takedown recurve bows about ten years ago when his blossoming *Flight-Rite*

spine tester business took off and required all his free time. Nonetheless, Alan still has all his bowmaking tools and equipment, and in fact is searching for the right someone with an interest in bowmaking to tutor so he can pass along the business of making his Spirit recurves. He still chases whitetails with his bow and even acquired some prime land in Iowa with his Uncle Roger where their family shares the lure of bowhunting giant bucks. www.spinetester.com.

Elburg's Archery—Harry Elburg—still lives in Madison, Indiana and works from his bow shop out back. However, Harry no longer makes composite bows. After decades of struggling with allergies aggravated by fiberglass and glue dust, he sold his composite bow building business a couple of years ago to a budding bowyer whom he trained. But Harry isn't about to give up making bows. No, it's too much in his blood and he's always loved the people he's met in archery. In fact, he's getting his shop ready to launch his new self-wood bow crafting business. He plans on making mostly osage bows—from longbows to recurves with sinew backing and perhaps an occasional yew wood longbow. Yeah, people change, but deep inside they remain the same. 812-866-5285.

Bruin Custom Recurves—Mike Steliga—of Antigo, Wisconsin, is still making bows, although some health issues and a new sawmill operation have forced him to cut way back to crafting bows part-time over the past several years. Over time, his recurve line has changed, and he now concentrates on a few select models. Of course, he still treks the tall woods after bears and whitetails. He can be reached at 715-623-6537.

Hoyt/USA—Earl Hoyt, Jr.—Perhaps the most innovative traditional bowmaker of all time and a true gentleman in every aspect of archery, Earl Hoyt, Jr. died February 24, 2001. After Earl passed away, Ann Hoyt sold their Sky Archery factory to Mathews, Inc. Hoyt/USA is now called simply Hoyt and makes hunting and target recurves. Mathews manufactures traditional bows that like most recurves today carry many of Earl's innovations. So yes, his pioneer bowmaking spirit lives on from all parts of the nation.

Pearson Archery—Even with their slogan, "America's Oldest Bowmaker —Since 1927," it appears that Ben Pearson Archery, now located in Brewton, Alabama, and offering quite a selection of compounds, no longer manufactures traditional bows. Nothing stays the same forever. Wonder what Ol' Ben would say?

Arkansas Stick—Terry Huges—It was reported that Terry sold his bowmaking gear around 1997 and moved on to other things in life.

Black Widow Bow Company—Ken Beck—Under the leadership and vision of Ken Beck, Black Widow has remained one of the most successful icons in the traditional bow business. For many archers, including the author, owning a Black Widow is the crown jewel of their bow collection. A few things have changed over the years, such as building a new, bigger bow shop in Nixa, Missouri. Also, Ken sold the business a couple of years ago to his core co-workers who helped build the company's reputation. However, Ken still mans the helm as the CEO at Black Widow where he helps steer the direction of old time bows into the 21st century. www.blackwidowbows.com. 417-725-3113.

Bighorn Bowhunting Company — G. Fred Asbell—Two decades saw a world of change at Bighorn Bowhunting. G. Fred Asbell sold the business in 1991 to King of the Mountain Sports, who later sold it to Bud Boker of Greely, Colorado, in 2001. Bud later died and the bow company along with him. G. Fred Asbell now lives in Michigan and performs instinctive shooting clinics at the headquarters of his long-time competitor, Black Widow Bow Company. Hmmm.

Wapiti Recurves, Longbows — J.K. Chastain—Keith Chastain is still crafting recurves and longbows at his shop in Lakewood, Colorado, with a strong core of repeat business. His designs have changed a little over the years with a few models coming and going. Keith notes that with the improvements in the quality of clear fiberglass about fifteen years ago, most of his bows nowadays have clear glass over the limbs. Now a senior member of Pope & Young, and inducted into the Colorado Bowhunters Hall of Fame, he has changed how much he hunts. He now spends about fifteen weeks a year bowhunting, instead of ten and is the only person on earth who has taken nine of the ten Colorado big game animals with his own crafted bows and arrows. www.worldclassbows.com 303-989-1120.

Scorpion Longbow — M.R. Hamilton—M.R. Hamilton's life took some twists for sure. While making his longbows from his remote mountainside home in Crestone, Colorado, he refurbished an old grand piano that he got in trade for helping an elderly lady. M.R. even had the old piano fitted with new strings, and tuned, and taught himself to play the thing, remarkably well. In no time he was playing piano for the local church, and before long became immersed in various church activities. He stopped making longbows, became minister of a church, got married, and moved to Missouri or back to his home state of Kentucky—somewhere.

Heritage Archery — Rocky Miller—Archery historian, Dave Doran or Oregon, reports that Big Sky bowmaker Rocky Miller quit making bows around 1997 and moved from Bozeman to New Mexico to become a flyfishing guide. If we know Rocky, he's also probably making custom flyrods in his spare time. Catch a big one for us.

Monarch Longbows — Byron Schurg—Byron still in lives in Missoula Montana, but his Monarch Longbow business has seen a number of changes, mostly unfortunate. He sold the business to noted bowhunter Monty Moravec, who ran it for a while before he took his own life in 1995.

Monty's father sold the business to someone else but the business eventually failed, and the name Monarch Longbow with it. However, Byron began a new longbow business with the Aspen Longbow Company in 1996. He built bows in earnest for years, but arthritis in his hands and back forced him to cut back to a handful of bows a year. It also hampered his hunting somewhat. But when he drew a prized Montana moose tag last season, he pushed aside the pain and took off into the mountains with one of his 60-inch longbows and arrowed a 41-inch moose. He's now recovering from back surgery and hopes to trek the mountains even more during the golden years ahead—and turn out as many Aspen Longbows as time and dexterity permit. 406-251-3300.

Kramer Archery—Ted & Lee Kramer—The passage of time has changed things at Kramer Archery. The patriarch, Ted, now in his 80s, is retired and no longer makes bows or performs trick shooting. His son, Lee, still lives in Montana but respiratory illness in 1998 forced him to quit building bows commercially because of the persistent ill effects of the various dusts generated during bowmaking. Nonetheless, Lee still does his trick shooting demonstrations when he can find time away from his computer business. "Yes, things have changed here," says Lee, "but our love for archery is something that will never end."

Robertson Stykbow—Dick Roberston—About fifteen years ago, Dick moved his home and bowmaking operation from Hamilton, Montana, to a bowhunter's dream location on a thousand acres of prime hunting ground in Forest Grove, located in central Montana. Like most bowyers that have continued their craft with distinctive quality over the decades, Dick now offers some new twists to his designs, including Laser Lams—where a computer assisted program laser etches realistic snakeskin patterns into the corewood laminations that go under clear fiberglass. One of the steadfast traditional bowyers over the years, Dick has seen a lot of budding bowyers come and go within the industry. But the one thing that hasn't changed is the genuine interest that spurs ranks of archers into looking for their basic roots in bowhunting with traditional gear. www.robertsonstykbow.com. 406-538-2818.

Trails End Recurves—Dale Dye—Still located where he retired as sheriff in Hamilton, Montana, and still crafting bows, Dale Dye is as sage as ever. He notes that his bows are pretty much the same except for introducing a shorter 58-inch model, plus all of them now are fitted with Fast-Flight strings. Because his long and growing list of customers are so pleased, he spends more time now making new limbs and refinishing bows for established customers instead of making new bows. The result is a waiting list for a new bow of over a year. But that doesn't seem to dissuade archers set on having one of his creations. Since the first edition of this book, Dale has ventured to Alaska three times with his recurve, where he's upended big things like moose and bears. He's also added a 150-plus whitetail to his shop wall. And even after twenty-five years of crafting his Trail's

End recurves, the warm rush of bowmaking still pumps through his veins. 406-363-2983.

Howard Hill Archery—Craig Ekin—Craig is still located in Hamilton, Montana, where he continues making the legendary lineup of Howard Hill longbows. He notes that they've developed some new models over the years such as their 5-lamination bamboo longbow and are now making one with carbon core material. Like many bowyers who have been in the craft this long, Craig has seen archers drop to more reasonable bow weights in the 55-pound range over the past fifteen years. Guess that goes with the old adage, "It's better to shoot a lighter bow good than a heavy bow poorly." www.howardhillarchery.com. 406-363-1359.

Martin/Howatt—Larry Hatfield—With over forty-five years of traditional bowmaking experience, Martin Archery only saw it fitting to come out with the "Hatfield Take-Down" recurve. Even after all those decades of bowmaking, Larry still leads the helm at the Howatt recurve factory in Yakima, Washington. www.martinarchery.com

Tim Meigs Custom Archery—Tim Meigs is truly one of the gentleman of the sport and perhaps the most seasoned bowyer in American. After an amazing fifty-three years of handcrafting traditional bows, Tim is starting to slow down just a little to half-time. He still produces his longbows from his shop in Carson City, Nevada. The biggest improvement he's seen over the decades is the improvement in the quality of fiberglass, especially the clear glass. Sorry, no Website for Tim. He's been too busy with making bows and chasing deer to get into that fancy computer stuff. But he can be reached by phone at 775-246-3633.

Mountainman Longbows—John Watson—Archery historian Dave Doran, or Oregon, reports that John had cut back on his bowmaking over the years and died from a heart attack incurred while mountain biking around 1999.

Don McCann Custom Archery—Don McCann—Don is no longer active as a traditional bowmaker-supplier and was reported to be working for Boeing. However, the company that manufactured his bows, Checkmate Archery, located in Abbotsford, British Columbia, is still making fine traditional bows today. They manufacture bows for Cascade Archery plus their own lineup of Checkmate bows. Their master bowyer, Larry Courchaine, who is now seventy and has been crafting his bows for thirty-five years, says it might be time to start slowing down. His two most popular models are his Take-down Hunter and one-piece Falcon.

Jim Brackenbury Bows—Jim Brackenbury tragically drowned in a riverboat accident in July 1991 on the John Day River. Even though Jim's vigor left this earth too soon, his company, bows, and spirit still live on in

Brackenbury Bows. After Jim's death, his stepsister's son, Gordon Porter, began building Jim's bows. He built them through the late 1990s and eventually sold the business to Bill Howland in 2001. Today, Bill tries to build the bows the same way as Jim, yet has refined the process with more modern techniques. For instance, he has retooled things so he can glue and cure limb composites with improved methods, plus refined some of the limb and riser shaping and alignment techniques. Bill has also refined things such as limb bushings and dual-pin metal-to-metal contact and alignment. Like many modern bowyers, he now builds bows to support high-performance bowstrings. The most popular models are the newer designed Quest recurve and Non-typical hybrid. "It's okay that more people are trying to use carbon in limbs," says Bill, "and pushing for the speed aspect in bowmaking. But in the end, we should remember that torsional stability in a limb and shootability are more important." www.brackenburybows.com. 509-468-3905.

Cascade Mountain Archery—Fred Anderson—Physical limitations from knee surgery forced Fred to quit making bows professionally in 2006. But he hopes that time and recovery will permit him to get back into his life's passion. He notes that perhaps there has been no better time to be in traditional archery because of the growing interest. However, he cautions that sometimes people are so driven to succeed that they forget their roots and the reasons why they shoot old-time gear. While his new knee joints mend, Fred plans on putting his finishing touches on his second archery book—one about the personal views of archery's founding leaders who took it from a crazy notion of modern man shooting ancient weapons to the widely loved pursuit it is today.

Don Adams Archery—Even after fifty years of spoke-shaving ancient Pacific yew into elegant English longbows, Don is still pursuing his passion of the old-world craft. His talents may be a lost art in most archery shops, but it lives on in Elmira, Oregon. It's logical that his historic bows haven't really changed much over the decades. Ancient yew has no modern replacement. And his customers are still from a worldwide base. Perhaps the only noted change is the new interest in Old English yew "war bows" similar to those that made headlines in the historic media with the discovery of crates of ancient yew longbows in the wreck of the Mary Rose. So in a traditional bowcrafting realm full of change across most of the nation, Don and his bows remain technically and historically . . . the same. www.donadamsarchery.com 541-935-3794.

The Spirit Longbow Company—John Strunk—Retirement may have taken the schoolteacher out of the local school in 1994, but that didn't take bowmaking teaching away from John. Today, he still not only makes his classic old-time bows, he now teaches self-wood and bamboo-backed bowmaking to others at his home and one the road. He was forced to quit making fiberglass-backed bows in the mid-1990s because of the allergic reactions to working with epoxy glues and fiberglass. However, he still crafts self-wood bows using good compression woods such as osage orange and yew, and backs them with bamboo. "So I'm not a retired a bowmaker," says John, "just retired from having someone else telling me it's time to go to work." John has noticed a change over the past twenty years with an increased interest in more archers handcrafting their own self-wood back bows. "Back in the 80s it was hard to find the bowmaking gear, information, and raw materials. But not now. Building your own bows helps you increase your enjoyment of archery beyond just the short hunting season to all year long." Call for classes or self-wood bows. 503-842-4944.

The Author—Dan Bertalan—After penning four books and broadcasting in syndicated radio and outdoor television for a few years, Dan focused his media talents into video production and outdoor education. Over the years he has produced nearly a hundred productions, including *Safe Treestand Hunting* and *How To Shoot Instinctively Better Than Ever*. Today, Dan directs his energies into developing multimedia that gets kids interested in archery, conservation, and the outdoors. His national award-winning educational productions, such as *Living with White-Tailed Deer*, are being distributed in schools across the nation to help educate our next generation about becoming responsible stewards of the land through balanced wildlife management. Dan's website, www.greatoutdoorsmultimedia.com, reveals in part how he now mixes his lifelong love of archery with inspiring kids to embrace our great outdoors. Dan still shoots his trusty recurve, but chooses to quietly slip through the shadows of bowhunting away from the limelight.

COMMON TRADITIONAL BOW DESIGNS

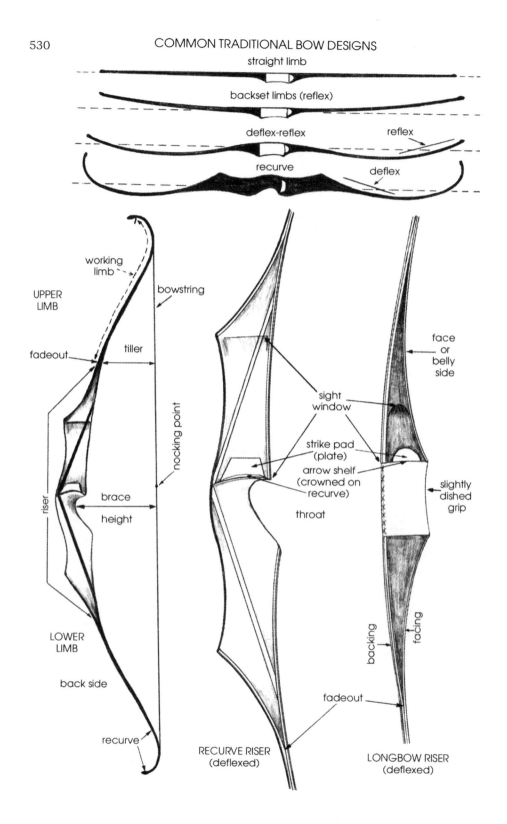

straight limb

backset limbs (reflex)

deflex-reflex

reflex

recurve

deflex

working limb

bowstring

UPPER LIMB

fadeout

tiller

nocking point

riser

brace height

LOWER LIMB

back side

recurve

face or belly side

sight window

strike pad (plate)

arrow shelf (crowned on recurve)

throat

slightly dished grip

backing

facing

fadeout

RECURVE RISER (deflexed)

LONGBOW RISER (deflexed)

Glossary

Actionwood — A limb core material made from laminated hard rock maple; laminations run perpendicular to the limb face and back; produced by the Old Master Crafters, Waukegan, Illinois.

alignment — The position of the bowstring relative to the centerline of both limbs. When the limbs are aligned, the bowstring follows the centerline of both limbs from tip to tip.

atlatl — A primitive armlike extension held in the hand to aid in throwing a spear.

back — The bow surface facing away from the shooting archer; the bow side opposite the bowstring.

backing — The material covering the outer layer of the bow back; fiberglass on modern laminated bows.

backset — A longbow design where unbraced limbs angle backward, away from the shooter, in a reflexed position, and the limb tips set backward of the riser; designed to put preload, or stress, into the braced limbs.

baleen — A calcareous mouth part of a whale used for bow backing material; most commonly used on self-wood longbows.

bamboo —A tropical grass used as a bow corewood. Dried and fashioned into limb laminations for making composite bows, mostly longbows.

belly — The bow surface facing the shooting archer; same side as the bowstring.

belly tip overlay — Material laminated to the belly of the limb tips, used mostly in recurves to provide extra material for fashioning the string groove and for strengthening the tip to reduce the possibility of limb twist

billet — A half bow-length piece of wood used in making self-wood bows. Billets are commonly split from a side by side position in the same log to obtain similar limb performance characteristics, and spliced in the handle section of a bow.

black locust — A native North American hardwood used for making bow risers and corewood laminations. Durable and resilient, also used for making self-wood bows.

bow form — A wooden or metal form used to press laminated bow composites into a specific shape; a bow form commonly represents the shape of the bow back and is part of a bow press.

bow length — The length of a bow, commonly measured from nock to nock along the back.

bow press — A device used for pressing bow composites to conform to the shape of the bow form.

bow stringer — Usually a cord with a small leather limb tip cup tied on each end used to aid in the stringing and unstringing of a bow.

bow weight — The drawing force, measured in pounds, required to draw a bowstring a specified braced distance, commonly 28 inches.

bowyer — A person who crafts, builds, or makes bows. A traditional bowyer crafts, builds, or makes recurves or longbows.

brace — To string a bow. A bow may be braced only slightly or to its recommended brace height.

brace height — The measured perpendicular distance from the braced bowstring to the low point of the belly of the grip. It may be adjusted up or down by twisting or untwisting the bowstring to slightly alter a bow's shooting characteristics.

broadhead — An arrow point with bladed cutting edges used for bowhunting.

brush button — A rubber button placed on the bowstring where the string touches the belly of the recurve to prevent brush from getting caught between the bowstring and limb.

bubinga — An African hardwood used in making bow handles.

butt end — The end of a lamination butted against another lamination (often paired) on the riser section. Also what commonly drags near the ground after a long hard day of bowhunting.

butt overlay — Backing material laminated over the butt end of a take-down limb where the limb attaches to the handle section.

cant — To hold the bow at an angle while drawing and shooting. Canting removes a portion of the bow handle and bowstring from an instinctive sight picture.

capping — Material overlaid on the back or belly of the handle for decorative and/or strengthening purposes.

center shot — A sight window cut to the depth of the bow's centerline so the arrow rests at or near the centerline of the bow. A center shot bow minimizes the effects of the archer's paradox.

centerline — A straight line from the center of the bow handle to the center of both tips, along the back or belly, which divides the bow lengthwise into halves.

chrysal — A hairline compressional fracture of the wood fibers in the belly of a self-wood bow.

clarified calfskin — A processed calfskin used for backing self-wood bows, commonly applied to protect the sapwood layer.

cocobolo — A dark, dense African hardwood used in making bow handles.

composites — The distinct components used in laminating a composite bow; commonly fiberglass facing and backing, corewood laminations, and a riser section.

compound bow — A mechanical device used for shooting arrows, utilizing a system of eccentric wheels, pulleys, and cables to control the draw/force relationship of the bending bowlike limbs.

core thickness — The thickness of a laminated limb's core materials; commonly measured at the butt end, between the facing and backing material.

corewood — Wood used in making limb cores on composite bows; commonly fashioned into a thin lamination.

crossbow — A gunlike weapon with a shoulder-stock and trigger that shoots arrowlike projectiles from a short bowlike mechanism.

crested — The crowned or peaked profile of an arrow shelf with a high point designed to enhance arrow flight.

cresting — the decorative painting on the feathered end of an arrow.

crown dipping — The dipping application of paint or finish on the feathered end of an arrow shaft.

crowned — The peaked or rounded profile of an arrow shelf with a high point designed to enhance arrow flight.

Dacron — Trademark for a synthetic polyester textile fiber used for making bowstrings.

deep-cored — A limb design with a relative core thickness greater than a flat limb design; commonly refers to a longbow with a thick limb core and "D" shaped cross section.

deflex — A bow design where the limbs, at the fadeouts, angle toward the belly. Designed to increase a bow's stability and decrease its hand shock.

deflex-reflex — A bow design where the unbraced limbs deflex forward toward the shooter then reverse attitude, reflexing backward away from the shooter. Reflexing replaces the braced limb stress lost by deflexing; a common longbow design.

delamination — The failure and separation of a glue joint in a laminated bow, sometimes caused by excessive heat or moisture.

dished grip — A bow grip concave along the belly; commonly fashioned on longbows to provide consistent hand placement.

draw weight — The pounds of pull exerted on the bowstring when drawn a specified braced distance; commonly measured at 28 inches of draw length.

dynamic position — A braced bow in a partially or fully drawn position.

epoxied — To glue together with epoxy.

epoxy — Any of the various usually thermosetting resins capable of forming tight bonds characterized by toughness, strong adhesion, and a high corrosion and chemical resistance.

exotics — Imported woods not indigenous to North America.

face — The bow surface on the same side as the bowstring and facing the shooting archer; also known as the belly.

facing — The material covering the bow face; fiberglass on modern composite bows.

fadeout — The tapered end of the riser enveloped by the limb composites; separates the limb composites into back and belly laminations.

fadeout wedge — The fadeout portion of the limb of a take-down bow; also known as a fadeout block.

Fast Flight — Trademark name of a non-stretching bowstring material used for making bowstrings. A Fast Flight bowstring shoots an arrow from a traditional bow approximately seven feet per second faster than a Dacron bowstring.

featherout — The thin feathered end of the fadeout.

ferrule — The cone-shaped portion of a broadhead that fits over the tapered end of an arrow and is secured in place with glue.

fiberglass — A composite material made of spun unidirectional glass fibers bonded in a high tensile strength, flexible epoxy matrix; approximately sixty-eight percent glass fibers by weight.

fistmele — A fancy and generally outdated word for brace height.

flatbow — A straight-limbed bow with thin-cored, relatively flat limbs. A longbow design styled after the Plains Indian flatbows.

Flemish bowstring — An older style of braided bowstring popular among longbow shooters.

fletch — To affix feathers or plastic veins to an arrow shaft, usually with glue and a fletching jig.

fletching — The feathers or plastic veins that help guide an arrow's flight.

flush cut — When bowstring nocks are cut to a depth that holds the string flush with the edges or back of the limb.

follow the string — When a self-wood bow develops a bend in the limbs in the direction of the braced position. Lemonwood and hickory longbows are noted for following the string.

Forgewood — A compressed wood arrow shafting material.

forgiving — Jargon for a bow that minimizes shooter inconsistencies.

fps — feet per second; refers to arrow velocity.

freezing — The mental inability to aim and hold on the center of the target; a form of target panic.

full cut — The part of the sight window cut deepest into the riser.

Fullerplast — A resistant two-part catalystic varnish used as a bow finish.

glass — A common slang word used to describe fiberglass.

glue creep — The intermolecular slippage of a laminated glue joint.

glue-up — The process of applying glue to the bow composites of a laminated bow.

gongola alves — An exotic hardwood used in making bow handles.

Gordon — Manufacturer of bow fiberglass.

grain — A small unit of weight commonly associated with arrows and broadheads equaling 0.002285 ounce, or 64.798 milligrams.

grip — The middle part of bow handle griped by shooter; on longbows, often covered with leather.

handle — The riser or middle section of a bow to which the limbs are attached. The middle section of a three-piece take-down bow.

hinged limb — A limb that bends predominantly near the handle section.

hued — A dimension of color; a particular gradation

Ishi — The last surviving Yana Indian. Discovered in California in 1911 and later befriended and treated by Dr. Saxton Pope.

lamination — One of the layers of a laminated bow limb; either corewood or fiberglass.

lay-up — The process of arranging the glued bow composites in a bow form.

limb length, working — The measurement from the end of the fadeout to the string nock along the back. The bending portion of the limb that does the work in propelling the arrow.

limb thickness — The measurement from the limb face to the limb back.

limb twist — The sideways bending of the recurve portion of a limb out of alignment. Some twisted limbs can be corrected. Contact your bowyer for advice.

limb width — The measurement across the limb face or back.

man-nee — Yana word for bow.

Micarta — A dense, fiber impregnated resin.

mike — Jargon for measuring with a micrometer.

mulie — Jargon for mule deer.

multibladed — Having more than two blades.

myrtlewood — A native wood used for making bow risers.

nock throat — The notched part of an arrow nock that holds the bowstring.

nock, arrow — The slotted end of an arrow that fits on the bowstring; commonly a plastic arrow accessory glued onto the tapered nock end of an arrow.

nock, string — The notched portion of a limb tip that secures the bowstring; it may also be a fashioned material such as animal horn attached to the tip of the limb on a self-wood bow.

nocking point — A metal or thread index placed on a bowstring to reference consistent positioning of the arrow nock.

osage orange — A native North American wood historically popular for making self-wood bows. Also used for risers and corewoods in laminated bows. Known for its resiliency and toughness.

overbowed — When an archer is attempting to master a bow too heavy in draw weight.

overlay — Material that is laminated to the belly, back, or side of a bow, usually on the tips or handle section.

paired laminations — Two corewood laminations cut consecutively from the same board to obtain similar grain and performance characteristics. Using paired laminations in opposing bow limbs helps achieve balanced limb characteristics.

parallel lamination — A corewood lamination uniform in thickness from the butt end to the tip end.

phenolic — A crystalline resin derived from phenol, impregnated with cloth-based material and used in some facets of bowmaking such as tip overlays and fadeout wedges.

polyurethane — A flexible resin coating used as a bow finish.

preload — A limb design feature measured by the amount of string tension at braced position.

psi — Pounds per square inch at atmospheric pressure.

push-pull — A bow stringing technique using the foot instep to hold the lower limb tip while pulling the handle with one hand and pushing the upper limb with the other hand.

recurve — A limb design in which the unbraced limb tips bend toward the back of the bow, and the braced bowstring lays against the belly of the tip.

reflex — A limb design in which the unbraced bow limbs angle toward the back of the bow, and the braced bowstring does not touch the belly of the tip. The opposite of deflex.

reverse handle — A handle design in which the bow handle sets flush with the bow belly and extends toward the back of the bow.

riser — The handle section of a one-piece composite bow, measured between the ends of the fadeouts.

riser thickness — The measurement from the back to the belly of the riser, normally thinning through the grip.

riser wedge — A decorative and/or strengthening material laminated between the belly and back sections of the riser. A wedge is usually either vertically straight, curved in the general profile of the riser back, or "V" shaped.

riser width — The measurement between the sides the rise, narrowing through the sight window.

rpm — Revolutions per minute.

sapwood — The often lighter-toned and softer layer of wood just under cambium layer (bark) of a tree. The sapwood is used as the natural backing on some self-wood bows such as yew.

shedua — A brown exotic hardwood known as African cherry, used in bowmaking.

shelf — The ledge at the base of the sight window where the arrow rests. Also know as the arrow shelf.

sight window — The cut out portion of the riser above the arrow shelf. It allows the arrow to pass near the bow centerline reducing the effects of the archer's paradox.

sinew — The fibrous tendon material from an animal leg or loin. It is used as a backing material on self-wood and primitive bows.

skived — A trimmed narrow edge, such as the edge on leather lacing.

snap shooting — The conditioned reflex of premature release of the bowstring, stimulated by the visual sight picture of the target; a form of target panic.

spine — The tensile strength of a material such as the stiffness of an arrow shaft or a lamination.

stabilizer — An extended weight attached to the bow to minimize bow torque and provide stability during shooting; not usually found on traditional bows.

stacking — Jargon for a bow that pulls an increased number of pounds or fraction of pounds per inch for each inch of draw.

static position — A bow in the braced position but not drawn.

stave — A full-length, unspliced piece of wood used for making a self-wood bow.

strike pad (plate) — The material covering the sight window where the arrow makes contact; commonly leather or animal fur on traditional bows.

string groove — A shallow groove in the belly of a recurve limb where the bowstring contacts the limb. It helps keep the string and limb in alignment.

swaged — The tapered shaping of an aluminum arrow foreshaft to directly accept an arrow point.

tamboti — An exotic African hardwood used for making bow risers.

tapered lamination — A lamination that tapers from the butt end to the tip end. A common lamination taper is .002" per inch.

Taxus brevifolia — The genius and species of yew wood used for making self-wood bows.

tensile strength — The resistance of a material to force.

throat, grip — The narrowest portion of the grip where the thumb and index finger encircle the grip.

tight radius recurve — A recurve limb exhibiting a pronounced and increased recurve in the outer half of the recurve.

tiller — The difference between the upper limb and lower limbs measurements from the bowstring to the belly at the fadeout. Bows are traditionally tillered to produce a stiffer lower limb; ie., the bowstring to belly measurement on the lower limb is less than the same measurement on the upper limb.

tiller board — A wall-mounted board used to visually inspect the bending of a bow's limbs in dynamic positions. Predominantly used by self-wood bowyers.

tillering — The adjustment of tiller by removing material from a bow limb or limbs. Most bows are tillered to approximately 1/4" positive measurement on the upper limb.

tip — The outer end of a bow limb.

tip overlays — Material laminated to the back of the limb tip, usually to strengthen the tips and to provide additional material for fashioning the string nocks.

tip wedge — A thin tapered piece of wood or fiberglass laminated in the outer portion of the limb tip for strength and rigidity; used mostly in longbows.

torque, bow — The unintentional twisting of the bow in the hand during shooting. Torquing the bow can cause inconsistent arrow flight.

trapezoidal cross section — A bow limb with a cross section in the shape of a trapezoid; commonly narrowing to the belly.

unbraced — A bow that is not strung.

Urac 185 — An animal-based glue used for gluing wood to wood contacts.

whip ended limb — a bow limb that bends predominantly in the outer portion, like a whip.

BOWHUNTING'S WHITETAIL MASTERS

By Dan Bertalan

LEARN TO HUNT LIKE NEVER BEFORE!

What the experts are saying about *Bowhunting's Whitetail Masters.*

"*Bowhunting's Whitetail Masters* is a winner. In a single text it serves up the experiences, tips and secrets of 12 of today's hottest whitetail hunters. It would take 12 books to replace this one. ...The blend of information and entertainment is excellent. " *Bill Krenz, Vice President,* Hoyt USA.

"Dan Bertalan is able to get inside the minds and hearts of his subjects as they reveal their passion for whitetails. His talents as an interviewer and as a writer can make readers feel they've gotten to know these 'Whitetail Masters' personally. You may not agree with all of them; but you can't ignore their success. Anyone who loves to pursue deer with stick and string should find this book engrossing." *Tim Dehn, Editor,* Bowhunting World.

"As usual, you've turned out an excellent book." *Dave Canfield, Editorial Director,* Bowhunter *magazine.*

"It's obvious that Dan Bertalan put as much time, thought and hard-nosed work into researching *Bowhunting's Whitetail Masters* as the masters themselves put into their deer hunts. I've read a lot of books on deer hunters, but few held my interest the way this one did throughout.

This is not only a book about top-notch deer hunters, but the methods they use to attain success. In reading it, one learns that master deer hunters don't get that way by accident. They know their quarry and the turf it inhabits. They then devise tactics that best employ their hard-earned knowledge.

Quite simply, the masters prove there are no shortcuts. The answers don't lie in super scents or high-tech delivery systems. Instead, they lie in the man himself.

Dan Bertalan has obviously spent many hours with these masters, delving into their personalities, theories, beliefs and experiences. The words that best describe this book are thorough, probing and insightful. It would be impossible to read it and not become a better deer hunter." *Patrick Durkin, Associate Editor,* Deer & Deer Hunting Magazine.

"One of the best books on whitetails and the bowhunters who pursue them I've ever had the privilege to read, and I read them all. Honestly — Pure enjoyment and that's from the heart." *Alan Foster,* Outdoor Writer.

"Not many of us have ever had the chance to hunt with America's top whitetail bowhunters. About all we could do was to admire their accomplishments from afar, gleaning advice and words of their wisdom from occasional magazine articles, books and videos. But now, thanks to Dan Bertalan's excellent new book, *Bowhunting's Whitetail Masters*, we have at our fingertips a collected wealth of information unselfishly provided by a dozen of this country's most successful deer hunters. It's all here, too — bowhunting techniques, success secrets, solid advice and candid comments — plus a rare glimpse at the men themselves. All told, this entertaining and informative book is the next best thing to meeting these experts and having them speak to us one-on-one. It's must reading for serious whitetail hunters." *M.R. James, Editor/Publisher,* Bowhunter.

The Masters: Bob Fratzke, Barry Wensel, Quince Hale, Noel Feather, Bill Meyer, John Hale, Roger Rothhaar, Gerald Shaffner, Russell Hull, John Kolometz, Mitch Rompola and Gene Wensel.

For more information, contact Envisage Unlimited Press, P.O. Box 777-110, East Lansing, MI, 48826-0777. Phone: 517-834-2276.

Bibliography

Bear, Fred. *Fred Bear's World of Archery*. Garden City, New York: Doubleday & Company, Inc., 1979.

Ekin, Craig. *Howard Hill: The Man and the Legend*. Hamilton, Montana: Charger Productions, Inc., 1982.

Jennings, Tom and Doug Kittredge. *How To Make Bows*. South Pasadena, California: Sportsman Publications, 1961.

Kroeber, Theodora. *Ishi in Two Worlds: Biography of the Last Wild Indian in North America*. Berkley and Los Angelas, California: University of Californian Press, 1961.

Massey, Jay. *The Bowyers Craft*. Girdwood, Alaska: Bear Paw Publications, 1987.

Pope, Saxton. *Hunting with the Bow and Arrow*. New York: G.P. Putnam's Sons, 1947.

Pope and Young Club. *Bowhunting Big Game Records of North America*. Placerville, California: 1987.

Rule, Margaret. "The Search for Mary Rose." *National Geographic* 163, No 5, (May 1983).

Bowyer's Addresses

Arkansas Stick, Rt 1 Box 77, Gurdon, AR 71743	501-353-2032
Assenheimer Bows, 1005 River Road, Bucyrus, OH 44820	419-562-7253
Bear Archery Inc., 4600 SW 41st Blvd., Gainesville, FL 32608-4999	904-376-2327
Ben Pearson Archery Inc., PO Box 7465, Pine Bluff, AR 71611	501-534-6411
Bighorn Bowhunting Co., 2709 Eisenhower, Loveland, CO 80621	303-962-9306
Black Widow Bow Co., PO Box 160, Highlandville, MO 65669	417-587-3358
Brigham Bowhunting, 146 Burrows St., Geneva, OH 44041	216-466-4219
Bruin Custom Recurves, W9664 Hwy D, Antigo, WI 54409	715-623-6537
Cascade Mountain Archery, E750 Krabbenhoft Rd., Grapeview, WA 98546	206-426-8634
Don Adams Archery, 24758 Warthen Road, Elmira, OR 97437	503-935-3794
Don McCann Custom Archery, 6411 366th St. Ct. East, Eatonville, WA 98328	206-832-3897
Elburg's Archery, Rt. 7 Box 301, Madison, IN 47250	812-866-5285
Fedora's Archery Shop, 115 Wintersville Rd., Richland, PA 17087	717-933-8862
Great Northern Longbow Co., 201 North Main, Nashville, MI 49073	517-852-0820
Heritage Archery, 12630 Glenna Dr., Bozeman, MT 59715	406-763-4896
Howard Hill Archery, 248 Canyon Creek, Hamilton, MT 59840	406-363-1359
Hoyt/USA, 475 North Neil Armstrong Rd., Salt Lake City, UT 84116	801-363-2990
Jim Brackenbury Bows, 8326 SE 252nd Ave, Gresham, OR 97080	503-666-1667
Kramer Archery, Box 62, St. Ignatius, MT 59865	406-745-4699
Martin/Howatt, Route 5 Box 127, Walla Walla, WA 99362	509-529-2554
Monarch Longbow Co. Inc., PO Box 5405, Missoula, MT 59806	406-251-3224
Mountainman Longbows, 5150 Tingley Lane, Klamath Falls, OR 97603	503-883-2114
Robertson Stykbow, PO Box 1432, Hamilton, MT 59840	406-363-2528
Rothhaar Recurves, 7707 Gun Lake Road, Delton, MI 49046	616-795-3832
Scorpion Longbow, PO Box 65, Crestone, CO 81131	719-256-4122
The Spirit Longbow Co., 5513 Third Street, Tillamook, OR 97141	503-842-4944
Tim Meigs Custom Archery, 18 Kit Kat Drive, Carson City, NV 89706	702-246-3633
Traditional Longbow Co., 477 Watermelon Hill Rd., Mahopac, NY 10541	914-628-5717
Trails End Custom Recurve Bows, 276 Grantsdale Rd., Hamilton, MT 59840	406-363-2983
Wapiti Recurves, Longbows, 490 South Queen Street, Lakewood, CO 80226	303-989-1120